U.S. WOMEN'S INTEREST GROUPS

**Greenwood Reference Volumes on
American Public Policy Formation**

These Reference Books deal with the development of U.S. policy in various "single-issue" areas. Most policy areas are to be represented by three types of sourcebooks: (1) Institutional Profiles of Leading Organizations, (2) Collection of Documents and Policy Profiles, and (3) Bibliography.

U.S. National Security Policy and Strategy: Documents and Policy Proposals
Sam C. Sarkesian with Robert A. Vitas

U.S. National Security Policy Groups: Institutional Profiles
Cynthia Watson

U.S. Agricultural Groups: Institutional Profiles
William P. Browne and Allan J. Cigler, editors

Military and Strategic Policy: An Annotated Bibliography
Benjamin R. Beede, compiler

U.S. Energy and Environmental Interest Groups: Institutional Profiles
Lettie McSpadden Wenner

Contemporary U.S. Foreign Policy: Documents and Commentary
Elmer Plischke

U.S. Aging Policy Interest Groups: Institutional Profiles
David D. Van Tassel and Jimmy Meyer, editors

U.S. Criminal Justice Interest Groups: Institutional Profiles
Michael A. Hallett and Dennis J. Palumbo

U.S. Educational Policy Interest Groups: Institutional Profiles
Gregory S. Butler and James D. Slack

U.S. Religious Interest Groups: Institutional Profiles
Paul J. Weber and W. Landis Jones

U.S. Health Policy Groups: Institutional Profiles
Craig Ramsey, editor

U.S. Consumer Interest Groups: Institutional Profiles
Loree Bykerk and Ardith Maney

U.S. WOMEN'S INTEREST GROUPS

Institutional Profiles

Edited by

Sarah Slavin

GREENWOOD PRESS
WESTPORT, CONNECTICUT • LONDON

Library of Congress Cataloging-in-Publication Data

U.S. women's interest groups : institutional profiles / edited by
   Sarah Slavin.
         p.   cm. — (Greenwood reference volumes on American public
   policy formation)
      Includes bibliographical references and index.
      ISBN 0–313–25073–1 (alk. paper)
         1. Women—United States—Societies and clubs—Directories.
   2. Pressure groups—United States—Directories.   3. Women's rights—
   United States—Societies, etc.—Directories.   I. Slavin, Sarah.
   II. Title: United States women's interest groups.   III. Series.
   HQ1904.U2   1995
   305.4'06'073—dc20   94–38500

British Library Cataloguing in Publication Data is available.

Library of Congress Catalog Card Number: 94–38500
ISBN: 0–313–25073–1

First published in 1995

Greenwood Press, 88 Post Road West, Westport, CT 06881
An imprint of Greenwood Publishing Group, Inc.

Printed in the United States of America

The paper used in this book complies with the
Permanent Paper Standard issued by the National
Information Standards Organization (Z39.48–1984).

10 9 8 7 6 5 4 3 2 1

CONTENTS

— / —

PREFACE

—————————————— / ——————————————

This volume, focusing on the national women's issues arena, is a reference work on organizations and a sourcebook on group development. The book offers not only accessible information but also systematically gathered data for testing theories of group formation, maintenance and demise, and response to socio-political change. It introduces the possibility, through content analysis, of rigorous comparison with groups in other issue arenas and eventually with women's issues groups from other countries.

Using the four-part questionnaire published in Appendix II, 106 contributors, including the editor, surveyed nearly 200 organizations ranging from the AIDS Coalition to Unleash Power Women's Caucus* to Zonta International.* Only a handful of organizations insisted on exercising rigid control over their profiles. Contributors applied documentary evidence; reviews of existing literature, including group publications; and interviews within and outside an organization to produce objective, balanced entries.

In 1988, before a New Directions in the Study of Interest Groups roundtable discussion at the American Political Science Association annual convention in Washington, D.C., a member of the audience approached me to say he had looked everywhere for women's groups lobbying at the national level and could not find them. Where were they? They are not to be found by relying solely on such generally useful distinctions as group oriented toward a cause versus non-profit occupational group. They have varying tax statuses, most often, but not exclusively, 501 (c) (3). Women's issues groups also present many types: church-related (thirteen of those profiled), civic (eighty-four profiled), elderly (four), professional/occupational (thirty-one), social (seven), sororital (four), sport (three), union (eight), and youth-serving (three) (McPherson, 1983, p. 525). This book further includes three not-for-profit and for-profit businesses, no vet-

erans' organizations but a related group, the National Military Family Association,* seven research groups, three partisan groups, two independent political
action committees, and six government agencies.

During a fall 1988 sabbatical leave, I undertook an extended search for wom-
en's interest organizations, my sampling unit. Besides *Washington Representatives,* 7th ed., edited by Arthur C. Close (Washington, D.C.: Columbia Books,
1983), the three-volume *Encyclopedia of Associations* (Detroit: Gale Research,
1987), and *Women's Organizations & Leaders Directory 1975–76,* edited by
Myra E. Barrer (Washington, D.C.: Today Publications & News Service, 1975),
the search included related scholarly literature. Most helpful in a generally sparse
field were Susan M. Hartmann *From Margin to Mainstream: American Women
and Politics Since 1960* (New York: Knopf, 1989) and J. Stanley Lemons, *The
Woman Citizen: Social Feminism in the 1920s* (Urbana: University of Illinois
Press, 1973).

Eventually this search expanded to lists: a ''Directory of Selected Organizations Interested in Women's Issues,'' prepared by the Congressional Caucus for
Women's Issues* (April 1989); lists distributed by the American Medical Wom-
en's Association* and National Women's Health Network*; the National Council
of Negro Women* and Council of Presidents* membership lists; ''Organizations
Supporting Reproductive Rights,'' *National NOW Times* (December–January
1986); ''International Black Women's Movement: Organizations in the United
States,'' *The Woman Activist* (October 1986); ''Key Women of Color Organizations,'' in ''Update on the Women of Color Program,'' National NOW [National
Organization for Women] Action Center, May 1989. Word of mouth also proved
helpful. Newspapers revealed the occasional group, for example, Feminists for
Life.* Programs of the Institute for Women's Policy Research* conferences, begun in 1989, revealed such groups as the National Institute for Women of Color*
(NIWC).

The organizations profiled in this volume present a nonprobabilistic sample.
I probably did not literally identify every unit in the population. (The 1993
Encyclopedia of Women's Associations Worldwide by Gale Research International includes over 3,400 women's groups; *National Women's Organizations,*
published in 1993 by NCRW, includes 477 national groups.) Specifically, I
sought to include virtually every major organization for women of color that I
identified, except the sororities; I chose four black sororities based on their
evident success, then included no other sororital organizations as none seemed
as fertile a source of leadership; regrettably, seven of twenty-four major women
of color groups are missing from the book. I selected from among church-related
groups mostly Catholic ones, along with two Jewish-related groups, two related
to moderate Protestant denominations, and two related to progressive ones. I
selected one or more groups from all organizational types except veterans'
groups but included a military families' group.

Although these choices were subjective, they seemed to represent organizational diversity and significant emphases in the women's issues arena. The in-

volvement of 105 other researchers allowed data collection to proceed at numerous sites, to try to heighten the generalizability of the overall findings beyond what the number of groups by type may permit (Sudman, 1976, p. 26). Overall, 20 of the 200 groups I tried to include were not available; the response rate, then, was 90 percent. The publisher set the sample size of 200. The findings, as the introduction indicates, compare well with those of earlier existing studies of women's issues groups and with the interest groups/social movement organization literature generally.

A women's issues group for this volume's purpose meets one or more of five criteria:

1. There is a reference to women—whether adults, youth, or children—in the organization's name, for example, Mothers against Drunk Driving* (MADD).

2. The group's members are only or mainly women; for example, in B'nai B'rith Women* (BBW), all members are women. BBW also includes a reference to women in its name, meeting two (and, in fact, ultimately all five) criteria. MADD by comparison has a membership that today divides about evenly between women and men; historically, its members were mainly women. MADD presently incorporates the first criterion and not the second one.

3. The group explicitly serves certain women's interests, for example, the National Citizens Coalition for Nursing Home Reform,* which serves nursing home residents, predominantly women. MADD serves women-in-between, that is, women giving care to children, parents, or a spouse with a chronic condition, in this case resulting from driving while drunk.

4. The group represents a traditional women's role, for example, the American Red Cross* and volunteers, the Consumer Federation of America* (CFA) (Veblen, 1899; reprint 1912), and MADD and caregivers. Men can and do assume these roles, but convention has assigned them to women. In such organizations as the Association of Family and Consumer Sciences* or American Library Association,* the role may center on an occupation or profession. In such groups as Dorothy Day's Catholic Worker,* it may reflect a phenomenon in women's history, such as, anarchism. Jane Addams, a settlement movement leader figuring prominently in the origin and development of several profiled groups, drew on Christian anarchism, including pacifism and an individualism that would return the fruits of human labor to their source.

5. The group may take a position on one or more issues distinctly of concern to women generally, for example, the Children's Defense Fund* or American Academy of Pediatricians* (which has social feminist roots). MADD supports crime victim rights, distinctly of concern to rape, incest, battering, and murder victims, the preponderance of whom are women, as well as to victims of Driving While Intoxicated and their significant others. One in three women will be raped, incested, or battered in their lifetime.

Why do these visible organizations often seem invisible to those seeking to research women's issues groups? At a 1993 State University of New York Conversation in the Disciplines conference, on a panel on women and political power, I mentioned as one organization presenting all five criteria the International Ladies' Garment Workers' Union* (ILGWU). Afterward, a woman from the audience protested ILGWU's classification as a women's issues group at all. First, she said, "ladies" refers to the garments, not the workers. *Webster's* defines a lady as "a woman of rank or distinction," hence, a reference to women in the ILGWU's name, standard number one. Perhaps, I asked, the protester felt concern that the organization's officers are mainly men? She shook her head no as I remarked that its membership is mainly women, standard number two, and then she commented that men make garments, too. "Generally in separate divisions," I recalled, indebted to economist Susan Davis for her ILGWU profile.

ILGWU indisputably incorporates standard number three, serving ladies' "garment workers" interests (by providing them with benefits comparable to higher-waged automotive workers). My antagonist tightened her lips. The group represents a traditional women's role (seamstress) *and* occupation (ladies' garment worker) *and* phenomena in women's history (which includes the Triangle Shirtwaist Company fire), standard number four. She stared at me and was unmoved. The group takes issue positions directly concerning women, as on Title VII, thereby incorporating standard number five. She shrugged at my inability to not see ILGWU as a women's issues group.

Nearly all the organizations profiled operate at the national level. There are a few exceptions, like Black, Indian, Hispanic and Asian Women in Action,* located in Minneapolis and functioning in Minnesota, which has a national perspective. As groups with national perspective, National Organization for Women—California* and National Organization for Women—New York City* demonstrate powerful intermediate and local structures within the National Organization for Women* (NOW) and also function independently. Because of population patterns and also intense community needs, matters with national implications, Hispanic women's organizations have grounded themselves largely at the regional or local level; several of the most important are profiled. Offering selected examples of the state and local commissions that spun off the President's Commission on the Status of Women* during the women's liberation movement's (WLM) onset, the Wisconsin Women's Council* originated as the Wisconsin Commission on the Status of Women.

Profiled groups include such ideologically disparate peak associations as Concerned Women for America,* a showpiece of the right wing, and NOW, a flagship of WLM, and such ideologically disparate single-issue groups as the National Abortion Rights Action League* (NARAL) and National Committee for a Human Life Amendment.* All have been active since 1960. Many have a longer history—the General Federation of Women's Clubs International,* founded in 1890, and National Association of Colored Women's Clubs,* in 1896. Fifty-three percent (ninety-five) of the women's issues groups profiled for this book have emerged since 1970, including all the Hispanic ones.

Certain groups focus on research or service. The Center for Women Policy Studies* and Institute for Women's Policy Research,* for example, are major players in the women's issues arena. To exclude service-oriented organizations virtually would be to exclude Hispanic, Native American Indian, Asian American, and half of African American women's groups, an inappropriate choice of perspective, and also to ignore their policy implications and the ongoing process of socializing interests. The collection also includes several groups working to elect/appoint women or to enhance women's election/appointment to policy-making posts, including three partisan ones and two unattached political action committees.

Appendix I profiles six government agencies (Walker, 1989) that have influenced agenda formation by women's issues groups significantly. The origin and development section of other group profiles, for example, the National Committee on Pay Equity* (NCPE), makes clear the extent to which their formation as an organization depended on a government agency, in NCPE's case, the Equal Employment Opportunity Commission during Eleanor Holmes Norton's directorship.

Exclusive of the government agencies, thirteen organizations profiled are now defunct. They belong in this collection because they either served interests that otherwise largely have gone unserved or helped set into motion such interest representation. An example of the former defunct groups is the National Welfare Rights Organization,* and of the latter, the Day Care Council of America.* These groups also offer a look at the end of organizational life cycles in the women's issues arena. A failure of material resources because the group was "ahead of its time" or was subsumed by groups it originally stimulated is common.

The introduction sets in context the entries that follow and offers theoretical perspective. Not surprisingly, women's issues entrepreneurs emerge as key to forming demand preferences. Federal tax law also plays a large part in structuring group responses. The search for social capital influences emphasis on so-called bystander publics, most notably movement by majority white groups toward other ethnic and racial groups. Incentives generally are first purposive, then solidary. A motive to experiment with consensus-based organizational structures seems evident; leaders may spend their "free votes" on this feminist-tending experimentation.

After this introduction comes the alphabetical array of the interest group profiles. Cross-references include former names of profiled groups and the names of groups that merged to form profiled groups. An asterisk after another group's name indicates the group is profiled elsewhere in the volume. A contributor's name is located at the profile's conclusion, and information about all the contributors ends the book.

The profiles present the following information:

1. The introduction suggests the group's scope and influence.
2. The origin and development section offers an organizational history, including key founders' names, participation by women from racial/ethnic minorities in the group's

formation and growth, key policy concerns, and, if relevant, the reason for the group's demise.

3. The organization and funding section provides information about structure, racial/ethnic representation among the leadership, membership and its incentives, and the budget, including tax status and any legal defense fund or educational foundation.

4. The policy concerns and tactics section outlines the source of decision making about policy and strategy within the organization, the group's preferred strategies and policy priorities, its ongoing support for choices from a proffered policy matrix, group perceptions about the direction policy is taking outside it, preferred allies, and expectations about opposition.

5. The electoral activity section indicates which organizations have political action committees and their organization, standards for endorsement, the extent of endorsements, and funding.

6. The further information section mentions selected group publications, most of which concern public policy.

The volume has two appendixes. Appendix I profiles six government agencies: the Citizens Advisory Council on the Status of Women,* Congressional Caucus for Women's Issues,* President's Commission on the Status of Women,* President's Task Force on Women's Rights and Responsibilities,* U.S. Department of Labor Women's Bureau,* and Wisconsin Women's Council.* Appendix II reprints the questionnaire contributors used.

No profile says all that there is to say about an organization but it does provide comparable data that are as up-to-date as possible. Yet the profiles offer data obtained cross-sectionally. Some profiles do not contain a full range of responses, usually because the organization was not forthcoming, and, to date, writing about the group or aspects of it has lagged. Even incomplete profiles may offer all or most information that currently is available on an organization.

This project has been seven years in the making. One of its contributors, Lynne White Scheider, died on October 4, 1992, in an automobile crash; another contributor, MaryAnne Borelli, sustained significant injuries in such a crash but thankfully survived them. Both White's CFA profile and Borelli's NARAL and Planned Parenthood Federation* profiles are published here. The young husband of one of our original contributors lost his life to a stroke; and Linda Mather helped pick up and complete her assignments. The editor regrets that the Seneca Falls Women's Peace Encampment, whose life was ending as the project progressed, and the Girl Scouts, who continue to exist, refused to be included.

Profiles contracted for the Black Women's Agenda, Indigenous Women's Network, National Federation of Republican Women, National Political Congress of Black Women, Native American Indian Women's Association, Sociologists for Women in Society, Top Ladies of Distinction, Women against

Violence against Women, and Women of All Red Nations did not materialize. Nor did I find contributors to profile the Breast Cancer Coalition, National Co-alition for Women and Girls in Education, National Consumers League, National Council of Women of the U.S., National Education Association, National Federation of Democratic Women, National Organization of Black Elected Legislators/Women, National Women's Law Center, and Women in Community Service. I wish I could have included them.

In support of this project, I received a State University of New York College at Buffalo Faculty of Natural and Social Sciences minigrant and a scholarship award from the vice president for academic affairs. Suzanne Tomkins served well as the project's research assistant. Rochelle Stevwing produced the mechanical for the questionnaire.

I thank my son Victor Hale Schramm and significant other, Barbara Shagawat, for their enduring patience during the project, and my contributors for their receptivity to suggestions about their profiles' organization and substance. I feel impressed by the ingenuity and tirelessness contributors often brought to their entries' completion. Joyotpaul Chaudhuri and Mattie L. Rhodes, in the Indian Women in Progress* and National Black Nurses Association* profiles, respectively, have provided valuable general overviews as well. Especially helpful throughout were Janet K. Boles, Flora Crater, Catherine East, Shirley Geiger, Barbara W. Gerber, Sarah Harder, Nancy Douglas Joyner, Karen M. Kennelly, Linda Mather, Nancy McGlen, Joan McLean, Jimmy E. W. Meyer, Charlotte T. Morgan-Cato, Barbara Bennett Peterson, Clyde Wilcox, and Laura R. Woliver.

Greenwood Publishing Group had the insight/foresight to make the project possible; and senior editor Mildred Vasan earned my vast appreciation for her patience. Carima El-Behairy did much of the manuscript's word processing; Heidi R. Slavin and Beth Schramm Podgorny completed it and have earned my gratitude for doing so.

The fact that a hit-and-run driver on May 4, 1993, took the life of my mother, Ruth Martin Slavin, as this project finally neared completion dimmed the satisfaction I otherwise might feel. Even so, I recognize the substantial effort that has brought the project to fruition and regret any errors of my own that detract from its usefulness.

REFERENCES

McPherson, Miller. "An Ecology of Affiliations." *American Sociological Review* 48 (August 1983): 519–32.

Sudman, Seymour. *Applied Sampling.* New York: Academic Press, 1976.

Veblen, Thorstein. *The Theory of the Leisure Class: An Economic Study of Institutions.* New York: Macmillan, 1912.

Walker, Jack. "The National Interest Group System." *VOX POP: Newsletter of Political Organizations and Parties* 8:2 (1989): 4.

INTRODUCTION

—————————————— / ——————————————

A Democratic administration, headed by U.S. president John F. Kennedy and acting in response to a political appointee, Women's Bureau* director Esther Peterson, in 1961 established the President's Commission on the Status of Women.* Increasingly, as the women's movement again rose in prominence, women's issues groups contributed to the process of setting a policy agenda and alternatives for the U.S. government. John Kingdon has written that "organized interests are heard more in politics than unorganized interests" (1984, p. 56). To be heard, as Kingdon suggests, women's issues groups struggled to maintain internal cohesion; led their constituents into the streets, for example, on the fiftieth anniversary of women's universal suffrage, if not with widespread economic consequences, then to generate political clout; and began looking toward electoral arenas to capitalize on women's finally having achieved parity with men in their voting rates.

By 1972, according to Ethel Klein, over one-fifth of Americans favored direct action for women's equality (1984, p. 125). Twenty years later, in 1992, 22 percent of the women's issues groups profiled herein strongly favored this same strategy to push their agenda items and alternatives. Twenty-six percent of the time, however, they strongly favored research strategies; 30 percent of the time, personal presentations to high national officeholders and staff; 31 percent of the time, legislative testimony; and 39 percent of the time, providing legislators and their staff with information. Only 19 percent of the time did they strongly favor administratively oriented strategies as compared, for example, with the 27 percent of the time they strongly favored legislatively focused letter-writing campaigns. As Jeffrey Berry would say, as lobbies, women's issues groups wanted "action out of Washington" (1989, p. 170), and they largely saw the U.S. Congress as a focal point for that action.

While women's issues groups have staked out varied interests, in 1992, 19 percent of them shared an ongoing interest in outcomes around the proposed equal rights amendment and around *Roe* v. *Wade* (1973). Thirteen percent of them acknowledged such interest in affirmative action, with nearly 12 percent describing the 1988 Civil Rights Restoration Act as one of three federal laws most important to them. It seems reasonable to recognize these redistributive interests as central to the women's liberation movement (see Costain and Costain, 1983, p. 214). Nor do these groups lobby alone. In keeping with their centermost concerns, 9 percent of them cite National Organization for Women* (NOW) as the group with which they most likely would collaborate, and 8 percent cite the American Association of University Women* (AAUW). Five percent each cite the more specialized National Abortion Rights Action League* (NARAL) and the National Women's Political Caucus* (NWPC)—this latter suggesting continuing concern with electoral strategizing (see also Heblom, 1983, p. 37).

Women's issues groups can identify their adversaries as well as their allies. Five and one-half percent nominate Operation Rescue* (OR) as one of three groups opposing their interests, and nearly 4 percent, the National Right to Life Committee* (NRLC) and Chamber of Commerce (CC). CC may be considered an externality group; but OR and NRLC are themselves women's issues groups. Robert Salisbury has found "friends and enemies" within a given issue arena, highlighting the diversity that may emerge (1987, p. 1227). Unexpectedly, specialization in the women's issues arena is characteristically confrontational (cf. Salisbury, 1987, p. 1229). But Salisbury makes the point that particular issues arenas will structure issues groups in ways leading to particularized relations of collaboration and opposition (p. 1230).

Proceeding at the level of the organization, this introduction first discusses the agenda-setting process as described by a content analysis of the profiles contained in this volume. It moves on to consider (1) social capital formation through issue specialization and central political processes, by means of litigation and by virtue of entrepreneurial behavior; (2) mobilization of such bystander publics as African American women by majority white women's issues groups, and including male nonbeneficiary constituents and lesbian potential constituents; and (3) exchange relations between organizers and constituents that cut across agenda items, exchange relations with isolated conscience constituents, exchange relations within membership organizations, and exchange relations owing to feminists.

AGENDA SETTING

In 1848 the Declaration of Sentiments and Resolutions was issued in Seneca Falls, New York, from the first U.S. women's rights convention (Griffith, 1984, pp. 52–57). In 1983, 135 years later, the Seneca Falls National Women's Center and Educational Institute (SFNWCEI) reissued the declaration, "to enable all women to rededicate themselves to the concepts first articulated in 1848 in the same place.'' Despite the achievement of the vote and demise of the feudal doctrine of coverture and impressive policy-making successes in the 1970s, women's equal station suffered. The reissued declaration said it suffered for reasons ranging from the paucity of women among lawmakers to domestic violence, from lack of pay equity and access to the primary labor market to the chilly classroom, from disregard for women's consciences to forced dependency.

A 501 (c) (4) nonmembership organization, the women's center was formed in 1982 to take educational initiatives supplementing those of the new Women's Rights National Park—one of the 4 percent of all national historic landmarks honoring women's accomplishments (*On the Issues,* 1993, p. 2)—and nonprofit Women's Hall of Fame in Seneca Falls. Previously, the founders had experienced educational community through Eisenhower College, which closed. Key founders included Rosemary Agonito, a philosophy instructor, and economist Corinne Guntzel. This majority white women's group had African American women among its founders: Constance Timberlake and Bobbie Ross. It sought to enhance its credibility with an advisory council of such notables as Maureen Stapleton, Helen Reddy, and Alan Alda. But, dispersed geographically by new academic assignments, shaken by Guntzel's subsequent suicide, and divided by disagreement over direction, the organization disbanded in 1987. It left its treasury to the Elizabeth Cady Stanton Foundation in Seneca Falls.

The short-lived SFNWCEI made a point: the passage of nearly one and one-half centuries has not proved sufficient to fulfill women's pursuit of ''their own true and substantial happiness'' in the United States. As the twenty-first century approaches, evidence has mounted to document the problem's pervasiveness.

There is relative deprivation. Perhaps most chilling is the status of the 1.2 million young women eighteen to thirty-four years old, one-third with children and a major share of the responsibility for them and over half living below the poverty line. Young women's earning power is not even 75 percent of young men's (*The Woman Activist,* p. 1). Nor is the overall problem limited by geography, as the United Nations Convention to Eliminate All Forms of Discrimination against Women attests. The United States has not ratified this convention, which the General Assembly adopted in 1979. One hundred one of the potential 183 signatories (55 percent) have, at the time of this writing, ratified it.

Whether through the Women's Campaign Fund* (WCF) to elect women to public office, the National Coalition against Domestic Violence* (NCADV), the American Federation of State, County and Municipal Employees* to achieve pay equity, the Association of American Medical Colleges Women in Medicine Program* (WIM) to enhance women's access to the primary labor market, the Association of American Colleges Project on the Status and Education of Women* to heat the chilly classroom, Network* to pursue peace and justice issues, or Wider Opportunities for Women* (WOW) to counteract forced dependency—the organizations profiled all address conceptualizations such as the reissued Declaration of Sentiments.

Moreover, a formal agenda exists, produced by the delegate-based Houston Women's Conference in 1977. The Council of Presidents* (CP), a group echoing the old Women's Joint Congressional Committee spirit, and National Women's Conference Committee* (NWCC), an oversight group authorized by the Houston conference, have significant efforts under way to manage the action plan's implementation at all governmental levels. CP's and NWCC's organizational members have committed themselves to implementing the agenda even-handedly, an improvement on coalition politics (Costain and Costain, 1983, p. 203). The National Association of Commissions for Women* (NACW) also may play a role in this endeavor by pooling the state and local commissions' ability to facilitate access to public officeholders (Rosenberg, 1982, p. 44). Further, Mary Lou Kendrigan has argued that "the women's agenda is the agenda of the Democratic Party*" (1992, p. 150).

The profiles reveal that, in practice, women's issues groups stress policy concerning abortion, aging, children, economics, education, the First Amendment free speech and press clauses, health and safety, housing, international relations, minority women, and public office holding. The most detailed practical agenda item for women's issues groups at the time of this writing is health and safety.

The Health and Safety Agenda Item

Besides widely generalized concern over teenage pregnancy and infant mortality, a significant source of emphasis in the health and safety agenda item, toward more national authoritative allocation of valued things, is acquired immunodeficiency syndrome (AIDS). Among the women's issues groups working on this issue, the AIDS Coalition to Unleash Power Women's Caucus* (ACT UP WC) has led the way in pressuring the National Institutes of Health to reassess entry standards to treatment groups that tend not to include women, and the Social Security Administration (SSA) to expand its disability definition to include women with human immunodeficiency virus (HIV)/AIDS, in order that related SSA funds may be allocated to them. The Gay and Lesbian Activists Alliance* is among the groups working to expand the Centers for Disease Control definition of AIDS to include women's symptoms. The Center for Women's Policy Studies* has founded a National Resource Center on Women and AIDS. The National Association of Negro Business and Professional Women's Clubs* (NANBPW) has entered a research-oriented action program with the National Jewish Center targeting AIDS and lupus, and the National Black Nurses Association* (NBNA) has a community-based AIDS education program.

Besides litigation over AIDS by its Gay and Lesbian Rights Project, the American Civil Liberties Union* (ACLU) Women's Rights Project has sought access for drug- and alcohol-dependent women to state-funded medical treatment. Sigma Gamma Rho* has been among the many women's issues groups promoting drug and substance abuse and alcohol awareness. A Citizen's Project to Remove Intoxicated Drivers* wants information about alcohol poisoning and addiction to appear in advertising.

WIM has worked more generally to reduce sexism in medicine. National Citizens for Nursing Home Reform* seeks to improve health care quality; and the Association of Black Nursing Faculty in Higher Education* seeks to improve black women's health care in particular. The National Council of Negro Women* (NCNW) has emphasized health career development for youth. The Congressional Caucus for Women's Issues* (CCWI) introduced a women's health equity package in 1990; and NOW has made this part of its 1993 action agenda.

The Organization of Parents through Surrogacy* works to advance infertile women's rights. The American College of Nurse-Midwives* seeks an environment in which women practitioners and pregnant women exert control over childbirth and maternal infant care. The National Women's Health Network (NWHN) seeks to reduce the high rate of cesarean-section births.

NWHN also promotes safe mammograms. The National Conference of State Legislatures Women's Network* (NCSL WN) has concluded a project to acquire Medicare coverage for mammograms for the highest-risk group, women over forty. (The U.S. Congress provided biennial coverage, in contrast to American Cancer Society guidelines of a yearly mammogram for women over fifty.) The National Council of Catholic Women* advocates mandatory mammogram insurance bills at the state level. The National Black Women's Health Project* (NBWHP) strives to acquaint legislators with the facts of accessible mammography for women with limited incomes.

The Links Incorporated* (TLI) has presented its Buffalo, New York, chapter with an award for an ongoing women of color and cancer project.

For years the United Autoworkers* (UAW) and the American Nurses' Association* (ANA) have called for national health insurance. WOW likewise supports a universal health care initiative, as has Women for Racial and Economic Equality.* The National Association of Social Workers* (NASW) has argued in favor of including mental health care in this package. The National Military Family Association* advocates expanding the Active Duty Dependent's Plan.

The American Red Cross* supports federal emergency medical assistance for communities affected by natural disasters. B'nai B'rith Women* (BBW) promotes assistance for women in between, and American College of Obstetricians and Gynecologists* support for bills for no-fault neurologically damaged newborns will have the same effect. The Older Women's League* has called for spousal impoverishment waivers that largely will protect old women, who tend to outlive old men, from the aftereffects of spending down to obtain Medicaid benefits during their husband's final illness.

The Unitarian Universalist Women's Federation* and American Medical Women's Association* have sought policy to contain violence against women. NCADV supports revision of the Immigration Fraud Act, which leads to threats of deportation against battered immigrant women who go to the police or seek a divorce before they have lived two years in the United States. The National Gay and Lesbian Task Force* (NGLTF) supports bias-related violence legislation. Mothers Against Drunk Driving* (MADD) seeks crime victim rights.

A Source of the Health and Safety Agenda Item

A 1974 Health Service Act attracted some women's issues groups' attention; and in 1974–78 the Mexican American Legal Defense and Educational Fund Chicana Rights Project* saw health issues as highly significant. The 1977 Houston conference called for improvement in women's health care. A failed presidential initiative in 1978 followed pressure by UAW. Much earlier still, the League of Women Voters* (LWV) focused on the health issue; and the International Ladies' Garment Workers' Union* (ILGWU) was the first union to provide its members with a health care center. But, despite these and other historical precedents for women's issues groups' involvement, overall this is a relatively new agenda item for them. Ellen Boneparth's fine 1982 edited volume on women's movement lobbying does not discuss a health-based agenda item. Nonetheless, the transition to a postindustrial society left women and their children disadvantaged in the health benefits arena (Kendrigan, 1992, p. 165). The general aging of the population and the tendency for women to outlive men only added to the potential constituency around the issue.

Constituents have shown their preference for the agenda item through support for new organizations such as NWHN (founded in 1976) and NBWHP (which became independent of NWHN in 1981) and through contributions, for example, to the Feminist Majority Foundation,* which mainly studies health issues and is an offshoot of the Fund for a Feminist Majority* (FMF). A rapidly growing organization (6,000 new members daily), the American Association of Retired Persons* (AARP) formed a Women's Initiative (WI) in 1984 and offers such material incentives as affordable health insurance to supplement Medicare and also a pharmacy service. AARP WI has 18 million potential constituents. The support so far given by constituents to the health and safety agenda item represented and shaped by women's issues groups, including the Breast Cancer Coalition, seems especially striking, coming as it does during an unfavorable economic climate, which can discourage investment in organizations to achieve such collective goods.

Women's issues groups' constituents' preference for the health and safety agenda item may come, as Salisbury has suggested it will (1969, p. 20), in response to organizers' expression or articulation of it. Organizers have fielded an ever wider array of health- and safety-related policy proposals within their organizations' targeted objectives to profit from exchange activity between them and their group's constituents. By 1992 this activity had yielded widespread recognition, for example, of the CCWI women's health research, service, and preventive care initiative (Rodriguez-Trias, 1992, p. 663) and publicizing analyses of women's health care needs by such state officeholders as New York Democratic governor Mario Cuomo.

Within the year, a letter to the editor of *Ms.* magazine by Representative Patricia Schroeder (D: CO) and now Senator Olympia Snow (R: ME), CCWI cochairs, sought "to set the record straight" on former *Ms.* editor and publisher Gloria Steinem's claim that CCWI functioned merely as a "clearinghouse." An editorial note following the letter in the May 1992 issue emphasized, among other things, a wider organizational role than CCWI's. Yet the influence and resources of an elite governmental organization such as CCWI may be critical to organizational movement against deprivation (McCarthy and Zald, 1977, p. 1215).

As Salisbury has suggested (1969, p. 21), it is appropriate to acknowledge the part played by organizers. Gelb and Palley's well-received study, *Women and Public Policies,* focused most on this role (1982, p. 4). One timely contemporary example came with Hillary Rodham Clinton's leadership of the National Health Care Reform Task Force to devise comprehensive health care reform for the Clinton administration. Her emphasis throughout on not only women but many aspects of the women's issues groups' health and safety agenda item was significant and represented an open "policy window" (Kingdon, 1984, pp. 174–76) for these groups. Clinton's background on interlocking directorates of women's issues groups, including past service as the Children's Defense Fund* (CDF) board president, puts her in a position to profit from exchange activity. (Six percent [eleven] of the groups here surveyed cite CDF as one of the three groups they most likely will collaborate with; because of the substantial diversity of this arena, a .06 collaboration score marks CDF as one of the most influential groups.)

Congresswoman Schroeder, coauthor of the 1992 *Ms.* letter, is one of six congresswomen most frequently shown by the profiles to be successful as an entrepreneur. The 180 profiles demonstrate one (6 percent [eleven] of the time) or a few (39 percent [seventy]) organizers' leadership from inception for half of these groups. These organizers cut across groups, that is, are not limited in scope only to one, helping to account for the regularity with which select target goals appear among women's issues groups.

Since 1960, the entrepreneuers, exclusive of the congresswomen, most often shown to be successful by the profiles include, in alphabetical order, Kathryn Clarenbach, Catherine East, Marian Wright Edelman (of CDF), Betty Friedan, Margaret Gates, Sarah Harder, Dorothy Height, Nan Hunter, Irene Natividad, Esther Peterson, Marguerite Rawalt, Bernice Resnick Sandler, Phyllis Schlafly, Nancy Seifer, Eleanor Smeal, Yolanda Tarango, and Harriet Woods. The other five congresswomen were Bella Abzug (D: NY), Shirley Chrisholm (D: NY), Geraldine Ferraro (D: NY), Martha Griffiths (D: MI), and Elizabeth Holtzman (D: NY). No single individual was mentioned more often than former congresswoman Chisholm. Certain historical organizers' names still recur: Jane Addams,

Mary McLeod Bethune, Crystal Eastman, Elizabeth Gurley Flynn, Marian Talbot, and Mary Church Terrell, along with Jeanette Rankin (R: WY).

SOCIAL CAPITAL FORMATION

The extensiveness of exchange activity results from the accumulation of what Salisbury has called "social capital sufficient to invest in the formation of durable organizations" (1969, p. 15). For this reason, one critical factor for these organizers has become tax law. Their choices about social capital are partly driven by public policy. More of the 180 women's issues groups are charitably oriented (40.5 percent [seventy-three]), as defined by section 501 (c) (3), than social welfare–oriented (14 percent [twenty-six]), as defined by section 501 (c) (4). On point is Richard Franke: "The funding of public interest groups has become so woven into the tax exemption equation that private interest groups involved in controversial issues have sought not-for-profit status" (1989, n.p.). Restrictions on 501 (c) (3) organizations are meant to curb substantial activity (basically, over 5 percent of a group's total activity) to influence legislation—whether by giving testimony or conferring with legislators and staff or advocating through publications or public appeals—and forbid campaigns for public office seekers. Previously, 501 (c) (3) groups could direct up to 30 percent of their activity toward lobbying. The restrictions limit 501 (c) (4) organizations to lobbying or political activity for charitable, educational, or recreational ends and without benefit of the tax-deductible contributions that 501 (c) (3) groups may receive.

In the last decade or so, restrictions on tax-exempt status, part of a campaign to "defund the left" (Peterson and Walker, 1986), led to scrutiny of organizations at the other end of the political spectrum and reform in the 1987 Revenue Act. Groups increasingly became sensitive to the presence of a social control agency (McCarthy and Zald, 1977), the Internal Revenue Service (IRS). Tandem, that is, 501 (c) (3)-(c) (4), organizations—formed to enlarge opportunities within nonprofit groups' limitations and thereby transfer resources to action—have come under scrutiny. More than anything else, fear of creating an image of engagement in "substantial" activity, with subsequent loss of tax-exempt status or at least the imposition of an excise tax, probably influenced some groups' reticence to respond to parts of this project's survey or provide requested clarification. Unguarded responses most typically came from less-experienced groups.

The most recent emerging regulatory tendency seems to narrow the meanings of "substantial" activity and influence on legislation. Further, IRS audits have decreased, and, in general, applications for nonprofit status have increased substantially. Calls for reform remain. These tendencies seem to explain the decision by organizers, in 20 percent of the profiled women's issues groups, to rely mostly, that is, for 50 percent or more of their funds, on membership dues for their capital. In the past, organizations such as NCNW placed great significance on their attainment of 501 (c) (3) status; and one more recently formed organ-ization, Catholics for a Free Choice,* even has retreated from its initial 501 (c) (4) to (c) (3) status. But the fiscal experiences of highly visible 501 (c) (4) peak associations like NOW and AAUW and the increasing emergence of tandem groups (now 26 percent of the total 102 nonprofits), with NOW a prime ex-ample, suggest that 501 (c) (3) status per se may not be the wave of the future for women's issues groups, when tandem organization promises the greater goal accomplishment.

Issue Specialization

For social capital's sake, networking among women's issues groups, as the late Jack Walker suggested (1983), likely will continue, with CP a leading ex-ample and its formation of a separate, smaller pro-choice network telling. For another example, AARP WI has a Women's Financial Information Program to network with a large number of community agencies on the international level. Indian Women in Progress* offers a particularly interesting example, lacking in bureaucracy and reliable funding sources. The Women's Work Force Network* has over 400 members, reaching more than 750,000 women and also bringing in fifty-five-dollar membership fees; the Women's Institute for Freedom of the Press* (WIFP) has 500 associates acquired through networking with several hundred groups but collects no membership fee.

Reflecting a general trend by social movements toward specialized organi-zation (Everett, 1992, p. 969), abortion politics, the most explosive of women's issues, appears increasingly limited to separate networks, for example, the Re-ligious Coalition for Abortion Rights,* and single-issue groups, for example, NARAL, which acts once it has created a network. Abortion politics cleaves women's issues groups, with the name of a leading U.S. Supreme Court deci-sion, *Jane Bray, Operation Rescue, et al.* v. *Alexandria Women's Health Clinic, National Organization for Women, et al.* (1990), indicative of the problem. The numerous friends of the court briefs in *Bray* pitted such organizations as NARAL and Planned Parenthood Federation* (PPF) against Feminists for Life* (FFL) and the Professional Women's Network.

Organizers cannot control conflict over the abortion issue. Among the profiled organizations, 30 percent see continuing interest in their position on either side of this issue. A group such as the Association of Junior Leagues International* (AJLI) has only 2 individual leagues of 267 in the United States formally taking a pro-choice position. For groups ranging from Church Women United* (CWU) to most labor unions, the abortion issue just is not conducive to capital formation for other purposes, although NOW-California* reports membership increases because of it, and women's issues political action committees (PACs) routinely place a candidate's abortion position among the criteria for endorsement. Fur-ther, in early 1993, CCWI's executive committee voted by a large margin to take a pro-choice position.

Groups active around the abortion issue find it costly and apply tactics such as letter-writing campaigns and signature advertisements to stretch their resources. One study of abortion politics has noted generally: "The ability of a group to advance or protect its interests depends on the abundance of its resources. Money has the enormous advantage of convertibility, and groups rich in dollars have a distinct advantage. But a large or intensely committed membership can compensate for lack of money" (Craig and O'Brien, 1993, p. 39). Networking among counterparts in abortion politics assumes greater importance than it usually would in this context.

At least for advocates (Marshall, 1985), a national equal rights amendment (ERA) is conducive to capital formation. Advocates even included half the evangelical women in one national survey (Wilcox, 1989, p. 149). Nineteen percent (thirty) of the present profiled groups have taken an ongoing commitment to the amendment's ratification. In the years since the proposed ERA expired, and it disappeared from most women's issues groups' agendas other than as a symbol; NOW, for instance, found ERA to be key to its mass mail fund-raising campaigns. During March 1992 an ERA Summit Group formed to network, along with CP, for ERA's ratification. Among the organizations supporting the summit group were Federally Employed Women,* LWV, the General Federation of Women's Clubs International* (GFWC), National Council of Jewish Women* (NCJW), National Woman's Party,* and NWCC. Congresswoman Maxine Waters (D: CA), the author of recent CCWI bylaw revisions, was strongly in evidence during this summit, as was Congresswoman Schroeder.

Central Political Processes

Besides networking, organizational efforts by government agencies and actors have assumed significance in the women's issues arena. They offer still another way to mitigate the effects of tax policy as well as to enhance economic opportunities more generally. An argument for the role of central political processes in promoting the women's movement may be made by observing the women's issues arena where 8 percent (fourteen) of the profiled groups formed with governmental assistance. The presence of six congresswomen, two governmental administrators (East and Peterson), one former state commission head (Clarenbach), one former state elected official and Democratic Party notable (Woods), and one Republican Party notable (Schlafly) among the twenty-two most mentioned contemporary organizers, that is, 50 percent of them, is strongly suggestive. The Costains, too, have reported this connection (Costain, 1982, p. 29; Costain and Costain, 1983, p. 199). These women may function as bridges, facilitating the integration of governmental institutions (McPherson, Miller, and Smith-Lovin, 1986, p. 75) with women-related concerns.

Finding public officials among these contemporary entrepreneurs (Kingdon, 1984, p. 214) also may help to explain the emphasis increasingly placed by women's issues groups on electing women to public office, if not through political action committees (PACs), then by educating members to involve themselves either as candidates or supporters of candidates outside the immediate group. One stunning example of the nonPAC strategy is found in Comision Femenil Mexicana Nacional*; still others, in United Methodist Women* and LWV. Viable approaches to electoral politics abound. The Gay and Lesbian Alliance Against Defamation* (GLAAD) monitors electoral candidates' remarks. The Young Women's Christian Association* (YWCA) mobilizes formidable voter registration projects. AARP VOTE has twelve staff and thousands of volunteers to inform elder citizens about the electoral process. Black sororities including Zeta Phi Beta* ready members for civic participation through a Black Women's Political Action Forum. The National Coalition of 100 Black Women* (NCBW) holds clinics to prepare workers to get out the vote. ERAmerica* finally involved itself in state-level races. Women's relatively depressed economic status works generally to reify this strategy and to limit the PAC one, which is, in any event, forbidden to 501 (c) (3) groups.

Women's issues groups overall do not present many PACs (see also Costain and Costain, 1983, p. 213). Eighteen of the 180 (1 percent) have a total of twenty-one national multicandidate PACs. Two of these are unattached. Reliance by the successful EMILY's List* on bundling suggests the degree of interest these groups set out to stimulate, which is understandable, given the gender gap's emergence (Klein, 1984, p. 163). WCF's refusal to fund more than one candidate per race suggests that these groups mean business. Growing out of a Women Elect 2000 project in Louisiana, the attached NOW/PAC's intention in the future to emphasize in-kind donations offers a tactical approach to limited economic wherewithal. Similarly, NASW Political Action for Candidate Election stresses professional skills in interpersonal relations, community organization, and volunteer action. Best funded are the five PACs attached to labor unions. NARAL PAC is among the top twenty wealthy ideological/single issue PACs; abortion figures prominently among the standards for endorsement of ten women's issues PACs. In fact, single-issue groups generally have found PACs to their taste (Hershey, 1984, pp. 154–55).

Klein has argued that the gender gap "placed women's concerns back on the public agenda" despite the Reagan administration's onset (1984, p. 28); and Barbara Burrell has shown that women and men candidates basically can raise the same amounts of money for their campaigns (1985). On one hand, in the manner of most PACs, the National Right to Life (NRL) PAC* prefers to endorse incumbents, whose issue stands are well established. The Consumer Federation of America* PAC endorses twice as many incumbents as challengers. On the other hand, because funding a female challenger is most cost-effective (Burrell, 1985, p. 264), NOW/PAC prefers open-seat candidates; and WCF, open- or new-seat candidates. Although WCF is the largest bipartisan national PAC to support women candidates, and NRL PAC, which will endorse either women or men, considers itself bipartisan as well, there is a tendency among these PACs to ally with the Democratic Party. The now-defunct Life Amendment PAC of the American Life Lobby* was an exception with its hit lists of pro-choice Democrats.

Women's economic status further declines as race and ethnicity are factored in. The presence in the women's issues arena of three African American women's groups focused on office holding—the National Black Women's Political Leadership Caucus* (NBWPLC), National Political Congress of Black Women, and National Organization of Black Elected Legislative Women—may reflect the situation and its own kind of politics. As Rhetaugh Graves Dumas has said, historically "it was only during periods of extreme stress that the value of the black woman's leadership outside of her women's groups could be realized" (1980, p. 204). However, the 1965 Voting Rights Act marked an opportunity for black candidates, including women, to attain elected office. Four percent (eight) of women's issues groups report significant ongoing interest in the act. The window of opportunity opened by the Voting Rights Act closed halfway through the seventies, leaving African Americans still underrepresented, and fewer African American women than men in public office, with white women no more or less likely than white men to perceive African American candidates as equally qualified with white ones for goal achievement (Williams, 1990, pp. 58–59)—hence, the need for such specialized organizations as these three, to accumulate social capital to extend their life spans,. This is particularly so, as they have no real counterparts.

Litigation

Karen O'Connor has written that resource-poor groups often litigate to overcome limitations in the legislative process (1980, p. 2). Such litigation can stimulate legislative and also executive action (Mezey, 1992, p. 4). Fifty of the 180 women's issues groups profiled (28 percent) cited litigation as a strategy they employ, with ten litigating strictly through amicus briefs to support a primary party to a suit. This finding suggests expansion by women's issues groups since 1980 of "outcome-oriented litigation" (O'Connor, 1980, p. 3), that is, an approach through test cases to building favorable case law. Eight organizations have a legal defense and education fund (LDEF), which somewhat systematizes the approach; seven associate regularly with an LDEF. Fifteen groups keep one or more attorneys on retainer; five have lawyers on their own staff. One group has a legal advisory board. Six groups rely on pro bono assistance. These arrangements with attorneys suggest a range to groups' abilities to be resourceful in the judicial arena, although their resources are evident. The consequence of the outcome in *Planned Parenthood of Southeastern Pennsylvania* v. *Casey* (1992) seemed to be lawsuits waiting to happen (Craig and O'Brien, 1993, p. 347), an opportunity for further growth in some women's issues groups' use of a litigation-based strategy. President Clinton's two appointments to the high court, though, may have slowed the tide.

Entrepreneurs

Organizers, that is, entrepreneurs, in the women's issues arena can be enormously talented. In 1990 *Business Week* recognized Alyce Faye Wattleton, PPF president 1978–92, as one of five top social service agency managers; and Byllye Avery, NBWHP founding president, has received a MacArthur Foundation "genius" award. Among the twenty-three most often mentioned organizers, about one-third have been salaried by the government and nearly half by their organizations. Smeal, a housewife, became NOW's first salaried president. The absence of at least extragroup subsidies (Salisbury, 1969, p. 26) may affect an organizer's inclination to continue her efforts, as the courses of the lives of Friedan and Seifer suggest. This situation may represent a maturation of the leadership as rational self-interested calculators, for Gelb's and Palley's earlier study found economic rewards less compelling (1982, p. 40). Ironically, this coming-of-age may not lead to materially well-compensated entrepreneurs, as excessive compensation for some executives in the nonprofit sector has helped stimulate policy proposals in the Congress for increased scrutiny and even outside approval of these salaries.

As might be expected, nowhere are the economic dimensions of organizer motivation more apparent than in NANBPW, a nonprofit business, or the Center for Surrogate Parenting,* a for-profit business; but the other-serving appearance of expressive activity in the women's issues arena can be deceiving. One strong historical case for this proposition is found in Bethune. As president of the National Association of Colored Women's Clubs (NACW), an office she assumed in 1924, she led the organization in raising $25,000 to purchase a headquarters building but ultimately invested her policy positions in NCNW, a new organization that she founded in 1935 and led as president for fourteen years. Her actions resulted in deep, enduring fractionation in the black women's club movement.

Satisfied leaders are important, though, because they make large contributions to group durability. NCNW remains a major player in the women's issues arena. To give a contemporary example, after serving two terms as chairone of NOW's board of directors and, in all, three as NOW's president, in 1987 Smeal invested her policy positions in forming FMF and has served as its president ever since. NOW's continuing influence cannot be denied; and FMF has been quite visible over its six-year life span.

Salisbury has observed that expressive groups characteristically break into factions (1969, p. 20); and this behavioral pattern seems to hold true for women's issues groups, too. For instance, Smeal's tenure in NOW depended on the outcome of an intense factional fight in the mid-seventies. The formation of both the Women's Equity Action League* (WEAL) and FFL occurred after factional fights among NOW leaders and active constituents over abortion. The WEAL leaders left voluntarily to pursue education- and employment-related goals; the FFL leaders were expelled. The NOW-New York City* (NOW-NYC) profile shows how bitter such divisions among elites can become. In the long run, an established group may benefit from the outcome of these divisions; but the losing faction will not necessarily benefit. This is because the established group was in place when adherents moved to reorient their loyalties. On one hand, WEAL finally folded; and FFL survives but is limited in size and impact. On the other hand, NOW-NYC, which was an established rather than a new group, survived and also seems recently to have reconciled with national NOW. The pending final separation of BBW from B'nai B'rith may pose a minimum of problems for BBW, because it, too, is an established group. The outcome of the Reproductive Freedom Project's departure from the ACLU seems less certain.

A material benefit group such as ILGWU does not demonstrate this kind of division. Its leadership is long lasting—and male. As is the case in the other American Federation of Labor-Congress of Industrial Organizations* affiliates profiled in this collection, active female members seeking elite decision-making posts enter a slow succession process. Women in these organizations likely will withdraw from activities that threaten their access to the material benefits membership confers—as UAW Women's Department* leaders did from NOW when it sought ERA's ratification before UAW changed its position opposing the proposed amendment. These loyal, active material benefit group members will, though, act to form a supplemental group of their own such as the Coalition of Labor Union Women* (CLUW), bringing with them their union's support; and their unions will contribute to other women's issues groups pursuing complementary goals but usually avoid the abortion controversy to avoid sacrificing resources. Under these circumstances, an innovative but independent group like Union WAGE* was hard-pressed to survive and, in fact, did not. Nine to Five,* however, connected with the Service Employees International Union* and survived.

All this begs the explicit question, To what actual extent do women's issues groups pursue ends deriving from their entrepreneurs' preferences? Among the 180, membership groups constitute 55.6 percent of the total. Only 5 percent of them poll the membership to help determine group policy preferences; and just 15 percent characterize their conventions as delegate-based assemblies. Twenty-eight percent of them do membership education rather than vice versa. Thirty-nine percent of them do public education. Only four groups (3 percent) claim their policy positions are limited by the membership. It seems par for the course that when Pamela Maraldo assumed PPF's presidency, she began working to move the nation's biggest source of contraception-related health care toward more explicit ties with national-level health care reform. Maraldo came to PPF from the National League for Nursing* (NLN). Overall, entrepreneurs have ample space to pursue their preferences.

MOBILIZATION

Someone has to pay the bill for engagement through one or more organizations in the socialization of conflict and policy-making process. The incentives most commonly seen as attracting potential constituents, in return for their contributions and/or membership fees, are policy advocacy, which is expressive or nontangible, and publications and information, which can be material or tangible but always is expressive. Fifty percent of groups profiled offered each of these particular incentives. Next most perceived as incentives were association with like-minded persons (by 42 percent of these women's issues groups) and conferences and meetings (35 percent). These are solidary incentives. One-fifth to one-quarter of these women's issues groups also see communication, representation of opinions to government, development of organizational skills, and even potentially controversial friendship ties as useful in attracting new members and contributors.

It falls upon the organizers to mobilize members and contributors from among potential constituents. Women in the United States are among the most participatory in voluntary associations (Almond and Verba, 1963, pp. 303–4; see also Pateman, 1980, p. 74), lending themselves to the task of integration to share preferences (Costain, 1982, p. 27). Unfortunately, mass constituents generally do not control vast resources, although it has been shown that volunteers donate more money than nonvolunteers (McCarthy and Zald, 1977, p. 1224). Altering this relatively limited access to resources may not be 501 (c) (4) women's issues membership groups' highest priority because, given the decision to forgo tax-deductible contributions, perhaps they do not expect much more—except through tandem organization. In any event, women's issues membership groups have access to a stable source of resources. As there are only so many members and limited membership fees to rely on, maintaining and maximizing access to them are the priority. (In this survey of women's issues groups, only TLI expressed openly its dissatisfaction with tax laws affecting charitable giving.) Based on incomplete information, at least 34 percent of these women's issues membership groups rely on fees of twenty-six dollars or more, 14 percent on twelve- to twenty-five-dollar fees. Thirty-three percent of these groups have memberships no larger than 1,000; 18 percent, no larger than 10,000; 25 percent, between 10,001 and 99,999; and 17 percent, 100,000 and above.

Bystander Publics

Under these circumstances, ''converting bystander publics'' (McCarthy and Zald, 1977, p. 1223) to maximize resource aggregation becomes a concern. Virtually every contemporary majority white women's organization profiled here has undertaken efforts to convert African American women, with 26 percent of the nongovernmental Anglicized groups engaging strongly in such efforts. Issues of gender, race, ethnicity, and class readily are shown to intersect; and Clyde Wilcox has shown black women to favor governmental initiatives against sexism partly because they support initiatives against racism (1990). African American women's contributions to white women's organizations and the women's movement are legion (Slavin, 1990; Evans, 1989, pp. 297–98; Giddings, 1984, pp.

302–3), although initially Anglo women's organizations were not quick to integrate African American women's shared preferences.

A parallel historical black woman's club movement was assured, and not only by the long-standing separation in the United States of white and black communities and institutions. Although Alpha Kappa Alpha* formed the first civil rights lobby, and black women occupied "the mainstream of civil rights activities in diverse contexts" (Bryan, 1988, p. 60), black clubwomen also have undertaken significant self-help programs—whether historically to assist newly freed persons, or contrabands as they were known, in a group such as the national Contraband Relief Association, or contemporarily, to improve their own health through NBWHP. One impetus to found NACW lay in championing African American women's reputations. The need to meet urban community needs—so pressing that one scholar has seen this activity as "holding back the ocean with a broom" (Gilkes, 1980)—motivated founders of such groups as the National Urban League Guild* (NULG). The U.S. government's only sporadic attentions, along with the need for an antiracist overview, worked to continue this self-help approach.

Further, African American women's groups do not show sustained interest in converting mainly white women's groups. None of the boards of directors of African American women's issues groups profiled here are said to include white women. In 1992 the National Association of Black Women Attorneys undertook a membership drive "to make our Organization one for **all minorities**" (form letter of April 1992 from Mabel D. Haden; emphasis added), a more typical development than African American women entrepreneurs actively seeking shared preferences with Anglo women. Understandably, the perception may be that outreach to Anglo women's groups will prove disappointing. Before a 1992 NOW-led march for reproductive rights, for instance, seven women of color groups joined in a letter to progressive groups to criticize NOW for not straightforwardly facing problems with inclusion, despite the march's cosponsorship by NCNW, NCBW, and the Women of Color Partnership. This would not be a situation likely to endear itself to community-minded organizers, because such divisiveness is diverting (Gilkes, 1980, p. 225).

Therefore, organizers for majority Anglo women's issues groups—seeking to convert potential African American women constituents into adherents of their own target goals for social capital purposes—have faced an uphill battle. The battle is portentous because black women demonstrate more liberalism on both ERA and feminist awareness than white women do (Wilcox, 1990). Virtually no contemporary majority Anglo women's issues group has failed to give some priority to this "conversion" process. Between 1987 and 1991, the Women's Research and Education Institute's* annual report, *The American Woman,* increased from two to five the chapters devoted to women of color, an act reflecting the high degree of interest in these potential constituents.

Besides such target goals as NCPE's advocacy of pay equity for people of color, this kind of prioritizing has necessitated consciousness-raising within majority white women's organizations and reform of dilatory structures and procedures. The National Women's Studies Association* (NWSA) nearly has prostrated itself in the process, turning on one occasion to the National Congress of Neighborhood Women* for help. The congress has found it must focus on the community, as opposed to national, level to maintain its gains here; and the 501 (c) (4) NWSA has directed almost no attention to the kinds of national issues it well might address, including academic freedom and censure in the award of federal grants by the National Endowment for the Arts.

Success stories do exist. For example, the National Assembly of Religious Women* has met its commitment to inclusion with 45–55 percent of those attending its conferences coming from racial/ethnic groups. The Houston women's conference was made up of a highly diverse group of delegates chosen through fifty preceding state-level conferences. Twenty percent of board members of the related National Women's Conference Center* come from racial/ethnic groups. An organization with a little over 7 percent of its board members from racial or ethnic groups and an uncertain proportion of its membership from them, the Association of Junior Leagues International* (AJLI) has hired an African American woman, Karen Hendricks, to direct its Washington, D.C., public policy office to serve as its registered lobbyist, suggesting concern with its noninclusive image overall and appreciation for an inclusive relationship as well as for Hendricks's substantial ability. Also at the elite level, in 1971, CWU elected an African American woman, Clarie Harvey, president; ALA followed with Clara C. Jones, in 1976. An African American consultant and former Equal Employment Opportunity Commission member, Aileen Hernandez, succeeded Friedan as NOW's second president.

The large traditional majority white women's organizations varied in their willingness as survey respondents to expose the internal struggles they have faced in reaching out to African American women, but all willingly described related contemporary programs. Even the YWCA, which has accomplished a good deal here, faced historical problems integrating "colored" YWCAs. ANA's affiliates discriminated by color; but ANA in 1949 absorbed the National Association of Colored Graduate Nurses. Nonetheless, NBNA emerged, 1971–72, outside ANA. Not until the mid-1960s did the Women's Christian Temperance Union* (WCTU) abolish its separate Sojourner Truth chapters, named after one of its founders. Today just 11 percent of the profiled women's issues groups remain all or mainly white.

Nonbeneficiary Constituents

Women's issues groups have sought to convert men, essentially nonbeneficiary constituents. In 1981, CCWI expanded to include men, prompted by financial needs exacerbated by House rules changes. NOW's male membership has grown overall to 11 percent, assisted in the past by a solidary incentive, masculine mystique task forces in the chapters that wanted them. Concerned

Women for America's* (CWA) male membership has reached 10 percent. In 1976, LWV converted to full voting status the men among its members; but only 3 percent of the members are men. Women in Communications* admitted men to membership in 1972; AAUW in 1987. TLI admits men, as "connecting links." Today only 40 percent of these women's issues membership groups are mainly or all women (90 percent, or more, female).

The conversion of men may take routes other than membership. Zeta Phi Beta,* for example, has affiliated with a fraternity, Phi Beta Sigma. NBWPLC created a men's auxiliary. ACT UP WC formed within the mostly male ACT UP New York. The National Organization for Men against Sexism* developed as an altogether separate organization; women serve in the leadership collective. Alternate routes work to bypass the conflict that can result from differences in women's and men's loyalties, allowing pressures toward cosmopolitanism to prevail (McPherson, Miller, and Smith-Lovin, 1986). BBW's and B'nai B'rith's impending final split suggests the extent to which this conflict can go; the National Welfare Rights Organization's* and Association of Intercollegiate Athletics for Women's respective demises suggest that failing to bypass it may prove deadly. The national scope of these women's issues groups also may facilitate this conversion process, although previous findings to this effect are not consistent (McPherson and Smith-Lovin, 1986, p. 65).

Lesbian Potential Constituents

Lesbians, their concerns torn between women's and homosexual issues, virtually inherit bystander public status. The profiles for Daughters of Bilitis* and the Mattachine Society* show the problems that arise from this situation. Despite the problems, NOW has moved toward full integration of preferences shared with lesbians and, in 1993, cosponsored the March on Washington. Attorney Patricia Ireland, NOW's current president, is herself a lesbian. Not quite 8 percent (13) of the predominately nongay/lesbian women's issues groups in this collection (172) do outreach to lesbians. The overrepresentation of lesbians among the leadership of profiled organizations with majority gay male members suggests not only the motivation gay male organizers experience to work with lesbians but also a lack of satisfaction presented by women's issues groups from the lesbian organizer's perspective.

EXCHANGE RELATIONS

The need organizations have to pay the bills influences the emphasis they may place in practice on First Amendment free speech and press-related policy, demonstrating yet again that exchange relations cut across women's agenda items. AAUW, for one, routinely places First Amendment issues on its agenda. The ACLU grew from just such concerns. NOW actively participated in the seventies' media reform movement (Slavin and Pendleton, 1983). Sensitivity to the link among means of communication, the civil liberties that undergird the U.S. political system and cost factors seems especially evident in American Women in Radio and Television's* advocacy for revision of the Federal Communication Commission's multiple radio ownership rules—contingent on women's inclusion as program beneficiaries. WIFP long has had as its motto: "Freedom of the press belongs to those who own the press." Support by GLAAD for positive imagery of women in sport demonstrates the crossover among speech-related activities for advocacy purposes, press as technology for doing outreach to a bystander public such as women in sport—some of whom, like women owning radio stations, command substantial resources—and positive imagery as a means of communication. Tennis-great Martina Navratilova's increasingly high profile in pursuing lesbian/gay rights suggests the wisdom of this approach. The media's constitutional and commercial interests nonetheless may render these approaches highly conflict-laden activity.

The Feminist Anti-Censorship Task Force* (FACT) has worked to defeat legislative initiatives to limit sexual imagery, partly because feminists themselves have interests in purveying sexual imagery but also doubtless because a favorable relationship with the press cuts costs. Despite conflict among feminists over the pornography issue (Gubar and Hoff, 1989), support for antipornography legislation tends to come from a group such as ALL, or for reform in violent and sexually exploitative programming, from CWA. Why? Because groups such as these have the potential to mobilize constituents through these policy stands. An organization like FACT even may rationalize resistance to antipornography preferences on grounds of the constituents involved. One women's issues groups project author expressed dismay that an organization she profiled took a stand on children's programming.

Isolated Conscience Constituents

FACT happens not to be a membership organization. Its funding sources include small fund-raisers and individual contributors, but its greatest appeal is to isolated conscience constituents. Isolated constituents tend to commit a group to generating the media's attention to reach them (McCarthy and Zald, 1977, p. 1229), which for FACT is fortuitous but also works to render FACT the media's captive audience. NOW began in much the same mode as FACT but moved within one year to setting up chapters such as NOW-NYC to bring isolated constituents together. NOW's early period is marked by reliance on media coverage (Freeman, 1975, p. 73) and also public service campaigns. Twelve and one-half percent of the 180 women's issues groups conduct these campaigns, thereby reaching out to isolated constituents. Like NOW, NWPC proceeded to form chapters; initially, neither group found this to be easy (Costain, 1982, pp. 22–23).

Early in the woman's club movement, GFWC and NACW took another, related approach to resource mobilization, federating already existing groups, as did LWV in 1920 with at least some preexisting suffrage associations (see also Schneider and Schneider, 1993, pp. 98–100). Not incidentally, Skocpol et al. have shown the significant influence federation has had on social policy enactment (1993). Overall, few (6 percent) of the profiled women's issues groups resulted from federating preexisting groups. Federation nonetheless is quick and offers more stable access to resources than reliance on isolated constituents does. The Mexican American Legal Defense and Educational Fund Chicana Rights Project,* for example, foundered when its isolated conscience constituents, especially the Ford Foundation, shifted to other preferences. NCADV itself withdrew from an isolated conscience constituent with incompatible preferences, Johnston and Johnston, destabilizing its own national domestic violence hot line: Not surprisingly, NCADV devotes noticeable amounts of attention to obtaining free media coverage. The ANA has federated since 1982, testimony to the relationship between success in the women's issues policy arena and stable access to social capital.

Contributions from outside an organization to enhance resource aggregation include foundation support (17 percent of these groups receive it in more than nominal amounts) and corporate donations (5 percent of the groups receive it). Such conscience constituents do not benefit directly; but women's issues group recipients do. For example, NANBPW received a $500,000 grant from W. K. Kellogg Corporation, which it characterizes as the largest ever received by a major African American women's group. NBWHP received $1 million, twice, to set up and continue three housing project community centers. FFM received $1 million from an "angel." Depending on the funding source involved, professionalization characterized from 63 percent to 89 percent of these recipients. AARP with its matrix management style and the highly professionalized Women in Governmental Relations* (WGR) remain models for emulation. It is said that where conscience constituents have sufficient resources, social movement industry can develop (McCarthy and Zald, 1977, p. 1225). In the women's issues groups case, social movement industry largely has developed without them.

Membership Organizations

Only 4 percent of the profiled women's issues groups have a declining membership, compared with 17 percent with dynamic memberships and 79 percent with a static number of members. Even allowing for occasional reports suggesting that some groups were not forthcoming in describing membership change—NWPC was one group for which conflicting reports were received—the numbers overall suggest stable, if not growing, memberships. Nonetheless, some groups are in decline and taking steps to try to counteract their losses. CWU, which has lost 56 percent of its units since 1970, has expanded its membership to include Catholic women among Protestants and abandoned its abortion position in the process; it also gives state and local units substantial policy-making input, presumably to stimulate constituent activists to help maintain membership levels. Two other declining traditional membership organizations, WCTU and NACW, have youth groups to influence future loyalty. The National Federation of Business and Professional Women's Clubs/USA,* the largest of the associations formed in the social feminist era, has lost 50 percent of its members since 1984; 61 percent of GFWC's units have disappeared since 1975. To enhance the outcome of exchange relations, both LWV and GFWC have increased dues, the latter by 100 percent in 1994, from two to four dollars. LWV increasingly has pushed local decision making as its membership has declined.

Organizations increasing in membership include not only such African American women's groups as Sigma Gamma Rho* (founded between 1915 and 1922) and Zeta Phi Beta* (founded in 1920) but also the Mexican American Women's National Association* (founded in 1974), National Conference of Puerto Rican Women* (founded in 1972) and Black, Indian, Hispanic and Asian Women in Action* (founded in 1983). GLAAD (1985) and NGLTF (1973) have increased their memberships, too. Professional groups with widely separated formation dates, such as AAP, NASW, NCSL WN, WGR, and the Women's Caucus for Political Science* (WCPS), are growing. AFSCME (1932) and NCPE (1977) are growing. So is CFA (1966). Likewise, NARAL (1969) and the National Abortion Federation* (1977) have grown. One traditional women's organization, Zonta International,* has grown, and NOW-NYC has as well; but constituent growth seems to favor issue specialization.

One resource controlled by the individual constituent is her own time. Depending on their life-cycle stage, potential constituents may decide they have limited time to give to voluntary associations, despite their propensity to participate—a factor that has much influenced AJLI in its mobilization efforts. Both type of employment and fact of motherhood can operate on choices here. In fact, it is known that, although women's political interest levels do not vary by whether they belong to the paid workforce, political participation increases after women take on gainful employment (Andersen and Cook, 1985). Through groups such as WCPS or NASW or the umbrella of the Federation of Professional Women's Organizations,* women have merged their employment with associational activity. The prominence of the abortion conflict suggests the ambivalence attending motherhood in this day and age, with *United Autoworkers v. Johnson Controls* (1991) a stark example of contemporary priorities.

The potential contituent controls her labor, along with her time. She may decide within her time constraints to volunteer. In making voluntarism her project as first lady, the late Patricia Nixon addressed this tendency—and NOW rebuked her, seeking, unsuccessfully, to distinguish the unpaid labor women traditionally have contributed and labor volunteered to achieve target goals. Women officeholders' organizations, perhaps better than most, display the fruitful role labor volunteered to achieve target goals can play. The fact that few of these 180 groups have a primarily service orientation suggests that the distinction NOW sought has made itself felt despite the controversy over saying so.

The continuance of service-based groups at all may reflect the presence of such an agenda item as housing, fraught with implications for resource-poor beneficiaries. TLI figures prominently as an outlet for the service-based ambitions of middle- to upper middle-class African American women, linking ends and constituents but disconnecting them when it comes to the service orientation itself.

Feminists

It is suggested that, as a group's resources grow, it turns increasingly to task specialization and, hence, leader and staff professionalization (McCarthy and Zald, 1977, p. 1234). It is true that the 180 groups here generally have highly formalized structures. Kathleen Iannello contends, though, that regardless of legal status, feminist organizations may develop modified consensus structures and decision-making procedures (1992). Ostensibly, these would promote independent action and mitigate against the leadership. Asking if organizations can avoid duplicating the hierarchy and bureaucracy of certain inherited systems (p. 13), Iannello concludes that feminist interventions have led to opportunities for consensus-based organization by distinguishing critical and routine decisions, maximizing skill and empowerment and minimizing authority, and clarifying goals. She bases her conclusions mainly on three case studies.

The women's issues groups project offers some evidence to support Iannello's conclusion. Many of these groups innovate in their offices. For example, ALA's Washington office features job rotation with differing levels of responsibility. NOW's National Action Center employs no executive director. At Network* and the National Assembly of Religious Women,* all staff receive the same pay. This is so for ACLU's Washington office also. Women Strike for Peace* stresses participation and consensus. The Federation of Feminist Women's Health Centers* (FFWHC) is unique among the profiled groups in its high degree of adherence to consensual structures and procedures, whereas profiled right-wing women's issues groups do not eschew hierarchical and bureaucratic systems. The groups ranged widely between FFWHC and the right wing show a propensity to introduce modified consensus into leadership hierarchies and staffing arrangements. Perceived risk to organizational efficiency—that is, how many resources it takes to produce what a group produces—seems not to deter this experimentation. Neither does the risk of being labeled feminist, which, after all, may serve to attract new, young members (Costain, 1982, p. 27).

McCarthy and Zald have argued that "the need for skills in lobbying, accounting, and fund raising leads to professionalization" (1977, p. 1234). But ALA, NOW, and Network* are all listed in *The 1990 American Lobbyists Directory.* One explanation for women's issues groups' willingness to experiment with consensual organization despite the need for, and cultivation of, lobbying skills lies in the extent to which tax law limits lobbying activities for many of them. They all routinely exercise care to avoid the appearance of exceeding these constraints; for example, only 8 percent (eleven) admitted to having registered lobbyists in their offices, when the lobbyists directory includes 13 percent (twenty-four) of them. Outside these constraints, they can afford to feel comfortable with experimentation. Where NOW, for example, allows only its four elected officers to lobby, NASW has a lobbying committee. AJLI, MADD, and others have the equivalent of public policy directors charged with this responsibility; AARP has a Spokespersons Program. NLN works with ANA lobbyists. NLN, ANA, AJLI, and AARP are found in the lobbyists directory.

Also, some women's issues groups have become or are becoming professionalized in their fund-raising activities and, by keeping them separate from consensual experiments, do not threaten resource mobilization. However, 37 percent of groups receiving foundation support and 11 percent receiving corporate help have not noticeably professionalized. As Gelb and Palley have said, based on their smaller sample, organized feminism is professionalized but refutes "the view . . . that bureaucratization . . . [will] replace a movement's initial momentum" toward change (1982, pp. 23–24). This is a different situation from what developed in the woman's club movement of the 1920s (Lemons, 1973, p. 41). Women's liberation movement organizations look institutionalized but escape certain of the limits of institutionalization.

As Iannello (1992) suggests, feminists well may stimulate this experimental motive. The twenty-three most-mentioned contemporary leaders include one prominent antifeminist and perhaps three nonfeminists; the remainder clearly self-identify as feminists. These women readily cross organizational boundaries. They and others like them, including constituent activists, would be important because relatively few women's issues groups are overtly feminist, even if they are receptive to feminism (Costain, 1982, p. 26; Gelb and Palley, 1982, p. 4). Smeal's FFM uses the word "majority" in its title in basically a Leninist sense: to confront control of major social, economic, and political institutions by a [male] minority. Gerda Lerner has shown that, historically, feminism functions as part of the larger women's movement (1971); it is not the movement per se. The National Black Feminist Organization,* founded in 1973 and disbanded about 1979, characterized itself as a feminist organization before NOW itself did. Las Hermanas* uses the word *mujerista* to describe its feminist activist stance but not in its name. In contrast to FFWHC or FACT, a feminist organization such as NCADV does not proclaim its identification in its name. In all, four of the profiled organizations do; most feminist organizations—including CLUW, Delta Sigma Theta,* NCJW, OWL, NWPC, the UAW WD, and UUWF—are, relatively speaking, more discreet.

Salisbury has suggested that leaders will spend surplus profits on personal choices and values (1969, p. 277). This appears to be one of those situations. The demise of a group such as the feminist Women's Housing Coalition may have resulted partly from a lack of surplus profits. Leaders' " 'free votes' " (p. 28) may or may not conform with constituents' wishes but help underpin group durability. Not incidentally, these particular free votes offer leaders a sterling opportunity to farm their constituents.

CONCLUSION

The status of women presents many disparities from men's status, and their status varies among women. Central political processes have yielded agendas of policy solutions to these problems, most significantly through the Houston women's conference. Alternative solutions have presented through other women's issues groups. Increasingly assuming tandem identities stimulated by federal tax law, these groups also include such elite governmental organizations as CCWI. Across the 1980s, the leadership of these groups may have become more based in rational, self-interested calculation than in public service. But, the profiled women's issues groups seem quite durable, with 47 percent (eighty-five) of them formed before 1970 and most of the rest coming in 1970–80, during the second half of what Berry calls "the advocacy explosion" (1989, p. 18). Established groups survive the factionalization typical of expressive organization, and the survival rate of these groups overall seems high. Further, half these groups are membership-based. Around 4 percent of them have declining memberships, but 17 percent have grown over the eighties, when these particular groups well might not have. It is well known that lasting organization results from satisfied entrepreneurs, and these profiles do not contradict that premise.

Growth among women's issues groups has come in the direction of specialization but not bureaucratization. Membership fees more than donations by conscience constituents characterize funding arrangements and help these groups maintain their independence. They network widely, if generally among themselves. Three percent of these groups also work closely with the Leadership Conference on Civil Rights, the National Association for the Advancement of Colored People, and National Urban League. Specialized networking has become de rigeur around the abortion issue. Continued success by majority white women's organizations in converting African American women—as so-called bystander publics—to shared preferences will strengthen central concerns, especially for amending the U.S. Constitution to guarantee equality of rights by sex. It also will help to maximize stable resource aggregation practices.

REFERENCES

Almond, Gabriel, and Sidney Verba. *The Civic Culture: Political Attitudes and Democracy in Five Nations.* Princeton, NJ: Princeton University Press, 1963.

Andersen, Kristi, and Elizabeth A. Cook. "Women, Work, and Political Attitudes." *American Journal of Political Science* 29 (1985): 606–25.

Berry, Jeffrey. *The Interest Group Society,* 2d ed. Glenview, IL: Scott, Foresman, 1989.

Boneparth, Ellen, ed. *Women, Power and Policy.* New York: Pergamon Press, 1982.

Bryan, Dianette Gail. "Her-Story Unsilenced: Black Female Activists in the Civil Rights Movement." *Sage* 2 (Fall 1988): 60.

Burrell, Barbara C. "Women's and Men's Campaigns for the U.S. House of Representatives, 1972–1982: A Finance Gap?" *American Politics Quarterly* 13 (July 1985): 251–72.

Costain, Anne. "Representing Women: The Transition from Social Class to Interest Group." In Ellen Boneparth, ed., *Women, Power and Policy.* New York: Pergamon Press, 1982, 19–37.

———, and W. Douglas Costain. "The Women's Lobby: Impact of a Movement on Congress." In Allan J. Cigler and Burdett A. Loomis, eds., *Interest Group Politics.* Washington, DC: CQ Press, 1983, 191–216.

Craig, Barbara Hinkson, and David M. O'Brien. *Abortion and American Politics.* Chatham, NJ: Chatham House, 1993.

Dumas, Rhetaugh Graves. "Dilemmas of Black Females in Leadership." In La Frances Rodgers-Rose, ed., *The Black Woman.* Beverly Hills, CA: Sage, 1980, 203–15.

Evans, Sarah. *Born for Liberty: A History of Women in America.* New York: Free Press, 1989.

Everett, Kevin Djo. "Professionalism and Protest: Changes in the Social Movement Sector, 1961–1983." *Social Forces* 70 (June 1992): 957–75.

Franke, Richard J. "Public Service—An American Tradition at the Crossroad. The Charles S. Hyneman Lecture." Urbana-Champaign: University of Illinois Department of Political Science, 1989.

Freeman, Jo. *The Politics of Women's Liberation.* New York: McKay, 1975.

Gelb, Joyce, and Marian Lief Palley. *Women and Public Policies.* Princeton, NJ: Princeton University Press, 1982.

Giddings, Paula. *When and Where I Enter: The Impact of Black Women's Race and Sex in America.* Toronto, Canada: Bantam Books, 1984.

Gilkes, Cheryl Townsend. "Holding Back the Ocean with a Broom: Black Women and Community Work." In La Frances Rodgers-Rose, ed., *The Black Woman.* Beverly Hills, CA: Sage, 1980, 217–31.

Griffith, Elisabeth. *In Her Own Right: The Life of Elizabeth Cady Stanton.* New York: Oxford University Press, 1984.

Gubar, Susan, and Joan Hoff, eds. *For Adult Users Only: The Dilemma of Violent Pornography.* Bloomington: Indiana University Press, 1989.

Heblom, Milda K. *Women and American Political Organizations and Institutions.* Washington, DC: American Political Science Association, July 1983.

Hershey, Marjorie Randon. *Running for Office: The Political Education of Campaigners.* Chatham, NJ: Chatham House, 1984.

Iannello, Kathleen. *Decisions without Hierarchy: Feminist Interventions in Organization Theory and Practice.* New York: Routledge, 1992.

Kendrigan, Mary Lou. "Progressive Democrats and Support for Women's Issues." In James MacGregor Burns et al., *The Democrats Must Lead: The Case for a Progressive Democratic Party.* Boulder, CO: Westview Press, 1992, 157–71.

Kingdon, John W. *Agendas, Alternatives, and Public Policies.* Boston: Little, Brown, 1984.

Klein, Ethel. *Gender Politics: From Consciousness to Mass Politics.* Cambridge, MA: Harvard University Press, 1984.

Lemons, J. Stanley. *The Woman Citizen: Social Feminism in the 1920s.* Urbana: University of Illinois Press, 1973.

Lerner, Gerda. "Women's Rights and American Feminism." *The American Scholar* 40 (Spring 1971): 235–48.

McCarthy, John D., and Mayer N. Zald. "Resource Mobilization and Social Movements: A Partial Theory." *American Journal of Sociology* 82: 6 (1977): 1212–41.

McPherson, J. Miller, and Lynn Smith-Lovin. "Sex Segregation in Voluntary Associations." *American Sociological Review* 51 (February 1986): 61–79.

Marshall, Susan E. "Ladies Against Women: Mobilization Dilemmas of Antifeminist Movements." *Social Problems* 32 (April 1985): 348–62.

Mezey, Susan Gluck. *In Pursuit of Equality: Women, Public Policy, and the Federal Courts.* New York: St. Martin's Press, 1992.

O'Connor, Karen. *Women's Organizations' Use of the Courts.* Lexington, MA: Lexington Books, 1980.

Pateman, Carole. *The Civic Culture: A Philosophic Critique.* In Gabriel A. Almond and Sidney Verba, eds., *The Civic Culture Revisited.* Boston: Little, Brown, 1980, 57–102.

Peterson, Mark, and Jack Walker. "Interest Group Response to Partisan Change: Impact of the Reagan Administration upon the National Interest Group System." In Allen Cigler and Burt Loomis, eds., *Interest Group Politics.* Washington, DC: CQ Press, 1983, 162–82.

Rodriguez-Trias, Helen. "Women's Health, Women's Lives, Women's Rights." *American Journal of Public Health* 82 (May 1992): 663.

Rosenberg, Rina. "Representing Women at the State and Local Levels: Commissions on the Status of Women." In Ellen Boneparth, ed., *Women, Power and Policy.* New York: Pergamon Press, 1982, 38–46.

Salisbury, Robert. "An Exchange Theory of Interest Groups." *Midwest Journal of Political Science* 13 (February 1969): 1–32.

———, John P. Heinz, Edward O. Laumann, and Robert L. Nelson. "Who Works with Whom? Interest Group Alliances and Opposition." *American Political Science Review* 81 (December 1987): 1217–34.

Skocpol, Theda, Christopher Howard, Susan Goodrich Lehmann, and Marjorie Abend-Wein. "Women's Associations and the Enactment of Mother's Pensions in the United States." *American Political Science Review* 87 (September 1993): 686–701.

Slavin, Sarah. Review of Cynthia Harrison, *On Account of Sex: The Politics of Women's Issues 1945–1968.* Berkeley: University of California Press, 1988. *National Political Science Review* 2 (1990): 264–67.

———, and M. Stephen Pendleton. "Feminism and the FCC." In John Havick, *Communications Policy and the Political Process.* Westport, CT: Greenwood Press, 1983, 127–47.

Walker, Jack L. "The Origins and Maintenance of Interest Groups in America." *American Political Science Review* 77 (June 1983): 390–406.

"Who's Sorry Now? Women of Color Protest Pro-Choice March." *Ms.* 3 (July/August 1992): 82.

Wilcox, Clyde. "Feminism and Anti-Feminism among Evangelical Women." *Western Political Quarterly* 42 (March 1989): 147–60.

———. "Race, Gender Role Attitudes and Support for Feminism." *Western Political Quarterly* 43 (March 1990): 113–21.

Williams, Linda. "White/Black Perceptions of the Electability of Black Political Candidates." *National Political Science Review* 2 (1990): 45–64.

"The Woman Activist" 20 (September 9, 1990): 1.

A
/

ACT UP NEW YORK
See AIDS COALITION TO UNLEASH POWER WOMEN'S CAUCUS

ACT UP WOMEN'S CAUCUS
See AIDS COALITION TO UNLEASH POWER WOMEN'S CAUCUS

AD HOC COALITION FOR LOW INCOME HOUSING
See NATIONAL LOW INCOME HOUSING COALITION

AIDS COALITION TO UNLEASH POWER WOMEN'S CAUCUS (ACT UP WC)
135 W. 29th Street
10th Floor
New York, NY 10001
(212) 564-2437
FAX (212) 989-1797

The leader and initiator of the struggle to access clinical trials for women and identify and develop treatments for women-specific symptoms of AIDS, the AIDS Coalition to Unleash Power (ACT UP) Women's Caucus (WC) seeks representation for women, people of color, and injection drug users in the institutional and citizen-level politics of HIV/AIDS.

ORIGIN AND DEVELOPMENT

Beginning in the summer of 1987, six lesbians active in ACT UP New York began ''dyke dinners'' as forums for discussing a tendency to bypass class, race, and gender issues endemic in the AIDS crisis, and their own status in a predominately men's organization. Amy Bauer, Jean Carlomusto, Maria Maggenti, Illith Roseblum, Gerri Wells, and Maxine Wolfe had been training AIDS activists in civil disobedience techniques or serving on ACT UP's outreach committee. An article in January 1988 *Cosmopolitan* stimulated them to take the lead in founding a women's caucus. The suggestion, by a psychiatrist, that women were not vulnerable to HIV through unprotected vaginal sex chilled the group, which knew not only the demographics of HIV/AIDS and women—2,000 cases, 26 percent apparently the result of unprotected vaginal sex—but also the tendency to view women as merely "vectors" transmitting infection to men or fetuses. The group also realized the lack of support mechanisms—interpersonal and funding—available to these women.

The women in the supper group felt concern that women with HIV/AIDS took even greater risks than most similarly situated men in becoming visible on the issues. Among other things, at stake was child custody. But all that *Cosmo*'s author found troubling were limitations placed by condom use on male sexual expression. Caucus founders feared that by relaying misinformation, he placed countless readers at risk. A subsequent meeting with the author revealed stereotypy and poor factual command. In response, ACT UP's new WC undertook informational picketing before *Cosmo*/Hearst headquarters. Despite a bitterly cold day, 150 picketers distributed 5,000 fact sheets to passersby at noon and netted wide coverage on television news and the talk show circuit. Carlomusto and Maggenti made a widely shown video, *AIDS Activists Say No to Cosmo*. The founders went on that spring to Shea Stadium and a Mets game, handing out 10,000 fact sheets and 5,000 condoms to warn the 22,000 attending and the millions watching via C-SPAN that "AIDS IS NOT A BALLGAME. HERE'S THE SCORE."

The issues surrounding women with HIV/AIDS reached social agendas literally, and the percentage of women in ACT UP increased. The WC reached out with a fact sheet and safer sex forum to the lesbian community, popularly regarded as inviolable by the pandemic, an unwarranted assumption. The U.S. Centers for Disease Control (CDC) had identified eighty-two lesbian and eighty-two bisexual women with HIV/AIDS; five lesbians belonged to no identified risk group. ACT UP's membership grew again. It was a short step to conventional political agendas as three federal institutions played particularly key roles in the crisis, besides CDC, the Social Security Administration (SSA), and National Institute of Allergy and Infectious Diseases (NIAID). Pressuring these agencies brought WC further into contact with women with HIV/AIDS and led to further integration of ACT UP. Many AIDS activists had become women with HIV/AIDS.

Caucus members stood at the center of a significant information flow that they set into motion and recognized the critical nature of sharing and expanding their knowledge base. Men in ACT UP were not informed about either institutional sexism or women and health. CDC then published no surveillance statistics on women's symptoms or injection drug users, but women experienced women-specific symptoms and primarily acquired AIDS by needle sharing. The WC reviewed the literature and learned lessons working with women with HIV/AIDS and health care delivery persons. It set out to provide women with a safe place in ACT UP; collect and distribute information about AIDS-related women's issues; press government for assurances, funding, epidemiology, study, treatment, and prevention—for women—along with accessible, quality health care; and put forward the voice and personae of women with HIV/AIDS.

The caucus's motivation has not lessened. Ninety-three percent of AIDS-related research subjects are white gay men who are not injection drug users. Yet tolerances for antivirals and drugs to treat opportunistic infections may vary. Nonsensitivity to women as independent persons is evident in drug trials emphasizing prevention of transmission from a woman to her fetus. Reproductive choice issues receive ambivalent attention. Stereotypes abound: African American women and Latinas among AIDS activists are assumed heterosexual and mothers; white female AIDS activists, lesbians and childless. The former presumptively have HIV/AIDS; the latter supposedly do not.

ORGANIZATION AND FUNDING

ACT UP Network connects a series of autonomous groups without a central structure; the groups are oriented toward change and do not worry about stability. The network has committees, including a 100-member women's action (formerly issues) committee that gets information out to women in peer education projects and HIV support groups. Women's caucuses have organized in ACT UP chapters other than New York. All function independently with their own processes and procedures. They have no standing committees but form ad hoc ones, for example, to produce a publication. The caucus has received all its revenues through ACT UP by making proposals to the coordinating committee or from the floor. It, too, has organized fund-raisers and passed the hat. In this way it has funded HIV + women's travel, housing, meals, and child care for meetings and actions.

POLICY CONCERNS AND TACTICS

As does ACT UP, the WC finds AIDS both a public health and a political issue and relies on political action to produce useful responses from the political system. Anticipated outcomes of its research-oriented activism include favorable impact on the public policy process and on popular images of persons with HIV/AIDS, of the pandemic, and of policy in both public and private sectors, for example, the pharmaceutical sector. The main strategy the caucus has adopted to influence policy making unites direct action and research.

The caucus has supplied congresspersons and staff with information, leading to hearings; made personal presentations to agency heads and staff; offered prepared and spontaneous testimony at agency hearings and conferences; commented on regulations and sought administrative review of incorrect agency decisions; undertaken public and member education with its own publications and mailings and through print and broadcast media, as well as educated the media; produced speak-outs, "die"-ins, and other high-profile demonstrations; collected information and disseminated research; and supported litigation, including one class action suit, with another pending.

The caucus has organized the distribution of clean needles, distributed condoms and dental dams outside public schools, investigated housing laws and shelter policies, and scrutinized the availability and coverage of private insurance policies and Medicaid.

The motivation behind this activism has related to CDC's failure to trace the communication of AIDS among women and to introduce to health care practitioners appropriate criteria for women's care. CDC's silence has meant a paucity of women-relevant entry standards for clinical trials and no bases for eligibility for social services, including disability payments; CDC's inattentiveness has hidden the epidemic's extent in the United States, delayed women's diagnosis and treatment, and contributed to a vastly shorter life span after diagnosis for women with HIV/AIDS than for men, a difference measured in months for women, years for men. When New York State assemblywoman Deborah Glick took leadership in obtaining endorsements, the WC received 300 endorsements of its "A Call to Change the CDC Surveillance Case Definition of AIDS." The women's committee also helped get endorsements with ACT UP-funded long-distance calls.

Although U.S. Public Health Service staff had sought a conference for three years, the first government conference on women and HIV came in 1990, ten years into the epidemic, after a sit-in by twenty-five women's caucus members. The national event brought together 1,500 conferees, mostly women, several hundred with HIV/AIDS. A unity statement by an alliance of women with HIV/AIDS and other, supportive activists led to formation of a women's health committee within the AIDS Clinical Trials Group, NIAID's AIDS division research arm.

The WC has become a recognized player. It has brought about racially and ethnically mixed participation, as well as wider participation by lesbians, in an issue arena previously dominated by white gay males. Its strategies have led to representation of women with HIV on NIAID research review panels and, one of many firsts, research into treatment for cervical cancer—a women-specific infection. The caucus has educated the public about these infections and, another first, seen that the CDC's proposed classification system include them. It continues to work for their inclusion in a new surveillance definition. Pending are new women-related research entry standards, including a gynecological examination. The caucus seeks an expanded new disability definition and is working to pass a bill allocating SSA payments for women with HIV/AIDS.

Caucus work also ranges from worldwide information distribution to international individual contacts and the international AIDS conferences. During the fifth one in Montreal, the caucus protested low lesbian visibility and presentations unfavorable to prostitutes. In Florence and Amsterdam it disseminated the

Women's Research and Treatment Agenda (WRTA), subsequently translated into Italian, Dutch, French, and Spanish. It distributed WRTA during the 1991 New Zealand HIV and Indigenous People's Conference. European women have urged the World Health Organization to change its AIDS definition so as to use caucus critiques. The Amsterdam conference's opening plenary speaker was a New York ACT UP member and woman with HIV, Marina Alvarez.

The caucus has coordinated with other organizations such as Legal Services and the American Medical Association. It works in coalition with the Women and AIDS Resource Network, Center for Women Policy Studies,* Women's Health Action Mobilization, Life Force, Health Force, and the Hyacinth Foundation and with hundreds of groups nationwide to change CDC's surveillance definition.

FURTHER INFORMATION

An array of documents put out by the WC identifies women's symptoms and AIDS policy and research issues and provides critiques found nowhere else. The caucus has issued yearly *Women's Treatment and Research Agendas.* In 1989 it produced *The Women & AIDS Handbook,* which South End Press published as *Women, AIDS and Activism* (1990). In June 1992 the National Institutes of Medicine Drug Forum on Gender Effects distributed the caucus-produced "Guidelines for the Ethical Inclusion of Women in Clinical Trials."

SARAH SLAVIN

ALAN GUTMACHER INSTITUTE
See PLANNED PARENTHOOD FEDERATION OF AMERICA

ALLIANCE OF UNITARIAN WOMEN
See UNITARIAN UNIVERSALIST WOMEN'S FEDERATION

ALPHA KAPPA ALPHA SORORITY (AKA)
5656 S. Stony Island Avenue
Chicago, IL 60637
(312) 684-1282

Alpha Kappa Alpha Sorority (AKA), the first African American women's Greek letter organization, will soon celebrate 100 years of "service to all mankind." The sorority has grown into a prestigious international service organization offering programs that make a difference in the lives of minorities, youth, the disadvantaged and homeless, senior citizens, and many others. It has an Educational Advancement Foundation.

The Mississippi Health Project (a mobile clinic), the establishment of a National Non-Partisan Council for Public Affairs (the first civil rights lobby), AKA's status of observer at the United Nations, its "adoption" of Africare villages, and its financial support of education are evidence of its commitment to caring.

ORIGIN AND DEVELOPMENT

AKA organized in 1908 at Howard University in Washington, D.C. Nine women are listed as its founding members—Ethel Hedgeman-Lyle, Beulah and Lillie Burke, Margaret Flagg Holmes, Marjorie Hill, Lucy Slowe, Martie Woolfolk Taylor, Anna E. Brown, and Lavinia Norman. Hedgeman-Lyle conceived the idea of the organization, proposing that the sorority be an instrument for enriching the social and intellectual aspects of college life. As a sorority, membership was meant to be selective and chosen. As members of an oppressed and underprivileged group just one generation removed from slavery, founders and early initiates felt conscious of their privileged position as college students. The decade of AKA's founding was a period of rising assertiveness in the black community, and self-help organizations and civil rights organizations were in formation.

Five years after its founding, AKA's existence was challenged by dissident members who left to form another organization. Nellie Quander, class of 1912, set about developing the sorority as a national body established in perpetuity. On January 29, 1913, AKA was incorporated under the provisions of the Code of Laws of the District of Columbia. AKA was expanded to other campuses and membership was extended to alumnae.

By the 1960s the sorority had celebrated more than fifty years of service and sisterhood. During these formative early years, basic programs were implemented that served as foundations for current programmatic developments. Racial consciousness was promoted through yearly programs commemorating the sorority's founding with programs on black history and culture; the official magazine, the *Ivy Leaf,* was published. Scholarship, community betterment, and general culture became early national efforts. Vocational guidance programs began in the 1920s and remained a major force until these services became standard in the public schools. International outreach first became apparent through the gradual evolution of AKA's foreign fellowship, which began in 1927, expanded to include awards to members living in Africa and other parts of the world for study in America, to the establishment of a chapter outside the continental United States in Monrovia, Liberia (West Africa).

The growing maturity of its membership, as college coeds became career women, led to new program emphasis. During the thirties public health in America's rural areas was improved through the Mississippi Health Project. For eight years, the sorority provided immediate short-term health care, including immunizations, vaccines, nutritional education, personal hygiene information, and dental care through mobile clinics. A national health-care project replaced this initiative and encouraged local efforts by chapters. The sorority later provided national health grants. One such grant funded a research project for sickle-cell anemia.

In the public policy arena, the growing social consciousness of AKA's maturing membership, coupled with the leadership opportunities many now held due to their educational advantages, led to the sorority joining forces with the NAACP and other fraternal groups in 1934 to promote anti-lynching and fair employment legislation. Shortly before that, the sorority affiliated with the Joint Committee on National Recovery to protect the interests of black industrial workers and sharecroppers, secure training opportunities for blacks with the Tennessee Valley Authority (TVA), and negotiate the placement of unemployed black artists, actors, and musicians. Five years later, under the guidance of founder and incorporator Norma Boyd, a lobbying effort—the Non-Partisan Lobby for Economic and Democratic Rights—was created to address issues of police brutality in Washington, D.C., local suffrage, the extension of the Public Works Program, a minimum wage for laundry workers, and support of the Costigan-Wagner Anti-Lynching Bill.

In December 1941, the name was changed to National Non-Partisan Council on Public Affairs. The lobby existed for ten years, using the services of paid staff and volunteers to address the elimination of discrimination in public life, disfranchisement, lynching, inequities in housing and hospitalization programs, and improvement in the status of black women. The council was also the first fraternal group accredited as an observer at the United Nations (UN).

AKA was a founding member of the Leadership Conference on Civil Rights and organized and supported for fifteen years the American Council on Human Rights (ACHR). Established in 1948, ACHR was an interfraternal organization whose objectives were cooperative social action to achieve broader opportunities in employment, adequate housing for the underprivileged on a non-discriminatory basis, and promotion of legislation for the attainment of the first two objectives. In 1963 the growing urgency of the civil rights movement led to the disbandment of ACHR and its funds being distributed to the Student Non-Violent Coordinating Committee, Leadership Conference on Civil Rights, and Prince Edward County Free School Association.

ORGANIZATION AND FUNDING

AKA has more than 870 undergraduate and graduate chapters located throughout the United States, Virgin Islands, Bahamas, West Africa, Great Britain, Germany, and Seoul, Korea. The sorority is divided into ten regions. Governing policies and procedures are voted upon democratically at biennial conventions known as boules. The boule is the sorority's official governing arm. The directorate is an elected voluntary executive board representing various regions and the organization's administrative and programmatic concerns. The international president, titled supreme basileus, sets the programmatic theme during her tenure. The current president is Eva L. Evans. There are also international elected and appointed standing committees. Within each region and state are additional appointments to carry out various programs. The international headquarters is located in Chicago. The paid staff is headed by an executive director, currently Alison Harris Alexander.

AKA's membership, predominantly African American, exceeds 140,000.

Members reflect the aspirations and achievements of today's women. Lifelong participation is encouraged, as witnessed by the ongoing participation of the 2nd Supreme Basileus Loraine Richardson Green (1919–23).

AKA members are, first, college women who find time amid the pressures of schoolwork to give community service and, second, professionals in every field who find personal satisfaction in extending themselves. AKA counts among its members Phylicia Rashad, Toni Morrison, and Althea Gibson. The sorority's honorary members represent women around the world, including international leaders Coretta Scott King, Leah Tutu, Dame Nita Barrow, Rosa Parks, and Mae Jemison.

The sorority is a tax-exempt organization supported by membership donations and dues. The Educational Advancement Foundation, a separate, tax-exempt fund, was established in 1980 to encourage and promote education and leadership. The foundation provides merit awards to female and male post-secondary scholars and mini grants to individuals and organizations submitting proposals that address AKA interests. The foundation is administered by an executive secretary and funded by contributions from AKA membership, revenues from merchandise sales, and funding from the public and corporations.

Besides AKA's traditional competitive programs of domestic travel grants for eligible high school junior and senior women and fellowships/internships for undergraduate members, current programs of the sorority focus on mathematics and science literacy, health, especially HIV/AIDS awareness, the black family, public policy, economic development, senior citizens, the arts and world community.

POLICY CONCERNS AND TACTICS

The International Connection Committee, like its predecessor, the National Non-Partisan Council on Public Affairs, is the national apparatus to identify and study issues, design membership communication strategy, and mobilize members. Established in 1980, its objectives are to increase the number of African Americans in elected and appointive positions in local, state, and federal government, work to help alleviate homelessness and poverty, maintain historically black educational institutions, and ongoing service as the legislative liaison for issues affecting AKA. Voter registration drives, local projects offering free health and social services, informational workshops, national conferences in association with other fraternal groups and national organizations, child care, cultural promotions and civic fund-raisers are the tools for AKA's charitable and community development efforts.

In 1994, AKA expanded its Washington, D.C., presence by appointing Sharon Worthy, 1990–94 International Connection Committee Chairperson, as the director of the AKA Washington Governmental Affairs Office.

Since 1965, AKA has administered, under contract from the federal government, a residential occupational training center, the Cleveland (Ohio) Job Corps, which currently houses more than 530 students and is coed. The grant is sup-

plemented by support from chapters. Through this effort the sorority has proposed to help at-risk males and females achieve their full academic, career, and
personal potential.

Locally, the chapters have continued to stress education by tutoring, building
self-esteem, and recruiting teachers as ways to increase the number of students
of color attaining degrees. Through the "Ivy AKAdemy," the sorority provides
quality out-of-school educational experiences and opportunities to supplement
the schooling of minority youth and adults. Currently the emphasis is on increasing mathematics and science literacy of students of African descent. The
sorority also promotes education through support of the United Negro College
Fund and the Hallie Q. Brown Collection of Rare Books at Central State University.

The UN Decade for Women (1975–85) served as a powerful vehicle to promote the sorority's participation in the Non-Governmental Organization Forum
in Nairobi, Kenya. Besides the promotion of community development overseas,
the sorority sought to educate its membership to a new relationship with women
abroad, emphasizing "our responsibilities as black women to understand the
problems of the Third World, assisting where we can support education, economic and political development, and the enhancement of women."

The African Village Development Program was launched in 1984, in conjunction with Africare, to provide rural Africa with financial assistance to attract
villagers who had migrated to the cities back to their villages. AKA chapters
provide funds for village development in many African locations, including Bur-
kina Faso, Chad, Mali, Senegal, and Zimbabwe. Africare provides the training
and tools. AKA projects have included a defluoridation process for water wells
in the Rift Valley of Ethiopia, supplying school clothes for Liberian refugee
children, vegetable gardens in Niger, and relief aid for Somalia.

The ongoing health care crisis in our society continues to be a major target.
Currently, the sorority focus is on training members as HIV/AIDS awareness
instructors to educate the African-American community about the disease.
AKA's resources are not limited to HIV/AIDS. Chapters also offer health fairs
and seminars to provide access to medical care. Medical screenings, dental care,
nutrition clinics, and physical fitness programs are routinely offered by numerous chapters as well as informational programs on teenage pregnancy, parenting,
and child wellness.

AKA supports programs to develop business knowledge and acumen through
money management training, investment clubs, seminars and promotions of
African-American business interests. During Black Dollar Month the entire
membership is encouraged to patronize black businesses and services. The AKA
Business Round Table was recently established to explore and promote entrepreneurial behavior among AKA members.

AKA's commitment to the black family remains intact. Of special interest is
the senior population. AKA is approaching four generations and the sorority is

pursuing providing a place for senior members and other seniors where they can be cared for.

Over the years, chapters have offered myriad services to their communities. They have participated in demonstrations urging change in South Africa and engaged in letter writing and telephone campaigns to maintain sanctions against South Africa; supported passage of the 1990 Civil Rights Act and A Better Childcare bill. Financial support of the nation's historically black colleges and universities continues to be a major emphasis. AKA gives continuing support to Africare, National Council of Negro Women, and NAACP Legal Defense Fund.

ELECTORAL ACTIVITIES

The sorority's nonprofit status prohibits partisan political activities. Individual members are encouraged to exercise their civil rights and demonstrate political acumen. Further, AKA members include elected and appointed government officials.

FURTHER INFORMATION

The national organ, issued quarterly and available to both members and non-members, is *Ivy Leaf*. A history book, *Alpha Kappa through the Years, 1908–1988,* and pamphlets detailing the sorority's programs are available. The AKA Archives, established in 1978, are located at and administered by the manuscript division of the Moorland-Spingarn Research Center at Howard University. The AKA library is located at the international headquarters.

CHARLOTTE T. MORGAN-CATO

ALPHA KAPPA ALPHA EDUCATIONAL ADVANCEMENT FOUNDATION
See ALPHA KAPPA ALPHA

AMERICAN ACADEMY OF NURSING
See AMERICAN NURSES' ASSOCIATION

AMERICAN ACADEMY OF PEDIATRICS (AAP)
141 Northwest Point Boulevard
Elk Grove Village, IL 60009-0927
(708) 228-5005
(800) 433-9016
FAX (708) 228-5097

The American Academy of Pediatrics (AAP) unites pediatricians to ensure for all young people the attainment of their full potential for physical, emotional, and social health. Today 50 percent of physicians completing residency training in pediatrics are female.

ORIGIN AND DEVELOPMENT

In 1855, the first U.S. hospital for sick children was founded in Philadelphia. The pediatrics (*pais* for child and *iatric* for a cure) specialty emerged in 1860. In 1880 the American Medical Association (AMA) organized a pediatric section. Section members founded AAP in 1930. The idea for AAP and much of the original organization belonged to several people, with no one individual acting as leader or chief organizer. Prominent among the founders were Isaac A. Abt, C. Anderson Aldrich, and Clifford G. Grulee. The organizers knew each other previously, not only from their AMA section but also from the American Pediatric Society, founded in 1888, and Central States Pediatric Society (CSPS). They felt moved to act by AMA's censorship in 1922 of the pediatrics section for unilaterally supporting the Sheppard-Towner infant and maternity act. The 1921 act represented a reversal for AMA and a significant win for the Women's Joint Congressional Committee and its subcommittee on the bill. Ordering that AMA sections restrict their activity to socializing and scientific papers, the AMA House of Delegates moved to forbid such independent action in the future.

Eight years later, AAP formed to represent infants, adolescents, young adults, and pediatricians. Within CSPS, which then had 300 members, sentiment favoring a national society had hardened to determination. A national organization offered advantages educationally, to help advance the field and consolidate the specialty, as well as to help it assume a position of national influence on health issues important to the group. A 1929 meeting in Portland, Oregon, centered on this prospect and attracted thirty-five well-known pediatricians. Grulee, Abt, and Aldrich sent out a letter afterward justifying a national organization and, based on the response, invited pediatricians to convene in Detroit in 1930. The meeting attracted thirty-four participants; they adopted a constitution, elected officers and an executive board, and appointed committees. The constitution has stood AAP in good stead. Subsequently the American Board of Pediatrics (ABP) evolved from AAP; it certifies physicians as pediatrics specialists. AAP's basic mission has not changed. Since the sixties, it has increased its involvement in legislative arenas and intensified its attention to socioeconomic issues.

ORGANIZATION AND FUNDING

AAP has fifty-nine affiliates, one or more in each state, with four in California and three in New York. It divides the United States into nine districts. Outside the United States it is represented through affiliations with pediatric societies in other countries, especially in Latin America. There are an annual convention and a spring meeting. The nine-member board of directors is not racially mixed. Nine percent of AAP's board members and officers are women; and 52 percent of the AAP affiliates' presidents are women. In 1991 Antoinette Eaton, professor of pediatrics, Ohio State University School of Medicine, became AAP's first woman president. The 1994 national president was George D. Comerci. AAP has over sixty internal sections and committees.

AAP headquarters is located in Elk Grove Village, Illinois. A Washington, D.C., office opened in 1970. Other officers are in Burlington, Vermont; Rochester, New York; and Palo Alto, California. The executive director is hired by the board and must be a pediatrician. The current executive director is James E. Strain. AAP employs 238 professional staff, including 15 in the Washington office, which may have up to two volunteers or student interns as well. Workers rotate jobs and experience different levels of responsibility. Ability is rewarded in the Washington office with merit salary increases. AAP has an attorney on retainer.

Membership is made up of individuals. AAP has 48,000 members, up in 1994 from 26,888 in 1985; 21,384 in 1980; 17,585 in 1975; 11,960 in 1970; 9,164 in 1965; and 6,775 in 1960. Annual dues are $320. Physicians must be ACP-certified to join. Members join largely to advocate important values, ideas, or policies and for publications and other information. Conferences and meetings and communication with peers or colleagues also provide incentives to membership. To a lesser extent, so do low-cost insurance, research-based information, representation of members' opinions to government, the chance to participate in the public affairs and exercise influence within AAP, and friendship ties and the chance to associate with similarly minded people.

Initially, AAP received financial help from member dues and registration fees from meetings. Most recently, its primary source of support has come from revenues from publications' sales or advertising (40 percent); dues (20 percent); conventions, conferences, or exhibitions (20 percent); interest and royalties; and nominal contributions from merchandise sales, government grants or contracts, corporate or business gifts or grants, gifts or bequests beyond dues from individuals and foundation grants. AAP is a 501 (c) (3) organization. Contributions to it are tax-deductible. Recently the budget was nearly $30 million. In 1980 the budget stood at $6.7 million, in 1970 at $1.6 million.

POLICY CONCERNS AND TACTICS

AAP policy usually is recommended by a committee or section composed of technical experts and approved by the executive board. Besides the board, executive officers' decisions and an annual chapter forum most affect policy discussions. The choice of strategy for a specific problem comes from a committee or task force assigned to the issue. Preferred strategies include giving testimony in congressional and state legislative hearings; supplying congresspeople, state legislators, and staff with information; making personal presentations to congresspeople, agency heads, and staff; testifying at agency/department hearings; offering written comments on proposed regulations; seeking administrative review of agency or department decisions; educating members with publications and encouraging them to write legislators and committees; and conducting and publishing research on issues. AAP also might contact public decision makers through an influential member. Occasionally, it engages in public education through press releases and files amicus briefs.

Child health services or preventive pediatrics in the community is an important part of government and extends to maternal health services. During the sixties, AAP experienced considerable internal conflict over its rapidly increasing interest in child health and welfare policy. At one point it looked as if the organization would lose a segment of its membership and that a new group would form. This cleavage did not come to pass, and the organization continued to expand its socioeconomic interests. In the process it involved itself with Project Head Start, a kind of compensatory education for preschoolers meant to provide them with an increasingly equal start in the education system: Head Start includes educational, health, nutritional, and social services. AAP also anticipated developing strong allied health care delivery staff projects. As its size and complexity grew, it reorganized to enhance the board's opportunity to engage in policy-making activity during the seventies. The 1975 Education for All Handicapped Children Act (P. L. 94-142) enhanced AAP's ability to care better for children with disabilities and spurred it onward in identifying appropriate means for accomplishing this charge. It strongly supported the United Nations International Year of the Child (1979).

AAP sees continuing importance in the 1964 Civil Rights Act, 1964 Food Stamp Act, 1968 Antidiscrimination in Housing Act, 1970 Food Stamp Reform and School Lunch Acts, Title IX of the 1972 Education Amendments, *Roe* v. *Wade,* 1974 Housing and Community Development and Social Services Acts, Child Support Amendments—1975 Social Security Act and 1976 Day Care Act, proposed human life constitutional amendment, 1978 Pregnancy Disability Act, 1982 Welfare Act, 1983 Social Security Act, and 1984 Child Abuse and Child Support Enforcement Acts.

AAP sees as the most important federal initiatives of the last decade the vaccine compensation law, Medicaid expansion to millions of poor children up to age nineteen and half a million pregnant women, litigation and repeal of the Baby Doe laws, and passage of the 1990 Americans with Disabilities Act (ADA). AAP played a key role in developing the vaccine law (vaccines have drastically changed pediatric practice over the years) and also addressing the children's issues entailed by ADA. It testified on behalf of Medicaid expansion. It litigated to defeat the Baby Doe laws. AAP long has had a great interest in the newborn period. It recently has taken positions on the guardianship of children born through surrogacy arrangements. AAP has developed an influential protocol for treatment of children subjected to sexual abuse—AAP estimates that almost 1 percent of children, girls and boys both, are abused sexually every year—and has in place guidelines to evaluate rape and also to prevent pregnancy in adolescents. AAP finds that almost 50 percent of rape victims are adolescents, the great majority of them young women, with an increasing incidence among young men. AAP further provides guidelines for HIV testing of assailants. In 1985, it provided "Guidelines for Infection Control in Schools in High-Prevalence areas" pertaining to children with HIV, furthering the provision of an education in the least restrictive environment to public school students with complex health needs. Members of legislative bodies, agency heads, and staff regularly solicit AAP views on policy matters.

Over the years AAP has worked with the American College of Obstetricians and Gynecologists,* Children's Defense Fund,* American College of Emergency Physicians, and American Heart Association.

ELECTORAL ACTIVITIES

AAP does not see women's issues as partisan and does not have a political action committee.

FURTHER INFORMATION

AAP publishes a monthly membership newsletter. *News and Comments,* and a monthly journal, *Pediatrics.* Besides research reports, it also produces such public education-oriented materials as magazines, books, and brochures.

SARAH SLAVIN

AMERICAN ALLIANCE FOR HEALTH, PHYSICAL EDUCATION, RECREATION AND DANCE
See NATIONAL ASSOCIATION FOR GIRLS AND WOMEN IN SPORT

AMERICAN ASSOCIATION FOR AFFIRMATIVE ACTION (AAAA)
8335 Allison Point
Indianapolis, IN
(317) 841-8038
FAX (317) 578-9073
For almost two decades the American Association for Affirmative Action (AAAA) has worked to create a nationwide network of professionals committed to effective affirmative action and equal opportunity programs.

ORIGIN AND DEVELOPMENT

The person most responsible for AAAA's creation was Betty Newcomb. In February 1973, she served as Ball State University's affirmative action officer and as a national board member of National Organization for Women* (NOW). During a Washington, D.C., meeting about the newly defined responsibilities of affirmative action officers coordinated by Bernice Sandler and funded by the Association of American Colleges Project on the Status and Education of Women,* Newcomb collected the names and addresses of participants interested in joining an affirmative action association. The next month, at an American Association of Higher Education meeting in Chicago, Ann London Scott, a NOW vice president and Title IX lobbyist, arranged for a workshop on the same subject. Again Newcomb collected names.

In April 1973, Newcomb wrote to all those whose names she had collected and to every university president asking if they or other campus representatives might be interested in participating in an affirmative action organization. The replies inundated her. In October, in Kansas City, she met with a steering committee to write bylaws, issue a newsletter, and name the new organization.

A year later in Austin, Texas, AAAA held its first conference. It celebrated the tenth anniversary of the Civil Rights Act of 1964 with Lady Bird Johnson as honorary host. Sue Fratkin, an administrator with the National Association of Land Grant Colleges and Universities, organized the conference. Serving on AAAA's first executive board with Newcomb were Fratkin, Sheila Nickson, Renedetta Stewart, and Gloria White. From the beginning, AAAA established a reputation for providing excellent workshops for its members.

AAAA's general goals have remained the same. They seek to foster the implementation of effective affirmative action and equal opportunity programs nationwide; establish and maintain ethical standards for the profession; provide formal liaison with federal, state, and local agencies involved with equal opportunity compliance in employment and education; promote members' professional growth and development; provide liaison with other organizations committed to the same purposes and objectives; and sponsor and conduct research to further AAAA's ends.

At its 1974 inaugural conference, more than half of the 400 in attendance were white, probably because of the large number of white men who were assistants to university presidents and present to recruit affirmative action officers. Minorities always have been well represented on the board, and over the years, the association has become increasingly minority in general membership. The percentage of women in the general membership has declined steadily, from 78 percent in 1970 and 66 percent in 1980, to 54 percent in 1990. Nevertheless, starting in 1992, the executive board, including President Gazella Summitt, was all women, except for the 1991 president, Robert W. Ethridge.

ORGANIZATION AND FUNDING

Divided into ten regional subunits and state and local chapters, AAAA has about 1,200 members. Besides state and local chapters, AAAA has officers in ten regions, which coincide with the ten regional divisions of the U.S. government. Each member of the board of directors represents a region and is elected at a regional meeting for a two-year term. The board also elects two at-large members for a two-year term. They are selected to achieve racial, sexual, and professional balance. The board of directors is mainly minority, with 83 percent African American, 6 percent Hispanic, and 6 percent white; at least 50 percent of the board always has been female. The president is elected for a two-year term by mail ballot of the membership and can serve no more than two consecutive terms. The past president serves on the board. While its officers are volunteers, AAAA does employ four staff people, including the executive director. The executive director is Roberta Seefeldt.

AAAA continues to attract members who are professionals in the field of equal employment opportunity/affirmative action and human resources. Members join primarily because of the training workshops offered, because they believe in AAAA's goals, and because membership will enable them to socialize and network with like-minded people. The communication that goes on with peers and the information exchange at AAAA national and regional conferences and meetings are strong incentives for membership.

AAAA was established and sustains itself through small contributions from many people. Annual dues have been set at $75, and the money from dues makes up about 80 percent of the group's financial base; the rest of the funding comes from conferences and perhaps 1 percent from corporate gifts. AAAA's financial base has grown steadily since 1974, when it had a budget under $3,000. In 1980, its budget was $19,000; in the early 1990s at approximately $200,000.

POLICY CONCERNS AND TACTICS

Official policy is set by committee work and subsequent approval by the board of directors or executive board. While membership discussion, membership polls, and committee recommendations are crucial, discussion by the executive officers and board members actually determines policy. AAAA and its members seek to influence policy directly in a number of ways: by directly lobbying U.S. congresspeople, testifying at federal executive department hearings, and educating the public through press releases and with information campaigns.

By a unanimous board vote, AAAA participated actively in support of the 1990 Civil Rights Act, which overturned a U.S. Supreme Court decision, *Martin* v. *Wilks* (1989), and also in the coalition supporting a 1991 act. It opposed, on the basis of his record, Judge Clarence Thomas's nomination to the U.S. Supreme Court; Thomas once headed the Equal Employment Opportunity Commission. AAAA has taken positions through amicus briefs on cases before the court such as *Richmond* v. *Croson* (1989), as well as *Martin* v. *Wilks.* Other policy issues of concern include joblessness and the impact that the closing of companies is having on women and minorities in particular. Quite often, public policymakers come to AAAA to get its view on policy matters.

AAAA coordinates with similar organizations such as Project Equality, National Institute for Employment Equity, and the American Contract Compliance Association. AAAA has cooperated with these organizations for over ten years.

ELECTORAL ACTIVITIES

AAAA does not have a political action committee.

FURTHER INFORMATION

AAAA uses a newsletter and direct mail to inform association members about changing legislative and judicial policy.

ROBERTA ANN JOHNSON

AMERICAN ASSOCIATION OF FAMILY AND CONSUMER SCIENCES (AAFCS)
1555 King Street
Alexandria, VA 22314

(703) 706-4600
FAX (703) 706-HOME

The American Association of Family and Consumer Sciences (AAFCS), formerly the American Home Economics Association (AHEA), has played an integral part in the diverse field's growth and development. Seeking to provide direction and commonality of purpose, AAFCS is dedicated to improving the quality of family life by research, education, development of public service programs, and monitoring state and national legislative issues.

ORIGIN AND DEVELOPMENT

Home economics emerged from late nineteenth-century social, economic and technological conditions. By the 1890s, both land-grant institutions and selected women's liberal arts colleges had introduced curriculum instruction in domestic economy. A series of conferences at Lake Placid, New York, 1899–1908, at Helvil Dewey's home, brought together educators to discuss program ends and enlarge upon subject matter. The first conference officially designated the field's name as home economics. AHEA was formally organized at the second conference, its purpose to improve home living conditions, institutional households, and the community.

Members are elementary, secondary, and postsecondary educators, administrators, extension agents, and professionals in government, business, and the nonprofit sector. They teach, conduct research, and design, develop, and administer programs in related areas such as foods and nutrition, clothing and textiles, housing, human development, child and family studies, and consumer affairs.

AAFCS has guided the evolution of home economics from the 1909 restricted concept of domestic economy associated with manual skills and domestic chores to education for the home to family education, which emphasizes all family members' responsibility regardless of sex. The field's mission and philosophy have become refined over the years; the interrelationship of family members and the relationship of family to society remain the field's central care.

ORGANIZATION AND FUNDING

There are fifty-three state affiliates, including the District of Columbia, Puerto Rico, American Overseas Group, and International Federation of Home Economics. AAFCS is governed by an elected board of directors and national delegate assembly whose duties include policy development, annual meetings, and budget approval. By 1990, AHEA had grown from a simple to a complex organizational structure complete with a six-member board of directors, seven professional sections, ten subject matter sections, and a foundation. Members' interests are addressed by committees, professional sections, and councils composed of individuals selected for service on the basis of expertise. The president is Peggy Meszaros. Originally based in Washington, D.C., in 1990 AHEA moved to Alexandria, Virginia. A professional staff of thirty-five and student interns are headed by an executive director. The present executive director is Mary Jane Kolar. Just as the membership is 95 percent female and ethnically mixed, so, too, are officers and board members.

Membership rose from 800 members in 1909 to a peak of 50,000 in the mid-1960s, leveling off at about 25,000 in the 1990s. Besides the opportunity for professional growth in sharing information and research at annual meetings, AAFCS is looked upon as a forum in which to advocate important values, ideas, or policies that impact on families as well as a conduit that represents members' opinions to government. Through AAFCS, members are afforded the opportunity to participate in public affairs.

AHEA became a 501 (c) (3) tax-exempt organization in 1967. Since the fifties, the majority of the $2.5 million budget has come from membership dues, followed by income from the convention. Government grants and gifts from corporations, businesses, and individuals are not included in the budget but are handled by the foundation.

POLICY CONCERNS AND TACTICS

Since the late sixties, AHEA policy has developed on internal and external tracks. Within, the board, public affairs committee, state chapters, and individuals present resolutions for discussion. The membership votes on selected resolutions at the annual meeting. The director of public policy represents national interests before the Congress, business community, and voluntary organizations. Monitoring legislative, judicial, and executive activities, the director provides information and technical assistance to home economic coalitions and state affiliates. In 1990, a Public Policy Hotline was established to provide a twenty-four-hour update for AHEA members.

Since inception, AAFCS has sought to meet family and home needs by means of an internal focus on the development of home economics in secondary schools, colleges, universities, and cooperative extension and an external focus on public policy impacting on the family. AHEA primarily was concerned, 1909–19, with educating women for domestic roles. It specified an undergraduate curriculum based on liberal arts subjects, with added course work either cultural or technical but family-centered. Policy activity was reactive. An elected AHEA representative from each state alerted women to proposed measures and kept congresspersons informed of women's legislative interests. Of particular interest was the 1917 Smith-Hughes Act, which provided federal moneys for vocational education.

In the 1920s, home economic concerns reflected social problems heightened by post–World War I adjustment. AHEA endorsed U.S. Bureau of Standards efforts to set standards for foods, apparel, and textile goods. AHEA did not support National Woman's Party* efforts on behalf of equal rights or take a stand on women's suffrage. From 1930 to 1940, amid the uncertainties and harsh realities of economic depression, war, and a changing lifestyle that brought women into the labor market, AHEA supported federal aid to housing and a

Maternity and Infant Welfare bill to enlarge upon the Social Security Act. It worked to establish truth in advertising.

In the forties, as AHEA's public policy involvement increased, a Washington Lookout Committee was appointed to feed information to AHEA's executive committee. By 1946, each issue of the *Journal of Home Economics* informed members about new bills in the Congress. Major new concerns included school lunches for underprivileged children, rent control, federal aid to education, and textile labeling. Members worked to effect change via participation ranging from local Better Business Bureaus and the U.S. Chamber of Commerce to agencies such as the Federal Trade Commission, Food and Drug Administration, Women's Joint Congressional Committee, National Consumer-Retailer Council, American Standards Association, U.S. Extension Service, Farm Security Administration, Farm Credit Administration, and Office of Price Administration. Home economics participated by invitation at the international level in the Food and Agriculture Organization. An AHEA Study committee in cooperation with Southern Negro Home Economics Workers Organization recommended in 1942 the AHEA-affiliated organization of black home economics in seventeen southern states, but apart from white state associations; this recommendation was vetoed in favor of commissioning plans to bring black home economics into AHEA.

During the fifties, a time for both outreach and self-analysis by the organization, AHEA acquired its own building in Washington. In 1952, the executive committee affiliated with sixteen organizations working to influence the Congress on issues such as juvenile delinquency and Social Security benefits for domestic help. Although AHEA membership was at an all-time high in the 1960s, student enrollment was down. To stem the tide, AHEA undertook further self-study to examine its history, past accomplishments, philosophy, objectives, curriculum, accreditation, structure, public policy, and future direction. Decisions implemented in the late 1960s through the 1970s remained in effect in the early nineties. Organizational changes did not negate AAFCS's basic objectives: improving the quality of life for the family and its individual members.

Currently, AAFCS is implementing several public service programs: school-age child care through Project Home Safe; teen pregnancy prevention through Project Taking Charge; minority participation in higher education through Project 2000; and family planning/women in development through Project Rural React.

One of five national organizations that form the Consortium of Family Organizations, a group addressing programs and policies affecting families, since 1985 AAFCS also has belonged to the Home Economics Public Policy Council (HEPPC), which grew out of concern for a unified home economics voice. The coalition established its policy agenda and initiates legislative action in priority areas identified by HEPPC, which seeks consensus among its constituent groups. A basic premise underlying HEPPC is that what is good for one segment of home economics is good for all home economics. Specific issues have been vocational education, particularly consumer and homemaking education, support for research efforts and the Cooperative Extension Service, child care with a special emphasis on school-age child care, teen pregnancy prevention, food safety and nutrition, and aging.

ELECTORAL ACTIVITIES

AAFCS is not a partisan organization and does not have a political action committee.

FURTHER INFORMATION

AAFCS is responsible for three major publications including *Journal of Home Economics,* a refereed professional research journal established in 1972; and *AAFCS Action,* a tabloid reporting AAFCS business and selected news items, established in 1974.

COLLEEN FREY

AMERICAN ASSOCIATION OF GROUP WORKERS
See NATIONAL ASSOCIATION OF SOCIAL WORKERS

AMERICAN ASSOCIATION OF NURSE-MIDWIVES
See AMERICAN COLLEGE OF NURSE-MIDWIVES

AMERICAN ASSOCIATION OF RETIRED PERSON'S WOMEN'S INITIATIVE (AARP WI)
601 E Street, NW
Washington, DC 20049
(202) 434-2277

Growing by 6,000 members a day, with a total membership of 32 million, the American Association of Retired Persons (AARP) is the nation's largest nonprofit organization serving the needs of those over fifty. The AARP's Women's Initiative (WI) has focused on problems facing midlife and older women.

ORIGIN AND DEVELOPMENT

In 1984, AARP created four initiatives targeting the major areas that affect older Americans' lives, one of them WI. Addressing key issues of pay equity and income security, access to quality health and long-term care, and fair treatment in employment, credit, taxes, and pensions, WI cuts across department lines, involving all AARP agencies, thousands of volunteers, and a significant proportion of the budget.

ORGANIZATION AND FUNDING

Professionally staffed regional offices support roughly 4,000 chapters and 400,000 volunteers in community service programs. Women constitute approximately 50 percent of AARP's governing board. WI's advisory committee of regional volunteers includes two men and five women. WI's liaison to the AARP board traditionally has been male and is currently Hispanic. Conscientious effort has been made to integrate the board ethnically and racially; attempts to attract volunteers from low-income levels have proved less successful. The presidency rotates by gender each term, with Louise Crooks, Robert Maxwell and Lovola W. Burgess as recent past presidents. Eugene Lehrmann is the current president. A staff of 1,300 works for AARP in Washington, D.C., under an executive director.

WI's director, Elizabeth Mullen, funds eight core staff and nine outreach staff, strategically placed in key departments. A matrix management style ensures that power penetrates all management levels through extended staffing and budgetary controls. AARP became the first nonprofit group to introduce matrix management into its administrative structure. The WI director uses the matrix style to enhance WI's ability to focus attention on women's issues across the organizational spectrum. Other than for the Spokespersons Program (SP), WI is non-operational. Although the director does not have the power to hire, fire, or promote, she uses diplomatic and budgetary skills to negotiate and improvise, shift priorities, and redirect resources.

Approximately 18 million women, 57 percent of AARP's membership, make up the WI's potential constituency. Extraordinary incentives to participate in AARP include a pharmacy service, investment program, travel service, group health/homeowners/auto insurance, and audiovisuals. Membership dues of five dollars constitute AARP's principal revenue source. Staff would not reveal budgetary information, including the WI's budget as a percentage of total AARP budget allocations. According to Director Mullen, WI has had an ongoing commitment to funding such external projects as the National Women's Law Center and National Citizens Coalition for Nursing Home Reform.* Recently, the pattern of support has shifted focus from general financial assistance to contractual funding for specific projects.

POLICY CONCERNS AND TACTICS

The policy formation process is initiated by regularly monitoring members' opinions by random polling and analyzing an annual opinion survey on key legislative issues. The national legislative council (NLC), composed of regional representatives, holds field hearings and regional forums. Advised by the executive council, state legislative councils, and congressional leaders, NLC starts each year by drafting federal legislative policy and guidelines for the state legislative committees. The board approves the draft. Given the numerical weight and concomitant ideological, economic, and geographic diversity of its constituency, WI has opted to stress a dual role: educator/resource center and coalition builder across a range of issues and groups. WI uses a broad range of strategies from finely honed legislative advocacy to the broad-based SP. This, WI's sole operational program, recruits and trains volunteers as spokespeople for women's contributions and concerns. In thirty-five states, forty-five spokespersons stay in contact through newsletters and ongoing "peer-to-peer" training sessions.

A Federal Affairs Department manages and coordinates AARP's lobbying with advice from the Public Policy Institute, a think tank. Each agency has eighteen to twenty staff divided into three parallel teams for economics, health, and consumer affairs. Volunteers present much legislative testimony, with technically difficult advocacy left to registered AARP lobbyists. Ten to twelve lobbyists work each state legislature. Despite a relatively lean staff, advocates produce statistics and analyses that rival the U.S. Office of Management and Budget in accuracy and credibility.

WI has forged links with every major women's organization. Recent partnerships include the Older Women's League,* International Federation on Aging, American Association of University Women,* and League of Women Voters.* In a three-year research project completed in the fall of 1990, Maxine Forman, senior program specialist, teamed with the Pension Rights Center to design six technical packets to be used by legal professionals as a guide to simplifying divorce proceedings.

Dramatic, innovative networking has evolved in the international arena. A joint venture with great growth potential is the Women's Financial Information Program (WFIP). It disseminates basic financial information through seminars cosponsored with hundreds of nonprofit, community-based agencies. In 1989 WI joined with the Pan American Health Organization to publish a status report on Latin American and Caribbean midlife and older women. WI also collaborates in a hemispheric effort to produce a cross-cultural protocol on older women and depression. To gain more equitable tax and vesting provisions, WI worked with over thirty groups; to promote long-term care coverage, it coalesced with over 100 organizations. WI's legislative goals have remained relatively constant as the scope of its strategic networking to achieve these goals has continued to expand.

The only group consistently challenging AARP WI analysis using an intergenerational conflict model was Americans for Generational Equity. It has closed its Washington office and no longer generates controversy.

ELECTORAL ACTIVITIES

Adhering to its nonpartisan policy, AARP never has supported candidates or sponsored political action committee activities. It enters the electoral process by informing older voters through workshops on key issues, candidate forums, and voter guilds. The director of AARP VOTE supervises twelve professional staff and over 700 volunteers in twenty-nine states.

FURTHER INFORMATION

In 1990, WI published the first issue of *WIN* (Women's Initiative Network) to bring closer cosponsors of WFIP and AARP WORKS. A high proportion of WI's budget goes to print the forty-one titles on its publication list.

PEGGY DOWNES

AMERICAN ASSOCIATION OF UNIVERSITY WOMEN (AAUW)
1111 16th Street, NW
Washington, DC 20036
(202) 785-7700
FAX (202) 872-1425

Founded in 1881, the American Association of University Women (AAUW) is widely viewed as the moderate leadership force of the women's liberation movement. Its mission is to promote equity for women, education and self-development over the life span, and positive societal change. It has an educational foundation and a Legal Advocacy Fund.

ORIGIN AND DEVELOPMENT

Seventeen college women gathered in Boston in 1881 to found an organization that would allow them to utilize their talents to better themselves, other women, and all humankind. Discrimination at that time on the basis of sex closed many doors for women, leaving them few opportunities to enter professions or use their educational skills for meaningful work. Those forward-looking women, among them Marion Talbot, envisioned a world in which all peoples would have an opportunity to develop their highest potential. As early as 1898, AAUW leaders publicly stated that "college training is a necessity and not a luxury for the average woman as well as for the average man."

AAUW's forerunner, the Association of Collegiate Alumnae, merged in 1903 with the Southern Association of College Women. This set the tone of advancing education and opportunities for women particularly, but always with an eye to improving society for all.

At the 1951 AAUW convention, Hallie Farmer, who headed the committee on legislative program, challenged members not to correlate "lobbying and sin." She equated lobbyists with heroines who significantly improved women's and children's lot and sought peace in the world. Early issues to which the organization committed itself included creation of a U.S. Education Department, federal aid for free public education, civil and economic rights for women, health and human service needs, and international cooperation.

AAUW's program activities fall in two major areas: concern for the development of, and equity for, women and education for women and girls. Since the 1960s, AAUW has emphasized support for the equal rights amendment (ERA) to the U.S. Constitution, educational equity, a woman's right to determine her own reproductive life, the right to privacy, and pay equity.

AAUW is a founding member of the International Federation of University Women (IFUW). Established in London in 1919 by three women—Virginia Gildersleeve, Rose Sedgwick, and Carolyn Spurgeon of the American, British, and Canadian federations, respectively—IFUW represents the international efforts of college-educated women to encourage world peace and prevent war's horror in the future. IFUW consists of sixty-nine member federations representing 250,000 college-educated women around the world. The IFUW added member federations from Bulgaria, Poland, Romania, and Zambia in the early 1990s.

Each member federation has a representative who serves on the IFUW Council. Decision making is vested in the triennial conference of federation delegates. IFUW maintains a paid executive director and small staff in Geneva, Switzerland. As a nongovernmental organization (NGO) of the United Nations (UN), IFUW has accredited NGO representatives to the UN Economic and Social Council in Geneva and Vienna, International Labor Organization in Geneva, and Educational, Scientific and Cultural Organization in Paris.

ORGANIZATION AND FUNDING

There are nearly 1,750 local branches and fifty-one state organizations throughout the United States. Over the years, the volunteer board of directors has fluctuated in size, from nearly thirty members to increase member representation, to a smaller group designed to function more efficiently and economically. The basic structure consists of a president; program, membership, and finance vice presidents; secretary; treasurer; ten regional directors; and directors of public policy and international affairs. The current president is Jackie De Fazio. Anne L. Bryant serves as executive director in the Washington, D.C., headquarters with a professional staff of close to 100 women and men. AAUW maintains a Lobby Corps of members residing in the greater Washington, D.C., area to lobby members of the Congress. Professional staff members located at headquarters provide training and research support for the volunteer lobby. AAUW maintains one paid registered lobbyist in Washington.

The association grew from 3,639 members in 36 branches in 1907 to 36,800 in 521 branches in 1931. By the early 1990s AAUW had about 150,000 members in 1,750 state and local branches throughout the United States. Originally, AAUW membership was open to any woman with the baccalaureate or higher degree from a regionally accredited college or university. Men were admitted to membership in 1987. College students who have not yet completed their baccalaureate degrees now are accepted as student affiliates. Most AAUW members belong to both their respective state AAUW and local branch. National dues are twenty-nine dollars annually. State and local dues vary, averaging an additional fifteen to twenty dollars. The category of members at large allows individuals to join at the association level. Nearly 850 colleges and universities have become institutional members.

An annual operating budget of over $5 million supports the program activities of all its members, membership in the IFUW, and the staff. Member dues account for three-fourths of the income. AAUW generates its remaining revenues from sales, investments, and program activities.

Over the years, AAUW has expanded structurally to include the AAUW Educational Foundation (1958), which carries out efforts begun with the first fellowship program in 1888 to fund highly qualified women in higher education, and the AAUW Legal Advocacy Fund (1981) to promote equal opportunities for women on college campuses.

Extensive branch fund-raising programs and contributions from members, corporations, and grants provide funding for the Educational Foundation. The foundation's endowed funds of over $74 million have made possible advanced study and research for over 5,000 American and international women scholars. The first international fellowship was awarded in 1917. One of AAUW's most famous awardees was Marie Curie, for whom members raised over $150,000 in 1931 to help purchase a gram of radium for her scientific research. In 1993, over 250 awards totaling nearly $2.8 million were made. There are more than ten applicants for every award given.

The association and the Educational Foundation have made great efforts in recent years to increase membership and program diversity. In early 1990, AAUW adopted a diversity statement: ''In principle and in practice, AAUW values and seeks a diverse membership. There shall be no barriers to full participation in this organization on the basis of gender, race, creed, age, sexual orientation, national origin or disability.'' The Diversity Working Group of the board of directors meets three time a year during board meetings to implement this policy. In February 1992, the board approved a motion that all committees and task forces of five or more members would include at least two members represented in the diversity statement. Panels making selections of American and international fellows for the Educational Foundation have followed a similar pattern. Recently the foundation awarded 30 percent of its most prestigious fellowships in the American and selected professions to women from racial and ethnic minorities.

POLICY CONCERNS AND TACTICS

AAUW always has taken active stands on educational, social, economic, and political issues on the local, state, national, and international levels. Voting delegates selected by the state organization or local branches assemble in biennial conventions to determine AAUW's public policy program. Activities on all levels reflect a need for educating members about issues, as well as training members in leadership, professional growth, and development. Members and committees generate and implement program and public policy ideas through local programs, projects, and lobbying and through the ''Every-Member Survey.'' They are urged to be thoroughly informed about issues before taking stands. AAUW has established a reputation for excellence in documenting its viewpoints for presentation before congressional committees and local governing bodies.

AAUW continues to support actions to make educational opportunities and equity for women and girls a reality. It fights sex discrimination on all levels; supports day-care and child-support amendments, and family and medical leave; encourages more women in elected and appointed office; worked for the Civil Rights Restoration Act and opposed Robert Bork's and Clarence Thomas's nominations to the U.S. Supreme Court; supports legislation that does not place restriction on a woman's right to choice; and promotes quality public education and eliminating gender bias in schools. A newly added Educational Foundation focus has been the Eleanor Roosevelt Teacher Fellowships to advance gender equity in the classroom.

In 1990, AAUW commissioned a poll of 3,000 children—boys and girls between nine and fifteen years old—to measure self-worth, career aspirations, and academic interests. The survey demonstrated that serious gender inequity exists and that high self-esteem in girls is reduced from 60 percent to 29 percent between elementary school and high school.

AAUW followed up the survey by sponsoring an Educational Equity Round-table, which brought together experts from education, corporations, governing bodies, and the media to focus on eliminating gender bias in girls' education. The event was part of a major effort to understand that gender bias in American schools is impeding women's and girls' educational advancement in the twenty-first century. As one significant outcome of that initiative, the Educational Foundation commissioned the Wellesley College Center for Research on Women to conduct a major thematic review of existing research on women's and girls' education. In conjunction with the release of *The AAUW Report: How Schools Shortchange Girls,* the Educational Foundation sponsored the National Educational Summit on Girls. Participants discussed the research findings and made commitments to take action to correct inequities. The association has adopted educational equity as a key programming and lobbying focus.

AAUW participates in coalition with women's and other organizations that share its goals, such as educational and women's roundtables, Planned Parenthood,* National Organization for Women,* and the United Nations Association of the USA.

FURTHER INFORMATION

AAUW members receive copies annually of the magazine *Outlook.* One especially well-received report has been Suzanne Howard's "But We Will Persist: A Comparative Research Report on the Status of Women in Academe" (1978).

NANCY DOUGLAS JOYNER

AMERICAN ASSOCIATION OF UNIVERSITY WOMEN EDUCATIONAL FOUNDATION
See AMERICAN ASSOCIATION OF UNIVERSITY WOMEN

AMERICAN ASSOCIATION OF UNIVERSITY WOMEN LEGAL ADVOCACY FUND
See AMERICAN ASSOCIATION OF UNIVERSITY WOMEN

AMERICAN BIRTH CONTROL LEAGUE
See PLANNED PARENTHOOD FEDERATION OF AMERICA

AMERICAN CIVIL LIBERTIES UNION (ACLU)

132 W. 43rd Street
New York, NY 10036
(212) 944-9800
FAX (212) 354-5290
FAX (202) 546-0738 (Washington, DC)

The American Civil Liberties Union (ACLU) was founded as a watchdog citizens' nonprofit organization in New York on January 20, 1920, largely to defend conscientious objectors against governmental limitations of free speech during World War I. This focus gradually expanded to encompass other aspects of the Bill of Rights. In 1971, the Woman's Rights Project (WRP) was formed to concentrate on women's constitutional rights as a "top priority" of the organization, but funding limitations precluded addressing problems of reproductive choice. A separate Reproductive Freedom Project (RFP) therefore was established in 1974. The Lesbian and Gay Rights Project (LGRP) was created in 1986.

ORIGIN AND DEVELOPMENT

ACLU's founding philosophy saw freedoms enumerated in the Bill of Rights as more a promise than reality for most Americans, requiring constant vigilance against potential government incursion. Among the founders were several notable women's rights activists, including Jane Addams, Crystal Eastman, Mary Ware Dennett, Elizabeth Gurley Flynn, and Jeanette Rankin; they all recognized that the rights of women, both as individuals and as an oppressed class, were a critical civil liberties concern. In 1928, ACLU defended Dennett's sex education pamphlet, declared obscene by the U.S. Department of Justice and Postal Service. This pioneer effort pinpointed the linkage between censorship of contraception information, limiting women's control of reproduction, and women's ultimate emancipation.

An ACLU committee on discrimination against women was founded in 1944 by Roger Nash Baldwin, the founding director, and chaired by New York lawyer Dorothy Kenyon. Kenyon, a board member and one of the first supporters on it of reproductive choice, was also instrumental in the organization's 1970 decision to endorse the equal rights amendment. This meant abandoning its position held since the 1940s that women's rights were best protected through the equal protection clause of the Fourteenth Amendment.

ACLU in 1965 was the first national organization to argue for women's right to terminate pregnancy and first to bring this to the Supreme Court in 1971. After the Supreme Court handed down its landmark decision *Roe* v. *Wade* in 1973, RFP was involved actively with the increasing case docket defending the principle of a women's right to reproductive choice based on the constitutional right to privacy. Earlier, ACLU filed an amicus brief for Estelle T. Griswold, executive director of Planned Parenthood League of Connecticut, in *Griswold* v. *Connecticut* (1965). In this case the Court recognized privacy as a constitutional principle inhering in the "penumbras and emanations" of various clauses in the Bill of Rights.

In 1964, the socialist feminist Harriet Pilpel was the first to raise the gay rights issue at the ACLU biennial conference; and ACLU formally embraced the principle in 1966. The Sexual Privacy Project was then established in 1973 to extend *Griswold* to adult consensual sexual activities. The AIDS crisis in the 1980s served as a catalyst for creating LGRP, headed by Nan Hunter from RFP, to address expanding instances of discrimination and privacy issues related to sexual orientation.

ORGANIZATION AND FUNDING

In 1992, the national board included twenty-nine women, with thirteen minorities. The board recently mandated that 25 percent of affiliate boards consist of minorities, with at least 50 percent women. ACLU is making a concentrated effort to achieve its affirmative action goals. ACLU's last president was a woman, Nadine Strosser, the first for this organization. The headquarters is in New York City; there also is a Washington, D.C., office. There has yet to be a woman executive director, a position held by Ira Glasser. ACLU maintains a substantial staff at its Washington, D.C., office to engage in lobbying activity.

WRP was directed since 1978 by Isabelle Katz Pinzler. Her replacement is Sara Mandelbaum. Janet Benshoof directed RFP from 1977 until June 1992. Benshoof, along with Kitty Kolbert and other staff members from RFP, decided to break away from ACLU and found the Center for Reproductive Law and Policy. The main reason stated for the move was that reproductive choice is an issue warranting a single organization specifically dedicated to its cause. Also, Benshoof and Kolbert wanted to expand their efforts to encompass a more broadly based feminist agenda addressing issues such as general women's health and to become involved in cases outside the United States, all beyond the scope of ACLU focus. The ACLU reestablished the RFP with Catherine Weiss as chief attorney.

ACLU, while nonetheless committed to civil libertarian principle of reproductive freedom, considered downsizing RFP, which under Benshoof consisted of eight attorneys, five of whom were women and three of whom were minorities. WRP has a permanent staff of three women attorneys, one of whom is African American. LGRP since 1987 was directed by Bill Rubenstein. His replacement is Matt Coles. Besides Coles, LGRP has on its staff three attorneys, one of whom is female. WRP and RFP set their priorities in accordance with national ACLU policy, aided by advisory committees. All projects are located at ACLU headquarters in New York City and funded solely by moneys from foundations that have chosen to support a project's work, with no membership dollars going to them. In 1992 WRP's budget was $361,000, LGRP's was $423,000, and RFP's was $2.03 million.

ACLU also maintains affiliate organizations in fifty-one regions, a few of which have their own WRPs or RFPs. Local affiliates and the national both solicit members, with 30 percent of local membership dues assessed to the national body. ACLU today has approximately 300,000 members, representing a broad cross-section of society. The organization does not break down its membership demographically, but women have always been a visible and significant force since ACLU's inception. Affiliates operate with relative autonomy, free to act as they see fit in accordance with policy set by the national board. While affiliates and national try to act in concert, instances arise when an affiliate is reluctant to become involved in an issue despite national's urging, as well as occurrences of the reverse scenario. National usually steps in at the local affiliate's request, although sometimes national itself may take initiative, particularly in precedent-setting cases such as the *Evan* case in 1991 in New York. Here ACLU succeeded in arguing for a lesbian's right to adopt her partner's biological child.

POLICY CONCERNS AND TACTICS

For civil libertarians, the Bill of Rights represents a series of entrenched, antecedent principles of personal liberty that are immune from continual redefinition by government or legislative action, public opinion, or democratic majoritarianism. ACLU seeks to defend four fundamental notions of civil liberty—freedom of expression, privacy, due process, and equal protection—in a nonpartisan fashion on behalf of anyone, irrespective of how unpopular the cause. Since ACLU cannot take on all the causes it conceivably might, staff attorneys in the projects make their decisions as to the relative importance of a case in conjunction with their advisory committees (where such exist), the legal director, and sometimes the executive director. By 1992, litigation, legislation, and public education were ACLU's primary roles, a shift from Roger Baldwin's original focus on just the last of these three.

Although ACLU has battled for a diverse array of individuals, the charge sometimes has been made that it is dedicated more to a liberal political agenda than a general defense of civil liberties. This allegation noticeably was raised by George Bush in his 1988 presidential campaign to discredit his liberal Democratic opponent. Michael Dukakis, as a "card-carrying member of the ACLU." It is worth noting, however, that in 1990, in Washington and Michigan, ACLU defended the free speech prerogatives of conservative right-to-life and Operation Rescue protesters enjoined by state courts from picketing family clinics and verbally harassing their clientele, nor are these isolated examples.

In the legal arena, ACLU has achieved considerable success for women's rights prevailing either in the capacity of an actual litigant or adviser to plaintiffs or through submission of amicus curiae briefs. WRP's first case to reach the U.S. Supreme Court was *Reed* v. *Reed* (1971). While not going to the extent of deeming gender a suspect classification demanding the strict scrutiny of race-based classifications, in *Reed* the Court held that Idaho's automatic preference of men over women similarly situated, as administrators of deceased persons' estates, violated the Fourteenth Amendment's equal protection clause. This was the first time the U.S. Constitution was held to forbid gender discrimination. Other early WRP triumphs include *Taylor* v. *Louisiana* (1975), where the court declared that a state law exempting women from jury service violated the Sixth Amendment right to trial by a jury of one's peers.

The 1992 legal docket for the three projects included cases at the federal and state levels dealing with the widespread practice of denying alcohol- and drug-dependent women access to state-funded medical treatment; gender bias in standardized testing; housing discrimination against families with children; governmental fetal protection policies; loss of maternal custody on grounds of neglect when a woman or her newborn child tests positive for drug abuse; lesbian family issues such as child custody, marriage, health benefits, and housing; discriminatory treatment of women, including lesbians, by the military; ROTC discrimination for reasons of sexual orientation on university campuses; discrimination against women, including pregnant women, by employers; parental notification laws for young women seeking abortions, as well as other cases concerning state laws controlling abortion.

The Reagan/Bush Court was particularly hostile to issues of reproductive choice, first by ruling that the issue was best addressed by individual states in *Webster* v. *Reproductive Health Services* (1989) and then by denying federal funds to family planning clinics that provide abortion counseling in *Rust* v. *Sullivan* (1991). ACLU felt concerned, unnecessarily, that Guam, Utah, Louisiana, and Pennsylvania statutes restricting abortions, if appealed to the Supreme Court, could result in the Court's overturning or seriously distinguishing *Roe,* a potentially dramatic setback for women's rights. Nonetheless, RFP pushed to have the Court review *Planned Parenthood of Southeast Pennsylvania* v. *Casey* during its 1992 term in an effort to force a definitive ruling on the subject. *Roe* was not overturned, although the decision extended state regulatory authority. President Clinton's Supreme Court appointments, especially of Ruth Bader Ginsburg, helped stem such decisions.

ACLU has shared cases with a variety of women's rights groups, including National Organization for Women Legal Defense and Education Fund,* Planned Parenthood,* Women's Law Project, National Women's Law Center, and the National Center for Lesbian Rights. Groups that have opposed ACLU on issues range from the National Right to Life Committee* to, occasionally, feminist coalitions. It is not always easy to predict whether the fault lines of a particular civil liberties issue will find ACLU on the same side as particular women's rights advocates. One example is ACLU's defense of the free speech rights of pornographers against efforts by certain womens' groups to have pornography banned as degrading to women. In 1983, ACLU participated in the Feminist Anti-Censorship Task Force,* which included writers Betty Friedan and Adrienne Rich, to defeat the Minneapolis and Indianapolis ordinances attempting to censor pornography; these laws were advocated strongly by feminists Andrea Dworkin and Catherine MacKinnon.

Aside from preparation of briefs for litigation, the projects also scrutinize and monitor state and national laws and work with U.S. congressional staff in crafting new legislation.

ELECTORAL ACTIVITIES

In accordance with ACLU policy of nonpartisanship, the projects and ACLU do not endorse candidates, contribute to campaigns, or engage in political action committee activity. However, in 1972, ACLU made an exception to its policy against taking stands on judicial appointments and opposed President Nixon's nomination of William Rehnquist to the Supreme Court. In 1987, after considerable debate, the board decided to alter policy to permit it to oppose Supreme Court nominees whose judicial policy was antithetical to civil liberties. It then campaigned actively against Reagan nominee Robert Bork. In 1991, although all board members decried Bush's appointment of Clarence Thomas, the board decided the wording of its policy did not permit active opposition. The policy was under examination again in 1992. As part of its public education agenda, ACLU tries to highlight civil liberties issues in election campaigns to increase public and candidate sensitivity to the topic.

FURTHER INFORMATION

The best resource is the annual reports published by ACLU and the projects, which provide comprehensive information on their activities. See also *In Defense of American Liberties: A History of the ACLU* (1990), written by Samuel Walke, the best single source of ACLU historical material written by a board member. The author wishes to acknowledge the assistance of Professor Philippa Strum, City University of New York.

PETER V. RAJSINGH

AMERICAN COLLEGE OF NURSE-MIDWIFERY
See AMERICAN COLLEGE OF NURSE-MIDWIVES

AMERICAN COLLEGE OF NURSE-MIDWIVES (ACNM)
818 Connecticut Avenue, NW #900
Washington, DC 20006
(202) 728-9860
FAX (202) 728-9897

In recent years many women's issues interest groups have included childbirth matters among their concerns. Such groups have worked to ensure that pregnancy is treated as a normal rather than a medical condition and that pregnant women, mothers, and infants receive quality health care. One organization active in these areas is the American College of Nurse-Midwives (ACNM). Although relatively young and small, ACNM has proved influential in promoting policies to support these goals.

ORIGIN AND DEVELOPMENT

Officially founded in 1955, ACNM had its roots in two organizations established earlier in the twentieth century. One branch evolved from the nurse-midwives section of the National Organization of Public Health Nurses* (NOPHN). Although nurse-midwives had created their own section in 1944, they had no provisions made for them when the parent organization merged with the National League for Nursing* (NLN) in 1952. Both NLN and the American Nurses' Association* (ANA) seemed reluctant to recognize the nurse-midwives; and several women who had been active in NOPHN—Hattie Hemschemeyer, M. Theophane Shoemaker, and Lillian Runnerstrom—decided to form their own organization. In 1954, seventeen nurse-midwives held an organizational meeting at the ANA convention and incorporated as the American College of Nurse-Midwifery. In 1960 it merged with the American Association of Nurse-Midwives, established in 1928 by Mary Breckinridge as an alumni association for women who had worked in the Frontier Nursing Service. In 1969 it changed its name to ACNM.

Its founders envisioned ACNM as a professional organization that would represent the needs of certified and student nurse-midwives. Its initial goals included setting standards for the practice of nurse-midwifery, evaluating and accrediting educational programs, certifying applicants, assisting certified nurse-midwives (CNMs) in establishing practices, promoting research and publication, communicating with other health care providers, and promoting public policy supportive of nurse-midwifery and quality health care for mothers and children. ACNM experienced great success in these areas, especially during the 1970s and 1980s, as the health care industry struggled with maldistribution of personnel and cost containment, and feminists advocated woman-controlled obstetrical care.

By 1990 the number of both educational programs and nurse-midwives in the United States had tripled. States that had prohibited or restricted CNMs amended their laws and legally recognized the practice of nurse-midwifery. In response ACNM broadened its activities. In the 1970s and 1980s, the group adopted a Code of Ethics, developed continuing education programs, and established a competency assessment program. It also worked on matters of concern to both practitioners and consumers. These included affordable malpractice insurance, third-party reimbursement for CNMs, and safe, affordable, family-centered maternity care for all women.

ORGANIZATION AND FUNDING

Members are organized in fifty-five chapters and six regions. The board is composed of the president, vice president, secretary, treasurer, and regional representatives. Officers and regional representatives are elected by active members and receive no salary. The current president is Teresa Marsic. Since 1960 some of the most visible officers have been Betty Bear, Judy Rooks, Angela Murdaugh, Elizabeth Sharp, Helen Burst, Agnes Reinders, and Lucille Woodville. Besides these elected officials, ACNM employs a chief operating officer, Ronald Nitzsche, and twenty staff members at the national headquarters in Washington, D.C. Committees, divisions, student interns, and volunteers also do much of the organization's work. ACNM also employs a legislative liaison who lobbies, testifies at congressional hearings, and disseminates information to candidates and political officeholders.

ACNM's membership growth kept pace with the growth of American nurse-midwifery. In 1955, 124 CNMs belonged to the organization. The number of members grew to 460 and 860 in 1965 and 1975, respectively. Between 1975 and 1985 membership tripled, reaching 1,500 in 1980 and 2,534 in 1985. By the 1970s ACNM represented the majority of American nurse-midwives. In 1971, 67 percent of CNMs belonged to the organization, and by 1977 the proportion had climbed to 78 percent. In 1982, 90 percent of all practicing nurse-midwives belonged to ACNM, in 1994, 97 percent.

Historically, 99 percent of members and 100 percent of the board of directors have been women. As of 1988, 96 percent of white and 88 percent of minority CNMs held membership in the group. Reasons that people join ACNM include a chance to communicate with peers and associate with like-minded people, to enhance professional knowledge through ACNM-sponsored publications and conferences, and to acquire an advocate to represent their professional opinions to government.

ACNM has 501 (c) (6) tax-exempt status. The ACNM Foundation is a 501 (c) (3). Members pay annual dues of $250. Significant expenditures include staff salaries and administrative expenses, grants for research and education, publication cost, legal and public relations fees, and committee and division expenditures.

POLICY CONCERNS AND TACTICS

The board and executive officers set policy for the group. ACNM members influence these decisions through communication with local chapter chairpersons, regional representatives, and board members. Officers regularly solicit rank-and-file advice through opinion polls and convention discussions. After adopting a course of action, the association uses a variety of strategies to influence public policy. ACNM has testified at congressional, state, and agency hearings; supplied legislators and department heads with information; published research findings and press releases; and conducted letter-writing campaigns to mobilize members, political officials, and the public on significant issues. A legislative committee informs the membership of relevant federal and state legislation, initiates letter-writing campaigns, and works with liaison in areas such as lobbying.

Since its founding, ACNM has worked consistently for the passage of laws pertaining to maternal and child health, such as the 1974 Social Services Act, 1978 Pregnancy Disability Act, 1982 Welfare Act, and 1983 Social Security

Act. Officers believe the organization's most important contributions in federal legislation have come in promoting CNM practice. ACNM support proved to be instrumental to passage of the 1980 Mandatory Medicaid Reimbursement Act, 1986 Risk Retention Act Amendment, and 1987 Mandatory Medicare Reimbursement Act. These acts provided for both reimbursement and self-insurance for CNMs and led the way to third-party payment of other non-physician health care providers.

Through this legislative program, as well as its efforts to establish standards, accredit educational facilities, and regulate nurse-midwifery practice. ACNM seeks to provide an environment in which both female practitioners and pregnant women can exert control over childbirth and maternal and infant care.

ACNM also works with other organizations on matters of mutual concern. For the last decade it frequently has allied itself with the Children's Defense Fund,* Washington Coalition of Nurses, and Southern Governors Task Force on Infant Mortality. Occasionally it joins forces with other groups. For example, ACNM and the American College of Obstetricians and Gynecologists* issued a joint statement on nurse-midwifery practice in 1971. This statement was jointly reconfirmed in 1994.

ELECTORAL ACTIVITIES

ACNM does not have a political action committee. While ACNM does not view women's issues as partisan and does not endorse candidates, it does identify "good friends" in public office and urges nurse-midwives to vote for "sympathetic legislators."

FURTHER INFORMATION

ACNM publishes the *Journal of Nurse-Midwifery* and an official newsmagazine, *Quickening.*

SUSAN RIMBY LEIGHOW

AMERICAN COLLEGE OF OBSTETRICIANS AND GYNECOLOGISTS (ACOG)
409 12th Street, SW
Washington, DC 20024
(202) 638-5577
FAX (202) 484-5107

The American College of Obstetricians and Gynecologists (ACOG) is the national organization that strives to have within its membership everyone who practices both obstetrics and gynecology or one of them exclusively. It makes itself extremely useful in creating national standards of care and in putting out technical bulletins and guidelines for the profession on new technologies and new problems, and it attempts to give the woman as a patient the rather comprehensive view of both the problems she faces and what is available to help her.

ORIGIN AND DEVELOPMENT

ACOG was founded in 1951. Among the founders were C. W. Beacham, M. D., Ralph A. Reis, and Herbert Schmidt. ACOG originally had ten members. They were informally members of the prior American Committee on Maternal Welfare, which met intermittently. The resultant college organization was modeled upon the Central Association of Obstetrics and Gynecology and used all the same requirements of that very successful professional gathering. The reason behind ACOG's founding nationwide was maternal mortality and maternal health committee work. In the late 1920s and all through the 1930s and 1940s, there were maternal mortality committees throughout the cities of the United States. All were famous for the work they did and for the type of postgraduate medical education that they offered to practitioners, hospital personnel, and medical students. The emphasis, once ACOG was founded, continued to be on maternal mortality and health, but ACOG did not ground its work in local committee meetings. It set up large programs for continuing medical education and national, published standards of care for the profession and for women patients. In 1990, the organization announced a national program to reduce fetal and infant mortality through careful perinatal mortality review.

Once ACOG's programs of patient care that reached physicians became successful, and most of those involved in the practice of obstetrics and gynecology became members. ACOG began to reach out to the patient herself, through printed material and television public service announcements. No videotape programs are used. In the past few years, ACOG has broadened its informational networking to include the general public and now puts out a weekly column on women's health that is published in over 1,000 newspapers in the United States.

ACOG continues to exist basically for the continuing education and updating of medical practitioners, to provide continuous information to the modern woman as a patient, and to educate the general public. Optimal physician training and concomitant technological excellence are perceived now as insufficient for successful outcomes when the patient is a woman who is alcoholic, bulimic or anorexic, a substance abuser, AIDS-infected or HIV positive, or infected with a sexually transmitted disease.

ORGANIZATION AND FUNDING

ACOG is governed by a board of seventeen members, one each from ten geographical districts into which it divides the United States, plus seven officers voted upon by the membership, including a president, vice president, one member from the public at large, and the chairman of the Junior Fellows. Junior Fellows is an in-house organization encompassing those trained individuals who are in active practice but have not yet passed their certifying boards. The public at-large member is a woman and always will be; a national vote of ACOG selects her from among selected nominations by physicians all over the country. The current president is William Andrews; the first woman president was Luella

Kline of Atlanta, who is still a current board member. The last president, Ezra C. Davidson, Jr., is African American, another first. Headquarters is in Washington, D.C.; and ACOG's executive director is Warren Pearse. Professional staff number 208.

Until 1965, ACOG's membership consisted of those who had practiced obstetrics and gynecology for five years. From 1965 onward, the organization has had a requirement for its fellowship of board certification in obstetrics and gynecology. In 1989, 2,489 women were board-certified. ACOG total membership is 23 percent female, who make up almost 50 percent of all board-certified obstetricians and gynecologists who belong. For those who work exclusively in nonpractice areas such as public health or research, there is an associate membership status.

In 1970, ACOG's budget was $1,900,000; in 1990, it was $5,300,000. Currently, ACOG's annual budget is $22 million, 27 percent of which comes from membership dues, which are $425 a year. Most income comes from creating and managing the educational programs and sales of published material. Ten percent of income is from federal grants on subjects that the governing board believes are important for ACOG to investigate, such as the National Cancer Therapeutic Program. The pharmaceutical houses contribute relatively small amounts, including $75,000 to support the weekly news column and $300,000 for special educational programs such as setting up self-assessment tests for women and men in residencies in order to start them on their career.

POLICY CONCERNS AND TACTICS

As a 501 (c) (3) organization, ACOG cannot do substantial lobbying. This is not to say that it is uninterested in equity legislation for women. It is there to help modify, develop, and write regulations for various laws concerning women's health. This is the reason its main office moved from Chicago to Washington, D.C. Decisions about what issues to treat through ACOG's Department of Government Relations are taken deliberately, through a Health Care Commission or Educational Commission, and approved by the executive board. Also influential are recommendations by professional staff. ACOG's most important strategies for influencing public policy include supplying congresspeople, agency heads, or staff with information, preparing comments on proposed regulations and seeking administrative review of agency or department decisions, educating the public through press releases, conducting and publishing research on issues, and fielding public service campaigns. Although ACOG's Department of Government Relations takes less than one-half of 1 percent of the overall budget, it is very much interested in women's issues such as *Roe* v. *Wade,* the Hyde amendments, proposed human life constitutional amendments, the 1978 Pregnancy Disability Act and health care reform. ACOG regards as most important the Title X regulations relating to abortion counseling, the 1986 Health Care Improvement Act, and Virginia's No-Fault Neurologically Damaged Newborn Act. ACOG has major group allies in, and develops programs with, the American Academy of Pediatrics* (AAP), the American Medical Association, and the American Academy of Family Physicians. All important projects that require such cooperative efforts are ad hoc coalitions. ACOG's chief adversary has been the U.S. Health and Human Services Department, which has blocked action on reproductive health care issues for women, including the areas of research service, population policy, and international health.

ELECTORAL ACTIVITIES

ACOG does not endorse candidates for political office or distribute partisan information.

FURTHER INFORMATION

The first issue of the *Standards of Care* was printed in 1957, six years after ACOG's founding. It now is in its seventh edition. ACOG began to publish printed perinatal guidelines as a joint program with AAP and has published over 100 technical bulletins defining acceptable current management for well-defined conditions in both obstetrics and gynecology. ACOG has published fifty committee opinions, giving a narrow consensus focus on current and important problems, such as defining the role of hysteroscopy, and in this area has done an enormous amount of work on ethical problems. ACOG also published very successful patient education pamphlets covering topics related to contraception, gynecologic problems, labor, delivery, and postpartum care, physiology and sexuality, pregnancy, special procedures, abuse, and women's health. Some of these are available in Spanish translation. In 1989 ACOG sold over 9 million of these pamphlets. In the same year ACOG produced 354 individual publications.

DOROTHY I. LANSING

AMERICAN COUNCIL ON EDUCATION COMMISSION ON WOMEN IN HIGHER EDUCATION
See AMERICAN COUNCIL ON EDUCATION OFFICE OF WOMEN IN HIGHER EDUCATION

AMERICAN COUNCIL ON EDUCATION OFFICE OF WOMEN IN HIGHER EDUCATION (ACE OWHE)
One Dupont Circle
Washington, DC 20036
(202) 939-9390
FAX (202) 833-4760

The Office of Women in Higher Education (OWHE) is a program office of the American Council on Education (ACE). It is advised by a Commission on Women in Higher Education (CWHE), composed of women presidents of ACE. ACE has completed seventy-five years of service as a national voice for higher education. It is a nongovernmental umbrella organization of institutions and associations dedicated to higher education. The current Office of Women was founded in 1973.

ORIGIN AND DEVELOPMENT

In 1920, ACE appointed a committee on the training of women for public service for a one-year period. In 1953, ACE established the Commission on the Education of Women to examine the role and levels of participation of women in higher education. This effort was funded initially by Katherine Sisson Phillips, founder of the National Association of Women Deans, Administrators, and Counselors (now known as the National Association of Women in Education*). The council terminated this commission in 1961 due to lack of funding and support from within.

The current OWHE formed in 1973. OWHE and CWHE came about because women presidents whose institutions belonged to ACE thought women's voices needed to be heard in ACE policy making, issue identification, and programming. These women and the men colleagues supporting them also thought that the number of women leaders throughout higher education should be increased. OWHE serves ACE member institutions by identifying and promoting women leaders and helping institutions meet women's educational needs and aspirations.

Since OWHE was founded, it has passed through three major phases. First, the office and the commission felt concerned with identifying a focus for OWHE that would enhance women's participation in higher education. Early issues addressed by OWHE included helping colleges and universities to interpret and implement Title IX of the 1972 Elementary and Secondary Act and other equal opportunity laws, regulations, and executive orders, especially regarding equal pension benefits.

The second phase focused almost entirely on advancing women leaders in higher education. The National Identification Program (ACENIP), formed in 1977, originally received funding from the Carnegie Corporation. Using a state-based structure, this program's goal is to increase the number of women in senior administrative positions. The women and men participating in this interlocking set of networks do so as volunteers, with each state determining the responsibilities and privileges of participation.

Another major component, which also formed in 1977, with a grant from the Johnson Foundation and the Fund for Improvement of Postsecondary Education, is the National Forum. This program is designed to afford outstanding women administrators, whose next move is a presidency, an opportunity to meet with each other and with high-level men administrators to establish a network and support for advancement. Over 900 women have attended these forums, and over 10 percent of them have become chief executive officers.

Once ACENIP was in place and working, it became possible to institute the third phase, which was marked by an effort to concentrate on institutional change. This phase really combined earlier efforts on legal issues and women's leadership and used the network of women leaders and supportive men colleagues to work on comprehensive strategies for changing institutions to educate women well and provide for this full and equal participation in higher education. To guide this effort, the staff, together with Carol Pearson, edited *Educating the Majority: Women Challenge Tradition in Higher Education.* The network used this book to promote "The New Agenda of Women for Higher Education," its last chapter.

OWHE also tracks women leaders' progress and reports on it. It serves a consulting function on a range of issues, with particular emphasis on academic searches. It coordinates ACE's Senior Executive Leadership Service, which assists in identifying talented women and men, majority and minority.

OWHE and the commission currently are engaged in an effort to reshape and reframe the ways in which colleges and universities think and act regarding women's issues. This process will inform the next phase of work, which will focus on making women's voices heard in the setting of institutional agendas and naming priorities.

ORGANIZATION AND FUNDING

OWHE's founding director, Nancy Schlossberg, was succeeded by Emily Taylor, who became a senior associate with OWHE in 1981. After Taylor, Donna Shavlik, who joined OWHE in 1973, served as director. Judith Touchton, with OWHE since 1977, began serving as deputy director in 1986. Additional staff include an executive assistant, program secretary, and program volunteer.

Foundation support accounts for approximately 25 percent of the office's funding, with the remainder coming from ACE program funding. ACE is a 501 (c) organization.

POLICY CONCERNS AND TACTICS

Staff determine new OWHE initiatives in conjunction with the commission or an advisory group of college and university presidents whose institutions are ACE members; the ACENIP network, numbering approximately 100; the ACE board of directors; and other ACE staff.

OWHE and ACE fully support all the equal opportunity laws, regulations, and executive orders pertaining to higher education, such as Titles IX, VI, and VII, executive order 11246 as amended, and the 1963 Equal Pay Act. OWHE does not interact frequently with government; it is responsive to requests such as nominations of women for major leadership roles in government. It works with other groups to promote women's leadership and sound public policy on women. For example, OWHE helped to found and continues to support the work of the National Coalition of Women and Girls in Education. This is a nongovernmental coalition of women's equity in education organizations. It has been instrumental in getting Title IX regulations issued, subsequently protecting and defending the Women's Educational Equity Act and Vocational Education Act and monitoring the enforcement of all the laws that affect equity for women and girls in education. OWHE also belongs to the National Council for Research on Women,* which it helped to found. This is an organization of all the major research and action centers that work on women's issues.

ELECTORAL ACTIVITIES

ACE and OWHE do not have a political action committee and do not see the issues that concern them as partisan.

FURTHER INFORMATION

OWHE publications include *Sexual Harassment on Campus: A Policy and Program of Deterrence, Educating the Majority: Women Challenge Tradition in Higher Education, Fact Book on Women in Higher Education, Women Chief Executive Officers in United States Colleges and Universities: Table XIII* (1992), and *Women in College and University Presidencies: A Descriptive Study.* ACE has two publications in which news about OWHE is published: *Higher Education and National Affairs,* a biweekly newsletter, and *The Educational Record,* a quarterly magazine.

LINDA MATHER

AMERICAN FEDERATION OF LABOR–CONGRESS OF INDUSTRIAL ORGANIZATIONS (AFL-CIO)
815 16th Street, NW
Washington, DC 20006
(202) 637-5000
FAX (202) 637-5058

The 14 million-member American Federation of Labor-Congress of Industrial Organizations (AFL-CIO) was created in 1955 from a merger of the AFL and the CIO. Within AFL-CIO, major affiliates with large numbers of women in their membership include the American Federation of State, County and Municipal Employees* (AFSCME), Amalgamated Clothing and Textile Workers (ACTWU), Service Employees International Union,* American Federation of Teachers, International Ladies Garment Workers Union,* and Communication Workers of America* (CWA). AFL-CIO has a political action committee (PAC), the Committee on Public Education (COPE).

ORIGIN AND DEVELOPMENT

By 1990 over one-third of union members were women, with black women (22.9 percent) more likely than Hispanic (14.5 percent) and white women (13.7 percent) to be unionized. The passage of Title VII of the 1964 Civil Rights Act, which made sex discrimination in employment illegal, was a milestone in AFL-CIO's treatment of women's issues. Title VII encouraged debate within unions and among feminists on how to advance women's rights. The AFL-CIO under President George Meany's leadership drew strong criticism for its record on women's issues. AFL-CIO was a major obstacle to calls for an equal rights amendment (ERA), and most of its affiliates continued to support protective legislation and contractual provisions that favored male workers.

Meany began the 1970s with public statements discounting the potential role of women in labor. The decade nonetheless brought noticeable changes in AFL-CIO's treatment of women. In 1973 it reversed its opposition to ERA. The establishment in 1974 of the Coalition of Labor Union Women* (CLUW)—an independent organization whose founding convention had substantial representation of women from AFL-CIO affiliates—sent a forceful message to the tradition-bound male leadership of AFL-CIO and its affiliates. The 1975 AFL-CIO convention passed a resolution declaring that AFL-CIO's civil rights committee's responsibilities included women's rights. There also were resolutions on child care policy, working women's rights, and the need to place minorities and women on the AFL-CIO executive council. In 1979, executive council election requirements were changed to promote affirmative action; and in 1980 Joyce D. Miller, a vice president of ACTWU and president of CLUW, became the first woman on that influential body. In 1981, Barbara B. Hutchinson, a vice president of the American Federation of Government Employees (AFGE) and the second director of its Women's Department, also joined the executive council, as its first black female member.

The 1975 convention was a pivotal event in the history of AFL-CIO's treatment of women's issues. Afterward, four women were appointed to the standing committee on civil rights (established in 1955); and in January 1976, Cynthia McCaughan joined the Civil Rights Department (CRD) as its coordinator of women's activities. She still holds the position. Because each standing committee has staff to assist its appointed membership, the Civil Rights Committee's responsibilities to women meant an increase in departmental staffing. By not creating a separate women's department, AFL-CIO chose a route different from that of affiliates that have, such as AFGE, AFSCME, and the United Automobile Workers.* Establishment of the position of coordinator of women's activities sent a clear signal, nevertheless, that AFL-CIO would begin to work with the women's liberation movement within and outside labor.

ORGANIZATION AND FUNDING

McCaughan is not the only staff member working with women's issues; there is substantial overlap of responsibilities among three staff members. A major function of CRD includes liaison activities with U.S. government civil rights officials, civil rights and women's rights organizations such as CLUW, the National Association for Advancement of Colored People and National Organization for Women,* civil and women's rights representatives of the affiliates, and civil rights and women's committees of AFL-CIO state and local central labor bodies. For example, McCaughan has served on the boards of the National Committee on Pay Equity,* Leadership Conference on Civil Rights (LCCR), and National Commission on Working Women.* Although the AFL-CIO constitution does not require it, some AFL-CIO state and local central labor bodies formally have established women's committees, such as the central labor bodies of California and Washington. CRD provides assistance to these committees when requested.

CRD's other activities include making information and literature available, assisting in resolving individual members' claims of rights violations by their respective unions, and conducting workshops and sponsoring conferences and meetings. Regardless of the activity, the guiding philosophy of CRD and its coordinator of women's activities has been to avoid isolation by emphasizing integration of women and women's issues into the labor movement generally. This philosophy also is reflected in AFL-CIO's departmental division of labor on women's issues. For example, the Education Department has cosponsored women's summer school programs; the Community Services Department has worked on issues related to women and poverty; and the Employee Benefits Department has assembled information on child care. An overall assessment of women in leadership positions in AFL-CIO yields mixed results. Women are directors of the important departments of education, employee benefits, and occupational safety and health and are well represented among AFL-CIO's regional representatives. AFL-CIO's executive council has not changed significantly, with only Joyce D. Miller and Lenore Miller among the thirty-three vice presidents in 1992. The executive council's 1992 racial composition was two blacks, one Hispanic, and thirty whites. Women then were presidents of only four affiliated unions, the only large one being the Retail, Wholesale and Department Store Union. Yet, just like men, women members of AFL-CIO are assessed a monthly per capita tax paid by their respective affiliates to AFL-CIO; the 1992 per capita tax was thirty-eight cents per member per month.

CRD's budget for 1990 was $470,786, compared with total AFL-CIO expenses of $58,798,031 for 1990; the proportion allocated to women's activities cannot be isolated, given CRD's overlap of responsibilities among staff members. The January 21, 1991, AFL-CIO secretary-treasurer's report, however, reports $110,000 in contributions to CLUW in 1990, which follows $100,000 in 1989.

POLICY CONCERNS AND TACTICS

The underlying source of AFL-CIO's decisions about policy priorities in lobbying consists of the affiliated unions' resolutions passed at the biennial conventions attended by the elected officials. Lobbying priorities also are determined by legislative staff's need to keep current with an ever-changing agenda of the Congress. AFL-CIO has a full-scale lobbying operation. As the umbrella organization for eighty-nine separate national or international labor unions, AFL-CIO's primary activities include lobbying government and engaging in political action as well as refereeing jurisdiction disputes among affiliates and providing a range of services to affiliated unions and members. AFL-CIO's Washington, D.C., office has twelve professional lobbyists, specialists on the basis of issues who are reluctant to isolate issues as women's alone.

AFL-CIO's lobbyists have devoted much attention in recent years to issues important to women, such as child care, parental and family medical leave, and civil rights legislation to reverse hostile Supreme Court opinions. AFL-CIO lobbyists were part of the coalition that helped pass the 1991 Civil Rights Act. Working with LCCR, AFL-CIO lobbyists invested much energy in counteracting the effects of rulings in employment discrimination cases such as *Wards Cove Packing Co.* v. *Antonio, Independent Federation of Flight Attendants* v. *Zipes,* and *Price Waterhouse* v. *Hopkins.* AFL-CIO's official policy on reproductive rights is to defer to its affiliates and their members in their individual judgments. Major lobbying adversaries of AFL-CIO on women's issues include the U.S. Chamber of Commerce and National Federation of Independent Business. Depending on the issue, AFL-CIO sometimes encounters opposition from other groups, as it did from the National Governors Association in 1990 on the issue of child care assistance.

ELECTORAL ACTIVITIES

AFL-CIO's electoral action capabilities are well known. Its PAC, COPE, contributed $837,927 to federal candidates during the 1989–90 election cycle, compared with $776,577 during the 1979–80 election cycle. Contributions generally go to Democrats on the basis of candidate endorsements by state labor federations and the projected closeness of electoral races.

FURTHER INFORMATION

In the fall of 1990, CRD began publishing a quarterly newsletter, *Equality Justice. AFL-CIO NEWS,* a weekly general membership newspaper, also provides useful information on activities of AFL-CIO and its affiliates on women's issues; it does not have a regular, designated column or section on women's issues.

RICHARD A. WANDLING

AMERICAN FEDERATION OF STATE, COUNTY AND MUNICIPAL EMPLOYEES (AFSCME)
1625 L Street, NW
Washington, DC 20036
(202) 429-5090
(202) 452-4800
FAX (202) 429-1293

The American Federation of State, County and Municipal Employees (AFSCME) is an American Federation of Labor-Congress of Industrial Organizations* (AFL-CIO) affiliated labor union representing the full diversity of workers found in state and local government, with the exception of teachers. This diversity includes workers in health care, corrections, social services, clerical services, state institutional care, and a variety of noninstructional positions in education. AFSCME has 1.3 million members; over half are women. It has a political action committee (PAC), PEOPLE, Public Employees Organized to Promote Legislative Equality.

ORIGIN AND DEVELOPMENT

AFSCME's origins are in the Wisconsin State Employees Association, founded in 1932. In 1936, AFSCME was recognized by the AFL as an independent union, and Arnold Zandler became AFSCME's first president. Zandler was unseated at the 1964 AFSCME convention by Jerry Wurf, who commonly is recognized as the individual most responsible for AFSCME's modern rise to power. With his aggressive personality, Wurf emphasized public employee activism, organizing, political action, and labor's involvement in civil rights issues affecting minorities and women. Beginning with the mid-1960s, AFSCME locals involved themselves in a number of high-profile labor confrontations. The best-known and perhaps most important confrontation involving women was a nine-day strike in 1981 by San Jose, California's, AFSCME local 101 over the issue of comparable worth. AFSCME's emergence as a major force in the labor community was ratified when Wurf became an international vice president on the AFL-CIO's Executive Council in 1969.

Wurf believed that rights issues affecting women and minorities were ultimately questions of "bread-and-butter justice." Under Wurf's leadership, AFSCME in the 1970s was the first AFL-CIO affiliate to support ratification of the equal rights amendment (ERA); AFSCME actively supported the founding and activities of the Coalition of Labor Union Women* (CLUW); and it established the AFSCME women's rights committee in 1979.

ORGANIZATION AND FUNDING

The president and the secretary-treasurer are elected for four-year terms by AFSCME convention delegates. AFSCME has some 3,300 locals and councils. The local is the basic unit of representation in AFSCME, and groups of locals then agree to associate together to form councils. The executive board consists of the international president, international secretary-treasurer, and thirty international vice presidents. The vice presidents, who serve four-year terms, are elected from legislative districts apportioned by membership size; the voting is done by delegates at a biennial convention. Five of the thirty vice presidents on the executive board are women, which at least compares favorably with AFL-CIO's two out of thirty-three but which is not proportionate to women's presence in AFSCME's membership. Women are well represented within the organizational structure of AFSCME, especially among the Washington office's regional representatives but also as directors or associate directors of key departments.

AFSCME's organizational structure includes the following key departments: Education, Community Action, Field Services, Legislation, PEOPLE, Political Action, Public Affairs, Public Policy, Research, Retirees, and Women's Rights. Each of these departments has the responsibility of implementing policy resolutions set at AFSCME's biennial conventions and the policy directives of the executive board. AFSCME officials extol the virtues of decentralization and see each department as playing an important role in serving locals, councils, and individual members.

Women also do well at the local level, AFSCME's basic unit. About half of all local elected officials, ranging from president to vice president and secretary-treasurer, are women. About one-third of the local union presidents are women. Since 1981, AFSCME's national president has been Gerald W. McEntee, a former organizer without the confrontational approach of his predecessor. He currently serves as chair of the AFL-CIO committee on the needs of the working family, which was established on his recommendation. William Lucy has been secretary-treasurer of AFSCME since 1972 and has left his mark on the labor movement by being a founder and president of the Coalition of Black Trade Unionists.

The Women's Rights Department (WRD) plays an important, but by no means exclusive, role in serving AFSCME's majority women membership. AFSCME has had a women's program for over fifteen years and a WRD for over ten years. WRD consists of a director, an assistant director, two coordinators, and two clerical workers. The current director is Catherine Collette. Major activities of WRD include conducting workshops and organizing conferences; providing technical assistance to locals and councils; preparing and distributing publications; serving as a spokesperson for AFSCME on women's issues; and participating in women's issues organizations and coalitions, such as the National Committee on Pay Equity* and the lobbying coalition that helped pass the 1991 Civil Rights Act. Women's success in AFSCME leadership seems likely to continue and even improve, supported by WRD leadership development programs. This success ultimately will mean more women on the international executive board.

An expanding membership base buttressed Wurf's activist presidency. Beginning in 1936 with a membership of 11,000, which included the attendance of twelve women as delegates at its founding convention, AFSCME has experienced a constantly upward movement in membership. This growth was facilitated by the increased participation of women, particularly working mothers in the paid labor force and rapidly expanding employment of both women and men by state and local governments. With 99,000 members in 1955, AFSCME increased to 237,000 by 1965 and 647,000 in 1975. In 1981, the year of Wurf's death, AFSCME had 957,000 members. While most AFL-CIO affiliates have declined or stagnated in membership, AFSCME has experienced some well-publicized successes in organizing. One of these highly visible successes was its May 17, 1988, election victory to represent 3,700 Harvard University clerical and technical workers, most of whom are women. AFSCME's financial support comes from membership dues, which financed a 1990 budget of $68 million. According to AFSCME's constitution, dues are to be no less than $8 per month, with adjustments made for members who work part-time.

POLICY CONCERNS AND TACTICS

Each AFSCME department has the responsibility for implementing policy resolutions set at AFSCME's biennial conventions and the executive board's policy directives. The board serves as AFSCME's policy-making body when a convention is not in session. AFSCME's international women's advisory committee meets periodically with the president and board to address concerns of women members. AFSCME pursues its agenda through lobbying. The Washington, D.C., office of the Legislation Department (LD), with its staff of seven professional lobbyists, monitors congressional voting and provides a legislative scorecard that rates the votes of members of the Congress on issues such as child care, parental and family medical leave, and health insurance reform. LD's lobbying focus ranges from civil rights reform to workplace issues and government taxation and spending.

AFSCME's contemporary record on women's issues probably most strongly is characterized by its use of litigation on comparable worth, which AFSCME during the last decade has viewed as the most important women's rights issue. AFSCME's most significant gain in eliminating wage-based discrimination in jobs dominated by women resulted from a favorable federal district court ruling in 1983 in *AFSCME* v. *State of Washington.* Although the ruling was overturned by the ninth U.S. Circuit Court of Appeals in 1985, AFSCME was able to negotiate an out-of-court settlement worth more than $100 million in pay adjustments for over 35,000 state workers.

AFSCME prefers to avoid litigation in favor of issue resolution through collective bargaining, as it did in San Jose, California, in 1981 following the nation's first strike over comparable worth. AFSCME locals also have used contract language to achieve gains for women in fighting sexual harassment, improving child care, and encouraging career mobility opportunities. These gains in contract language, in turn, are touted by AFSCME organizers. Organizing continues to be a major strategic and budgetary priority of AFSCME.

Lobbying allies include AFL-CIO and LCCR. AFSCME also may, depending on the issue, work with governmental lobbies such as the National Association of Counties. AFSCME lobbying extends well beyond the Congress because it has to deal with fifty different sets of state and local laws, particularly respecting collective bargaining. Major adversaries of AFSCME on women's issues have included the U.S. Chamber of Commerce, Eagle Forum,* and National Federation of Independent Business.

ELECTORAL ACTIVITIES

AFSCME is organizationally and financially equipped for the electoral arena. The Washington, D.C., and regional staff of the Political Action Department specialize in mobilizing AFSCME's membership. In 1971, AFSCME established its PAC, PEOPLE, which is funded by voluntary membership contributions. PEOPLE contributed $1,548,970 to federal candidates during the 1989–90 election cycle, compared with $338,035 during the 1979–80 cycle. Local and council affiliates have been encouraged to form state PEOPLE chapters, and state versions of PEOPLE have actively supported endorsed state government candidates with money and members in campaign support roles. Most of PEOPLE's support, whether at the federal or state level, goes to Democratic candidates.

FURTHER INFORMATION

During the 1980s and ending in 1991, WRD published the *AFSCME WOMEN'S LETTER* on a quarterly basis. The newsletter has been replaced by a department, "Not for Women Only," in AFSCME's bimonthly general membership magazine *The Public Employee.* The change was due to budgetary reasons and AFSCME's desire to reach a wider audience.

RICHARD A. WANDLING

AMERICAN FRIENDS SERVICE COMMITTEE, NATIONWIDE WOMEN'S PROGRAM (AFSC NWP)
1501 Cherry Street
Philadelphia, PA 19102-1479
(215) 241-7000 AFSC
(215) 241-7160 NWP
FAX (215) 864-0104

The American Friends Service Committee (AFSC), a religious, nonprofit organization, engages in numerous educational, humanitarian, and social change efforts. The Nationwide Women's Program (NWP) of AFSC seeks to combat sexism, which NWP views as a fundamental cause of social violence, exploitation, and oppression.

ORIGIN AND DEVELOPMENT

AFSC has its roots in the Religious Society of Friends, the Quakers. Quakerism was founded in turbulent seventeenth-century England by George Fox, who preached that every human being has infinite worth and that living in the spirit of God "takes away the occasion of all wars." Quakers in the United States formed the AFSC in 1917 in order to provide conscientious objectors to war a means of alternative service. The devastation produced by World War I gave AFSC an opportunity to provide medical service, famine relief, and reconstruction assistance to civilians in France, Germany, Austria, Poland, and the Soviet Union. For their decades of relief efforts on behalf of victims of oppression and war, the AFSC and Friends Service Council of London received the Nobel Prize for Peace in 1947.

Stemming from a 1973 Women's Gathering, NWP crystallized as an organization within AFSC between 1975 and 1977. NWP's efforts for women's equality, power, freedom, and justice draw on the rich historical legacy of Quaker feminism and service—a legacy suggested by such women as Margaret Fell, Mary Dyer, Sarah and Angelina Grimke, Alice Paul, and Elise Boulding. Among its many accomplishments, the NWP organized Quaker participation in the United Nations International Women's Decade, for example, world conferences in Copenhagen (1980) and in Nairobi (1985).

ORGANIZATION AND FUNDING

AFSC international headquarters is located in Philadelphia. The organization is headed by a 160-member corporation. All 160 belong to the Religious Society of Friends. Corporation officers include a chairperson, treasurer, and executive secretary. The corporation appoints a board of directors to oversee AFSC's policies, programs, and administration. Organized into nine regional offices (each with its own executive secretary and board) and more than forty program offices, AFSC's approximately 400 staff members (from a variety of religious, ethnic, and occupational backgrounds) carry out program and administrative tasks with the help of numerous volunteers. NWP provides resources and program development assistance for each AFSC region and for each AFSC division: International, Peace, and Community Relations.

NWP and AFSC are not membership organizations. Like other AFSC programs and divisions, NWP has a small paid staff. It includes a program coordinator, program associate, administrative assistant/office manager, and managing editor for a publication. The program coordinator currently is Saralee Hamilton. Numerous interns and volunteers provide additional staffing. A multiracial NWP committee of twenty to twenty-five women is appointed by the AFSC board to advise the staff and to provide general oversight for NWP's activities. Approximately 60–65 percent of the NWP committee are women of color.

As a nonprofit organization, the bulk of AFSC funds are derived from individual contributions and bequests. NWP works with an annual budget of less than $200,000: approximately three-fourths of that total comes from AFSC.

POLICY CONCERNS AND TACTICS

Important themes of NWP's work in recent last years have been (1) women, poverty, and economic power (WPEP); (2) women and global corporations (WGC); (3) feminists against militarism (FAM); (4) lesbian feminism; (5) reproductive rights; and (6) women, development, trade, and debt. Women's struggles, movements, and empowerment in the developing nations and in the United States are of central concern.

NWP has produced information resource packets for use on International Women's Day and during National Women's History Month. Other packets have covered such issues as women fighting poverty and empowering women in the workplace. Program resources have been made available to treat the topics of women's health, reproductive rights, domestic violence, apartheid, and the plight of women farmworkers.

In 1989–90, NWP sponsored pilot workshops on economic literacy for women as part of its WPEP. Its FAM project sponsored Voices of Hope and

Anger, a women's speaking tour about U.S. military bases at home and abroad. The WGC project documented the various ways in which corporate policies and militarism exploit women and produced in 1979 a widely used packet of resources entitled "Women in Global Corporations: Work, Roles and Resistance."

NWP also seeks to raise women's concerns within AFSC. It works to ensure that feminist perspectives are included in all phases of program design for all levels of the organization. It provides resources to enable AFSC to engage women's constituencies in its work. Especially important is the fact that NWP communicates and cooperates with over 100 domestic and international women's groups. For example, NWP has worked with a prenatal nutrition program in Chile, an employment program for women in West Virginia, and a support network for homeless women in Boston. Finally, NWP assists the AFSC affirmative action efforts as they relate to women staff members.

ELECTORAL ACTIVITIES

Like AFSC, NWP is not a traditional interest group. It does not engage in lobbying or in partisan politics.

FURTHER INFORMATION

NWP publishes a quarterly bulletin, *Listen Real Loud: News of Women's Liberation Worldwide.* See also Rachael Kamel, *The Global Factory* (AFSC, 1990).

LEONARD WILLIAMS

AMERICAN JOURNAL OF NURSING COMPANY
See AMERICAN NURSES' ASSOCIATION

AMERICAN LIBRARY ASSOCIATION (ALA)
50 East Huron Street
Chicago, IL 60611
(312) 944-6780
FAX (312) 440-9374

The oldest and largest nongovernmental organization committed to widely accessible libraries, the American Library Association (ALA) provides standards for library education accreditation and seeks to protect the professional status of a women-dominated field. Representing librarians, libraries, and supporters such as trustees, publishers, and other vendors, ALA early recognized the special responsibilities libraries have in meeting society's educational, social, and cultural needs, chief among them the preservation of intellectual freedom. It sees itself as the primary advocate for the U.S. people in their quest for excellence in library and information services.

ORIGIN AND DEVELOPMENT

ALA was founded in 1876 during the U.S. centennial, after unproductive meetings during the Civil War at librarians' conferences. An Amherst College librarian, Melvil Dewey, took leadership in founding it. William F. Poole of Chicago Public Library and Justin Winsor of Boston Public Library were among the founders. Thirteen women attended ALA's first conference. Early in the twentieth century, women entered librarianship in large numbers; Theresa West Elmendorf became the first women to serve as ALA president, 1911–12.

In 1909, ALA had a committee on federal and state relations. During World War I, it aided the U.S. War Department by providing services for troops statewide and abroad through public contributions. After 1920, having grown in membership and stature, ALA expanded its purview. It founded a library and library school in Paris, which led to extensive international connections, including participation in the United Nations Educational, Scientific and Cultural Organization. ALA's organization of Mexico City's Benjamin Franklin Library became a precedent for U.S. Information Agency libraries worldwide. One of only two amendments to ALA's 1879 charter alludes to its international stature.

ALA seeks to support and improve libraries of all kinds and to maintain access to their resources. It introduced means of classifying and cataloging resources so that readers might benefit from their availability and fought for libraries in schools, hospitals, and prisons. Open shelves, lending libraries, and public libraries supported by tax revenue were ALA reforms. It promoted the first act of Congress, passed in 1956, to provide federal aid to public libraries, an ALA goal since the 1930s.

In 1935, the organization refused to convene in cities where racial discrimination would limit its members. Its first black president, Clara C. Jones, served 1976–77.

ALA works with its affiliates and other national associations, such as the Special Libraries Association (SLA) and Association for Library and Information Science Education, in establishing central postures on library-related legislation. ALA has contact with such federal agencies as the Library of Congress, Education Department, National Commission on Libraries and Information Science, and National Endowment for the Humanities.

In 1971, ALA established its Social Responsibilities Roundtable (SRR) Task Force on Women (now, Feminist Task Force) to consider problems of sex discrimination and affirmative action; in 1991, women's salaries continued to lag behind men's in the field, and women were underrepresented on library school faculties. SRR now also includes a Gay and Lesbian Task Force. Social responsibility issues have included whether library services shall be provided without fee. ALA also participated in the boycott of conference sites called by the National Organization for Women* in states that had not ratified the equal rights amendment (ERA).

ORGANIZATION AND FUNDING

ALA has fifty-seven state and regional chapters in the United States and territories and international members in eighty-five countries. It has a 173-member representative council that meets twice yearly to set policy and air issues. From its membership is elected a thirteen-member executive board. One-quarter of the board is African American and Hispanic; board participation is encouraged of persons from a variety of backgrounds. Executive officers include a president, president-elect, past president, and treasurer elected by the personal membership by mail ballot.

The board administers eleven internal divisions and seventeen roundtables such as the Ethnic Materials Information Exchange and International Relations Roundtable, reflecting various types of library interests and different functional areas. In addition, there are numerous committees, such as the Committee on the Status of Women in Librarianship (COSWL), and twenty-two affiliated organizations, such as the ALA Black Caucus. Marilyn L. Miller is the current president. Seventy-five percent of officers and board members are women.

Besides its long-standing headquarters in Chicago, in 1943 ALA opened an office in Washington, D.C.; it maintains an editorial office in Connecticut for its academic library selection guide, *Choice*. The executive director of the Chicago office is Linda F. Crismond. Nationwide, ALA employs 100 professional staff; in Washington it has 4. Washington workers rotate jobs and experience different levels of responsibility; they are rewarded by promotion, salary increases, public recognition, and enhanced opportunities. The Washington office has a student intern and, besides two registered lobbyists, uses volunteers to testify before the Congress. There is an attorney on retainer.

ALA has 54,730 individual and institutional members worldwide, 1,654 outside the United States. Over half the international members are from Canada. Around 75 percent of members are women, which reflects the proportion of women in the profession. ALA has increased in size two and one-half times since 1963, when its membership stood at 22,000, and by two-thirds since 1984, when it had 37,000 members. Part of this growth resulted from a chapter relations office, which recruits members by raising awareness of the association and its benefits. It also can be attributed to the increasing importance of information to society, ALA's success in meeting its mission, and the organization's increasing visibility. Members join primarily to associate and communicate with like-minded colleagues; they have a chance to advocate important policies and to attend the annual convention and midwinter meetings, as well as to receive publications at discount and group insurance. Organizational skills development, public affairs participation, exercise of influence within ALA, and its representation of opinions to government, along with continuing education and research, also help attract members.

A nonprofit 501 (c) (3) organization, ALA derives 40 percent of its financial support from membership dues, which depend on membership type; for a first-time member, dues are $38. Personal dues range from $19 to $75, organizational dues from $70 to $900, and special dues from $150 to $1,000. A large publisher, ALA receives another 40 percent of its income from publication sales. Conventions account for most of its remaining revenue; relatively small amounts deriving from government grants or contracts, individual gifts or bequests (which are largely deductible), foundation grants, and sales of merchandise and insurance. With an endowment of $5 million, ALA has a budget of about $26,000,000 and revenues of over $26 million.

POLICY CONCERNS AND TACTICS

The executive board serves as the management board and makes recommendations with respect to policy and operation. Council determines the association's policies, often upon recommendation of its committees and overall ALA membership votes. To achieve legislative policy goals, ALA most typically testifies in congressional hearings and supplies congresspersons and their staff with information; it encourages members to engage in letter-writing campaigns. ALA also makes personal presentations to decision makers or encourages third parties to do so, testifies at administrative hearings, and offers comments on proposed regulations. It monitors voting records and engages in a large educational role, reaching members through publications and the public through press releases, conducting and publishing issue-oriented research, and mounting public relations or public service campaigns. Every year it pushes for adequate federal funding for libraries.

ALA has filed amicus briefs, for example, in *Webster* v. *Reproductive Health Services* (1990), challenging, among other things, First Amendment limitations legislated by an abortion control statute against health care providers and counselors. It also has litigated directly, for example, in *ALA* v. *Thornburgh,* a challenge to the 1988 federal Child Protection and Obscenity Enforcement Act, which placed heavy burdens on librarians. The Freedom to Read Foundation (FRF), a separate corporation that works in close liaison with ALA, was one of several plaintiffs in *Village Books* v. *Billingham* (1989); the case challenged a city ordinance treating pornography as a per se violation of women's rights.

ALA substantially influenced passage of the 1992 reauthorization of the Higher Education Act, 1990 reauthorization of the Library Services and Construction Act, and the 1991 High Performance Computing Act, which established the National Research and Education Network. ALA entered the nineties committed to the Omnibus Children and Youth Literacy through Libraries Initiative, recommended by the White House Conference on Library and Information Services. It urged libraries to develop guidelines on patron behavior and library usage after a recent court holding that a homeless man has a First Amendment right to receive information through a public library. It opposed the U.S. Education Department's 1991 prohibition against race-based college scholarships and the nation's entry into the Persian Gulf War and accompanying press regulation.

Among the policies that ALA has found of continuing importance are the 1964 Civil Rights and Equal Opportunity Acts, the affirmative action executive orders, ERA, and the 1974 Office of Economic Opportunity Act. The 1983 Social Security Act, 1984 Pension Equity Act, and 1986 Age Discrimination Act also have provoked ALA's interest. To express its overall stance on women's equality, the association took part in the 1989 march on equality but has not taken a stance on abortion rights per se.

COSWL seeks to help women in librarianship through association policies such as comparable wages for comparable work, affirmative action monitoring, and required salary ranges in ALA advertising. It sponsors a speaker's bureau and advisory material. In 1989, it organized the ALA delegation for the women's equality march and urged ALA involvement in the *Webster* case. It collaborates with both the Federation of Organizations for Professional Women* and National Women's Studies Association.*

ALA is a member of the International Federation of Library Associations and Institutes and sends representatives to a variety of organizations. It is affiliated with twenty-two organizations, including such groups as the American Association of Law Libraries, American Indian Library Association, Association for Library and Information Service Education, Chinese-American Librarians Association, Literacy Volunteers of America, Medical Library Association, National Association of Spanish-Speaking Librarians, Oral History Association, and Urban Libraries Council. It finds coordination with similar organizations to be advantageous. It has established National Partners for Libraries and Literacy with some sixty-two organizations, including the General Federation of Women's Clubs.*

ELECTORAL ACTIVITIES

ALA neither sees women's issues as partisan nor has a political action committee.

FURTHER INFORMATION

ALA publications include the monthly newsmagazine, *American Libraries,* which reaches over 55,000 readers; semimonthly review periodical *Booklist* and bimonthly *Booklinks* for educators; and *Choice,* which comes out eleven times yearly. In 1989, COSWL published a five-year cumulative sequel to *On Account of Sex: An Annotated Bibliography on the Status of Women in Librarianship* and continues to track this literature. A new edition of *Sisters Have Resources Everywhere Directory* was recently published. ALA publishes books and pamphlets; additional periodicals, some through its divisions; and films and videos. In 1990, ALA brought out forty new titles, and in 1991, fifty-one new titles.

SARAH SLAVIN

AMERICAN LIFE LEAGUE (ALL)
P.O. Box 1350
2721 Jefferson Davis Highway
Number 101
Stafford, VA 22554
(703) 609-2049

The American Life League (ALL) (before 1992, the American Life Lobby) describes itself as the "largest Christian pro-life organization." ALL supports only the amendment which would constitutionally prohibit all abortions by stating that "the paramount right to life is vested in each human being from the moment of fertilization without regard to age, health or condition of dependency."

ORIGIN AND DEVELOPMENT

Founded in 1979, soon after Judie Brown left her position as director of the Washington, D.C., office of the National Right to Life Committee* (NRLC), ALL frames its opposition to abortion in the context of the importance of religion and the restoration of family values. Critiques on secular humanism and attacks on Planned Parenthood* are common themes. Brown has welcomed media attention and in her numerous television appearances and print interviews, talked about the need for restoring absolute values.

This approach has evoked conflict among competing movement leaders and organizations, which challenge the media portrayal of Brown as a typical abortion opponent, reject her explicit reliance on religious discourse in arguments about abortion law and public policy, and, above all, contest her claim that ALL embodies a "pure" pro-life principle. ALL does, though, best fit media stereotypes of the antiabortion movement as comprising Christian fundamentalists who disfavor government intervention in the economy but favor government intervention to protect public morals by supporting prayer in the schools, suppressing pornography, restricting abortion, and the like.

Brown's own moral traditionalism and the explicit religiosity of her opposition to abortion found a ready niche both in movement and in national party politics. Within the movement Brown is considered independent and impatient, as well as unlikely to compromise her principles. She has testified against abortion laws supported by main players in the abortion controversy—such as NRLC and the National Conference of Catholic Bishops (NCCB)—because they are less restrictive than the "paramount right to life" amendment. Within the Republican Party, strategies seeking to expand the party base beyond fiscal conservatives found Brown's fledgling organization an early beachhead into conservative religion. In turn, Brown used Republican strategists to supply institutional and financial resources she lacked. Coming from a blue-collar background, she relied on NRLC Washington contacts with Paul Weyrich, Howard Phillips, and John Terry Dolan and the start-up contribution and direct mail techniques of Richard A. Viguerie.

Reasons for ALL's waning are mostly the inverse of its waxing. Its movement niche became crowded. When the Reagan presidency secured the religious Right, its ALL alliance deflated in value. The alliance between moral and fiscal conservatives on abortion was loosened, if not unhinged, by the 1989 U.S. Supreme Court decision *Webster* v. *Reproductive Health Services,* which upheld Missouri's state laws prohibiting abortions performed in state-funded hospitals (save for medical reasons) and permitting late-term determination by physician of fetal development. After *Webster,* the Republican national chairman declared the party's "umbrella" would now include explicitly pro-choice Republicans. Post-*Webster* Republican strategists openly began to question whether the party could afford to maintain simultaneously its opposition to abortion and to welfare costs, when one-third of women obtaining abortions fell below the poverty line. Finally, within the pro-life movement, ALL peaked and then declined as newly formed antiabortion groups within conservative Protestantism, such as the Christian Action League, Baptists for Life, Presbyterians for Life, and so on, provided explicitly religious movement niches of their own.

In January 1992, ALL, citing a recession-caused decline in contributions, requested its members to promise scheduled monthly contributions. These and other signals suggest that ALL, if it survives, will play an increasingly marginal role in abortion politics. Few activists any longer envision the legal prohibition of all abortion; religious fundamentalists and evangelicals now have already greatly distanced themselves from antiabortion activists. Still an antiabortion celebrity, Brown undoubtedly will continue her role in the movement as "moral purist." But her appearances are now cameo rather than starring.

ORGANIZATION AND FUNDING

ALL peaked in the mid-1980s, when Brown claimed a membership of around 300,000. In 1986, ALL (or its no longer extant political action committee) had offices not only in Washington, D.C., but also in New York City; Houston; Sacramento, California; and Stafford, Virginia. Its budget then was just under $3 million. By 1990, all but the Stafford offices had closed. At its peak, ALL staff numbered about thirty, busy with fund-raising, direct mail appeals, publication of ALL materials, data processing, and telephone receptions. As is the case with many social movement organizations, a major part of ALL's resources are expended on sheer survival.

Judie Brown has been ALL's sole president, and her husband, Paul Brown, its chairman. ALL holds no annual convention, and in the mid-1980s there were only two other members of the executive board, Secretary Susan Sassone and Treasurer Walter Avery. ALL's national advisory board includes religious activists, among them Beverly LaHaye and Phyllis Schlafly.

POLICY CONCERNS AND TACTICS

ALL rates its most important strategy as the education of its membership. Least important strategies include contacting public decision makers through influential members; personal presentations to congresspersons, agency heads, or staff; and filing court cases. Publicly ALL has criticized the Roman Catholic hierarchy for supporting abortion legislation that does not prohibit all abortions, such as the subsequently defeated 1983 Hatch amendment, and for linking opposition to abortion with opposition to capital punishment, military spending, and cuts in poverty programs. This "consistent ethic of life" perspective is the position of the NCCB and several other pro-life organizations, such as Just Life, Feminists for Life,* and Common Ground. ALL has also frequently criticized Republican allies for putting what Brown believes to be important issues appealing to working-class and middle-class moral conservatives, such as anti-abortion, prayer in the schools, and antipornography legislation, on the back burner in favor of its economic growth policies.

Considering itself the protector of the right to life "purity of principle," ALL does not stress coalition politics. ALL has actively testified *against* legislation proposed by NRLC because it would not prohibit all abortions. ALL finds little worth in such laws as the Pennsylvania Abortion Control Act, largely upheld by the Supreme Court (1992), judging that such restrictions as parental consent for minors, a twenty-four-hour waiting period, and ratification by the doctor about alternatives to abortion would accomplish little in stopping legal abortion. ALL's uncompromising hostility to legal abortion is infertile territory for the growth of coalitional skills.

ELECTORAL ACTIVITIES

Originally challenging NRLC for dominance in the pro-life movement, the first ALL initiative was the formation of the Life Amendment Political Action Committee (LAPAC). It was headed by Paul Brown. At that time, NRLC had no political action committee (PAC), and the only other directly political pro-life movement initiative was Women for the Unborn, by Ellen McCormack, a Long Island housewife who sought the Democratic Party presidential nomination in a dozen 1976 Democratic primaries and again in 1980. LAPAC published hit lists of prominent pro-choice Democratic liberals and filed an unsuccessful suit against every Roman Catholic diocese because church officials would not allow LAPAC to distribute single-issue campaign literature listing pro-choice candidates to vote against. Critics charged that less than 20 percent of LAPAC's funds went to political campaigns. By 1990, LAPAC made no more headlines and is now defunct.

FURTHER INFORMATION

ALL publishes a newsletter, *ALL about Issues;* in 1986, subscribers numbered 100,000.

JAMES R. KELLY

AMERICAN LIFE LOBBY
See AMERICAN LIFE LEAGUE

AMERICAN MEDICAL WOMEN'S ASSOCIATION (AMWA)
801 N. Fairfax St., Suite 400
Alexandria, VA 22314
(703) 838-0500
FAX (703) 549-3864

The American Medical Women's Association (AMWA) is a national organization of over 13,000 women physicians and medical students. AMWA is dedicated to promoting women's health care and enhancing the professional development and personal well-being of its members.

ORIGIN AND DEVELOPMENT

Originally named the Medical Women's National Association (MWNA), AMWA was established in 1915 by Bertha van Hoosen and a group of women physicians who met for dinner during an American Medical Association meeting in Chicago and decided to form the first national association of women physicians. In its early years, AMWA's most notable cause finally provided for the appointment of women physicians and surgeons in the Medical Corps of the Army and Navy under Public Law 38, passed on April 16, 1943. During World War I, a time when women physicians were denied commission as officers, the MWNA started the American Women's Hospitals Service Committee (AWHS), a committee which continues to support programs and provide medical services for the underserved both in the United States and abroad. In the 1920s and 1930s, "MWNA was a strong advocate for improved prenatal and child health care services through subsidized public health clinics and preventive health care education" (AMWA Annual Program; 1990). In 1937, the MWNA was renamed the American Medical Women's Association and initially served as a forum for the presentation of papers.

For many years, AMWA had no formal program to encourage women physicians to join its efforts. News about the organization traveled through professional networks. In the 1970s, AMWA had about 2,000 members. A new executive director, Carol Davis-Grossman, made a concerted effort to recruit members, and membership doubled in the early 1980s. By the late 1980s, with medical students being granted the privilege of joining, voting, and holding office, AMWA grew to about 8,000 members.

In recent years, AMWA has promoted women's health care issues and served as the leadership training ground for women physicians who have then served as leaders of other major national medical associations.

ORGANIZATION AND FUNDING

AMWA's national officers consist of a president, president-elect, and vice-presidents in finance, membership, career development, communication, and programs. In 1992, two new officers were added, a speaker and a vice-speaker for the House of Delegates. These officers lead a twenty-six-member elected Board of Directors, which manages and directs the organizational policy. In addition, the Board leads a structure consisting of nineteen committees, twenty-five subcommittees, six task forces, and three ad hoc committees. This committee structure allows many AMWA members to become involved at the national level.

In 1957, a branch system of regional and community networks of membership was established. AMWA is divided into ten regions, each with an elected Regional Governor. Each region is comprised of local chapters, called branches, in the state or area. Currently, there are eighty physician branches and 150 student branches. Regions and branches sponsor AMWA activities and programs for members in their locale.

Each branch is represented proportionate to local membership size in AMWA's national House of Delegates, which is responsible for electing officers, establishing association policy, and amending by-laws. Resolutions passed by the national House of Delegates form the foundation of AMWA's legislative agenda and often are used as the basis of position papers. A student network, composed of two National Student Coordinators, fifteen Student Regional Coordinators, and more than 150 student branches at medical and osteopathic schools supplements the organizational structure.

AMWA's national staff consists of twenty full-time and three part-time employees as well as two consultants. Eileen McGrath currently serves as the Executive Director.

AMWA has over 11,000 members (6,000 regular members, 2,400 medical interns and residents, and 2,600 medical students). AMWA membership includes membership in the Medical Women's International Association, founded in 1919.

The current annual income of the association is about $1.5 million; about 65 percent of the income is generated by membership dues and 35 percent is generated equally by interim and annual meeting fees, fundraising, and the Product Acceptance Program. The Product Acceptance Program, administered by AMWA's Scientific Evaluation Council, is a visibility and income generating program which allows companies to have their products evaluated in terms of improving women's health for possible endorsement by AMWA.

POLICY CONCERNS AND TACTICS

In 1988, AMWA moved its headquarters from New York City to the Washington, DC area to have more impact on federal policy. AMWA has joined in *amicus curiae* briefs and developed a legislative alert network through AMWA state directors. AMWA members have been recognized by national media sources, have helped create health care policy by serving as members of task forces led by the U.S. President, and have testified before the U.S. House of Representatives and Senate committees on behalf of women's health care issues.

The association has been particularly instrumental in advocating and supporting programs related to women's health. AMWA's agenda of women issues has included breast cancer, reproductive health, osteoporosis, smoking cessation, health care reform, and cardiovascular disease in women. AMWA is also concerned about domestic violence, AIDS prevention and education, gender discrimination, and sexual harassment. AMWA offers Continuing Medical Education (CME) credits though several annual educational programs to train physicians in better detection, diagnosis, and treatment of women patients with increased sensitivity and improved patient/physician relationships.

AMWA has been a part of a number of coalitions of organizations, mainly women's and medical organizations, which support or endorse legislation. Frequent allies include the American College of Obstetrics and Gynecology,* the American Psychiatric Association, and the American Nurses Association.* AMWA, along with other associations, officially endorsed the Family and Medical Leave Act, Freedom of Choice Act, and International Family Planning Protection Act.

FURTHER INFORMATION

The *Journal of the American Medical Women's Association,* a scholarly journal of research, is published six times a year along with *What's Happening in AMWA,* a quarterly newsletter. AMWA also offers low-interest medical education loans to Student Life Members, makes several important awards of recognition annually, and offers an informal mentor program. AMWA maintains archives on women in medicine in the Archives and Special Collection on Women in Medicine at the Medical College of Pennsylvania and at the Medical Archives at New York Hospital/Cornell Medical Center in New York City.

CAROL J. AUSTER

AMERICAN NURSES' ASSOCIATION (ANA)
600 Maryland Avenue, SW
Suite 100 West
Washington, DC 20024
(202) 554-4444
FAX (202) 554-2262

The American Nurses' Association (ANA), a membership organization, is the only American constituent member of the International Council of Nursing. In recent years, an economic and general welfare program has emerged as a major ANA function, particularly for nurses in larger states where collective bargaining is the norm. ANA has a political action committee (PAC) and a research foundation.

ORIGIN AND DEVELOPMENT

ANA grew out of efforts by the Society of Superintendents of Training Schools for Nurses of the United States and Canada (later, National League for Nursing* [NLN]) to form a national organization for nurses. First, the superintendents formed a coalition of nursing schools' alumnae associations. In 1896, ten representatives of the associations met to found the Nurses' Associated Alumnae of the United States and Canada (NAA), which in 1912 became ANA.

ANA campaigned early for state registration of nurses and establishment of the designation registered nurses (RN). Although the first licensing laws were enacted in 1903, not until 1923 were they on the books of all states, as well as the District of Columbia and Hawaii. Controlled by ANA but independent of board action, the establishment in 1900 of the *American Journal of Nursing* aided the ANA's campaign. NAA set up constituent state organizations to encourage local members to lobby for the registration acts. This action forced the separate alumnae associations to band together and led to organizations in states without associations. The result was a more professional organization that deemphasized alumnae activities.

One issue over which nurses divided early in their history was the women's rights movement and suffrage campaign. The *American Journal of Nursing* debated the issue, with pro-suffrage forces led by Lavinia Dock and Lillian Wald. The journal's editor, Sophie Palmer, believed suffrage was not a nursing matter and that "editorial policy must be neutral." Not until 1915 did ANA finally vote to support the Susan B. Anthony amendment. Dock in 1923 began a campaign for an equal rights amendment (ERA) once the suffrage amendment was ratified and the National Woman's Party* organized around it. As a whole, nurses were slow to follow suit, with an ANA committee opposing ERA as late as 1950. Nurses did not want to lose the benefits they believed women had achieved through protective labor legislation.

Most early nurses did private duty as independent contractors, and private duty nurses and nursing administrators dominated ANA for much of its early history. Various ANA affiliates ran employment registries for nurses in cities across the country emphasizing the dominance of private duty nurses.

Like most other occupations, nursing often drew a color line. Most early hospital training schools refused to admit black students; by 1891 separate schools appeared. A 1925 study found education facilities for black nurses to be inadequate, with little hope for improving them. The National Association of Colored Graduate Nurses (NACGN) organized in 1908, but its growth was slow. ANA never drew a color line for membership, although many ANA state affiliates discriminated. In 1946, the House of Delegates recommended that state and district associations eliminate racial bars to membership as early as possible, and to pressure recalcitrant states further, ANA provided individual membership for professionally qualified nurses excluded from state associations. Encouraged by these efforts, in 1949, ANA proposed that it absorb the NACGN, which accepted the proposal. In 1951, the two groups merged. In the 1960s, as black consciousness rose, a separate affiliated group, the Council for Black Nurses, again organized. At least since World War II, a significant number of African American women have occupied ANA leadership roles.

Collective bargaining was slow to become part of ANA. Students staffed most hospitals. Not until the 1930s did the number of staff nurses begin to grow and the number of private duty nurses to decline. ANA members in California during World War II started efforts toward collective bargaining but had to abandon them because ANA did not allow its constituent societies to act as bargaining agents. This changed in 1944, and in 1946 the House of Delegates adopted an economic security program that included collective bargaining, but it also adopted a pledge not to strike. The 1947 Taft Hartley Labor Management Relations Act exempted nonprofit hospitals from bargaining with employees. Without the right to strike and a need for hospitals to negotiate, nurses were compromised in bargaining. Opposition to the right to strike proved an emotional issue, and the pledge was not repealed until 1968. Official recognition in 1974 of the right to strike and organize came when the Labor Relations Act was extended to nonprofit health care institutions.

ANA increasingly has become an organization of rank-and-file nurses who are members because ANA is their bargaining agent. State nurses' associations became the bargaining units, and although at first not effective, they have gained expertise to mount an effective campaign both for bargaining rights and against rivals, including American Federation of Labor-Congress of Industrial Organizations* unions with nursing local and independent unions. The result has been a change in the nature of membership with the exodus of nurse administrators. Nurse educators still are disproportionately influential in ANA but are being replaced by nurses belonging to bargaining units. Many advanced specialty nurses have left to join specialty organizations such as the American Association of Critical Care Nurses, with 56,000 members and much smaller specialty groups.

ORGANIZATION AND FUNDING

Throughout its history ANA has had different organizational structures. In 1982, it adopted a modified federation structure with membership composed of state nurses' associations. The individual nurse belongs to a constituent state organization, with each state free to establish its own membership plan provided membership is limited to registered nurses or recently graduated nurses who have not yet passed the state board examination.

ANA is governed not only by its House of Delegates but also by its board of directors. Elected by the state associations, the House of Delegates meets annually to transact business and establish programs and policies. It elects the board of directors and officers, the majority of its nominating committee, and some cabinet members. Elections for national officers are held at the biennial, ANA's national meeting, which is held in even-numbered years. The current president is Virginia Trotter Betts. In intervals between delegates' meetings, the board transacts general business. A fifteen-member body consisting of ten directors and the association's officers—president, two vice presidents, secretary, and treasurer—has staggered terms in office. Offices are contested with organized campaigns at the biennial. In 1951, ANA established a full-time lobbyist in Washington, D.C.

ANA has standing committees, many written into the bylaws, and has organized deliberative bodies known as cabinets to which delegates assign specific responsibilities for nursing education, practice, research and service, economic and general welfare, and human rights. ANA also has councils, groups with a clinical or functional focus that provide a forum for discussion, continuing education, consultation, certification, and other services for specialty groups. An ANA subunit, the American Academy of Nursing, established in 1973, recognizes professional achievement and excellence; fellows are entitled to list Fellow of the American Academy of Nursing, FAAN, after their names.

Slightly more than 10 percent (200,000) of registered nurses, mostly in bargaining units, belong to ANA. One reason for low membership of nurses not in bargaining units is high cost of dues, over $250 a year, in local (district), state, and national associations. As it has changed, ANA has moved tentatively to retain and expand membership, including certifying some nurse specialists not yet certified by a specialty group. The certification program has weakened as more groups have grown sufficiently large to do their own certification. Philosophical disagreement has increased between ANA and some of its rivals as to who will certify. As nursing organizations have grown in complexity, they overlap in function, with some confusion as to which organization is supposed to do what.

The American Nurses' Foundation carries on nursing research; it solicits, receives, and administers funds for ANA projects and publications.

POLICY CONCERNS AND TACTICS

As the early nurse practice acts were written, a long-range agenda emerged to strengthen the policies related to licensure to give nurses increased autonomy in their practice and to protect them from competition from untrained nurses. This remains a political agenda for state constituents. At the national level, ANA long has involved itself in legislative activities, establishing its first committee in 1923. Originally confined to health, nurses, and nursing, it gradually has extended this mandate. ANA was an early supporter of national health insurance, which organized medicine has opposed. In 1984, independent of its political action committee (PAC), ANA endorsed Mondale-Ferraro because Geraldine Ferraro was on the Democratic ticket. ANA continues to support health-related federal entitlement programs such as Medicare and Medicaid and to support federal aid to nursing education and nursing research, and it is a strong lobby for women's issues at both the national and state levels.

ELECTORAL ACTIVITIES

In 1974, ANA established its own PAC, Nurses Coalition for Action in Politics (N-CAP), to solicit funds and politically educate nurses. N-CAP has become ANA PAC. It also provides funds to candidates favorable to nursing and of a progressive bent. It helps to fund only campaigns for federal office, including president. It endorsed President William Clinton in 1992 and the Mondale-Ferraro ticket in 1984. Over 30 percent of its funds go to like-minded challengers, among them women and people of color. In the 1990 cycle, it directed $287,000 to campaigns.

FURTHER INFORMATION

ANA's Washington office publishes a legislative newsletter twenty-four times a year. *Capital Update* highlights ANA's lobbying activities. The *American Nurse,* the official newspaper sent to members, also includes monthly updates about legislation, as does the *American Journal of Nursing (AJN)*. ANA exercises indirect control of *AJN,* which is published by the American Journal of Nursing Company, the stock for which is owned by ANA. Other publications include *Facts about Nursing,* various reports, and convention proceedings.

VERN L. BULLOUGH AND BONNIE BULLOUGH

AMERICAN NURSES' ASSOCIATION POLITICAL ACTION COMMITTEE
See AMERICAN NURSES' ASSOCIATION

AMERICAN NURSES' FOUNDATION
See AMERICAN NURSES' ASSOCIATION

AMERICAN RED CROSS (ARC)
17th and D Streets, NW
Washington, DC 20006
(202) 639-3200
FAX (202) 347-1794

Known best for providing relief to people who are victims of natural and man-made disasters and armed conflicts and for its volunteer blood donors program and certification courses in health and safety, the American Red Cross (ARC) is a volunteer-led citizens' group that operates at the grassroots level. ARC's conception of its humanitarian service mission mirrors the traditional female role; and women played a pivotal role in its founding. Groundwork for ARC's acceptance in the United States was provided by the Women's Central Association of Relief, organized in 1861 to coordinate union military relief activities during the Civil War. The International Red Cross's founder was himself influenced by the pioneering efforts of Florence Nightingale to alleviate the unsanitary conditions of military hospitals in the Crimean War. Clara Barton, who founded the American Association of the Red Cross in 1881, recognized that relief work could provide more meaningful occupation for women than the existing options of teaching and clerical work, while also observing women's acceptable roles of caregiver and volunteer.

ORIGIN AND DEVELOPMENT

As part of the International Red Cross created at the Geneva Conference in 1864 by Jean-Henry Dunant, ARC was committed to care for all casualties during war, whether allies or enemies. Barton authored an amendment enlarging the organization's mandate to dispense aid to victims of natural disasters. She envisioned ARC as a spontaneous, grassroots organization to rally public funds and support in times of national emergency. As humanitarian enterprises proliferated during the Progressive era of the early 1900s, the public demanded that philanthropic organizations adopt more efficient business methods. Shortcomings in ARC's administrative organization were revealed during the Spanish-American War when Red Cross voluntary efforts and U.S. military services duplicated and at times obstructed each other's relief efforts. When Barton resisted outside supervision, a split developed within ARC between her supporters and a faction led by Mabel T. Boardman and Anna Roosevelt Cowles (sister of President Theodore Roosevelt), who felt that ARC must become efficient and financially accountable in order to maintain the public's confidence.

In 1900, ARC received a charter from the U.S. Congress officially sanctioning the organization's exclusive obligation to provide services to U.S. armed forces members and relief to disaster victims worldwide. This charter effectively forced reform in that its governing body became a central committee with direct governmental representation. Barton resigned in 1904. The central committee was enlarged in 1947 into a board of governors with greater local representation. Although ARC never has received direct federal funding, its historically close, significant relationship with the government persists to this day. U.S. presidents are honorary heads of the organization and appoint representatives from cabinet-level agencies to serve on its board of governors.

Recognizing the limitations of a mission focused only on war and disaster relief, in the early 1900s, officials began to expand and diversify. Early developments, for example, included the establishment in 1910 of a relief commission to create pensions for widows and orphans of men killed in mine disasters and led to enactment of national workmen's compensation laws. The ARC established the Red Cross Nursing Service in 1909 and the Nutrition Service in 1919, which have involved professional women in large numbers. ARC emergency relief programs have expanded into a variety of prevention activities, including parenting and lifesaving skills, first aid, small craft and water safety programs, and immunization and blood pressure screening for the elderly.

ARC is supportive of women's concerns in many ways; for example, many chapters with sufficient local resources provide temporary housing and social services to help women provide for their families and emphasize development of financial and social ability to remain in permanent housing through assistance with government benefits, child care, referral to educational and career training, support groups, and workshops on health, parenting, human sexuality, nutrition, budgeting, and cultural and recreational activities.

Help for seniors provided by some chapters includes twenty-four-hour emergency housing and case assistance for crime victims and seniors without essential services such as heat or electricity. Some provide short-term rental assistance to prevent eviction and escort and transportation services after hospital discharge, as well as help with arranging housekeeping or home care. Some chapters provide a personal emergency response system and a Telephone Club and Good Neighbors to Seniors Visiting Program for seniors living alone. By assisting the elderly to live independently and offering emergency help and companionship, ARC relieves the burden of "women-in-between," who are often responsible not only for their families but for their aging parents.

Locally, where resources are available, ARC also meets the special needs of latchkey children, black and Hispanic youth, Asians, Native Americans and other minorities, people with disabilities, and the victims of spouse abuse. At World War II's conclusion, ARC expanded its blood service for the military into a civilian blood service that now supplies one-half of the nation's donated blood to hospitals. This program recently has expanded to include tissue transplantation services such as bone tissue for orthopedic procedures, skin tissue for burned patients, temporal core bone to restore hearing, and heart valves for heart defects.

The American Red Cross also runs the Holocaust and War Victims Tracing Center, serving those who were separated from their families during World War II. Through an arrangement with the International Committee of the Red Cross, the center assists those trying to discover the fate of those lost during the war in Europe and the Soviet Union.

ARC has responded to changing health needs and technologies, trains its volunteers to cope with toxic chemical and radiation disasters, and has developed educational programs on HIV/AIDS, with an emphasis on youth, persons requiring bilingual programs, and specialized training for health care providers and foster families of children with HIV/AIDS, as well as AIDS home care courses for family and friends who become caregivers. A volunteer emergency services organization, ARC continues to define its mission as improving the quality of human life, enhancing self-reliance and concern for others, and helping people prepare for, and cope with, emergencies.

ORGANIZATION AND FUNDING

As an independent, community-based organization, ARC's services and programs are largely formulated by 1,900 local chapters and based on community needs. The public is encouraged to contact local chapters for help and information. The national headquarters in Washington, D.C., formulates policy and provides guidance through an all-volunteer board of governors. The current chair of the Board is Norman Augustine. Former secretary of the U.S. Departments of Transportation and Labor, Elizabeth H. Dole serves as president. Volunteers and paid staff at the national level also provide educational and technical assistance for local projects. In 1993 there were 1,417,986 volunteers and 25,394 career staff. ARC is an equal opportunity organization, with women and minorities well represented at all levels, including chapter boards of directors and the national board of governors. Volunteers are becoming increasingly diversified and include working women, African Americans, Hispanics, Asian Americans, youth and young adults, retirees, and business executives. All volunteers and contributors are considered members.

Direct public support and revenues are major sources of funding. Public support consists of individual and corporate contributions and moneys raised through federated fund-raising organizations. Depending on the nature of the contribution, funds can be either unrestricted by the donor or restricted for a specific purpose such as disaster services or program building. Revenues are derived from investment income or "cost-recovery programs"; for example, through fees from hospitals to reimburse expenses related to collecting, processing, and distributing blood and blood products.

Total ARC public support and revenue from all sources for fiscal 1992–93 came to $1.796 billion. Total expenses were approximately $1.675 billion; expenses incurred for biomedical services made up 60 percent of expenses, and disaster services ($224.2 million) made up 15 percent of expenses. Other expenditures included health services (8 percent), armed forces services (5 percent), management and general expenses (4 percent), community volunteers and international services (5 percent), and fund-raising (3 percent).

ARC leaders explain their ability to operate at a modest 7 percent of contributions in terms of the large numbers of unpaid staff; for every paid employee there are fifty volunteers. A not-for-profit enterprise, ARC does not pay blood donors and benefits from tax-exempt status and from free advertising provided by the Advertising Council of America and the media. Excess of revenues over expenses are applied to accumulated net assets, to replace capital equipment and maintain an adequate disaster services reserve fund.

POLICY CONCERNS AND TACTICS

Policy is set by the board of governors after preliminary work by board committees. Policy issues for board attention usually develop from professional staff or within the board itself. Delegate assemblies and membership polls have the least influence on policy decisions. ARC does not attempt per se to influence public policy through direct political or legal action. Instead, it exerts indirect influence by supplying congresspeople and the membership with educational newsletters about pertinent issues. It encourages members to write legislators, relying particularly on influential individuals to communicate its agenda. Members are interested in the maintenance of income tax deductions for charitable contributions. Staff in the Blood and Transplantation Services work with the Federal Drug Administration in formulating guidelines to assure distribution of the safest possible blood and tissue products. Recent legislation of interest has included the Coastal Barrier Reef Protection Act as part of a flood prevention effort and an increase in Federal Emergency Medical Assistance to communities affected by natural disasters. ARC also coordinates its efforts with allied organizations such as the Independent Sector, the National Assembly, and United Way of America. ARC is also a participant in the Federal Response Plan.

ELECTORAL ACTIVITIES

ARC does not see as partisan the issues that concern it and does not have a political action committee.

FURTHER INFORMATION

ARC publishes a variety of continually supplemented and updated educational materials. American Red Cross workbooks are the texts for ARC lifesaving training courses. Workbooks are illustrated and contain detailed, step-by-step instructions in lifesaving procedures, including infant and child CPR, adult CPR, standard first aid, basic water safety, basic first aid training for children, and community CPR. Other workbooks that focus on health education have as their goal the improvement of the quality of human life and enhancing self-reliance and concern for others. They include *Nutrition and Better Health, High Blood Pressure Control, Babysitting,* and *Preparation for Parenthood.*

ARC also publishes a series of brochures about AIDS, including: *Women, Sex and AIDS, Men, Sex and AIDS, Teenagers and AIDS, Children, Parents and AIDS, School Systems and AIDS: Information for Teachers and School Officials, Drugs, Sex and AIDS,* and *Your Job and AIDS: Are There Risks?* Other programs and materials about AIDS include "AIDS Prevention for the Workplace," "AIDS Prevention Program for Youth," and a video presentation, *Beyond Fear.*

JOAN SAYRE

AMERICAN WOMEN IN RADIO AND TELEVISION (AWRT)
1101 Connecticut Avenue, NW
Suite 700
Washington, DC 20037
(212) 429-5102
FAX (202) 223-4579

American Women in Radio and Television (AWRT) has served as the advocate and voice of women broadcasting professionals for over forty years, seeking to advance their influence in the electronic media and allied fields by educating, advocating, and acting as a resource to its members and the industry. There is an education and research foundation.

ORIGIN AND DEVELOPMENT

AWRT spun off from the National Association of Broadcasters (NAB) when NAB discontinued its women's division, the Association of Women Broadcasters, in 1950. NAB did so by dismissing Dorothy Lewis, who had directed NAB's women's activists since 1942. Organized in 1951 at a convention of 282 women from the broadcasting industry, AWRT lists its key founders as Agnes Law from CBS, Edythe Meserand of WOR New York, and Jane Barton, the New York State program director for radio and television.

AWRT first was conceived at a NAB meeting in Washington, D.C., on October 21, 1950. The NAB board voted approval of the new organization, offering complete cooperation and assistance, such as the use of office space, a secretary, mailing list, and budget, until the new organization worked out the details of separate operation. By 1951, a steering committee of eleven women, with Law as chair, was formed. Plans developed for the organizing convention at the Hotel Astor, New York City, April 6–8, 1951; and a proposed constitution and bylaws were prepared with the then-tentative name. The women attending the first AWRT convention gave approval to the name, constitution, and bylaws and elected officers and a board of directors. Meserand, who chaired the first convention, became AWRT's first national president. Headquarters offices were established in Grand Central Station in New York City until 1969, when the offices moved to Washington, D.C.

AWRT has sought through more than four decades ''to advance the impact of professionals in the electronic media and allied fields.'' Yet the organization's formal objectives reveal its evolution from strictly occupational interests to concern with the electronic media's quality around the world and with women's status in the electronic media and related areas, and to involvement in community issues and the marketplace of ideas. Its mission has changed only in becoming more explicit in its meaning to members and the industry.

ORGANIZATION AND FUNDING

Members are served by forty-nine chapters in twenty-three states, down from sixty-three chapters in 1984. AWRT is a tightly structured organization, with published procedures and manuals for different roles and units within it as well as the usual bylaws. AWRT considers its chapters to be the organization's ''backbone.'' An annual delegate assembly votes on bylaw changes. The elected president is unsalaried; currently serving in that capacity is Sally H. Forman, the president of a government relations firm in Washington, D.C., providing clients with professionally tailored services to meet their specific legislative, regulatory, and public relations goals. Ten vice presidents, five other officers, six at-large directors, and the executive director join the president to make up the board of directors. One of the twenty directors is African American. AWRT has thirty-three standing national committees, three task forces and three joint AWRT/foundation committees. Since 1985, it has kept headquarters in Washington, D.C. The Washington office has four paid professional staff members, led by Executive Director Donna Cantor. In the past, the office had an internship program.

AWRT extends membership to qualified professionals in the electronic media and allied fields. It has approximately 2,600 current members; 5 percent are male. This total shows a decrease from 1980's total membership of 3,000. One

AWRT brochure, *A Career Investment,* urges members to think of themselves, their employers, community, and professionalism by remembering AWRT as advocate, mentor, and support network. AWRT services for attracting members include publications, conferences and meetings, advocacy of issues, communications with peers and colleagues, and representation of member opinions to government and networking. Chapter activities include local meetings, internships, and career development activities to encourage women to enter the field. A job bank, Careerline, offers listings of current job openings of interest to members.

Women entering a broadcasting organization at the ground floor might not be eligible for membership. Eligibility for membership is reserved to women broadcasters, executives, managers, administrators, and account executives, along with women in creative roles in radio and television, cable, advertising, and related areas. There is some flexibility on these matters since membership guidelines state that job descriptions do not matter as much as the worker's actual responsibilities. Because of its clearly defined occupational focus, the group makes no particular efforts to target lower-income, disabled, older, or lesbian members. AWRT presents annual awards for programs that place women's image, positions, and welfare in a favorable light, thereby contributing to women's advancement. Besides the prestigious Silver Satellite Award, there are national commendation awards, achievement awards, and even a chapter-of-the-year award.

As a 501 (c) (6) organization, AWRT receives funding from a variety of sources, including dues. Dues are $125 yearly; employers pay many members' dues. Conventions, conferences, and exhibitions; grants from corporations and businesses and from other foundations and individuals; and occasional fundraisers round out AWRT's sources of revenue, along with proceeds from a travel agency, discount car rentals, group rate insurance plans, and magazine discounts.

In 1960, in a first for broadcasting organizations, AWRT started the 501 (c) (3) Foundation of American Women in Radio and Television. Its board of trustees is similar in size to AWRT's and has a predominantly male board of honorary trustees. The foundation has eleven standing committees. Its goals differ from AWRT's in breadth. One foundation project is the Soaring Spirits program, which provides more than 100 U.S. hospitals with appropriate television programming for their younger patients. The project, which received a Presidential Citation Award for Private Sector Initiatives, is an example of how the foundation encourages mainstream and nonpolitical donors to contribute by emphasizing professionalism and social service in broadcasting. Foundation revenue must be applied to appropriate ends within the donor's intention and must not jeopardize the foundation's tax-exempt status.

POLICY CONCERNS AND TACTICS

AWRT has a long and detailed list of procedures for staking out positions on national issues. Policy is set by both the board and the membership. AWRT's interests are well within the mainstream of industry and government. It seeks out issues also of interest to the broadcast and advertising industries and related organizations. Strategies used to influence public policy include congressional testimony and testimony at agency and department hearings, written comments about proposed regulations, personal presentations to government personnel, and similar activities at the state level. Members are encouraged to write the Congress or the Federal Communications Commission (FCC) on issues AWRT targets. The U.S. Transportation and Labor departments also have heard from AWRT.

AWRT has a government relations committee, chaired by its vice president for government relations, Melodie Virtue. This committee reviews and analyzes current legislation, proposed regulations, and executive branch activities; reports regularly to the membership on areas of concern and encourages members' response and participation; suggests programming on government issues for chapter, area, and national functions; and provides guidelines for members and chapter involvement with state broadcasters' associations.

Legislation most of interest is broadcasting-related. Current policy issues of interest include the FCC rules on radio ownership and female employment in broadcast and cable systems. Among the regulatory rules of recent interest to AWRT are the dual network rule, network station ownership rule, and the multiple network affiliation rule. The new Cable Consumer Protection Act also holds great interest for AWRT. It cites as significant to its ongoing activities the 1963 Equal Pay Act, 1974 Women's Educational Equity Act, Child Support Amendments to the 1975 Social Security Act, 1976 Day Care Act, 1978 Pregnancy Disability Act, and 1986 Age Discrimination Act.

In late 1992, AWRT commented favorably on the FCC's proposal to permit owners to exceed the present national radio limitation of eighteen AM and eighteen FM stations, suggesting an outward limit of three AM and three FM stations per group owner. AWRT's support was contingent upon the establishment by the owners of a program to encourage underrepresented group presence as broadcast station owners and inclusion of women as beneficiaries of these programs.

Likely AWRT allies in activism are the National Women's Political Caucus* and National Organization for Women.*

ELECTORAL ACTIVITIES

Although AWRT plays many other roles that bring it into contact with the government, it expressly forbids political campaign endorsements and remains uninvolved in electoral politics.

FURTHER INFORMATION

A newsletter, *News and Views,* is published eight times yearly. A membership directory appears irregularly. With the U.S. Labor Department's Women Bureau,* AWRT publishes a categorization of electronic media industry jobs.

VALLAURIE CRAWFORD

ASSOCIATION FOR INTERCOLLEGIATE ATHLETICS FOR WOMEN (AIAW)

An organization designed by women, for women, the Association for Intercollegiate Athletics for Women (AIAW) provided women student-athletes with hitherto unknown opportunities and representation. Besides lobbying extensively in Washington, D.C., for retention of a strong Title IX and its enforcement by the Office for Civil Rights, the AIAW became the largest intercollegiate organization in the United States. In 1982 the AIAW was forced out of existence by the National Collegiate Athletic Association (NCAA), the men's primary governing organization.

ORIGIN AND DEVELOPMENT

Girls and women historically have experienced discrimination in sports. The need for intercollegiate opportunity ultimately led to the AIAW's establishment. When informed in 1966 by the NCAA that creating a new national athletic governance organization for women would not conflict with its mission of guiding men's athletics, the Division for Girls and Women in Sport (DGWS), a branch of the American Alliance for Health, Physical Education and Recreation* (AAHPER), appointed the Commission on Intercollegiate Athletics for Women (CIAW). Frances McGill, DGWS chair, assisted Phoebe Scott, Maria Sexton, and Katherine Ley in forming the CIAW. The CIAW developed an organizational framework for the conduct of women's intercollegiate athletics that led to the initiation of seven national championships between 1966 and 1972. Recognizing the need for a regulatory organization based on a dues-paying institutional membership, the AAHPER in 1971 established the AIAW to replace the CIAW. Carol Gordon and Carole Oglesby were instrumental in this movement to a membership organization. The first delegate assembly met in November 1973.

One basic tenet of the AIAW's philosophy justified athletic programs in educational institutions because students accrued benefits through their sporting experiences; sports gave women the opportunity to grow as scholars, athletes, and human beings. To many in the AIAW, the philosophy focused on providing an educationally sound and fiscally prudent model for intercollegiate athletics programs while striving for equal opportunity for collegiate women athletics. Additionally, the organization was characterized by a democratic governance system that fairly represented student-athletes' and minority views. The AIAW provided broadly based programs, that is, a variety of sports where coaches and athletes were treated similarly, maximum opportunities for student-athlete participation in postseason play, and a due process and appeals system for not only individual institutions but also each individual in the organization. The AIAW also tried to avoid the commercialism of big-time athletics and any tendency to exploit student-athletes.

In the AIAW's decade of existence, a revolution occurred in women's collegiate sports. On average, universities offered 2.5 intercollegiate sports for women in 1973; by 1979 this number had jumped to 6.48, compared with 7.4 for men. By 1981, women constituted one-third of the total intercollegiate athletic population. During this period the AIAW grew from a charter membership of 278 to 973 active members.

The most significant catalyst for the explosive growth of women's athletic opportunities was Title IX of the 1972 Education Amendments, which prohibited discriminatory practices in educational institutions receiving federal funding. Although applicable to all educational programs, the inclusion of athletic programs in Title IX generated the most intense debate and set the stage for the decade-long struggle between the AIAW and the NCAA. Men's athletics representatives first mounted an intense but unsuccessful lobbying action to exempt all athletics from Title IX; they then attempted to exempt the revenue-producing sports of football and basketball. Thanks in large part to the AIAW's lobbying efforts, these efforts failed in 1974 and 1975. In 1976, NCAA filed suit against the U.S. Health, Education and Welfare Department (HEW) to challenge the legal force of its regulations. A court dismissed the suit; the NCAA appealed its decision in 1980. Throughout, the AIAW lobbied strongly in support of HEW's authority to issue and enforce the regulations.

In 1978, the Amateur Sport Act reorganized sports throughout the nation and assured women reasonable representation on all sports governing boards, including the U.S. Olympic Committee and all national governing boards (NGBs) of sports. Representatives in the AIAW were instrumental in the passage of this legislation. One AIAW function was to encourage all NGBs to incorporate increased representation of women into their governance structures. The AIAW then worked to ensure that one AIAW representative would be invited to the meetings of each NGB.

ORGANIZATION AND FUNDING

AIAW's ultimate authority lay with a delegate assembly that convened annually. Delegates, who had one vote per institution, debated and voted on all policies and procedures. Between assemblies, an executive board fulfilled the organization's functions. The board included a president, the past president, and president-elect; ethics and eligibility committee and rules standards committee chairs; a commissioner of national championships from each division (of which there finally were three); a vice president from each division; the DGWS' president; a student representative; and one elected representative from each of the nine geographic regions in the nation. The chair of the committee on the status of minority women was a voting member of the executive board. In 1981, the delegate assembly voted to have 20 percent minority representation on all national committees. Each region had a regional executive board responsible for organizing regional championships in all sports. In almost all the states, a state board managed state championships. The group's first elected president was Carole Oglesby.

The national office, located in Washington, D.C., was staffed by an executive director and, at its zenith, eight support personnel. Ann Uhlir served as executive director at the height of the AIAW's influence. The organization's office proved instrumental in the successful retention of a strong Title IX, as well as passage of the Amateur Sport Act. Leadership opportunities for women coaches and administrators existed not just in Washington but throughout the country. By 1980, there existed over 1,200 leadership opportunities for women coaches or administrators in the AIAW at the state, regional, and national levels. The vast majority of those in leadership positions were women.

The AIAW worked to make its postseason championships inclusive. Through state and regional championships, it provided opportunities for participation in approximately 450 competitive events. These opportunities gave teams with little hope of qualifying for a national championship experience in postseason competition.

In 1972–73, the AIAW offered only one championship in each sport; by 1975–76 the association had moved to separate championships for large colleges and small colleges; by 1980, it had created a three-division championship structure. Had AIAW continued in 1981–82, it would have offered forty-one national championships in nineteen sports.

The AIAW based dues on membership division: $700 for Division I, $600 for Division II; $500 for Division III. It relied to a significant degree on this income, which represented 45 percent of the association's total operating budget of $1 million in 1980–81. Fifty percent of dues came from Division I programs. Scholarships, television contracts, and championship income generated the rest.

AIAW's first television contract came in 1975 with Sugarman Productions. This two-year, $50,000 contract allowed the company access to all the AIAW championships. In 1977–78, NBC purchased television rights to Division I women's basketball and gymnastics national championships. ESPN, the sports cable network, acquired rights to selected Division II and III national championships. By 1980–81, NBC showed ten women's national championships and ESPN, two.

POLICY CONCERNS AND TACTICS

As early as 1974, Walter Byers, NCAA executive director, predicted that NCAA would become involved in women's athletics. At a 1975 joint meeting, the AIAW actually suggested that both groups be dissolved and a new unified organization formed; but NCAA did not agree to this suggestion. Further talks on reorganization stalled over strong disagreement on equal representation of women in a merger.

The day prior to the 1975 NCAA convention, the AIAW learned that the NCAA membership would be asked to vote on starting women's championships. The NCAA council argued that legally, it had to do this to comply with Title IX. A full membership vote of the NCAA defeated all such proposals in 1975 and years to come, until a 1980 proposal of championships for five Division II and five Division III sports prevailed. Another men's governance organization, the National Association for Intercollegiate Athletics (NAIA), a longtime AIAW supporter, also started women's championships because, with the proposed NCAA action, its survival, too, was at stake.

In 1980 the NCAA unfolded a massive campaign not only to move into Division I championships but also to integrate women into the NCAA's governance system. Despite tremendous support for the AIAW and its principles by female and male athletic administrators of women's programs, the NCAA received support from several visible women administrators. This support, coupled with financial inducements for those joining, started tipping the balance in the NCAA's favor. During 1980 the AIAW made numerous appeals to the chief executive officers (CEOs) at institutions of higher learning and also to physical educators through the AAHPER system to support its continuation as an alternative model of intercollegiate sports. Generally, CEOs refrained from entering the struggle between the AIAW and the NCAA.

The 1981 AIAW delegate assembly overwhelmingly supported a resolution urging NCAA delegates to delay the initiation of women's championships, defeat the governance plan, and instruct the organizations to merge in a manner acceptable to both. The 1981 NCAA convention initially defeated by 128 to 127 a resolution to begin women's championships. With lobbying by key individuals in the NCAA, a motion to reconsider passed, and championships for women subsequently won approval, 137 to 117.

Institutional mergers of men's and women's athletics programs during the 1970s largely had eliminated women from decision-making roles in athletic programs. In 1981, under the direction and influence of these decision makers in men's athletics, institutions began to shift their women's programs into the NCAA. The best teams were some of the first to move because the NCAA paid their expenses to championships. AIAW had not paid championship expenses, so the NCAA used this financial leverage to improve its position. The loss of most of the top twenty teams led to AIAW's demise by affecting its commercial appeal and severely impairing its revenue base. Regardless of most women's preferences, their programs finally moved into the NCAA. Eighteen months after NCAA's vote to initiate Division I women's championships, the AIAW went bankrupt. It sued the NCAA for violation of the Sherman Anti-Trust Act, but the U.S. District Court in the District of Columbia ruled in 1983 that plaintiff had ''failed to prove the specific intent necessary to sustain its claim of attempted monopoly.''

In its ten years of existence, the AIAW had a significant influence on intercollegiate sports. Part of the AIAW's strength came through its participation, along with that of DGWS and A AHPER, in informal, regular coalition meetings of representatives from numerous women's organizations based in Washington, D.C. The power and influence each of these organizations possessed proved to be mutually beneficial to all. Of major significance during the 1980s was the AIAW's role, through heavy lobbying in Washington, in Title IX's maintenance in its original form. Another important legislative achievement was the passage of the Amateur Sport Act, which completely restructured amateur sports. The AIAW's primary contribution was the creation of an alternative model of inter-collegiate athletics, a model that was fiscally sound, nonexploitive, democratic, and academically based. Although the AIAW no longer exists, its concepts and ideas are beginning significantly to influence athletics governance today. In the long term, AIAW ideas may have a substantial effect in reforming NCAA.

FURTHER INFORMATION

Members received the AIAW *Handbook*, an annual document outlining reg-ulations governing the membership.

CHRISTINE H. B. GRANT

ASSOCIATION FOR THE STUDY OF ABORTION
See NATIONAL ABORTION FEDERATION

ASSOCIATION FOR THE STUDY OF COMMUNITY ORGANIZATION
See NATIONAL ASSOCIATION OF SOCIAL WORKERS

ASSOCIATION FOR WOMEN IN SCIENCE (AWIS)
1522 K. Street, NW
Suite 820
Washington, DC 20005
(202) 408-0742

Composed of individual scientists, professors, researchers, and students work-ing in academe, scientific institutes, businesses, and government agencies, the Association for Women in Science (AWIS) networks with other women's groups to monitor scientific legislation and the status of women in science. Its goal is to improve the educational and employment opportunities for women in all fields of life, in the sciences, mathematics, and engineering, to promote equal opportunities for women to enter the scientific workforce and to help their mem-bers realize their career ideals.

ORIGIN AND DEVELOPMENT

Traditionally, women have faced opposition and special problems while pur-suing careers in science. The problems of women scientists began as women entered the professional scientific arena in the early part of the twentieth century. The scientific community's biases based on gender expectations limited women in their access to intellectual and economic equity. The woman scientist faced segregation, double standards, underrecognition, and male territoriality.

The idea for a new organization to counter these difficulties arose from the intellectual and professional ideals of a few key founders, such as Anne Briscoe, Adele Pool, Joy Ozer, and other biologists who met regularly at annual meetings of the Federation of American Societies for Experimental Biology, where AWIS was formed. The first meeting of AWIS in April 1971 elected officers, collected dues, and prepared press releases. Twenty years later, a beginning membership of 40 had risen steadily to 5,000.

Shortly after its founding, in 1971, it collaborated with other women's groups to bring a class action suit against Elliott Richardson the secretary of the Department of Health, Education and Welfare (DHEW), and Robert Q. Marston, director of the National Institutes of Health (NIH), for failure to pursue affirmative action policies. The move followed a meeting in November 1971 with Robert Marston and a representative for the secretary of DHEW. The women's organizations were given a list of 413 vacancies on study sections and advisory groups of NIH; after this they compiled a list of 1,000 women who could fill these vacancies. The list of women was submitted as part of the documentation of the lawsuit opening the way for plaintiffs to enter a phase to discover the extent of the discrimination. In 1974, AWIS filed another suit against the DHEW for not enforcing Title IX of the Education Act Amendments of 1972 (prohibiting sex discrimination in educational facilities receiving federal funds) and Titles VII and VIII of the Public Health Services Act (prohibiting sex discrimination in health training facilities). In February 1977, AWIS was granted standing by the court to bring the suit. In June the judge issued an order to set up procedures and timetables for handling complaints. The Reagan administration did not enforce the order. AWIS and the other plaintiffs went back to court to file a motion of contempt of court. This was followed by a new consent order in 1982.

AWIS supported the equal rights amendment and the Women in Science and Technology Equal Opportunity Act in 1979 and more recently the Educational Equity Act, which has specific legislation encouraging girls in math and science. Most important, members benefit from networking with professional peers in the advocacy of shared values and ideas.

In keeping with its goal to improve the educational and employment opportunities of women in the sciences, the organization's name changed in 1975 from the Association *of* Women to the Association *for* Women in Science. AWIS became an affiliate of the American Association for the Advancement of Science. In 1974, AWIS established the Educational Foundation to provide advice and support to women involved in equal opportunity legislation.

ORGANIZATION AND FUNDING

The first chapter was founded in 1974. Presently, sixty-three chapters in thirty-six states correspond with the central office in Washington, D.C. AWIS has representatives in several countries as well as international affiliates such as European Women in Science and Humanities. Ten executive officers include a president, Penelope Kegel-Flom; president-elect, Jalsh Daie; past president, Ellen Weaver; vice president, Shelia Pfafflin; treasurer, Aliz Robinson; secretary, Lynne Freidmann; and four councillors. The national office has a total of seven to ten staff members. The executive director is Catherine Didion.

The organization is financially self-supporting through the collection of dues, which range from $15 to $65, depending on the applicant's income and student status. In 1989, AWIS received tax-deductible status, 501 (c) (3). Membership dues are now tax-deductible. The 1994 annual budget was $300,000, more than double the budget under the previous executive board. AWIS sponsors conventions, conferences, and exhibitions, including an annual reception held in conjunction with the American Association for the Advancement of Science meeting.

The AWIS Educational Foundation started in 1974 provides recognition and scholarships to women Ph.D. students. AWIS Educational Foundation Predoctoral Awards of at least $1,000 each are given to women who are working toward a Ph.D. in the life, physical, or social sciences or in engineering. The scholarship money has come primarily from individual donations. A major change occurred in June 1990, when AWIS was awarded its first large grant. The Sloan Foundation provided $400,000 for AWIS to carry out an extensive mentoring project and $200,000 for AWIS to address the issues of women science faculty.

The Federation of Organizations for Professional Women (FOPW) evolved from AWIS. In April 1972, at its annual meeting, AWIS conceived of this umbrella organization. It is a nonprofit, nonlobbying volunteer organization, composed of several hundred individual members and thirty affiliate organizations, including the Association for Women Geoscientists, American Medical Women's Association,* Women's Program of the American Psychological Association, and American Association of Women Business Owners. The executive board has members appointed from each affiliate, five councils, and an alternate. The president is Viola M. Young-Horvath. Its mission, which changes with the times, is to identify the needs of professional women and to provide support and assistance.

The newly formed sex discrimination issues committee has been concerned with cases of sexual discrimination and harassment. FOPW set up a legal defense fund to assist in the litigation of two women physicians who filed suit against the NIH in 1990 for sexual discrimination and harassment. A support group was formed and meets monthly to discuss these pervasive issues.

POLICY CONCERNS AND TACTICS

The various presidents of AWIS have chosen to emphasize different programs to achieve the stated goals. The membership is polled on critical issues and priorities. Appropriate AWIS activities and actions are determined by the executive board after the listed issues are reviewed at the national office. The councillors and committee chairs have significant input into the decision-making process. The various state chapters are conspicuously represented on the executive board and committees.

AWIS's greatest interest is in federal laws affecting equal rights for women within the work environment, such as equal pay, affirmative action, employment opportunities, educational equity, and civil rights. A legislative task force formed in 1982 worked on passage of the Civil Rights Restoration Act and the 1990 Civil Rights Act. AWIS worked to help establish the committee on equal opportunities in science and technology at the National Science Foundation (NSF), which led to the creation of NSF Visiting Professorships for Women.

AWIS has collaborated for years with Graduate Women in Science, the American Association for the Advancement of Science, and American Association of University Women* on common issues. The executive board notes that the professional climate is becoming unfavorable to women in the sciences due to the current conservative policies and a difficult economy.

ELECTORAL ACTIVITIES

AWIS organized a national conference, Taking the Initiative! A Leadership Conference for Women in Science and Engineering, with support from the Department of Energy (DOE) and the National Aeronautics and Space Administration (NASA), held in Washington, D.C., May 12–14, 1994. Midcareer women scientists and engineers were invited to participate in a program that focused on the development of leadership skills as a crucial aspect to achieving the full integration of women into the sciences. The conference's program concentrated on creating a leadership culture in science and engineering by generating visions for change and developing clear strategies and directions for women, as well as motivating and inspiring fellow female scientists and engineers.

FURTHER INFORMATION

AWIS Magazine, previously called the *Newsletter of the Association of Women in Science* and first published in 1971, features bimonthly book reviews, chapter news, grant information and deadlines, legislation news, and employment advertisements. AWIS has published a number of resources, including *A Hand Up: Women Mentoring Women in Science. A Hand Up* contains advice and reflections from accomplished women scientists designed to dispel many of the myths about mentoring and to encourage scientists to become mentors to young women seeking advice and guidance. *Mentoring Means Future Scientists,* which presents and analyzes the results of the AWIS Mentoring Program, was published in 1993. In addition, in 1992, AWIS published an updated edition of *Grants at a Glance,* a 100-page book of funding information listing over 400 awards, fellowships, and scholarships for women at all levels in a wide variety of scientific fields.

ELLEN GIARELLI

ASSOCIATION OF AMERICAN COLLEGES PROJECT ON THE STATUS AND EDUCATION OF WOMEN (AAC PSEW)
1818 R Street, NW
Washington, DC 20009
(202) 387-3760
FAX (202) 265-9532

Influenced by the activities of the women's liberation movement in the early 1970s, the Project on the Status and Education of Women (PSEW) was founded in 1971 by the Association of American Colleges (AAC). Located in Washington, D.C., it is the oldest national project for women's equity in higher education.

ORIGIN AND DEVELOPMENT

Inexorably linked with Bernice Resnick Sandler, the executive director from 1971 to 1991, the project started with Sandler's commitment and enthusiasm for the myriad of women's issues raised and addressed in the seventies. Sharing in the optimism of the time. Sandler first focused her efforts and PSEW's on legal issues such as the federal programs Title VII and Title IX. PSEW has continued to interpret and translate legal concerns for an academic audience.

PSEW also chose to address a variety of issues related to women in higher education and gradually shifted its focus from federal to institutional policy. Early topics included sexual harassment and the recruitment of minority women. Frequently, PSEW has crystallized emerging issues, as in its work on date rape and peer harassment. It also has introduced concepts such as the "chilly classroom." The original paper *The Classroom Climate: A Chilly One for Women?* has had a distribution of 65,000. No poll has ever been taken to validate the effects of such agenda setting on women's education; however, few in the field will dispute PSEW's influence in identifying issues and in providing a network for response and reaction. PSEW handles about 15,000 requests for information per year. In 1990, more than 40,000 copies of PSEW papers sold.

By assuming the broad goal of serving women's needs in higher education, PSEW seized the opportunity to attend to issues related to all segments of the college community, including students, faculty, and administrators in many disciplines. A recent topic concerns women in the sciences as students, as faculty, as mentors. PSEW works from a variety of perspectives, both in and out of the classroom. It serves both as a clearinghouse and as a liaison among the academic community, women's organizations, and federal and state policymakers.

ORGANIZATION AND FUNDING

Staff has ranged from two to twelve. Bernice Sandler, director since PSEW's founding, left it in June 1991. The stated reason for her leaving was that AAC had set new priorities for PSEW. Sandler now is senior associate at the Center for Women Policy Studies* (CWPS) and serves as editor of *About Women on Campus.* A new director was not named. Correspondence on PSEW is directed to Caryn McTighe Musil at AAC. Sandler's responsibilities at PSEW included fund-raising, writing, staff supervision, answering queries, meeting with federal officials and representatives of women's organizations, and traveling to institutions throughout the country. Sandler's collaborative style epitomized PSEW's tenor and was largely responsible for its success as a clearinghouse. All requests for information received a response. Ongoing research projects conducted at institutions were accepted for inclusion in PSEW's library. Ideas and concerns generated on campuses helped to provide foci for consideration by PSEW.

PSEW was first on a variety of issues, including the first set of papers on minority women in higher education, first chart analyzing the major sex discrimination laws, first analysis of Title IX, first comprehensive paper on returning women as graduate students, first paper on the relationship of returning women and the availability of child care, first set of questions for search committees to determine a candidate's concern with women's issues.

Financed in varying degrees by, on one hand, government and foundation grants and, on the other hand, income from publication sales and newsletter subscriptions, PSEW most recently received about half of its revenues from each source.

POLICY CONCERNS AND TACTICS

PSEW identified campus issues such as date rape through its newsletter and sought to define related needs, share activities, and likewise provide readers with resources. Usually, topics of concern are generated by institutions. For example, questions from the audience following a speech by Sandler on faculty harassment led to a report on peer harassment. Matters discussed in recent issues of the newsletter include women in sports, child care, campus violence, gender studies, and minority women.

Many subscribers relied on the newsletter both to keep them apprised of current issues as well as to provide contacts in other institutions who could help with solutions. Although other newsletters on women's issues have developed since PSEW's founding, most are discipline-specific and do not have the same breadth. *On Campus with Women* refers, as its title suggests, to all issues relating to all women at institutions of higher education. PSEW's mailing list included about 17,000 people.

The format of all other PSEW publications centers on problem solving; that is, they present the problem, the evidence, some solutions, and a list of resources. A PSEW publication, *Relating to Each Other: A Questionnaire for Students,* exemplifies this pragmatic approach. Four pages of questions seek to give students information about their perceptions and interactions with the other sex. Colleges and universities can use this student input to assess the everyday environment of their students. Taken together, PSEW publications contain over 180 recommendations for change.

ELECTORAL ACTIVITIES

PSEW is not a partisan organization and does not have a political action committee.

FURTHER INFORMATION

Subscriptions to the quarterly newsletter, *On Campus with Women,* are available from the Publications Desk of the Association of Women Colleges. A number of the PSEW publications are now available from CWPS. For a publication list, send a SASE to Publications, Center for Women Policy Studies, 2000 P Street, NW, Suite 508, Washington, DC 20036.

LINDA MATHER

ASSOCIATION OF AMERICAN MEDICAL COLLEGES WOMEN IN MEDICINE PROGRAM (AAMC WIM)

2450 N Street, NW
Washington, DC 20037
(202) 828-0575
FAX (202) 828-1125

A valuable informal and formal network meeting once a year in conjunction with the Association of American Medical Colleges (AAMC), the Women in Medicine Program (WIM) assists women medical students and physicians who are women, including those on medical school faculties, with career development and education issues, while contributing to a national agenda on their behalf.

ORIGIN AND DEVELOPMENT

In 1960, the proportion of medical school applicants who were women was 7 percent. By 1975, the proportion of women applicants had grown to 20 percent. For the only time in history, women's representation in the first-year classes (22 percent) exceeded the seats usually made available for those applying. In the early 1970s, a number of women deans in medical college admissions and student affairs began meeting informally during meetings of the Group on Student Affairs (GSA) of the AAMC. These assistant deans increasingly recognized, along with other higher education administrators (as is clear from the Association of American Colleges Project on the Status and Education of Women* at about this time), that these women students faced problems of sexism, needed women role models on the faculty, and had other special needs and interests that deserved to be addressed. Many areas of the United States had inadequate numbers of doctors; therefore, doctors of either sex were very welcome. The demand for women doctors has only intensified as women consumers actively seek women physicians, especially as gynecologists, and as attention focuses on the fact that many women's health concerns have received inadequate attention and research compared with men's.

The objective of the women deans was a discussion of affirmative action problems. Although not included in the governance of AAMC, GSA became operative for professional development purposes and affirmative action had bearing here. GSA has traditionally and continues to be instrumental in AAMC's policy and program development for all issues related to students and to provide professional development opportunities for all levels of student services and student affairs personnel. AAMC is more than 102 years old and has as its purpose the improvement of the nation's health through the advancement of academic medicine. An association of dues-paying medical schools, teaching hospitals, and academic societies, AAMC works to set a national agenda for medical education, biomedical research, and health care.

The women deans' lobbying the AAMC president in 1976 resulted in AAMC's assigning staff support to coordinate efforts aimed at improving the environment for women faculty and students at the nation's medical schools. In order to extend these efforts to all medical schools, the position of women liaison officer (WLO) was created. In 1977, the WLOs had their own AAMC annual meeting program. By 1978, 100 medical schools and thirty academic societies had appointed a WLO. Teaching hospitals sought guidance in developing parental leave policies and on child care issues, so in 1990, AAMC began offering its Council of Teaching Hospital members the opportunity to appoint a WLO. By 1994 125 of the 126 medical schools, thirty-five of eighty-five academic societies, and 200 of 400 teaching hospitals had at least one WLO.

ORGANIZATION AND FUNDING

WLOs do not elect a chair, and thus their organization has no formal "head"; however, it is professionally staffed and forms a valuable network that meets yearly in conjunction with AAMC's annual meeting. Many WLOs also attend Women in Medicine (WIM) sessions held in conjunction with GSA regional meetings. Thus, WIM has brought into focus issues and needs of women students that medical schools were not well positioned to address on their own.

In 1987, the focus of support for WIM shifted from the Office of the President to the Division of Institutional Planning and Development; and 50 percent of a staff associate's time was assigned to these responsibilities. This new director for women's programs, Janet Bickel, took as one of her first actions the expansion of the five-member WIM planning committee to the eight-member coordinating committee, selected from the most active WLOs (regional representation is sought) and including one woman student and one department chairperson. Previously, staff had formed and convened this committee to plan for the annual meeting program. Now the coordinating committee also assists in developing other projects and programs, such as those discussed under policy concerns, and continuing efforts to communicate updated descriptions of the activities, ideas, and resources that WLOs initiate at their institutions.

POLICY CONCERNS AND TACTICS

Although by 1994 the proportion of women in the applicant pool exceeded 42 percent, and women constituted almost 40 percent of entering students, problems remained to be addressed. While sexist teaching materials and language have not been entirely eliminated, great strides forward have occurred, and many students complete medical school without an incident they would label as "discriminatory." However, sexism remains as much a problem in medical education as in other professional schools, perhaps more so, because the body is the constant focus of discussion and because of large status and power differences among the various levels and types of health professions trainees and faculty.

WIM also has compiled a great deal of information about programs for women at medical schools. The quarterly newsletter, *Women in Medicine Update,* features this information and multiple approaches to addressing sexism in education. Issues related to combining family responsibilities with professional and educational ones are another continual focus. AAMC published *Medicine & Parenting: A Resource for Medical Students, Residents, Faculty and Program Directors* in 1991. This handbook summarizes what is known about maternity and parental leave policies and also includes sections on child care resources and on adding flexibility to faculty policies and a bibliography.

WIM annually compiles a set of statistics on women in medicine. In 1988, these were brought together in a status report published in the *New England Journal of Medicine.* The journal of the American Medical Women's Association,* also in 1988, presented examples of WIM's faculty salary equity studies. *Humane Medicine*'s spring 1990 issue asked if women physicians filled the role of a change agent or were consigned to second-class status in the medical profession. WIM's most popular effort is its annual professional development seminar for junior women faculty. Always oversubscribed, it includes twelve workshops on topics such as conflict management, building a research program, and writing for professional journals. Addressing the paucity of women in leadership positions, in 1993 a new professional development seminar for senior women was offered. Its workshops include committee leadership, critiquing grants and manuscripts, managing job searches, and understanding the organizational culture. The visibility and value of AAMC's WIM program continue to increase.

ELECTORAL ACTIVITIES

Neither AAMC nor WIM is involved in electoral politics or operates a political action committee.

FURTHER INFORMATION

WIM publishes *Women in Medicine Update,* a quarterly newsletter with a circulation of 1,000 among WLOs, medical school deans, women assistant and associate deans, section chiefs, and academic department chairs. In 1993, AAMC published the second edition of its handbook, *Building a Stronger Woman's Program: Enhancing the Educational and Professional Environment,* which describes WIM offices and programs and includes discussion of considerations for starting a program, sexism, salary equity, and future directions, along with a women in medicine bibliography.

JANET BICKEL

ASSOCIATION OF BLACK NURSING FACULTY IN HIGHER EDU-CATION (ABNF)
5823 Queens Cove
Lisle, Illinois 60532
(708) 969-3809
FAX (708) 969-3895

The purpose of the Association of Black Nurse Faculty (ABNF) is to inform and maintain a group whereby black professional nurses with similar credentials, interests, and concerns may work to promote certain health-related issues and educational interests for their benefit and the black community.

ORIGIN AND DEVELOPMENT

Sallie Tucker-Allen founded ABNF with a group of interested black nurse educators in March 1987 in the state of Illinois. This group came together in response to a need to address the professional needs of black nursing faculty in higher education. It provided an opportunity for black faculty members to meet and share similar experiences and support one another.

Black women have worked in higher education for over a century. Issues related to sexism and racism impact on the growth and success of black women in academe. Areas such as support, retention, research, teaching, and tenure are affected by the climate surrounding black women at predominantly black, and certainly white, institutions. Doctoral preparation for faculty appointment is preferred by most institutions of higher education. Statistics on earned doctorates in 1985 reveal that black women constituted 1.9 percent of full-time faculty in higher education. Black women make up 0.6 percent of those at full professor rank, 1.4 percent of associate professors, 2.7 percent of assistant professors, and 3 percent of instructors, lecturers, and others. National Data Guide in 1985 placed the number of black nurse faculty members in baccalaureate and higher degree programs at 580. A 1990 descriptive study by Sallie Tucker-Allen, Ruby Steele, and Sonia Baker reported that black nursing faculty members are primarily female and employed predominantly in the southeast region of the country at white institutions. Black nurse faculty employed at these predominantly white institutions encounter numerous barriers and are subsequently not fully integrated or socialized into the academic milieu of higher education. Much of the problem relates to the lack of inclusion in such scholarly activities as fellowships and merit awards and invitations by fellow white peers to publish jointly. These activities serve as a benchmark for academic success and professional advancement. Black faculty who have tenure are employed most often at historically black institutions; black faculty are employed more in nontenured tracks at white institutions.

ABNF's formation occurred as a result of these concerns. Its function/purposes are to provide a center for communication among black nursing faculty whereby they are able to (1) assist members in professional development and encourage and support research; (2) support black consumer advocacy issues such as access to quality health care for blacks, increased awareness of cultural diversity in health care and, subsequently, the need to foster improvement of health care for black Americans and other disadvantaged minority groups; (3) act and speak on health issues such as a multicultural focus in health promotion, illness prevention, and delivery of health care to black children and the elderly; and (4) encourage guidance and networking in employment and recruitment activities.

ORGANIZATION AND FUNDING

The association's annual business meeting is conducted at an annual conference, usually in the summer; ABNF's governing structure comprises a board of directors and an executive committee of officers elected by the membership. Committees include by laws, finance, program, public policy, research, and publication/communication. Founding officers were President Sallie Tucker-Allen, Vice President Sonia Baker, Secretary Sandra Sayler-Cross, and Treasurer Katie McNight. Business is conducted from Lisle, Illinois. At the annual meeting ABNF presents professional awards to outstanding nurse educators. Members also have the opportunity to present research papers and posters. The association has held four annual conferences.

Membership consists of registered nurses with an earned graduate degree in nursing currently licensed to practice in at least one of the states, possessions, or territories of the United States and teaching nursing in an institution of higher education. Most members are of African American descent. Members include approximately 40 percent of all black nursing faculty in accredited baccalaureate and higher-degree programs.

Financial support for this nonprofit group comes primarily from membership dues (currently fifty dollars annually).

POLICY CONCERNS AND TACTICS

ABNF investigates legislation that may have an effect on the black community and/or black faculty in the health care arena. ABNF has taken a stand against a proposal by the American Medical Association regarding the development of a new type of health care provider called the registered care technologist to alleviate a nursing shortage. ABNF opposed the development of this category of health care provider, because it would undermine the role of the professional nurse. This provider would be totally controlled by the medical profession yet monitored by the professional nurse. In many cases the role of this provider would be conflictive with the nurse's current role. ABNF has supported nurses' choosing unionization and collective bargaining and taken the position that the only appropriate representation for nurses is the state nurses' association.

ABNF also has spoken out against the closing of traditionally black baccalaureate nursing programs in North Carolina. ABNF's concern here is with the potential banishment of black baccalaureate nursing programs. Most of the predominantly black nursing programs are in the southern region of the United States. The University of North Carolina board of governors made a decision to shut down its "weakest" schools to save the taxpayers money. Three of the black nursing programs in this system faced impending closure. ABNF felt concerned as to whether these programs received equal treatment, adequate resources, and nurturance to promote their growth. In view of the current nursing shortage and underrepresentation of blacks in education and nursing practice, it is hard to accept the possibility of closing any of these programs. ABNF maintains that there is a need for the traditional black nursing program located in North Carolina. These programs are the main means for dealing with underrepresentation of minorities within the health care system. At the time of this writing, no closing date for these programs was projected. ABNF has initiated a "Come Blow Your Horn" campaign to help fight these closings.

ABNF belongs to the Nursing Organization Liaison Forum of the American Nurses' Association* and also works closely with the National Black Nurses Association.*

FURTHER INFORMATION

Published four times a year, *The ABNF Newsletter* facilitates official communication. It is distributed to all members and other subscribers. It includes topics of current interest, along with information about coming conferences and workshops, book reviews, research abstracts, and job announcements. ABNF also publishes a membership directory, a useful tool in establishing linkage with peers in the field. *The ABNF Journal* is the official bimonthly refereed journal; the first issue came out in the spring of 1990. The journal focuses primarily on research related to black health care.

MATTIE L. RHODES

ASSOCIATION OF COLLEGIATE ALUMNAE
See AMERICAN ASSOCIATION OF UNIVERSITY WOMEN

ASSOCIATION OF COLLEGIATE SCHOOLS OF NURSING
See NATIONAL LEAGUE FOR NURSING

ASSOCIATION OF JUNIOR LEAGUES
See ASSOCIATION OF JUNIOR LEAGUES, INTERNATIONAL

ASSOCIATION OF JUNIOR LEAGUES, INTERNATIONAL (AJLI)
660 1st Ave.
New York, NY 10016-3241
(212) 683-1515
FAX (212) 481-7196

The Association of Junior Leagues, International (AJLI) is a women's organization that joins together Junior Leagues (JLs) from different cities. More than 192,000 JL volunteers act through analysis, direct service, advocacy, and public education to meet community needs and promote social changes. This is a multicultural, multinational organization whose primary goal is to promote voluntarism and empower community leadership. It has remained one of the most influential women's organizations in the United States.

ORIGIN AND DEVELOPMENT

Mary Harriman Rumsey and her friend Nathalie Henderson Swan founded the first Junior League in New York City in 1901 to help immigrant families and give educated young women from upper and middle classes an opportunity to do meaningful work. Rumsey also recruited her friend Eleanor Roosevelt, who became an early and important member of the New York JL. At that time, when women did not have the vote, league members learned through their volunteer involvement with the tenement housing movement that their collective voice could have an impact. Early league members were especially effective in getting landlords to abide by existing laws. As they raised funds for the settlement movement, league volunteers also broadened their own horizons. Demand for their services developed so rapidly that by 1907 the league's focus had grown, and the Junior League for the Promotion of Settlement Movements became the Junior League for the Promotion of Neighborhood Work. Soon more Junior Leagues started in other cities.

The Association of Junior Leagues (AJL) began in 1921 in order to provide collective consultative services to the increasing number of member JLs. By 1960, there were 195 JLs in the association, and that number is still increasing. In 1988 *Time* magazine recognized the AJL as "a powerful force for social change"; and in 1989, President George Bush bestowed upon it the President's Volunteer Action Award.

In 1989, the delegates, recognizing the need to enhance the league's international image and to make it easier to conduct business in foreign countries, passed a resolution to change their name to the Association of Junior Leagues, International. This name change went into effect in 1990. The AJLI experience offers a wide variety of training in areas of public speaking, serving as board members and meeting community needs and leaders. The early emphasis on a mix of service work, research, education, and advocacy continues, with an increased emphasis on collaborative efforts with other groups having similar concerns.

ORGANIZATION AND FUNDING

There are 286 JLs in the AJLI: 275 in forty-seven states of the United States, 9 in Canada, 1 in Mexico, and 1 in Great Britain. In 1990, AJLI restructured the organization, reshaping job responsibilities, redefining services, closing field offices, and committing to a comprehensive approach to community action and policy-based program development. There are 27 elected directors in AJLI. All AJLI members and board members are women. Currently, 5 members of the board of directors are members of racial/ethnic minority groups. AJLI does not specifically encourage board participation by women with disabilities or by women from lower-income strata. It does, however, encourage a multicultural membership; and there have been Hispanic, African American, and Asian American presidents of individual JLs. AJLI has a president elected by the member leagues to a two-year term of office. The current president is Nancy H. Evans. Besides the president, there are also four other officers elected by the entire membership to the executive board: two vice presidents, a secretary, and a treasurer. In June 1991, AJLI appointed Holly Sloan as its paid executive director. AJLI always has employed a staff leader but did not use the term executive director until the early 1970s. The Washington, D.C., office, opened in 1986, has a paid staff of four and facilitates legislative efforts between AJLI and the federal government. It also coordinates relationships with other international voluntary organizations and supports networking activities among the Junior Leagues.

Each individual JL with its own members and organization is linked directly to AJLI. Through her membership in a local JL, a woman becomes part of the larger association. AJLI constantly reevaluates the effectiveness of the contract between it and member leagues. In the nineties, more women are working and have less time to volunteer. With the number of individual JLs and members increasing, AJLI must adapt to meet members' diverse needs and coordinate with them effectively in their communities. Making meeting times convenient for working and minority women is one such adaptation tried by several local JLs. Many sustaining members have chosen to remain active; AJLI has added sustaining directors to its board and provided continuing education programs for them. Individual JLs have opened their membership to any women wanting to join, although some retain strict entry requirements such as high dues, extensive hours of volunteer work, several letters of recommendation, and inconvenient meeting times. Requirements as to who may join the local JLs are under constant revision.

JL began with contributions from early members and supporters. Today a little less than 80 percent of its revenue comes from membership dues; about 20 percent derives from the sale of publications and advertising; and 5 percent comes from a combination of merchandise sales, commissions from insurance rates, corporate and business gifts and grants, gifts or bequests beyond individual dues, and foundation and foundation grants. AJLI has tax-exempt status; and contributions are tax-deductible. Among the community-minded organizations from which AJLI has received support are Blue Cross/Blue Shield, BMW of North America, March of Dimes, Allstate Insurance Company, which supported the Woman to Woman Alcoholism Prevention Program, and the Charles Stewart Mott Foundation, which supported the Teen Outreach Program. Currently, dues go to both the individual JLs and AJLI. Each local JL is free to set its own dues, but twenty-seven dollars per member of this amount is passed on to AJLI annually.

POLICY CONCERNS AND TACTICS

In addition to the bylaws and certain operational policies, the Junior Leagues have authority for the external policies of the Association, which directs all AJLI international community program and advocacy efforts. Through the AJLI Strategic Plan, the Leagues determine the priorities from which the Board of Directors determines objectives. Then, the staff has responsibility for determining the activities which implement those objectives and priorities. Because individual JLs and AJLI are nonpartisan and multi-issue, they can mobilize widely based coalitions and directly impact hundreds of localities.

AJLI has effectively influenced public policy, especially in the area of children's rights, voluntarism, and family preservation. To influence desired legislation, AJLI holds regional training conferences and topical forums. JL volunteers and staff lobby the Congress on behalf of league concerns; individual JLs also lobby state and local government. Only volunteers testify before the Congress and in committees; but staff members help prepare testimony. AJLI also supplies information to congresspeople and their staff, makes personal presentations, and encourages its members to write their legislators. AJLI provided substantial leadership for the passage of the 1980 Adoption Assistance and Child Welfare Act, 1984 Child Abuse Act, and 1988 Civil Rights Restoration Act. It provided widespread backing for the Family Violence Prevention and Services Act because its numerous members around the country who had extensive experience working with battered women and family violence were a persuasive force on lawmakers. While these and other issues continue to be top priorities, AJLI also is concerned about what it perceives as an overall ''watering down'' of previously passed legislation and data collection requirements.

Because AJLI represents the collective voice of all its member JLs, its opinion carries weight in Washington. More than most other women's organizations, AJLI has been able to mobilize its members in their communities' service and around several social issues, especially in the area of protection for women and children. When individual and volunteer league members from different states, who do not represent any special interest groups, call their legislators, they can have a big impact on whether a bill passes.

For over ten years AJLI has coordinated with other organizations such as the Children's Defense Fund,* Independent Sector, and American Academy of Pediatrics* to increase and support AJLI's impact on legislation.

ELECTORAL ACTIVITIES

AJLI considers women's issues to be nonpartisan and does not support candidates.

FURTHER INFORMATION

To inform and educate its members and others about its positions, AJLI releases research reports, membership newsletters and legislative alerts. In all,

AJLI publishes over 80 titles on many topics covering leadership, public relations, trends analysis and major issues of concern to AJLI, such as parental leave or homelessness. Individual JLs also may have their own publications on local affairs.

ELEANOR E. ZEFF

ASSOCIATION OF UNIVERSALIST WOMEN
See UNITARIAN UNIVERSALIST WOMEN'S FEDERATION

ASSOCIATION OF WOMEN IN SCIENCE
See ASSOCIATION FOR WOMEN IN SCIENCE

ASSOCIATION OF WOMEN IN SCIENCE FOUNDATION
See ASSOCIATION FOR WOMEN IN SCIENCE

BLACK, INDIAN, HISPANIC AND ASIAN WOMEN IN ACTION (BIHA)
122 W. Franklin Avenue
Suite 306
Minneapolis, MN 55404
(612) 870-1193

The goal of Black, Indian, Hispanic and Asian Women in Action (BIHA) is the empowerment of black, Indian, Hispanic, and Asian communities at all levels through implementation of projects created to educate, inform, and advocate for communities of color in the areas of family violence, chemical dependency, education, physical and mental health, and employment, to achieve social change, healthy families, and advancement of socioeconomic status. BIHA teaches culturally specific mechanisms to enable service providers effectively and acceptably to serve clients in need of protection against family violence throughout the state of Minnesota. Its focus on family and social issues includes not only battering and sexual assault but also ageism and AIDS.

ORIGIN AND DEVELOPMENT

BIHA was established in March 1983 in recognition of a lack of communication and information sharing within and between communities of color regarding family violence. Specifically, it was an outgrowth of the Advisory Committee of the Minnesota Department of Corrections Battered Women's Unit. The original small group of founders consisted of women of color who were members of the advisory committee. Among the black, Indian, and Hispanic women involved in the initial planning and organization were Ruthie Dallas, Eulalia Reyes De Smith, Janet Anderson, Maryann Walt, and Donna Anderson. BIHA unveiled the scope and extent of family violence and brought together women of color concerned about this problem from all over Minnesota. BIHA has provided a forum for translating the issues of family violence to both communities of color and society as a whole, educating the public on the diverse cultural values involved in specific social service and police actions essential to protect women. BIHA also was formed to investigate why organizations of women of color had not submitted grant requests to funding sources about their concerns in this area, and a task force was formed to determine the circumstances behind the lack of applications.

After its formation in 1983, BIHA started networking with groups through a newsletter and offered information on issues, programs, and activities aimed at solving domestic violence and assistance in grant writing. BIHA recognizes the racism faced by women of color and seeks at all levels to dispel racism and all its manifestations. Its general goals are to provide information, education, and networking with women of color for the betterment and sustenance of healthy families, and these goals have remained constant since the organization's inception.

BIHA started doing seminars in 1983–84 on battered women and in 1985 developed a cultural awareness manual and ran sensitivity training workshops. By 1987–88, the organization had received funds to produce educational videos on family violence for black, Indian, and Hispanic communities. In the same year, it expanded its focus to include problems of sexual assault, child abuse, chemical dependency, ageism, and AIDS. Currently, BIHA provides training on these issues insofar as they affect communities of color. In 1989–90, BIHA received funding for videos to educate the Southeast Asian community about family violence.

ORGANIZATION AND FUNDING

The original program director was Rochelle Lopez, who served for two years. The current head, titled director, Alice O. Lynch, has served since 1986. BIHA has its headquarters in Minneapolis, at the Minnesota Church Center, where it maintains a full-time staff of two and one part-time person. It has an attorney on retainer. The director is responsible to the board of directors. Women occupy 90 percent of the board positions. The board is racially mixed and about equally represented by African Americans, Native American Indians, Hispanics, and Asian Americans. Efforts are made to integrate persons from lower-income stratas, persons with disabilities, and older women.

From the beginning BIHA has received support from the Minnesota Department of Corrections. In addition to financial support from government grants (40 percent), BIHA receives private foundation grants (30 percent), and gifts or corporate grants and donations (20 percent), as well as membership dues, revenue from conventions, conferences, and exhibitions, and merchandise sales. It has tax-exempt status, and contributions are tax-deductible. The 1993 budget was $172,000, up from $64,000 in the organization's early stages. Annual dues are $5 for individuals, $25 for supporting organizations, and $100 for corporations and foundations.

Women make up 95 percent of BIHA's membership, and men may join. Membership in 1990 was 200, up from 100 in 1985. BIHA membership overlaps with that of many other women's community groups. Membership benefits include information on issues related to women, development of organizational skills, conferences and meetings, advocacy of important values, ideas, or policies, networking with colleagues and peers, consciousness-raising sessions, research, legal assistance, representation of members' opinions to government, opportunity to participate in public affairs, friendship ties, opportunity to exercise influence within an organization devoted to the special needs of women of color, and an opportunity to associate with similarly minded people.

BIHA has a nonprofit educational and research foundation, which uses the same name—BIHA Women in Action.

POLITICAL CONCERNS AND TACTICS

The board of directors represents the membership in lobbying and political activities. Polls of the membership are taken to set policies and endorsements. Communication with the membership is through a newsletter, meetings and seminars, and an annual report. Program services are offered through a network support group for people of color, a speakers bureau composed from the membership of the four racial communities that make up BIHA, video projects, a resource library, the newsletter, community forums, and workshops. To influence public policy, BIHA supplies U.S. congressional staff with information and makes personal appeals to congresspeople, testifies in state legislative hearings, and supplies state legislators and staff with information, testifies at departmental hearings, makes written comments on proposed regulations, seeks administrative review of agency or departmental decisions, educates the public through press releases, conducts research and coordinates with other groups taking similar positions on issues. BIHA supports the outcome and enforcement of all significant federal sex- and race-related initiatives including areas of special legislation related to women of color, especially the Welfare Act of 1982, Social Security Act of 1983, Pension Equity Act of 1984, Child Abuse Act of 1984, Child Support Enforcement Act of 1984, the Age Discrimination Act of 1986, and the Civil Rights Restoration Act of 1988.

Groups with which BIHA coordinates include Casa de Esperanza, the Institute on Black Chemical Abuse, and the Domestic Abuse Project, Minneapolis Department of Corrections. BIHA also collaborates with the National Institute of Women of Color* and has designated March 1 of each year as Women of Color Recognition Day.

ELECTORAL ACTIVITIES

The goals and issues BIHA presses for are partisan issues; they tend to receive support from Democrats. BIHA does not have a political action committee. Candidates of color, though, are supported.

FURTHER INFORMATION

BIHA publishes a newsletter and has a series of videos about family violence in communities of color, *Broken Promises.* It also has a publication, *What Is Abuse? What Can I Do about It?*

BARBARA BENNETT PETERSON

BLACK WOMEN'S HEALTH PROJECT
See NATIONAL WOMEN'S HEALTH NETWORK

B'NAI B'RITH
See B'NAI B'RITH WOMEN

B'NAI B'RITH WOMEN (BBW)
1828 L Street, NW
Suite 250
Washington, DC 20036
(202) 857-1300
FAX (202) 857-1380

B'nai B'rith Women (BBW) supports Jewish women in family, community, and social settings, working to continue Jewish values and protect Jewish people worldwide, promote young people's emotional health and security, and empower women within and outside Judaism.

ORIGIN AND DEVELOPMENT

When BBW formed in 1897 as a Jewish service organization, it was a local women's auxiliary for B'nai B'rith (BB) lodge and had as its mission filling Jewish women's needs in the family. Founded in 1843, BB also is a service organization. The words B'nai B'rith mean "Sons of the Covenant" in Hebrew, and BB was a men's organization. Many local women's auxiliaries formed after 1897. In 1940, a national organization formed to coordinate these local groups' activities and the seven autonomous U.S. districts that encompassed them. Key founders included Lenore Underwood Mills, Lena Orlow Ginsburg, Anita Perlman, and Ida Cook Farber. BBW's constituency included women Jewish by birth or conversion or married to a Jew. As time passed, its goals gradually became distinguished from BB's. In 1957, it abandoned its early name, B'nai B'rith Women's Supreme Council, and in 1962, it incorporated as a separate organization within BB.

In 1965, BBW held its first biennial convention with local chapter delegates, created a public affairs program, and passed its own resolutions. In 1974, the delegates adopted a completely new constitution, which phased out the districts and introduced regions with a volunteer and staff structure supported by a national budget. B'nai B'rith Women Canada (BBWC) evolved from BBW in 1976. In 1988, after 145 years, BB decided to admit women to full membership and threatened to expel BBW when it insisted on maintaining its automomy and refused to submit to BB. In 1990, BBW entered into an agreement with BB that declared BBW an independent organization affiliated with BB. This contract will be renegotiated in 1995. Presently, BBW seeks to realize its own ends through strategic long-range planning. It has increased its community activism, emphasizing the interests of Jewish and non-Jewish women, especially domestic violence and interfaith marriage.

ORGANIZATION AND FUNDING

BBW has 600 local affiliates and twelve regions and also is represented in Canada. A biennial delegate convention elects the executive board's sixteen at-large members and the organization's officers; it can amend the constitution and passes public affairs resolutions. All delegates are eligible for some form of subvention of convention expenses. The fifty-three-member board of directors is not racially mixed. All its members are women. In 1992, Joan Kort served as president. In 1957, the group opened a Washington, D.C., office. It also has offices in Rockville, Maryland; West Palm Beach, Florida; Houston; Philadelphia; Los Angeles and Burlingame, California; Chicago; Cleveland, Ohio; Kansas City, Missouri; New York City, Elmont, and Mamaroneck, New York; and Toronto, Ontario. BBW's current executive director is Elaine Binder. It employs fifty-two paid staff, thirty of them at the executive level, with twenty-nine in Washington and sixteen of these at the executive level. Ability in the Washington office is rewarded by bonuses and promotion to a higher level of responsibility.

Membership is on an individual basis. Currently, BBW has 100,000 members, a decline from 110,000 in 1985, 120,000 in 1980, 130,000 in 1975, and 150,000 in 1970. In 1965, there were 140,000, and in 1960, 133,000 members. All members are women. BBW has discussed its status as an all-women group and will remain as it is. Annual dues are a minimum of thirty dollars. Members join for the sake of friendship ties and the chance to associate with similarly minded people. Communication with peers and advocacy of important values also work as incentives to membership and, to a lesser extent, conferences and meetings and organizational skill development. BBW has on the drawing board a comprehensive member benefit package.

In its early stages, BBW received financial help from BB and small contributions from many people. Today 40 percent of its financial support comes from gifts or bequests beyond dues from individuals and 40 percent from fund-raising events, with 20 percent from membership dues. Conventions, conferences, and exhibitions; merchandise sales; and corporate or business gifts or grants provide negligible support. Since 1962, BBW has been a 501 (c) (3) organization. Contributions are tax-deductible. In 1992, BBW had a $6 million general fund. In 1980, it had a $3,700,000 fund, a large increase over $1,700,000 in 1970 and $1,300,000 in 1960 due to nationalization of the interim structure.

POLICY CONCERNS AND TACTICS

The regional boards, national planning committee, and officers may recommend policy to the national executive board. Other than for constitutional change, the board has the authority to adopt policy. The delegate assembly also influences these policy decisions; to a lesser extent executive officers and membership polls are influential. Strategy choices are discussed by the program/public affairs director with the executive director, and the latter also talks with the relevant national task force and officers. Other organizations might be consulted. As preferred strategies, BBW finds reasonably important conducting and publishing issue-oriented research, educating the membership with publications, and encouraging members to write legislators and committees. To a point, it contacts public decision makers through an influential member, works to educate the public through press releases, especially regarding its contributions to young people's mental health, and participates in direct action political demonstrations.

BBW encourages local groups to engage in high-impact activities at the community level and grants awards for the implementation of such projects. Through these it seeks to promote personal levels of consciousness of Jewish life and values. It also works to assist "women in the middle"—caretakers for offspring and elderly parents alike. One major funding recipient is the organization's Jerusalem-based Residential Treatment Center for emotionally disturbed boys. BBW has also sponsored a Scholar Exchange Program since 1990 from the Yale University Child Study Center. BBWC has a "safe house" system for victims of domestic violence; Holiday Inn, large Canadian grocery store chains, and other corporations sponsor this service project. BBW helps to support the BB Youth Organization for high school students of both sexes from orthodox, conservative, and reform persuasions and Hillel Foundation, which BB International commissions.

BBW has as a goal advocacy on the national, state, and local levels for women's issues. It supports ratification by the United States of the United Nations Convention to Eliminate All Forms of Discrimination against Women. It finds of continuing interest the 1963 Equal Pay Act and 1964 Civil Rights Act, 1965 Administration on Aging Act, Voting Rights Act, Act of 1972 in which sex discrimination was added to the Civil Rights Commission jurisdiction and 1972 Equal Employment Act, equal rights amendment (ERA), *Roe* v. *Wade*, 1974 Equal Credit Opportunity Amendments, 1975 Social Security Act, 1976 Day Care Act, human life constitutional amendment, and, to a lesser extent, the Hyde amendments, 1978 Pregnancy Discrimination Act, 1984 Pension Equity and Child Support Discrimination Act, 1984 Pension Equity and Child Support Enforcement Acts, 1986 Age Discrimination Act, and 1988 Civil Rights Restoration Act.

BBW supported the family and medical leave bill twice vetoed by President Bush and pending bills on abortion and violence against women, this latter sponsored by Joseph Biden (D-DE). It seeks ratification by the United States of the United Nations resolution to end all discrimination against women.

BBW would applaud any federal pro-choice, pro-Israel, or pro-child initiatives passed over the last decade. It believes the worst federal actions were antiabortion ones and the failure to ratify ERA and to support children's programs. It finds the laws and amendments passed in the 1980s worse than legislation passed in the 1970s.

BBW most likely would coordinate with the National Abortion Rights Action League* (NARAL), National Council of Jewish Women* (NCJW), and BB Anti-Defamation League (ADL), which files numerous amicus briefs annually, particularly in cases of race discrimination and church-state conflict. BBW has worked with NCJW and BBADL for thirty or more years, with NARAL since the seventies. It plans to heighten its relationship with BBADL even more and has fourteen members on the BBADL commission. Currently, BBW and BBADL have an exhibition on Jewish women's diversity in the United States traveling to ten large cities. BBW sees as its regular adversaries right to life and anti-ERA groups.

ELECTORAL ACTIVITIES

BBW does not see women's issues as partisan and does not have a political action committee.

FURTHER INFORMATION

BBW has a membership newsletter, *Women's World,* published eight times yearly.

SARAH SLAVIN

B'NAI B'RITH WOMEN CANADA
See B'NAI B'RITH WOMEN

B'NAI B'RITH WOMEN'S SUPREME COUNCIL
See B'NAI B'RITH WOMEN

BUSINESS AND PROFESSIONAL WOMEN'S FOUNDATION
See NATIONAL FEDERATION OF BUSINESS AND PROFESSIONAL WOMEN'S CLUBS OF THE U.S.A.

BUSINESS AND PROFESSIONAL WOMEN'S POLITICAL ACTION COMMITTEE
See NATIONAL FEDERATION OF BUSINESS AND PROFESSIONAL WOMEN'S CLUBS OF THE U.S.A.

C
———————— / ————————

CALIFORNIA NOW PAC
See NATIONAL ORGANIZATION FOR WOMEN—CALIFORNIA

CAMPAIGN SUPPORT COMMITTEE
See NATIONAL WOMEN'S POLITICAL CAUCUS

CATHOLICS FOR A FREE CHOICE (CFFC)
1436 U Street, NW
Suite 301
Washington, DC 20009–3916
(202) 986–6093
FAX (202) 332–7995

Catholics for a Free Choice (CFFC) is a national educational organization that supports the right to legal reproductive health care, especially family planning and abortion. CFFC also works to reduce the incidence of abortion and to increase women's choices in childbearing and child rearing through advocacy of social and economic programs for women, families, and children. CFFC also seeks to develop sexual and reproductive ethics that are based on justice, reflect a commitment to women's well-being, and respect and affirm the moral capacity of women and men to make sound and responsible decisions about their lives.

ORIGIN AND DEVELOPMENT

In the early 1970s, a small group of Catholic laity founded CFFC to oppose Catholic Church efforts to reinstate restrictive abortion laws in New York. Founding members included Patricia McQuillan Fogarty, Joan Harriman, and Meta Mulcahy, three Catholic feminists who were members of the local New

York chapter of the National Organization for Women (NOW). As feminists they sought to apply the tenets of the women's movement to the struggle for gender equality within the Church. Since New York had repealed its antiabortion law in 1970, the state had been the scene of major protests by pro-life forces led by Terence Cardinal Cooke and the New York Catholic archdiocese. CFFC began to defend New York's policy of legalized abortion, and this broadened into a national defense of legal abortion in the wake of the 1973 Supreme Court decision in *Roe v. Wade*. In response to *Roe*, CFFC was officially chartered as a corporation in New York in 1973.

From 1973 to 1976, CFFC remained a small group housed in New York, having little money, no staff, and no ongoing programs. The group had intermittent contacts with other pro-choice organizations such as Planned Parenthood,* NOW,* and the National Abortion Rights Action League* (NARAL). It was also an affiliate of the Religious Coalition for Abortion Rights (RCAR), an association of over 25 national religious organizations joined together to protect the option of legal abortion.

In 1976, the organization (CFFC) moved to Washington and hired Ginny Andary as a part-time lobbyist. From 1976 to 1979, Andary worked through the pro-choice coalition and visited members of Congress to make them aware of the existence of pro-choice Catholic opinion. The organization operated with a small budget ($15,000 to 20,000) mostly provided by grants from a Unitarian Universalist Church in New York.

In 1979, a new CFFC director, Patricia MacMahon, secured a large educational grant ($75,000) from the Sunnen Foundation in Missouri and initiated CFFC's publications program. During her tenure, the CFFC Board of Directors also decided there was no reason the organization should continue as a lobby, since its strength was not in numbers but in the power of ideas and in the articulation of an alternative Catholic perspective on abortion policy. They therefore shifted the organization's status from a 501(c)(4) lobby to a 501(c)(3) tax-exempt, educational organization. This made CFFC eligible for foundation grants and placed the organization on a more secure financial footing. Finally, MacMahon expanded the CFFC Board of Directors and invited Frances Kissling, who was then executive director of the National Abortion Federation (NAF), to join the Board. By 1982, MacMahon had retired and Kissling had become the new executive director of CFFC.

Under Kissling's leadership, CFFC's funding increased and the organization became increasingly prominent throughout the 1980s. In 1981, CFFC held a press conference at the U.S. Senate to protest the National Conference of Catholic Bishops' testimony supporting the Hatch Human Life Amendment. In 1982, CFFC held a briefing for Catholic members of Congress, sponsored by then-Representative Geraldine Ferraro (D-NY). The purpose of the briefing was to provide assistance to Catholic lawmakers in coping with the abortion issue in electoral and legislative politics. When Ferraro became the Democratic Vice-Presidential candidate two years later (in 1984), several Catholic bishops recalled the 1982 CFFC Congressional briefing and accused Ferraro of misrepresenting Catholic teaching on abortion.

The ensuing controversy over Ferraro's pro-choice policy position provided the context for what is perhaps CFFC's most controversial media intervention, a full-page paid advertisement in *The New York Times* on October 7, 1984. The ad described a diversity of opinion on abortion within the American church, decried clerical attacks on political candidates over the issue, and called for dialogue. This public statement triggered a series of repressive actions by Vatican agencies against the ad's signers; the subsequent controversy kept CFFC in the media spotlight for a considerable period of time.

ORGANIZATION AND FUNDING

CFFC is an educational organization with a board of directors, an operational staff of approximately ten people, a. headquarters in Washington, D.C., and a network of twenty-eight state affiliates. It is a non-profit, tax-exempt organization which is primarily foundation-financed. Its 1992 budget is over one million dollars (compared with $750,000 in 1991, $232,000 in 1982, and $15,000 in 1979). Sponsors include the Ford Foundation, the George Gund Foundation, the Ms. Foundation, the Packard Foundation, the Sunnen Foundation, the Alida Dayton Foundation, the Brush Foundation, and the Veatch Program of the North Shore Unitarian Church.

CFFC's Board of Directors is a small board of approximately thirteen members drawn from law, business, academia, and the world of Washington governmental analysts. The board formulates policy, deliberates about funding, and oversees the activities of the organization. Scholars and writers who have served on the board include John Giles Milhaven from Brown University, Rosemary Radford Ruether of Garret-Evangelical Seminary in Illinois, feminist theologian Mary Hunt, novelist Mary Gordon, and Patricia Hennessey, a New York lawyer who is a cooperating attorney with the ACLU Reproductive Freedom Project. CFFC's staff includes Frances Kissling (President), Denise Shannon (Executive Vice President and Program Director), Greg Lebel (Vice President for Public Policy), Maggie Hume (Newsjournal Editor), Jane Reilly (National Network Coordinator), and several staff assistants.

POLICY CONCERNS AND TACTICS

As a national educational organization, CFFC's efforts are directed primarily towards ordinary citizens, Catholic and non-Catholic, who contact the organization seeking information and assistance in thinking about abortion. The organization spends a good deal of its time trying to persuade anyone who will listen that "pro-choice Catholic" is not a contradiction in terms. Concretely, this means that a significant portion of its budget is allocated to its publications program and to communications and public relations. CFFC publishes *Conscience*, a quarterly newsjournal with a circulation of 12,000. In addition, the organization has developed a line of publications such as *Abortion: A Guide to*

Making Ethical Decisions, which are designed to assist women callers seeking information.

CFFC also provides educational materials to more specialized audiences. It runs a press clipping service focusing on the Catholic Church and abortion-related issues, and serves as a media clearinghouse for Catholic and non-Catholic activists. The organization holds Congressional briefings periodically and has developed materials advising politicians how to approach the abortion topic. In 1990, in the wake of the Supreme Court's decision in *Webster*, CFFC published its *Guide for Pro-choice Catholics*, a compendium of articles and essays designed to assist pro-choice Catholic politicians and candidates whose right to make independent policy judgments about abortion was being challenged by the bishops. Six thousand copies of this publication were mailed to state legislators across the United States.

CFFC also conducts more specialized projects directed at particular audiences. In the mid-1980s, it inaugurated "Bishops Watch," a program monitoring the extent to which dioceses incorporated women into their ministries and offices. CFFC's Hispanic Project does educational outreach among Hispanic Catholics in the United States. Indeed, CFFC has developed an international focus, helping to organize pro-choice Catholics in countries such as Poland, Ireland, Mexico, and Uruguay.

On the domestic front, in the wake of the *Webster* decision returning some abortion regulation to the states, CFFC has sponsored a Grassroots Organizing Project to assist pro-choice Catholic activists in the development of a network of state affiliate organizations. To date, representatives from twenty-seven states have attended training conferences held in 1990 and 1991. CFFC's Washington headquarters acts as a resource center for these state affiliates.

Finally, CFFC has filed amicus briefs in several abortion cases which have reached the Supreme Court. It first filed a brief with other members of RCAR in *City of Akron v. Akron Center for Reproductive Health* (1983). In the *Webster* case, CFFC filed its own brief, written by Board member and attorney Patricia Hennessey; material from this brief was quoted directly by Justice John Paul Stevens in his dissenting opinion in *Webster*.

As a non-profit, tax-exempt organization, CFFC is non-partisan and does not have a political action committee. It has developed close ties with Catholic and Protestant groups such as the National Coalition of American Nuns (NCAN), the Women's Ordination Conference (WOC), the National Assembly of Religious Women* (NARW), Catholics Speak Out, WomenChurch and the Religious Coalition for Abortion Rights* (RCAR). It also works with a secular pro-choice coalition which includes Planned Parenthood, NARAL, NOW, the National Abortion Federation,* and other feminist activists. However, CFFC has refused to be identified as simply the Catholic extension of the pro-choice movement. Instead, CFFC has consistently sought to combat the occasional, latent anti-Catholicism of the movement and to insist upon the necessity of a moral and ethical framework in deliberations about abortion.

SOURCES

Interview with CFFC officers, Frances Kissling (President), Mary Jean Collings (Director of Public Affairs), and Denise Shannon (Director of Communications), Washington, D.C., January 25, 1991.

Interview with Mary Jean Collins (Director of Public Affairs) and Jane O'Brien Reilly (National Network Coordinator), Catholics for a Free Choice, Washington, D.C., April 27, 1992.

Frances Kissling, Address at Conference of the CFFC Grassroots Organizing Conference, June 2, 1990.

CFFC, *The Abortion Issue in the Political Process: A Briefing for Catholic Legislators*, Washington, D.C., 1982.

CFFC, *Guide for Prochoice Catholics*, Washington, D.C., 1990.

Mary E. Hunt and Frances Kissling, "The *New York Times* Ad: A Case Study in Religious Feminism," *Journal of Feminist Studies in Religion*, Vol. 3, No. 1 (Spring 1987), pp. 115–127.

Richard Doerflinger, "Who Are Catholics For a Free Choice?" *America*, November 16, 1985, pp. 312–317.

Joe Feuerherd, "Kissling's Crusade for Catholics' Free Choice," *National Catholic Reporter* February 8, 1991.

Maureen E. Fiedler, "Dissent Within the U.S. Church: The Case of the Vatican '24,'" in Mary C. Segers, ed., *Church Polity and American Politics: Issues in Contemporary American Catholicism* (New York: Garland Publishing, 1990), pp. 313–333.

MARY C. SEGERS

CATHOLIC WORKER (CW)
36 East First Street
New York, NY 10003
(212) 777-9617

A movement of Christian radicalism, the Catholic Worker (CW) espouses as a way of life voluntary poverty and works of mercy and nonviolence to build a decentralized, noncapitalist society. Dorothy Day's newspaper, *The Catholic Worker,* as well as the movement begun by Day and Peter Maurin, draws on some anarchist tendencies present in pre–World War I radical movements. Although Day was jailed for thirty days after a 1918 suffrage protest in Washington, D.C., she wrote in 1967, "I went to jail in Washington upholding the rights of political prisoners. An Anarchist then as I am now, I have never used the vote that women won by their demonstration before the White House."

ORIGIN AND DEVELOPMENT

The problem of how to define CW has existed since writer Day (1897–1980) and French worker-philosopher Maurin (1877–1949) founded the movement during the Great Depression years. Day addressed this problem in a May 1970 "On Pilgrimage" column in *The Catholic Worker* newspaper. She wrote that

"The New York Times usually identifies us as people who run some kind of mission on the Bowery. The *Daily News,* more discerning for once, looked us squarely in the eye and identified us as a group of pacifist-anarchists."

First published in New York City on May Day in 1933, the purpose of *The Catholic Worker* was to "make known the encyclicals of the popes in regard to social justice." The introductory issue featured stories about strikes and unions, the fight for new social legislation in Washington, D.C., and the plight of the Negro. A Communist before her conversion to Catholicism, Day wanted to reconcile her advocacy for workers with her Christian faith. After the first issue, Maurin withdrew his name from the masthead. As a Christian agrarian, he wanted unemployed laborers to find work in farming communities.

He set forth his ideas in a series of *Easy Essays,* in addition to "clarification" discussions with Day and anyone willing to listen. Maurin's idea that "we need houses of hospitality to give the rich the opportunity to serve the poor" was quickly adopted; the first house of hospitality was an empty barbershop beneath Day's apartment on East Fifteenth Street. There was a place for people to be seated in the large kitchen where Day, Maurin, and young Catholics who were attracted to a way of life among the poor served meals.

In May 1936, the house at 115 Mott Street was used to house and feed striking merchant seamen of the National Maritime Union. Headquarters, Day wrote, "were a tribute to the seaman's dignity as a man free to form associations with his fellows, to have some share in the management of the enterprise in which he was engaged." During the 1930s and 1940s, more than a dozen houses of hospitality appeared in Chicago, St. Louis, Boston, Milwaukee, and other cities. These houses functioned autonomously, yet Day's leadership and their shared views on voluntary poverty and pacifism held the disparate houses together.

The May 1992 *Catholic Worker* listed houses of hospitality in the United States, Canada, and elsewhere. The Dorothy Day Catholic Worker House in Rock Island, Illinois, engages in resistance protest against the Rock Island Arsenal; the Thomas Merton House in Bridgeport, Connecticut, offers a soup kitchen; Bethany House of Hospitality in Oakland, California, is an AIDS hospice; Strangers and Guests House in Maloy, Iowa, is an organic farm community; Zacchaeus House in Binghamton, New York, offers hospitality for women with children; and Alderson Hospitality House in Anderson, West Virginia, offers welcome and support to visitors and inmates at the Federal Women's Prison.

During World War II, some workers in the houses of hospitality argued that the struggle against Nazism fit the criteria for a just war. Day gave an unyielding response. In a letter to workers in far-flung houses she offered two choices: conformity to the principles of absolute Christian nonviolence or disassociation from the movement.

The Catholic Workers strengthened their pacifist stand during the cold war years by refusing to participate in nuclear civil defense drills. Day maintained an arduous schedule of speaking tours and visits to CW houses while still writing her "On Pilgrimage" column for the newspaper. Day also was an ally and supporter of Clarence Jordan's interracial Kiononia Farm in Americus, Georgia, and a boycott of California fruit growers by the United Farm Workers.

Day's last stay in jail was during the 1973 United Farm Workers strike led by Cesar Chávez in Fresno, California. Day believed that the union was attempting to build a new social order, whereas trade union leadership had settled for improved wages and benefits. In her prayer for the strikers (which Day hoped *Catholic Worker* readers would say), she asked, "Dear Pope John—please, yourself a 'campesino,' watch over the United Farm Workers. Raise up more leader servants throughout the country to stand with Cesar Chávez in this nonviolent struggle."

CW was one of the very first groups to oppose U.S. involvement in the Vietnamese conflict. As the group had done during World War II, it provided counsel for those willing to declare themselves conscientious objectors. Almost every issue of *The Catholic Worker* has news and letters from diverse peace and justice groups. Some of these groups, such as the National Coalition to Abolish the Death Penalty, Fellowship of Reconciliation, and the War Tax Refusers Support Committee, are fairly well established protest groups. The newspaper also has news of new and small groups, such as the Co-Creators of Peace and Justice—a group of artists striving to live in a radically nonviolent way.

ORGANIZATION AND FUNDING

Despite its name, the movement and newspaper have no formal ties to the Catholic Church hierarchy. The movement has two houses on the Lower East Side of New York City. St. Joseph House is at 36 East Third Street, and the Maryhouse is located at 55 East Third Street. The Peter Maurin Farm, home to 90 people, is located in Marlboro, New York. Meals for approximately 90 are served three times a day, seven days a week all year at St. Joseph House. In addition, a morning meal for about 250 to 300 people is served four days a week year round. Sandwiches, tea, and soup are served six days a week, all year. A special holiday breakfast for 400 to 500 people is served on Thanksgiving, Christmas, and Easter. At St. Mary House, lunch for fifteen to twenty women is served six days a week year-round. Vegetables and fruit grown at the Peter Maurin Farm are shared with the needy, mostly in Newburgh, New York.

A September 1991 editorial, "Why We Are Not Tax Exempt," explained that all gifts to CW go into a common fund used to meet daily expenses. CW believes that works of mercy are acts of conscience done without having to ask government permission—as in applying for a federal tax exemption. In the 1993 Annual Financial Report for Charitable Organizations—filed with the New York Department of State—CW listed $300,000 in direct public support from contributions from subscribers and other supporters. Major expenses are food, printing, postage, and insurance applications. All Catholic Workers are volunteers; there are no employers and no employees.

POLICY CONCERNS AND TACTICS

The women and men of CW seek to follow the gospel teaching to live lives of voluntary poverty and nonviolence. Each house makes up policy as it goes along. Father John Shanahan, a priest in the diocese of Toledo, Ohio, who came to St. Joseph House on a sabbatical visit in 1990, wrote about wondering for years about Christian anarchism, which was often mentioned but never defined. The idea seemed to Father John a contradiction in terms. Once he arrived at St. Joseph House, he learned that "there is no boss or anyone to tell you what to do. It is assumed that you will be guided by the ten commandments, the spirit of charity, and a sense of personal responsibility."

The "Aims and Means" statement printed each May during CW's anniversary month in *The Catholic Worker* attempts to describe the ideas of Day and Maurin that guide the movement. The statement covers economics, labor, politics, morals, and the arms race. In contrast to the control and power of the technological state with its military might, CW advocates a philosophy of personalism. Personalism offers the freedom and identity of each person as the basis, focus, and goal of all metaphysics and morals. As taught by Peter Maurin, the philosophy gives workers the opportunity to turn away from selfish individualism toward the good of others. This they do by taking personal responsibility for changing conditions instead of asking the state or any other institution to give out charity.

In contrast to the technological state, CW advocates a decentralized society with family farms, rural and urban land cooperatives, and worker ownership and management of factories. A personalist revolution can come about by nonviolent action. CW opposes the deliberate taking of life for any reason. Any fight against violence is to be undertaken with the spiritual weapons of prayer, fasting, and noncooperation with evil: refusal to pay taxes for war, to register for conscription, and to comply with any unjust legislation; participation in nonviolent strikes and boycotts, protests, or vigils; withdrawal of support for dominant systems, corporate funding, or usurious practices.

ELECTORAL ACTIVITIES

CW does not have a political action committee, nor does it engage in direct mail, telephone, door-to-door, or special events solicitation and fund-raising.

FURTHER INFORMATION

Day originally decided to sell *The Catholic Worker* for one cent, or twenty-five cents a year by subscription. The one-penny charge has become a trademark. Even now the newspaper, which is published eight times a year, still costs a penny an issue. As of 1990, *The Catholic Worker* published an average of 93,000 copies per year.

MARTHA JOY NOBLE

CENTER FOR SURROGATE PARENTING (CSP)
8383 Wilshire Boulevard
Suite 750
Beverly Hills, CA 90314
(213) 655-1974
FAX (213) 852-1310

The Center for Surrogate Parenting, Inc. (CSP), functions as a case manager for individuals interested in a surrogate parenting arrangement and, in the process, lobbies in California for comprehensive legislation in the area of reproductive technology.

ORIGIN AND DEVELOPMENT

Founded in 1981 by William Handel as part of his law practice in the firm of Sherwyn and Handel, CSP incorporated as a private for-profit organization separate from the law firm in 1986. It was created to serve the needs of couples where the wife is infertile and where medical efforts at curing infertility have been exhausted or where couples are interested in pursuing nonmedical avenues to construct or expand their families. These needs became particularly apparent in the 1970s with the rising incidence of female infertility revealed among women who had chosen to delay pregnancy into their late twenties and early thirties. CSP also sought to serve the needs of women desiring to become surrogate mothers in order to carry children for infertile couples.

The center provides comprehensive case management between infertile couples and women willing to act as surrogates. To qualify for the center's programs, the couple must provide a letter from the wife's physician stating that she is infertile or that pregnancy would threaten her life. Couples contracting with CSP tend to be middle-class professionals or businesspeople who have undergone years of infertility treatment. They pay a fee of $13,600 to CSP for its services. If the surrogate does not carry health insurance, the couple must purchase it for her. The couple also incurs legal fees, and total costs may run as high as $45,000. Surrogates contacting CSP tend to be married women in their late twenties with an average of two years of college and an average family income of $36,000. They already must have children in order to qualify for the program. Surrogates receive a fee of $10–$12,000. No CSP clients have broken contracts, nor has CSP been named as a defendant in litigation.

ORGANIZATION AND FUNDING

Located in Beverly Hills, California, CSP employs a staff of fourteen, including attorney Handel, administrator Ralph Fagen, staff psychologist Hilary Hanafin, and three licensed mental health professionals. Handel and Fagen constitute the board of directors. The staff is composed of two males and nine females. One staff member is Filipino, and all other staff members are Caucasians. The staff is organized into management, legal, and psychological teams.

The center's funds are derived from fees paid by clients. Financial data regarding CSP's income or financial holdings are unavailable.

CSP provides a comprehensive approach to surrogacy. Besides acting as a resource for individuals and couples requesting information on surrogacy, it selects, screens, and matches surrogates with infertile couples. It provides legal and administrative assistance, financial supervision, and psychological services. It does not provide direct medical services. Couples and surrogates use their own physicians. CSP currently has three programs: a traditional surrogate parenting program (TSPP), an in vitro fertilization/embryo implant with host surrogate program (IVF/E), and an egg donor program (EDP).

TSPP brings together couples where the wife is infertile and women interested in acting as surrogates. The surrogate is artificially inseminated with the husband's sperm, and after delivery, the wife adopts the child. A licensed psychotherapist interviews surrogate candidates to assess their motivations for becoming surrogates. Group counseling is required from the month of acceptance through the postpartum period. Prior to beginning medical procedures, surrogates are required to review the contract with an independent legal counsel. Medical exams are performed on the husband, wife, and surrogate. Additionally, all three must be screened for the HIV (AIDS) virus. As of August 1994, CSP had participated in the births of 236 children and twenty-three ongoing pregnancies through TSPP. IVF/E offers surrogate parenting through in vitro fertilization (IVF) and embryo implantation. Eggs are removed from an infertile wife, fertilized with her husband's sperm, and implanted in a "host surrogate" who has no genetic relationship to the fetus. The biological mother's name is entered on the birth certificate, and thus adoption is not necessary. Host surrogates undergo a screening process that is similar to the process for traditional surrogates. As of August 1994, ninety-three children had been born through this program, and there were sixteen ongoing pregnancies. EDP allows women to donate ova to a couple. Egg donors are specifically solicited, screened, and matched with prospective recipients. The ova are fertilized through IVF with the husband's sperm and then implanted in the wife. As of August 1994 nine births had occurred through the egg donor program.

POLICY CONCERNS AND TACTICS

Policies at CSP are developed after discussion by the management, legal, and psychological teams. CSP has involved itself in lobbying activities at the California state legislature. It sponsors comprehensive legislation dealing with new fields in reproductive technology. Commercial surrogacy continues to raise controversy. Supporters argue that surrogacy is one mechanism for creating families for couples who might otherwise remain childless due to the woman's infertility. They also argue that women are capable of making rational choices about their reproductive capabilities and therefore should have the right to serve as surrogates or contact surrogates. Opponents counter with the argument that surrogacy constitutes baby selling and therefore commodifies women and children. Opponents also argue that commercial surrogacy encourages socioeconomic exploitation because contracting couples typically have higher income and education levels than do surrogates. Moreover, opponents contend that the process may be traumatic for the surrogate's family, particularly her other children who see their half-sibling given to another family.

CSP works with other organizations interested in surrogacy. It is not directly affiliated with, but cooperates with, the National Association of Surrogate Mothers (NASM) and the Organization of Parents through Surrogacy (OPTS), both of which are based in California and both of which are pro-surrogacy.

ELECTORAL ACTIVITIES

CSP is a nonpartisan organization and has no political action committee.

FURTHER INFORMATION

CSP publishes a semiannual newsletter and acts as a source for individuals and couples requesting information on infertility.

JANNA C. MERRICK

CENTER FOR WOMEN POLICY STUDIES (CWPS)
2000 P Street, NW
Suite 508
Washington, DC 20036
(202) 872-1770
FAX (202) 296-8962

The first national policy institute to focus specifically on the social, legal, and economic status of women, the Center for Women Policy Studies (CWPS) is an action-oriented, research-based organization that has helped place on both federal policy and women's movement agendas issues such as equal credit opportunity, violence against women, and AIDS. To advance the agenda for women's equality and empowerment, CWPS has combined not only advocacy with research but also policy development with public awareness. As part of its official purview, CWPS holds that sex and race bias throughout society must be addressed simultaneously. CWPS programs look at the impact of combined race plus sex bias on women of color, women from diverse socioeconomic backgrounds, women with disabilities, women of different ages, and women of diverse sexual orientation.

ORIGIN AND DEVELOPMENT

Margaret Gates, an attorney specializing in consumer issues, and Jane Roberts Chapman, an economist working on employment training issues, founded CWPS in 1972 after a year of planning. The two had met in 1970 at a National Organization for Women*-sponsored meeting of feminists in Washington, D.C., about employment discrimination against women. They recognized the need for a feminist policy center that would produce the action-oriented research needed to support the advocacy efforts of other women's organizations in Washington. With the late writer, Nancy Gager Clinch, Chapman and Gates developed plans to establish CWPS as the first national policy institute to focus specifically on the social, legal, and economic status of women.

At first, CWPS focused on issues relating to employment policy, such as moving women into nontraditional jobs and credit discrimination. Its first major grant, from the Ford Foundation, funded a study of credit discrimination against women; this grant also was Ford's first in the women's policy arena. CWPS began its credit project in 1973, a time when sex discrimination in the extension of credit was deemed good business practice. But CWPS's research and policy analysis showed that women's credit performance was as good as men's. Chapman and Gates testified before the U.S. Congress and conducted briefings for feminist organizations. Their efforts contributed to passage of the 1974 Equal Credit Opportunity Act. They continued advocacy work to ensure that the Federal Reserve Board issued effective implementing regulations.

CWPS also focused on issues of equal justice under the law, emphasizing treatment of rape victims by the criminal justice system; this interest stemmed partly from Gager Clinch, who had conducted research and written in the area. Rape and other forms of violence against women were hidden problems, not yet part of public agendas. With the exception of women in law schools and activists in the growing rape crisis center movement, few others had confronted these issues, particularly in the context of federal policy. Unfortunately, attempts to persuade funders and other policy analysts that rape should be considered a policy issue initially were unsuccessful.

CWPS sought to bring federal resources to bear; a 1973 grant from the now-defunct Law Enforcement Assistance Administration of the U.S. Department of Justice enabled the center to develop program guidelines for police, prosecutors, hospitals, and community groups on the treatment of rape victims. During the remainder of the 1970s and into the 1980s, CWPS conducted major policy research on issues of violence against women. In 1976, it established the National Resource Center on Family Violence.

For the U.S. observance of International Women's Year in 1976, CWPS conducted research on the legal and economic impact of marriage on women, including a state-by-state survey and analysis of domestic and inheritance law, judicial practices, and the economic impact of divorce on women. The center also made an early contribution to research and policy development for older women. When CWPS began its work, sexual harassment of women in the workplace was denied as a problem and, along with other forms of violence against women, was seen as a fact of life; the center convened a seminar and published an early report on these issues. CWPS also has confronted the "invisible" problems of women in prison, both as workers and inmates.

ORGANIZATION AND FUNDING

An initial grant from Ralph Nader's Public Citizen made it possible to lay the groundwork for CWPS's agenda for the 1970s; this funding also permitted the employment of attorney Marilyn Sloane on a half-time basis for one year. Established in Washington, D.C., CWPS applied for tax-exempt status and created a board of directors that consisted of the codirectors and their mentor, the feminist scholar Jessie Bernard. The board of directors now consists of eight members, four of whom are women of color, and one of whom is a man. Board members include chair Felicia Lynch, Rayna Green, Charlotte Bunch, Jean Hardisty, Irene Lee, Stephen Moskey, Irene Natividad, Leslie Wolfe, and Jessie Bernard. There also is a fifty-seven-member national advisory council, which includes men; nearly half its members are women of color. In 1987, the board of directors hired Leslie R. Wolfe as the center's new executive director, with a mandate to expand programs and position CWPS for continued success into the 1990s and beyond. CWPS professional staff at the Washington-based headquarters consists of eight women, five of whom are women of color. To continue building a cadre of women of color policy analysts and leaders, CWPS launched a new internship program in 1991 in collaboration with Spelman College in Atlanta to bring undergraduate women of color to Washington, D.C., for summer internships that combine public policy, leadership development, and community service experiences.

CWPS's overall budget for 1993 was $500,000. Its 1993 funders included the MetPath Foundation, George Gund Foundation, Equitable Foundation, American Express, Ford Foundation and others. CWPS also has an Associates Program with a $50 annual fee.

To honor its founding board member and role model, CWPS conducts an annual Jessie Bernard Wise Women Awards program, which honors women whose contributions reflect Bernard's vision of feminist enlightenment.

POLICY CONCERNS AND TACTICS

With support from the Ford Foundation, the center convened a long-range planning meeting in March 1988. To define continuing barriers to equal education and work preparation for women and girls and to develop national educational equity goals to eliminate the barriers, CWPS established an Educational Equity Policy Studies Program (EEPS) in 1988. Keeping issue interrelationships in the forefront, the center uses several projects to explore connections among educational opportunities, economic status, family roles, and employment options. A National Agenda for Equity in Math, Science and Technology Education identifies strategies and programs that work to recruit and retain women and girls of color in related educational and career opportunities.

Another EEPS project confronts bias in, and misuse of, standardized testing. CWPS founded and cochaired the Bias in Testing Task Force of the National Coalition for Women and Girls in Education. A joint project with the Springside

School in Philadelphia compared single-sex and coeducational settings on pedagogical, curricular and structural grounds to determine what exactly promotes academic success, aspiration and achievement in girls. The center also conducts policy-relevant research on how women of color define and experience work and family roles and workplace diversity policies and practices and is exploring higher education as a route to economic self-sufficiency for low-income women.

The Law and Pregnancy Program brings policy recommendations about complex reproductive rights/health issues to policymakers and advocates of pro-choice and women's rights. In a context of women's equality and reproductive autonomy, this program focuses on the new reproductive technologies and efforts to define a legal status for the fetus. It also generated resource collections and policy reports in this area and worked with key organizations, including the Women's Legislative Network of the National Conference of State Legislatures* and the Center for the American Woman and Politics, to reach policymakers.

To address critical issues for women in the AIDS crisis from women's diverse perspectives, CWPS established the National Resource Center on Women and AIDS (NRCW A) in 1987. NRCW A develops policy options to ensure that women's needs are met in biomedical and behavioral research, clinical trials of AIDS treatments, development of HIV prevention strategies and risk reduction education, and delivery of health care and social services. NRCW A assists national women's organizations to put women and AIDS on their agendas and to advocate on women's behalf. An action kit is available with a video, *Fighting for Our Lives: Women Confronting AIDS,* which features local women and AIDS projects developed by and for women of color. As part of the Women's Health Equity Act, NRCW A worked with the Congressional Caucus for Women's Issues* on legislation focused on women and AIDS.

The Violence Against Women Program focuses on defining violence against women as bias-motivated hate crime and also examines issues related to girls as both victims and perpetrators of violence. The center convened the first national conference by, for, and about women in their twenties in 1989; this Feminist Futures Conference involved 500 young women.

ELECTORAL ACTIVITIES

CWPS is not a partisan organization and does not have a political action committee.

FURTHER INFORMATION

CWPS has an extensive publications program begun by its founders; it includes more than thirty publications (1993), including book-length studies and policy papers. NRCW A publishes an annual guide to Resources on Women and AIDS and a series of policy papers on current issues. The center also publishes materials on women in higher education, including some previously published by the Project on the Status and Education of Women of the Association of American Colleges.* CWPS research has been published independently.

LESLIE R. WOLFE

CHILDREN'S DEFENSE FUND (CDF)
122 C Street, NW
Washington, DC 20001
(202) 628-8787
FAX (202) 783-7324

The Children's Defense Fund (CDF) is a twenty-two-year-old advocacy organization whose goal is to assure that no child in America will "grow up homeless, sick, undereducated or without hope for the future." The fact that children's issues have achieved status as mainstream items on the U.S. political agenda is in large measure due to CDF's work. CDF also has been a major catalyst in local and state efforts to meet children's needs.

ORIGIN AND DEVELOPMENT

CDF has deep roots in the social movements of the 1960s. It grew out of the Washington Research Project, begun by Marian Wright Edelman in 1968 to work on issues related to civil rights and poverty. A young black civil rights lawyer in Mississippi, Edelman was an active board member of the Child Development Group of Mississippi (CDGM), a community agency that ran a Head Start program and provided health care and other services to the families of the children it enrolled. When CDGM nearly lost its funding, due to attacks by conservative white southern U.S. senators, Edelman decided that her focus should be on the policy process in Washington, D.C.

Edelman's early work in Washington suggested to her that class and racial divisions might be bridged by placing children's needs at the center of the political dialogue. If people were not interested in the needs of minorities or the poor, perhaps they would show greater sensitivity to children. In 1973, Edelman founded CDF with foundation grants. CDF was successful in lobbying to increase funding for Head Start during the Nixon administration but failed in its efforts to expand the number of poor children covered by Medicaid during the Carter administration.

During the 1980s, CDF played a major role in the expansion of Medicaid eligibility for pregnant women and children. Its carefully documented reports on the increasing poverty of American children and the inability of many pregnant women and children to get access to health care attracted congressional and media attention. CDF was also instrumental in creating coalitions of interest groups and members of the Congress supportive of expansion. By the decade's end, Medicaid eligibility was separated from eligibility for AFDC and expanded to phase in coverage for all children up to age nineteen living in families with incomes at or below the poverty level. This legislation made 3 million children and 500,000 pregnant women eligible for Medicaid who were not previously.

CDF also has worked successfully for legislation guaranteeing equal opportunities in education to children with disabilities, establishing rights to services for foster children, expanding children's rights to financial support from parents not present in the home, expanding tax relief for low-income working families, and prohibiting housing discrimination against families with children. In 1986, CDF staff drafted the Act for Better Child Care in consultation with a large number of organizations. After a long legislative process, new comprehensive child care programs and federal moneys for them were authorized in the fall of 1990.

CDF is now one of Washington's most respected, influential public interest advocacy groups. Members of the Congress respect its research accuracy and capacity; and its president is considered to be a "superstar" among lobbyists.

ORGANIZATION AND FUNDING

CDF is a staff rather than a membership organization. It has mailing lists of tens of thousands of people who buy its publications, make contributions, and/ or work in child welfare or health or any of the areas in which CDF acts. It has a nineteen-member board of directors, nine of whom are women. The full board or its executive committee meets at least four times a year to set general policy. Edelman is CDF's president, and James D. Wiell is CDF's general counsel.

CDF's main office is in Washington, D.C. It has a staff of over 100. CDF also has offices in Ohio, Texas, and Minnesota that engage in a broad range of advocacy strategies for children at the state level. Additionally, CDF has a District of Columbia project and an office in a rural county in South Carolina where it sponsors a demonstration project aimed at reducing infant mortality and teen pregnancy. CDF's activities are divided among five departments: Administration and Finance, Development, Communications, Program and Policy, and Government and Community Affairs.

Recently revenue sources have included foundations (52 percent), more than 10,000 individuals (16 percent), special events (8 percent), publication sales (7 percent), corporate donors (5 percent), conference registrations (3 percent), and others such as unions, honoraria, and attorney's fees (9 percent). CDF's budget is almost $10 million. It has legal status as a charity, and contributions are tax-deductible.

POLICY CONCERNS AND TACTICS

CDF engages in a wide range of strategies at the local, state, and federal levels. It does its own surveys of state activities affecting children, often collecting more state data than does the U.S. government. It aims not only to educate government officials and their staffs in Washington but to reach and mobilize the public. CDF's media staff issues press releases, gives briefings, tapes commentaries on specific issues, and works with local groups on media campaigns. Staff has worked with black media leaders to campaign to meet the critical needs of black children and initiated a similar effort with the Latino media. From 1988 to 1989 alone, 13,000 articles cited CDF staff or studies or were written about CDF's work. CDF staff drafts legislation and testifies before the Congress. CDF is very active in policy implementation from the process of commenting on proposed federal regulations to publication of manuals on new federal programs for state and local officials, service providers, and advocates. Staff provides direct technical assistance to both government and private organizations.

CDF maintains close ties with the grass roots. Every year it runs a three-day conference on policy issues and skill building that is attended by about 1,500 advocates from around the United States. Its community organizing/advocacy work includes the Child Watch Projects. In 1981, to document the impact of the Reagan administration's budget cuts on children, CDF and other national organizations trained local volunteers to collect information in their cities. In 1984, CDF initiated an Adolescent Pregnancy Prevention Child Watch. Two thousand volunteers in seventy-two communities learned to collect and use data to communicate the causes and consequences of adolescent pregnancy in their communities. In an effort to personalize children's issues and national policy by having community leaders visit and experience the suffering of homeless, institutionalized, poor, and sick children, CDF's current Child Watch Project is collaborating with retired persons', church, women's, Hispanic, and black organizations.

Coalition building is a major political strategy. As a staff organization representing a constituency that cannot vote or take political action (and many of whose parents have extremely limited political resources), CDF seeks to work with membership groups that represent voters. CDF has worked with major church groups, professional associations, organizations of service providers, and single-issue groups such as those concerned about education or foster care. In coalition with CDF on the child care bill were unions and women's groups. CDF also has worked with the American Association of University Women,* League of Women Voters,* National Council of Negro Women,* National Organization for Women,* National Women's Law Center, Women's Equity Action League,* and the Women's Legal Defense Fund. It has developed cooperative relationships with business leaders and groups representing the elderly. The American Association of Retired Persons,* for example, supported CDF legislation prohibiting housing discrimination and expanding Medicaid eligibility.

ELECTORAL ACTIVITIES

CDF is nonpartisan and does not endorse candidates. It does publish, as part of the lobbying process, annual records of congressional votes on children's issues and occasionally sponsors forums where candidates for elected office discuss their positions on these issues.

FURTHER INFORMATION

CDF annually issues *The State of America's Children*, reviewing the status of U.S. children and an analysis of how the president's proposed budget will affect children, including proposals to pay for the programs that CDF recommends. Six annual reports are published as part of *The Adolescent Pregnancy Prevention Clearinghouse. CDF Reports* appears monthly and describes CDF's work and that of other children's advocacy groups at the local and state levels. Edelman writes a weekly column on children and public policy that appears in black newspapers across the country and another column that appears in church-related publications.

ALICE SARDELL

CHURCH WOMEN UNITED (CWU)
475 Riverside Drive
New York, NY 10115
(212) 870-2347
FAX (212) 870-2338

Representing an ecumenical constituency, Church Women United (CWU) is a prominent Christian women's organization that has taken leadership in demanding women's rights in church and society as well as in encouraging women's spiritual growth.

ORIGIN AND DEVELOPMENT

As women responded to the ecumenical movement within Protestantism, a group came together in 1941 calling itself the United Council of Church Women (UCCW). It had a preexisting framework, the hundreds of local groups that women already had formed across denominational lines in order to carry out effective mission work both at home and abroad. UCCW also inherited two specific projects, the World Day of Prayer and May Fellowship Day. Since 1920, the World Day of Prayer had united thousands of Protestant women, calling them together through over 7,000 local units to pray for home and foreign missions and to raise money, mainly for Christian colleges in Asia. May Fellowship Day, begun at the height of the Great Depression, raised concern and money for a ministry to migrant workers. Once this network became the UCCW, it began to grow into the preeminent Christian women's group—today including not only Protestant but also Roman Catholic and Eastern Orthodox women—called CWU.

The new UCCW immediately responded to the challenge of World War II. At its first national gathering at Cleveland in 1942, delegates called for a day to be set aside in the fall to study peacemaking; this day became World Community Day, the third of UCCW's special days. Its first project was a ballot sent to 90,000 churchwomen asking two questions: should the United States work to form the United Nations (UN), and would these women be willing to continue wartime rationing into the postwar period to help war victims? These questions illustrate the two lasting strengths of UCCW: its idealistic belief in social change and its practical willingness to work for that change. Over 80,000 women voted yes to both proposals.

When the National Council of Churches was founded in 1950, it incorporated UCCW as one of its departments and renamed it United Church Women (UCW). By placing itself at the heart of the Protestant ecumenical movement, UCW entered a time of dynamic growth and influence. Because its leadership was able to speak out in a more radical voice than the denominational women's groups, it became the cutting edge for Protestant women. Working to improve race relations and to support the UN were its main challenge for the next fifteen years. Meanwhile the organization built up its grass roots, training women for leadership on the state and local levels. Black women became more than tokens on the national board, and in 1971, a black woman from Jackson, Mississippi, Clarie Harvey, was elected president for a three-year term. Chapters formed in Puerto Rico, the Philippines, and South Korea.

Contributing to early stirrings of the women's liberation movement, in 1966, UCW separated from the National Council of Churches and became Church Women United. Backing the trend toward women's ordination and a greater voice for laywomen, CWU brought together female theologians and laywomen to formulate a stronger basis for demanding women's rights in the churches. More political than when it was founded, CWU worked for passage of the equal rights amendment and gave a five-year focus to eliminate poverty among women and children. It created new liturgies that expressed women's unique spiritual gifts and contributions to the churches.

CWU's greatest impact has been in the fight against racism. In the 1950s and 1960s in the South, CWU groups, together with the Young Women's Christian Association,* were often the first and sometimes the only place where black and white women could meet, work, and pray together. CWU has remained faithful to its antiracism goal by sponsoring continuing racism workshops at its leadership training conferences. CWU has chosen to sit out another major social struggle, the debate over abortion rights: To welcome the many Roman Catholic women who joined after Vatican II, it chose to be silent about a woman's right to choose. It thus extended its ecumenical base outside Protestantism at the expense of appealing to many young Protestant women. Today, between 25 percent and 40 percent of local leaders are Roman Catholic.

In contrast to its early views during World War II, CWU today is more critical of the role that the U.S. government and corporations play in the world. Long, close association with women from around the world has made CWU aware of the ways in which the United States is a threat to small countries, and its policies reflect these international contacts.

ORGANIZATION AND FUNDING

CWU reached its greatest growth around 1970, with over 3,000 local units, represented in every state. Today it is down to about 1,700 units due to the aging membership. With an average age in the sixties, CWU is seeking ways to serve and interest younger churchwomen whose lifestyle involves both family and job and who have less time than their mothers for volunteer work. Its volunteer officers, the administrative committee, include a president, currently Ann Baker Garvin, an African Methodist Episcopal laywoman; first and second vice presidents; a secretary-treasurer; and committee chairs of finance, personnel, nominations, communication and interpretation, and ecumenical development (leadership development, revitalization, and diversity). CWU is advised by an executive council, including eight regional coordinators and representatives from the state presidents and an even larger common council whose annual conferences are like a town meeting. A top priority is to keep these groups racially inclusive. CWU's main office is located in New York City. It has a staff of one professional and an intern in Washington, D.C.

CWU has a budget of about $1.3 million, raised from offerings on its three special days from denominational gifts; it does not have dues and is tax-exempt. Its pronouncements reach about half a million women.

POLICY CONCERNS AND TACTICS

Always responsive to grassroots opinion, CWU is striving to become even more flexible in its structure. Because the Common Council uses a mail ballot, the administrative committee hears from state units directly. It is considering ways that local units can have input into national policy statements while they are being formulated. The Washington office maintains a mail network that it alerts to congressional issues on women, advocating letter-writing campaigns. It also works with IMPACT, the interdenominational information agency, especially on issues about the poverty of women and children.

CWU always has operated with two overreaching goals: to encourage women's spiritual growth (as seen, e.g., in the liturgies for the World Day for Prayer and for its national assemblies, which are a rich mine of innovative ritual) and to broaden women's ecumenical contacts. In 1990 its immediate goals were in the health care arena in order to meet older women's needs, about which it held a conference in 1988; interracial cooperation was another goal, on which it published study booklets and "Women Doing Theology," a third. CWU has made an extensive contribution to women's theology through its Celebrations, which challenge traditional theology, and its pamphlets called *Wellsprings,* which focus on social action, women's rights, inclusive language, poverty, peace, and the biblical basis of faith.

With ongoing commitment to global witness through the UN and the World Council of Churches, CWU continues to speak out for its diverse constituency. It works closely with the women's units of many denominations and cooperates with Jewish women's groups. CWU is thus a major voice for women in the churches.

ELECTORAL ACTIVITIES

A nonpartisan organization, CWU has no political action committee.

FURTHER INFORMATION

The official magazine of CWU is *Churchwoman,* with a circulation of about 6,000; it is sent to all local officers and to outside subscribers. CWU also publishes *Wellsprings* (occasional pamphlets).

ANNE L. BARSTOW

CITIZEN'S PROJECT TO REMOVE INTOXICATED DRIVERS (RID)
P.O. Box 520
Schenectady, NY 12301
(518) 372-0034

The first, most aggressive national grassroots antidrinking-and-driving organization, A Citizen's Project to Remove Intoxicated Drivers (RID) seeks to provide victim support, monitor the criminal justice system, heighten public awareness that driving while intoxicated (DWI) is not a victimless crime, and influence a sane national alcohol policy (SNAP). The Stop DWI movement became a women's movement because women tend to assume victims' care or the burden of their loss and are the majority of arena activists.

ORIGIN AND DEVELOPMENT

RID formed in February 1978 in Schenectady. The previous November, public affairs television talk show host and producer Doris Aiken learned that a drinking driver had killed Karen and Timothy Morris. Karen and Timothy were the Aiken children's ages, seventeen and nineteen; the driver was twenty-two. The local district attorney did not intend to prosecute, maintaining his office represented the people of New York, not the Morris survivors. Aiken founded RID to represent the people, also having learned that plea bargains enabled drinking drivers to continue for an average 3.5 years before they were convicted. Twenty-five thousand people died annually in alcohol-related crashes; but the drivers kept driving. In 1979, when four groups independently founded to combat DWI merged to form New York State RID (RID-NYS), Aiken received significant assistance from Janet Beise, Fran Helmstadter, Bonnie Schwalm, and Diane Harris.

Between 1980 and 1981, RID-NYS persuaded the state legislature to pass thirteen relevant bills. Twenty-eight religious, volunteer, and business groups, such as the Greater Rabbinical Organization in New York, American Association of University Women,* and Highway Users Federation, joined the effort. Aiken monitored legislators' votes and facilitated networking among RID chapters, which led to more state-level organizations. The educated middle-class activists, including professionals and retirees, quickly grasped the legislative process and the fact that bills pending since 1977 had not passed because of lawyer legislators. RID argued that some of them might have conflicts of interest and threatened to tell local media. It took as a symbol one lighted candle and held the first of many public candlelight rallies. Through its efforts, the campaign against driving drunk became a public agenda item.

By 1982, with help from a National Highway Traffic Safety Administration (NHTSA) start-up grant, RID had 75 chapters in twenty-two states. It incorporated as a national organization. Aiken became national president. By 1983, RID had 155 chapters in thirty-five states, having benefited from print and broadcast media coverage, including appearances on such programs as "Donohue" and "CBS Morning News." Soon the movement reached 95 percent of the U.S. population by strategic use of media markets. The same year, nineteen states passed license revocation laws. A Harris poll showed that over 75 percent of the public favored sobriety checkpoints, another RID agenda item. Despite the American Civil Liberties Union's* opposition, in *Michigan* v. *Sitz* (1990), the U.S. Supreme Court found checkpoints constitutional. For five years running, traffic fatalities in the state with the most powerful RID representation, New York, declined 23 percent, and states with strong RID chapters showed continually improved records, the nation's best.

Unlike Mothers against Drunk Driving* (MADD), which received backing from Anheuser Busch, RID refused alcohol industry funding. Students against Drunk Driving (SADD) also accepted it, from the Miller Brewing Company. In 1984, RID joined a coalition, Stop Marketing Alcohol on Radio and Television (SMART), promoted by the Center for Science in the Public Interest (CSPI), and earned the National Association of Broadcasters' (NAB) wrath. These advertisements produced $900 million in revenue a year for the industry. RID ceased to appear on network television.

SMART abandoned the proposed ban in favor of counteradvertising. The broadcast industry still boycotted RID, helped by the Federal Communications Commission's rescission in 1987 of the fairness doctrine. MADD and SADD were not boycotted because they did not support the ban. RID lost twenty chapters, its name recognition dropped, and the Harvard School of Public Health showed news coverage of the movement to have dropped precipitously. RID has recouped its losses since, supporting an increased beer excise tax, tightened availability laws, and mandatory testing, among other initiatives.

ORGANIZATION AND FUNDING

RID has 150 chapters in forty states, up from 135 chapters in 1985, and is represented in France. Although a chapter's name must include RID, and it must support the national's goals, local chapters experience legal and financial independence and must specify when they speak for themselves. The nine-member national board includes no minorities. It is two-thirds women. RID helps to pay active chapter heads' and coordinators' conference and board meeting expenses. Aiken has been reelected president biennially. Schenectady headquarters employs five professional staff. Workers rotate jobs and experience different levels of responsibility.

The chapters keep their own membership lists. Women are 70 percent of the members, up from 60 percent in 1980 and 50 percent in 1970. Individual members pay dues of $20; chapters, $50; corporations, $100. Chapters dues are voluntary. Active chapters with limited means may get a dues scholarship from the national. Members join to advocate important policies and help victims. Also offering incentives are publications, information, and research; consciousness-raising sessions and the chance for peer communication; friendship ties; and chapter autonomy. RID helps members develop organizational skills and presents their opinions to government. Members may exercise intragroup influence and participate publicly. They associate with like-minded people and meet at the annual conference and regional meetings such as the 1988–89 NHTSA-funded Public Awareness Community Tactics Project.

Churches, volunteer associations, corporations and businesses, small individual contributions, and memorial funds helped RID get started financially. Since then, 40 percent of funds have come from government grants or contracts, 20 percent from membership fees, 20 percent from merchandise sales, and 15 percent from foundation grants; the remaining 5 percent comes from publication sales and advertising, conferences, corporate or business grants, and fund-raising events. A 501 (c) (3) organization, RID had a total budget in 1991 of $90,000, up from $15,000 in 1980 and $1,000 in 1978. Chapters keep the money they raise; and much of RID's income returns to them in programs and grants.

POLICY CONCERNS AND TACTICS

Annual or as-needed board meetings set RID policy. Chapters forward recommendations and ideas for consideration. Executive officers' decisions influence policy discussions. To develop strategy, RID networks with groups affected by an issue and seeks to increase public awareness to get feedback. RID's agenda is deterrence-oriented. It also believes that the crime victim's most important right is to be heard. Preferred strategies include direct action and demonstrations, membership education through publications, and public education through press releases. RID also testifies in congressional, state legislative, and agency/department hearings, encourages members to write letters, fields public service campaigns, and conducts research. It monitors voting records, has a computerized report card service, and comments in writing on proposed regulations.

RID works to influence elected and appointed officials and personnel with the job of protecting the public from DWI's risks and impact and to encourage victims' participation in the criminal justice process. It court-watches to let judges know their courts are under surveillance; keeps systematic track of, and makes public, judges' conviction rates; and has filed amicus briefs arguing issues such as the admission of evidence at sentencing and relief from full-blown trials at test refusal hearings.

Aiken has become increasingly feminist, seeking heightened regulation of ads stressing commercial linkage of beer consumption, demeaning depictions of women, and men's depiction in stereotypically masculine activities that, combined with alcohol, risk serious injury or death. The leading cause of death for men aged fifteen to twenty-three is an alcohol-related crash. One-third of 500,000 respondents to a 1987 *Weekly Reader* survey believed more than anything else that television and the movies make drinking and drugs seem like fun; only one-quarter cited peer pressure. The American Automobile Association Foundation for Traffic Safety supported Aiken's analysis.

Defense attorneys have tried to excuse defendants—such as the one who killed an honors student by severing her spine and breaking her neck and who then left the crash scene in Manhattan in 1986—by telling the jury to imagine itself in the bar with a crowd, fooling around. "It's a beer-chugging contest. It's not against the law, it's a little silly." This defendant, his cousin, and brother also butted heads in the bar; defense compared the defendant to the Chicago Bears' quarterback. The jury convicted the defendant on two counts of a lesser offense on a list of possibilities available to it.

In a victim impact statement (VIS) at the sentencing stage, the victim's brother Eric said that although the attorney suggested the defendant was only having fun, he ignored the fact the defendant became increasingly lethal with each swallow of beer. On September 9, 1987, the criminal court judge gave the defendant two consecutive maximum sentences, one and one-third to four years each. RID monitored the case and initiated a joint letter with MADD to the judge at the sentencing stage.

In 1992, Congresswoman Patricia Schroeder (D-CO) introduced a bill to require alcoholic beverage containers to display information such as alcoholic content; RID long has argued for such legislation. With CSPI in 1992, it petitioned the Federal Trade Commission (FTC) to ban product placement of alcohol in music videos, on television generally, and in movies. The FTC previously had refused to outlaw such placements, which often aim at entry-level drinkers.

Public officials often seek RID's views. It sees as the most important recent federal policies the Supreme Court's decisions in *Payne* v. *Tennessee* (1991), upholding the VIS in capital cases where juries do the sentencing, and in *Sitz*, the 1982 Howard-Barnes Act encouraging state anti-DWI initiatives, 1985 Bankruptcy Amendments defining drunk driving as willful and reckless and forbidding discharge of debt incurred as a result of it, a 1989 act providing warning labels on alcoholic beverages, and amendments to the Highway Safety Act providing states with incentives to raise the drinking age to twenty-one. RID filed amicus briefs, testified, or lobbied for all these policies. Over the last decade it found least useful the fairness doctrine's demise and the Supreme Court's *Grady* v. *Corbin* decision (1990) that the Fifth Amendment's double jeopardy clause forbade prosecution for reckless manslaughter and related charges based on conduct constituting traffic offenses such as DWI, for which the defendant had already had been prosecuted. (In 1992, RID enabled a bill preventing quick pleas to minor offenses when death or serious injury is involved.)

RID has collaborated with NHTSA for ten years, CSPI for five, and the

National Coalition to Prevent Impaired Driving for three. It belongs to the National Alcohol Tax Coalition, which includes the National Council on Alcoholism, American Association of Retired Persons,* and Parent-Teacher Association. RID and MADD stay in contact, coordinating, for example, local initiatives, and referring victims to each other when the referring organization does not have a local chapter. RID also collaborates with the Connecticut Federation of Women's Clubs,* Stop Advertising Alcohol at Youth, and Women's National Safety Leaders.

ELECTORAL ACTIVITIES

RID does not see its issue agenda as partisan and does not have a political action committee.

FURTHER INFORMATION

RID has a monthly newsletter, bulletins called *RID in Action,* and a DWI victim rights handbook compiled by William Aiken, RID vice president and the founder and national coordinator's spouse. Recent national action alerts have concerned a rally for the Sensible Alcohol Family Education (SAFE) bill sponsored by then Senator Al Gore (D-TN) to mandate alcohol warnings on all alcohol ads, including radio and television; a campaign to defuse a General Accounting Office audit and investigation orchestrated by the brewing industry to undercut a health campaign for SAFE; a push for SNAP to raise taxes on wine and beer equal to those on spirits and forbid promotions on college campuses and using athletes, stars, and youthful heroes to promote beer drinking; and a national push for prompt administrative suspensions of licenses and lower legal entry Blood Alcohol Content.

SARAH SLAVIN

CLEARINGHOUSE ON WOMEN'S ISSUES (CWI)
P.O. Box 70603
Friendship Heights, MD 20813
(301) 871-6106
(202) 363-9795

The Clearinghouse on Women's Issues (CWI) meets to educate and inform individual members and national and local organizations about such issues as equal opportunity for women socially, economically, and politically; discrimination by sex and marital status; equal pay; reproductive freedom; and women's health issues.

ORIGIN AND DEVELOPMENT

In 1974, a small group of well-known, well-connected women, including Abigail McCarthy, Arvonne Fraser, Caroline Ware, Catherine East, and a few others, saw a need for an organization to serve as a channel to disseminate information on a variety of issues of mutual concern to women of all ages. The founders knew each other through congressional contacts—some worked in congressional offices—and political organizations. The equal rights amendment (ERA) moved these predominantly professional, white middle-class women to act. Small contributions from many people enabled them to get under way.

In 1975, the group set out to implement its charter. Mary Kaiserling served as president for four years. After a temporary lull caused by change of residence of some activists, Daisy Field brought the group back. Subsequently, she served as chair for four years. A national women's organization, labor unions, and occasionally a government agency or private organization have provided meeting space over the years. Attendance at the meetings on the fourth Tuesday of each month in downtown Washington varies with the subject under discussion. Well-known speakers also stimulate attendance increases. Meetings are held nine times yearly. The group's goals have not changed: workplace equality, equal legal rights, educational advancement, improved status for homemakers, attention to older women's problems, the elimination of prejudice and discrimination in all areas of society, women and health, protection of human and civil rights, emphasis on the problems of low-income women, and the national and world plan of action.

ORGANIZATION AND FUNDING

CWI has no local or state chapters or affiliates. The six-member board of directors is not racially mixed. All the directors and officers are women. An effort is made to encourage board participation by persons from lower-income strata, persons with disabilities, and older women. The group's nonsalaried president is Elaine L. Newman. The president achieves office after nomination by a committee and election at a meeting. There are no Washington office, no executive director, and no professional staff.

Members come from a range of individuals and organizations. There are approximately 400 members, half of them organizations. Women make up virtually the entire membership; and the organization expects to maintain its status as an all-women group. Since 1985, the membership has remained around 400; prior to 1985, no membership records were kept. Members join for the information offered, many just to get the newsletter, and others for the meetings and a chance to associate with similarly minded people. Networking goes on around the meeting tables.

CWI is a 501 (c) (3) organization. Its revenue comes entirely from membership dues, $18 for individuals and $35 for organizations. Dues and contributions are tax-deductible. The budget is approximately $4,000; in 1980 it was $3,000.

POLICY CONCERNS AND TACTICS

The board sets policy for CWI. Its preferred strategy to influence public policy is to encourage members to write legislators and committees. CWI also monitors elected officials' voting records.

Federal laws of continuing importance to CWI include the 1964 Equal Pay

Act, 1964 Civil Rights and Equal Opportunity Acts, affirmative action executive orders, and, to a lesser extent, the 1968 Antidiscrimination in Housing Act and 1974 Housing and Community Development Act. Also of concern are the Act of 1972 in which sex discrimination was added to the Civil Rights Commission jurisdiction, the 1972 Equal Employment Act, and Title IX of the Education Amendments along with ERA, *Reed* v. *Reed, Frontiero* v. *Richardson, Craig* v. *Boren, Roe* v. *Wade,* the 1974 Equal Credit Opportunity and Women's Educational Equity Acts, the Child Support Amendments to the 1975 Social Security Act, 1976 Day Care Act, 1978 Pregnancy Disability Act, 1982 Welfare Act, 1983 Social Security Act, 1984 Pension Equity and Child Abuse and Child Support Enforcement Acts, 1986 Age Discrimination Act, and 1988 Civil Rights Restoration Act. CWI opposes the Hyde amendments and human life constitutional amendment.

CWI finds the Civil Rights Restoration and Age Discrimination acts to be the most important initiatives of the past decade. The worst initiatives, in its estimation, have restricted abortion in the District of Columbia due to budgetary constraints. Overall, CWI believes that initiatives of the eighties were worse than those of the seventies.

CWI collaborates with groups from the Council of Presidents,* labor unions and their women's departments and Federally Employed Women,* the Congressional Caucus on Women's Issues,* and Catholic and Jewish religious groups, although the National Council of Catholic Women* might object to issue positions CWI might take. CWI sees as adversaries Concerned Women for America* and such opponents of ERA as Eagle Forum.* CWI frequently finds itself in opposition to these groups. Persons who disagree with CWI may express their views but may not work within CWI.

ELECTORAL ACTIVITIES

CWI sees women's issues as nonpartisan and, as a 501 (c) (3) organization, does not get involved in electoral politics.

FURTHER INFORMATION

CWI publishes a newsletter which summarizes the speaker's remarks from the previous meeting. It also informs members about pending legislation and issues of sex discrimination, health, women's economic status and progress, and so on.

SARAH SLAVIN

COALITION OF LABOR UNION WOMEN (CLUW)
15 Union Square W.
New York, NY 10003
FAX (212) 255-7230

The Coalition of Labor Union Women (CLUW) is the largest national organization of trade union women in the United States. It represents the first interunion organization with an agenda for women and a major voice bringing women's issues to unions. Given the high percentage of working women, its organization has empowered labor to increase pressure for change on behalf of working people generally and for society as a whole. There also is a separate CLUW Center for Education and Research (CER).

ORIGIN AND DEVELOPMENT

CLUW was organized by national trade union women leaders—chiefly Olga Madar of the United Auto Workers (UAW) Women's Department,* the first large union to support the equal rights amendment (ERA). Madar had prevailed upon UAW to come out in support of ERA; and other unions followed suit. There were some union women who opposed ERA because enactment would do away with protective legislation in the states, which regulated hours of work, amount of weight to be lifted, and other work conditions. Working on ERA, however, developed a strong alliance between trade union women and feminists and increased the formation of women's union committees. From these committees came the organizers of CLUW to consolidate the voice and issues of trade union women.

Working closely with Madar was Addie Wyatt of the United Food and Commercial Workers Union, who with Madar organized a series of events leading to the founding midwest conference in Chicago, June 1973. The 3,200 women and men in attendance came from all over the country. The founding conference sought to represent the multicultural workforce on common issues. Approximately one-third of those in attendance were African Americans. CLUW's belief in labor women's potential for change was reflected in the goals it adopted at the founding conference: (1) organize the unorganized; (2) implement affirmative action; (3) increase women's participation in their unions; and (4) increase women's political participation.

The original structure of CLUW included eight officers: Madar, president; Wyatt, national vice president; Joyce Miller of the American Clothing and Textile Workers Union (ACTWU), East Coast vice president; Clara Day of the Teamsters, midwest vice president; Dana Dunhan of Communication Workers of America,* southern vice president; Elinor Glenn of Service Employees International Union, West Coast vice president; Gloria Johnson of the International Union of Electrical Workers, treasurer; and Linda Tarr-Whelan of the American Federation of State, County and Municipal Employees,* secretary. The structure then, as now, represents a conscious effort to represent as many major unions as possible and also their multicultural composition.

CLUW's governing twelve-member National Officers Council, including the nonpaid president, CLUW's general council, and a national executive board (NEB) of 300 members all are elected at the biennial convention. The council meets at least quarterly to act on business between conventions. NEB includes council members, state vice presidents and chapter presidents, union delegates, and CLUW chapter delegates. Union chapter delegates are elected in proportion to their membership in CLUW. NEB meetings are held three times per year.

CLUW has grown into an organization of more than 18,000 members, with seventy-two chapters in thirty-three states, composed not of trade union organizational membership but rather of individual trade unionists. Its present annual budget of about $200,000 is up from $120,000 in 1980. Funds from many American Federation of Labor-Congress of Industrial Organizations* (AFL-CIO) industrial unions and dues helped it get established. About 40 percent of CLUW's revenues comes from trade unions; another 40 percent comes from members' dues. Dues are $20 annually, but less for workers from the lowest pay scales. Less than 20 percent of revenues comes from grants or contracts from government agencies. One percent of revenue comes from publication sales, advertising, conventions, and exhibitions.

Old ways of thinking about women workers are being challenged by CLUW through its CER, established in Washington, D.C., in 1978. A separate nonprofit, tax-exempt entity, the center provides information for use by labor leaders, CLUW members, educators, and others in making constructive changes in the workplace and labor movement. Operating policies for CER's activities are set by a fourteen-member board of directors composed of the CLUW national officers council. The board meets four times per year.

CER's activities have expanded from its initial project in 1978, examining the status of women in leadership positions within the labor movement, through subsequent development of an empowerment of union women program. In 1990, a one-year grant from the North Shore Unitarian Veatch Program provided $35,000 start-up money for a reproductive rights project. Refunding for the following year came from other sources. The Ms. Foundation for Women granted $25,000, and the Jessie Smith Noyse Foundation, $10,000. Funding pays for one full-time paid project director, Cathy Parent, and expenses, plus one-half clerical position.

The center maintains a comprehensive library of collective bargaining, legislative, legal, and educational resources on working women's issues. Center representatives have participated in national, regional, legal, and educational conferences on working women's issues, including technological change and the empowerment of union women to have both job rights and protection. The interconnection is seen as essential. Protective legislation of the past was used to deny women access to jobs and economic opportunities.

Data pertaining to relevant issues are collected and stored at the center for different groups for the purpose of education, research, and information. For example, union members and leaders, economists, authors, members of the press, business representatives, state and local government agencies, lobbyists, attorneys, and others seek, through the center, information and resources on issues affecting working women.

POLICY CONCERNS AND TACTICS

The board of directors and executive officers deal directly with policies and directives; the delegate assembly and membership polls have the most influence. CLUW pays the expenses of delegates not subsidized by their unions. CLUW seeks not only to educate members with publications and the public through press releases but also to encourage members to write legislators and their committees and, when necessary, to participate in direct action and political demonstrations. CLUW also is becoming more aligned with other women's groups. CLUW gives testimony to congressional and state legislative hearings and makes personal presentations to congresspeople, agency heads, and their staff.

CLUW supports passage of laws opposed to wage discrimination and political, economic, and sexual inequality. CLUW defends reproductive and family rights. CLUW has learned from its history that control over job rights begins with control over family rights, specifically, reproductive ones.

CLUW has felt propelled beyond the narrow confines of traditional party politics toward direct action and political demonstrations. CLUW in alliance with civil rights, religious, and women's rights activists held in 1988 in Washington, D.C., the American Family Celebration, a demonstration calling for a national family policy. In 1981, it joined with the whole labor movement and others in a massive march on Washington, calling for job rights, specifically, plant closing regulatory legislation to impact multinational corporations, a proposal particularly of concern to unionized women textile workers. The export of textile production to underdeveloped countries has created high unemployment among women textile workers in the United States.

Federal laws that have evoked CLUW's strongest support include the 1963 Equal Pay Act; 1964 Civil Rights and Equal Opportunity Acts, affirmative action executive orders, Act of 1972, in which sex discrimination was added to the Civil Rights Commission's jurisdiction; 1972 Equal Employment Act; and *Roe* v. *Wade*. CLUW also testifies at middle-level administrative hearings, makes written comments on proposed regulations, contacts public decision makers through influential members, and fields public relations campaigns. CLUW often is solicited for its view on policy matters when the issue is of importance to labor and women in particular, including child care and parental leave. CLUW has used the courts to a limited extent to influence policy. Its attorney on retainer filed an amicus brief with the U.S. Supreme Court in the *Vinson* v. *Meritor Savings Bank* sexual harassment case (1986).

On issues of common concern, CLUW often coordinates with the AFL-CIO, National Organization for Women,* and Children's Defense Fund,* believing that coordinated alliances sustain independent political empowerment for women in general and CLUW specifically. CLUW's adversaries, represented by the Chamber of Commerce, National Right-to-Life Committee,* and National

Right-to-Work Committee, have traditionally worked against CLUW's issue positions.

FURTHER INFORMATION

Among CLUW's publications are *Women and Health Security* (1975), *Commitment to Child Care* (1977), *Effective Contract Language for Union Women* (1979), *LEAD: A New Perspective on an Old Problem* (1981), *A Handbook for Employment of Union Women* (1982), and *Bargaining for Child Care: A Union Parents Guide* (1985).

CLUW sends out *CLUW News* and has many publications, including *The Women's 1992 Voting Guide, Is Your Job Making You Sick? A CLUW Handbook on Workingplace Hazards* (1992), the updated *Bargaining for Family Benefits: A Union Member's Guide*, and *Pride at Work: Organizing for Lesbian and Gay Rights in Unions.* CLUW has materials on sexual harassment, including a poster and card, and videos available in a number of topical areas, including sexual harassment.

MARY CHIANTA CANZONERI

COMMITTEE ON PUBLIC EDUCATION
See AMERICAN FEDERATION OF LABOR-CONGRESS OF INDUSTRIAL ORGANIZATIONS

COMISION FEMENIL MEXICANA NACIONAL, INC. (CFMN)
379 South Loma Drive
Los Angeles, CA 90017
(213) 484-1515

A prominent issues organization founded to address Latina needs, the Comision Femenil Mexicana Nacional (CFMN, or the National Commission of Mexican Women) takes leadership in networking and exercises considerable influence regionally, nationally, and internationally over service provision, regulation of sterilization procedures and education on adolescent pregnancy, and issues affecting public policy on child care, taxes, and immigration.

ORIGIN AND DEVELOPMENT

A group of Latinas attending the National Hispanic Issues Conference in Sacramento, California, formed CFMN in 1970, desiring to create an organization that could address the local needs of Latinas. Needs identified at the time were training women to take leadership positions within the Chicana movement and in their communities, which were concentrated in California, with scattered representation in Arizona, Colorado, Illinois, Massachusetts, New Mexico, New York, Texas, Virginia, and Washington, D.C. Twenty-six women are honored as founders, including past presidents Francesca Flores, Anita Ramos, and Gloria Molina. CFMN considers itself the first action- or issues-oriented organization of national scope dedicated to meeting the needs of Latinas. A resolution adopted at the 1970 assembly called for establishment of a commission to train women for assuming leadership within their ethnic community and in society at large, to publicize Latina achievements, to assess their needs, and to identify solutions to problems confronting Latinas and their families.

Operating with a volunteer staff from its strongest base in southern California, CFMN first sought to assist poor working mothers and to secure positions through which it could influence policy in this regard. Appointment of a Latina to the California State Commission on the Status of Women in 1971 was CFMN's first victory. Next came the Chicana Service Action Center (CSAC), opened in Los Angeles in 1972 under the leadership of CFMN president Francesca Flores. Initially subsidized by the U.S. Department of Labor (DOL), the center offers job training and placement and conducts a battered women's shelter in East Los Angeles. A plan of action, formed in 1973, provided for a "womanpower" counseling program, job referrals, job placements, and supportive services. Nationally recognized, CSAC has continued to receive funding from such sources as DOL and the Comprehensive Job Training Partnership Act and from the City and County Manpower Programs of Los Angeles. A women's Pre-Apprenticeship Program was added in 1976 to prepare women for skilled construction trades. Other innovative CSAC programs are the Handy Women's Project and the Mural Program.

Shortly after the 1973 conference that provided CFMN with a constitution and its overall strategy, President Yolanda Nava guided the commission to the establishment of a Centro de Ninos to meet child care needs. Projects begun in the 1980s that have influenced further CFMN development are Casa Victoria, a group home opened in 1985 as a residential treatment setting for adolescent girls on probation in Los Angeles County, and the Teenage Pregnancy Child Watch. CFMN opened the former agency and took a leading role in establishing the latter.

Participation in the International Women's Conference in Mexico City in 1976 and the National Women's Conference in Houston, Texas, the following year brought CFMN, under the presidencies of Molina and Sandra Serrano Sewell, into new prominence. CFMN led in developing the Hispanic women's plank at the Houston meeting and presented the Latina portion of the minority resolutions to assembled delegates. In 1978, it adopted a pro-choice abortion stance following participation as a delegate organization in the national equal rights amendment extension march in Washington, D.C., and meetings with legislators regarding women's rights issues.

International involvement was extended in the 1980s through representation at the United Nations World Conference on Women in Copenhagen, Denmark, in 1980 and at the United Nations Decade Conference for Women in Nairobi, Kenya, in 1985. President Beatriz Olivera-Stotzer served as a panelist at Harvard University's Kennedy School of Management following the Nairobi meeting, analyzing the impact of the Nairobi experience from the Latina vantage point. CFMN was a charter member of the International Network of Women Journalists. Collaboration with the latter group led to hosting a meeting of the international editorial board and the translation, editing, and publication of *Together We Are Stronger,* a volume of materials collected at the Copenhagen meeting.

ORGANIZATION AND FUNDING

CFMN's structure and goals evolved as a result of its initial leadership and projects. It has twenty-two chapters, located in central and southern California, Colorado, Arizona, Illinois, and Texas. Additional at-large membership in Massachusetts, New Mexico, New York, Virginia, and Washington, D.C., makes it the largest and most representative organization of its type among Latinas in United States. It has 2,300 members. CFMN's first national conference, held in 1973 under the presidency of Ramos, attracted 800 women whose backgrounds revealed the broad appeal of the group: homemakers, farmworkers, trade unionists, welfare recipients, educators, students, advocates, and community activists. A constitution drawn up at this conference provided for a plan of action to be implemented by local chapters.

CFMN continues to function with a volunteer staff, although a grant proposal in 1992 involving preparation of a national white paper on children's issues includes introduction of a paid executive director. A board of directors sets policy and budget, conducts planning, and oversees commission projects. It is composed of President Maggie Cervantes, other commission officers, chairs of the Casa Victoria management committee and several other committees, and nine at-large members. Although commission leadership and service goals encompass a broad spectrum of Latinas, the majority of directors are Mexican American.

CFMN has financed its projects, many of which are managed by a private staff, through a combination of government grants and private donations, the latter secured through fund-raising events and direct solicitation. Membership dues are minimal, $5 ($3 for senior citizens and students) and cover less than 5 percent of the total budget of around $100,000.

POLICY CONCERNS AND TACTICS

CFMN has functioned to carry out such political action as advocacy, training members for electoral campaigning, congressional testimony, voter registration projects, demonstrations, and informal contacts with legislators. To achieve its goals, CFMN also has used legal action, most conspicuously in the case of *Madrigal* v. *Quilligan* (1975). President Molina acted for the commission in entering an amicus curiae brief in this landmark California case. As a result, sterilization practices at Los Angeles County-University of Southern California Hospital were modified to require bilingual consent forms and a mandatory seventy-two-hour waiting period.

CFMN has advised the Children's Defense Fund* on programming affecting the Hispanic community, particularly strategies for community education on adolescent pregnancy. A summit meeting of presidents of national Latina organizations, convened in 1985 by CFMN president Olivera-Stotzer and the Mexican-American Women's National Association* (MANA), resulted in formation of the Coalition of National Hispanic Women's Organizations, which includes the American G.I. Forum-Women of the United States, National Association of Cuban-American Women, and National Network of Hispanic Women,* as well as CFMN and MANA. Members have worked on legislative reapportionment issues through Californians for Fair Representation and in a variety of community projects and coalitions.

ELECTORAL ACTIVITIES

CFMN has declined to form a political action committee. However, the 1981 national conference focused on ways to develop political campaign skills and strategies among the membership. Molina went on from the CFMN presidency to win election to the California State Assembly in 1982, to the Los Angeles City Council in 1987, and in 1991 to the Los Angeles Board of Supervisors. Numerous other members have moved into elective and appointive positions at local, state, and national levels. Commission members have served on boards of directors for the National Council of La Raza, National Hispanic Council on Aging, Federal Council on Aging, National Conference of Puerto Rican Women,* MANA, Association of Mexican-American Educators in Support of Bilingual Education, and the Women's Public Policy Research advisory board. In California, they have served as commissioner of the California Youth Authority and held seats on the Governor's Hispanic Advisory Committee, State Commission on Alcoholism, Task Force on the Feminization of Poverty, Equal Employment Opportunity Commission, and many others. Members have held the presidency as well as board posts in the Mexican American Legal Defense and Education Fund.* Involvement in the arts has been significant through the contemporary Chicana artists and commission members, Esperanz Martinez and Judith Hernandez. Influence in print and electronic media has been secured as members of media policy boards. CFMN has provided its members with both motivation and training for these roles and for electoral campaign staffing.

FURTHER INFORMATION

The 1985–86 annual report, sixteenth anniversary edition, is particularly useful.

KAREN M. KENNELLY, CSJ

COMMITTEE FOR ABORTION RIGHTS AND AGAINST STERILIZATION ABUSE (CARASA)

Despite a short life and small membership, the Committee for Abortion Rights and against Sterilization Abuse (CARASA) raised awareness and left a legacy: by 1980 there were regulations and guidelines associated with performing sterilization procedures. In addition, the attempt to prohibit the use of federal funds through the Medicaid program ultimately was resolved in favor of states' rights.

CARASA concentrated on informing people about these issues and feeding into the network of reproductive rights groups nationally.

ORIGIN AND DEVELOPMENT

CARASA was founded in response to a political and legislative backlash against abortion funding in the late 1970s and in the wake of evidence that policies of the U.S. government had resulted in a high rate of sterilization of Puerto Rican and Native American women. In the summer of 1977, women's groups in New York City came together to plan a response to amendments to pending civil rights legislation, introduced by Senator Henry Hyde (R-IL), that would have prohibited the states from funding abortions for poor women. The Hyde amendments galvanized and momentarily overcame the ideological differences among several leftist and feminist groups, including Bread and Roses, the Socialist Democrats, Communist Party, socialist feminist study groups, and lesbian rights groups.

Leftist feminist scholars at the core of CARASA's organizers, including Meredith Tax, Ellen Ross, and Rosalind Pechesky, were able to show that federal population control policies had led to sterilizations without the knowledge or consent of the Puerto Rican and Native American women receiving them. For example, to the extent that policymakers understood poverty as stemming from overpopulation, sterilization, rather than the ongoing provision of other contraceptives, was often the preferred option. Evidence indicates Native America women were unaware of the sterilization while Puerto Rican women most likely concurred since it resolved the thorny problem, for Catholics, of using birth control on an ongoing basis. The sterilization of Puerto Rican women without their knowledge or consent was still a major problem, particularly in Puerto Rico itself. Widespread concern in New York City, with its sizable Puerto Rican population, followed the publicity surrounding charges of forced sterilization.

The coalition of left-wing and feminist groups, concerned about its narrow demographic base, changed itself into a committee, hoping to attract individuals from more varied backgrounds. CARASA never succeeded in expanding its membership base much. In 1977, at its founding, it was 99 percent white women, and by 1980, at the peak of its membership, it was still 85 percent the same. In 1980, CARASA had 1,000 members. By then, however, it allied its efforts with thirty-nine other reproductive rights groups nationwide through the Reproductive Rights National Network. Ultimately, the factionalism that has hampered national organization and unity among left and left liberal groups undid CARASA. Along with the right-wing backlash of the Reagan years, infighting over the correct electoral politics worked its destruction among the individuals most active in CARASA.

ORGANIZATION AND FUNDING

While it existed, CARASA had a committee structure that united eight chapters in New York and New Jersey. Individuals in the chapters rotated jobs, and officers were elected by members. Ideas percolated from chapter committees up to the steering committee for CARASA, which was composed of representatives from each committee. The steering committee had the most centralized power and authority. Officially, a series of local and committeewide meetings and votes set policy. Finally, a poll of the membership determined policy. But fractional blocks within CARASA evidently influenced the organization's policy and initiatives greatly. This process apparently drove many out of CARASA.

Funding came from annual dues of five to twenty dollars, based on the individual's ability to pay, plus publication fees. Particularly well thought of was a published historical treatment of religious and cultural policies toward abortion, as influenced by economic trends and shifts, including the shift in the Catholic Church's position on abortion in the nineteenth century, when the combination of imperialism (and therefore increased contact with the Third World) and the emergence of various Protestant churches vied for Christian membership and attendant power.

POLICY CONCERNS AND TACTICS

The primary activity of CARASA was to research the issues of reproductive choice, both historically and currently among different income and religious groups, and to assess the impact of pending legislation and policy on women. This information then was disseminated through newsletters and publications. Many more people were on the CARASA mailing list than were actively involved in the organization. The strategy was to influence public policy on reproductive issues by educating the public through publications and press releases and by organizing letter-writing campaigns to the U.S. Congress and its relevant committees and to organize and participate in political demonstrations around these issues. The organization researched and published information on women's reproductive issues to educate the public and, through its letters, to influence pending legislation. To maximize their efforts, activities were coordinated with similar organizations nationally, such as the Reproductive Rights National Network (no longer existing) and the Reproductive Rights Coalition (still operating in New York City).

ELECTORAL ACTIVITIES

CARASA did not support either of the two major parties or establish a political action committee. Most of the members' political development traced back directly to the 1960s' political movements (antiwar, women's, and civil rights movements), and after years of researching and writing about imperialism, capitalism, and so on, many moved further left politically. Left factionalism and liberal and left splits contributed to stalemate in supporting the mainstream candidates, as well as ultimately undermining the very existence of the organization.

FURTHER INFORMATION

One CARASA publication in particular, *Women under Attack: Abortion, Sterilization Abuse, and Reproductive Freedom,* published in 1979, was widely used and regarded within the national reproductive rights network, as well as among students taking the emerging women's studies courses on U.S. campuses.

SUSAN DAVIS

COMMUNICATIONS WORKERS OF AMERICA (CWA)
501 Third Street, NW
Washington, DC 20001
(202) 434-1100
FAX (202) 434-1482

Representing workers in telecommunications, printing, broadcast, health care, and clerical jobs—a segment of the paid workforce with a significant proportion of women—Communications Workers of America (CWA) continues to be a significant player in the labor union movement. It is an American Federation of Labor-Congress of Industrial Organizations* (AFL-CIO) affiliate and has its own political action committee (PAC), the Committee on Political Education (COPE).

ORIGIN AND DEVELOPMENT

The telecommunications industry has been known for the long hours and difficult work required of its often female employees. Despite its "Ma Bell" image, AT&T at the time exploited young women operators and other female employees, who worked difficult jobs, frequently under rigorous supervision. CWA's precursor, the National Federation of Telephone Workers was formed in 1938 at meetings in Chicago and New Orleans. In the spring of 1947, a major national strike took place. Women played an active role in the walkout during the strike. CWA formed that June. Early pioneers of the CWA union included Francis Smith of Michigan and Mary Gannon of Washington. The union's founding president was Joseph A. Beirne.

During the national strike, AT&T and the government endeavored to damage the union. For example, New Jersey Republican governor Alfred H. Driscoll seized AT&T properties and helped push an antistrike bill through the New Jersey state legislature. Despite serious obstacles, CWA became a powerful union in the telecommunications industry. In 1949, it joined the CIO. The AT&T System saw this change as an opportunity to exploit rifts in the union; but CWA continued its affiliation with CIO through CIO's 1966 merger with AFL. It remains an AFL-CIO union.

CWA includes a Women's Activities and Community Services Department, which coordinates work with United Way, blood drives, fund-raising for charities, and other community activities. Many CWA locals have women's committees. The national women's committee meets twice a year to consider issues of concern to working women and includes rank-and-file union members from eight districts. CWA participated actively in the fight to ratify the equal rights amendment, and the CWA was a leader in founding the Coalition of Labor Union Women.*

On January 1, 1984, the 70,000-member International Typographical union joined CWA to become the union's printing, publishing, and media workers section. Its public and health care bargaining unit includes the largely female Nurses United (NU).

ORGANIZATION AND FUNDING

There are more than 1,250 CWA-chartered local unions throughout the United States and Canada, representing more than 10,000 different communities. CWA holds over 1,000 collective bargaining contracts with corporations, including American Telephone and Telegraph, the Regional Bell operating companies, General Telephone, United Telecom and other independent telephone systems, NBC and ABC television networks, state governments, and newspapers. Morton Bahr became CWA's third president with his election in July 1985; Glenn E. Watts served as president from 1974 to mid-1985. The three-member executive committee and the sixteen-member executive board implement policies and administer the union. The CWA executive committee of top officers includes President Bahr, Secretary-Treasurer Barbara Easterling, and Executive Vice President M. E. Nichols. Other members of CWA's board, which governs the union between annual conventions, are vice presidents from local districts and five vice presidents heading special bargaining units—communications and technology; telecommunications; public and health care workers; printing, publishing, and media workers; and broadcast and cable television workers. Three women serve on the executive board. CWA's international office is located in Washington, D.C. The CWA staff consists of more than 200 workers.

CWA has more than 700,000 members employed in telecommunications, health care, printing and news media, and public employment, among other fields; and this membership is about 50 percent female. Membership has grown in minority representation, and today approximately 20 percent are African American and 6 percent Latino/Latina. The greatest regional concentration of minorities is in the northern urban areas. NU president Debora Hayes, whose local 1168 in Buffalo, New York, is the largest health care local in the international union, notes that its members chose CWA because "we needed an organization that could teach us how to organize ourselves, to bargain strong contracts, and to represent ourselves in the workplace. We felt through CWA we could do all of these things, and we are very satisfied."

CWA, through its membership base, has an annual budget over $5 million.

POLICY CONCERNS AND TACTICS

On the national level, CWA has supported pro-labor legislation, such as striker protection and telecommunications and trade policy. Contemporary areas of concern include technology and workplace issues such as drug testing to monitor employee behavior, employer eavesdropping and surveillance, and other privacy-based concerns. CWA has lobbied strongly for the Privacy for Consumers and Workers Act, which would provide employees with disclosure on electronic monitoring of worker's performance and telephone eavesdropping by management. CWA supports AFL-CIO COPE initiatives, including family and women's issues such as the Family Medical Leave Act, which President Bush vetoed twice, and comparable worth legislation.

Most of NU's political activity centers around the Buffalo Council of the AFL-CIO and Western New York CWA Council. Many health care unionists, including NU, would like to take a more active role in support of reproductive choice issues than they do currently but find the issue is not cut-and-dried in labor communities, which include pro-life sentiment. CWA has been active in the Postal, Telegraph and Telephone International (PTTI), representing 5 million telecommunications workers in the United States and other nations. CWA has provided assistance to communications workers internationally through Operation South America's School for Latin American unionists. CWA often works with the AFL-CIO COPE. Democratic National Committee,* and Jobs with Justice. Opponents include antilabor and management lobbies.

ELECTORAL ACTIVITIES

CWA has formed a number of state-level legislative political action committees (PACs). On the national level, as part of AFL-CIO COPE, CWA has endorsed Democratic presidential candidates. Its PAC, CWA-COPE, provides support to House and gubernatorial campaigns. CWA-COPE has two officers plus an assistant treasurer. There are eight regional vice presidents, each responsible for expenditures in his or her region. Decisions are made at the request of local union leadership. With other large membership organizations, CWA claims its PAC funding decisions are made from the "bottom," as the national PAC acts on the recommendations of its locals.

Standards used in funding decisions vary. Incumbents have priority because they have a legislative track record. Challengers who have held elective office have previous voting records to examine, too; but CWA-COPE has its own candidate screening process. PAC money is raised through CWA members' voluntary contributions. CWA works most often with AFL-CIO COPE and many other PACs, such as from women's organizations and environmental groups.

FURTHER INFORMATION

Available to CWA members only, CWA publications include *The Alert, Journeys and Capital Comments, The State Worker,* Local Editors News Service, and *CWA News.*

MARTHA BAILEY

CONCERNED WOMEN FOR AMERICA (CWA)
370 L'Enfant Promenade, SW
Suite 800
Washington, DC 20024

(202) 488-7000
FAX (202) 488-0806

Concerned Women for America (CWA) is devoted to protecting traditional Judeo-Christian family values through prayer and action.

ORIGIN AND DEVELOPMENT

Founded in 1979 by Beverly LaHaye and eight other women, CWA's original impetus in forming was opposition to the equal rights amendment (ERA). LaHaye believed that individuals such as Betty Friedan and ERA supporters did not speak for all women. An organization was needed that promoted the traditional family values most women held to, because LaHaye perceived they were threatened by ERA. Once ERA failed ratification in 1982, CWA broadened its concerns. A pro-family approach to abortion, pornography (including the protection of children from involvement in pornography), education, and the radical redefinition of the family currently dominates CWA's policy agenda. Moral issues, fiscal responsibility, and religious freedom issues also occupy this agenda.

CWA strongly supports the right to life of the unborn and believes that the public education system should be more focused than it is on the basic academic skills necessary to train students to enter college or the workplace. CWA is strongly opposed to the modern trend of outcome-based education and has worked diligently to defeat it in many of the local school systems. CWA actively opposed H.R. 6 and Goals 2000, two radical education bills that the Congress passed in 1994. CWA is committed to sex education programs teaching children and the community that abstinence is the only sure way to prevent an unwanted pregnancy or AIDS. CWA strongly supports the Religious Freedom Restoration Act of 1993 and family-friendly budget programs, as well as a balanced federal budget.

ORGANIZATION AND FUNDING

Currently CWA has chapters in forty-eight states totaling 1,200 Prayer and Action Chapters. There is a board of trustees whose president is LaHaye. Originally located in San Diego, California, CWA moved its headquarters to Washington, D.C., in 1985. The national office is the hub of information and education to the grassroots chapters and broadcasts "Beverly LaHaye Live," a national daily radio program, educating listeners on issues affecting the family, and reaches out to families through its monthly newsmagazine, the *Family Voice*. The 32-page magazine includes up-to-date information on national issues as well as field updates; CWA's legislative department represents the organization's interests to the Congress. Legislative staff analyzes and monitors key pieces of legislation on family-related issues.

Perhaps CWA's most crucial activity takes place in the Field Department. The Field Department is responsible for establishing, training, directing, and educating members across the nation.

CWA has a membership of over 600,000, which includes an estimated 100,000 male members. The national operating budget is over $13 million; its primary source of funding is donations from members. CWA also sells publications.

POLICY CONCERNS AND TACTICS

When developing organizational policy, CWA works through its mission statement. The mission statement is used as a guidepost for a traditional Judeo-Christian approach to family and women's issues. The executive officers provide the greatest input to decision making; professional staff and employees also contribute. The board of trustees is involved in financial decisions and overall organizational concerns.

The strength and main focus of CWA are educating the grassroots membership. CWA mobilizes support through publications, press releases, alerts, "Beverly LaHaye Live," and press conferences. It promotes citizen involvement by encouraging its members to write to legislators and committees. CWA also participates in coalition-building activities. Among its allies are the National Right to Life Committee* (NRLC), Eagle Forum* (EF), Traditional Values Coalition, the American Family Association, and the Family Research Council.* These alliances rank high among indicators of CWA's influence. These coalitions also exhibit CWA's strong pro-family focus, as do its identified adversaries. CWA considers the National Abortion Rights Action League,* National Organization for Women,* American Civil Liberties Union,* and People for the American Way to be its strongest foes. Further, CWA has opposed these groups on numerous occasions.

CWA's most important legislative, judicial, and constitutional concerns include the Freedom to Access to Clinic Entrances law, *Roe* v. *Wade,* ERA, the 1988 Civil Right Restoration Act, and 1993 Religious Freedom Restoration Act, CWA considers the Hyde amendments to be the most important policy enactments of the last decade and extends its focus on women's issues to the 1963 Equal Pay Act and the Civil Rights and Equal Opportunity acts of 1964.

ELECTORAL ACTIVITIES

CWA does not involve itself with the electoral process through a political action committee.

FURTHER INFORMATION

CWA's Research and Publications Department publishes a monthly newsletter and research reports. CWA also produces pamphlets, books, and curricular materials, including literature distributed by direct mail. "Concerned Women Live," a one-hour national radio broadcast hosted by LaHaye, focuses on political, family, and social issues.

                                                            TERRI SUSAN FINE

CONGRESSIONAL CAUCUS FOR WOMEN'S ISSUES (CCWI) and WOMEN'S POLICY, INC. (WPI)

409 12th Street, SW
Suite 705
Washington, DC 20024
(202) 554-2323
Fax (202) 554-2346

The Congressional Caucus for Women's Issues (CCWI) is a congressional member organization meets to coordinate advocacy by congresswomen and their staffs on issues for women and families. Prior to 1995, when the new Republican majority in the House of Representatives abolished congressional funding for legislative service organizations, the CCWI had an office in the Rayburn House Office Building, a staff of 6, a budget of $240,000, a monthly and weekly publication. The advocacy functions of CCWI remain on the Hill under co-chairs Nita Lowey (D-NY) and Constance Morella (R-MD), but the informational services have been transferred to a new organization, Women's Policy, Inc. WPI was founded by the former CCWI staff with the support and encouragement of the congresswomen and has applied for non-profit tax status.

From 1977 through 1994, the women's caucus organization operated as an interest group within the House of Representatives. Caucus leaders testified at hearings; members lobbied other members of Congress; and the staff distributed information to congressional offices and the media. CCWI served as a contact point for an array of feminist interest groups; it played a key role in developing and advocating policy proposals, and in obtaining funding for its priorities. Its severed parts now operate in a more hostile political environment and face the challenge of developing financial support in the private sector.

ORIGIN AND DEVELOPMENT

Elizabeth Holtzman (D-NY), Margaret Heckler (R-MA) and Shirley Chisholm (D-NY) founded CCWI's predecessor, the Congresswomen's Caucus (CC) in 1977. Although several Democratic congresswomen had met periodically, the reluctance of Lenore Sullivan (D-MO), the senior woman in the House, to support a feminist women's caucus and the fear among many congresswomen of identification with Bella Abzug (D-NY), the most outspoken feminist in the House, delayed the founding of a formal organization until after both left the House in 1976.

Officially known as legislative service organizations, House members formed caucuses to fulfill their goals of representation, personal power, policy promotion and reelection. Caucuses provided a training ground for members seeking leadership opportunities, developed comprehensive approaches to issues that cross committee boundaries, and built support coalitions in the decentralized House. More than 100 caucuses were active in the early 1990's, but only 28 had separate staff budgets and House office space. The women's caucus established itself in a lounge on the 4th floor of the Rayburn House Office Building. Holtzman and

Heckler were the driving forces behind it and they spoke on behalf of women across the country as the first bipartisan co-chairs.

CC advocated the Equal Rights Amendment and the appointment of women to senior governmental positions. CC members met frequently with Carter administration officials and spearheaded the drive to extend the time limit for ratification of the Equal Rights Amendment. Holtzman and Heckler participated in the July 1978 ERA demonstration on Capital Hill. CC also served as a support group for the small number of women then in Congress.

In late 1981, the congresswomen invited congressmen to join CC and, the following year, changed its name. This expansion was prompted by a House rules change that required all caucuses to rely entirely on member contributions, or move out of House office space. Prior to the expansion, CC had faced: (1) recurrent financial problems that had led it to raise money from sources outside the chamber and from sympathetic congressmen; (2) the reluctance of some congresswomen to join CC and identify with its feminist goals; (3) the conservative tide among the public evidenced by the 1980 elections; and (4) the frustration of activist congresswomen with the inability of CC to be a stronger advocate for women.

Also in 1981, CC became the House coordinator for the Economic Equity Act (EEA), a package of bills initiated by Senator David Durenberger (R-MN). EEA sought to further the economic interests of homemakers, widows, employed women, and married or single mothers through separate proposals dealing with pensions, individual retirement accounts, insurance classifications, tax deductions and tax credits. Until 1995, CCWI coordinated the development, introduction and consideration of a revised EEA package of bills with individual sponsors in every Congress.

Under the leadership of Co-Chairs Pat Schroeder (D-CO) and Olympia Snowe (R-ME), the 98th Congress (1983–84) was particularly productive for CCWI. Public opinion polls showed President Reagan to be much less popular with women than with men. Republicans feared a women's vote and the Democrats were anxious to exploit their gender gap advantage. Although an EEA bill to eliminate gender classifications in insurance and annuities was defeated, the Congress passed and President Reagan signed EEA bills for child support enforcement, sponsored by Barbara Kennelly (D-CT), and private pension reform, sponsored by Geraldine Ferraro (D-NY), before the 1984 election.

ORGANIZATION AND FUNDING

At the time of the expansion, the congresswomen retained control of CCWI by creating an executive committee for themselves. In the 103nd Congress (1993–94), 42 congresswomen, 35 Democrats and 7 Republicans constituted the executive committee. Five Republican congresswomen and one Democratic woman did not belong. The number of congressmen in CCWI was 109. By mid-1995, 38 of the 48 congresswomen belonged to CCWI and an additional 25 congressmen received informational services as subscribers to WPI's weekly newsletter. Among congresswomen, the non-members are: Democrat Furse (OR), Republicans Chenoweth (ID), Cubin (WY), Dunn (WA), Myrick (NC), Ros-Lehtinen (FL), Sea-strand (CA), Smith (WA), Vucanovich (NV), and Waldholtz (UT).

In 1994, women paid $1,800 annual dues and participated in setting policy; the men paid $900. In 1995, CCWI cannot charge dues and, since congressional offices are restricted in the use of their budgets, WPI is essentially limited to fees of $500 or less. It charges $495 for its nonpartisan information services, which are available to policy advocates, reporters, and other interested individuals on the same basis as congressional offices.

In addition to the bipartisan co-chairs, CCWI has vice co-chairs Eleanor Holmes Norton (D-DC) and Nancy Johnson (R-CT), and a secretary, Cynthia McKinney (D-GA). Beginning with the 104th Congress (1995–96), co-chairs are selected for each new Congress. Congresswomen may be reelected to the post, but may not serve more than two years consecutively. The vice co-chairs are also limited to one Congress in that position, but may then become the co-chairs in the subsequent Congress. Of the previous co-chairs, Olympia Snowe left the House and was elected to the Senate and Pat Schroeder was expected to become the first woman to chair a full standing committee since Lenore Sullivan retired nearly 20 years before. With the Republican ascendancy, Jan Meyers (KS) had that honor instead.

The CCWI staff in the 103rd Congress consisted of Lesley Primmer as executive director, Susan Wood as deputy director, four other staff members and two or three college student interns. In 1995, Lesley Primmer became President of the Board of Directors of WPI with Susan Wood as Treasurer, Constance Morella and Nita Lowey as board members, and Majorie Sims, formerly senior legislative assistant for CCWI, executive director and a non-voting board member. There are also a writer/editor and three college interns. Each CCWI member/subscriber assigns at least one of her/his legislative assistants to cover women's issues and serve as liaison to CCWI and WPI.

CCWI meets in the Lindy Boggs Women's Reading Room in the Capitol, a space long reserved for the use of the congresswomen. WPI's office is located 12 blocks from the Capitol. Office space for the first two years and furnishings have been donated by the American College of Obstetricians and Gynecologists.

Back in 1981, the Congresswomen's Caucus had only 10 members and only 2 of them were Republicans. By admitting men it moderated its image and soon became one of the largest House caucuses, with membership of 117 men and 15 women in the 98th Congress. In 1994, total House membership was 151 plus 10 Senators who paid $900 a year to subscribe to the newsletter. Although predominately liberal in orientation, the caucus continued to include members on both sides of the abortion issue and from both political parties.

Prior to the expansion, annual dues and contributions from clerk-hire funds were insufficient; and staff salaries were often delayed. Dues from the congressmen, though nominal, provided 75 percent of the 1992 budget of about $170,000, but the influx of congresswomen in 1993 brought that percentage down to less than 60 percent.

The Women's Research and Education Institute,* which split off from CC in

1978, receives foundation grants, but CCWI cannot. WPI is actively soliciting foundation and corporate support under the names of the Co-Chairs of CCWI. WPI is publishing "The Source on Women's Issues in Congress" as the weekly successor to the monthly "Update." WPI plans a quarterly magazine, in-depth special reports, and a fax bulletin service, and will explore additional on-line services in the future. It also seeks individual charitable donations and plans an annual gala dinner starting in 1996.

POLICY CONCERNS AND TACTICS

When CC was founded, all policy decisions had to be unanimous. The rule was modified, shortly before the decision to admit men, because of the delays and frustrations it caused. In practice, policy ideas were developed after discussion between the co-chairs, among the executive committee, and with feminist interest group leaders. In the case of the Family and Medical Leave Act, Schroeder and Mary Rose Oakar (D-OH) proceeded with the concept along with several male members, the Women's Legal Defense Fund, Association of Junior Leagues,* Coal Employment Project, Children's Defense Fund* and CCW staff. Snowe became co-sponsor only after small businesses had been exempted.

The relationship of trust between Schroeder and Snowe enabled CCWI to maintain bipartisanship despite the recent partisan importance of women's issues. Publicity and credit for accomplishments went most often to the co-chairs and other members, rather than to CCWI as an organization. The CCWI staff functioned as an extension of the personal and committee staff of its members. The rule that forced the staff off the Hill seems certain to make it more difficult for feminist congresswomen and their interest group allies to coordinate efforts on new legislation or to protect gains already won.

In 1985, describing the family and medical leave bill as pro-family rather than for women, CCWI coordinated development and consideration of the bill, which was then vetoed twice by President Bush and signed by President Clinton in 1993. CCWI played a limited role in the passage of the childcare bill in 1990, because of disagreement within the executive committee. The two civil rights bills enacted during the Reagan and Bush presidencies were advanced by the Leadership Conference on Civil Rights and CCWI in response to Supreme Court decisions undermining laws prohibiting educational and employment discrimination.

Although abortion has been the driving issue for many feminist groups in the last few years, CCWI had a primarily informational, rather than advocacy, role on abortion rights until January 1993. The 1992 elections added 22 new pro-choice women to the Executive Committee while two pro-life women departed from Congress and therefore from the Caucus. The new executive committee voted overwhelmingly to support the Freedom of Choice bill to codify the Roe v. Wade Supreme Court decision on abortion rights. In the 103rd Congress, CCWI was committed to removing restrictions on abortion funding and including abortion services in health care reform.

CCWI members actually began to focus on health equity issues prior to 1990. In July 1990, the Women's Health Equity Act (WHEA), a package of bills dealing with health research, medical services and preventive care, was first introduced. A number of key provisions of the WHEA became law in June 1993 as part of the National Institutes of Health Revitalization Act. These provisions addressed issues dealing with research on breast and ovarian cancer, menopause, osteoporosis, contraception and infertility, and provided statutory authority for the NIH Office of Research on Women's Health.

The Violence Against Women Act, a CCWI priority since its introduction in 1990, was enacted as part of the Omnibus Crime Bill before the 1994 elections. The Economic Equity Act package in the 103rd Congress included 30 bills dealing with such areas as employment discrimination within the congressional and federal workforce; childcare; child support enforcement; and Social Security reform divided into four titles: Workplace Fairness, Economic Opportunity, Work and Family and Economic Self-Sufficiency.

In April 1993, CCWI introduced omnibus legislation on women and education entitled the Gender Equity in Education Act (GEEA). Inequities faced by girls are to be addressed through teacher training, sexual harassment awareness training, math and science programs, dropout prevention programs for pregnant and parenting teens, and non-discrimination within collegiate athletics. Portions of GEEA were added to the Elementary and Secondary Education Act, which was enacted into law in October 1994.

CCWI found packages of related bills developed with feminist interest groups an effective way of attracting and sustaining public, media and congressional attention for eventual legislative results. Programs that are authorized must also be funded through the separate appropriations process, making the annual budget a continuing priority for CCWI. CCWI may be able to put together a women's health equity package for this Congress, but most of the 1995 activity on women's issues has been aimed at preserving existing programs.

ELECTORAL ACTIVITY

As a legislative service organization, CCWI was forbidden from engaging in electoral politics. WPI must be non-partisan and has taken no policy positions. Nevertheless, electoral politics may be an incentive for membership in them both. Congresswomen can fulfill constituent expectations for leadership on women's issues through CCWI activity; and male subscribers to WPI can use their membership to stress their commitment to women's issues, especially if they ever face a female opponent. Individually or through their political parties, male supporters can arrange for congresswomen from their party to campaign for them. Membership can also indirectly help raise money, solicit endorsements and sign up volunteers from feminist groups. WPI envisions feminist political organizations, political consultants and individual candidates for public office subscribing to its information services.

PUBLICATIONS

The Source is published weekly, when Congress is in session. A $495 subscription from WPI includes the weekly newsletter, a projected quarterly journal and special reports when published. The fax service will be an additional charge and the journal, entitled *The Women's Policy Quarterly*, will also be available to individual subscribers for about $35 per year.

JOAN HULSE THOMPSON

CONGRESSIONAL UNION
See NATIONAL WOMEN'S PARTY

CONSULTATION OF OLDER AND YOUNGER ADULTS FOR SOCIAL CHANGE
See GRAY PANTHERS PROJECT FUND

CONSUMER FEDERATION OF AMERICA (CFA)
1424 16th Street, NW
Suite 604
Washington, DC 20036
(202) 387-6121

The Consumer Federation of America (CFA) is a coalition of 250 local, state, and national pro-consumer organizations ranging from ten-member grassroots groups to the 29 million-member American Association of Retired Persons* (AARP). CFA supports issues that assist disadvantaged consumers, including women. CFA has been instrumental in the passage of legislation in fair credit and banking practices, fair packaging and labeling, and product safety that has benefited women as consumers. The CFA political action committee (PAC) endorses candidates whose voting records show continued support for CFA-backed issues.

ORIGIN AND DEVELOPMENT

In 1966, a coalition of labor unions, rural cooperatives, farm organizations, and senior citizen, women's, and church groups united through their support of proposed legislation known as the "truth bills"—Fair Packaging and Labeling and Truth-in-Lending. The coalition sponsored a conference to show consumers' increasing awareness and to establish a communication link for their organizations. Esther Peterson, then President Johnson's special assistant for consumer affairs, urged the coalition to federate and continue the conferences, which have since become the basis for CFA's annual consumer assemblies.

Several organizations and leaders played a key role in CFA's establishment, including Rhoda Karpatkin of Consumers Union, Jake Clayman of the Industrial Union Department, Jack Sheehan of the Steelworkers, and the Reverend Robert McEwen of Massachusetts. Peterson's constant, encouraging presence was paramount to the organization's founding. In April 1968, fifty-six charter organizations elected officers and formally adopted policies, CFA's official beginning.

Since its founding, CFA's goals have remained philosophically the same: to advocate for consumer interests before the Congress and federal regulatory agencies and to inform consumers of public policy impacts. Its goals have expanded to state policy making and more extensive consumer education. The issues of fair labeling and truth in lending that spurred CFA's formation indicate the type of issues that continue to be on its agenda. Credit card disclosure, consumer banking reforms, consumer health and product safety, utility rates and practices, and the consumer impact of industry deregulation (telephone, airline) have remained key issues.

ORGANIZATION AND FUNDING

CFA has no local chapters and maintains its only office in Washington, D.C. An executive director, salaried since 1968, is hired by a racially mixed board of directors. Stephen Brobeck has served as executive director since 1982, following Erma Angevine, Carol Tucker Foreman, and Kathleen O'Reilly into the post. CFA employs fifteen full-time professionals to accomplish its research and advocacy goals. Three staff members are attorneys, and seven staff members are registered to lobby. An average of two interns serve CFAs at any one time.

By 1970, the number of member organizations in CFA grew to 75. Membership more than doubled by 1980 and today stands at approximately 250 organizations. More than 50 million consumers are represented by the member organizations. Member organizations represent diverse population groups, but the majority of people represented are Caucasian. Women are thought to constitute roughly 50 percent of the people represented by member organizations.

Membership dues range from $50 for grassroots consumer organizations to $10,000 for the Consumer's Union. Dues constitute about 10 percent of CFA's close to $1 million budget. The bulk of CFA's funding derives from conferences (roughly 40 percent). Contributions from organizations/businesses, foundation grants, publications sales, and speaking honoraria make up the remainder. In 1991, the group's income totaled $1,035,769, and its expenses, $961,524.

POLICY CONCERNS AND TACTICS

What makes CFA different from other consumer organizations is its "bottom-up" organizational approach. Member groups send representatives to participate in seventeen policy committees that provide resolutions for members to discuss and vote on at the annual delegate consumer assembly. These committees make recommendations to the CFA board of directors, who then determine regulatory and legislative priorities.

The strategies needed to advocate these priorities are the responsibilities of CFA staff. Testifying in congressional and agency hearings, supplying congresspersons and staff with information, and participating in direct action political demonstrations are frontline strategies that staff utilize to influence public policy. Providing research results to the media and the public and providing issue-specific publication, are educational efforts aimed at increasing public support for CFA-supported issues. Although CFA has lawyers on staff, it does not file suits to advocate for consumer protection but joins other organizations that have have suits pending. Organizations with which CFA has joined include Public Citizen-Litigation Group. An example of such collaboration occurred in 1987, when CFA joined the National Association of Attorneys General and other groups filing a motion with a district court to request a hearing between the Consumer Products Safety Commission (CPSC) and all-terrain vehicle (ATV) manufacturers. CPSC and ATV manufacturers had generally reached an agreement to end sales of ATVs, but CFA and its cohorts supported legislation that provided consumer refunds and established an age limit (sixteen) for ATV use.

Some of the success of CFA's efforts is reflected in legislation and regulation that address consumer needs in the areas of banking (check processing time, interest rate caps on variable rate mortgages), indoor air quality (radon, the ban on smoking on airline flights), utility rates (local and long-distance telephone rates), product safety (choking standards for toys, all-terrain vehicles standards). Some bias may exist toward issues that especially assist disadvantaged consumers, particularly in low- to moderate-income groups. Because women frequently meet these criteria, many of CFA's positions are supportive of them.

ELECTORAL ACTIVITIES

CFA views its issue agenda as nonpartisan and supportive of all consumers' interests. CFA PAC, formed in 1976, endorses congressional candidates on the basis of yearly and lifetime voting records. Endorsements are offered not for every race but for candidates who have supported issues on CFA's agenda through the years or who have taken a leadership role in a particular issue of concern. Incumbents generally receive twice as many endorsements as do challengers. Party affiliation and gender are not criteria for endorsement.

LYNNE M. WHITE

CONSUMER FEDERATION OF AMERICA POLITICAL ACTION COMMITTEE
See CONSUMER FEDERATION OF AMERICA

COUNCIL OF COLLEGIATE WOMEN ATHLETIC ADMINISTRATORS
See NATIONAL ASSOCIATION OF COLLEGIATE WOMEN ATHLETIC ADMINISTRATORS

COUNCIL OF PRESIDENTS (CP)
c/o Chris DeVries
American Nurses' Association
600 Maryland Avenue, SW
Suite 100 West
Washington, DC 20002
(202) 554-2222
FAX (202) 554-2262

The Council of Presidents (CP) of national women's organizations coordinates public policy action by over fifty groups representing diverse constituencies in the women's liberation movement. A sophisticated delivery system that provides a kind of national machinery outside the government, CP facilitates practical working relationships.

ORIGIN AND DEVELOPMENT

CP was formed initially for the exchange of information among a small group of leaders of the largest organizations. The Women's Vote Project (WVP), first organized in the 1982 elections around the theme ''It's a Man's World Unless Women Vote,'' was the council's genesis. However, the vote project named no issues, and its sixty groups avoided areas of potential conflict. Presidents of the largest groups began meeting monthly over lunch to strategize on action in the Congress: Kathy Wilson of the National Women's Political Caucus* (NWPC), Judy Goldsmith of National Organization for Women* (NOW), Mary Purcell of the American Association of University Women* (AAUW), and Dorothy Ridings of the League of Women Voters* (LWV).

In overorganized Washington, D.C., there was no shortage of groups coalescing, often temporarily, to lobby on specific issues, but there also was no forum where leaders responsible to diverse nationwide constituencies could shape large strategies that would build momentum and impact. There was further need to extend connections beyond largely white middle-class feminist organizations to include leaders from an increasingly diverse women's movement.

WVP served as the bridge between the single unifying focus of the equal rights amendment (ERA) and the plethora of single-issue coalitions in District of Columbia to a broad and diverse connection of constituencies and issues. It was not able to move to the next stage to mobilize a women's vote; a new and more inclusive vehicle was needed. In 1985, Sarah Harder (AAUW) and Irene Natividad (NWPC) were elected presidents of it; and with the impetus of Nairobi and the Reagan stalemate, the first enlarged meeting was called in September.

A wide cross-section of groups ready to engage in advocacy through the new council presented itself at the September meeting. During its first year CP met monthly, with attendance of around twenty groups. The organization included representatives from the Black Women's Agenda, National Federation of Business and Professional Women's Clubs/USA* (BPW/USA), National Association of Commissions on Women,* Women's Equity Action League,* National Council of Negro Women* (NCNW), Mexican American Women's National Association,* Project for Equal Education Rights,* B'nai B'rith Women,* National Center for Policy Alternatives, Wider Opportunities for Women* and National Institute for Women of Color.*

CP supports and reinforces the work of such organizations to increase impact on a progressive national public policy agenda. While it avoids loyalty oaths, its member groups support the principles of the 1977 National Plan of Action adopted at the federally sponsored National Women's Conference held in Houston, Texas, as part of the United Nations Decade for Women. Agendas and priorities vary, but no participating organization works against an issue in that plan.

CP first adopted a legislative priority in 1985. Its groups united on passage of the Civil Rights Restoration Act (CRRA), using the criteria of timeliness, critical need, strong member support, and the potential to mobilize what was needed for action in the Congress. Working with the civil rights community, member groups next organized to help defeat in the Senate President Reagan's nomination of Robert Bork to the Supreme Court. In 1987, when the 100th Congress convened, sixteen CP organizations agreed upon a congressional agenda. The same criteria were used to arrive at a manageable set of federal policy priorities most strongly shared by participating organizations. These include CRRA, the Family and Medical Leave bill, comparable worth, welfare reform, increases in the minimum wage, child care, reproductive health care, and reintroduction of ERA. By the 102d Congress, the agenda had added as items universal health care, including prevention and research, employment opportunities through job training, economic equity through Social Security, pension and insurance reform, equity for women and girls in education reform and funding, and the elimination of violence against women.

These priorities acknowledged the varying readiness of targeted legislation for actual passage. However, the focus also provided allied organizations with access to congressional leadership and the press that they had not achieved separately. Importantly, it spurred orchestration of new national outreach strategies that allowed varying membership constituencies to achieve the greatest impact. Collaboration with the Congressional Caucus for Women's Issues* offered new opportunities to assess support and timing in an effort to move legislation.

ORGANIZATION AND FUNDING

Since 1985, when it formalized and expanded its membership, CP has worked in Washington. Rotating the responsibility for convening meetings, CP operates without staff. CP also has operated effectively with no governing structure per se and no budget. The new leaders who have taken over most of the founding organizations continue to find in CP a functional vehicle. Each group is invited to send agenda items and a high-ranking leader to the monthly or bimonthly Washington meetings.

After the *Webster* v. *Reproductive Health Services* (1989) decision, when the pro-choice agenda predominated, CP attendance suffered. The related November 1989 march and other actions nationwide spawned a powerful pro-choice coalition in which smaller organizations were not seen as key players. With the addition of the National Abortion Rights Action League* and Planned Parenthood,* it also fostered a resurgent interest in CP and its Women's Agenda (WA), with meeting attendance rising to about fifty and a cooperative election strategy emerging around the agenda. As issues or actions are proposed, supporting groups assist in developing strategies and reaching out to involve their 15,000 local citizen groups, representing every U.S. congressional district.

Membership is open to the head of an organization that accepts CP's premise and priorities and that fits the following organizational criteria designed to affirm CP's focus and nonpartisan character: (1) a freestanding women's organization, with its board of directors and leaders representing a national constituency and perspective; (2) a membership composed predominantly of women, its general purpose including the promotion of public policy and legislative strategies affecting women; and (3) an organization whose primary purpose is not to elect candidates from a single party.

Of the current fifty-plus groups participating in CP, six are large, multistructured, multi-issue organizations with affiliates in every state: AAUW, the General Federation of Women's Clubs,* LWV, NCNW, BPW/USA, and the Young Women's Christian Association of the U.S.A.* Fifteen represent particular racial or ethnic backgrounds, including the Jewish Women's Caucus, National Association of Negro Business and Professional Women,* National Conference of Puerto Rican Women,* National Political Congress of Black Women,* Organization of Chinese American Women,* American Jewish Conference and Hispanic Women's Council.* Seven represent special constituencies such as older women, girls, displaced homemakers, or unions. Seven have organized around issues of health and reproductive choice. Seven advocate for women professionals; and three organize women in politics. Six are policy centers devoted to women's issues, and two represent coalitions of advocates operating in state capitals.

POLICY CONCERNS AND TACTICS

CP has created a strategy that mobilizes the resources and expertise of the women's movement to achieve policy gains. For the 1988 elections, CP launched this nonpartisan strategy under the banner of WA. Reaching back to 1982, the strategy was built on the experience of WVP coalitions, primarily in voter registration drives. WA serves as a new means to produce a set of issue priorities—a kind of chorus on a shared song sheet that invited organizations to add their verses. It was the first time since the 1977 action plan that so many groups had signed onto a multiple-issue document. More than forty organizations pledged to press the agenda with national, state, and local candidates for office regardless of the candidate's party affiliation. CP cosponsored the first Women's Agenda Conference, in Des Moines, Iowa, where 2,000 women and the Democratic presidential candidates gathered in January 1988. BPW/USA sponsored a subsequent Women's Agenda Conference in Kansas City, Missouri, during January 1989 but did not center on CP's WA and the national strategy to implement it.

The first WA included five broadly framed areas that identified major issues to be addressed in 1989 and beyond: (1) family policies assuring access to housing, child and elder care, family and medical leave, and equitable education;

(2) economic opportunity, including occupational preparation, comparable worth, increases in the minimum wage, and welfare reform; (3) comprehensive health care and safety, including long-term care, minimum health coverage, and reproductive health care; (4) a federal budget-balancing adequate defense with global economic and human development; and (5) equality under the law including ERA, protection of civil rights, and reproductive choice.

To address WA, CP continues to organize meetings with leaders of the Congress and administration as well as through media and public information campaigns. Based on expertise, resources, and the premise of diversity, groups are identified to lead and coordinate issue campaigns, often linking with specialized advocacy coalitions. Existing organizational staff and volunteers are assigned to these collaborations.

CP makes every effort to transcend partisan divisions and has established a record of success in marshaling support from both parties on its issues. It claims significant contributions to the passage in the Congress of CRRA, welfare reform, increases in the minimum wage, child care and family medical leave policy, and the 1990 Civil Rights Act. President Bush unfortunately vetoed the last two enrolled bills.

ELECTORAL ACTIVITIES

CP is a nonpartisan organization that does not endorse candidates for election. It does not have a political action committee.

SARAH HARDER

CRATER'S RAIDERS (CR)
2310 Barbour Road
Falls Church, VA 22043
(703) 573-8716
FAX (703) 573-8716

Crater's Raiders (CR) was a successful lobbying organization for a two-year period in the early seventies when part of the women's liberation movement turned its energy and experience to getting the U.S. Congress to pass the equal rights amendment (ERA). A small group, CR generated one of the most powerful lobbying efforts in congressional history.

ORIGIN AND DEVELOPMENT

Alice Paul called for a national campaign for the proposed ERA—to many women, their bill of rights—in 1923 in Seneca Falls, New York. Its original wording derived from the 1848 Seneca Falls Declaration of Sentiments and Resolutions. Paul, president of the National Woman's Party* (NWP), convinced members of the Congress to introduce an amendment to cover all women's legal deprivations. Passage was hindered by opposition of proponents of protective legislation for women, which ERA would have made unconstitutional; Frances Perkins, U.S. secretary of labor, and Mary Anderson, director of the U.S. Women's Bureau, threw their resources behind ERA's defeat. However, in 1946, 1953, and 1959, lobbied by NWP, the National Federation of Business and Professional Women's Clubs* and General Federation of Women's Clubs,* the Senate Judiciary Committee had reported ERA favorably.

In 1968, to learn more about women's legal condition, Flora Crater, a long-time Democratic Virginia party activist, found a reference to Paul and called NWP to talk. Crater understood the problem to be transmission of priorities from one generation of feminists to the next, to move women into the future. A group of "new" feminists determined to do what they could to monitor, lobby, and hold the Congress accountable for ERA; they convened the first National Organization for Women (NOW)* chapter in Virginia.

CR was made up of thirty-five women, mostly housewives in the Washington, D.C., area with time to spend at the Capitol. They were committed amateur lobbyists. Crater and the late Carol Burris, who chaired NOW's ERA Task Force, provided CR's leadership. The push for passage in 1970 began during the August 26 Women's Strike for Equality March. On that day, Senate sponsors received the U.S. President's Commission on the Status of Women* legal memorandum on ERA. To show appreciation, CR also presented pink paper roses to Senate sponsors; these became the logo of *The Women Activist* (*TWA*), an action bulletin for women's rights started by Crater for women. In January 1971, *TWA*'s first issue thanked readers for their quick response to efforts sparking a national ERA movement.

ORGANIZATION AND FUNDING

Entirely a volunteer organization, CR had no professional staff or executive director. Action was directed from Crater's home. In all, CR spent around fifty dollars to help get ERA out of the Congress and to the states for ratification. It spent the money on coffee. Its thirty-five members paid no dues.

POLICY CONCERNS AND TACTICS

CR members testified in congressional hearings, supplied congresspeople and their staff with information, and made personal presentations to the same. They encouraged women at large to write congresspeople and themselves participated in direct action. Through *TWA,* they published research critical to the ratification effort and coordinated efforts with like-minded organizations. They undertook public education as well.

One especially important effort went toward building a constituency supportive of ERA within congressional districts. In 1971, CR sent a congressional district profile for completion to a mailing list of 700 organizations at the district level, including labor unions and individuals. There was space to list the representatives' record vote when the ninety-first session acted on ERA. Additionally named were the two U.S. senators, governor, and members of the legislatures in the counties, cities, and towns within respondent's congressional district and the women's and civil rights organizations, labor unions, and human rights councils at the local level. State and local information was necessary to spread the word at the grassroots. This profile worked as a learning tool for respondents.

CR began to push House members, especially the ERA sponsors, to sign a discharge petition. It mailed fact sheets to organizations on a 500-member mailing list. In July, CR began a telephone campaign with twenty-five women calling House members. It began lobbying senators and followed meetings of the Senate Judiciary Committee, urging a favorable vote on S.J.R. 61 in the Subcommittee on Constitutional Amendments. The resolution was reported out to the full committee. By then CR could count the required number of votes on the discharge petition sponsored by Congresswoman Martha Griffith. It began a second telephone campaign to be sure signers would be there to vote. ERA passed the House on August 10.

CR shifted to the Senate, assigning callers and lobbyists to specific senators. It got 1,500 signatures on a petition at the Women's Strike for Equality March rally and presented it to Senators Mike Mansfield (D-MA) and Hugh Scott (R-PA), along with the pink paper flowers. An ERA teach-in was organized at the Capitol. Through September, CR continued action memos to women and organizations, particularly calling attention to new hearings that they could attend and at which they could testify. Val Fleischhacker arranged press conferences for unions now supporting ERA. CR also distributed to senators pertinent testimony and rebuttal to Senator Sam Ervin's (D-SC) dilatory amendments.

In October, CR held a press conference on delay in the Senate and day and night vigils October 6–13, the day the vote occurred. When it came, twenty-six members listed as sponsors voted against ERA; twenty-five were absent. The remaining forty-nine senators supported ERA. The vote failed by three; and CR explored other ways to get a vote on the resolution. It opposed a proposed substitute by Birch Bayh (D-IN). CR asked draft-age women at George Washington University to develop a position on the draft, the issue that had defeated the resolution.

Among the organizations that worked with CR were the American Federation of Teachers, B'nai B'rith Women,* Federally Employed Women,* Women's International League for Peace and Freedom,* National Education Association, National Association of Colored Women's Clubs,* NWP,* Presbyterian Task Force for Women,* Republican Party National Committee and Democratic Party National Committee* members, the Young Socialist Alliance, and Zero Population Growth.

The January 1971 *TWA* enclosed another profile. Enclosing the ERA FACT sheet, which still is used with updates, the February issue reported ERA's introduction, listed sponsors, and gave each senator's vote in the ninety-first session. It also called on the Congress to reform the filibuster rule. Women were asked to write about this reform. The March issue noted CR's opposition to the seven-year period within which states had to ratify ERA. NWP's Paul believed this restriction would prevent its ratification.

Workshops for women lobbyists included the information kit and instructions on how to lobby. CR also began what proved to be its most effective tactic, regular meetings to develop lobbying strategy and assignments. Held in the cafeteria in the Longworth House Office Building, the meetings continued every Wednesday for a year. Typically fifteen to twenty women attended at once. Women activists lobbied door-to-door in the three House office buildings, urging sponsorship and a favorable vote when ERA got to the floor. CR encouraged women to take a delegation to see their member during the August recess and to get petitions signed and mailed to TWA for hand delivery.

In April H.J.R. 208 was voice-voted out of subcommittee. CR called on women in the districts of the House Judiciary Committee (HJC) members to write. During a standoff between opponents and proponents, CR gave their names and called for mail. When HJC voted by a close margin to include a crippling amendment, *TWA* reported on those voting right and wrong. Granted to the debate by the House Rules Committee was an open rule with four hours of debate, which meant members could strike out the problematic amendment to ERA with a simple majority. *TWA* sent out an insert listing House members leaning that way. In the Senate the bill could be called up for a vote on the decision of the proponents and leadership.

The proficiency of the volunteer lobbyists is measured by their tally the evening of the House vote: 254 for, 114 against. They were correct on votes for and nearly so on votes against. For the Senate vote, CR volunteers stepped up their lobbying. Women in the states were asked to get a commitment that their senators would vote for closing debate if a filibuster developed.

Another action plan went out in TWA. It included assignment of specific senators to specific women to keep information current and CR apprised of any change, a telephone chain to disseminate information, and calls to senators to inform them of the favorable vote by their Judiciary Committee. Women made sure their senators opposed all amendments to ERA. The Senate committee finally reported ERA out without any amendment, and with instructions that there would be a time limit of sixteen hours on the resolution with two-hour limitations on each proposed amendment to it. ERA passed the Senate on March 22, 1972.

The ERA Summit conference moderated by Allie Corbin Hixsen from Kentucky advocated a three-pronged strategy. The first prong is a move to ratify in the three necessary states—thirty-five of thirty-eight had ratified by the extension deadline. The ERA Summit holds that the Congress was arbitrary in setting a ten-year deadline for ratification, a requirement enumerated in the Constitution. The decision to make this move was inspired by the 1993 ratification of the 103-year-old Madison Amendment. The other two prongs include a 1994 resolution introduced in the Congress affirming the effort to capture three more states and the suggestion the amendment might be re-introduced entirely and without a time limit.

ELECTORAL ACTIVITIES

CR engaged in no electoral activity.

FURTHER INFORMATION

TWA still is published ten issues per year for seventeen dollars.

FLORA CRATER

D
/

DAUGHTERS OF BILITIS (DOB)

The Daughters of Bilitis (DOB) was the first organization of lesbians, then called "female homophiles," formed in the United States. Intended as a self-help organization, providing a safe social structure for lesbians, that is, a safe place to "come out," DOB became a national organization with chapters involved in both homophile—gay rights—and women's liberation movements and sometimes in local political activity.

ORIGIN AND DEVELOPMENT

Four lesbian couples founded DOB in San Francisco in 1955. The idea for the group came from a Filipina woman named Marie (for reasons of desired anonymity at the time, no last name was used); other founding members among the leadership of the group until the late 1960s included Del Martin and Phyllis Lyon, later the authors of *Lesbian/Woman* (1983). The name for the group came from a poem by Pierre Louys called "Song of Bilitis"; Bilitis was assumed to live on the island of Lesbos during the same period as Sappho.

DOB felt concerned with raising the self-esteem and self-awareness of lesbians, educating the public about homosexuality, participating in research projects to change public perceptions about lesbians, and working to replace laws and practices discriminatory to homosexuals. Due to its belief that women need a place to work on these issues by themselves, DOB limited its membership to women.

While DOB sponsored many social events for members, as the group increased its focus on social issues, many members grew dissatisfied with the limited scope of purely social activities. As members increasingly addressed social issues and their own social consciousness rose, members broke off to form other organizations more amenable to their needs. Several new organizations, Hale Aikane, Quatrefoil, and NOVA, resulted from this schism within the organization. In 1970, after serious internal disagreements over direction and identity, the national organization of DOB ceased to exist, leaving chapters across the country to function on their own. The founding San Francisco chapter disbanded in the late 1970s, leaving only the Boston chapter functioning in the 1980s.

DOB activities proved critical to the development of both the so-called homophile or gay rights movement and the women's liberation movement. DOB's activities would be considered socially conservative by the standards of gay and women's rights activists of the AIDS era. They served an important role in educating DOB members, interested professionals, and the public on social and homosexual rights issues of the time through public discussion sessions, DOB's own library, and the publication of its newsletter/magazine, *The Ladder.*

Many of DOB's topics focused on lesbians' legal rights and relevant court cases of the day, including those concerning job losses due to one's homosexuality being made public, and the ability of the police freely to raid lesbian and gay bars. Other issues discussed were more relevant to gay men, such as the vagrancy laws used to arrest and detain men or the laws requiring those jailed for homosexual acts and then returning to the community to register as sexual psychopaths.

Although group members often knew much more about the topic than the experts, they also brought expert speakers on homosexuality to educate themselves. DOB's research function attempted to fill this gap in knowledge by providing healthy, functioning homosexual research subjects. DOB cooperated with researchers on topics such as the psychological adjustment of homosexuals and initiated a series of surveys itself on issues such as the attitudes of mental health professionals toward gay people.

While *The Ladder* was aimed at the individual lesbian, it served a crucial role in the development of a lesbian group identity by reporting on lesbians' political, legal, social, literary, and cultural activities. A monthly feature, "Lesbiana," provided an important outlet for developing lesbian literature by publishing the work of many writers not distributed elsewhere and through annotative listings of new lesbian literature. Some of the well-known writers whose early work appeared in *The Ladder* included Lorraine Hansberry, May Sarton, Jane Rule, Rita Mae Brown, Isabel Miller, Mary Renault, and Marian Zimmer Bradley. One of the early editors of *The Ladder,* Barbara Grier, also went on to cofound Naiad Press, one of the first and now among the largest lesbian presses operating today.

The Ladder also served an important role in the political education and consciousness-raising of DOB members, many of whom joined just to receive it. In its early years, *The Ladder* featured reports on bar raids, police harassment, employment discrimination, and court cases relevant to the civil liberties of lesbians. The 1960s saw a distinctive shift toward an emphasis on lesbians as women rather than homosexuals and the influence of the women's liberation movement. Thus, the latest events of the women's liberation movement and writings of many of its influential thinkers, including Jill Johnston, Kate Millett, and Monique Wittig, often were to be found in *The Ladder.*

ORGANIZATION AND FUNDING

DOB began publishing *The Ladder* in 1956, a year after its own launching, and incorporated as a nonprofit corporation in California in 1957. Eventually the organization expanded its base and developed into a national organization with a national board and up to fifteen chapters during its existence. These began with the New York and Rhode Island chapters in 1958 and later added chapters in cities such as Chicago, Boston, New Orleans, Reno, and Melbourne, Australia. DOB held its first national convention, billed as the nation's first lesbian convention and criticized as separatist by some gay men, in 1960 in San Francisco.

The organization was described as a democratic organization whose policies were determined by the paying membership. The organization also had several influential and lasting leaders over the years, including Martin, Lyon, and Grier (pseudonym, Gene Damon). The influence of Martin and Lyon was particularly strong, lasting until the end of the 1960s. Martin was not only one of the founding members but also the first national president after a national governing board was created in 1960. Lyon was the first editor of *The Ladder,* operating for a time under the pseudonym Ann Ferguson.

Membership dues and subscriptions to *The Ladder* funded the organization. Lack of funding reportedly kept some chapters from increasing their activities or from moving their offices into expanded facilities.

POLICY CONCERNS AND TACTICS

While DOB served a role in developing the political consciousness of the lesbian community and provided political education to that community, in today's terms it was a politically conservative group in its tactics. DOB began its political involvement as a group by educating its members, editorializing for particular homosexual rights bills, and bringing attention to discrimination laws. Various chapters, such as the New York City chapter in the 1960s, also utilized confrontational tactics such as marching or picketing, which the national organization specifically disavowed.

The organization also was peripherally involved in the legal strategies around several important bar raid cases. Two issues of *The Ladder* discussed briefs filed in a case focusing on the rights of homosexuals to congregate in public bars. The case centered on a police raid on a lesbian bar in Oakland; the Court ruled that homosexuals have the same rights as others to gather in a public place.

The accepted focus of the national organization was education. *The Ladder* advanced this goal by continually providing political education in the guise of news about civil liberties issues, legal cases, and other political activities that affected the lives of lesbians, women, or gay men. *The Ladder*'s shift in the late 1960s toward a more feminist approach represented an ongoing debate within the DOB over two growing social movements, the gay rights/homophile movement in the 1950s and 1960s and the women's liberation movement of the 1960s and 1970s. One dispute revolved around the allegiance of DOB members as women or as homosexuals. As the homophile movement, then the women's movement, grew, this issue continued to be a source of conflict within the organization.

DOB's policy concerns revolved around issues important to lesbians as women and as gay people. Initially, job security, career advancement, family relationships, and the problems of coming out, so important to individual lesbians, were uppermost in the membership's interests. Some early disagreements within DOB revolved around dress, behavior, secrecy, and how to relate to gay men and to the straight world. Because of this concern with protecting personal identity, many women used pseudonyms within the organization.

There were also ongoing disagreements on the importance of gay men's issues to the group and about maintaining separate identities as women and lesbians. This discussion took the form of serious dissension about how feminist an approach DOB should take and how much importance to attach to feminist issues at the expense of purely gay issues. The choices within DOB were presented as lesbian alignment with the women's liberation movement as women or with the predominantly male gay rights movement as lesbians or an emphasis on the social needs of the individual lesbian. Differences over this issue led to divisions between the old guard, preferring less confrontational tactics and activities, and the new, who preferred a lesbian feminist approach in *The Ladder* and were supportive of more confrontational tactics. This disagreement ultimately led to a confrontation in 1970 after the editors of *The Ladder* left with DOB's membership list and the subscription list for *The Ladder*.

ELECTORAL ACTIVITIES

Individual chapters often involved themselves in some electoral politics at the local level. Originally, DOB became involved in politics when it became a campaign issue in the 1959 San Francisco mayoral election. Assessor Russell Wolden challenged incumbent Mayor George Christopher by criticizing him for allowing San Francisco to be labeled as the national headquarters for homosexuals. By 1965, this interest in politics had become institutionalized, with homosexual organizations in San Francisco, including DOB, showing their interest in local politics by regularly interviewing candidates for city/county supervisor and sponsoring public forums on elections. Up to 250 members and one-third of the candidates invited attended some of these sessions.

FURTHER INFORMATION

One of the most influential legacies of DOB was the publication of its newsletter/magazine *The Ladder,* the first continuing publication for lesbians in this country. Publication began in October 1956 and lasted until 1972, ending after funding substantially diminished following the fight within DOB over the magazine's growing feminist direction.

GENIE L. STOWERS

DAUGHTERS OF THE AMERICAN REVOLUTION
See NATIONAL SOCIETY, DAUGHTERS OF THE AMERICAN REVOLUTION

DAY CARE AND CHILD DEVELOPMENT COUNCIL OF AMERICA
See DAY CARE COUNCIL OF AMERICA

DAY CARE COUNCIL OF AMERICA (DCC)
Signifying a strengthening commitment to provide publicly funded quality care for children, the Day Care Council of America (DCC) had as its primary goal the generation of broader public understanding of, and support for, affordable day care services for children. It functioned as a national information clearinghouse about day care services and offered consultation on program planning and organizational techniques.

ORGANIZATION AND DEVELOPMENT

Responding to the growing number of women entering the labor force and the growing interest in children's issues during the 1960s, the Day Care and Child Development Council of America (DCCDC) was founded in 1967. The establishment of DCCDC represented approximately twenty-six years of work. DCCDC's origins date to 1958, when the Intercity Committee on the Day Care of Children was formed in New York City. Working to provide information about day care services, the intercity committee received grants from the U.S. Health, Education and Welfare Department (HEW) in the late 1950s and incorporated as the National Committee for the Day Care of Children in 1960.

Under Elinor Guggenheimer's guidance, the national committee continued gathering more support for its goal, federally funded day care. Throughout the early and mid-1960s, it worked extensively to influence federal legislation and provide information on day care. It joined with the Child Welfare League of America and the U.S. Children's Bureau to develop day care proposals for the Kennedy and Johnson administrations. By 1967, the national committee moved its headquarters from New York City to Washington, D.C., and changed its name again to reflect its broad mission.

Under Therese Lansburgh's and Ted Taylor's direction, DCCDC expanded. Competition for federal funding increased; and in 1970 it faced a financial crisis. It recovered by expanding its bases of support and starting a grassroots approach to expanding day care services. DCCDC obtained grants from HEW's Office of Child Development and the Office of Economic Opportunity. As federal funding again became strained in 1978, the organization cut back staff and services. In

1981, the group changed its name, this time to Day Care Council of America, to reflect a narrow scope of services and goals. Struggling through the first four years of the eighties, the council ceased operation in 1985.

ORGANIZATION AND FUNDING

Oversight for DCCDC came through its board of directors; from inception, the board included women and minority groups. Jule Sugarman was serving as the acting executive director when the organization ceased operation in 1985. The Washington headquarters had a staff that varied in size, depending on DCCDC's financial condition. DCCDC opened its only regional office in Atlanta in 1973.

The membership was composed of local citizen community groups, individuals, and service agencies concerned with children. Membership fluctuated during the early years from 1,150 in 1970 to approximately 6,000 in 1978. The membership was diversified; it included day care professionals and laypeople, was racially mixed, and had members from all income levels. However, the early eighties saw a sharp decline in membership and resources, perhaps due to success at establishing locally funded day care programs throughout the nation. In 1983, membership decreased to 5,000 and a year later, membership reached its nadir at 1,000.

Individual contributions to DCCDC were tax-deductible; however, some funding for DCCDC's activities came from grants from the federal government, private foundations such as the Ford Foundation, and corporations. DCCDC also provided consulting services, held conferences, and sold publications to generate revenue. The organization's annual operating budget during the midseventies hovered near $500,000.

POLICY CONCERNS AND TACTICS

DCCDC and its predecessors worked for years to promote the development of universal, publicly funded day care. Policies were developed by staff in conjunction with the board of directors. The primary strategy used by DCCDC was to work with federal agencies concerned about children's issues. DCCDC worked diligently to support child care legislation. It supported the adoption of the Federal Interagency Day Care Requirements in 1968. During 1970, it advocated legislation before the ninety-second Congress, notably testifying about the importance of child care with local control and parental involvement. The legislation was supported by other groups interested in child welfare, including the American Academy of Pediatrics.* The legislation passed through the Congress but was vetoed by President Nixon, who objected to the legislation's administrative provisions. DCCDC continued to promote the passage of legislation, supporting the 1975 Child and Family Services Act cosponsored by John Brademas (D-IN) and Walter Mondale (D-MN).

In an effort to expand its membership and provide more information on its mission, DCCDC began a field service program in 1971. The program consisted of husband-wife teams of day care professionals who conducted seminars and recruited members for the organization. A further outreach program in 1971 was aimed at migrant children; DCCDC received support for this program from the Colorado Migrants' Service. DCCDC also worked to promote child welfare programming in Appalachia.

DCCDC allied itself with other organizations interested in child welfare, including the Child Welfare League of America, Coalition for Children and Youth, and Children's Defense Fund.* While the agencies had common goals, they often competed for federal funding, with CDF being the most successful. DCCDC was affiliated with the Community Coordinated Child Care program and with the Connecticut Social Welfare Conference.

ELECTORAL ACTIVITIES

DCCDC's board expressed its intention in 1973 to establish a separate political organization in order to preserve the council's tax-exempt status. It is unclear whether this group ever was constituted formally and if it was, whether it had any impact.

FURTHER INFORMATION

A primary source of information for many in the day care industry, DCCDC published a newsletter for its many members under a number of names including *Voice for Children.* The group also published a directory for child care advocates that provided information on federal agencies and national organizations interested in children's issues. The council sporadically published child care bulletins that addressed specific issues. During its peak period, DCCDC published *Hotline,* a newsletter chronicling pending legislation related to child care, and operated the Children's Embassy, a public information center in Washington.

SARA ANN GROVE

DELTA SIGMA THETA SORORITY
1707 New Hampshire Avenue, NW
Washington, DC 20009
(202) 986-0000
FAX (202) 986-2513

"Our concern for the welfare of humankind everywhere," explains Delta Sigma Theta national president Yvonne Kennedy, is why "we've always been a public service sorority rather than a social sorority." Since 1913, five generations of African American women have built an impressive tradition of leadership in confronting the pressing social issues of their times. From women's suffrage and antilynching in the 1910s to AIDS research and teen pregnancy in the 1990s, human needs at home and around the world have been the focus of Delta Sigma Theta service.

Delta Sigma Theta has afforded minority women crucial leadership training and opportunities. Some, like former congresswomen Shirley Chisholm and Barbara Jordan and former cabinet member and ambassador Patricia Roberts Harris, have parlayed their skills and expertise into exemplary public service careers. Others have achieved distinction in a variety of fields, for example, Nikki Giovanni in letters, Leontyne Price in music, Charlayne Hunter-Gault in public affairs reporting, and Eunice W. Johnson in publishing. Because the vast majority of Deltas are educators, their impact has been immeasurable. As highly visible models of middle-class female leadership in the black community, they have underscored—especially to young people—the importance of individual action and social responsibility. Outside the black community, Deltas have built bridges of interracial cooperation and understanding through their activities on predominantly white campuses and through their work as professionals and civic leaders.

ORIGIN AND DEVELOPMENT

The first African American sorority, Alpha Kappa Alpha was founded in 1908 as a local sorority at Howard University. Inspired by the women's suffrage movement—which was gaining momentum a short distance from their campus in the nation's capital—some of its members were moved to reflect upon their own civic rights and responsibilities. Eschewing their sorority's social and fraternal emphases, twenty-two members took action to reconstitute the group, changing its focus to public service. They reorganized under a new name, Delta Sigma Theta, and took steps to become a national Greek letter sorority. The Alpha Chapter was chartered by Howard's trustees on January 1913. One month later, the organization was legally incorporated in the District of Columbia.

ORGANIZATION AND FUNDING

Soon Delta Sigma Theta chapters began forming on other campuses. Its first national convention was held in 1920, when members christened *The Delta Journal* their official publication and authorized the formation of alumnae chapters. Regional conferences began in 1925. In 1930, a Grand Chapter was chartered, incorporating the entire body into a single national entity with authority to charter new chapters. The Grand Chapter grants three types of charters, creating undergraduate campus chapters, undergraduate citywide chapters, and alumnae chapters. Today, more than 800 chapters span the United States, Europe, the Caribbean, and the Far East.

Although membership is open to academically qualified collegiate women of all races, creeds, and nationalities, most members are African American women. Honorary membership has been extended over the years to women of outstanding achievement, including Mary McLeod Bethune, Alice Dunbar Nelson, Mary Church Terrell, Lena Horne, Ruby Dee, Judith Jamison, and Marian Wright Edelman. Today, Delta Sigma Theta has more than 175,000 undergraduate and alumnae members worldwide.

Since 1953, the organization has maintained a national office in Washington, D.C. Patricia Roberts Harris served as it first executive secretary; today Roseline

McKinney holds that position. A paid staff of thirty, supplemented by volunteers and student interns, keeps the organization running.

An elected board of forty governs the organization. These include the national officers (who are appointed), two representatives from each of the seven geographic regions of the United States, and the national committee chairs. The second vice presidency is always filled by an undergraduate member. The national executive board determines policies and initiates projects and programs for the constituent chapters to carry out.

Because Delta Sigma Theta is a membership organization, dues provide its main source of income. Individual chapters also raise money for special projects. Grants and corporate gifts provide additional funding. The current budget is reported as $2 million. The national board makes financial decisions.

POLICY CONCERNS AND TACTICS

Delta Sigma Theta's founders pledged its members to "concerted action in removing the handicaps under which we as women and as members of a minority race labor" and to "promoting social and race betterment." The founders' feminist activism—which included marching in a suffragist parade and meeting with President Woodrow Wilson in the White House—provided a sound and lasting philosophical foundation for the organization's evolving social concerns. An equal concern for minority civil rights is evident in the organization's long-standing affiliation with the National Association for the Advancement of Colored People, the National Urban League,* and National Council of Negro Women.* In recent years, these concerns have expanded to include international human rights.

Specific issues and areas of concern have changed with the times; as goals are reached, new problems are identified and new goals established. Yet, one important thread of continuity persists: educational advancement and academic excellence for women continue to be seen as essential. Scholarship programs and tutorial assistance have always supported these aims. Through its emphasis on academics and leadership, Delta Sigma Theta has prepared its members to assume professional and civic positions of influence.

Today, Delta's programs address domestic and international problems in the areas of education, employment, health, and social welfare. Recent projects—aimed primarily at women and young people—have dealt with career counseling, literacy, drug abuse, single parenting, and rehabilitating female offenders. Few of society's ills escape the group's thoughtful action, which might include providing direct services, combining with other organizations in joint efforts, providing financial assistance, or influencing public policy.

ELECTORAL ACTIVITIES

A nonpartisan, nonpolitical organization, Delta Sigma Theta is not involved in electoral politics, nor does it have paid lobbyists. Nonetheless, it has taken an active role—alone and in concert with other organizations—in affecting public policy decisions through public education efforts, letter-writing campaigns, voter registration drives, and ad hoc lobbying.

FURTHER INFORMATION

DST's official publication since 1920 is *The Delta Journal.*

LINDA NIEMAN

DEMOCRATIC NATIONAL COMMITTEE (DNC)
430 South Capitol Street, SE
Washington, DC 20003
(202) 863-8000
FAX (202) 863-8081

Women on the Democratic National Committee (DNC) and throughout the Democratic Party (DP) have as their general goals the election of Democratic women to political office along with Democratic candidates believing in rights for all, including women, and equitable integration of women into every aspect of DNC and the party platform's principles and constituency.

ORIGIN AND DEVELOPMENT

The goals of DNC/women were incorporated during 1972 as the women's liberation movement grew to include electoral politics as well as issues such as the equal rights amendment (ERA). In 1972, National Women's Political Caucus* (NWPC) members pressured for 50 percent representation among delegates and with the help of the McGovern-Fraser Commission got that percentage in 1976. Both years, NWPC was well represented among the delegates. Women's electoral politics focused not only on the election of women and men supporting these general goals but also on economic gains for women. Since that time, DNC has championed issues such as child care, equal employment and educational opportunity, and pay equity.

DP ideals tend toward egalitarianism and include the abolition of special privilege. Currently, DP members believe that government is a legitimate vehicle for solving social and economic problems, although from its first platform in 1840 through 1915, the party affirmed principles of limited and decentralized government. Only with the renomination of President Woodrow Wilson in 1916 did the Democratic Party incorporate progressive concepts of positive government.

During the San Francisco 1920 national convention, which nominated Governors James M. Cox and Franklin Delano Roosevelt for president and vice president, respectively, several planks supporting efforts to strengthen women's status were offered. These urged the elimination of sex discrimination in civil service positions and the quick ratification by the states of the Nineteenth (suffrage) Amendment. By 1944, DNC affirmed its support for an equal rights amendment in response to the National Woman's Party* encouragement, although Republicans supported ERA more strongly than Democrats. Democrats had committed themselves to protective legislation, which ERA would render unconstitutional. At India Edwards's behest, the Democratic Party supported legislation assuring equal pay for equal work regardless of sex.

Women have participated in this partisan organization since its first national nominating convention in 1832. As guests, Democratic women early observed or provided support to each DNC quadrennial effort to elect a national ticket and shape a party platform of issues and principles. Democratic women yielded this supportive role in 1860, when they became active lobbyists for a women's suffrage plank in the committee's platform. As early as 1896, women served as reporters, mainly covering women's events along with reporting on candidates' wives at convention time. Women's issues emerged as the focus of the first recorded demonstrations by women in 1916, when they vocally promoted planks for peace, child care, civil rights, ERA, and freedom of choice. These early roles—observer, supporter, lobbyist, reporter, demonstrator—were, however, external to DNC activities.

In 1924, Eleanor Roosevelt was asked to develop and present the women's planks to the national platform as well as to serve as party treasurer. She set an example for women as partisan insiders by touring New York state's fifty-two counties, endeavoring to place female leadership in each area so that local Democratic clubs could be established. DP had a women's division; and Eleanor Roosevelt in 1934 saw that social feminist Molly Dewson became part of it. Women became especially active in the party during the Franklin and Eleanor Roosevelt era. Dewson deserves credit for much of this, having seen that women received patronage appointments and served equally with men in party committee leadership posts.

By 1948 and 1952, with the encouragement of Harry S Truman and Volunteers for Stevenson, the number of active Democratic women increased visibly. Notables included Mrs. Roosevelt, India Edwards, who did public relations for the DNC/Women's Division and chaired it, U.S. treasurer Georgia Neese Clark, ambassador to Norway Eugenia Anderson, and Mary McLeod Bethune of the Civil Defense Advisory Board. Yet it took the turbulent 1968 Chicago convention before new rules established guidelines for delegate selection, which stipulated larger quotas of women, young people, and minorities than the various state delegations heretofore had affirmed. In 1972, Shirley Chisholm and Patsy Mink campaigned for delegates, and both congresswomen, especially Chisholm, had committed delegates when they came into the convention, a first.

ORGANIZATION AND FUNDING

DP is organized by national, regional, state, and local committees that, since 1986, have mandated gender equality. Geographically, the organization outside the United States is represented by Democrats abroad and within, by division into four regional units. State committees are active in the fifty states, with gender equity their practice. County, city, town, and ward/precinct committees are viable substate units throughout most of the country. All official subunits, entities, caucuses, and special interests within DNC are integrated since 1986 into the basic structure as programmatic concerns. The national convention is a delegate assembly representing state and local party organization; it meets every four years to nominate the party's candidate for president and vice president. Between the quadrennial gatherings, DNC conducts national business.

DNC professional staff in the District of Columbia numbers 150, presently augmented by twenty-seven interns. Alice Travis serves as director of DNC programs, including women's. The staff, although specialists in one area, such as speech writing or campaign fieldwork, may rotate positions as well as serve as generalists when needed. Organizationally, the trend is to encourage increased responsibility by DNC staff members, women and men both, along with an increase in rewards.

DNC total membership is 404, with parity for women and men.

Funding for DNC's operation and its programmatic arms is raised through diverse sources, including individuals, political action committees (PACs), and private foundations. Both large contributions from a few persons as well as small contributors are sought. The committee does not have tax-exempt status under the U.S. Internal Revenue Code, nor are its contributions tax-deductible. Information about the total budget is not available.

POLICY CONCERNS AND TACTICS

The gender gap in party registration, with women most likely to register Democratic and since 1980 more likely than men to vote, has challenged DNC to represent Democratic women's interests. It has continued through the party platform to carry a standard for ERA, the Republican Party having since left the fold, and has become the sole party committed to women's right to choose. The nomination and election of a Democratic president, Clinton, in 1992 brought children's issues and health care to the fore; soon after, Hillary Rodham Clinton visited the Congressional Caucus for Women's Issues* and also the minority caucuses to assure them of her intent as she worked to shape future health policy in United States.

ELECTORAL ACTIVITIES

The major American political parties are in business to label and elect candidates. In 1980, DP nominated the first woman to run on a major party ticket, for vice president; she was U.S. congresswoman Geraldine Ferraro (D-NY). Besides established fund-raising units such as the Senate Campaign Committee, several independent PACs have been set up to encourage and elect Democratic women. Nationally since 1985, EMILY's List* has raised campaign funds successfully for exclusively Democratic women supporting a pro-choice position. National Organization for Women's* (NOW) NOW/PAC and NOW/Equality/ PAC maintain close ties with DNC; NOW endorsement standards virtually eliminate Republican women from consideration. As a state-level PAC, Women's Impact Network is organized for the Massachusetts Coalition of Democrat

Women to identify Democratic women candidates supporting the Democratic state platform.

FURTHER INFORMATION

DNC has publications, but none related to women's issues per se.

FRANCES BURKE

DEMOCRATIC PARTY
See DEMOCRATIC NATIONAL COMMITTEE

DIVISION OF GIRLS AND WOMEN IN SPORT
See NATIONAL ASSOCIATION FOR GIRLS AND WOMEN IN SPORT

E
/

EAGLE FORUM (EF)
316 Pennsylvania Avenue, SE
Suite 203
Washington, DC 20003
(202) 544-0353
FAX (202) 547-6996

A direct outgrowth of Phyllis Schlafly's 1972 Stop ERA campaign, the Eagle Forum (EF) has been the preeminent conservative women's political organization since its founding in 1975. It acts both as a political action committee (PAC) and nonprofit organization, setting the agenda for conservative women in the United States. EF also has a legal defense and education fund (LDEF) and education and research foundation.

ORGANIZATION AND DEVELOPMENT

Defeated in 1967 as a candidate for National Federation of Republican Women President, in 1975, Schlafly recognized the opportunity to redirect the efforts of Stop ERA's grassroots organization to work on a complete conservative agenda. Historically, EF's most significant contribution has been the equal rights amendment's (ERA) defeat. Since 1982, EF has concentrated its efforts on education issues, pro-life and antitax campaigns, lobbying for a strong defense, and ending discrimination against traditional family values. It does not lobby against gay rights.

ORGANIZATION AND FUNDING

The holder of a Radcliffe College master's degree and recipient in 1978 of a Washington University law degree, Schlafly continues to head EF in the unpaid position of president and is listed on Federal Election Committee records as the treasurer as well. Women hold all the officer positions and all the seats on the board of directors. EF's national headquarters is located in Schlafly's hometown of Alton, Illinois, with local chapters in all fifty states and Australia. The bulk of the staff and policy making comes from the Washington, D.C., office. EF LDEF and EF PAC both operate from the Washington office. No information is available on the number of lobbyists it employs. The forum utilizes both volunteers and student interns.

EF does not consider itself a women-only group. Self-described as a nonquota organization, demographic information such as race, income strata, and sex about the 80,000 members is not available. They join in order to advocate on ideas and policy important to them and to represent their opinions to government. Membership gives them a chance to participate in public affairs and develop organizational skills. Members appreciate attending conferences and receiving information. Members contribute to the annual budget through annual dues of twenty dollars, fifteen dollars for subscriptions to the monthly newsletter, and gifts and bequests from individuals. The *Phyllis Schlafly Report* also serves to raise funds and offer merchandise and supplemental publications to 40,000 subscribers. The remainder of the budget comes from foundation grants.

EF is a nonprofit 501 (c) (3) organization and has established a lobbying group under Section 501 (c) (4) of the Internal Revenue Service Code. It downplays the level of its political organization and is reluctant to release any specific information on its size and structure or membership and funding.

POLICY CONCERNS AND TACTICS

With membership feedback, Schlafly continues to set policy for EF. Recommendations by professional staff, board of directors' discussions, executive officers' decisions, and informal polls of the membership are the primary influences on policy. The wide array of issues addressed by the forum necessitates a broad range of tactics, including congressional and state legislative testimony, personal recommendations to legislators and information provisions for their staff, contributions to political campaigns and vote monitoring, comments on regulations and pressure for administrative review, letter writing, press releases, and demonstrations.

Schlafly is a master of grassroots politics. Under her direction, EF pioneered the use of telephone trees to mobilize supporters. During the Stop ERA campaign, Schlafly had supporters lobby legislators with home-baked goods such as small loaves of bread and handwritten notes with messages such as ''I was bred to be a lady and like it that way.'' Personal appearances are carefully staged. In 1973, the galleries full of supporters, husband Fred prominently seated nearby, Schlafly was escorted with the greatest courtesy to the front of the Missouri House chamber to give testimony against ERA; thereafter, Professor Joan Krauskof of the University of Missouri Law School was excused from testifying because her specialty was criminal and not domestic law. Schlafly and her supporters debate only if they are allowed to speak last. They emphasize their support for the 1964 Equal Pay Act.

In 1985, EF sent 250,000 letters to supporters, urging them to use the Hatch amendment to the General Education Provision Act to force public schools to exclude sex and death education, discussions of organic evolution, instruction on the ideas of nuclear policy, globalism, and occultism from their curricula. Both Schlafly and the forum continually publish new materials and editorials to expose supporters to new issues and ideas. EF has established programs to teach supporters everything from the basics of public relations and accessing local media to a Head Start reading program for their children. The annual Full-time Homemaker Award recognizes a woman considered to embody the best of traditional family values.

Policymakers regularly solicit EF for opinions on legislative matters; it regularly gives public opinions on legislation. It considers ERA and *Roe* v. *Wade* to be the federal laws that most concern it. It mobilized, for example, in 1986 to stop a state ERA campaign in Vermont; and Schlafly's picture with picketing supporters near the steps of the U.S. Supreme Court appeared in newspapers nationwide after announcement of the decision in *Casey* v. *Planned Parenthood* (1992). These two issues provide the basis and continuity for EF's policies and tactics. It does not lobby against gay rights or for antigay policies.

Coordination with similar groups is identified by the forum as one of its most important strategies. During EF's most public campaign, Stop ERA, participants in rallies were requested to carry signs without the names of their affiliate organizations, thus eliminating the potential political damage of having groups such as the John Birch Society participating. EF has identified feminism and feminist groups, for example, National Organization for Women* and National Abortion Rights Action League,* as major contributors to the degradation of the nation's moral fiber.

ELECTORAL ACTIVITIES

Despite Schlafly's prominence in Republican politics, including frequent appearances at national conventions as a delegate or alternate, EF does not view women's issues in partisan terms. EF PAC was founded on September 26, 1978, originally under the name Stop ERA PAC. The name changed after the amendment's defeat. Candidates are chosen for support on an individual basis by the office staff and Schlafly. Ideological compatibility, that is, conservatism, is the basis for candidate support, with candidate selection based on individual cases.

FURTHER INFORMATION

EF publishes the *The Phyllis Schlafly Report* and a newsletter.

MEGAN ISAACS

EAGLE FORUM POLITICAL ACTION COMMITTEE
See EAGLE FORUM

EAGLETON INSTITUTE OF POLITICS CENTER FOR THE AMERI-CAN WOMAN AND POLITICS (CAWP)

Rutgers, the State University of New Jersey
New Brunswick, NJ 08901
(908) 828-2210
FAX (908) 932-6778

A unique research, education, and public service entity, the Center for the American Woman and Politics (CAWP) serves as a catalyst for women participating in government and politics as well as for those studying and monitoring their status and chances for success and as a resource—accumulating, analyzing, and interpreting data. It functions genuinely as a connection between the political institutions and academe. It is among groups most deserving credit for the 1992 year of the woman in American politics.

ORIGIN AND DEVELOPMENT

In 1971, CAWP formed within the Eagleton Institute of Politics (EIP) at Rutgers University (RU), early in the move to establish women's studies as the academic arm of the women's liberation movement. Founded in 1956, EIP pursued interests in practical politics and the public policy process. The institute received its name from Florence Peshine Eagleton, a New Jersey suffragist serving thereafter as president of the state's League of Women Voters.* Eagleton and her spouse agreed that the estate of the partner dying first would go to the other's favorite cause. Eagleton's husband predeceased her. She left RU the money to advance "learning in the field of practical political affairs and government to the end that the study of the actual administration of government processes, especially in the municipality and the state, may be encouraged and the active participation of American citizens therein may be fostered and stimulated and that knowledge of the meaning of democracy may be increased through the education of young women and men in democratic government."

Faculty at EIP introduced the idea for CAWP in the early 1970s; and staff and a distinguished advisory committee guided it at inception. Start-up funds came from the Ford Foundation and continued for six years. During this period CAWP hosted a Carnegie Corporation-funded conference bringing fifty women legislators together in Pennsylvania's Pocono mountain resort area. Never before had elected women in the United States met to gain insight into their own experiences and ideas. The first substantive book on women and politics, *Political Woman* (1974) by Jeane J. Kirkpatrick, a distinguished political scientist who served 1980–85 as U.S. ambassador to the United Nations, was based on a survey of these conference participants. Kirkpatrick later reported to a Mt. Vernon College women and politics class that some male colleagues found her interest to be incomprehensible. Subsequently, Bonnie Cook Freeman reported that women in politics were widely considered political primitives.

In 1973, Douglass College at RU pioneered an in-residence program for politicians, beginning with two women state legislators, Audrey Beck (D-CT) and

Louise Connor (R-DE). The year after—with the sponsorship of Ford, and the Mary Reynolds Babcock and Laurel foundations—there were Florence Eagleton grants to underwrite the study of women volunteers in politics. An information clearinghouse followed in 1975, along with the first national census and survey of women public officials at the national, state, county, and municipal levels. These findings appeared in a directory and abstract thereafter. CAWP also undertook a study for a National Commission on the Observance of International Women's Year committee to document women's presence on the boards and commissions of thirty-nine states and joined the National Women's Education Fund (NWEF) and several journalists in documenting women's electoral campaigns. By 1976, CAWP reflected EIP's strengths, including graduate fellowship programs, research, and public service.

CAWP's goal of representing female political activists and officeholders as well as students of women and politics has not changed. It went on in the seventies to extend its grant program, continued the census and survey, and started looking into the impact of women serving on school boards. This last effort yielded a report, among the first of many. CAWP also had a bibliography published; its directory and abstract went into a second edition; and it began compiling fact sheets. The U.S. Housing and Urban Development Department funded its research into women as municipal managers and also associations of women officeholders. This research led to a series of practicum-oriented workshops at meetings of such public officials as the National League of Cities and International City Management Association, to a leadership conference of women's organizations, and to additional reports. CAWP's documentation of organization among women in public office also has continued, and it has assisted with the organization process, especially in New Jersey.

Throughout the eighties, CAWP enlarged the compass of its inquiry and direct facilitation of women in politics, compiling information and recruiting to its staff such well-known scholars as Susan J. Carroll for her expertise on women state legislators and Katherine E. Kleeman for her expertise on women's organizational networking. New Jersey governor Thomas Kean helped celebrate CAWP's tenth birthday in 1982. Five years later its interests extended to women in international leadership positions, a focus open for future development. Today CAWP also seeks to educate U.S. secondary and college students about women's public leadership opportunities.

ORGANIZATION AND FUNDING

CAWP has no officers or board. Since 1971, Ruth B. Mandel has served as its director. There are nine staff at the center's headquarters in New Brunswick, New Jersey. Workers take a fixed level of responsibility and do not rotate jobs. The center has student interns.

CAWP is not a membership organization.

In 1985, the center set up an endowment fund and in 1991 undertook a $5 million campaign to further assure its development. The Program for Women

State Legislators (PWSL) has attracted an impressive array of funders, among them such benefactors as the American Express Philanthropic Program, the Robert Wood Johnson Foundation, and Philip Morris Companies, such donors as Nestle USA and RJR Nabisco; such sustainers as Abbott Laboratories, Chevron Corporation, and Sandoz Pharmaceuticals Corporation; such supporters as the American Federation of State, County and Municipal Employees,* the Boeing Company, Fannie Mae Foundation, and Miller Brewing Company; such contributors as the American Association of Retired Persons Women's Initiative,* American Federation of Labor-Congress of Industrial Organizations,* American Trucking Associations, Association of Trial Lawyers of America, Avon Products, the Coca-Cola Company, the Hershey Food Corporation Fund, Johnson & Johnson Family of Companies, Mobil Oil Corporation, Monsanto Company, National Education Association, Rockwell International, and United Parcel Service; and such friends as Ford Motor Company Fund. Contributions to CAWP are tax-deductible. Its annual budget is around $750,000.

POLICY CONCERNS AND TACTICS

The director, in consultation with staff, sets policy for CAWP. As a think tank, its preferred strategy is conducting and publishing research. Besides surveying, it maintains a data bank and library. It sponsors such educational programs as conferences and seminars for women officeholders, distributes information and interpretation to government and the media, and spectacularly links academe with practical politics.

CAWP has a particular interest in women state legislators, believing them critical to not only policy making but also increases of women among officerholders generally. In 1983, 1987, 1989, and 1991, it sponsored well-attended national forums for these women; the 1991 assembly attracted 450 women from forty-seven states, one-third of all the women legislators, compared with 330 from forty-six states (33 percent) in 1983. Beginning in 1987, the forums provided internships for students. In 1990, PWSL convened a midwestern forum. There also have been three conferences. With Charles H. Revson Foundation backing, in 1981, CAWP began contrasting women's and men's behavior in this context.

CAWP has undertaken other comparisons, including appointments by Presidents Carter and Reagan and Reagan's male and female appointees. It also has looked at state government appointments of women compared with all state appointees, another first. It has interviewed women who have run on a major party line for the U.S. Senate and assisted in documenting the role of women at the national presidential nominating conventions. Its 1983 kit on ''Bringing More Women into Public Office'' contrasted women's and men's paths to elected and appointed office.

Under Coors National Hispana Leadership Initiative auspices, in 1988, the center helped to train Hispanic women for leadership. With the social work program of Rutgers at Camden, in 1989, CAWP helped establish a yearlong Hispanic Women's Leadership Institute training program. It has continued.

CAWP also plays a role in framing and defining issues. *Roe* v. *Wade* and related policies stimulated it in 1991 to issue a report on their influence in four state gubernatorial campaigns. A separate report analyzed the abortion issue in New Jersey and Virginia alone. CAWP's position, established as early as 1983, is that women make a difference. Legislators often come to CAWP for its views on public policy as well as for the names of other officeholders and organizations sharing their position. The center is featured in the press as well and undergrids many scholarly studies.

In 1978, CAWP helped establish a consortium, the Public Leadership Education Network (PLEN), with NWEF and the women's colleges. It has since worked with PLEN on summer leadership programs for young women. In 1986, it worked on a women's election project with the National Women's Political Caucus* (NWPC) and Women's Campaign Fund.* It has undertaken programming with U.S. Information Agency sponsorship. Throughout PWSL, CAWP has collaborated with such groups as the Children's Defense Fund,* NWPC, the Democratic* and Republican national committees, National Conference of State Legislators Women's Network,* National Order of Women Legislators,* and National Organization of Black Elected Legislative/Women.

ELECTORAL ACTIVITIES

CAWP does not see women's issues as partisan or have a political action committee (PAC). Since 1982, its scholarly interests have included PACs that largely or entirely endorse women candidates.

FURTHER INFORMATION

CAWP has a quarterly newsletter, *News & Notes: About Women Public Officials,* for associations of women officeholders. Its extensive publications list includes books, directories, research reports, fact sheets, and bibliographies. The books include Mandel's *In the Running: The New Woman Candidate* (1983) and Carroll's *Women as Candidates in American Politics* (1985). Recent reports focus on the impact of women officeholders, the relationship between gender and policy making, and changes in state legislatures' agendas as women have increased their presence in these chambers proportionately. There is a subscriber information service that distributes packets of information three times yearly for twenty dollars. There also is a documentary film, *Not One of the Boys;* a discussion guide accompanies the film.

SARAH SLAVIN

EDUCATIONAL ADVANCEMENT FOUNDATION
See ALPHA KAPPA ALPHA

EMILY'S LIST
The Southern Building
805 15th St. NW, 4th Floor
Washington, DC 20005
(800) 683-6459

An acronym for "Early Money Is Like Yeast" (it makes the dough rise), EMILY's List is a grassroots fund-raising network. It is partisan and helps only pro-choice Democratic women candidates. Both the organization and its president, Ellen Malcolm, have become respected players in Democratic and political fundraising circles.

ORIGIN AND DEVELOPMENT

Malcolm and a small group of women activists and political consultants founded EMILY's List in 1985. Included in this group were Betsy Crone, Joanne Howes, Marie Bass, Lael Stegall, Kathleen Currie, and Judith L. Lichtman. Those involved in starting EMILY's List witnessed the narrow defeat of Harriet Woods in her 1982 race for the U.S. Senate. Donations from traditional sources, such as labor, national Democratic Party political action committees (PACs), and big donors had come late to Woods's campaign. As a result, in the crucial closing stages of the campaign, she had to pull off the air her effective campaign television advertisements. Eventually, Woods raised enough money to get them back on, but her momentum had slowed. Incumbent Republican senator John Danforth eked out a narrow 51 percent–49 percent victory.

The founders did not want any other viable Democratic women running for the Senate to face that dilemma ever again. EMILY's List and its network of donors would make early contributions to campaigns. Early money would enable candidates to mount sophisticated campaigns and fund-raising efforts quickly. The founders strongly supported the bipartisan Women's Campaign Fund* and National Women's Political Caucus,* but they believed that the political differences over women's issues between the two major parties had become too great, so they wanted to concentrate their efforts on electing progressive Democratic women.

EMILY's List is a non-lobbying political action committee (PAC) that operates as a donor network rather than as a traditional PAC. Members join with a minimum contribution of $100. They are asked to make additional gifts (of at least $100) to two or more recommended candidates each election cycle. These contributions go directly to individual candidates. This "bundling" technique allows maximization of the amount of money channeled to candidates. To help members decide which pro-choice candidates to support, EMILY's List provides candidate positions on key issues and offers assessments of each candidate's political situation.

In 1986, EMILY's List helped Congresswoman Barbara Mikulski become the first Democratic woman elected to the U.S. Senate in her own right. From 1986 to 1990, EMILY's List was instrumental in the election of seven new Democratic women to the U.S. House: Nita Lowey (NY), Jolene Unsoeld (WA), Jill Long (IN), Patsy Mink (HI), Rosa DeLauro (CT), Maxine Waters (CA) and delegate Eleanor Holmes Norton (DC). In 1990, it helped Ann Richards (TX) and Barbara Roberts (OR) win elections and become governors. In special elections in 1989 and 1990, EMILY's List helped Jill Long (IN) and Patsy Mink (HI) win congressional seats.

ORGANIZATION AND FUNDING

EMILY's List maintains an office in Washington, D.C. During its first election cycle, 1985–86, it was staffed by volunteer president Ellen Malcolm and several consultants and fundraisers. Membership grew to 1,200. During the 1987–88 election cycle, EMILY's List employed one full-time and one part-time staff members. Malcolm, along with the consultants, continued to supplement the staff. Membership increased to 2,025. The majority of new members joined in response to direct mail appeals or attendance at one of a series of membership meetings held in twenty-eight different cities across the country. Operating costs at this time totaled $317,356, or 35 percent of the total amount of money spent by EMILY's List and its members to elect candidates. Members contributed about 80 percent of the funds used to finance EMILY's List. Labor groups supplied the rest.

Because of expanded fund-raising, research, and reapportionment projects during the 1989–90 election cycle, EMILY's List staff grew to seven full-time and one part-time staff member. They were assisted by a number of unpaid volunteer interns. Rosa DeLauro served as the organization's first executive director but soon left to run successfully for the Congress; Wendy Sherman became the second executive director.

For the two-year cycle, EMILY's List raised $1.39 million and spent $1.21 million for its operations: programs, in-kind contributions to candidates, direct candidate contributions, and operating costs. EMILY's List members contributed the bulk of these funds. Labor groups provided $121,000. In addition to the money earmarked for operations, EMILY's List members contributed $1.36 million directly to candidates. Operating costs were $402,240 or 16 percent of the total $2.57 million spent to elect candidates during this time period.

In 1992, a combination of factors—including the all-white male Senate Judiciary Committee's treatment of Anita Hill's accusations of sexual harassment against Supreme Court nominee Clarence Thomas and the national anti-incumbent mood—produced an outpouring of support for women candidates. EMILY's List experienced an explosion in members and money. By the end of that year, membership reached 24,000 and direct and bundled contributions to candidates surged to $6.2 million.

POLICY CONCERNS AND TACTICS

EMILY's List has conducted several research projects. Highlighted in the 1989 report, "Campaigning in a Different Voice," was a discussion of how

gender affects voters' perceptions of candidates. It was noted that these perceptions work both for and against women candidates. On one hand, voters often
consider women candidates to be "outsiders" to the political system—free to
promote change and more understanding of ordinary people. On the other hand,
because women candidates are not thought of as "insiders," they are considered
less skilled and effective at making tough decisions and understanding how
government really works.

In 1991, a follow-up study was prepared for EMILY's List by Greenberg-
Lake: Analysis Group. A debriefing of Democratic women candidates who had
run in 1990, their managers, pollsters, media consultants, and other consultants
revealed that women candidates continued to face a "credibility gap." In an era
of "antipolitics," women candidates as outsiders seemed to represent the change
that voters wanted in government. But voters were still wary about electing more
women to office. Participants in the briefing noted three areas in which their
candidates' credibility had been challenged: qualifications and competence to do
the job, toughness to handle the job, and the ability to run viable campaigns. If
women candidates were going to be elected, they would have to walk a thin
line—convincing voters that they had the skills, experience, resources, and
strength to hold office while at the same time not giving up their unique outsider
image.

EMILY's List also commissioned Greenberg-Lake: Analysis Group to do a
1990 study on how candidates' pro-choice positions affect voters' perceptions.
Results from eight focus groups and a national poll confirmed that pro-choice
stands could have positive results for Democratic candidates. The findings revealed that Democratic candidates who were pro-choice reinforced their support
from women voters and also increased significantly their support from younger
voters, suburban and independent voters, single voters, and middle-income voters. The study concluded that the electoral advantage of pro-choice Democratic
candidates is ten points over pro-life Republican candidates. Pro-choice Republican candidates outrun pro-life Democratic candidates by five points.

During the 1993–94 cycle, EMILY's List held a series of political training
sessions for fundraisers, campaign managers, and press secretaries. It also
launched a communications program for 1994–95 that focused on seven research
topics: Effectiveness of Women in Congress; Negative Campaigning and
Women Candidates; Crime and Women Candidates; Women and Money: Donor
Patterns; Women and Money: Fundraising Patterns; Spouses of Women Candidates; and Women Candidates and Gay Baiting.

ELECTORAL ACTIVITIES

Democratic women candidates seeking support from EMILY's List undergo
extensive evaluations. Staff conduct their own research into races and also solicit
information from other PACs. Some of the PACs consulted regularly include
the Women's Campaign Fund,* AFL-CIO Committee on Political Education,*

the Democratic Party* and Democratic Congressional Campaign Committees, and NCEC.

EMILY's List communicates recommendations of Democratic women candidates who are pro-choice and considered viable through special candidate mailings. Each member is free to decide which candidates to support and what amount of money to contribute. Checks are made payable to the candidate's campaign and mailed to EMILY's List. It records contributions, then forwards them to the campaign. In addition to members' contributions, EMILY's List makes in-kind and direct contributions to candidates.

In the 1985–86 election cycle, EMILY's List members contributed $350,000 to two U.S. Senate candidates, Harriett Woods (MO) and Barbara Mikulski (MD). Of the $150,000 donated to Mikulski's winning campaign, $60,000 represented nearly 20 percent of the candidate's early money.

In 1988, EMILY's List turned its attention primarily to helping candidates for the U.S. House of Representatives. EMILY's List and its members contributed $600,000 to candidates during the 1987–88 election cycle: $70,000 from EMILY's List in technical assistance and direct campaign money, $530,000 from members for nine recommended House candidates. A joint mailing with Peace PAC raised another $35,734 for select candidates endorsed by EMILY's List.

In 1990, EMILY'S List continued to support congressional candidates and for the first time contributed to women candidates running for governor. Of nearly $1.5 million spent to elect candidates during the 1989–90 election cycle, EMILY's List contributed $90,000 directly and through technical assistance, and members contributed another $1,386,800 directly to candidates. EMILY's List also began to focus on the effects of redistricting on the 1992 federal elections. It encouraged viable women candidates such as Florida state senators Karen Thurman and Gwen Margolis to run in targeted new congressional districts and in districts with redrawn boundaries.

In the 1992 elections, record numbers of women decided to run for seats in the U.S. Senate and House. EMILY's List capitalized on its reapportionment research and experience gained in past election cycles to target key races and raise significant money for the candidates in those races. At an event held at the National Democratic Convention EMILY's List raised $750,000 for seven pro-choice Democratic women running for the U.S. Senate. That event was the largest single fund-raiser ever held for women candidates. By the end of 1992, EMILY's List had raised over $3.7 million, more than twice as much as it had raised in all of 1991. EMILY's List members received profiles of seven pro-choice Democratic women running for the Senate: Congresswomen Barbara Boxer (CA), Carol Moseley-Braun (IL), Dianne Feinstein (CA), Geraldine Ferraro (NY), Josie Heath (CO), Patty Murray (WA), and Lynn Yeakel (PA). It also recommended thirty-five women candidates running for the U.S. House. It was especially active in Florida and California, which had gained several new congressional seats. EMILY's List recommended eight women House candidates in California and six in Florida, a state that had never elected a Democratic woman to Congress. Included on the overall list of recommended Senate and House candidates were many women of color. This list included Carol Moseley-Braun (IL), Corinne Brown (FL), Eva Clayton (NC), Anna Eshoo (CA), Anita Perez Ferguson (CA), Eddie Bernice Johnson (TX), Carrie Meek (FL), Gloria Ochoa (CA), and Lucille Roybal-Allard (CA). In addition to its activity at the federal level, EMILY's List made direct contributions totaling $195,135 to 174 pro-choice Democratic women candidates running at the state and local level.

During the 1993–94 election cycle, EMILY's List had two equally important fundraising goals: raise money for pro-choice Democratic women incumbents facing tough reelection campaigns and for the growing number of new women candidates seeking higher office. In addition to raising money for recommended candidates, EMILY's List members worked to keep ''bundling'' by non-lobbying political committees legal in the campaign reform legislation introduced during the 103rd Congress.

FURTHER INFORMATION

To help potential candidates decide whether they should run, EMILY's List wrote and published *Thinking of Running for Congress? A Guide for Democratic Women.* It also produces ''Notes from EMILY,'' a quarterly newsletter.

JOAN E. MCLEAN

ERAMERICA

ERAmerica was the longest-lived and most visible of the national coalition organizations formed to ratify the equal rights amendment (ERA).

ORIGIN AND DEVELOPMENT

Formally announced on January 18, 1976, the group remained active until the deadline to ratify ERA expired on June 30, 1982. The need for a coordinating ratification campaign was noted by the consulting firm of Bailey, Deardourff, and Eyre in its report on strategies to the National Federation of Business and Professional Women's Clubs* (BPW) in December 1974. In 1975, representatives of several major proponent groups, including BPW, the League of Women Voters* (LWV). National Organization for Women* (NOW), National Women's Political Caucus* (NWPC), Women's Equity Action League* (WEAL), American Association of University Women* (AAUW), and National Education Association (NEA), began planning the formation of a new activist umbrella coalition.

The National Commission on the Observance of International Women's Year, established by President Gerald Ford on January 9, 1975, ranked ERA ratification as its top priority. Under the leadership of its ERA subcommittee cochairs actor Alan Alda and Congresswoman Margaret Heckler (R-MA) and staff member Meriwyn Heath (who also served as BPW's national ERA coordinator), the commission also was instrumental in ERAmerica's formation as an independent, nongovernmental body with a single purpose—to wage a nationwide bipartisan political campaign. (Responding to this linkage, antifeminist leader Phyllis Schafly in March 1976 accused ERAmerica of using federal International Women's Year money for its own organization.)

ORGANIZATION AND FUNDING

On February 25, 1976, ERAmerica opened its national headquarters in Washington, D.C., with office space and furniture donated by NEA. Democrat Liz Carpenter and Republican Elly Peterson agreed to serve as national cochairs to provide, for public relations purposes, an image of nonthreatening bipartisan leadership. In the campaign's last stages, state First Ladies Sharon Percy Rockefeller (West Virginia) and Helen Milliken (Michigan) replaced Carpenter and Peterson, respectively, as national cochairs.

Although ERAmerica was officially an alliance of over 200 national organizations, including professional, civic, religious, labor, and women's groups, the core (predominantly women's) groups numbered fewer than thirty. Few provided major, continuing financial support. For example, in early 1976, LWV was asked to contribute $10,000 in seed money to ERAmerica; instead it gave $1,000 and lent staff member Mary Brooks as a field organizer for more than three months. Similarly detailed were Heath (BPW) and Joan McLean (NWPC). By late 1976, NOW, an original coalition member, had withdrawn to wage an independent campaign.

Despite these setbacks and persistent financial problems, ERAmerica remained active for six years, with Sheila Greenwald, followed by Suone Cotner, serving as paid executive director. Incorporating, opening the national office, staff organizing, and campaign strategizing were the responsibility of a small, all-female planning committee drawn from the core groups that initially founded ERAmerica. The size of the paid, mostly female staff in Washington, D.C., ranged from three to eight, and the annual budget varied between $100,000 and a high of $350,000 in 1976–77. In some years, ERAmerica and some male consultants utilized unpaid interns and paid field directors; and for six months in 1976, it hired Jane Wells of Texas as national campaign manager.

ERAmerica received cash donations from groups and individuals. The in-kind services of NEA and cash contributions from AAUW, Coalition of Labor Union Women* (CLUW), and, in particular, LWV and BPW were most notable. ERAmerica sponsored several successful fund-raising events and engaged in ongoing direct mail appeals for money. A fund-raiser held at the International Women's Year Conference in Houston in November 1977 collected $100,000 and attracted many celebrities, including Lady Bird Johnson, Betty Ford, Rosalyn Carter, and Coretta Scott King. Those attending an ERAmerica gala in Washington in 1979 also received an invitation to a White House reception hosted by the Carters.

POLICY CONCERNS AND TACTICS

A board of varying size that met monthly formally set ERAmerica policy. In practice, the staff, in consultation with the national cochairs and a steering committee composed of representatives from the major supporting organizations, presented policy to the board. ERAmerica used almost all conceivable tactics to achieve its goal, including testimony and lobbying in the Congress and state legislatures; mass demonstrations and rallies; letter-writing campaigns and petition drives; appearances by celebrities such as Erma Bombeck, Marlo Thomas, and Alda and Helen Reddy; and radio spot advertising, newsletters, research reports, and other public education techniques. In 1981, it hired prominent political consultant Joseph Napolitan to analyze the ERA campaign.

One tactic, extending the deadline for ERA ratification from March 1979 to June 1982, was not universally favored by coalition members. As Liz Carpenter recalled in a 1991 interview, the extension was NOW's idea, not ERAmerica's. It was feared that an extension campaign in the Congress would divert resources and attention from state ERA ratification at a time when victory might be possible. Extension efforts in 1977 also took the pressure off newly inaugurated president Jimmy Carter to convert anti-ERA legislators during the period when presidential influence is traditionally at its peak. Further, extension exposed amendment proponents to charges of unfair procedures, that is, changing the rules in the middle of the game. This was especially harmful since legal scholars were themselves divided concerning the constitutionality of extension. The primary tactical advantage of extension rested in the upcoming 1980 election year and the promise of additional leverage for proponents.

In some observers' and participants' view, ERAmerica lacked the financial resources and authority to play a central role in ratification. Instead, it served primarily as a national clearinghouse for information on the amendment, coordinator of proponents' Washington press conferences, and participant in, or sponsor of, events organized and financed by other pro-ERA groups. Others believe that ERAmerica became a valuable adviser and motivator for the fifteen state groups. Beginning in 1976, ERAmerica coordinated efforts to target funds to those states with the strongest chances for ratification. After several ratification failures in 1977, ERAmerica and its core Washington-based support groups assumed an increasingly direct role in the leadership of state ratification campaigns.

In retrospect, the failure to ratify ERA may rest less in the tactical shortcomings of ERAmerica than in the inherent limitations of coalition organizations. ERA was only one of several important issues for coalition members and the priority of none. As the LWV-commissioned study noted, the suffrage and ERA campaigns differed in their organizational structure from the movement to ratify the suffrage amendment led by an independent membership organization, the National American Woman Suffrage Association* (NAWSA). Not only was ERAmerica never a membership organization, but it never commanded adequate resources or influence to do what the NAWSA did. Nor could ERAmerica draw strength and motivation from a single leader analogous to the legendary suffragist, Carrie Chapman Catt, a pragmatic politician as well as a hands-on manager.

ELECTORAL ACTIVITIES

As originally conceived, ERAmerica was to wage a national campaign for ratification similar to a political campaign but without a political action committee. Although ERAmerica spokeswomen publicly urged uncommitted candidates to support ERA and encouraged its supporting groups to judge candidates on the basis of their stance on this issue, ERAmerica became directly involved in state legislative elections only late in the ERA campaign. They had some success, particularly in Florida, Indiana, North Carolina, Oklahoma, and South Carolina, and concede that the coalition should have tried this tactic earlier. Certainly, ERAmerica was well situated to engage in electoral targeting. By 1982, a complete record of each legislative vote on the ERA, along with the record of each legislator in nonratifying states, had been compiled by Field Director Jane Campbell.

FURTHER INFORMATION

Historically, ERAmerica had a newsletter and published a pamphlet for ERA lobbyists to hand out to legislators, the general public, and so on. It occasionally issued such research reports as law briefs for ERA.

JANET K. BOLES

F

/

FAMILY RESEARCH COUNCIL (FRC)
700 13th Street, NW
Suite 500
Washington, DC 20005
(202) 393-2100
FAX (202) 393-2134

The Family Research Council (FRC) is an advocacy group dedicated to ensuring that public policy reflects the needs and interests of the family. The council directs its resources toward providing policymakers and the public with information in support of traditional family values.

ORIGIN AND DEVELOPMENT

The council was founded in 1983 by a group of individuals who knew one another professionally and were concerned that no group existed to speak for Judeo-Christian family values. The founders, among them Jim Dobson, Jerry Regier, and Dave Larson, had an interest in public policy and had traveled to Washington, D.C., to testify on policies related to families. No one individual acted as the chief organizer. Regier became FRC's first president. In 1988, the council merged with the Colorado-based Focus on the Family to become one of its divisions. The council became independent again in October 1992.

The council began as a small enterprise with a $1.7 million budget and a single policy analyst. Since then it has grown to a $3.5 million operation that includes legislative and media divisions. The legislative division monitors legislative proposals and makes contacts with members of the Congress and their staff. The media division issues news releases and fact sheets to the print media, radio, and television.

FRC is primarily concerned with public policy that supports the traditional family. The council encourages any legislation that makes it easier for two parents and their children to live and spend time together and opposes legislation that interferes with such a lifestyle. For example, FRC supports reform to reduce the tax burden on families; a more specific example is the council's endorsement of the expansion of the Young Child Tax Credit to facilitate greater parental involvement in the lives of their children under the age of six. The council also supports divorce and welfare reform to discourage single parenthood and opposes legalized abortion. The council discourages government intervention in ways that would interfere with parents' choices about how to raise their children. For example, they support parents' right to choose where their children should be educated.

ORGANIZATION AND FUNDING

The council recently formed a board of directors, which, at present, includes only nonminority men. Currently, there is no effort to encourage participation of people from lower-income strata, people with disabilities, or women. There recently was some discussion of developing a subboard structure that would serve as a training ground for individuals who would eventually be asked to join the board. Gary Bauer has served as FRC president since 1988, and Charles Donovan has served as executive staff director for the past three years. The staff consists of twelve professionals, about four or five volunteers a year, and twelve interns per year who work out of the single office in Washington, D.C. There is one lobbyist.

The nonprofit council was founded with the assistance of private foundation grants, as well as individual contributions, both large and small. It is not a membership organization but rather is supported by gifts or bequests from individuals (about 60 percent) and foundation grants (about 40 percent). Currently, there are about 150,000 names on the council's mailing list to receive its publications and make donations. Most of those on the list are married couples with children, and an estimated 10 percent of them are minority. FRC is exempt from taxation under 501 (c) (3).

POLICY CONCERNS AND TACTICS

Policy positions are determined at meetings of professional staff. If staff cannot agree, the president makes the final decision. Initial policy recommendations generally are proposed by one of the policy analysts, and then the issue is discussed at a staff meeting. The newly formed board also will begin to play a role in the policy development process. Like policy positions, strategies to be used for particular issues are decided through discussion among professional staff.

Strategies considered most important for influencing public policy really center on providing information to policymakers to shape their opinions and votes and providing information to the public, who, in turn, are encouraged to apply pressure to policymakers. They have a "legislative hotline" providing current information on pending family issues (phone (202) 783-HOME). The policy-making arena to which the council devotes most of its attention is the Congress. Besides direct lobbying, it widely distributes its publications and encourages those supporting the council's agenda to write to their representatives. FRC also issues press releases with data that support its policy positions. The council does not conduct much original research but disseminates the results of other research that supports the positions. Strategies of lesser, but still significant, importance include testifying in congressional hearings, making personal presentations to members of the Congress, and monitoring the voting records of elected officials. The council has developed a nationwide Resource Network, which includes professionals from various academic fields who are available to provide expert testimony on relevant issues when such testimony is needed.

FRC occasionally directs its attention to issues at the state legislative level, but much less frequently than at the federal level. It does not yet contribute to campaigns, nor is it active in the judicial arena. It does not engage in litigation, although it occasionally files amicus briefs.

Any legislation that affects women and children is considered important by the council, but those pieces of legislation that it considers as most directly within their purview include *Roe* v. *Wade,* the 1976 Day Care Act, Hyde amendments, and the proposed human rights constitutional amendment. Of somewhat lesser importance are the 1963 Equal Pay Act, the Child Support Amendments to the 1975 Social Security Act, 1978 Pregnancy Disability Act, 1984 Child Abuse Act, and 1984 Child Support Enforcement Act. FRC's views very often are solicited by members of legislative bodies, agency heads, and their staff.

For the past several years, FRC has worked with Eagle Forum,* Concerned Women for America,* and the Heritage Foundation on issues of mutual concern. It is most likely to find itself in opposition to the American Civil Liberties Union,* Children's Defense Fund,* and Fund for the Feminist Majority,* although they are not adversaries on every issue.

ELECTORAL ACTIVITIES

FRC does not have a political action committee but has considered setting up one. It does not see the family issues that concern it as partisan ones, nor does it see women candidates as necessarily more sympathetic to its positions. While the council has not been in a position to support candidates yet, it anticipates looking for candidates who see family as society's cornerstone and share the belief the government should ensure that the family is not damaged by public policy. Most likely, the candidate would be conservative.

FURTHER INFORMATION

FRC's publications include periodicals, reports and issue packets, and books. A monthly newsletter, *Washington Watch,* focuses on current issues concerning the traditional family before Congress, federal courts, and the White House and is free to the general public. In addition, the council has a bimonthly publication called *Family Policy,* which provides an in-depth look at research trends and policy initiatives. This publication is offered free of charge to every congressional office on Capitol Hill and a wide range of media contacts, and the public is offered a subscription for a suggested donation of fifteen dollars per year.

In addition, on an irregular basis, the FRC publishes *Insight,* which provides background on policy issues before Congress, the administration, or federal agencies. A recent seventeen-page issue of *Insight,* for example, analyzed the Employment Non-Discrimination Act, which would prohibit discrimination in employment on the basis of sexual orientation. *Insight* and other policy papers are released initially to opinion leaders in government, business, and the mass media and are made available to the public for a suggested donation of fifty dollars per year.

The FRC also offers "issue packets" available for a suggested donation of $7.50. Each issue packet includes ten to fifteen documents concerning specific issues. Examples are family stability, health care, the homosexual agenda, teen sex, and family law and ethics.

Special "Family Policy" reports are also available from FRC for donations ranging from $2.50 to $15. Recent reports include "Outcome-Based Education: Dumbing Down America's Schools"; "The Family Friendly Corporation: Strengthening the Ties That Bind"; and "Home Remedies: Family-Based Guidelines for Health Reform."

Finally, FRC president Gary Bauer wrote *Our Journey Home* (1992); former FRC vice president Kay James wrote *Never Forget;* and Executive Staff Director Charles A. Donovan coauthored a book with Robert G. Marshall, *Blessed Are the Barren: The Social Policy of Planned Parenthood.*

KATHERINE C. NAFF

FEDERALLY EMPLOYED WOMEN (FEW)
1400 I Street, NW
Suite 425
Washington, DC 20005
(202) 898-0994

Federally Employed Women (FEW) remains the only extragovernmental group dedicated to promoting the interests of the 900,000 women employed by the government. Set up to inform federal women of their rights under executive order 11375 of 1967, FEW both trains and helps promote women within the federal government and introduces and supports legislation to assist women in federal service. FEW has a legal education fund.

ORIGIN AND DEVELOPMENT

In early 1968, a conference was held for executive women in Washington, D.C. Among those in attendance were thirteen women relatively high in the federal employment structure (GS 11 to GS 15). Allie Lattimer, a lawyer for the General Services Administration (GSA), became FEW's first president. Lattimer informed the others she had been named coordinator of GSA's Federal Women's Program (FWP). The others did not know such a program existed. None of their agencies had FWP coordinators despite an order to appoint them the previous year.

When President Johnson signed 11375, he asked the Civil Service Commission to carry it out by seeing to it that all federal agencies appoint a FWP coordinator, develop an action plan to combat sex discrimination, and submit periodic progress reports on compliance. Lattimer actually had attended the conference expecting to meet coordinators from the other agencies and found the agencies had not begun to comply with the directive.

Concerned that FWP would not be implemented unless they pressed for it, the thirteen resolved to continue to meet, find out more about the mandate, and organize to ensure its implementation. By the spring of 1968, another ten persons, including one man, had been recruited for the effort. They met in each other's homes over the spring and summer and by fall conceived the organization's basic outline and structure.

Originally, the group named itself the Organization of Federally Employed Women, or TOO FEW. But, because it wanted to organize women in the lower GS grades as well, and because women constituted the majority of the federal workforce in the lower grades, TOO FEW seemed inappropriate. The new organization incorporated under the name FEW.

By the midseventies FEW lobbied for increases in the number of women political appointees and amendment of Title V to limit the preferential treatment of veterans, a losing battle. The passage of Public Law 92-261, which brought federal employees under the equal employment opportunity provisions of the 1964 Civil Rights Act, gave the group confidence to pursue these goals. Although the legislative arenas addressed by FEW varied, strong enforcement of current regulations and passage of new laws to help women achieve equity in the workplace have continued to be FEW's central theme. The 1990s are dominated by the same agenda FEW pursued since 1968: enforcement of existing laws for federal employees.

ORGANIZATION AND DEVELOPMENT

FEW has organized the chapters on regional bases. Currently, there are eleven regions, overseen by an elected regional manager who is responsible for coordinating chapter activities and organizing new chapters within the regions. The founders set up a steering committee, with one member from each federal agency to establish chapters everywhere there were federal employees. The first FEW chapter was chartered in January 1970 for the Central Cincinnati area. It quickly was followed by chapter formation in New Jersey, Alabama, and Chicago. Ultimately, there were chapters in thirty-four states, the District of Columbia, and four foreign countries, including Spain, Japan, South Korea, and Okinawa.

FEW is governed by a board of directors composed of national elected officers, chairs of standing committees, regional managers, and regional representatives selected on a proportional basis. The organization's administration is carried out by an executive committee made up of elected officers and chairs of standing committees. Several special assistants to FEW's president address specific concerns. There are special assistants in the areas of cultural awareness, the equal rights amendment (ERA), military women, persons with disabilities, and FWP. The current president is Jean Christiansen. Karen R. Scott serves as executive director.

A full-time legal and legislative staff seeks to ensure that the rights of individuals as well as of all women in federal service are protected and promoted. FEW's legislative efforts led it first to hire a full-time legislative director. In the early years, FEW's legislative program focused on enforcement of equal employment opportunity laws as well as on the provision of training and information programs that the steering committee believed critical if women were to achieve upward mobility in the federal services. Members pressured their respective agencies to set goals and timetables that President Johnson had suggested specifically for female employees. FEW also pressed for expansion of part-time professional opportunities, assessment of the need for child care in all agencies, and the collection of required statistics.

Under the legislative director, FEW's legislative activities are assisted by the chair of a legislative committee. FEW's full-time legislative staff monitors the federal agencies' policies and practices to determine if they conform to the requirements and, if they are found deficient, confers with the Equal Employment Opportunity Commission (EEOC) or the agency itself over the matter. FEW's legislative team primarily concerns itself with compliance by the seven federal agencies with statutes, executive orders, and regulations established to provide equal employment opportunity in the federal sector.

FEW does not publish its total membership.

FEW's annual revenue has varied from $200 to $500,000. The primary source of funding comes from FEW's training programs. Biannual training conferences are conducted at the regional level to increase women's knowledge of the system in which they work and help them develop career plans and reach their full potential in advancing their federal careers. Additionally, a national training program is held each July and rotates from region to region.

Focusing on the needs of federally employed women only, FEW established a legal defense and education fund in 1977 to provide legal assistance to individuals where questions of equal opportunity or advancement in government employment have arisen. The fund also undertakes research in areas involving government employment such as discrimination, training, and funding.

POLICY CONCERNS AND TACTICS

FEW frequently has been asked to testify before the Congress on issues of importance to its constituents and women generally, including the 1971 Women's Educational Equity Act and Post Secondary and Equal Employment Opportunity Acts, 1974 Health Service Act, 1978 Civil Service Reform and Veteran's Preference Acts, and, more recently, the Family and Medical Leave bill, 1988 Civil Rights Restoration Act, and ongoing initiative for ERA.

One way FEW has operated to achieve its goals is the establishment in 1979 of the Coalition for Constructive Modification of the Veteran's Preference Act. The coalition lobbied heavily against the inequality inherent in the preferential hiring of veterans over nonveterans, which, in effect, has made veteran status a prime qualifying factor for job applicants. It advocated changing the law to allow a one-time five-point preference for Vietnam veterans. During this lobbying effort, FEW hired its first congressional liaison.

Also during the seventies, FEW worked instrumentally to eliminate the two restrictions on women's employment in law enforcement: the prohibition of women federal employees from carrying firearms and the Federal Bureau of Investigation's minimum height requirement. Additionally, in 1975, FEW successfully lobbied to pass legislation admitting women into the U.S. military academies.

FEW is responsible for flexible work schedules in federal employment. In 1978, FEW lobbied for a pilot program allowing federal employees to work flexible hours within a day as well as flexible days within a week. The program was reauthorized for an additional three-year period in 1981. Its success resulted in the permanent authorization of flexitime in 1985. FEW's activities include a project on Workforce 2000.

Pay equity remains a legislative priority. Wage differentials between men and women in the federal workplace are due largely to outdated standards for assigning value, and hence compensation, to the occupations women traditionally hold. Federal legislation has been pending since 1984 to reevaluate the federal government's wage system; but the Congress has continued to postpone addressing the issue. Further, the discrepancy in annual salary for women and men in federal employment has improved by only 3 percent since 1976.

Another ongoing area of concern for FEW is concentration of women in the lower grades. Some improvement has occurred since 1968; but the majority of women (over 70 percent) remain concentrated in grades 1 through 6. FEW data showed the percentage of top positions going to women actually had declined: 14 percent in the Ford administration, 22 percent in the Carter administration, and 8 percent in the Reagan administration. In 1990, only 22 percent of all government supervisors were women, and fewer than 9 percent of all senior level executives.

In 1978, the Civil Service Reforms Act charged the EEOC with responsibility for approving agency goals and timetables in affirmative action plans. But not until 1978 did EEOC issue an order to move women and minorities up the career ladder, and it gave the agencies five years to shift their affirmative action focus from emphasis on hiring women and minorities at entry-level grades. FEW has maintained that giving EEOC another five years to accomplish something mandated twenty years ago is not acceptable. FEW especially is concerned that the government be a showcase for the nation in eliminating sex discrimination in employment and compensation. In early October 1991—just before the hearings began on Clarence Thomas's appointment to the U.S. Supreme Court—FEW published a pamphlet entitled *Combating Sexual Harassment: A Federal Worker's Guide*. The pamphlet was purchased by federal agencies as well as individuals, and within ten months was already in its fifth printing.

FEW has forged an alliance with EEOC. In 1980, it joined the steering committee of the National Committee on Pay Equity* and worked with federal employee unions on the issue of contracting work out. In 1984, FEW joined the Women's Vote Project*; and members succeeded in registering 10,000 new voters. FEW also has allied with the Office of Personnel Management, Department of Defense, and the Public Employees Roundtable.

ELECTORAL ACTIVITIES

Federal employees are prohibited from campaigning for individuals for public office.

FURTHER INFORMATION

FEW's News and Views is a bimonthly newspaper put out by the organization.

SUSAN DAVIS

FEDERALLY EMPLOYED WOMEN LEGAL DEFENSE AND EDUCATION FUND
See FEDERALLY EMPLOYED WOMEN

FEDERATION OF FEMINIST WOMEN'S HEALTH CENTERS (FFWHC)
1680 North Vine Street
Suite 1105
Hollywood, CA 90028-8837
(213) 957-4062
FAX (916) 957-4064

The Federation of Feminist Women's Health Centers (FFWHC) seeks to further the networking and communication of women-controlled clinics through loans, grants, and consultation.

ORIGIN AND DEVELOPMENT

During the early 1970s, a radical new approach toward women's health care led to the proliferation of feminist women's health centers. The hallmark of these new women-controlled clinics was education. Demystification of women's bodies and health care began with the self-help clinic. The clinics taught women to perform their own pelvic exam using a plastic speculum, exposing many of them to a first complete view of their own bodies.

In 1975, several of these centers founded FFWHC in order to coordinate their activities, promote and achieve common goals, foster improved communications, and pool resources. The group of women responsible for the foundation of many of the original feminist women's health centers—Carol Downer, Dido Hasper, Linda Curtis, and Lorraine Rothman—set the basic agenda and made up the original board of directors. FFWHC's goals remain the same: to secure reproductive rights for women and men, educate women about the normal healthy functions of their bodies, and improve the quality of women's health care.

ORGANIZATION AND FUNDING

Member clinics, which span the continent from Atlanta, Georgia, to Portland, Oregon, agree to meet as often as necessary. One annual session is dedicated to the discussion of global and national issues that affect all women. The annual meeting ends with theory and strategy discussions. Members make the commitment to remain in contact during interim periods through regular correspondence. Members also travel regularly as a group to conferences.

An elected council and board of directors steer the federation. All positions on the board are held by white women. The federation has one office, its headquarters in Hollywood, California. The executive director is Carol Downer.

The federation has no plans to change its focus from women's issues or its women-controlled status. Women compose 99 percent of the membership of thirty. FFWHC encourages participation from persons of color, older women, lesbians, persons with disabilities, and persons from lower-income strata. The federation gives the impression of a close-knit, if far-flung, extended family. Friendship ties, association with similarly minded persons, and communication with peers and colleagues are listed among the most important benefits of membership. Consciousness-raising sessions, conference attendance, and an opportunity to participate in public affairs, exercise influence, and function as an advocate and gain organizational skills and information also work as incentives to belong. FFWHC participates in the individual member clinics' community activities and provides extra support to members during times of crisis or difficulty. Member clinics regularly exchange staff, furthering personal ties and connections within the organization.

FFWHC has tax-exempt status under 501 (c) (3) of the Internal Revenue Service Code, and contributions are tax-deductible. In 1986, the council expanded membership categories from the clinics alone to include other women's health projects and individual supporters; the revenues generated by this mix of organizations and individual memberships range from $25 to more than $200. The remainder of the federation's income comes from book sales.

POLICY CONCERNS AND TACTICS

Policy is set by the executive directors of the member clinics, the council, and board of directors. Consultants are provided to member clinics on the malpractice insurance crisis, internal organization, administration, clinic protocols and standards, and clinic harassment by pro-life groups.

FFWHC's focus on ensuring reproductive rights for women has led it to play an active role in the fight to sustain *Roe* v. *Wade.* Individual clinics have operated on the front lines of the abortion controversy, with numerous attacks from Operation Rescue.* The majority are picketed weekly. In 1984, Los Angeles FWHC was bombed; in 1990, Redding, California, FWHC was a victim of arson. Thus, unimpeded access to abortion and to member clinics has become the federation's highest priority. In conjunction with member clinics, FFWHC has developed a network of volunteer escorts, gained restraining orders against pro-choice protesters, and won antitrust suits.

FFWHC has coordinated its efforts with numerous groups. It has worked together with the National Women's Health Network,* National Abortion Federation,* and National Black Women's Health Network* for fifteen years, promoting natural barrier methods of birth control, such as the cervical cap, and developing protocols for various practitioners, including lay health workers. The federation participated in both the Washington, D.C., and Los Angeles National Organization for Women* marches for women's lives. It considers the National Right to Life Committee,* Catholic Church, and Operation Rescue* to be adversarial groups.

ELECTORAL ACTIVITIES

Because of its tax-exempt status, FFWHC does not participate in electoral politics.

FURTHER INFORMATION

FFWHC has published three books: *A New View of a Woman's Body, Women Centered Pregnancy and Birth,* and *How to Stay out of the Gynecologist's Office.*

MEGAN ISAACS

FEDERATION OF ORGANIZATIONS FOR PROFESSIONAL WOMEN
See ASSOCIATION FOR WOMEN IN SCIENCE

FEDERATION OF ORGANIZATIONS FOR PROFESSIONAL WOMEN LEGAL DEFENSE FUND
See ASSOCIATION FOR WOMEN IN SCIENCE

FEMINIST ANTI-CENSORSHIP TASKFORCE (FACT)
c/o Carole S. Vance
Associate Research Scientist in Anthropology and Public Health
Sociomedical Sciences
Columbia University School of Public Health
600 W. 168th Street
New York, NY 10032

The Feminist Anti-Censorship Taskforce (FACT) has made a major impact on American politics. Its public education and advocacy efforts and the controversial nature of its subject have allowed this relatively small group of articulate women to mobilize and reach millions of Americans.

ORIGIN AND DEVELOPMENT

A group of feminist activists and scholars, in response to antipornography ordinances introduced in Minneapolis and Indianapolis, formed FACT in 1984. (The mayor of Minneapolis vetoed the bill, which was drafted by radical feminist Andrea Dworkin and jurist Catharine MacKinnon.) FACT had no single leader or chief organizer; key founders included Lisa Duggan, Kate Ellis, Nan Hunter, Barbara Kerr, Ann Snitow, and Carole Vance. FACT's founders wanted to educate feminists about the hazards presented by censorship of sexual imagery and the mistaken belief that sex discrimination will vanish if sexually explicit material is uprooted. They also sought to educate the public to distinguish feminism from antipornography activism and to recognize the diversity among feminist positions on pornography and sexual imagery and on the most effective tactics for fighting sexism and sexual violence against women.

Public opinion has favored acting on pornography but not been clear about what form this action should take. During 1984–86, FACT members wrote and spoke widely as various municipalities introduced antipornography ordinances. In Suffolk County, New York; Los Angeles; Cambridge, Massachusetts; Madison, Wisconsin; and Seattle, Washington, traditional morality groups endorsed the often-conservative legislators introducing these ordinances. Feminists organized successfully in each of these areas to defeat them. FACT sees itself as representative of feminists opposed to censorship of sexually explicit and erotic materials and favoring an expansionary and safe sexual culture for women.

ORGANIZATION AND FUNDING

Besides the founding New York group, chapters have been formed in several cities and states where antipornography ordinances were under consideration, including San Francisco, Madison, Seattle, Los Angeles, and Cambridge. FACT is a grassroots action group structured in a relatively informal way and so lacks elected officers, board, dues, or a big budget. FACT New York acts as a clearinghouse for local FACT groups.

FACT is not a conventional membership organization. It works with a large network of local supporters who participate in briefings, demonstrations, and events. Services offered by FACT that attract member support include publication, advocacy, communication with colleagues, research/information, and representation to government on these issues.

What funding the group has comes from small fund-raisers and individual contributions. FACT does not have tax-exempt status.

POLICY CONCERNS AND TACTICS

Policy and action are set through discussion and consensus. FACT ranks highest on political strategies: education through publications, organizing members to act, issuing press releases, doing research, and engaging in demonstrations and direct action. FACT also sees as important strategies testimony before government hearings, comments on proposed legislation, and lobbying.

A specialized information and advocacy tool used by the group is the amicus brief, filed in connection with a 1984 challenge on First Amendment grounds against the Indianapolis ordinance. The case was *American Booksellers Association* v. *Hudnut*. U.S. District Court for the Southern Division of Indiana judge Sarah Evans Barker found in favor of the challenge and against the ordinance, which defined as sex discrimination and, therefore, a violation of women's civil rights, trafficking in pornography (''the graphic sexually explicit subordination of women, whether in pictures or words''), coercing someone to perform it, forcing it on a person, or engaging in assault or physical attack because of it. The ordinance was a version of a law advocated by Dworkin and MacKinnon.

Many feminist activists, including Adrienne Rich and Betty Friedan, signed the FACT brief. It outlined the reasons these feminists opposed restrictions on sexual imagery and how such laws could be used to restrict information on sexuality, abortion, and birth control, as happened in the late nineteenth and early twentieth centuries. Allied with the American Civil Liberties Union,* FACT is not convinced that acts are affected by images and expresses concern that allegations by women to the contrary characteristically support victimology. In 1985, the Seventh Circuit Court of Appeals upheld Judge Barker's ruling that the Indianapolis ordinance was unconstitutional and the finding that even if pornography is harmful sex discrimination, it is protected speech. In 1986, the Supreme Court summarily affirmed the appeal court's ruling.

Despite the defeat of the antipornography ordinances against which FACT formed to mobilize, the issue of ''pornerotica'' is far from resolved. FACT members have continued to work to defeat legislative initiatives to limit sexual imagery. These efforts increasingly are sponsored by moral conservative and religious fundamentalist groups. Despite a lack of interest in empowering women or addressing sexism, the groups have tried to update their traditional antisex agenda by drawing on terms and arguments used by antipornography feminism. FACT has organized responses to, and spoken about, the U.S. attorney general's Commission on Pornography, which endorsed censorship on a broad scale, and about right-wing assaults on the National Endowment for the Arts and new efforts legally to restrict both books and images. FACT has attained such an authoritative position that public policymakers seek its help or comments several times a year.

Federal policy that FACT sees as of ongoing importance includes the equal rights amendment, *Roe* v. *Wade,* Hyde amendments, and a human life amendment. The 1974 Women's Educational Equity Act also remains important to it.

Three likely FACT allies are National Organization for Women* and the National Coalition against Censorship and Writers' Guild. Likely adversaries are the American Family Association, Women against Pornography, and National Federation for Decency. Internationally, the group is loosely affiliated and co-operates with other feminist anticensorship groups in Canada and England.

ELECTORAL ACTIVITIES

FACT takes no role in electoral politics and has no political action committee.

FURTHER INFORMATION

FACT has a newsletter for members and issues research reports. In 1986, FACT published a collection of feminist anticensorship essays, *Caught Looking: Feminism, Pornography, and Censorship* (4th ed., 1992). The *University of Michigan Journal of Law Reform* (Fall 1987–Winter 1988) published the FACT amicus brief filed in the *American Booksellers* case.

VALLAURIE CRAWFORD

FEMINIST MAJORITY FOUNDATION
See FUND FOR FEMINIST MAJORITY

FEMINISTS FOR LIFE (FFL)
811 East 47th Street
Kansas City, MO 64110
(816) 753-2130

Feminists for Life (FFL) seeks to eliminate abortion but otherwise to advance feminist policies. Each state chapter decides its specific policy agenda and tactics, so long as they fit pro-life guidelines. It has a separate education project, Feminists for Life Education Project.

ORIGIN AND DEVELOPMENT

FFL was founded in 1972 by two Ohio women, Pat Goltz and Cathy Callahan. At the time, both women belonged to National Organization for Women* (NOW). They met in a judo class and discovered their shared pro-life sentiments. Subsequently, one of them was expelled from NOW, and the other eventually left the organization. The idea of expulsion became central to the organization's mythology that it needs a special feminist organization for those opposing abortion because they are not welcome in NOW. The U.S. Supreme Court's decision, *Roe* v. *Wade* (1973), led to increased organizational activity by FFL.

The organization was fairly diffuse for the first decade or more, relying on part-time volunteer help. Subscribers received a newsletter; and a few chapters formed in midwestern states such as Ohio, Minnesota, and Wisconsin. A few sympathetic organizations, for example, Pro-Lifers for Survival, helped inform potentially sympathetic citizens. In the mid-1980s, several events occurred that led to increased organizational development. Perhaps most important was the articulation by Roman Catholic cardinal Bernadin of his "seamless garment ethic," which endorses life-sustaining policies "from womb to tomb." The seamless garment doctrine includes an opposition to abortion, capital punishment, euthanasia, and nuclear weapons programs and support for life-sustaining programs such as infant nutrition, prenatal health care, and so on. Liberal pro-life Catholics formed a number of organizations to support the seamless garment agenda, and these organizations in the seamless garment network proved fertile recruiting for FFL. In 1985, FFL got its first full-time president, Rachel McNair. At the time, the group had five state chapters. With full-time direction and a growing network of sympathetic political organizations, FFL grew rapidly.

ORGANIZATION AND FUNDING

FFL has a decentralized organizational structure, with thirty-six state chapters. New chapters form with help through technical assistance and with other resources from sympathetic organizations. In some states, new chapters have benefited from advice from a large number of pro-life groups such as the National Right to Life Committee,* which provided information on setting up tax-exempt status and the foundation. In other states, primarily Catholic and liberal Protestant peace and justice networks, especially in such pacifist churches as Quakers and Mennonites, have provided aid. The board consists of the officers and a representative from each state chapter. There are now two women of color heading state chapters, and so on the board. All of the officers and most of the board of directors are women. The board meets twice a year. The FFL's president is elected by the board of directors for a two-year term. The national office is located in Kansas City, Missouri.

Currently, the organization has 3,500 members, a nearly fourfold increase since 1984. Its members come from a variety of religious groups, with Catholics and various pacifist denominations strongly represented in the Washington, D.C., chapter. Approximately 80 percent of the membership is female. FFL feels disappointed in its success in attracting minorities to the organization, although some state chapters do attract women and men of color as members, and FFL seeks to develop outreach in minority communities.

As a nonpartisan group, FFL has tax-exempt status with the Internal Revenue Service. The organization is classified as 501 (c) (4). Most of its funds come from membership dues of fifteen dollars per member, with provisions for lower dues for students and others with limited means. FFL also sells publications and other materials. With other interest groups, FFL has negotiated an innovative fund-raising deal with the private sector. In this case, a long-distance telephone provider pays funds to the organization when the group's members sign up with the provider. The organization also has entered an arrangement with a company that makes checks. These come with the organization's logo on them, and a portion of the purchase price goes back into the FFL treasury. FFL is in the process of hiring a vice president for resource development to work on getting more grants from corporations, foundations, and so on. Presumably she will work from her home state.

The separate education project has 501 (c) (3) status. As a tax-exempt foundation, it can accept large donations but cannot lobby or engage in political activity. The project has organized Consistent Life Ethic conferences, and sponsored workshops in various states on the death penalty, racism, sexism, teenage pregnancy, and abortion. It has developed materials for high schools on sexual harassment awareness. It runs radio spots on various issues and develops booklets and pamphlets on policy issues.

POLICY CONCERNS AND TACTICS

The executive board takes responsibility for general policy making. The chapters initiate most political activity; state chapters differ in their priorities and tactics. The Minnesota chapter has actively lobbied the state legislature and written bills that sympathetic legislators have introduced. Other states have focused primarily on sponsoring forums and public debates, both with pro-choice feminists and with pro-life antifeminists. The Washington, D.C., chapter uses demonstrations. Some state chapters have made family leave a top priority, while others have focused primarily on abortion limitations.

A tactical effort in the large pro-life effort, the top priority of several FFL state chapters, is passage of Right to Redress legislation at the state level. This type of legislation would expand the grounds on which women who have abortions later may sue the doctors who performed them, for example, for subsequent psychological damage, and would allow family members to file wrongful death suits. FFL thinks that this sort of bill could pass in some states where limitations on the legality of abortion are politically impossible at this time. Because of the potential for such lawsuits, FFL believes Right to Redress legislation would drastically reduce the availability of abortion.

Besides family leave, FFL's set of official resolutions includes part of the "seamless garment" position, such as opposition to the death penalty. It also endorses boycotts of sellers of pornography and opposes sexual harassment and domestic violence. It opposes RU-486. It supports "non-harmful attempts at contraceptive control," although it opposes methods such as the intrauterine device that destroy fertilized embryos and pose potential health risks to women. The contraceptive issue is a bit more divisive than opposition to RU-486. The group's position on conception control is different from that of many pro-life organizations, which either are neutral toward, or opposed to, all forms of contraception.

Because of its feminist positions and generally liberal positions on issues other than abortion, FFL often is found in coalition with peace and justice groups. Part of the seamless garment network, FFL sees its allies as groups such as JustLife, a political action committee in the network. Who its adversaries are depends on the issue. On abortion, clearly it opposes the National Abortion

Rights Action League* and other pro-choice groups. On family leave, it more often has opposed conservative groups, including some that are pro-life.

ELECTORAL ACTIVITIES

FFL is nonpartisan, and does not involve itself directly in elections. It does not endorse candidates or provide financial aid. It has no political action committee. The organization does inform its members when someone from the organization runs for office.

FURTHER INFORMATION

The national organization publishes a quarterly newsletter, *Sisterlife.* Most state chapters also publish newsletters: Minnesota publishes the *Minnesota Feminist* eight times a year, and the Washington, D.C., chapter publishes a newsletter six times a year. In addition, members may subscribe to the *Monthly Greensheet,* a national publication that has topical information. Some state chapters also do small topical mailings. Finally, the organization has a recorded weekly update on issues that members can hear by calling (816) 561-1365. This is not a 900 number, so the organization does not profit from calls. Interested members are advised to call on evenings or weekends when rates are low.

CLYDE WILCOX

FEMINISTS FOR LIFE EDUCATION PROJECT
See FEMINISTS FOR LIFE

FOCUS ON THE FAMILY
See FAMILY RESEARCH COUNCIL

FOUNDATION OF AMERICAN WOMEN IN RADIO AND TELEVISION
See AMERICAN WOMEN IN RADIO AND TELEVISION

FUND FOR THE FEMINIST MAJORITY (FFM)
1600 Wilson Boulevard
Suite 704
Arlington, VA 22209
(703) 522-2214
FAX (703) 522-2219

The Fund for the Feminist Majority (FFM) seeks to further a national feminist agenda by encouraging women to fill leadership positions in business, education, media, law, medicine, and government. FFM works both to empower women and to influence public policy on women's issues. It has an educational and research foundation, the Feminist Majority Foundation.

ORIGIN AND DEVELOPMENT

Eleanor Smeal, a former president of National Organization for Women*
(NOW), founded FFM in 1987. A talented organizer and dedicated feminist,
Smeal also had chaired NOW's board of directors. Cofounders Peg Yorkin and
Katherine Spillar also were NOW activists. Spillar served as president of NOW's
Los Angeles chapter, while Yorkin gained Smeal's attention as producer of
NOW's televised twentieth anniversary show.

Driven by the belief that most Americans, male and female, are feminists
(i.e., advocate or demand equality for women in all levels of society), Smeal,
Yorkin, and Spillar founded FFM in order to educate, inform, and encourage
this majority to act in order to empower women in the workplace as well as in
government. Thus, FFM believes that the feminist majority already exists and
just needs to be mobilized.

FFM's primary goal, which has remained unchanged since the group's founding, is to inspire unprecedented numbers of feminists to seek leadership positions. FFM develops creative new strategies to empower women through action.
FFM incorporates these strategies into what it calls the "Feminization of Power
Campaign."

ORGANIZATION AND FUNDING

The board comprises minor officers and others appointed as a result of their
experience, activity, and dedication to feminist principles and goals. Approximately 10–20 percent of the women on the board are minorities. Yorkin chairs
the twelve-member board of directors. Smeal holds the salaried position of president. Spillar serves as FFM's national coordinator, spending a great deal of
time conducting research and traveling around the country organizing FFM efforts. FFM has a small, versatile staff. Smeal is assisted at the group's Arlington,
Virginia, headquarters by a professional staff of eight persons and an average
of ten to fifteen volunteers or student interns. FFM employs twenty additional
professional staff in Los Angeles and Boston, its offices other than that in Virginia. Those in the Los Angeles office are concerned primarily with direct action
organizing, while activity in Boston is centered on the Feminist Majority Foundation. Those working in the headquarters office experience some shifting of
duties on an as-needed basis.

To facilitate its establishment, FFM received financial backing, some in the
form of large contributions from a few individuals; it also received small individual contributions. Since its founding, FFM has received 10 percent of its
revenues from the sale of merchandise; 5 percent from fund-raising events such
as concerts, parties, or theatrical events; roughly 1 percent from publication sales
or advertising; less than 1 percent from foundation grants; and an unknown
percentage from gifts or bequests. Figures on FFM's total budget are unavailable. It is a tax-exempt 501 (c) (3) organization.

The foundation conducts research and publishes studies on chiefly health-related issues of concern to women. The foundation works in conjunction with over 2,000 scientists, deans of medical schools, and other health professionals in order to educate the public on such matters as the safety of RU 486 (the abortion pill), conduct research on breast cancer, and explore other matters concerning the reproductive health and rights of women. The foundation also publishes studies on the "glass ceiling" that exists in many professional fields, preventing women from rising above certain levels in the corporate and academic worlds. All in all, the foundation seeks to educate the public on issues critical to equality and women's well-being.

POLICY CONCERNS AND TACTICS

Policy is set by the board of directors, which meets on a quarterly basis. The decisions of FFM's executive officers serve as the primary influence on policy formation; board discussions and professional staff recommendations also influence this process. Strategies for specific problems are developed in a cooperative manner by the president, national coordinator, and key staff members. Among the most important strategies adopted by FFM are testifying in congressional hearings (mainly by Smeal), networking that leads to verbal encouragement of potential female candidates for office, offering information and advice to female potential candidates (although due to its tax status, FFM is prohibited from contact with candidates after they file), and participating in clinic defense demonstrations in order to counteract Operation Rescue* efforts to deny women access to abortion clinics.

FFM's main criterion in encouraging women to become candidates for political office is that they support the feminist agenda (i.e., that they are pro-choice and have been active in their support for across-the-board equality for women). FFM also encourages minority women to run for office. Party affiliation is of little concern to FFM; it does not matter as long as the potential candidate supports feminist issues.

A significant number of federal laws passed since 1960, ranging from the 1963 Equal Pay Act to the 1988 Civil Rights Restoration Act, are seen by the fund as having intrinsic importance to the organization and its goals, primarily because of their promotion of across-the-board equality for all individuals. Of similar importance are the proposed equal rights amendment and the Freedom of Choice bill promoted to reduce leeway given the states to regulate abortion by *Casey* v. *Planned Parenthood* (1992).

FFM identifies with organizations such as NOW, Planned Parenthood,* and the National Women's Law Center since they share similar goals and concerns. Identified as adversaries to the group's goal of empowering women are Concerned Women for America,* Operation Rescue,* and Lambs of Christ. FFM also cites economic policies promoted by the Reagan and Bush administrations as having been particularly devastating to women.

ELECTORAL ACTIVITIES

The nonpartisan FFM does not have a political action committee.

FURTHER INFORMATION

FFM produces the *Feminist Majority Report,* a quarterly newsletter. It also communicates via direct mail and provides organizing kits, fact sheets, videos, and books upon request.

SARAH SLAVIN

G

---/---

GAY AND LESBIAN ACTIVIST ALLIANCE (GLAA)
1734 14th Street, NW
Washington, DC 20009
(202) 667-5139

The Gay and Lesbian Activist Alliance (GLAA) of Washington, D.C., is organized to advance the civil rights of lesbians and gay men in the nations's capital. The Gay and Lesbian Education Fund (GLEF) is a related nonprofit foundation with a separate board of directors dedicated to educating the heterosexual population about lesbian and gay issues.

ORIGIN AND DEVELOPMENT

GLAA was founded in 1971 by activists who had worked on the Frank Kameny for Congress campaign in 1970. Kameny was an openly gay man who, in 1961, founded the Washington, D.C., chapter of the Mattachine Society,* the first nationally based gay activist organization. While the impetus for GLAA was based upon the political campaign of one individual, many took responsibility for the group's development. Along with Kameny, Paul Kuntzler and Joel Martin played instrumental roles in GLAA's initial development. They modeled the organization after the Gay Activists' Alliance in New York City but did not officially affiliate with that organization.

Throughout the late 1970s and early 1980s, GLAA continued its earlier activism by working toward such policy goals as obtaining civil rights protection for lesbians and gay men in the District, replacing repressive police practices, and ensuring more appointments for lesbians and gay men on local appointed boards.

In 1986, one of the earliest acts by GLAA's first woman president, Lorri L.

Jean, was to change the name from Washington Gay Activists' Alliance to the more women-focused Gay and Lesbian Activist Alliance in order to symbolize the desire for greater involvement and incorporation of lesbians and their concerns. In 1988, another prominent woman leader, Mindy Daniels, became vice president and then, in 1990, president. Under Daniels's leadership GLAA continued to increase the focus on lesbian issues such as child custody and the definition of families. Yolanda Inchauteguiz, a Latina and GLAA's secretary as of 1992, has worked to involve more ethnic lesbians and gay men in the organization by coordinating and working in coalition with other groups in the District and by working specifically on issues of interest to ethnic lesbians and gay men.

Although GLAA is over twenty years old, its basic goals have not changed. The civil liberties of lesbians and gay men remain the group's central focus.

ORGANIZATION AND FUNDING

In 1990, GLAA, with only the one chapter in Washington, had approximately 280 members. The organization is run totally by volunteers, although occasionally interns work in the office.

Approximately 35 percent of the membership by 1990 was female. The proportion of women had increased considerably since the seventies and eighties, when the membership was only 10 percent female. In 1990, when Daniels was elected GLAA's president, she was the only woman among otherwise male officers. In 1991, the organization's board of directors was totally white European. With the involvement of Inchauteguiz, the number of both lesbians and people of color on the board increased, and additional outreach efforts were made to incorporate more lesbians, people of color, people with special needs, older lesbians, and gay men.

Like any activist organization, GLAA finds funding difficult to achieve. Primarily based on small contributions from many people, 40 percent of GLAA's financial support comes from membership dues ($15 per person), 40 percent from fund-raising and special events, and 20 percent from gifts from individuals. The 1989–90 budget was approximately $15,000. GLAA was funded for only $5,000 in 1980 and $2,000 in 1971, so the group has made progress over the last two decades in generating revenue. As GLAA has a primary political mission, it does not have nonprofit, tax-exempt status.

GLEF, a nonprofit arm of GLAA with a separate board of directors, was established in 1981. While affiliated with GLAA, the organization is more an educational foundation whose purpose is to raise money and provide grants for efforts designed to educate the heterosexual community about the lesbian and gay community and its issues.

POLICY CONCERNS AND TACTICS

Characteristically political, GLAA's members seek to express their political and policy views through organizing toward a greater lesbian and gay participation in society. GLAA's origins from the early Mattachine Society and Frank Kameny's congressional campaign are present in the continued focus upon lesbian and gay civil rights issues, but the tactics have changed with the political climate and the growing power and sophistication of the gay rights and women's liberation movements. GLAA works toward its policy goals primarily through legislative and agency strategies, such as testifying, contacting decision makers to provide information, formulating legislative policies, and monitoring and advertising legislators' voting records.

Direct action tactics are employed depending on the direction of the existing leadership. One successful demonstration campaign focused on the Big Brothers organization and their discrimination policy against gays. In the early 1970s, demonstrations targeted at Big Brothers fund-raisers and other public events began and continued for over fifteen years. Finally, in 1989, the organization changed its policy to allow gay people to act as Big Brothers as long as the child's parents approved. Another campaign, organized in 1991, protested violence and abuse against lesbians and gay men by the police. After incidents of harassment and violence at a Halloween event, the community organized a successful "take back the night"-like event, the "Gay/Lesbian/Queer Walk without Fear" march.

Legal and educational strategies are less important to GLAA, while the related GLEF exists primarily as an educational tool focused on lesbian and gay issues and aimed at the heterosexual community. One significant GLEF effort was the 1991 Metro Bus campaign. This campaign placed antidiscrimination advertisements with the slogan "Every Time You Think 'Dyke' or 'Faggot' Remember, We Belong to Someone's Family. Perhaps Yours" on buses throughout the District of Columbia.

GLAA works primarily on issues of interest to lesbians and gay men in the capital areas. Primary among these interests in the past was the inclusion, in 1977, of protection against discrimination based on sexual orientation in the District's Human Rights Act under the home rule charter. Other issues have included continued work against the District's now-defunct sodomy laws, other vice-related crimes, monitoring of legislation in these areas, and relationships with the local police. At the federal level, GLAA's major concerns in 1990 involved family medical care, the definition of family, family leave, and child custody issues. In addition, many individual members of GLAA are heavily involved in coping with the AIDS epidemic; they work specifically on pediatric AIDS and issues involving women with AIDS (such as the Centers for Disease Control definition of AIDS).

To accomplish its goals, GLAA often works in coalition with other groups interested in similar aims. GLAA has participated in coalitions with such groups as the Gertrude Stein Democratic Club, D.C. Coalition of Black Lesbians and Gay Men, ENLACE (a gay Latino group), the Log Cabin Club (gay Republicans), Gays and Lesbians Opposing Violence, and the Sexual Minority Youth Assistance League.

ELECTORAL ACTIVITIES

GLAA is nonpartisan and does not have a political action committee. Its main electoral efforts are educational; the group surveys local political candidates and rates them on their stands on lesbian and gays issues. These ratings, published in a local gay newspaper, provide an important service to the lesbian and gay community in guiding their electoral efforts.

FURTHER INFORMATION

While the group does not publish a formal newsletter, it distributes a president's letter and periodic action alerts to its members.

GENIE L. STOWERS

GAY AND LESBIAN ALLIANCE AGAINST DEFAMATION (GLAAD)
150 West 26th Street
New York, NY 10036
(212) 807-1700
FAX (212) 807-1806

The Gay and Lesbian Alliance against Defamation (GLAAD) is dedicated to documenting and eliminating negative images of lesbians and gay men in America's media and raising the visibility of lesbians and gay men in television, radio, and the print media.

ORIGIN AND DEVELOPMENT

GLAAD was established in November 1985 during a period of intense press coverage of AIDS-related public policy issues in New York City. Starting in the summer of 1985, the *New York Post,* in both its editorial pages and news columns, waged a campaign against gay bathhouses—still open then in New York—and ultimately against a lesbian or gay lifestyle. With such headlines as "AIDS Dens in New York" and detailed reports of various sexual practices, the initial founders of GLAAD believed that the *Post* had created an environment of hate toward lesbians and gay men. They, along with members of the evolving Anti-Violence Project, pointed to a rise of hate crimes against lesbians and gay men in New York during this period as evidence of the *Post*'s influence. This new media attention followed years of invisibility for gay men and lesbians in the New York and American media. The refusal of the *New York Times* to include the word "gay" in its style manual, for example, was seen as a symbolic denial of both personal and political identification of lesbians and gay men. The first organizational meeting of GLAAD was held at Duane Methodist Church in Greenwich Village, in November 1985. Over 300 people attended. The meeting coconveners included writers Marcia Paley and Darrel Yates Rist and activist Jewel Gomez.

ORGANIZATION AND FUNDING

Initially, GLAAD was a volunteer advocacy organization. By 1991, there were over 7,000 dues-paying members of GLAAD based on a mailing list of 17,000 in cities throughout the United States, including Washington, D.C., Los Angeles, and San Francisco among other media centers. A board of directors representing a broad racial, gender, and professional mix oversees finances. In 1987, the first executive director, Craig Davidson, was hired, and in 1988 a more permanent staff assembled. Ellen Carton is the current executive director.

Funding through 1986 was based largely on contributions taken at GLAAD events and demonstrations or through benefactors. By the summer of 1986, GLAAD's revenues were $2,000. A direct mail campaign and explicit solicitation to large contributors were begun thereafter. By 1991, GLAAD was a tax-exempt educational foundation under Internal Revenue Service regulations with a budget of over $450,000, and a full-time staff of four and one part-time employee.

POLICY CONCERNS AND TACTICS

GLAAD's board oversees its wide policy goals. The board's policies are influenced by GLAAD members, with long-term goals and tactics drawn from both activists and media professionals. GLAAD uses briefings, demonstrations, media contact, and media support and serves as a sounding board for entertainment and news professionals in developing their story lines and news stories. It maintains a phone tree to inform members of particularly negative images of lesbians and gay men that occur in the media.

Since its founding in 1985, GLAAD has claimed a series of important accomplishments. Among these are the approval of the word "gay" for use in the *New York Times* style manual; an apology by William F. Buckley, Jr., for his article in the *Times* that supported tattooing HIV positive individuals; after litigation, inclusion of "Gay and Lesbian Organizations" as a heading in NYNEX-sponsored *Yellow Pages;* and, in cooperation with other groups, the pink and lavender lighting of the Empire State Building on Lesbian and Gay Pride Weekend in New York. (The lights atop the Empire State Building typically celebrate important days in New York. On July 4, for example, the building is lit in red, white, and blue; and on Nelson Mandela's visit to the city, the colors were black, red, and green. On St. Patrick's Day it is lit in the colors of Ireland.) GLAAD also has pursued greater visibility throughout the New York metropolitan area press of lesbian and gay issues and lifestyle. In the media capital of the United States, GLAAD's impact on New York-based media often is reflected in the national news journals, network news programming, and business press. GLAAD's greatest accomplishment, however, has been as a sustained resource for some in the entertainment and news media who desire advice on how to portray lesbians and gay men in a nonstereotyped and positive manner.

With little financing initially, the mainstay of GLAAD's tactics for several years was direct, grassroots political actions. The first protest sponsored by GLAAD was against the *New York Post* in November 1985. It received wide media attention. Early GLAAD activists pursued a strategy called "swift and terrible retribution," where demonstrations were called outside the offices of media organs that had published or broadcast negative images or remarks concerning lesbians and gay man. In addition, rallies and letter-writing campaigns were conducted. Many of those initially associated with GLAAD during its grassroots days were among the early members of the AIDS Coalition to Unleash Power/New York* (ACT-UP/NY) when it was formed in 1987. Grassroots activities remain an important aspect of GLAAD's tactics, with a 1991 boycott against WNET, the New York/New Jersey Public Broadcasting System affiliate, for the underrepresentation of lesbians and gay men in its programming as an example.

As GLAAD became more influential within mainstream media and more fiscally established, it broadened its strategies to include influencing media representation of lesbians and gay men at the development and production stages of entertainment and news products. It particularly moved toward obtaining positive imagery in television programming. These efforts resulted in the first, if hesitant, inclusion of positive and stable same-sex relationships on some network sitcoms and drama programs, such as NBC's "L.A. Law" and "Melrose Place," as well as daytime dramas. GLAAD currently is moving toward influencing advertisers to include positive gay images in their ads and for advertisers to purchase ad pages in newspapers and magazines primarily aimed at progressive women and the lesbian and gay community. A recent national print campaign by Absolut Vodka and inclusion of a gay couple in a K-Mart national television campaign are examples of success. In addition, GLAAD is concerned with the imagery of women in sports, the stereotyping in film of lesbians as violent, and the general representation of *all* women in media. It was at the forefront of opposition to the imagery of lesbians in the 1991 film *Basic Instincts* and has established "lesbian invisibility" as one of its major policy concerns for the next several years.

ELECTORAL ACTIVITIES

As a nonpartisan and tax-exempt organization, GLAAD does not directly involve itself in electoral or campaign activity. It does, however, monitor potentially negative and inaccurate comments about lesbians and gay men by candidates or the media covering the candidates. Local GLAAD chapters throughout the United States viewed and assessed local television and radio commercials where referenda on gay rights went to voters. The campaigns against a state equal rights amendment in Iowa and state initiatives against lesbian and gay equal protection ordinances in Oregon and Colorado were critical issues to GLAAD in 1992. In addition, GLAAD/New York and GLAAD/Los Angeles cooperated in a "sample specific" exit poll aimed at tracking the lesbian and gay vote in the 1992 presidential election.

FURTHER INFORMATION

The New York City chapter of GLAAD has established a *MediaGram* system so members can protest negative imagery immediately. GLAAD nationally produces several organs targeted toward different groups: "GLAAD Tidings" is distributed for inclusion in lesbian and gay publications across the country; "Naming Names" is produced and distributed for inclusion in broadcast, radio, and cablecast shows; *The GLAAD Media Guide to the Gay and Lesbian Community* serves as a comprehensive resource for media and public relations professionals.

ROBERT W. BAILEY

GAY AND LESBIAN EDUCATION FUND
See GAY AND LESBIAN ACTIVIST ALLIANCE

GENERAL BOARD OF GLOBAL MINISTRIES, UNITED METHODIST CHURCH
See UNITED METHODIST WOMEN

GENERAL FEDERATION OF WOMEN'S CLUBS INTERNATIONAL (GFWC)
1734 N Street, NW
Washington, DC 20036-2990
(202) 347-3168
FAX (202) 835-0246

An international service-oriented women's organization and the largest non-denominational women's club in the world, the General Federation of Women's Clubs (GFWC) unites and advances women's clubs' common interests in the arts, conservation, education, home life, and international and public affairs. It has a Women's History Resource Center.

ORIGIN AND DEVELOPMENT

In 1868, newspaperwoman Jane Cunningham Croly, the first woman syndicated columnist, founded Sorosis, a women's literary club that would "manage its own affairs, represent as far as possible the active interests of women, and create a bond of fellowship between them." Jennie June (Croly's pen name) felt concern for middle-class women's use of their leisure time. The New York Press Club's exclusion of women from a reception honoring Charles Dickens had turned June into an organizer. In 1889, she founded the Women's Press Club of New York and, on Sorosis's twenty-first birthday, in 1890, convened the national conference in New York City that founded GFWC. By then an influential eastern club, Sorosis issued the invitations; and sixty-one women's literary clubs responded. GFWC's purpose was to unite "women's clubs to enhance community service by volunteers throughout the world." Ella Dietz Clymer and Charlotte Emerson Brown were among the founders, Brown serving as GFWC's first president. State, local, and regional federations followed; GFWC's increasingly civic-minded agenda passed along a pyramidal structure inspired by the Women's Christian Temperance Union.*

In 1892, GFWC supported passage of an eight-hour workday bill for women and children and in 1906 again took a stand for working-class women, but the federation was not always working-class-minded and could display nativist sympathies. It also avoided admitting black women's clubs after two years of maneuvering. Until the National American Woman Suffrage Association hit its stride, GFWC was the largest women's organization in the Progressive movement. It grew from 20,000 members in 1890 to 150,000 in 1900. In 1910, it generated 1 million letters for the 1906 Pure Food and Drug Act. In 1914, it had 1,700,000 members. It supported civil service reform, conservation, and protective legislation and helped found the Women's Joint Congressional Union (WJCU) to serve as a clearinghouse for lobbying. In 1914, GFWC endorsed the suffrage amendment, eight years after it first was suggested the group do so.

In 1920, social worker and suffrage leader Alice Ames Winter became president and strengthened GFWC's lobbying role. Its issue agenda now included citizenship for women independent of their husband's, uniform marriage and divorce laws, prohibition, and establishment of a U.S. Education Department. Despite internal conflict, GFWC supported the child labor amendment, which was not ratified. It set up an active Indian welfare committee, which helped to heighten Native American women's organizational skills and influence. A GFWC letter-writing campaign helped pass the 1921 Sheppard-Towner Maternity and Infancy Protection Act. In 1922, Ames established an international relations committee. In 1925, GFWC belonged to a National Conference on the Cause and Cure of War.

An increase in literary interests and decrease in political action during the twenties did not deter Women Patriots in 1928 from accusing GFWC of being a Communist dupe that should have its charter revoked. To the contrary, the federation had brought many urban and small town middle-class women into leadership roles and self-awareness that otherwise they might not have achieved. In 1930, GFWC withdrew from WJCU but, during the Great Depression, fought a series of measures that in law prohibited more than one of a married couple from holding a government job and, in fact, deprived women of their jobs. It also protested wage differentials that appeared in National Recovery Administration codes. GFWC's extensive community-based interests brought into existence three-quarters of the public libraries in the United States in 1933, laws regulating child labor, and the National Park Service.

In 1922, GFWC had opposed an equal rights amendment (ERA) but by 1940 supported it. The amendment nearly passed the Congress one year later. In 1959, GFWC helped defeat moves to delete ERA from the Democratic Party platform.

It supported passage of the 1963 Equal Pay Act with the proviso that the act did not make ERA a moot issue. In the midsixties it conducted leadership training programs with the National University Extension Association Community Development Division. Another of its letter-writing campaigns helped get ERA out of the Congress and to the states for ratification.

As a mass constituency-based organization, GFWC plays a critical role in the polished U.S. women's organizational network that emerged in the seventies. It still promotes libraries, for example, through an "Adopt-a-Library" program with literacy-based concerns. In recent years, among other things, it began an alcohol and substance abuse program for women and young people and a youth suicide prevention program, with child care and the environment continuing interests. GFWC's international interests emphasize relief activities, projects serving persons in great need, and the arts. The U.S.-based international affairs department has cultural exchange, international understanding, and international trade and aid divisions. The latter includes support for international relief organizations and study of international trade and its effects on a global economy.

ORGANIZATION AND FUNDING

GFWC has 8,500 local clubs in all fifty states, the District of Columbia, and Puerto Rico. In 1984, it had 11,000 chapters; in 1975, 14,000. International clubs are found in Australia, the Bahamas, Bermuda, Brazil, Canada, Chile, Columbia, Costa Rica, Egypt, Germany, Greece, India, Indonesia, Israel, Jamaica, Japan, Korea, Liberia, Sweden, Taiwan, Thailand, Uganda, and Uruguay. GFWC board members are state presidents and junior directors elected to office on the state level. No information on the board's racial mix is available, but efforts are made to encourage participation by persons from lower-income strata, persons with disabilities, and older women. Board members' expenses to the delegate assembly are paid. The executive committee includes the president and president-elect, first and second vice presidents, recording secretary, treasurer, and parliamentarian. The international president/chief executive officer is elected by the biennial convention delegates, who also vote on resolutions and discuss programs and projects. Phyllis Dudenhoffer serves as president.

The organization opened a Washington, D.C., office in 1922 in a building that the U.S. Interior Department has since declared a National Historic Landmark. GFWC has six internal departments, each divided into multiple programs. It employs an executive director, Judith Maggrett, and a total of twenty professional staff, down from twenty-three in 1984. There is an intern. GFWC keeps an attorney on retainer.

In 1991, GFWC had 10 million members worldwide, 350,000 of these in the United States; in 1990 it had 400,000 U.S. members; in 1984, 500,000; and in 1980, 600,000 members stateside. In 1975, there were 11 million members overall. (Because GFWC has neither per capita dues nor an individual membership list outside the United States, these figures are based on average number of persons in those groups.) GFWC believes its membership decreases reflect increased numbers of women's membership organizations. Its membership is 100 percent female; and the organization plans to keep it this way. Members join primarily to advocate important values and for friendship ties, but also for information. Many wish to develop their organizational skills. Although in the eighties interest in volunteerism diminished, it has heightened recently among women taking early retirement and seeking to apply their marketing skills and among younger working women wanting something for themselves.

At its founding, GFWC managed with small contributions from many people. A 501 (c) (3) organization, its total budget today is $1,300,000; in 1980, it was $900,000. The increase largely reflects inflation. Membership dues provide 60 percent of revenues. The long-standing membership dues of $2 per person increased twofold to $4 in 1994; it was a hard-fought increase. Women also pay a membership fee between $15 and $100 to their local club, part going to their state federation. Affiliates' dues are $15–20. Besides dues, there is an endowment; GFWC has investments in stocks, bonds, money markets, and real estate. It receives grants for projects from corporations such as Shell Oil, Procter and Gamble, and Allstate Foundation. Corporate gifts or grants account for 20 percent of revenues. Five percent of remaining revenues come from publication and merchandise sales, insurance sale commissions, conventions, government grants, and individual gifts or bequests. The federation is in the midst of a five-year fund-raising drive, the Second Century Endowment Fund.

Located at the GFWC headquarters, the Women's History Resource Center, founded in 1984, has archives and a special collection library. Holdings range from local to international club records and statistics and from the history of volunteerism and the club movement to the Good Housekeeping United Nations (UN) Decade for Women collection. They are open to the public.

POLITICAL CONCERNS AND TACTICS

The GFWC convention adopts resolutions reflecting basic concerns of the day. It is the organization's most important source of influence on policy, although professional staff recommendations also are influential, and executive officers' decisions followed by board discussion play a role. Basically, GFWC develops strategy by consulting experts in the field, contacting other special interest organizations about working cooperatively, and then preparing a program design, for which it seeks funding. It alerts its clubs nationwide. GFWC supplies information to congresspeople and staff and, to a lesser extent, to state legislators and staff and monitors elected officials' voting record. It educates its members with publications and encourages them to engage in letter-writing campaigns. Sometimes it testifies in congressional hearings. To develop national publicity, it may field public relations or public service campaigns.

GFWC finds important to its present-day organization ERA, the Equal Pay Act, and 1964 Civil Rights and Equal Opportunity Acts. The 1965 Administration on Aging Act and Voting Rights Act remain of interest, as do the affirmative action executive orders, 1972 Equal Employment Act, and the act to add sex discrimination to the Civil Rights Commission jurisdiction. To GFWC, the most important new pieces of legislation of the last decade were the 1984 Child Abuse Act, literacy legislation, and 1990 Americans with Disabilities Act (ADA). It has used its numerous grassroots contacts to influence the Congress in these areas.

Recent issue concerns have included the Family and Medical Leave bill that President Bush twice vetoed and President Clinton signed, Family Preservation Act, literacy appropriations, highway safety (particularly, state legislation to curb drunk driving), state-level volunteer protection legislation, reauthorization of the National Institutes of Health bill that contains provisions for increased research on women's health and encourages women to enter health research professions, and ratification by the United States of the U.N. Convention to End All Forms of Discrimination against Women (pending since 1970). State federation women press not only for issues on which GFWC has resolutions but also for recycling and conservation. They actively support child welfare and many other issues connected with their volunteerism. The categories in 1922–94 GFWC project awards are suggestive, for example, solid waste management, energy, promotion of National Library Week, Elderhostel, promotion of ADA, a world hunger crusade, and highway safety.

For 100 years GFWC has worked in coalition with environmental and health care/aging organizations and groups concerned with crime prevention and drug and alcohol abuse. It belongs to a working group seeking ratification of ERA. A member of the Council of Presidents,* GFWC also works with the American Association of University Women,* B'nai B'rith Women,* Church Women United,* NA'Amat/USA, and National Woman's Party.*

ELECTORAL ACTIVITIES

GFWC does not see women's issues as partisan and has no political action committee.

FURTHER INFORMATION

Nine times yearly, the organization publishes *Clubwoman* magazine, with a subscription fee of six dollars, and it distributes legislative issues bulletins.

SARAH SLAVIN

GENERAL FEDERATION OF WOMEN'S CLUBS WOMEN'S HISTORY RESOURCE CENTER
See GENERAL FEDERATION OF WOMEN'S CLUBS INTERNATIONAL

GIRLS' CLUBS OF AMERICA
See GIRLS INCORPORATED

GIRLS INCORPORATED (GI)
30 East 33rd Street
New York, NY 10016

(212) 689-3700

FAX (212) 683-1253

A national network of local organizations, Girls Incorporated (GI) advocates for girls, fostering skills and attitude development so that they may become self-sufficient young women. It has a National Resource Center.

ORIGIN AND DEVELOPMENT

The first local girls' club, founded in 1864 in Waterbury, Connecticut, served farm girls working in mills and factories. Nineteen primarily New England and New York clubs incorporated in Springfield, Massachusetts, in 1945 as Girls' Clubs of America (GCA). GCA was a social and educational organization, seeking to enrich girls' lives by developing their homemaking skills. In 1960, the organization, under the direction of Gertrude DonDero, moved its national office to New York City. In that same year, the Western District office opened under the direction of Martha Newsome.

The organization's mission shifted in 1974, when Edith Phelps took the helm. Phelps was the first executive director to join GCA who had training for work with adolescents and their concerns. Under Phelps's leadership, long-range programming about alcohol abuse and pregnancy prevention started. In 1976, the organization joined the Collaboration for Youth. Members of GCA testified at congressional hearings on juvenile justice and youth employment, issues with which GI is very involved today. In 1980, GCA established the National Resource Center in Indianapolis as the research and planning arm of the organization. The group changed its name in 1990 to reflect the broad mission of helping women and girls in the 1990s.

Found primarily in urban areas, GI assists 250,000 girls and young women ages six to eighteen in approximately 125 cities. Alliances with the National Federation of Business and Professional Women's Clubs* and American Association of University Women* permit GI to serve an additional 100,000 girls. Fifty-six percent of the girls participating in GI-sponsored activities come from households earning $15,000 or less per year, and 53 percent come from single-parent families; 46 percent are members of minority groups.

The organization sponsors programming in a wide variety of areas, including prevention of teenage pregnancy and substance abuse and encouragement for girls to enter careers in math or science. GI's programs for adolescent girls are nationally recognized; many of these programs have received financial support from federal agencies and private foundations.

ORGANIZATION AND FUNDING

In local communities, local chapters of the United Way support GI, which is administered by local boards of directors. In 1990, there were approximately 200 affiliates nationwide. GI is led by a forty-three-person board of directors; Donna Brace Ogilvie is the current chair of the board. Hillary Rodham Clinton serves as the honorary chair. The organization also has nineteen honorary directors, including Marian Wright Edelman of the Children's Defense Fund* and Frances Hooks of the National Association for the Advancement of Colored People. The board of directors is chosen through a nomination process, with affiliates having the opportunity to support members. The organization strives to include minorities in leadership positions. The current president of GI is Alice H. Ball. GI has its national headquarters in New York City and regional service centers in Atlanta, Santa Barbara, and Indianapolis. It also maintains a Washington, D.C., office to monitor public policy issues affecting girls. The New York office develops programming and assists local affiliates by serving as an information clearinghouse. Approximately fifty staff members work at headquarters, including executive director Isabel Stewart. The organization has no paid lobbyists or staff attorneys. The affiliates are staffed by approximately 2,500 professionals and over 8,000 volunteers.

GI has tax-exempt status under section 501 (c) (3) of the Internal Revenue Code. Funding comes from individual contributions; grants from government, foundations, and corporations; and membership dues. Membership dues come from affiliates and are based on their annual expenditures. In 1990, the organization received $1.7 million from individual, corporate, and foundation contributions; approximately $380,000 from government grants; and approximately $358,000 from membership dues. GI operated in 1990 on a total budget of approximately $3.7 million. GI also received $740,000 from the settlement of a lawsuit with Boys Clubs of America in 1990.

Local chapters of the United Way support GI on the local level. Occasionally, local chapters have received grants to develop specific programs. For example, in 1985, the Omaha chapter received a $150,000 grant from the National Center on Child Abuse and Neglect to develop a national training program on child sexual abuse. GI of Santa Fe, New Mexico, has received three grants totaling $80,000 for programs involving substance abuse prevention and gang prevention and for Friendly PEERsuasion. The gangs of Santa Fe declared the GI center a neutral site, and the organization is attempting to resolve conflicts between rival gangs.

GI maintains a National Resource Center in Indianapolis. Besides serving as the most extensive information center on issues pertaining to girls in the United States, the center researches and reports on a wide range of areas, including drug abuse, pregnancy prevention, and education. The center is assisted by twenty-one associates who analyze programming and review research. Information is available to all interested comers.

POLICY CONCERNS AND TACTICS

The board of directors of GI determines what issues to emphasize by engaging in long-range planning. Concerns focused on by GI in the 1990s are generally continuations of programs started in the 1970s. The Washington, D.C., office reports on public policy affecting girls and supports issues pertaining to girls, including parental notification, choice, and juvenile justice. GI is monitoring the Women's Educational Equity Act as well as the percentage of women in the Job Corps. GI engages in little lobbying because of its staff size and financial resources. The Washington, D.C., office sends action alerts to affiliates to keep them informed about current policies. The Washington office is involved in coalitions such as the National Coalition for Women and Girls in Education, National Youth Employment Coalition, and Ad Hoc Committee on Juvenile Justice. Through these networks, GI pursues changes in public policy.

The issues GI addresses reflect the dramatic changes for women in society. In 1945, local chapters provided instruction in cooking and sewing. Over the years, the programming adapted to the concerns facing girls and the transition to womanhood, such as sexuality and career choices. Specifically, in 1981–86, GI addressed the issues of unemployment and poverty facing young women if they relied on men. As GI moves through the nineties, it is working to develop science and math skills in young women to help them achieve economic independence. GI has five major programs to assist girls in their development: Preventing Adolescent Pregnancy, Friendly PEERsuation, Operation SMART (Science, Math, and Relevant Technology), Teen Connections, and Sporting Chance.

Preventing Adolescent Pregnancy not only educates girls about sex but also works with their parents or guardians to improve communication about sex. Health Bridge, a component of the pregnancy prevention program, introduces girls to reproductive health care services in the community and also promotes awareness of other community-based health services, including dental and vision care. Teen Connections is another large-scale program designed to promote health concerns among young women and focuses on exercise, smoking, and diet. Sporting Chance works to build girls' competitiveness, encourages teamwork, and promotes involvement in sports.

Friendly PEERsuasion addresses the impact of substance abuse on girls' and women's lives. The program encourages girls to avoid the use of drugs and alcohol. Funded in part by the U.S. Department of Health and Human Services and International Business Machines, Friendly PEERsuasion trains girls aged eleven to fourteen about substance abuse; these girls then talk to younger girls about the problems associated with substance abuse.

ELECTORAL ACTIVITIES

GI has no political action committee because its tax-exempt status is prohibitive.

FURTHER INFORMATION

GI publishes an annual report, as well as a newsletter, *Girl's Ink.* Each of GI's programs is discussed in pamphlets. The National Resource Center publishes curriculum guides about its programs for use by affiliates. GI also sponsors seminars for affiliates dealing with program implementation.

SARA ANN GROVE

GIRLS INCORPORATED NATIONAL RESOURCE CENTER
See GIRLS INCORPORATED

GRANDMOTHERS FOR PEACE INTERNATIONAL (GFP)
9444 Medslead Way
Elk Grove, CA 95758
(916) 684-0394

Grandmothers for Peace (GFP) is an organization of grandmothers and other women committed to eliminating nuclear weapons and promoting peace.

ORIGIN AND DEVELOPMENT

Barbara Wiedner founded Grandmothers for Peace in 1982 in Sacramento, California. Wiedner decided to start the organization while jailed for protesting nuclear weapons stationed near her home. She felt motivated by the threat of nuclear war and her grandson's response to her protest: "My grandma loves us so much she's going to jail to save us from 'the bomb.'" Weidner realized then the important role grandmothers could play, giving their grandchildren hope and relieving their fears.

The desire to protect their grandchildren's future continues to motivate GFP members. In their Statement of Principle, the members proclaim that grandmothers worldwide feel fearful their grandchildren may not have a future. They trace their motivation as peace activists to this fear and call upon other grandmothers to draw on love and become active in creating peace through nuclear disarmament.

GFP's goal has been to protest against nuclear weapons and to work toward their elimination. To this end, members have worked on a number of related issues including a nuclear test ban. The organization also has sought actively to establish better ties with grandmothers and other women around the world, including the former Soviet Union. In partial reflection of their increasingly international focus, they changed their name in 1990 from Grandmothers for Peace to Grandmothers for Peace International.

GFP's most notable member and leader is its founder. Weidner's contributions to peace have been recognized in several ways. In 1990, the American Association of Retired Persons* selected her to receive its award as one of ten outstanding senior volunteers in the United States. She also serves on the Board of Directors for Women for Meaningful Summits.*

Since its founding, GFP has grown fiftyfold. Expanding its concern beyond nuclear weapons, GFP has had notable success in linking grandmothers in several nations in the cause of peace.

ORGANIZATION AND FUNDING

GFP has eleven chapters, mostly in California but also in New York City, Minnesota, Nevada, and Wisconsin. A Grandmothers for Peace group in Moscow connects loosely with the United States organization, as do chapters in Norway, Australia, and Africa. An eleven-member board of directors, appointed by the executive director, is almost entirely female and white. GFP is staffed entirely by volunteers working out of its one office in Sacramento. The executive director, founder Weidner, also receives no salary.

Composed of mainly grandmothers and other women but including a men's auxiliary, GFP expanded from ten members in the beginning in 1982 to 1,000 members and five chapters in 1986. By 1991, it claimed 5,000 members, eleven chapters, and 3,000 subscribers to its newsletter from forty-seven countries. The newsletter and the opportunity to work with like-minded women are the main motivations for joining the organization.

Sixty percent of the money to support the organization comes from individual membership dues of twenty-five dollars. Additional funds are raised through contributions from individual donors and other limited fund-raising activities. GFP does not have tax-exempt status; donations over twenty-five dollars can be considered charitable contributions if forwarded to the Agape Foundation with whom GFP has a working relationship. Besides the newsletter, the largest share of the money goes to fund the founder and executive director's representation of GFP at many peace summits and meetings. During the 1990s, the organization's financial difficulties sometimes have limited the board's ability to finance the newsletter's publication, but for the time being these problems appear to be resolved.

POLICY CONCERNS AND TACTICS

The board of directors, along with the executive director, who is a member of the board, sets policy and determines the choice of strategies to affect its agenda. Since its founding, GFP has participated actively in protests against nuclear weapons and the testing of nuclear weapons, although in recent years it also has concerned itself with stopping the war in the Persian Gulf, peacemaking in the Middle East, and redirecting national spending priorities away from military to domestic needs. A Statement of Action lists among GFP's strategies vigil keeping at military bases, munitions factories, and research sites and nonviolent civil disobedience as required. To this end, members have staged demonstrations at the Nevada Nuclear Test Site.

Another political strategy has been letter-writing campaigns. One such effort, directed to members of the U.S. Senate, supported the Intermediate Nuclear Force treaty. Another letter-writing campaign aimed at former president George Bush came in opposition to the Persian Gulf War. GFP also has circulated petitions to influence French president François Mitterand to stop testing nuclear weapons. To date, it has collected nearly 8,000 signatures.

A third activity, keeping members informed of peace actions, relies upon the newsletter. Through its subscribers, GFP cosponsors demonstrations, assuring itself that grandmothers have a visible presence. The newsletter also reports the executive director's travels to peace meetings representing the organization and grandmothers generally. Her trips to the Middle East and the former Soviet Union have been particularly notable.

ELECTORAL ACTIVITIES

GFP generally has stayed out of partisan political activities, neither endorsing candidates nor forming a political action committee. In 1988, it did make an effort to influence the presidential election through an apron campaign. All members were urged to send their aprons to headquarters, to be forwarded to the Democratic and Republican party national offices as tangible proof of GFP's commitment to supporting the candidate that members individually believed would find a way to peace.

FURTHER INFORMATION

GFP's publishes its newsletter, *Grandmothers for Peace International* (formerly *Grandmothers for Peace and Grandmothers for Peace Newsletter*), and sends periodic mailings to its members.

NANCY E. MCGLEN

GRAY PANTHERS
See GRAY PANTHERS PROJECT FUND

GRAY PANTHERS PROJECT FUND (GP)
2025 Pennsylvania Avenue NW
Suite 821
Washington, DC 20036
(202) 466-3132
FAX (202) 466-3133

The Gray Panthers Project Fund (GP), an intergenerational organization, focuses on eliminating exploitation, profiteering, and disregard for human needs in the U.S. political economy. It also seeks specific policy and programmatic reforms such as those affecting Medicare, nursing homes, education, and the criminal justice system. These interconnected issues are of immediate and lasting consequence for an older, predominantly female population. The Margaret Mahler Institute makes grants to persons over seventy.

ORIGIN AND DEVELOPMENT

Nearly 90 years old at the time of this writing, GP's official national convener Margaret E. Kuhn, otherwise known as Maggie, has played a key role in the organization's image and growth. In 1970, when Maggie and five female friends were forced to retire from their professions, they met monthly to discuss both their own situation and their overall societal concerns. Calling themselves the Consultation of Older and Younger Adults for Social Change, they organized initially to oppose ageism, including mandatory retirement policies, and the war in Vietnam. Preparing for the 1971 White House Conference on Aging, the group helped organize a Black House Conference, demonstrating the official meeting's lack of black representation.

Within a year the group, which included both retired people and college students, had grown to 100 people. A television talk show host interviewing Maggie in 1972 dubbed the group the Gray Panthers; and the organization officially adopted the name. In 1973, GP joined the Retired Professional Action group, a Ralph Nader Public Citizen Group. Working to reform the hearing aid industry, the newly expanded organization now included about 3,200 members. Incorporated as the Gray Panthers Project Fund, the organization convened a national convention in 1975 to approve Articles of Agreement setting forth its goals and elected national officers soon afterward.

ORGANIZATION AND FUNDING

Until 1972, decisions were made by the group as a whole during bimonthly meetings. The organization was loosely structured, unorganized, and informal. A swelling, geographically dispersed membership convinced the group to elect a national steering committee, later entitled the national board of directors, at the biennial national convention. In 1990, the board had twenty-two members elected by a majority of convention delegates and balanced regionally as well as by age and ethnicity. Convention delegates represent chapters and networks. The board's primary responsibilities are to select the year's issue program and devise strategies for its implementation. An executive committee consisting of the board officers and committee chairs conducts GP business when the board is not in session. Maggie is a permanent member of both the board and the executive committee. The current board chairperson is Charlotte Flynn.

Initially located in a Philadelphia church basement, utilizing a work-study college student as its only staff member, GP moved to various Philadelphia locations as it developed. A Washington, D.C., office was set up in 1985, but most functions were not centralized there until 1990. The *Gray Panther Network,* an official GP publication, and Maggie's office have remained in Pennsylvania.

National staff implement policies and programs. Full-time paid staff until recently included an executive director, office coordinator, secretary/bookkeeper, administrative assistant, and fund-raiser; but GP was down to two paid staff in late 1992. The executive director is Jule Sugarman. The *Network* editor works part-time at home. There are also volunteer positions such as informational specialist and student interns. Recently, GP recruited a program specialist as the group's lobbyist, a function previously assumed by the executive director.

Based on the principle of grassroots politics, most GP activity centers in local organizations, or networks. There are sixty-five networks located in twenty-two states and the District of Columbia. Press coverage of Maggie and the Panther media tactics helped the group swell to 27,000 members nationwide by 1981; it reached approximately 70,000 by the end of 1990. Despite serious attempts to recruit people of diverse ages and ethnic and social backgrounds, the membership is white, middle-class, and middle-aged to older. The paucity of African American, Hispanic, youth, and low-income associates concerns Maggie and the executive committee. A preponderance of women active at all organizational levels reflects the fact women outnumber men at older ages.

GP received nonprofit status in 1974. A 501 (c) (3), (4) organization, it receives most of its revenues by direct mail solicitation of members, as well as from dues, subscriptions to *The Network,* and publication sales. Sixty percent of the $20 annual dues accrues to the local networks. A limited amount of money is received from corporate or government grants. The total 1992 national budget was $250,000, down almost 60 percent from 1989. Maggie supports her own personal activities through speaking fees.

The Margaret Mahler Institute awards money to anyone over seventy for an unlimited variety of purposes. Individuals have received grants to go to school, publish, and even produce a song.

POLICY CONCERNS AND TACTICS

Local networks choose their own issues and tactics but work on at least one national Panther proposal. Specific requests to direct additional efforts to national questions are heeded. Local issues range from organizing older people in Grateford Prison, Philadelphia, to tutoring junior high school students in Denver. Developed in task force position papers, national Panther policies and programs—which convention delegates vote on as resolutions—guide the organization over the two years between conventions. In 1990, proposals ranged from changes in Social Security financing and improvements in public schools to implementation of universal health care and nonviolence in U.S. foreign policy strategies. Overall, the organization does not select mainstream policies; its purpose is to stimulate political leaders and other groups to move in radically new directions.

GP utilizes diverse strategies in order to influence local, state, and national policy. It has found street theater, including demonstrations, protest marches, rallies, and picketing, particularly effective in attracting media attention to its action agenda. GP employs traditional techniques as well: petition drives, letter writing, and telephone campaigns. Its leaders have testified at hearings, especially those held by the U.S. Senate and House committees on aging. GP encourages public debate by sponsoring conferences and hearings of its own, through publication and distribution of pamphlets and position papers, funded research (the Margaret Mahler Institute), and a national speakers bureau.

On several occasions GP has initiated suits against federal agencies. It obtains counsel through the National Senior Citizens Law Center and has filed amicus briefs, for example, in cases presenting issues pertaining to pension benefits and physicians' fees schedules.

GP always has seen as a priority a national health service to restructure the health care delivery system radically. Similarly, it has focused on ageism (e.g., the 1986 Age Discrimination Act) and lobbied to eliminate mandatory retirement, preferring flexible leave policies for everyone regardless of age. The group supported the Family Leave bill vetoed twice by President Bush and finally signed into law by President Clinton. Additional concerns include comprehensive housing policy. GP held three regional forums on housing and homelessness in 1990. It seeks redirection of military funds to such areas as education, mass transportation, and other social programs; judicial system reform; environmental protection; elimination of poverty and hunger; and full employment.

At the 1988 convention GP reaffirmed its support both for the equal rights amendment and for reproductive rights. The group also has helped its members participate in women's rights marches in Washington, D.C. Local networks have worked to ensure that states with equal rights laws enforce them. *The Network* offers continuing coverage of women's rights issues.

GP increasingly works in informal coalitions, including the American Medical Student Association, National League for Nursing,* Children's Defense Fund,* and the American Public Health Association. Issues that GP studied initially have fostered the development of separate groups such as the National Shared Housing Resources Center, Older Women's League,* Pension Rights Center, Caucus and Center for the Black Aged, and National Citizen's Coalition for Nursing Home Reform.* These organizations maintain close ties with the Panthers.

ELECTORAL ACTIVITIES

GP does not have a political action committee. It purposely eschews electoral politics so that it can focus on issues rather than particular candidates.

FURTHER INFORMATION

GP publications include the bimonthly *Gray Panthers Washington Report* and *Health Watch,* the quarterly *Gray Panther Network: Age and Youth in Action,* and *Gray Panthers Media Watch Guide.*

LAURA KATZ OLSON

H
/

LAS HERMANAS
Center for Women in Church and Society
Our Lady of the Lake University
411 SW 24th Street
San Antonio, TX 78207-4689
P.O. Box 15792
San Antonio, TX 78212-8992
(210) 434-0947

As the singular Catholic Hispanic women's organization in the United States, LAS HERMANAS seeks to maintain solidarity with the Hispanic community in its struggle for justice and liberation, instigating necessary change in church and society through action motivated by faith.

ORIGIN AND DEVELOPMENT

LAS HERMANAS formed in 1971 as a national organization of religious Hispanic women during a period of Chicano resistance. Two Chicana sisters, Gloria Gallardo and Gloria Ortega, founded the organization in Houston, Texas. These women were both members of religious orders and Chicano movement activists. They felt moved to action by the fact that the majority of Hispanics, particularly Mexican Americans, are Roman Catholic, yet the church did not then have a single Hispanic bishop. They also felt moved by the experience of young Hispanic women and men joining a convent or seminary only to find they were not allowed to work with their people. Historically, Hispanic women entering religious life in U.S. communities left their people and cultural identity at the convent door. The Chicana religious faced gender discrimination, church paternalism, and a restrictive view of women in Mexican American culture.

Gallardo and Ortega began their efforts by writing the bishop of every U.S. diocese, requesting the names of Spanish-speaking sisters in their area. The bishops' response was limited. The Leadership Conference of Women Religious* (LCWR) proved more helpful; and within a short time, the letter inviting women to come to Houston went in the mail. Fifty predominantly Mexican American women from eight states arrived in Houston in April 1971. These women represented twenty religious communities, and in some cases their religious superiors even accompanied them. Also represented at the first meeting was PADRES, an organization of Mexican American priests striving to organize ministries with Mexican American activists. The group decided to form a national organization called LAS HERMANAS and to convene its first meeting that November in Santa Fe, NM, the oldest Catholic diocese in the country. Gallardo and Ortega served as the provisional president and vice president.

Guidelines established at that first meeting determined the organization's agenda for more than twenty years. These include establishing an information clearinghouse to increase awareness of the Hispanic community's needs, working for social change, training members and community in leadership skills, and exerting pressure on the Catholic hierarchy. At the second national meeting in Chicago, during August 1972, LAS HERMANAS established a team form of government, drawing on the experience of women just returned from the Latin American Pastoral Institute (IPLA). At the early national meetings, the membership question received extensive debate. Initially open only to native Spanish speakers as full members in order to build their self-identity, since 1975, LAS HERMANAS has opened itself to all Hispanic Catholic women regardless of country of origin. In 1978, the first laywomen were elected to serve on the national team.

The IPLA experience helped to shape the agenda for Hermanas activities throughout the nation by establishing important Latin American ties. The national office worked diligently on Proyecto Mexico (Mexico Project), a project designed to get women religious out of U.S. seminary kitchens and into direct contact with people in the parishes. Hermanas felt deeply committed to promoting *communidades de base* (small group communities: part of the Latin American movement to promote political theological consciousness). The United Farmworkers received strong support at national meetings and in boycotts and demonstrations; LAS HERMANAS also took part in founding the Mexican American Cultural Center (MACC) in San Antonio and served on its board of directors in the early period.

Another group very influential in shaping the Hermanas agenda was Sisters Uniting. This group brought LAS HERMANAS into the mainstream of the Catholic religious structure and provided a forum for delivering its message. Through contact with the various groups of women religious, LAS HERMANAS began to develop its own feminist activist stance, today known as *mujerista*. As did private foundations, churches, and small contributions from many people, these congregations helped LAS HERMANAS get established by providing financial assistance. LAS HERMANAS identifies itself as a national organization of Hispanic Catholic women committed to a constituency of Hispanic communities and specifically Hispanic women, many of whom struggle economically. These are women of action and prayer (*en accion y orcion*).

LAS HERMANAS has worked to develop Hispanic women's leadership capabilities in order best to meet the needs of the Hispanic community at large and has supported Hispanic women in their desire to maintain and/or gain appreciation for their cultural identity and religious expressions and values. Increasingly, the group has focused on the Hispanic woman as the community's change agent and has brought a feminist perspective to its analysis. It deserves credit for contributing national leadership from Hispanic women's standpoint to theological thought. Today, LAS HERMANAS continues to provide a vehicle for the promotion and development of the unique faith perspective that Latinas bring to this nation and its churches. The organization nurtures an activism based on shared life experiences. This compels members to engage in the continuing struggle for the liberation of all people and the articulation of a prophetic vision that is given voice through the ministries of its members.

ORGANIZATION AND FUNDING

LAS HERMANAS has chapter affiliates in several states. A biennial delegate assembly elects the leadership and identifies priority issues; the organization pays assembly-related expenses for low-income individuals. All of the five- to seven-member board of directors are Hispanic women. An effort is made to recruit persons from lower-income strata, persons with disabilities, and older women to the board. The National Leadership Team includes Maria Carolina Flores, Dolores Flores and Rocio Salfur. The national office was located in San Antonio in 1988. The organization employs one part-time professional staff member.

Until recently, individuals made up the membership. Currently, membership is a mix of organizations and individuals. There are 700 members. Members all are women; and the organization expects to remain a women-only group. Members receive publications and information, attend conferences and meetings, and build networks and friendship ties, as well as advocate Hispanic values, ideas, and policies in church and society. Members find that LAS HERMANAS functions as a forum to express and advocate their concerns.

Forty percent of LAS HERMANAS revenues stems from religious congregations, 10 percent from conferences, and 30 percent from foundation grants, with the rest coming from membership dues and publication sales. Individual members and affiliates pay $20 annual dues; corporate members pay $200. This is a 501 (c) (3) organization; contributions are tax-deductible. Grants largely go for scholarships for self-development courses and training for Hispanic laywomen. Information about the size of the budget is not available. The organization typically has felt plagued by a lack of funds.

POLICY CONCERNS AND TACTICS

Based on indications of the national assembly, the board of directors with the national coordinators sets policy. Sometimes the membership is polled. Once LAS HERMANAS decides to become active on an issue, it seeks to educate the membership and asks for voices on the issue. Preferred tactics include giving testimony in congressional and state legislative hearings: supplying congresspeople, state legislators, and their staff with information; testifying at agency/department hearings; and educating the members with publications.

Within the Catholic Church, LAS HERMANAS has developed a tradition of challenging church officials. For example, in 1985, the national leadership team gave testimony to a consultation committee for the U.S. Bishops' pastoral letter on women about Hermanas perceptions of Hispanic women's oppression in church, society, and family life—concluding with a line from Matthew 7:9–12: "Would one of you hand your child a stone when they ask for a loaf?" The team then handed a stone to each bishop at the meeting, asking that the six place the stones on their altar when celebrating the Eucharist, in remembrance of Hispanic women's struggle. It has articulated the Hispanic women's agenda in meetings of, for example, the Women's Ordination Conference (WOC), challenging the racism of feminist organizations. It has joined such grassroots actions as a farmworkers' picket line at a local grocery store, challenging economic structures long inimical to Hispanic needs. It has protested U.S. Catholic institutions' exploitation of Mexican sisters as domestic workers and provided scholarships to encourage apostolic training.

Federal initiatives that LAS HERMANAS finds of continuing interest include the 1963 Equal Pay Act; 1964 Civil Rights, Equal Opportunity and Food Stamp Acts; the Voting Rights Act, affirmative action executive orders; 1968 Antidiscrimination in Housing Act; 1970 Food Stamp Reform and School Lunch Acts; act of 1972 adding sex discrimination to the Civil Rights Commission jurisdiction; 1972 Equal Employment Act; Title IX of the 1972 Education Amendments; the proposed equal rights amendment; 1974 Housing and Community Development and Office of Economic Opportunity Acts; Child Support Amendments—1975 Social Security Act; 1976 Day Care Act; 1982 Welfare Act; and 1984 Child Support Enforcement Act. The organization believes the most important federal initiatives of the last decade to be welfare reform in 1990 and the 1991 Civil Rights Act and day care legislation.

LAS HERMANAS finds the worst federal initiatives to have been legislation on low-income housing that resulted in drastic cuts, the 1980s Tax Reform Act, and general lack of legislation affecting the health care industry. It attributes these initiatives to supply side and Republican economic theories. It believes the initiatives of the eighties were worse than those of the seventies due to the growing gap between rich and poor people characteristic of the Reagan period.

Because LAS HERMANAS has limited resources, it seeks like-minded organizations to work with on the issues. Throughout its history, it has often collaborated with the National Assembly of Religious Women,* National Black Sisters Conference,* and National Council of La Raza. Among the other groups it works with are LCWR, WOC, the Religious Network for Equality for Women, United Farm Workers, and Network.* Hermanas were founding members of Mary's Pence, a Catholic women's organization to raise funds for poor women's needs, and the Women-Church Convergence.

ELECTORAL ACTIVITIES

LAS HERMANAS is nonpartisan. It does not have a political action committee, and historically has confined its political activism to issues of importance to women in the Roman Catholic Church and the social context.

FURTHER INFORMATION

LAS HERMANAS provides a quarterly newsletter, *INFORMES,* for its membership.

YOLANDA TARANGO

HISPANIC WOMEN IN HIGHER EDUCATION
See NATIONAL NETWORK OF HISPANIC WOMEN

HISPANIC WOMEN'S COUNCIL (HWC)
5803 East Beverly Boulevard
Los Angeles, CA 90022
(213) 725-1657
FAX (213) 725-1504

The Hispanic Women's Council (HWC) is dedicated to engaging its membership in development and maintenance of programs of direct assistance to Hispanic women and youth. HWC has an endowment fund that supports a scholarship program.

ORIGIN AND DEVELOPMENT

Like many women's organizations, HWC formed over afternoon tea. It evolved in 1973 from the Latin American Affairs Office in Los Angeles City Hall. Founder Cecilia Sandoval, executive director Lourdes Saab, Grace Martinez, Rebecca Sancion, Eva Heslington, and others invited speakers and arranged for food and entertainment at monthly gatherings, which helped coalesce a group desiring to unite to promote Hispanic women's interests.

Initially inspired by this general mission and without specific programmatic goals, the council operated for several years with a simple structure and diverted to other community organizations the small sums of money it raised. It ultimately dedicated itself to helping women through programs for Hispanic women and youth. Programmatic components fall into the categories of educational opportunities, leadership and career development, youth outreach, and communication-advocacy.

ORGANIZATION AND FUNDING

HWC has rejected invitations to establish chapters outside Los Angeles County in favor of remaining an active local force. Members gather in general assembly to take action on issues from time to time, depending on their seriousness and controversial nature. An annual retreat makes possible board training, enhanced networking, building community and members' organizational skills, evaluation, and planning. A corporate advisory board also assists the council in its work. A fifteen-member board of directors is elected for two-year terms. HWC encourages board participation by persons from lower-income groups. Committees chaired by a board member mainly implement programs. They include career development, education, and scholarships. The current president is Blanca Scot. Since 1981, HWC has had a salaried executive director, program coordinator, administrative staff person, and senior aide. There is an attorney on retainer.

Council membership is generally between forty and sixty working women, professionals, housewives, students, mothers, and grandmothers, with all members expected to be active on committees. The active membership always has been less than 100. A desire to preserve an inclusive approach to membership has led the council not to take an official position regarding abortion rights.

Twenty percent of the funding for this 501 (c) (3) incorporated organization comes from a combination of individual ($35), sustaining ($75), and corporate ($2,500) membership dues. Corporate and foundation contributions provide another 20 percent of the funding; net profits from an annual fund-raising dinner provide 60 percent. The total budget is under $200,000.

In 1976, the council began an endowment fund. It awards scholarships to adult Los Angeles County Hispanic women enrolling in a college or vocational school. Contributions from individual and corporate donors also support the Nati Cano music awards to talented artists.

POLICY CONCERNS AND TACTICS

A well-developed communication and advocacy program facilitates the projection of council issue positions through individual activity as panelists, speakers at public hearings, and meetings and advisory committee membership. Promotion of a positive image for Hispanic women is sought through both print and electronic media. HWC educates members with publications and encourages letter writing to legislators and committees. Public policymakers weekly solicit HWC's views on policy matters.

The council's compact structure and philosophy of direct assistance enabled it to respond quickly to meet needs generated by the 1992 Los Angeles riots. Its assistance has taken the form of aid to Hispanic families and advocacy. Special donations totaling $50,000 were received in support of HWC's postriot programs.

HWC finds important to its endeavors the 1963 Equal Pay Act and 1964 Civil

Rights and Equal Opportunity Acts, along with the Voting Rights Act and affirmative action executive orders. Also significant for HWC are the 1972 act adding sex discrimination to the Civil Rights Commission's jurisdiction, the 1974 Equal Credit Opportunity Act, child support amendments to the 1975 Social Security Act, the 1976 Day Care Act, and 1978 Pregnancy Disability Act.

A youth outreach program attracts Hispanic youth ages eleven to seventeen from low-income communities; it has as its aim to demonstrate the relationship among education, self-worth, and quality of life. The newest council program, a Youth for Education & Success group, started in 1987 for girls ages eleven to fifteen, emphasizes self-esteem, personal development, and motivation to realize self-potential. Older career and leadership development programs include women and work seminars targeted to low-income women entering or reentering the workforce, as well as to women seeking advancement to higher levels of management. A job fair brings together women from college and business environments.

Affiliation with the National Council of La Raza provides opportunities for expanded networking, as does collaboration with the National Hispanic Media Coalition. HWC regularly works locally with Comision Femenil* and the Latin American Professional Women's Association on issues of common concern.

ELECTORAL ACTIVITIES

HWC does not see its issue agenda as partisan and does not have a political action committee.

FURTHER INFORMATION

Hispa News, a quarterly newsletter with a circulation of over 800, highlights HWC aims and activities for corporations and the community at large.

KAREN M. KENNELLY, CSJ

HOUSTON AREA WOMEN'S CENTER (HAWC)
3101 Richmond
Suite 150
Houston, TX 77098
(713) 528-6798
FAX (713) 535-6363

The Houston Area Women's Center (HAWC) provides rape crisis services; shelter and counseling for abused women and children; and referral, education, and advocacy for women experiencing victimization. It serves approximately 80,000 women and children annually.

ORIGIN AND DEVELOPMENT

The major force in creating HAWC was a group of women concerned about a variety of women's issues who came together in 1976 through Nikki Van

Hightower, women's advocate for nonpartisan mayor Fred Hofienz. Formally incorporated early in the following year, HAWC took in an information and referral service begun under the civic group Women in Action. A source of data to educate government and the public, this information service became a vital part of HAWC. Initially, the center hired program staff and developed volunteer services without an executive director or administrative staff. After a year and a half of growth, Van Hightower became the first executive director; she already had served as the first president of the board.

In 1977, HAWC began a community education program, speaking to civic organizations and churches, and in 1978, opened a shelter for battered women. The rape crisis program, begun in 1980, proved the most difficult to organize because it had to open essentially in complete form with a twenty-four-hour phone and trained volunteers; it also was the most difficult program to fund. A number of women played key roles in the early development of HAWC programs—Toby Myers with the shelter, Adelyn Bernstein in the referral service and rape crisis center, and Susan MacManus in finance. HAWC contributed to the development of similar programs in the area. It began a now-independent women's shelter in Montgomery County and provided technical assistance in beginning shelters in Galveston and Pasadena and a rape crisis center in Fort Bend County. Clients began the Formerly Battered Women's Coalition.

In the first years, HAWC had to overcome at least four major problems: a significant turnover in participants as some found they preferred acting alone or felt loyalty to an old organization; conflict between the organizers' strong feminist perspective and practical necessities such as raising funds in a conservative southern community; an inability to fit programs such as treating alcoholism, which has many causes not specific to women, into the center; and problems inherent in establishing any organization, such as raising money and combining volunteer and paid staff. It took two to three years to establish the organization firmly.

The core of early movers were Anglo women, and for several years, despite effort, HAWC did not attract strong involvement, either as leaders or clients, from the minority community. Minority women served on the boards but generally did not stay long. Many from the Hispanic and Jewish communities believed that abuse was not a problem in their community. The center now has staff positions aimed at outreach to Hispanic and African American communities, and its clientele has become more a cross-section of the Houston population. One-quarter of the clients are Hispanic.

Education and advocacy, information and referral, aid to domestic violence victims, and rape crisis assistance have become central to the organization. Since its creation, HAWC has changed its approach somewhat. It now does less advocacy and focuses more on service provision. Originally the center sought to help women decide what they should do; now it seeks to empower women to make their own decisions.

ORGANIZATION AND FUNDING

HAWC is governed by a thirty-two-member board of directors, which sets general policy and selects a full-time paid executive director to provide day-to-day direction. Over time, women have been 75–80 percent of board members, Hispanics and African Americans about 15 percent each, and Anglos about 70 percent. Most board members are affluent, although some lower-income persons have served, along with some with disabilities, a substantial number of older women, and a number of lesbians. In 1994, Caroline Vetterling served as board president and Ellen Cohen as executive director. In 1994, the center had fifty-eight paid staff and approximately 500 volunteers.

Membership is primarily a fund-raising device, and members do not play a formal role in governance. Members and volunteers are primarily women, although the center never has wanted to be seen as a women-only organization. Because of the nature of its programs, all its clients outside education and information are women and children.

The Houston and Brown Foundations, Women in Action, Women's Club of Houston, and the University of Texas School of Public Health made important contributions of money or space in the center's early years. HAWC's budget grew from $467,694 in 1981 to 1,924,625 in 1994. Funds come from three principal sources: in 1994, 24 percent from United Way, 27 percent from government grants and contracts, and 49 percent from contributions, grants, and membership dues of $25. Additionally, HAWC receives volunteer services worth approximately $1 million per year. HAWC has tax-exempt 501 (c) (3) status, and contributions are tax-deductible. A development department does planning and fund-raising. A thrift shop sells donated items to the public.

POLICY CONCERNS AND TACTICS

The board has overall policy responsibility. The executive director is a key figure in policy development; staff and volunteer input is quite important; and programs often have considerable independence, although less presently than earlier in the center's history. Suggestions generally come to, or originate with, the director. She passes them to a public policy committee made up of staff, board members, and members at large. The committee makes recommendations to an executive committee and the board. Individual programs have councils, which vary greatly in strength and actual role.

The organization has gained media recognition for its expertise. Political leaders often call for information and response to events. In cooperation with groups such as Aid to Victims of Domestic Abuse, the Texas Council on Family Violence, and National Coalition against Sexual Assault, the center lobbies the Texas legislature and local government agencies. In 1991, for example, it was instrumental in creating a coalition to lobby for changes in the Texas family code to provide prompt and more uniform court handling of abuse in custody and visitation cases. Respondents credit the center with a major role in the improvement of the Houston Police Department's handling of sexual assault and domestic violence. The organization feels particularly proud of the increased willingness of women victims of violence in Houston to speak out. The group has experienced no consistent, organized opposition, although it has occasional conflict with antichoice groups that see it as pro-choice and with fundamentalist religious groups that advocate male domination of women.

In 1994 HAWC's programs dealing with domestic violence and sexual assault included the following:

—A 45-bed shelter for abused women and their children, providing emergency housing to 850 clients;

—Non-resident services, which counsel battered women and children not living in a HAWC shelter and that helped 1,156 clients to identify and utilize community resources;

—A rape crisis center operating a 24-hour emergency hotline, which answers 285 calls a month and that accompanies rape survivors through the hospital and criminal justice systems and provides counseling for survivors, family, and friends totalling 1,597 new clients;

—The Houston Area Women's Center Hotline, which offers over 1,000 referral resources in over fifty-three categories such as legal, counseling, health and emergency housing, and that handles 30,896 calls annually.

A community education program provides in-service training for police, medical personnel, and clergy, and a speakers bureau.

ELECTORAL ACTIVITIES

HAWC does not believe that rape and domestic violence issues are partisan in nature. Further, a partisan approach probably would harm service delivery by impeding volunteer recruitment and fund-raising. HAWC has no political action committee, deals with both political parties, and makes no endorsements.

FURTHER INFORMATION

HAWC publishes a quarterly newsletter, *Catalyst,* and brochures on a variety of topics, such as sexual assault, child abuse, services available to women and children, and HAWC programs. Publications are increasingly available in English and Spanish.

ROBERT E. BILES

I
/

INDIAN WOMEN IN PROGRESS (IWP)
P.O. Box 805
3404 S. McClintock
Tempe, AZ 85282
(602) 829-7221

Indian Women in Progress (IWP) is an intertribal group. Its core activities have involved the enhancement and survival of Indian ways.

ORIGIN AND DEVELOPMENT

IWP began to be active in 1979 in New Mexico and Arizona. It is an example of a minority women's network that has worked on a variety of issues and projects without creating a bureaucracy and without waiting for stable funding. Outside of tribes, intertribal women's organizations in Arizona include two National American Indian Women's Association chapters (NAIWA), the One Feather Network, IWP, and other occupationally related groups. NAIWA is an intertribal organization with decentralized chapters in each state. The presence of two NAIWA groups in Arizona involves differences in leadership and linkages. One NAIWA group remains affiliated through the national organization, while the second NAIWA incorporated as an Arizona organization. The One Feather group provides support for Indian women working in non-Indian institutions.

Native American organizations face some environmental factors that are different from those faced by other kinds of women's organizations. The indigenous American Indian factors that account for the differences include the following: American Indian women are comparatively the farthest removed from the mainstream middle-class organizational environments; Indian environments include diverse tribal structures in addition to challenges of ethnicity, class, and gender; they have to deal with the politics, policies, and issues of incredibly complex sets of federal-state-tribal intergovernmental relations, which also vary with reservation/off-reservation and other analogous distinctions.

Indian women's organizations in Arizona are part of a very large group of Indian tribal and intertribal organizations serving the large, diverse reservation and off-reservation state Indian population. The twenty-one tribes of Arizona each have women's groups with diverse functions, personalities, and organizational features. Women's groups' influence is tribe-specific since the cultural authority patterns of tribes vary. Indian Women in Progress has been influential in articulating issues of cultural survival in key areas of resources, education, and the arts in Arizona.

ORGANIZATION AND FUNDING

Many Indian organizations involve networks rather than formal mainstream features of charters, bylaws, and structures. This does not always minimize their effectiveness, which depends on other factors as well as resources, objectives, and will. Thus, IWP remained unincorporated in its early years. It has moved toward incorporation since 1990. The group's president is Jean Hoktilusteel/Hill Chaudhuri of the Musogee/Creek tribe.

Group members have come from many tribes, including Navajos, Apaches, Pueblos, Pimas, Yaquis, Choctaws, Sioux, Chippewas, Cherokees, and Creeks. There have been both reservation and off-reservation Indians involved in the group's activity.

POLICY CONCERNS AND TACTICS

IWP minimizes involvement in any regular service delivery systems and, therefore, does not duplicate the work of tribal entities or urban Indian centers. The organization prefers to be involved, selectively, in key public policy and public educational issues. It also produces plays, dances, and traditional storytelling and is involved selectively in counseling, particularly for, but not limited to, women.

Recent organizational involvements can illustrate the organization's nature. Since 1987, IWP has worked with issues surrounding the closing of the U.S. Indian Affairs Bureau boarding school in Phoenix, the 106-acre Phoenix Indian School. IWP provided tutoring in math, English, and several other subjects to students for about a two-year period. It also first tried to prevent the school's closing. Although boarding schools in Indian country are things of the past, the school's abrupt closing resulted in the dislocation of services to several groups: students from the tribes without high schools of their own, students from broken homes, and others needing special attention. IWP was not successful in preventing the school's closing but was successful in postponing it by a year, allowing more time for adjustments.

IWP then opposed the backdoor decision making whereby the approximately

106 choice acres of urban property were being taken out of Indian education and about to be placed in the hands of the Barron Collier organization, a private developer from Florida, in return for limited governmental control of surface rights to Collier swampland in Florida. IWP picked up the support of the Sierra Club and several other concerned groups. Although the group aligned itself against the entire congressional delegation of Arizona and part of Florida, IWP was able to mobilize considerable public opposition to the complex land swap, which was supposed to be a done deal from the beginning.

The Congress approved a swap in 1988, but IWP's work assisted in the movement toward Phoenix's retaining the right to create a public park on the 106 acres. Since this partial victory, IWP's energies have turned toward controlled usage that there might be a meaningful, active, and ongoing Indian heritage center as part of the property.

Apart from the Phoenix Indian School preservation project, IWP put on a four-day festival in the quinticentennial year in order to celebrate 500 years of Indian giving to the world. This was *not* a celebration of Columbus's contributions to genocide. The four-day festival included a musical comedy and satire titled *Indians Discover Christopher Columbus.* IWP festival activities included demonstrations of various forms of Indian talent and a mock trial of Columbus staged by law students.

IWP also has organized medicine men's conventions and sweat lodge ceremonies for women and engaged in sustained advocacy of improved spiritual counseling for Indians caught up in the Arizona correctional system. IWP has put on other plays besides the satire on Columbus and has been involved in traditional Indian storytelling with full songs, music, costumes, and other accompaniments.

The group has been nondiscriminatory in its alliances with Anglos, Hispanics, and blacks sharing similar goals.

ELECTORAL ACTIVITIES

IWP does not see Native American women's issues as partisan and does not have a political action committee.

FURTHER INFORMATION

At this time IWP has no publications for public dissemination.

                                                            JOYOTPAUL CHAUDHURI

INSTITUTE FOR WOMEN'S POLICY RESEARCH (IWPR)
1400 20th Street, NW
Suite 104
Washington, DC 20036
(202) 785-5100

The Institute for Women's Policy Research (IWPR) produces high-quality research supportive of policy initiatives undertaken by advocacy organizations.

ORIGIN AND DEVELOPMENT

In 1987, Heidi Hartmann, an economist, and Teresa Odendahl, an anthropologist, wanted to start a new policy-focused women's research organization. They wrote and circulated a proposal for seed money to the Ford, Carnegie, Rockefeller, and MacArthur foundations.

The launching of IWPR in 1987 culminated several years of discussion and attempts by women's groups around the country to fill their research needs. As the need for an organization to respond to the need for women-centered, policy-oriented research became clearer, Hartmann and Odendahl set out to determine the consensus of colleagues and the women's community at large. In a series of meetings, organized by IWPR and a variety of cohosts, including the Pettus Crowe Foundation, American Council on Education,* Villers Foundation, Boston Foundation, National Institute for Women of Color* (NIWC), Sophia Fund, Shalan Foundation, and Abelard Foundation, women recounted legislation, litigation, and policy developments where gaps in research and information were filled too late or not at all. For example, the National Committee on Pay Equity* (NCPE) cited the need for an institution with the technical skills to analyze raw data and critique reports published by government agencies or other services, because these may be misleading on ideas critical to women's economic success.

With these objectives in mind, the founders formed a steering committee of about ten women. This group included representatives from the Organization of Pan Asian American Women, NIWC, National Displaced Homemakers Association (NDHA), National Organization for Women Legal Defense and Education Fund* (NOW-LDEF) and the NOW-LDEF Project on Equal Education Rights,* and NCPE. The committee guided the organization through incorporation. A board of directors formed in December 1987.

IWPR formed to bridge the gap between women's scholarship and practical social change projects, produce and disseminate research for the women's liberation movement and other progressive social change groups, make research accessible to women advocates, and advance social change by providing solid, credible research that policymakers listen to. IWPR specializes in the use of quantitative techniques that help advocates and policymakers understand costs and benefits in terms their impact on people, especially women and their children.

ORGANIZATION AND FUNDING

All of the officers are women, as are 92 percent of the board members. While the majority of board members are white, there is an effort to recruit women of color. IWPR also does outreach to lesbians and older women. The board is self-perpetuating, with current members recruiting new members. The board elects the officers; Anna Padia chairs the board. The board breaks down into three committees: executive, personnel, and research.

The institute has a Washington office, which opened in November 1987. Hartmann has served as executive director since the institute was formed. There are four other paid staff members: one director of research, one research associate, and two research assistants. Since the institute is a research organization, it does not rely on volunteers. It has four interns at a time. These interns stay for a school year, or nine months.

IWPR has 700 members. From the beginning, women have constituted 90 percent of the membership. They pay dues in order to be on the mailing list and to receive quarterly mailings, which include research notes, research briefs, and other research materials. Annual dues are $50 for an individual, $100 for corporations, and $100 for affiliates.

About 700 individuals donate money each year. In 1987, the organization had a budget of $75,000. In 1991, that budget had grown to $500,000. The institute has tax-exempt status under the Internal Revenue Code section 501 (c) (3). Sixty percent of its revenues comes from foundation grants, 20 percent from membership dues and gifts or bequests from individuals, and 20 percent from grants or contracts from government agencies.

POLICY CONCERNS AND TACTICS

The board, program advisory committee, executive officers, and professional staff all influence organizational policy and choice of strategies to implement it. IWPR considers itself interested in all political activities that concern women's issues. Major issues that have concerned IWPR in recent years have included the 1978 Pregnancy Disabilities Act, the Family and Medical Leave (FML) bill that President Bush vetoed twice and President Clinton signed, and 1991 Civil Rights Act.

IWPR figures out what research advocates/policymakers need and then provides it. Staff members testify in congressional and state legislative hearings; supply congresspeople, state legislators, and staff with information; make personnel presentations to congresspeople, agency heads, and staff; educate the public through press releases and fact sheets; and conduct and publish research on major social issues such as women in the workforce, health care, housing, and child care. Sometimes institute staff testify at agency/department hearings and offer written comments on proposed regulations.

IWPR considers itself unique because it works closely with advocacy groups to produce or disseminate research to support specific policy initiatives. IWPR's work on FML demonstrates the manner in which it proceeds. Released in both a full report and an executive summary, *Unnecessary Losses: Costs to Americans of the Lack of Funding and Medical Leave* found that women, families, and taxpayers bear large costs in the absence of leave, including earning losses and increased costs for unemployment compensation, welfare payments, Supplemental Security Income, and so forth. Advocates and policymakers such as the media, the Congress, the Coalition on the Homeless, and political candidates have used IWPR's findings widely to continue informed national and state policy debates on family and medical leave.

At the national level, IWPR testified on FML before the Senate Children, Families, Drugs and Alcohol Subcommittees of the Labor and Human Resources Committee. The institute had its report delivered to every member of the Congress before the votes on FML. Locally, IWPR testified before the Housing and Economic Development Committee, District of Columbia, to support a proposed district bill. The Maryland Citizen Action Coalition used IWPR estimates in its testimony before the Maryland Assembly committee. The Massachusetts Nurses' Association used specifically designed IWPR estimates on the cost of not having paid parental leave in its testimony before that state's Disability and Dependent Care Commission.

In coordinating with similar organizations, IWPR works not only with advocacy groups but also sometimes with other research groups. It has worked with organizations such as NCPE, NIWC, and NDHA.

ELECTORAL ACTIVITIES

A research institute, IWPR does not engage in electoral politics, nor does it see women's issues as partisan ones. It does not have a political action committee.

FURTHER INFORMATION

IWPR has put out publications in such areas as family and medical leave; work, family, and health issues; employment equity issues; women and poverty; women, housing, and homelessness; child care; and young women.

MARY LOU KENDRIGAN

INTERCITY COMMITTEE ON THE DAY CARE OF CHILDREN
See DAY CARE COUNCIL OF AMERICA

INTERDEPARTMENTAL COMMITTEE ON THE STATUS OF WOMEN
See CITIZEN'S ADVISORY COUNCIL ON THE STATUS OF WOMEN

INTERNATIONAL LADIES' GARMENT WORKERS' UNION (ILGWU)
1710 Broadway
New York, NY 10019
(212) 265-7000
FAX (212) 765-3298

The International Ladies' Garment Workers' Union (ILGWU) has set many precedents in the U.S. labor movement in providing services to its predominantly female membership. ILGWU was the first union to provide education programs for its members; it also established the first union-sponsored health center, pension plan, immigration program, and vacation facilities for members and their families. It has a Campaign Committee and participates in endorsements by the Committee on Political Education* (COPE).

ORIGIN AND DEVELOPMENT

Neither organized by women nor seeking expressly to promote women's interests, immigrant workers laboring in New York City sweatshops founded ILGWU in 1900. The small group of cloak makers, all male, started a movement to organize in an era when the garment industry was notorious for poor wages and working conditions. Garment workers often have come from the ranks of the most recent immigrants. Whole immigrant families worked night and day sewing garments in dimly lit, poorly ventilated tenements. Fifteen hours a day were typical and even longer during the busiest seasons. If industrial homemakers did not work weekends and holidays when asked, jobbers (subcontractors) quit sending them work.

In garment shops, where hundreds worked in air filled with dust and fluid fumes, fire was a constant hazard, and the atmosphere was prisonlike. Management locked the doors so no one could leave without permission and did not allow employees to talk or sing as they worked. One company fined workers looking out the window or laughing. Shop workers constantly were played off tenement workers, driving down wages and allowing deplorable working conditions. Most employees were women. While there were, and are, men in the industry, they largely work in tasks separate from the female majority.

At first the union was weak, lacking legal standing in an era when union activity was prosecuted as criminal conspiracy. But in 1909–11, two large, successful strikes and one major tragedy provided a turning point in ILGWU history. In 1909, 20,000 shirtwaist makers, mainly women and young girls, marched out of the shop to demand better conditions. They demonstrated and picketed for two months, eventually winning a wage increase and maximum workweek of fifty-two hours. In 1910, 50,000 cloak workers, mainly men, refused to work until there were industrywide uniform wages, a shorter workweek, and paid holidays.

In March 1911, the Triangle Shirtwaist Company had a devastating fire in which 146 young women lost their lives. The public felt outraged that faulty wiring and poor ventilation caused it and that workers could not escape because they were locked into the building's top two floors. The owner collected insurance on the loss, but no compensation was available for the deceased workers' families. The fire prompted New York to force changes on industry. Established were a state Board of Sanitary Control to supervise health conditions in shops and tenement work sites and an arbitration board to hear workers' complaints against employers.

After these events, thousands of garment workers flocked to ILGWU. By 1914, the union began innovations in member services not seen in other unions. It opened an office where members could get physical exams; this grew into a union health center that offered a complete range of medical services. In 1915, it started a workers' vacation resort, Unity House in the Pennsylvania Poconos, where workers and their families still go to relax.

The union suffered setbacks in the 1920s, when the business and political establishment clamped down on unions again. Membership declined from 100,000 to under 25,000. Fortunately, Franklin Roosevelt, elected president in 1931, was not timid about promoting working people's interests; and his labor secretary Frances Perkins found over 1,000 plans to combat unemployment waiting for her attention when she took office. During the 1930s, many issues ILGWU had struggled over were resolved in workers' favor: a federal minimum wage, overtime pay for work in excess of forty hours a week, restrictions on child labor, a Social Security system, and workers' right to organize without fear of employer retaliation. In this climate, despite the Great Depression, ILGWU thrived.

During the 1940s, ILGWU pioneered two more union firsts, financing a pension fund for its members and negotiating the first employer-financed health insurance plan. The next twenty years generally were prosperous; and although wages never have been high in the industry ($7.55 an hour in 1987), ILGWU negotiated contracts that gave members job security, health and retirement benefits, and the vacations and sick leave policies usually found only among higher-waged industries such as steel and automobile.

Since 1975, ILGWU has turned its attention from organizing and improving garment, textile, and apparel workers' lot to protecting its past gains and lobbying for trade policies to save its workers. Two developments challenged gains. The first was the flood of cheap imports, which cost 350,000 jobs in women's and children's apparel alone during the 1980s. American firms were moving their assembly operations to Taiwan, Thailand, and Costa Rica, where workers earn a fraction of what U.S. workers earn, laws regulating working conditions are nonexistent, and union activity is illegal.

Second, the Reagan years were difficult. One of the administration's first attacks on the labor movement was to lift the industrial homework ban. By 1989, the U.S. Labor Department had exempted six industries—knitwear the largest—and women's apparel was slated to be next. Within months jobbers returned to the industry, and unregistered sweatshops emerged. Failure to raise minimum wage—important in industries like those ILGWU represents, because wages are close to the minimum—and to enforce child labor laws and unfair employer labor practice laws also took their toll.

The Congress twice during the eighties failed to override Reagan's veto of the Textile and Apparel Trade bill, which would have limited growth in imports to the rate of growth in domestic consumption. The administration maintained that the U.S. consumer's interest lay in not restricting cheaper imports. Data collected by ILGWU indicate the cost savings accrued to manufacturers and retailers, not consumers in the form of lower garment prices. Reagan's Caribbean Basin Initiative (CBI) also presented a setback to these workers. CBI provided free access to the U.S. market as long as apparel imports' fabric had been made and cut domestically. U.S. garment workers, earning on average $250 weekly, hardly can compete with workers in Honduras and Costa Rica earning

$25 a week. The United States has lost 100,000 garment jobs to CBI countries since 1983. The Bush era with its free trade emphasis offered little hope for relief.

ORGANIZATION AND FUNDING

Every three years ILGWU holds a national convention, to which members of the hundreds of local chapters elect delegates. Programs, policies, and any changes in the union's constitution are decided on by convention vote. Election of the general executive board also is held. While ILGWU membership always has been predominantly female—in 1988, 95 percent of more than half a million textile and other apparel workers—union leadership always has been firmly in white men's hands. The president, secretary-treasurer, and fourteen of nineteen vice presidents are all men. The current president is Jay Mazur. ILGWU headquarters in New York City houses 200 paid staff. The executive director is Edgar Rumney. There are seven attorneys on retainer.

Due to plant closing and membership loss, the organization and staff of hundreds of ILGWU locals in the United States, Canada, and Puerto Rico have been consolidated and downsized. For example, in 1986–88, seventeen new locals formed, thirty-five went out of existence, and twenty-one merged with other locals. Most recent organizing successes have occurred in nongarment industries. ILGWU has organized security personnel, workers in retail and health care, tanners, warehouse employees, and production workers in optical devices and waterbeds. ILGWU is organized much like other unions that are large and geographically dispersed. Full-time organizers seek to unionize nonunion shops.

Even where women occupy senior-level positions at the national or local chapter level in ILGWU, they do not reflect the ethnic or national background of the rank and file they serve. The Coalition of Labor Union Women* has tried to change this situation without success. In New York City, for example, where most garment workers are Chinese or Puerto Rican, the sole female union official is white. This situation presents potential for exploitation of union members. Irregularities most easily occur where turnover is relatively high, employees are recent immigrants who do not fully understand their rights, and representatives of their interests come from the outside instead of the rank and file.

The demographic characteristics of current and potential members always have required consideration. During the century's first 25 years, members were largely Eastern European Jewish and Italian immigrants. By 1940–60, the newest members tended to be Puerto Ricans, Portuguese, Slavs, and French Canadians. Between the two world wars, as manufacturers moved to the deep South to escape northeastern unions, the rural southern black population became organized. Since 1970, new garment workers mainly have come from Latin America and Asia. Organizing is complicated because newcomers often do not speak English and tend to feel unsure of their rights and insecure in their status. In 1986, the Immigration Reform Control Act, which provided amnesty for those living illegally in the United States since before 1982, affected many ILGWU members; and the union created a service to help undocumented members with counseling and legal representation.

ILGWU's funding comes from union dues and real estate and other investment holdings accumulated over the years. In 1989, for the first time, income from investment assets was placed in the hands of outside professional investors.

POLICY CONCERNS AND TACTICS

The general executive board, consisting of the president, general secretary-treasurer, and nineteen vice presidents, meets every four months to determine goals and strategies and assess overall operations for ILGWU. In 1975, ILGWU pioneered a union first in publicizing the union's plight in the wake of runaway shops, antiunion sentiment, and the emerging job threat from imports. It developed television ads that initially focused on how imports were made in countries that used child labor, paid poverty wages, operated in government subsidized plants, and did not allow workers to form unions. The networks found these ads too controversial and began refusing to air them. In 1976, ILGWU found a new angle. Its ads promoted "America Helping America by Buying American" and thereafter embellished the union label with the American flag. By 1982, both unions and corporations in the steel and auto industries began developing their own "Buy American" campaigns.

ILGWU's tactic during contract negotiations has been to seek "master agreements" with firms wherever possible. A master agreement exists, for example, with Maidenform to cover that firm's employees in New Jersey, West Virginia, and Florida installations. Without this agreement, a firm may play workers in one plant off those in another in competing for contracts, thereby driving down wage and benefit levels. As of 1990, ILGWU also had master agreements with Bobbie Brooks, Jonathan Logan, Leslie Fay, and Calvin Klein.

While legislative process has been disappointing in recent years, there were some successes. The 1988 Omnibus Trade bill, although not as strong as initially proposed, did include provisions dealing with unfair trade practices and workers' rights and protection among our trading partners. It also included some assistance for dislocated workers. In 1988, ILGWU, singly, successfully urged the National Labor Relations Board General Counsel to reverse its positions on remedies for undocumented workers discharged in violation of the National Labor Relations Act. In 1989, it joined as amicus curiae in a pending Title VII case, brought by the Equal Employment Opportunity Commission, where the employer was claiming that undocumented workers are not covered by the antidiscrimination provisions of the 1964 Civil Rights Act. Substantial legislative efforts focused on the North American Free Trade Agreement and the inclusion of provisions to combat job and income losses among its members, because employment was expected to accelerate when it passed.

ILGWU traditionally has joined in coalitions with other unions to press the Congress for legislation affecting not only its members but all working people.

Domestically ILGWU has joined forces with other American Federation of Labor-Congress of Industrial Organizations* (AFL-CIO) affiliates who have become increasingly international in focus with labor markets' globalization. It is an active member of the International Textile, Garment and Leather Workers Federation, a coalition of 160 unions from eighty countries with a combined membership of 5 million workers. This alliance seeks to join democratic labor movements in industrialized nations of the North with the emerging labor movement in less industrialized countries of the South.

ELECTORAL ACTIVITIES

ILGWU has a Campaign Committee (CC), which, despite the organization's membership loss, reports rising contributions from both active and retired members. CC uses funds to investigate candidates' voting records and public pronouncements, with the goal of electing progressive-minded candidates to public office. Local chapters endorse the progressive candidates. At the national level ILGWU participates in AFL-CIO's campaign endorsements and COPE.

FURTHER INFORMATION

ILGWU publications include a monthly newspaper for members and retirees, *Justice,* and the *General Executive Board Report to the Convention,* which appears every three years, most recently in 1992.

SUSAN DAVIS

INTERNATIONAL LADIES' GARMENT WORKERS' UNION CAMPAIGN COMMITTEE
See INTERNATIONAL LADIES' GARMENT WORKERS' UNION

INTERNATIONAL PAN-PACIFIC AND SOUTHEAST ASIA WOMEN'S ASSOCIATION
See PAN-PACIFIC AND SOUTHEAST ASIA WOMEN'S ASSOCIATION—U.S.A.

INTERNATIONAL RED CROSS
See AMERICAN RED CROSS

INTERSTATE ASSOCIATION OF COMMISSIONS FOR WOMEN
See NATIONAL ASSOCIATION OF COMMISSIONS FOR WOMEN

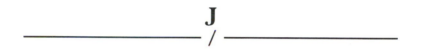

JANE ADDAMS PEACE ASSOCIATION
See WOMEN'S INTERNATIONAL LEAGUE FOR PEACE AND FREEDOM, UNITED STATES SECTION

JUNIOR LEAGUE
See ASSOCIATION OF JUNIOR LEAGUES, INTERNATIONAL

JUNIOR LEAGUE FOR THE PROMOTION OF NEIGHBORHOOD WORK
See ASSOCIATION OF JUNIOR LEAGUES, INTERNATIONAL

JUNIOR LEAGUE FOR THE PROMOTION OF SETTLEMENT MOVEMENTS
See ASSOCIATION OF JUNIOR LEAGUES, INTERNATIONAL

L
---/---

LEADERSHIP CONFERENCE OF WOMEN RELIGIOUS OF THE UNITED STATES OF AMERICA (LCWR)

8808 Cameron Street
Silver Spring, MD 20910
(301) 588-4955
FAX (301) 587-4575

The Leadership Conference of Women Religious (LCWR) seeks to promote understanding and living of religious life through personal and communal assistance with leadership service in congregations, to accomplish Christ's mission in today's world; through dialogue and collaboration among religious congregations in church and the larger society; and through the development of models to initiate and strengthen relationships with social justice organizations, to maximize conference potential for effecting change.

ORIGIN AND DEVELOPMENT

The Vatican's Congregation of Religious requested in 1951 that each country in the world organize a national conference of its religious congregations of men and women. It requested the union of men and women in one national conference; LCWR's founding women, including Sister Madeleva, Mother Mary Gerald Barry, Mother Kathryn Marie, and Mother Gertrude Clare, rejected the offer in favor of two separate conferences. This was a unique response, because they wanted to keep their independence from the men.

In 1952, the religious congregation of women's leaders convened its first congress at Notre Dame, Indiana, to share mutual goals, problems, and necessary adaptations to continue effectively their mission in the church. Women leaders felt especially concerned with their members' health and education as well as their involvement in foreign mission activity. An emphasis on the unity and cooperation of all U.S. religious women with the hierarchy, clergy, and Catholic associations emerged. These meetings culminated in 1956 in the organization of the Conference of Major Superiors of Women, canonically established in 1959 by decree of the Roman Congregation for Religious. After the 1959 decree, the group's title changed to the Leadership Conference of Women Religious of the United States of America.

LCWR's role has become more comprehensive in recent years. It began developing programs for its members' benefit on local, regional, and national levels in areas such as health, retirement, education, and social justice issues. By fostering communication and cooperation among its members, these programs conserved the resources of personnel, finances, properties, missions, hospitals, and schools. Communication through the programs extended beyond the membership to others in the Catholic Church, especially to laywomen and the society at large. Encouraged were new apostolates and ministries such as chaplains to campuses and prisons, soup kitchens, shelters for homeless persons, social work, and sensitivity to elderly concerns. The sisters agreed upon a priority of service to poor people and dedicated their finances, personnel, and efforts to this "primary option."

ORGANIZATION AND FUNDING

In all, LCWR operates on three levels, the national, regional, and local. Fifteen regional groups meet twice yearly in geographical locations. The fifteen regions are similar to the regions of the National Conference of Catholic Bishops. The local group generally forms within a diocese. Local LCWR members usually meet bimonthly to reflect together and study and make decisions that are of mutual interest or affect local congregations. The national organization sponsors a national assembly that is the conference's fundamental legislative body. Held annually in various cities, the meeting usually serves two functions: providing a prayerful, reflective experience to facilitate insight about a topic or situation affecting religious life and the church in the United States, and attending to legislative affairs, including election of officers, resolution formulation and approval, and policy and directive establishment.

An eight-member national board is directed by the organization's officers. LCWR has a unique structure for its governing body. Although the president is by law the chief executive officer, the presidency consists of three members operating as a team: the vice president, president, and immediate past president. Elected each year, a new vice president commits herself to a three-year term— one as vice president, one as president, and the third as past president. This structure allows for collaboration at the highest levels of governance and models the effectiveness of collegiality and shared leadership. President Anita de Luna is the first Hispana elected to the post. A national secretariat serves as a permanent headquarters and maintains a professional staff to assist and enable the conference's work. The present executive director is Sister Janet Roesener.

LCWR includes women religious who administer their religious congregations in the United States. The conference membership consists of approximately 800 sisters, representing 300 religious congregations of women and 104,429 women religious. An associate membership includes major superiors of religious congregations of women residing outside the United States with members within it, prioresses of contemplative congregations and major officers of related national organizations such as the Leadership Council of Male Religious and National Organization of Women Religious.

Founded as a nonprofit, tax-exempt group, LCWR exists financially by the contributions of its members. Dues usually are assessed at about $200 per member but can be reduced upon request depending on financial ability. The annual budget is usually around $140,000.

POLICY CONCERNS AND TACTICS

Concerns for social justice led to collaboration with Network,* a national Catholic social justice lobby with a LCWR staff member acting as liaison to its board of directors. LCWR in 1971 gathered at Trinity College in Washington, D.C., to write its vision for Network, which was grounded in the gospel tradition of commitment to poor people while working to transform the structures that cause oppression. In 1988, Network board and staff rearticulated a commitment to gather women religious and other religious persons to address sources of injustice by lobbying. LCWR's member congregations support these lobbying activities through financial grants.

Some policies LCWR seeks to bring about with its grants include improved housing for welfare women, child care, health care, and boycotts of companies held to discriminate against women and children, like Nestle and Folgers. LCWR also sponsors, conducts, and coordinates study and research on such matters of interest and concern to its members as retirement needs, financial assistance, and ministry opportunities. This action, in turn, provides a repository of resources and information for members to share.

In 1989, LCWR set as its goals work for women's liberation through social and ecclesial structural transformation and work to eliminate the sin of racism in members, their congregations, and institutions and in other church and social structures. LCWR has introduced inclusive language in church rituals, raised the salary of women religious, addressed their retirement and introduced antidiscrimination clauses in their colleges, schools, and hospitals.

ELECTORAL ACTIVITIES

LCWR does not see women's issues as partisan, because it would lose its tax-exempt status if it did, and does not have a political action committee.

FURTHER INFORMATION

A quarterly newsletter is sent to all members, along with minutes and correspondence with the Vatican. Each region communicates with its members bimonthly.

MARIANNE C. FERGUSON

LEADERSHIP DEVELOPMENT EDUCATION AND RESEARCH FUND
See NATIONAL WOMEN'S POLITICAL CAUCUS

**LEAGUE OF REPUBLICAN WOMEN OF THE DISTRICT OF COLUM-
BIA (LRW)**
1155 Connecticut Avenue, NW
Suite 400
Washington, DC 20036
(202) 785-8534

The League of Republican Women (LRW) of the District of Columbia has
three primary goals: to educate the general public about politics, including the
relationship of the economy to government and its operation; to encourage citizen participation in the political process at the national and local levels; and to
encourage women, especially minorities, to become involved in the political
arena.

ORIGIN AND DEVELOPMENT

Established in 1912 under Virginia White Speel's leadership, LRW, with
many other women's organizations during that period, worked to establish wom-
en's suffrage. When the Nineteenth Amendment was ratified in 1920, the
group's mission shifted. It sought to promote women's involvement in political
life primarily by providing educational programming designed to encourage
women's participation. Incorporated in 1923, making it one of the first women's
organizations in the United States to take this step, over the course of the next
decade, LRW was the focal point when issues involving women arose before
the Congress. The league did not join the National Federation of Republican
Women (NFRW) when the group formed in 1938. By 1940, the District of
Columbia Federation of Republican Women (DCFRW) joined NFRW as a federated club, while LRW still remained an independent organization.

Reduced in size and scope by the formation of NFRW and DCFRW, the
league maintained its mission of educating women about political issues and
continued to support Republican candidates for citywide office. As the population in the counties surrounding the District grew, the organization reached out
to include Republican women in the suburbs; however, the Rock Creek, Maryland, Women's Republican Club and the Alexandria, Virginia, Republican
Women's Club diminished the number of potential members.

LRW has been recognized during its history for hosting luncheons at the
Mayflower Hotel, with featured speakers from within the party and the Washington community. Examples of these speakers are Mary Catherine Gibson,
NFRW president from 1957 to 1961, who encouraged LRW membership recruitment efforts; and then-senator Richard M. Nixon, who urged the women to
support military withdrawal from Korea and economic sanctions against China.
In addition to its luncheons, LRW activities have included civil defense classes,
campaign schools, and political debates.

In 1992, LRW submitted its application to join NFRW and DCFRW. Two of

LRW's bylaws did not comply with those of NFRW, and a compromise was sought.

ORGANIZATION AND FUNDING

An eleven-member board of directors governs LRW. Four committees direct the numerous activities of the organization: the political activities committee, membership committee, program committee, and international community affairs committee. The political activities committee arranges education briefings, a long-standing league tradition. The membership committee sponsors a new member reception every year and encourages members to recruit other women for the organization. The program committee assists the political activities committee in arranging luncheon speakers; it also alerts members to campaign workshops sponsored by the Republican Party. The international community affairs committee coordinates more educational programs, with an emphasis on international affairs rather than partisan politics. Anne Heuer, an investment adviser, has served as president of the organization since 1993. The organization maintains an office in the District but does not employ any staff members or interns.

Prior to NFRW's and DCFRW's formation, the league had about 1,500 members; presently, it has 210 members from the District and its suburbs. The majority of members are professional women with full-time employment. The membership includes attorneys, cabinet members' wives, and federal employees. Two league members were elevated to visible positions in the former Bush administration. Barbara Franklin was appointed commerce secretary, and Cathi Villilpando, U.S. treasurer. During its eightieth anniversary in 1992, LRW began a two-year informational mailing to the approximately 14,000 registered Republican women in the District proper. The league also recruits new members from the District's suburbs in Maryland and northern Virginia, primarily by word of mouth.

LRW has tax-exempt status and is classified under the Internal Revenue Service Code as a 501 (c) (4) organization. The group's primary source of revenue is interest from its endowment, approximately $100,000. Members pay nominal dues: $25 for a regular membership, $35 for a contributing membership, and $50 for a sustaining membership. The group also raises a small amount of money through ticket sales to its luncheons and receptions. The organization's annual budget over the last decade has fluctuated between $25,000 and $35,000; rent of office space and operating costs constitute the organization's expenses.

POLICY CONCERNS AND TACTICS

The primary mission of LRW is education. The organization has a strong tradition of providing women with the opportunity to hear senior members of the president's cabinet or the Congress. In 1924, U.S. Attorney General Harlan Fiske Stone spoke to the group about the evolution of the Constitution, at a campaign school conducted for Republican women. Today, the league maintains its interest in promoting women's awareness of current issues in a similar manner. During 1991, the group hosted former secretary of state Alexander Haig to discuss foreign policy.

LRW also mounts voter registration drives and encourages citizens, including men, to participate politically. One present league project, cosponsored with the District of Columbia American Legion Auxiliary, is the establishment of a District of Columbia Girls' State program.

ELECTORAL ACTIVITIES

While LRW generally supports Republican candidates for local positions, it cannot provide any candidate funding due to its tax-exempt status. It urges members to give support to Republican candidates on an individual basis and to volunteer to work for other Republican organizations such as the District of Columbia Republican Committee. For example, LRW members worked with the committee in supporting Maurice Turner in the 1990 mayoral contest.

LRW encourages members to express their opinions on a variety of issues. During the 1991 U.S. Senate confirmation hearings on Judge Clarence Thomas's nomination to the U.S. Supreme Court, LRW urged members to express support for him. Although LRW could not express an opinion, it sought concerted individual efforts from members.

FURTHER INFORMATION

During the 1920s, LRW published addresses by its speakers in small booklets, some of which can be found in the Library of Congress. Today, LRW publishes the *League Bulletin* on a bimonthly basis.

SARA ANN GROVE

LEAGUE OF WOMEN VOTERS CARRIE CHAPMAN CATT MEMORIAL FUND
See LEAGUE OF WOMEN VOTERS

LEAGUE OF WOMEN VOTERS EDUCATION FUND
See LEAGUE OF WOMEN VOTERS

LEAGUE OF WOMEN VOTERS OF THE UNITED STATES (LWV)
1730 M Street, NW
Washington, DC 20036
(202) 427-1965
FAX (202) 429-0854

The League of Women Voters (LWV) believes that government policy, programs, and performance must flow from, and create, well-defined channels for citizen input and review. It works to enhance citizen participation generally in federal, state, and local government decisions and to increase citizen participation in the election process itself. LWV has an Education Fund.

ORIGIN AND DEVELOPMENT

The National League of Women Voters (NLWV) emerged as an auxiliary of the National American Women Suffrage Association (NAWSA) in 1920. It was founded at the culmination of the seventy-two-year struggle to gain woman's suffrage. In 1946, NLWV was reconstituted as the League of Women Voters of the United States.

The league's initial mission was to promote political education of the newly enfranchised women citizens. The early members worked toward forming a link with the political parties that would give women the opportunity to take part in governing. Over the years the transition to LWV was completed with very few problems. There have been focuses ranging from political education to more substantive issues relevant to the needs of local LWVs. However, the league's original goals have not changed much. It seeks "to promote political responsibility through informed and active participation of citizens in government" and to "take action on governmental measures and policies in the public interest."

Many of the original members were part of the 2 million individuals active in NAWSA. President Maud Wood Park, the first president, was a graduate of Radcliffe College and a lecturer there in economics and political science. As president, Park assisted in the adoption of thirteen platform planks. Heading the list was the Sheppard-Towner bill for infant and maternal health. Also of concern was a constitutional amendment to abolish child labor, adequate funding for the Children's Bureau, a federal department of education, federal aid for combating illiteracy, and raising teachers' salaries. Many of the state leagues were successful in redressing these and other women's grievances. In addition to state-level successes, the league was able to see the following national bills passed: the 1921 Sheppard-Towner Act and the 1922 Cable Act, which allowed women to retain their U.S. citizenship after marrying foreign nationals.

Even with these legislative victories, the league continued to be plagued with crises and internal struggles. From 1924 to 1934, it experienced political and educational experiment and continuous self-questioning. In the early 1920s, one major goal of the league was to train women for their new civic role. This training in formal political education soon was abandoned for methods more pragmatic and experimental. Since women no longer needed politicization, emphasis on political education no longer was seen as the primary focus of the league. The total abandonment of political education occurred as NLWV was reconstructed as LWV in its 1946 convention. Its primary objective was to promote citizen responsibility by means of informed and active political participation.

By 1950, the league had reached organizational maturity. It had developed as a fundamentally grassroots organization with approximately 1,200 local leagues organized in all fifty states. From 1950 to 1970, membership fluctuated between 120,000 and 150,000. Actions were not confined to national questions but extended to state and local concerns. Within the broad framework of its principles, state and local leagues worked on issues pertinent to their specific needs. Much of the influential action of the league occurred at the local level, where league organization was strongest during these two decades. During this period local leagues became increasingly supportive of measures to improve the coordination, effectiveness, efficiency, and economical operation of local governments. The focus of debate and concern, thus, shifted from the national to the local level.

The contemporary focus of concern is still on the local level and still seeks to educate and empower women. There has been no overall change in the goals of LWV. President Carrie Chapman Catt made a five-year plan to teach women to use the ballot, and that has continued to be the focus. One of the first issues was health and maternity leave. LWV advocated the 1993 family and maternity leave act. In addition, educating citizens about how government works was an original idea and continues to be an important aspect of LWV. During the June 1992 convention the following four major issues were adopted: first, health care. LWV wanted to design a process of consensus on what kind of health care would be best. It is believed that most members would like to see the development of some kind of national health care system. Electoral reform, right to privacy and reproduction, and a focus on waste management and pollution control completed the 1992 issue agenda.

ORGANIZATION AND FUNDING

There are 1,200 local leagues, 50 state leagues, and leagues in Puerto Rico, the Virgin Islands, and District of Columbia. Local and state chapters are independent entities and set up the rules that govern a particular chapter. Each state and local board can send a delegate to the national convention. The number of delegates sent often depends on the available resources of each local and state league. In June 1993 there were 1,100 delegates at the convention. Most officers at the local, state, and national levels are unsalaried volunteers who do the bulk of the organization's work at the local level. The board recently has been streamlined to fourteen elected directors. This board is racially and geographically mixed and serves until the conclusion of the next regular biennial convention. President Becky Cain serves for a two-year period and is elected by delegates to the convention. The national office in Washington has about fifty paid staff members. The executive director is Gracia Hillman.

LWV always has been open to all women eighteen and over. Men have been able to join since the league's inception but were not able to vote until 1976. After ERA passed from the Congress to the states in 1972, members did not believe they could prohibit men from voting. Most of the male members were political scientists or lawyers curious about the league's functioning. They make up close to 3 percent of the national membership. There are approximately 110,000 members. They join and participate in LWV for a wide variety of reasons. The league's concerns are widespread and diverse, ranging from citizen rights to international concerns, natural resources, social policy, and health care.

The league believes that government policy, programs, and performance must flow from, and create, well-defined channels for citizen input and review. Members may join at any level—local, state, and national. People get involved because the league provides them with information about issues and provides them with an opportunity to meet the people who work in the community and to improve skills such as leadership training through speaking and writing events.

Financial support comes from member dues paid to the local leagues, which, in turn, forward part of the dues to the national. Each local and state league decides what its dues will be. For example, in Colorado, dues are set at $45. Across the country, dues range from $35 to $55. The rest of LWV's budget comes from contributions from individuals and corporations and grants for specific league projects supported by foundations and government entities. As of June 1992 there were two budgets: the Educational Fund budget, set at $3,198,819; and the regular LWV fund, set at $2,645,800.

In 1974, the Carrie Chapman Catt Memorial Fund (in 1980, renamed the Overseas Education Fund International) was established to encourage and assist citizens of other countries to participate actively in the political process. The fund was meant to sponsor leadership training programs in foreign countries. The organization's goal was to form groups similar to the league in other countries. In 1991, the members voted to rename the fund the Education Fund and shift its concern from the international arena to the domestic arena. The Education Fund develops and promotes educational programs about public policy with financial support from foundations, corporations, government agencies, and individuals. Independent state and local chapters design and operate their own education fund. For example, LWV in Colorado has concentrated on school finance, supporting the 1973 School Finance Act and amendments to that law that increased funding equity for districts. LWV in New York, through its Foundation for Citizen Education, provides a voter's guide to fair campaign practices. LWV also has supported funding for disadvantaged students and for districts with rapidly rising and falling enrollments.

POLICY CONCERNS AND TACTICS

Choices of strategies to apply to LWV's issue agenda often are determined regionally. The position the league takes on public policy issues is influenced heavily by member participation and agreement. The members decide what issues the league addresses and what action the league takes on issues. Consequently, many decisions are made on the state and local levels and heavily depend on local and state needs. At the biennial convention, state and local delegates voice their concerns. The league studies issues, informs citizens and legislatures about the results of its research, sponsors candidate debates and public forums about vital issues, monitors the workings of legislative bodies and commissions, lobbies for the passage of laws and works toward the defeat of those opposed by members, and cooperates with other organizations working toward the same goals. In addition, it registers millions to vote, monitors government activities from local school boards to the U.S. Congress, teaches citizens about their rights and responsibilities, and helps put laws on the books that citizens and members care about.

During the height of the women's liberation movement in the seventies, LWV strongly supported the equal rights amendment, Title VII of the 1964 Civil Rights Act, the 1974 Equal Credit Opportunity Act, and Title IX of the 1972 Education Amendments. During the 1980s, the league adopted positions on arms control and on military policy and defense spending. The league supports negotiation of a bilateral, mutually verifiable freeze on the testing, production, and deployment of nuclear weapons, followed by arms reduction. The league has played a key role in legislative efforts to ban U.S. testing of antisatellite weapons against objects in space.

In 1970, the fiftieth anniversary convention of the league reformulated its program to incorporate environmental quality concerns. Since that time there have been numerous actions by the league at state levels to work on issues relevant to state environmental needs. Adoption of environmental concerns enabled several states to support attempts in the early 1970s to enact an environmental policy act. In the mid-1970s, the league successfully supported legislation that required consideration of natural resources. State leagues also respond to alerts disseminated by the national league on issues of environmental legislation.

During the Decade for Women, 1975–85, LWV was one of the ten organizations to be recognized as a nongovernmental organization at the United Nations. This recognition provided it with the ability to further its concerns about leadership training in various countries. The league works frequently in lobbying coalitions with other like-minded groups, including the American Association of University Women,* National Women's Political Caucus,* and Common Cause.

ELECTORAL ACTIVITIES

LWV is political but strictly nonpartisan. It does not support or oppose any political party or candidate, financially or otherwise. League officials believe that this ensures its members' voices are heard above party politics.

FURTHER INFORMATION

One of the main emphases of LWV's publications during 1992 was to summarize ballot issues. Publications are written to inform the members of issues in a pro/con format. All publications are written in clear language, so that an ordinary person can understand the debate over the issues. Other typical publications include a packet for elementary teachers to inform their students about voting and government and a citizen's guide to government workings.

ONEIDA MASCARENAS AND ANNE COSTAIN

LEAGUE OF WOMEN VOTERS OVERSEAS EDUCATION FUND INTERNATIONAL
See LEAGUE OF WOMEN VOTERS

LA LECHE LEAGUE INTERNATIONAL (LLLI)
1400 North Meacham Road
Schaumburg, IL 60173-4840
(708) 519-7730, (800) LA-LECHE
FAX (708) 519-0035

La Leche League International (LLLI) encourages improved understanding of breastfeeding as a significant factor in healthy development for babies and their mothers and to assist breast-feeding mothers the world over through education, information, encouragement, and personal support.

ORIGIN AND DEVELOPMENT

A group of seven women belonging to the same church founded LLLI in 1956. Betty Wagner, Mary Ann Cahill, Edwina Froehlich, Mary Ann Kerwin, Viola Lennon, Marian Tompson, and Mary White sought to make breastfeeding an easier and more gratifying experience for mother and child alike. Gregory White, a founder's husband, and Herb Ratnor have offered medical information, support, and referrals to the group since its inception. Because of the sensitivity of using the word breast-feeding in the 1950s, the founders searched for an appropriate name for their organization. The Shrine of Our Lady of La Leche, established in St. Augustine, Florida in about 1620 by Spanish settlers as a sign of their love for the Nursing Mother of Christ, served as the inspiration for the founders' decision to choose this "La Leche," the Spanish word for milk, as the organization's name.

Over the past thirty-five years, LLLI has grown dramatically. While in 1956 there were only seven accredited leaders, by 1966 there were 786 accredited leaders, partly due to the public interest and international contacts which resulted from Karen Pryor's 1963 *Reader's Digest* article about LLLI. By 1976 there were 10,568 leaders; by 1986 there were 24,104 leaders; and by 1994 30,100 leaders had been accredited by LLLI's Leader Accreditation Department. LLLI grew from one group in 1956 to nearly 3,000 groups by 1993. The only policy pursued is that of helping mothers to breast-feed their babies. This policy has not changed since the group's founding.

ORGANIZATION AND FUNDING

The organization is made up of three director-headed divisions: United States-East, United States-West, and all other countries of the world. These divisions are comprised of thirteen regions—ten in the United States and three elsewhere in the world—and about forty areas. Each area is headed by a district advisor to oversee groups in the area; each group is headed by two accredited volunteer leaders. There are currently 1,021 groups in the East, 955 groups in West, and 1,030 in other countries. A seventeen-member board of directors, which includes the chair, the first and second vice chairs, the secretary, the treasurer, and a five-member executive committee, oversees LLLI's policy, philosophy, and budget. The current chair is Paulina deSmith. The national office, which recently moved to Schaumburg, Illinois, is run by six professional staff and about forty support staff. Founder Betty Wagner, who served as executive director since 1972, stepped out of that role in 1991 to head the capital campaign; LeAnn Deal is the current executive director. In addition, a health advisory council composed mainly of physicians, a legal advisory council, and a management advisory council comprise the LLLI professional advisory board.

The network of over 8,000 active accredited leaders and about 50,000 members (United States—35,000; other countries—15,000) reaches more than 100,000 mothers in sixty countries. Members receive a discount on purchases from the LLLI catalog and the opportunity to participate in LLLI-sponsored special events, including conferences. Other incentives to become a member and attend meetings are to share ideas about breast-feeding and child rearing with other women. There are also family picnics and couples' evenings which help families connect with others at the same stage of life. Babies and toddlers are welcome to attend LLLI meetings and other LLLI-sponsored events.

The current annual income of this tax-exempt organization is about $2 million; 60 percent of the income is generated by sales of educational materials, 20 percent by membership dues, and 15 percent by contributions. The remaining 5 percent comes from a variety of sources.

POLICY CONCERNS AND TACTICS

Although the board of directors is the most influential, volunteers throughout the United States and around the world have potential input into policy decisions. Despite its membership growth, LLLI has resolved to remain unified as a single-issue organization and has functioned largely as an organization focused on the dissemination of educational information about and support for breast-feeding. LLLI holds lactation consultant workshops and annual seminars for physicians to educate health professionals about breast-feeding and cooperates with community organizations and agencies by sharing educational information and combining in-service training. LLLI serves as a United Nations (UN) consultant and is a registered Private Voluntary Organization of International Development.

More recently, LLLI has become more involved in breast-feeding as a political and social issue, particularly in developing nations. In cooperation with UN Children's Fund (UNICEF), LLLI has helped prepare a UNICEF booklet entitled "Protecting, Promoting, and Supporting Breast-feeding." LLLI took part in an international letter-writing campaign asking groups and individuals to write their nation's leaders asking for ratification of the Convention on the Rights of the Child and also for breast-feeding adoption as a major strategy of the World Summit for Children. LLLI believes that providing mothers the support and opportunity to breast-feed is a political issue because (1) it saves governments, particularly in developing nations, money otherwise spent on formula, (2) it helps ecologically, and (3) it has a positive impact on a nation's health. LLLI believes that breastfeeding supports the concept of family by bringing mothers in particular closer to their babies.

Along with the World Health Organization, UNICEF, UN Population Fund, and UN Educational, Scientific, and Cultural Organization (UNESCO), LLLI was one organization to participate in the 1990 UN World Summit for Children. LLLI strongly advocated Section II.B.vi of the United Nations Declaration on Children, which resulted from the World Summit and sought to empower women to breast-feed their infants for four to six months and to continue the practice with accompanying food into the child's second year. They hoped to empower women by showing the importance of breast-feeding to women, their children, family and country, and ultimately the world.

An accredited member of the U.S. Healthy Mother/Healthy Baby Coalition, LLLI is also a part of the National Breast-feeding Coalition and World Alliance for Breast-feeding Action. LLLI works closely with the American Academy of Pediatrics (AAP) and often has AAP members and members of the American College of Obstetricians and Gynecologists speak at seminars. LLLI shares interests with the UN, UNICEF, and WHO.

ELECTORAL ACTIVITIES

LLLI does not see these women's issues as partisan nor does it have a political action committee.

FURTHER INFORMATION

Members receive a bimonthly magazine, *New Beginnings.* In serving as the world's largest resource for breast-feeding information, LLLI has distributed more than 3 million publications annually and has sold over 2 million copies of LLLI's basic manual, *The Womanly Art of Breastfeeding,* which is available in nine languages and Braille.

CAROL J. AUSTER

LESBIAN AND GAY RIGHTS PROJECT
See AMERICAN CIVIL LIBERTIES UNION

LIFE AMENDMENT POLITICAL ACTION COMMITTEE
See AMERICAN LIFE LEAGUE

THE LINKS FOUNDATION, INCORPORATED
See THE LINKS, INCORPORATED

THE LINKS, INCORPORATED (TLI)
1200 Massachusetts Avenue, NW
Washington, DC 20005
(202) 842-8686
FAX (202) 842-4020

A volunteer service organization, The Links, Incorporated (TLI) engages in educational, intracultural, and civic endeavors to enrich the lives of persons educationally disadvantaged and culturally deprived in the United States and abroad. It has a charitable and educational foundation.

ORIGIN AND DEVELOPMENT

Sarah Scott and Margaret Hawkins founded TLI in Philadelphia in 1946. The idea for "links in friendship's chain" was theirs. They also knew African Americans needed an outlet for community service and volunteerism. TLI is a group of better-educated, upwardly mobile African American women seeking to assist those less fortunate, today through four program facets: the arts, youth services, national trends and services, and international trends and services. TLI is a United Nations nongovernmental representative.

ORGANIZATION AND FUNDING

TLI has 241 chapters in thirty-nine states, the District of Columbia, Nassau, the Bahamas, and Frankfurt, Germany. There are four area directors. The biennial assembly tends to constitutional and procedural matters and ratifies specific contributions to charitable organizations. TLI pays assembly expenses for speakers and program participants, board members, and staff. The board of directors has fifteen members. Marion Schultz Sutherland serves as TLI president. Since 1985, TLI has had a headquarters building in Washington. Mary P. Douglass has served as chief administrative officer for the last decade. Anywhere from one to ten volunteers or student interns serve in the office, taking a fixed level of responsibility. The organization has an attorney on retainer.

TLI has 8,500 members or links, an increase of 4,000 over 1985. Members all are women and will remain so. They join for friendship ties but also to communicate with their peers and advocate important values along with community service. To a somewhat lesser extent, conferences, representation of members' opinions to government, and the chance to exercise influence within TLI also offer incentives to membership. Besides Links, TLI has Connecting Links and Heir-O-Links. Eighty percent of TLI revenues come from annual membership dues of $60, and 20 percent from conventions, with incidental contributions from publication sales, corporate or business gifts or grants, and individual gifts or bequests. Contributions are not tax-deductible, because TLI is a 501 (c) (4) organization. It has a budget of $700,000, an increase over $600,000 in 1980, $300,000 in 1970, and $200,000 in 1960. In 1972, because African American people's needs can be so great, TLI decided to create an endowment fund to underwrite future scholarships and programs. To get the fund under way, members paid $30 apiece for each of the two following years. New members pay a $100 capital endowment assessment. A fund development committee is exploring corporate contributions to the tax-exempt permanent trust receptacle.

Incorporated in 1979, The Links Foundation, Incorporated (TLFI), shares officers with TLI; and all TLI members are TLFI members, too. The death of TLFI director Doris Chambers set into motion a search for her successor. TLFI is a 501 (c) (3) organization. With funding from the U.S. Health and Human Services Department Office of Substance Abuse Prevention, TLFI undertook a major demonstration/research project, LEAD (Links Erasing Alcohol and Drug Abuse), to prevent teenage pregnancy, alcohol and substance abuse, and sexually transmitted diseases among at-risk African American youth in targeted cities; subsequently, funding was renewed, and the project expanded to include children K–12.

TLFI also has a grants-in-aid program that has contributed in excess of $1 million to the United Negro College Fund (UNCF) and in excess of $107,000 to the National Urban League,* among other recipients. In 1990, it granted the Black Women's Agenda and Women's Finance Trust of Zambia $10,000 each. Out of $300,000 awarded, the 1992 National Assembly granted the National Association for the Advancement of Colored People (NAACP) Legal Defense and Education Fund (LDEF) $100,000 and instituted a "Sojourner" program to make funds available for emergency requests during the fiscal year.

POLICY CONCERNS AND TACTICS

Policy is set by the executive board and ratified by chapter delegates at the assembly. The board of directors, including officers, and membership polls exercise the most influence in discussions of TLI policy. Professional staff recommendations and the delegate assembly also function as important sources of influence. Ad hoc committees recommend strategy for specific problems. Preferred strategies include supplying congresspeople, state legislators, and staff with information; making personal or third-party presentations to members of the Congress, agency heads, or staff; offering written comments on proposed regulations; encouraging members to write legislators and committees; and participating in direct action political demonstrations. TLI also works to educate its members through publications.

TLI intends to devote much of its effort in the nineties to "reversing the creation of a permanent underclass of African American with little hope or aspirations." It will do this by promoting economic development and through public education around African American people's needs, as well as by supporting appropriate public policies. During 1990–92, besides economic development, it addressed issues of unemployment, health and wellness, education, women and empowerment, environmental concerns, persons with disabilities, minority concerns, civil rights, and older Americans.

Individual chapters undertake umbrella programs such as that of Durham, North Carolina, Links. The chapter literally constructed a three-bedroom house. A single woman-headed family now makes this house its home. Buffalo, New York, Links received an award for three continuing service projects, including one addressing women of color and cancer.

TLI has under consideration a proposal to include in its programming the

1989 World Summit for Children recommendation that the nineties be the decade for children's rights. TLI contributes to the Africare Southern African Initiative, including specific relief projects and development support. Besides in Africa, TLI works to assist global friends in Caribbean countries. It supports Human Rights Day observances, an African Water Wells project, and development of improved awareness on the Haitian refugee issue.

Federal laws of continuing importance to TLI include the 1963 Equal Pay Act; 1964 Civil Rights and Equal Opportunity Acts; 1965 Administration on Aging Act; Voting Rights Act; 1968 Federal Jury Reform and Antidiscrimination in Housing Acts; affirmative action executive orders; 1970 School Lunch Act; act of 1972 adding sex discrimination to the Civil Rights Commission jurisdiction; 1972 Equal Employment Opportunity Act and Title IX of the Education Amendments; the proposed equal rights amendment; *Roe* v. *Wade;* 1974 Equal Credit Opportunity, Housing and Community Development, Legal Services, and Office of Economic Opportunity Acts; 1974 Social Services and Women's Educational Equity Acts; Child Support Amendments—1975 Social Security Act; 1976 Day Care Act; proposed human life amendment; 1978 Pregnancy Disability Act; 1983 Social Security Act; 1984 Pension Equity, Child Abuse, and Child Support Enforcement Acts; 1986 Age Discrimination Act; and 1988 Civil Rights Restoration Act. TLI believes the worst changes in federal laws over the last decade came in tax laws affecting charitable giving.

TLI collaborates with UNCF, NAACP LDEF, the National Merit Scholarship Fund, and various foundations, sororities, and fraternities.

ELECTORAL ACTIVITIES

TLI does not see women's issues as partisan and does not have a political action committee, preferring to focus its efforts and resources on social services.

FURTHER INFORMATION

TLI publishes six newsletters, including *Link to Link,* the president's newsletter, and a semiannual Links journal. There also is a quadrennial directory. Audiotapes and videotapes from the national assembly are available for ten dollars and twenty-five dollars, respectively. New members of the organization may purchase an organizational history. There is a national resource list on HIV/ AIDS.

CHARLOTTE T. MORGAN-CATO

LOW INCOME HOUSING INFORMATION SERVICE
See NATIONAL LOW INCOME HOUSING COALITION

M
/

MANA, A NATIONAL LATINA ORGANIZATION
1101 17th Street, NW
Suite 803
Washington, DC 20036
(202) 833-0060

One of the most successful Latina feminist organizations, representing a broad range of political, professional, and occupational backgrounds, the volunteer nonprofit MANA establishes an important presence in national and international issues affecting Mexican American and Latina women and their communities throughout the United States.

ORIGIN AND DEVELOPMENT

A diverse group of fifty Mexican American women founded the Mexican American Women's National Association in 1974. Among them were Texan Blandina "Bambi" Cardenas Ramirez, a Rockefeller fellow working out of U.S. senator Walter Mondale's (D-MN) Washington, D.C., office, Californians Gloria Lopez Hernandez and Sharleen Maldonado, and Coloradan Bettie Baca Fierro. MANA, from the word *hermana,* or sister, provided testimony at the 1975 International Women's Year (IWY) hearings and sought equal representation on both the staff and delegation of the U.S. IWY team to the Mexico City conference. For this effort it earned early recognition among Chicana/Chicano rights activists.

By the time MANA elected Texan Evangeline "Vangie" Elizondo, a U.S. General Service Administration employee, as its first president in October 1975, the group had formulated the groundwork for its existence. It sought to provide a national forum by which Chicanas would have a voice in national issues of concern, provide leadership development opportunities, further parity relationships between Chicanos and Chicanas in professional, family, and community roles, support activities of organizations responsive to the quest for Chicana equality, develop communications networks for Chicanas across the United States, and stimulate public awareness for Latinas' and Chicanas' concerns. MANA intended to create a Chicana voice in the nation's capital by expanding Chicana political leadership and to represent the estimated 3 million Chicanas in the United States by developing equality with men. Under the 1977–79 leadership of Elisa Sanchez, a Silver City, New Mexico, native and National Council of La Raza leader, MANA grew into national prominence and has called attention to common issues faced by poor and underrepresented Hispanic communities throughout the United States.

Sanchez, as well as those who followed her—Wilma Espinoza of Colorado; Raydean Acevedo of California; Veronica Collazo and then Gloria Barajas of Texas; Rita Jaramillo, New Mexico; Irma Maldonado, California; Judy Canales, Texas; and Elvira Valenzuela Crocker, Kansas—increased the organization's effectiveness and credibility through continued and strong advocacy for Latinas. Whether the issues have been the equal rights amendment, reproductive rights, pay equity, health, welfare, education, civil or human rights, the census, the economy, or immigration, MANA has spoken in behalf of this country's Latinas.

ORGANIZATION AND FUNDING

The 501 (c) (3) organization is supported by membership dues and contributions from individuals, corporations, and foundations. MANA's growing membership is spread through thirty-six states with several chapters in California, Colorado, Kansas, Michigan, Missouri, New Mexico, Oregon, Texas, Virginia, and Washington, D.C. Its members are Cuban, Puerto Rican, and Central and South American, as well as Mexican American. Its members are homemakers, college students, government employees, professionals in all kinds of fields—and everything in between.

MANA elects officers every two years. Between annual meetings, generally held in the summer, it is governed by a twelve-member board of directors that meets twice a year, and an eight-member executive committee that meets monthly.

Its programs have been geared to the development of Latinas of all ages. MANA's legacy grows annually as its members take leadership roles in the private and public sectors across the country. Teenage Latinas are increasingly running for leadership positions in their schools and winning. Young and more mature women are being appointed and elected to public office and moving into senior corporate and government positions. MANA pursues its goals through:

• The Hermanitas Program, a teenage stay-in-school effort that exposes Latinas to career opportunities and provides self-development and leadership training. MANA members serve as mentors to the teenagers. The program is developing Latinas who are increasingly involved in their schools as elected leaders, staying in school through graduation, and seeking higher education in larger numbers.

- The Raquel Marquez Frankel Scholarship Program, named after one of its past leaders, geared to traditional and nontraditional college-bound Latinas. MANA is developing a cadre of future professionals and leaders through its financial assistance program. Scholarship recipients have gone into the fields of science, medicine, education, law, and engineering—paving the road to new leadership roles for Latinas.

- Economic Equity Project, which provides training and educational materials for MANA members and other Latinas on the subjects of employment, education, health, pay equity, and politics. The materials are geared to arm Latinas so that they can become their own best advocates.

- Leadership training through its local, regional, and national conferences, workshops, and meetings. The conferences are keyed to develop personal, professional, and leadership skills.

- Las Primeras, a national recognition program that honors women of achievement who are first in their fields and provides important role models for younger Latinas.

POLICY CONCERNS AND TACTICS

MANA has demanded Chicana representation in different administrations and supported Chicano appointments that work to defend Mexican American rights. MANA also supported the Southwest Voter Registration Project in 1979 to urge Hispanas to register to vote, recognizing the importance of Hispanas working together with other Latino groups to bring about political and economic change in their communities.

ELECTORAL ACTIVITIES

MANA does not have a political action committee.

FURTHER INFORMATION

MANA publishes and distributes its quarterly newsletter among its membership. The ''MANA Profile,'' a public relations reference tool, outlines its history and purpose.

CHRISTINE MARIN

MARGARET MAHLER INSTITUTE
See GRAY PANTHERS PROJECT FUND

MARGUERITE RAWALT LEGAL DEFENSE FUND (MRLDF)
c/o Mary W. Gray
Mathematics Department
American University
Washington, DC 20016
(202) 885-3120
FAX (202) 885-3155

The Marguerite Rawalt Legal Defense Fund (MRLDF) prefers cases advocating issues once considered to be priorities by the Women's Equity Action League (WEAL). WEAL chose to focus on equity issues, particularly economic equity, and because it perceived education as a major route to this goal, from the beginning it concentrated on educational opportunities. WEAL also pioneered in techniques such as the use of interns and intensive lobbying.

ORIGIN AND DEVELOPMENT

In 1972, feminist attorney and WEAL founder Marguerite Rawalt began the LDF that now bears her name. The fund was part of WEAL, which formed in 1968 when attorney Elizabeth Boyer found the National Organization for Women* too radical in its support of abortion and lesbian rights and in its protest activities. WEAL began with a forty-four-member national advisory board of such professional women as Sandra L. Bem, Jessie Bernard, Cynthia Fuchs Epstein, Ruth Bader Ginsburg, LaDonna Harris, Herma Hill Kay, Pauli Murray, Estelle Ramey, Alice Rossi, Jill Ruckelshaus, and Sarah Weddington and several congressmen and congresswomen. Once bylaws were formulated and a board of directors formed, Boyer served as the organization's first president. WEAL's fourth president, Arvonne Fraser, set up a Washington legislative office; and WEAL LDF undertook research and passed out information about gender discrimination.

In 1974, encouraged by board member Bernice Sandler, WEAL undertook litigation to require the U.S. Health, Education and Welfare Department (later, the Education Department) to enforce affirmative action requirements in higher education in what became a series of cases: WEAL v. Weinburg followed by WEAL v. Califano and WEAL v. Adams. For nearly twenty years the federal government operated under guidelines and timetables imposed by the WEAL suit's outcome. WEAL also received the opportunity to be kept informed about the progress of specific enforcement activities. Subsequently, the group presented Sandler with its Elizabeth Boyer Award. WEAL filed an amicus brief in Pittsburgh Press v. Pittsburgh Commission on Human Relations (1973). Attorney Marcia Greenberger prepared many of the LDF's briefs, and Rawalt filed still others.

WEAL's advocacy techniques featured lobbying, congressional testimony, and other public presentations as well as litigation. An extensive intern program—including college and high school students, older women returning to the workforce, and retirees—implemented its broad agenda. WEAL supported ratification of the equal rights amendment and stressed the need to introduce gender equity into tax laws, especially the Social Security system. The group took leadership through its LDF in persuading the British Parliament to open Rhodes scholarships to women. It also monitored the progress of U.S. government and private scholarship and fellowship programs, including the White House Fellowship program, toward funding substantial numbers of women. It had a federally funded program, Sprint, to promote opportunities for women in high school and college sport.

WEAL's long-standing foundation program on women in the military provided a unique focus on progress from admission to the service academies, to increased access to specialties, to provision of gynecological services in Veterans Administration hospitals. The program also including improvement of employment opportunities and other benefits for military spouses and women civilian employees of the armed services. The goal of official recognition of women in combat was not achieved, but substantial progress occurred in all other phases of the program.

MRLDF continues in operation, but WEAL ended operations in 1990, after other women's organizations had adopted similar issues and tactics. Although WEAL's membership never exceeded more than about 10,000, its leverage through an active presence on the Washington scene was substantial.

ORGANIZATION AND FUNDING

MRLDF has a board consisting of a chair and four other members. The current chair is Mary W. Gray, former president of WEAL.

Not a membership organization, MRLDF is a tax-exempt organization. Each year the interest on the foundation assets provides money for grants. The foundation has assets of approximately $125,000.

POLICY CONCERNS AND TACTICS

WEAL officers preferred cases advocating those issues considered WEAL's special purview, especially those involving higher education. Grants today are made in support of litigation expenses other than attorneys' fees. In its early days the LDF might have provided legal services as well; the attorneys would have donated their services but after a while, they found this not to be a feasible proposition on an ongoing basis. LDF does not itself bring actions nowadays, although it files or joins amicus briefs.

MRLDF is a leading advocate of pension and insurance equity. Pension equity was achieved through *Arizona Governing Committee* v. *Norris* (1986), a case in which WEAL filed an amicus brief. Insurance equity has not been achieved. MRLDF worked with more than 300 groups in the earlier movement to reverse *Gilbert* v. *General Electric Company,* leading to passage of the 1978 Pregnancy Discrimination Act. In keeping with its emphasis on higher education, WEAL played a part in producing an amicus brief in *Mississippi University for Women* v. *Hogan* (1982), J. O'Connor's first opinion on the U.S. Supreme Court, holding that the university's nursing school had to admit a male applicant. Many groups have not emphasized this area of litigation because of its uncertainty and expense. In 1981, WEAL joined a Lawyer's Committee for Civil Rights Under Law amicus brief concerning Title VII. Throughout the eighties, it was found among the friends of the court on nearly all major women's rights cases. One group it often has collaborated with is the Center for Law and Social Policy.

ELECTORAL ACTIVITIES

MRLDF does not engage in partisan activity and does not have a political action committee.

FURTHER INFORMATION

MRLDF does not have publications.

MARY W. GRAY

MARY MCLEOD BETHUNE MEMORIAL MUSEUM-NATIONAL AR-CHIVES FOR BLACK WOMEN'S HISTORY
See NATIONAL COUNCIL OF NEGRO WOMEN

MATTACHINE SOCIETY (MS)

The Mattachine Society (MS) was an organization dedicated to the rights of the homosexual minority in the United States. It illustrated that a cohesive base for organizing around gay rights was possible in the United States and may be credited with beginning the homophile movement, a broad-based movement to integrate homosexuals into society and afford them equal rights on a par with heterosexuals.

ORIGIN AND DEVELOPMENT

Until the early 1970s, women remained a woefully small percentage of MS, and virtually no MS programs focused specifically on women's issues. In July 1950, (Henry) Harry Hay, a native of England and dedicated Communist, had gathered together a group of eight gay men concerned about the treatment of homosexuals. The organization, originally known as International Bachelors Fraternal Orders for Peace and Social Dignity, sometimes referred to as Bachelors Anonymous, was described as "a service and welfare organization devoted to the protection and improvement of Society's Androgynous Minority." Reasons for organization included fighting against persecution of minorities, ending government indictment of "androgynous civil servants," securing the employment of and asserting the rights of "Androgens"—10 percent of the population—to their "place in the sun" along with other minorities. Although MS began as a vehicle to support political candidates, it broadened its focus to encompass many aspects of homosexual rights.

Hay based his figure of 10 percent on the Kinsey reports. Alfred Kinsey's *Sexual Behavior in the Human Female* (1968) asserted that at least 7 percent of women are exclusively homosexual. Hay, in fact, considered women when he conceived MS but believed that women's issues might be addressed by "supplementary subsidiaries" such as "International Spinsters Orders."

MS took its name from the medieval European guild organization, Mattassins, which on April 1 each year would parade in costumes and masks and poke fun at the church hierarchy and monarchies. Because they celebrated a religious festival, these revelers were exempt from prosecution for voicing unpopular views. It is assumed by recent historians of the period that the flamboyancy of the Mattassins' antics drew many homosexuals to its ranks.

The founders understood that they needed a political analysis on which to base their organizing and actions, and for this, they looked to their own lives. They understood that to equate man or masculine *only* with husband and father and to equate woman or feminine *only* with wife and mother served heterosexuality's purposes and did not generate an adequate sense of value for homosexuals. A new set of values had to be found. This new structure was finally identified as a legitimate social minority within the dominant culture. By the early autumn of 1951, the membership pledged: "We are resolved that our people shall find equality of security and production in tomorrow's world. We are sworn that no boy or girl, approaching the maelstrom of deviation, need make that crossing alone, afraid and in the dark ever again." Geraldine Jackson, one of the few women members, remembered that people believed they were doing something tremendously worthwhile.

A new philosophy of liberation emerged after a year. Despite personal support and popularity, the founders relinquished leadership to the conservatives. The new leaders stated that sex variants were not a cohesive homosexual minority but the *same* as all others in society except in the object of their sexual preference. Individualism, sensitivity to dominant mores, and expertise came to predominate. MS quit cultivating the grass roots in favor of participating as research subjects. This more conservative attitude prevailed for the next twenty years in America's homophile movement. The policy in the organization's newsletter *Mattachine Times,* of devoting half its pages to women's issues and women writers, often came under attack for giving so much space to a minority of the readership.

The *Mattachine Review,* which produced a major bibliography with over 1,000 entries, published biographical articles on writers such as Radclyffe Hall and Walt Whitman, historical articles on homosexuality in Europe, and political pieces including the draft of a new model penal code released by the American Law Institute in 1965. Much space went to developments in English law, including the 1957 Wolfenden Report, and to the positive opinions of psychologists such as Evelyn Hooker. The *Mattachine Review* published articles and letters from gays and lesbians around the United States and detailed their lives, loves, political concerns, and frustrations. When *The Ladder,* a Daughters of Bilitis* publication, appeared in 1956, many women's articles were submitted here rather than to *Mattachine Review.*

The Mattachine Society of the Niagara Frontier (MSNF) appears to have bridged the historical gap between the predominantly male-led homophile movement and the new wave of gay liberation and lesbian feminist organizations of the post-Stonewall era. The forces of the women's liberation movement finally proved too strong, however, to be ignored by the women of Mattachine. This last Mattachine Society in the United States finally became a paper organization by the early 1980s.

ORGANIZATION AND FUNDING

Because of Hay's familiarity with the Communist Party, MS's structure initially reflected a combination of party and Masonic guild structure, which was useful in the division of tasks. Chapters were founded throughout California, and these attracted a few women, but women rarely rose to positions of leadership. Within MS's first year of existence, the founder's Communist leanings and affiliations came under scrutiny. Senator Joseph McCarthy (R-WI) headed the House Committee on Un-American Activities, and it had subpoenaed Mattachine's lawyer to testify. He refused. But the growing conservative factions in Mattachine became nervous. Under the new leadership of Kenneth Burns, Marilyn Rieger, and Hal Call, Mattachine became a simple membership organization led by a coordinating council.

In January 1970, MSNF, an independent organization, as were all those formed outside California, was founded in Buffalo, New York. From the outset many women in the public gay and lesbian bar community became involved. These women quickly rose to leadership positions, including the presidency, assumed in 1971 by Bobbi Prebis. In 1972, MSNF sponsored Madeline Davis as the first openly lesbian delegate to the Democratic National Convention in Miami, Florida. At its organizational peak, during the first six months, MSNF had over 200 members.

MSNF had no recorded budget. Moneys were collected as projects necessitated. In later years, an annual budget was submitted primarily for running the only solely community-supported gay center in the United States. (Los Angeles's center was supported by grants.)

POLICY CONCERNS AND TACTICS

Throughout the fifties and sixties, Mattachine chapters founded in Chicago, St. Louis, Washington, D.C., and New York City worked on issues of jobs and housing discrimination and gay bar raids and supported political candidates sympathetic to the gay cause. Under MSNF's watchful eye, the Buffalo Common Council passed one of the few gay rights ordinances in the country. MSNF worked for legal change, used "expert" testimony, and debated the police department and state legislators; it also participated in the first New York State march on the capital in Albany in 1971, had a major counseling effort, and for many years ran the only self-supporting gay and lesbian community center in the country. After a time, specifically women's issues—lesbian mothers' custody fights, lesbian health, child abuse in lesbian lives, and so on—as well as a growing consciousness about sexism became overpoweringly compelling and ultimately led to a split in the movement.

ELECTORAL ACTIVITIES

MS did not see lesbian and gay issues as partisan, although it recognized that liberal Democrats would have more sympathy for gay issues than others. At election time, all candidates were surveyed.

FURTHER INFORMATION

The *Fifth Freedom* was MSNF's monthly publication. It contained articles, drawings, photos, interviews, and news briefs of local and national interest.

                                                                MADELINE DAVIS

MEDICAL WOMEN'S NATIONAL ASSOCIATION
See AMERICAN MEDICAL WOMEN'S ASSOCIATION

MEXICAN AMERICAN LEGAL DEFENSE AND EDUCATIONAL FUND CHICANA RIGHTS PROJECT (MALDEF CRP)
634 S. Spring Street
11th Floor
Los Angeles, CA 90014
(213) 629-2512
FAX (213) 629-8016

The Chicana Rights Project (CRP) marked an attempt by the Mexican American Legal Defense and Educational Fund (MALDEF) to use litigation and advocacy to improve the status of poor Hispanic women. A small program, it lasted only nine years; however, MALDEF continued to pursue its goals through other programs.

ORIGIN AND DEVELOPMENT

Inspiration for CRP came from a group of San Antonio Hispanic women political activists who approached MALDEF about using litigation to help solve problems confronting poor Hispanic women. A central figure in the group was Patricia Vazquez, a staff member for Congressman Harry B. Gonzalez (D-TX). The national president of MALDEF, Vilma Martinez, played a central role in CRP's early development.

CRP began in 1974 and ended in 1983 because of lack of outside funding. Project participants argue that it died from general cutbacks in civil rights funding and from apathy about the problems of minority women by the funding sources. It simply could not maintain sufficient funding in the face of the strong competition for dwindling grants. Participants believed that, in part, they competed with women's groups that were not focused on minority issues. Believing in CRP's goal's, MALDEF decided to give priority to suits involving women's needs and to handle the types of cases CRP pursued through other programs. Subsequently, over half of MALDEF's clients in the San Antonio office have been women.

ORGANIZATION AND DEVELOPMENT

CRP functioned as part of a nonprofit, nonmembership organization focusing on litigation and advocacy on behalf of Hispanic Americans. MALDEF is governed by a board that selects a president and general counsel to provide day-to-day direction for the organization.

CRP originally had two attorneys—the project director and a staff attorney—and a full-time paralegal. The first project director was Patricia Vazquez, followed in 1979 by Carmen Estrada. All the attorneys for CRP were women. Originally, both attorneys worked in San Antonio; later, one went to San Francisco, the national headquarters of MALDEF at the time. By 1983, CRP had only one attorney. As in MALDEF, throughout the project, CRP placed primary reliance on paid staff.

CRP began with a grant from the Ford Foundation and continued to be influenced by the foundation. Despite an aggressive effort, CRP eventually ended because of the inability to obtain additional funding. CRP did receive a few small grants from, for example, Levi Strauss and the Catholic Church. After grants dwindled, MALDEF paid salaries and expenses for the last eighteen months of CRP's existence. MALDEF has tax-exempt status; and at the time of the project, contributions were tax-deductible. CRP's annual budget reached approximately $50,000 for three years; it declined to around $25,000 at the end.

POLICY CONCERNS AND TACTICS

MALDEF traditionally has encouraged strong staff initiative and decentralization. If a CRP attorney believed that a client had a case that fit CRP's goals, that the case could be won, and that there were sufficient funds, the attorney would attempt to ''sell'' the case to the project director, who, in turn, sought approval of the national office. The project director made program decisions once an initiative was approved.

The primary tactic used by CRP was to file a lawsuit. As did MALDEF, the project preferred cases likely to have wide impact and, thus, did not serve primarily as a simple legal aid agency. Because of the traditionally weak status of CRP's clients, opposing parties seldom accepted negotiation and compromise. Generally, cases proceeded to a court ruling. Because they lacked funds and personnel, the attorneys made heavy use of amicus briefs and coattailed on suits filed by others. Underfunding meant a heavy caseload for the small staff, a source of frustration.

CRP's clients came from among indigents denied access to public services, particularly health and job training, and government employees victimized by discrimination. CRP lawyers found that health and employment issues were of vital importance to poor Hispanic women and that many of the abuses they suffered were susceptible to legal attack. CRP filed about a dozen cases a year. Some of its victories included changes in admission requirements for Comprehensive Employment Training Act (CETA) job training in San Antonio that admitted more Hispanic women than previously and admission of more women into training for nontraditional jobs in New Mexico, compulsion of various private employers not to discriminate against women in hiring, increasing access to prenatal care in California and Texas, and stopping the Laredo, Texas, hospital district from requiring immigration documents before admission to the emergency room and from dumping poor patients.

CRP participants view it as successful; they also note it faced problems. Besides the limited number of cases its small funding permitted, CRP found that discrimination against Hispanic women in education was more difficult to attack legally than were problems in employment and health. Thus, it elected not to pursue education issues. In some instances CRP lost cases but contributed to the development of eventual solutions. For example, sterilization of poor minority women without informed consent was a problem in charity hospitals and welfare programs in the Southwest. CRP appealed a Los Angeles sterilization case begun by Legal Services lawyers. It lost; but the case and attendant publicity contributed to the development of federal regulations in keeping with CRP's goals. In other instances, CRP lost decisions that would be won or even unnecessary today. For example, CRP challenged the Texas State Employment Commission's rejection of unemployment compensation for women who lost work because they were pregnant. A later U.S. Equal Employment Opportunity Commission rule required essentially what CRP had sought.

Originally, CRP put out a monthly action alert to Hispanic organizations and published pamphlets explaining women's legal rights, but with little money and personnel, it came to concentrate on litigation. CRP did not attempt to lobby the executive or legislative branches of government but rather focused on influencing policy through litigation. It did, however, respond to requests for information from political leaders and the media.

CRP made a strong effort to coordinate its work with other organizations, most often in the Texas area with the League of United Latin American Citizens (LULAC), American G.I. Forum, and Image. There also was cooperation by both the San Antonio and San Francisco offices with the American Civil Liberties Union* and the U.S. Legal Services program. Through the initiative of the Ford Foundation, CRP developed a working relationship with two other women's rights organizations, Equal Rights Advocates of San Francisco and the National Women's Law Center in Washington, D.C. On such issues as reproductive choice, CRP received support from mainstream women's organizations. However, on what CRP considered the critical issue of access to basic public services such as hospital emergency care, CRP received little cooperation for several years. Nonminority women generally had access to the facilities, and their organizations failed to perceive that there was a problem. By the 1980s, mainstream women's rights organizations began hiring minority attorneys and sharing some of CRP's concerns. CRP had no specific group as an adversary.

ELECTORAL ACTIVITIES

Neither CRP nor MALDEF operated a political action committee. CRP lacked the personnel, resources, and orientation to engage in electoral politics. CRP viewed both major parties as unresponsive to its clients and saw partisan activity as inconsistent with nonprofit status.

FURTHER INFORMATION

CRP produced a number of pamphlets in English and Spanish aimed at explaining women's legal rights in laypersons' terms. Topics included job training through CETA, health and immigration issues, and women's rights in Texas. Several CRP publications are archived in the Benson Latin American Library of the University of Texas.

ROBERT E. BILES

MOTHERS AGAINST DRUNK DRIVERS
See MOTHERS AGAINST DRUNK DRIVING

MOTHERS AGAINST DRUNK DRIVING (MADD)
511 East John Carpenter Freeway
Number 700
Irving, TX 75062
(214) 744-MADD
FAX (214) 869-2206/2207

Mothers Against Drunk Driving (MADD) seeks to end impaired driving and support victims of that violent crime by having society become accountable for responsible alcohol consumption, particularly when associated with driving. MADD's members often are married women victimized by an alcohol-related crash.

ORIGIN AND DEVELOPMENT

Founded in 1980 as Mothers Against Drunk Drivers, MADD grew from a small group of concerned citizens led by Candy Lightner. The founders did not know each other from previous organizational activity. A drinking driver killed Lightner's thirteen-year-old daughter, Cari, on May 3, 1980, and this tragedy, combined with the opinion of police that the driver would not be incarcerated, moved her to call Congressman Robert Takeo Matsui (D-CA) about the situation. She had a lot to discuss: the driver not only had previous alcohol-related arrests and a valid license but thereafter was arrested again. (Convicted that time, he served two and one-half years.) MADD's mission statement called for mobilizing victims and allies to turn public opinion on "impaired driving as unacceptable and criminal, . . . to promote public policies, programs and personal accountability."

Lightner applied her savings and insurance proceeds to MADD's expenses during its first year; and volunteers staffed the organization's office in Fair Oaks, California. After repeated daily visits to Governor Jerry Brown's Sacramento office, Lightner persuaded him to establish a statewide commission to study the drinking and driving problem. He appointed Lightner to it. MADD set out to counsel victims and sought mandatory sentences for first-time offenders and both sentences and license suspensions for repeat offenders. It then had four California chapters.

Another early organizer was Cindy Lamb of Maryland, whose daughter Laura, in 1979, at five and one-half months, became the youngest person with quadriplegia when a repeat offender crashed into the family truck; Laura died at age six. Lamb founded a MADD chapter in Maryland in 1980. By 1981, MADD had twenty-five chapters in five states and a $26,000 budget. Nine states had passed laws to curtail drinking driving; and arrests in Maryland increased 10 percent after state troopers went on overtime to provide additional highway patrols. California enacted some of the strictest laws nationally to stiffen sentences; arrests and deaths in the state decreased. The California Supreme Court paved the way to more serious charges by finding drinking driving to be socially malicious behavior.

In 1982, although he favored state-based solutions, President Ronald Reagan established a national Commission on Drunk Driving and appointed Lightner to it. By then MADD had 89 chapters in twenty-nine states and had received a $60,000 National Highway Traffic Safety Administration (NHTSA) grant. Nearly 60 percent of the states had reformed their laws. In many, a blood alcohol content (BAC) of 1 percent or more in a driver became a per se criminal violation. Maryland kept logging increases in arrests and posted a 20 percent reduction in highway deaths. MADD chapters began youth education programs; and the national chapter began an annual poster and essay contest. Lightner persuaded the Congress to give the states monetary incentives to raise the drinking age; four states did. In 1983, NBC produced a movie about MADD and Lightner. A little over a year later the group has 184 chapters in thirty-nine states.

Lightner kept after a national minimum drinking age law. The presidential commission recommended that states with a drinking age below twenty-one be denied federal highway funds. By mid-1984, a national act became a reality, and with President Reagan's support. U.S. Transportation Department (DOT) secretary Elizabeth Dole announced drunk driving no longer was tolerable and acknowledged MADD's role in raising awareness on the issue. The 1986 Budget Reconciliation Act made the minimum age law permanent.

From 1980 to 1985, Lightner filled the roles of MADD president, executive director, and chief executive officer. MADD received funding from foundation grants, government agencies, and other organizations, corporate assistance, and many small individual contributions. In 1983, it moved to Texas to take advantage of Dallas office space provided by Allstate, a corporate sponsor; its East

Coast chapters had become so plentiful that the group needed to centralize geographically. In 1984, it changed its name to the present one, to emphasize the problem and act of impaired driving rather than the individual driver. By the period's end it had 325 chapters in forty-seven states.

In 1985, after an inquiry into MADD's fund-raising practices by the Council for Better Business Bureaus and the National Charities Information Bureau, Lightner and the national board of directors parted ways. Lightner found herself at last able to begin healing. The board assumed control over program implementation, agreeing that Lightner should receive the title of founder and consultant. By 1989, the board began hiring professionals to direct its 150-member staff; and MADD worked to balance the influence of autonomous grassroots volunteer activists, the board, and paid staff. These roles still are undergoing clarification and definition to improve operational efficiency, because in this arena intense volunteers and staff are susceptible to burnout.

Two organizations—Businesses against Drunk Driving and Students against Drunk Driving—have evolved from MADD. Its well-focused mission, to stop drunk driving and give victim support, has not changed, but it has become more elaborate. It has helped each of the fifty states strengthen penalties for drinking driving. Combined with Driving Under the Influence (DUI) laws passed in California in 1982, among many things, MADD can take credit for reducing the incidence of DUI-related crashes and recidivism among drivers convicted of DUI. In 1985, *Time* magazine named founder Lightner its "Man of the Year." In 1986, *Ladies Home Journal* named her one of its Top One Hundred Women in America, and the Young Women's Christian Association* gave her its Woman of the Year Award.

ORGANIZATION AND FUNDING

MADD has 420 local chapters and thirty-one state offices, largely located in state capitals. It also is represented in Canada, the United Kingdom, Australia, and New Zealand. There are yearly leadership conferences and an annual conference for state chairpersons/administrators. Fifteen of the twenty-five-member board of directors are women. Board members elected from all parts of the United States include one African American and one Hispanic. Board participation is encouraged of persons from lower-income strata and persons with disabilities. Two-thirds of the board must come from the grassroots level; one-third fills at-large positions, mainly as corporate representatives. Half of the six executive officers are women. The bylaws require that the national president be female and a victim of an alcohol-related crash. MADD's current president and national spokesperson is Milo Kirk.

In 1986, the group opened a Washington, D.C., office. Hired by the board, the national's current executive director is Robert J. King. There are 360 professional staff nationwide, two in Washington. Workers take a fixed level of responsibility and do not rotate jobs. They are rewarded by increases in remuneration or retainer. One person in the organization holds the job title of lobbyist.

In 1992, MADD counted 3.2 million individual members and supporters, up from 20,000 in 1984. In 1980, women made up 100 percent of members; most recently they are half of them. Discussion has centered on status in the past as a women-only group, and a decision was taken to change it. Dues are $20 for individuals and $150 for corporations; senior citizens join for $10, families for $30. Victims do not pay dues. Members join to advocate important values, ideas, and policies and have their opinions represented to government. These are people with a common goal. Members participate in consciousness-raising sessions, associate with like-minded people, and have a chance to exercise influence in MADD. Chapter leaders often are victims. Members stress information dissemination and educational efforts. Some seek to develop organizational skills.

MADD is a 501 (c) (3) organization. Its budget totals about $50 million, up from $375,816 in 1982. Eighty-eight percent of this revenue comes from tax-deductible individual contributions, which may by earmarked for a given purpose. In equal amounts, dues, merchandise sales, government grants or contracts, corporation or business grants or gifts, bequests, foundation grants, fund-raisers, interest income, and in-kind donations account for the rest of the budget.

POLICY CONCERNS AND TACTICS

The volunteer board sets policy. Professional staff recommendations and executive officers' decisions also help determine MADD's agenda. To an extent, conferences and membership polls play a part in agenda building. Once the board has a position, staff develops appropriate guidelines for reaching it and timetables and so on for implementation; they draw on volunteer support and perceive it as limited.

MADD engages in a panopoly of strategies that include giving testimony to congressional and state legislative hearings; supplying congresspeople, state legislators, and staff with information; making personal presentations to legislators, agency heads, or staff; testifying at agency/department hearings and offering written comments on proposed regulations; educating the membership with publications and encouraging it to write legislators and committees; educating the public through press releases; participating in direct action political demonstrations; conducting and publishing research on issues as well as participating in public and private studies; and fielding public service campaigns such as that underwritten with State Farm Insurance Companies and Jayne Fitzgerald Productions in 1986. MADD had ongoing contacts with public policymakers seeking its views.

MADD files amicus briefs and finds most important its brief concerning the constitutionality of sobriety checkpoints. In *Michigan* v. *Sitz* (1990), MADD argued that these checkpoints provide, without exception, the most effective means to protect the public against impaired drivers. In *Sitz* the U.S. Supreme Court broke its long-standing tradition of accepting only one brief per amicus to take two, from national and Michigan MADD. Other MADD amicus briefs have supported video camera use to document offenders' behavior. The judiciary has upheld this usage by law enforcement officials as admissible evidence.

In 1990, MADD set out to achieve a 20 percent decrease in alcohol-related traffic fatalities by 2,000. It identified a set of initiatives to pass within five years in five areas: youth issues, enforcement, sanctions, self-sufficiency, and responsible marketing and service. The initiatives include a .00 BAC for persons under twenty-one, a prohibition on marketing alcoholic beverages to underage youth, and criminalization of alcohol provision by adults to them; preliminary breath testers, mandatory BAC tests after crashes causing death or serious injury, and open container restrictions; mandatory confinement of repeat offenders, a prohibition on plea bargaining, and integrated systems for tracking drinking and driving convictions; application of offender-generated fees and fines and alcoholic beverage taxes to program funding; and responsible alcohol advertising, alcohol warning labels, and state guidelines prohibiting "happy hours." MADD further supports state constitutional amendments for crime victims and sanctions against impaired drivers with minors in the vehicle.

MADD the organization focuses on prevention, and members typically see strict penalties as an optimal solution. Among federal laws of continuing importance to the group is the 1968 Federal Jury Reform Act. MADD sees as the most important federal legislation of the last decade the 1984 amendment to the Highway Safety Act offering states incentives to increase the drinking age and a 1989 Omnibus Anti-Drunk Driving bill. Also of great interest have been administrative driver's license revocation and .08 BAC limits at the state level. MADD has involved itself daily to make key input on these policies.

MADD considers the worst initiative of recent years the 1991 Intermodal Surface Transportation Infrastructure Act, which provided weak funding for drunk driving initiatives. It regrets that the Random Drug Testing bill for commercial drivers took a long time to pass. It finds DOT engineer-oriented, keeping funds in construction instead of such key safety areas as drinking driving. Similarly problematic have been transportation unions opposing random testing. A 1991 New York City subway crash by an alcohol-impaired operator, which killed 5 people and injured over 200, resulted in provisions in the 1992 transportation appropriations act to amend drug testing rules to include alcohol testing and to extend the rules to mass transit workers.

Overall, MADD sees an improvement in the eighties over policy of the seventies, when most cities spent less on law enforcement, and arrests for public drunkenness decreased. It does not consider the problem of drinking driving to have been resolved.

Since its founding, MADD has worked with NHTSA and the Offices of Victims of Crime and of Substance Abuse Programs, along with Remove Intoxicated Drivers* in some states, SADD, Advocates for Highway and Auto Safety, and National Federation of Parents for Drug-Free Youth (NFPDY). In 1986, it participated in the National Association of Broadcasters Operation Prom/Graduation Task Force with the American Floral Marketing Council, National Restaurant Association, NFPDY, National Federation of State High School Associations, and NHTSA, among other groups. Its adversaries include the Distilled Spirits Council, National Beer Institute, and National Beer Wholesalers Association, which it finds always work against issues of concern.

ELECTORAL ACTIVITIES

MADD does not see its issues as partisan and does not have a political action committee.

FURTHER INFORMATION

MADD has a newsletter, *MADD in Action,* published three times yearly. Twice a year MADD publishes a magazine for victims, *MADDVOCATE,* and victim support material and has a journal for public sale/consumption. It also publishes research reports, for example, in September 1991 a ''National Tracking Study to Identify the American Citizen's Attitudes and Behavior Regarding Drunk Driving.''

SARAH SLAVIN

NATIONAL ABORTION AND REPRODUCTIVE RIGHTS ACTION LEAGUE (NARAL)
1156 15th Street, NW
Suite 700
Washington, DC 20005
(202) 973-3000
FAX (202) 973-3096

The National Abortion and Reproductive Rights Action League (NARAL) argues for abortion rights and responsible reproductive health policies. With this message to display the philosophical breadth of the pro-choice movement, NARAL hopes to enhance its strength in legislative and electoral politics. NARAL consists of three legal entities: NARAL; The NARAL Foundation, a 501 (c) (3) organization; and a political action committee, NARAL-PAC.

ORIGIN AND DEVELOPMENT

Established in 1969 at the first conference on abortion laws and originally named the National Association for the Repeal of Abortion Laws, NARAL was the first national organization of the pro-choice movement. Its founders sought to coordinate the efforts of state level abortion rights groups and to lobby aggressively for abortion legislation. Among those on the planning committee that established NARAL were Lawrence Lader (Chair), Ruth Proskauer Smith (Vice Chair), Betty Friedan, and Bernard Nathanson (later a prominent member of the pro-life movement).

Although abortion rights have remained its first priority, NARAL has expanded its mission and adapted its political strategies to political circumstances. From 1969–73, NARAL coordinated lobbying campaigns in the states, encouraged litigation against restrictive legislation, and conducted public demonstrations. With the 1973 *Roe* v. *Wade* ruling, NARAL changed its name and increased its Washington presence, orchestrating congressional lobbying to create a pro-choice coalition including Planned Parenthood Federation of America* (PPFA), the Religious Coalition for Abortion Rights* (RCAR), and American Civil Liberties Union.*

Like *Roe, Webster* v. *Reproductive Health Services* (1989) greatly altered NARAL's political style. The organization returned somewhat to its pre-1973 state-based lobbying campaigns, grassroots organizing, and public relations work. Immediately after *Webster,* consultation with pollsters led NARAL to select the "Who Decides?" message, which redefined reproductive choice as an issue of individual liberty, a slogan for its campaigns. In 1992 the organization began to stress its concern for more responsible reproductive health care policies, including sexuality education, family planning, prenatal care and freedom from coercive reproductive policies. Given the diversity of opinion among pro-life organizations regarding these issues, the unity of the pro-choice coalition is a valuable political resource. NARAL remains at the forefront of congressional lobbying for the Freedom of Choice Act.

ORGANIZATIONS AND FUNDING

The early NARAL was a loose coalition of state-based interest groups; affiliate and national responsibilities gradually were designated. Affiliates work with field managers and must adopt the national NARAL mission, though they have their own boards and fund-raising activities. In turn, the national organization provides grants and staff for state-level groups. NARAL's growth suggests that this power balance is workable and generally satisfactory. Before 1973 NARAL had 23 affiliates; by 1983 there were 40; and in 1994 NARAL claimed 36 state affiliates.

The 21-person Board of Directors, chaired by Melonease Shaw, sets NARAL policy and strategy at its three annual meetings. The board has eight committees. The president is Kate Michelman; previously Michelman's job title was executive director. This structure keeps the organization focused and yet flexible, a necessity in a national office with a professional staff of only forty. Two are registered lobbyists, and three are attorneys. The annual budget is approximately $6.3 million.

Affiliates provide NARAL with a core of activists. NARAL membership is held by individuals and has increased steadily from 2,000 members before 1973 to more than 500,000 in 1994. Over two-thirds of the membership are women, with most male members as part of a married couple. Aware that its support in society needs to become more diversified, NARAL currently seeks to recruit members and staff from varied ethnic, racial, and socioeconomic backgrounds. The national organization, meaning to set an example, has established an educational program on membership and staff recruitment/retention.

Most people join NARAL principally to endorse the pro-choice agenda and to support lobbying and policy research. Members also believe NARAL can effect change through litigation and media campaigns.

POLICY CONCERNS AND TACTICS

Effective in the Congress, NARAL in the early 1990s was also known for grassroots organizing. Many NARAL activists have participated in the well-known pro-choice marches on Washington. NARAL often works with RCAR, the National Organization for Women,* and United States Students Association in organizing such events. When NARAL lobbied to defeat the Supreme Court nomination of Robert Bork, the list of allies also included People for the American Way, Alliance for Justice and Leadership Conference on Civil Rights. Employment-related health issues have led NARAL to work with the American Federation of State, County and Municipal Employees,* American Federation of Government Employees, Service Employees International Union* and the American Federation of Labor—Congress of Industrial Organizations.* That NARAL takes political action by first creating a network reflects its institutional character and history. Its leadership often comes from other pro-choice organizations; past director and current president Michelman formerly was a PPFA affiliate executive director. From its earliest days, NARAL activities have depended upon the support of others.

To reach pro-choice activists and others, NARAL conducts well-researched, forceful media campaigns. Their advertisements reveal a solid understanding of media markets and public attitudes. The *New York Times* and *Washington Post* are used to mobilize pro-choice citizens and communicate with decision makers. During the week before the *Webster* argument, these papers were part of a $25 million print-radio-television campaign. NARAL uses smaller markets and local papers to capitalize on situations where the abortion issue is already before the public. Thus, NARAL placed a number of advertisements in the Wichita papers during the Operation Rescue* demonstrations; NARAL also has invested in media campaigns on behalf of Democrat Douglas Wilder's election as Virginia's Governor and against U.S. Senator Jesse Helm's (R-NC) re-election and Republican Dick Thornburgh's unsuccessful senatorial campaign in Pennsylvania.

NARAL files amicus briefs in cases of national or state significance. NARAL attorneys, for example, submitted two briefs in the *Webster* case. In mid-1992, NARAL was active in several cases pending in the state and federal courts. There is a close relationship between NARAL's lobbying and litigation efforts.

ELECTORAL ACTIVITIES

NARAL PAC registered with the Federal Election Commission on August 5, 1977. During the 1977–79 election cycle, the PAC contributed $51,257 to campaigns; by 1989–90, contributions rose to $384,225. NARAL PAC is among the 20 wealthiest ideological and/or single issue PACs. It requires that candidates be unreservedly pro-choice to receive an endorsement. Funding is further contingent upon whether pro-choice issues play a role in the election, which must be winnable by the NARAL candidate. During the primaries, NARAL PAC usually will not endorse one pro-choice candidate over another. If a pro-choice candidate is an incumbent, NARAL might issue an early endorsement.

Although NARAL explicitly avoids articulating a partisan preference, 86–89 percent of its campaign donations from 1977 through 1990 went to Democratic candidates, but it is also true that the Republican party platform added a pro-life plank during the Reagan years. Developments during the Reagan and Bush administrations, particularly *Webster* and the Supreme Court nominations, have obliged NARAL to equal pro-life organizations in holding officials electorally accountable for their abortion position.

In the 1987–88 election cycle 117 congressional candidates were funded, with 72.4 percent of the donations going to House candidates (an average donation of $1,936), the remainder to Senate candidates (average donation $4,069). By 1991–92, a total of 163 candidates received NARAL PAC funding, 144 House candidates receiving 80 percent of the funds (an average donation of $2,727), and nineteen Senate candidates awarded average donations of $5,241. Only 56.9 percent of all 1987–88 donations went to incumbents. This number dropped in 1991–92, when only 42.4 percent of campaign donations went to incumbents. In contrast, 65 percent of union PAC financing and 81 percent of business PAC donations go to incumbents. The donations point to NARAL's financial strength, but its heavy financing of challengers suggests that the pro-choice PAC is still identifying its Washington supporters.

FURTHER INFORMATION

NARAL has an extensive list of publications and also issues a newsletter, "NARAL News."

MARYANNE BORRELLI

NATIONAL ABORTION COUNCIL
See NATIONAL ABORTION FEDERATION

NATIONAL ABORTION FEDERATION (NAF)
1436 U Street, NW
Suite 103
Washington, DC 20009
(202) 667–5881
FAX (202) 667–5890

ORIGIN AND DEVELOPMENT

The National Abortion Federation (NAF) is a professional association of abortion providers whose mission is to "preserve and enhance the quality and accessibility of abortion services" in the United States (NAF Annual Report 1991). It is a membership association representing providers of abortion services— physicians' offices, clinics, feminist health centers, and Planned Parenthood affiliates. NAF's goals are to set standards of performance for abortion providers, to coordinate continuing medical education and professional development, to serve as a voice in the policy arena for providers, and to ensure quality care and respect for women as the recipients of abortion services. In more recent years, the organization has also had to address issues such as a shortage of physicians to perform abortions, anti-abortion violence, and harassment of providers by anti-abortion demonstrators.

NAF was formed in 1977 from the merger of the National Abortion Council and the National Association of Abortion Facilities, two early organizations of abortion providers, with the Association for the Study of Abortion, a long-standing non-profit research organization in the field. The original founders and first board members included Frances Kissling, first executive director; Jeannie Rosoff, president of the Alan Guttmacher Institute; Christopher Tietze, statistician on abortion at the Population Council; Joan Babbott, a physician; and several rerpresentatives from Planned Parenthood. The impetus for forming NAF was the need for provision of safe, legal abortion services in the United States in the aftermath of the Supreme Court's 1973 *Roe* v. *Wade* decision. Since abortion was a controversial medical service provided by relatively few hospitals, free-standing abortion clinics developed to meet the needs of women. Also, because abortion had been illegal, clinicians had little experience in how to administer such facilities, provide appropriate counseling, and ensure high standards of medical care. NAF was founded to set standards for the performance of abortion services and to serve as a general mechanism for support and solidarity in a field in which providers of services were often marginalized.

NAF has grown from approximately 60 members in the beginning to a current roster of 300 institutional members and 75 individual members. The primary membership is institutional; most NAF members are clinics, health centers, and doctor's offices which provide abortion services or are involved in reproductive health issues in some way. Members include, for example, Preterm, Inc. (Boston), Women's Medical Services, P.C. (the only provider in the state of South Dakota), and the Alan Guttmacher Institute. There is also provision for auxiliary membership where persons can show their support by joining as individual members.

ORGANIZATION AND FUNDING

A twenty-member Board of Directors (including President, Vice President, Secretary, and Treasurer) oversees the policy, activities and budget of NAF. NAF also retains outside consultants for publications, development, and legal affairs. The national office, located in Washington, D.C., is run by four professional staff and approximately six support staff.

The current annual income of the organization is about $900,000; 40 percent of the income is generated by grants and contributions, 35 percent is generated by membership dues, 18 percent is generated by continuing education conferences, and the remaining 7 percent comes from a variety of sources (e.g., sale of publications, an annual auction, and group purchasing fees). Institutional members benefit from a variety of services, such as: savings on medical supplies through group purchasing; help with violence and disruption; discounts on publications and meetings; advice from legal experts; updates on legislative and regulatory changes; referrals from a national toll-free abortion hotline; and continuing medical education on reproductive health issues. In addition, the organization strives to articulate the concerns and interests of abortion providers in public policy settings.

POLICY CONCERNS AND TACTICS

NAF is a 501 (c) (3) nonprofit, tax-exempt organization which has elected to lobby within the limits of the law. It can and does testify before federal and state legislatures and regulatory agencies, but it has no separate lobbying arm and no PAC.

Although women are the recipients of provider services, NAF is not so much a women's interest group as a professional association which sets standards for abortion providers and furnishes them with a broad range of necessary services. In recent years, its continuing medical education conferences, which are accredited, have been very successful. NAF continues its public affairs work, monitoring court cases, contacting media, and maintaining its Washington regulatory watch for federal agency guidelines. It also maintains a Legal Clearinghouse which analyzes key federal health regulations and prepares a model pleadings book for clinics' use.

NAF's most recent efforts include a project to help teenagers and abortion providers comply with judicial by-pass regulations in various states, and a second project to address the growing shortage of abortion providers (83 percent of all counties in the United States have no abortion provider). NAF is also a major source of data and information for providers; it has a computerized data base on reproductive health, contraception, sexually transmitted diseases, and abortion. The Federation makes two annual awards: the Christopher Tietze Humanitarian Award to a worthy person in NAF who has made a significant contribution to women's reproductive health, and the C. Laylor Burdick Award, which honors the dedication and commitment of the "unsung heroes" providing abortion care. By uniting abortion service providers into a professional community dedicated to health care, NAF works to overcome the stress and marginalization these providers face and to maintain the legitimacy of abortion as a medical service.

For non-professionals, NAF is chiefly known for its referral service. It runs a national, toll-free hotline for information and referral to qualified providers (1–800–772–9100, 9:30 to 5:30 Eastern Standard Time). This consumer hotline answers from 5,000 to 10,000 calls a year, and is staffed by trained interns at NAF's Washington office. NAF also provides fact sheets, data and educational materials to non-members and to the general public.

SOURCES

Interview with Susan Shermer, Deputy Director of NAF and Training and Education Director, September, 1991.

Interview with Frances Kissling, currently president of Catholics for a Free Choice, formerly a founder and first executive director of NAF. September 1991.

"Making Choice Real," NAF, Annual Report 1990.

NAF Fact Sheets, 1989 and 1990.

"Abortion: A Matter of Women's Health," NAF, Annual Report 1991.

Interview with Patricia Anderson, NAF Membership Director, July 1992.

MARY C. SEGERS

NATIONAL ABORTION RIGHTS ACTION LEAGUE POLITICAL ACTION COMMITTEE
See NATIONAL ABORTION AND REPRODUCTIVE RIGHTS ACTION LEAGUE

NATIONAL AMERICAN WOMAN SUFFRAGE ASSOCIATION
See LEAGUE OF WOMEN VOTERS

NATIONAL ASSEMBLY OF RELIGIOUS WOMEN (NARW)
529 South Wabash
Suite 404
Chicago, IL 60605
(312) 663-1980
FAX (312) 663-9161

The National Assembly of Religious Women (NARW) is a movement of women of faith committed to the prophetic tasks of working inclusively, giving witness, raising awareness and engaging in public action to achieve justice. Since its origins in 1970, NARW has sought to address the issues of systemic injustice as they are impacted by racism, sexism, classism, and heterosexism in society, church, and world.

ORIGIN AND DEVELOPMENT

A grassroots membership organization, NARW's members came initially from women in Catholic religious congregations. Key founders in 1968 included Marjorie Tuite, Kathleen Keating, Rosalinda Ramirez, Linda Chavez, and Yolanda Tarango. Founding members knew each other from working on various social justice issues. Two factors contributed to founding NARW—Vatican II in the Roman Catholic Church, during which people were urged to heed poor people's needs, and concern about ongoing discrimination and exploitation of women in all social institutions. Private foundation grants, large and small contributions, and funding from religious congregations of women and men helped NARW get under way. In 1978, membership extended to all Catholic feminist women and women from other faith traditions sharing NARW's vision and justice agenda. Known in 1970 as the National Assembly of Women Religious, the organization's name changed to reflect membership changes. NARW subsequently became the cofounder of several other organizations including Network,* Women's Ordination Conference, Call to Action, Chicago Religious Task Force on Central America, and the Interfaith Task Force on Central America.

Since its beginning, the group's agenda has emphasized a ministry of justice that challenges members to use their organized power to effect systemic change. NARW has addressed an agenda including workers' rights, economic rights, homelessness, and opposition to militarism and U.S. intervention in other nations' affairs. This agenda has been strengthened further by insistence on empowerment and individual participation in decisions affecting a woman's life. NARW strives to use social analysis as a tool for change, to do theology as women of faith, and act collectively to build a world of peace with justice.

In the 1970s, NARW mobilized thousands of women across the United States in ministry for justice workshops. In 1989, an NARW packet about women and homelessness accompanied a successful skills training workshop in leadership development for staff and residents living and working in shelters, to enable them to conduct small group sessions to bring about a sense of community and actions toward systemic change. Shelters from numerous areas across the United States participated in this project. In 1991, NARW received funding from United Way to work extensively with homeless women throughout the Chicago area.

In July 1987, 200 women from diverse racial, ethnic, and economic backgrounds came together for a national NARW conference, Circle of Justice: Creating Inclusive Community. It initiated programmatic efforts to overcome barriers that keep women separated in the struggle for justice. That October, NARW's vision statement made explicit its commitment to work inclusively as women from diverse races or ethnicities, economic backgrounds, and sexual identifications. In 1988, through a membership survey, NARW women named two program priorities: creating inclusive women's communities and continuing their dissent within the Catholic tradition. The board affirmed these priorities in 1989; they now set the direction for NARW's work.

NARW's efforts at becoming a multicultural and antiracist grassroots/community-based organization continually deepen. The results of this commitment have received recognition as significant and unique among women's groups working for social justice from a faith perspective. These accomplishments are evidenced partly by the organization's diversified leadership and membership. In place is a set of criteria for the board to critique its efforts to become increasingly antiracist. Programmatic efforts and publications are planned and developed from the beginning by multicultural groups of women with end results reflecting this diversity. Since 1987, approximately 45–55 percent of those attending NARW national conferences have been women of African American, Native American, Latina/Hispanic, Asian, and Pacific Island heritage.

To assist members in efforts to work in solidarity, NARW developed an inclusive community project. Its major components include small group sessions guided by an eight-session packet focusing on experiences and issues related to race, class, gender, and sexual identity and facilitation of two related workshops. The project's ultimate goal is to enable women to work together in relationships of mutuality and respect in order radically to transform systems and structures based on domination, exploitation, and discrimination wherever they are found. Participants in the project develop an action plan that confronts the various "isms" as they are found both relationally and structurally in participants' groups.

ORGANIZATION AND FUNDING

The board of directors ultimately is responsible for NARW and consists of fifteen to twenty-five members. Membership on the board reflects diversity, which is necessary to accomplish the organization's goals and actualize its commitment to working inclusively. NARW members nominate women for the board and elect board members from a slate of nominees selected by the elections committee. Members of the national coordinating team serve on the board with a voice and vote. The national team consists of a coordinator, development coordinator, and administrative coordinator. NARW's national office has three paid staff. The national coordinator is Judy Vaughan.

NARW has approximately 3,000 members, all women. Men may become associate members. Membership is up from 1,100 in 1986, down from 5,000 in 1970. Besides in the United States, NARW has members in Canada, France, Germany, and Latin America. Throughout its twenty-two-year development, NARW constantly has evaluated membership to determine how most effectively to respond to the critical needs of our day and work for radical social change. Members join to advocate important values, communicate with their peers, and engage in education and action for justice. In the process, members experience friendship ties and association with similarly minded people.

Fund-raising efforts for NARW include membership fees of $20, two direct mail appeals, a sustaining pledge program, the sale of publications, and resources, grants, and foundation support. Dues constitute 20 percent of revenues; sales, 20 percent; grants, 20 percent; funds from churches, 20 percent; and gifts, 20 percent. Contributions are tax-deductible. The organization's total budget is $180,000, up from $56,000 in 1980 and $32,000 in 1970. A 501 (c) (3) organization, NARW has initiated a plan to increase its membership base so that it becomes the largest sustained contributor to the budget.

POLITICAL CONCERNS AND TACTICS

Since inception NARW has been a multi-issue organization with a focus on systemic injustices that most directly impact upon women's and children's lives. Through education and analysis, NARW makes connections among issues and advocates for change. The board sets this policy; and the coordinating committee makes decisions between board meetings. Professional staff and board discussion influence choices of strategies.

Besides educating the membership with publications, and the public through press releases, NARW participates in direct action. It advocates many different forms of action for systemic change, including interim legislative work. It sees as most significant movement building for radical social transformation but does some testifying in congressional and state legislative hearings and may supply congresspeople, legislators, and staff with information. It monitors voting records and files amicus briefs as in recent reproductive rights cases. Sometimes NARW encourages letter-writing campaigns. It sees legislative action as a good networking tool and consciousness-raising device but in the end not necessarily useful for systemic change.

Of importance to NARW are the 1964 Civil Rights and Food Stamp Acts, affirmative action executive orders, act of 1972 in which sex discrimination was added to Civil Rights Commission jurisdiction, the equal rights amendment, *Roe v. Wade,* the 1982 Welfare Act, and 1988 Civil Rights Restoration Act. It includes among the worst changes over the last decade reversals in civil rights and affirmative action and the rolling back of *Roe* v. *Wade.* Recently, it supported a national health care plan, reinstatement of federal funding for low-income housing, and initiatives useful to working women and their children.

NARW works in coalition with organizations, groups, and community-based efforts that have similar values and priorities. Significant values include the importance of grassroots/community-based participation; inclusivity, especially related to race, ethnicity, culture, class, and sexual identification; the call to be prophetic; and action to achieve justice. In becoming active on an issue, NARW identifies and meets with allies, develops a campaign, including use of NARW resources, and brainstorms and deliberates with groups committed to addressing the issue. Groups NARW has worked with include Coalition for the Homeless, the American Friends Service Committee,* Day Center for Justice, Las Hermanas,* Women for Economic Security, National Farm Worker Ministry, National Health Campaign, Children's Defense Fund,* National Committee on Pay Equity,* United Methodist Women,* Black Women's Health Network,* Women's Alternative Economic Network, and La Mujer Obrera.

NARW's adversaries include Catholics United for Faith and Family, Operation Rescue,* and organizations and institutions that support militarism, racism, economic exploitation, and homophobia.

ELECTORAL ACTIVITIES

NARW does not see women's issues as partisan and does not have a political action committee.

FURTHER INFORMATION

Probe, NARW's eighteen-year-old bimonthly publication, serves as the membership's educational and networking tool. Completed in January 1989, around

1,200 copies of a packet, *Homeless Women: Creating Community, Creating Change,* have been sold or distributed to shelters, transitional residences, and day programs for homeless or near-homeless women. In 1988, NARW produced a resource packet, *Economics: Women's Cry for Change;* more than 1,000 copies have been sold or distributed to date.

JUDY VAUGHAN

NATIONAL ASSEMBLY OF WOMEN RELIGIOUS
See NATIONAL ASSEMBLY OF RELIGIOUS WOMEN

NATIONAL ASSOCIATION FOR GIRLS AND WOMEN IN SPORT (NAGWS)
1900 Association Drive
Reston, VA 22091
(703) 476-3450
FAX (703) 476-9527 and/or
(703) 476-3400

The National Association for Girls and Women in Sport (NAGWS) is part of the American Alliance for Health, Physical Education, Recreation and Dance (AAHPERD). Primarily a professional education organization, its members are concerned with improving women's athletic programs and sport knowledge and getting more women into sport leadership positions at all levels of education and the Olympics.

ORIGIN AND DEVELOPMENT

In the 1890s, recreational physical education programs became popular in women's colleges to help women withstand the rigors of academic life. NAGWS began in 1899 as a committee to establish separate rules for girls' basketball. Alice Foster headed this committee when it developed into a rules-governing body. Clara Baer and Senda Berenson were other professionals who helped develop rules for girls' basketball. At a time when marriage was the favored female career, the idea of women's liberation was just emerging with the woman's club movement, 90 percent of women with leadership positions in women's athletics remained single to devote themselves full-time to their profession and work for women's rights in sport.

Although NAGWS has had several name changes, its affiliation with AAHPERD has continued. For years it served as both the primary rule-making body for girls' and women's sports and a counter to men's athletic groups. In 1972, when NAGWS was called the Division of Girls and Women in Sport (DGWS), Congress passed Title IX of the 1972 Education Amendments. This decision improved gender equity in sports in most areas except leadership. The National Collegiate Athletic Association (NCAA) interpreted Title IX as a mandate for its governance of both men's and women's sports. The percentage of women coaching women's teams fell from 90 percent in 1972 to 48.3 percent in 1992.

Because of court decisions in the 1980s involving the Association for Intercollegiate Athletics for Women* (AIAW) and NCAA, NAGWS now controls the rules for women's volleyball.

To maintain its effectiveness NAGWS has changed during the last decade. It has developed an Applied Strategic Plan focusing on long-term projects promoting advocacy, leadership, and coaching and participated in attempts to pass legislation to widen opportunities for women in sport. The Knight Foundation Commission on Intercollegiate Athletics, set up by NCAA to look at athletic reform with a focus on women's athletics, found that women playing intercollegiate sports trail men in scholarships, equipment, facilities, travel, and coaching. One of NAGWS's goals is to advocate for gender equity in sport.

NAGWS now sponsors coaches' institutes and the National Girls and Women in Sport Day, held in all fifty states in February. On this day in 1991, it initiated the Pathfinder awards to honor a member in each state who advocated for girls and women in sport. Recipients are selected by state committees in each state. The Pride Award is for minority women in sport. Two women, Alpha Alexander and Robertha Abney, have received it. The Nell Jackson Memorial Award is dedicated to an African American female coach, and the first recipient was Dorothy Richey, a member of the NAGWS board of directors.

ORGANIZATION AND FUNDING

NAGWS is affiliated with the National Riding Commission and the National Boards of Officials and has joint committees with the National Association for Sport and Physical Education (NASPE), also a part of AAHPERD. NAGWS is one of six national associations forming AAHPERD. As do each of the six, NAGWS has an independent volunteer board of directors that sets policy in its specific interest areas but that also acts in compliance with AAHPERD guidelines. NAGWS's board has as members the executive committee, including the president, past president, president-elect, a representative to the AAHPERD board of governors, and seven vice presidents. The vice presidents are in charge of professional development and leadership; publications and communications; advocacy and liaison; minority representation, including physically limited women, mature women, and ethnic minority women in sport; coaching enhancement; officiating enhancement; research division; and student representation. The board has one student representative, who oversees a student committee. All eleven board members are female, and two are from minority groups. Women over fifty have served on the board, but currently no women with disabilities serve. President Roberta Abney was elected by the membership to a two-year term. The executive director is Mary Hill, assisted by paid staff members.

To join NAGWS, individuals first must join AAHPERD. This paid membership automatically bestows membership in any two of the six associations, including NAGWS. In 1960, women made up 98 percent of NAGWS membership whereas today they form about 90 percent of it. The 9,000-plus members are teachers, coaches, athletic trainers, officials, athletic administrators, students, and athletes. Every year AAHPERD holds a convention to approve the actions of its various boards, vote on a president, and discuss issues and upcoming policy; the convention provides opportunities for communication by members to AAH-PERD and information exchange among members. All six affiliated associations participate. Convention participation allows NAGWS some publicity and a forum in which to promote the importance of women's athletics. AAHPERD is an influential organization, and educators and students in physical education and related fields as well as prospective professionals find membership helps their careers.

About 80 percent of NAGWS funding comes from its $85 annual dues. The sale of publications produces another 20 percent of revenue; before outside sports organizations made most of the rules for women's collegiate sports. NAGWS earned more money from the sale of its rule books. Even today, the NAGWS Volleyball Rulebook earns about $10,000 a year. NAGWS is a non-profit organization; and its operating budget for 1993–94 was $102,000, not including salaries. NAGWS also gets funding and grants from corporations and foundations for specific projects. It received $35,000 in 1993–94 from the U.S. Olympic Committee (USOC) to use for women's leadership development through the Olympic movement and for coaching education in cooperation with various national governing bodies of the USOC. In 1994, NAGWS hired a private contractor for marketing and fund-raising.

POLICY CONCERNS AND TACTICS

Members of NAGWS and its volunteer board, with the approval of AAH-PERD, influence strategies to achieve desired policies. NAGWS has a vested interest in seeing the Congress pass legislation for women in sport. It testifies in congressional hearings; consults for Title IX questions; makes personal presentations to members of the Congress, agency heads, and staff; writes comments on proposed regulations; educates its members with publications; conducts and publishes original research on issues; and seeks administrative review of agency and departmental decisions. NAGWS members played an important role in passing civil rights legislation such as Title IX of the 1972 Education Amendments, the 1978 Amateur Sport Act, and 1988 Civil Rights Restoration Act. Because NAGWS has a 501 (c) (3) status, that is, is tax-exempt, it acts directly only for bills affecting girls and women in sport. NAGWS is not the only rule-making body for women's sports, but it remains in the forefront of the fight for women's equality in sport.

Although unique, NAGWS collaborates with similarly inclined organizations such as the National Coalition for Women and Men in Education, Coaches Advisory Roundtable of the Women's Sports Foundation, National Association of Collegiate Women Athletic Administrators,* the Young Women's Christian Association of the U.S.A.,* and various other associations.

ELECTORAL ACTIVITIES

NAGWS has no political action committee.

FURTHER INFORMATION

NAGWS publishes a quarterly newsletter for its members and two journals and has a guide and rule book for public sale. Recently, it published a history entitled *A Century of Women's Basketball* and a *Title IX Tool Box* to help women take advantage of this law. It sponsors publications about women and athletics, especially about minority women in sport. Currently, NAGWS has about a dozen books for sale.

ELEANOR E. ZEFF

NATIONAL ASSOCIATION FOR SURROGATE MOTHERHOOD
See ORGANIZATION OF PARENTS THROUGH SURROGACY

NATIONAL ASSOCIATION FOR WOMEN IN EDUCATION (NAWE)
1325 18th Street, NW
Suite 210
Washington, DC 20036
(202) 659-9330
FAX (202) 457-0946

Since its founding in 1916, the National Association for Women in Education (NAWE) has sought to provide professional support for women educators through programs, services, advocacy, and scholarly publications.

ORIGIN AND DEVELOPMENT

NAWE had its origins in a 1903 meeting called by Marion Talbot, then the University of Chicago's dean of women (1892–1925). Previously, Talbot had participated in founding the Association of Collegiate Alumnae, which became the American Association of University Women,* and took part in the 1908 conferences preceding the American Home Economics Association's* formation. Although annual meetings continued to be held after 1903, NAWE, then called the National Association of Deans of Women, was not formally established until July 6, 1916. At that meeting, held at the Teachers College of Columbia University, Dean Kathryn Sisson McLean (Phillips) of Ohio Western University was elected the organization's first president.

In the first decade, membership grew from 50 to 980. Of this founding group, 13 percent were women of color, indicating a long-standing organizational commitment to membership diversity. Among the early African American members were Ruth Brett Quarles, Hilda Davis, and Lucy Diggs Slowe. Slowe was Howard University's first dean of women in 1922, a position she held until her death in 1937. In 1923, she became the first president of the National Organization of College Women, a group representing African American women college graduates, and in 1929, president of the National Association of Deans of Women and Advisors to Girls in Negro Schools (ADWAGNS). Davis followed in Slowe's path, becoming dean of women at Shaw University, an African American college in Raleigh; associate professor in English at Talledega College; and finally the second president of ADWAGNS after Slowe's death. Quarles served as assistant dean at Spelman College (1936–38), dean of women at Dillard University (1938–42), dean of students at Bennett College (1942–44), and associate personnel director at Tuskegee Institute (1945–49). She also followed Hilda Davis as president of ADWAGNS (1944–46).

During the first decade, twenty-four state associations were formed, and plans for a permanent headquarters office got under way. In 1934, the national office was set up in the National Education Association building in Washington, D.C.; a biennial convention pattern was established; and plans for a quarterly journal were under discussion. Between 1934 and 1960, the organizational membership grew, stabilizing at about 2,000 as the conference and journal attracted women administrators of varied job titles. As a result the organization's name changed over the years, first adding "counselors" in 1956 and "administrators" in 1967, to represent more accurately the group's constituency. In 1991, the organization assumed its present name. Throughout its history NAWE has been committed to the education and advancement of women in leadership positions in higher education. In its publications, programs, services, and advocacy NAWE has created a network through which members communicate.

ORGANIZATION AND FUNDING

Currently, NAWE has members in fifty states and nine countries and twenty local/state affiliates. Its fourteen-member volunteer executive board includes representatives of the caucuses for ethnic women, graduate students, and new professionals. These caucuses represent the concerns of their constituencies and present special programming for and about those concerns at the annual conference. Thirty percent of the current board and 20 percent of the entire organizational membership are African American. The president of the association, Lynne Davis, heads the board while the executive director, Patricia Ruckel, sits in an ex officio capacity and takes responsibility for the day-to-day operations of the national office in Washington, D.C.

Among the incentives for membership are publications. NAWE now holds a national conference in a different city each year. It also sponsors a separate national meeting for some 450 college women student leaders annually.

The principal funding for the organization has been, and continues to be, in the form of membership dues and fees related to the annual conference. Dues are $55 for new members and $65 for renewals. An 501 (c) (3) tax-exempt status organization, NAWE has an annual budget over $300,000. The board oversees the Ruth Strang awards, which fund two research projects annually; Strang served as editor of the association's journal from 1935 to 1960 and provided an important part of the intellectual leadership in the early years of

NAWE's development. These grants are competitive, refereed, open to non-members as well as members, and provide $750 per award.

POLICY CONCERNS AND TACTICS

Policy is set through resolutions developed by the members at the annual meeting or through mail ballots, in consultation with the board, president, and executive director. NAWE's key activities center on professional networking, enhancing organizational skills, and the publication of relevant research.

NAWE has supported the passage of civil rights and affirmative action legislation, the Family and Medical Leave bill, equal rights amendment, and other bills that would enhance equity and opportunity for women in education, including Title IX, funding for the Women's Educational Equity Act, and scholarships for part-time women students.

Historically, NAWE has collaborated on advocacy issues with a number of other organizations, including the National Association of Student Personnel Administrators, Intercollegiate Association of Women Students, American Council on Education,* Center for Women Policy Studies,* American Association of University Women,* National Coalition of Women and Girls in Education (NCWGE), and Federation of Professional Women's Organizations.* In 1963, NAWE president Helen B. Schleman (dean of women at Purdue University) became a member of the first President's Commission on the Status of Women.*

ELECTORAL ACTIVITIES

NAWE does not see its concerns as partisan. It does not have a political action committee but works with NCWGE (which represents over fifty women's organizations) to promote many legislative and executive issues related to equity for women and girls.

FURTHER INFORMATION

NAWE has a quarterly academic journal, *Initiatives;* a quarterly newsletter, *About Women on Campus;* monographs; and a membership directory. Some of the recent issues of "Initiatives" have focused on African American women in higher education, sexual harassment, and Catholic women's colleges. The newsletter includes information on campus climate, the academic workplace, and other educational equity issues, along with job announcements and news about conferences, publications, workshops, and awards of special interest to women.

PATRICIA ANNE CARTER

NATIONAL ASSOCIATION FOR THE REPEAL OF ABORTION LAWS
See NATIONAL ABORTION AND REPRODUCTIVE RIGHTS ACTION LEAGUE

NATIONAL ASSOCIATION OF ABORTION FACILITIES
See NATIONAL ABORTION FEDERATION

NATIONAL ASSOCIATION OF BROADCASTERS
See AMERICAN WOMEN IN RADIO AND TELEVISION

NATIONAL ASSOCIATION OF COLLEGIATE WOMEN ATHLETIC ADMINISTRATORS (NACWAA)
Women's Sports Foundation
Eisenhower Park
East Meadow, NY 11554
(516) 542-4700
FAX (516) 542-4716

The National Association of Collegiate Women Athletic Administrators (NACWAA) provides opportunities for leadership, development, and networking among individual women with an administrative role in intercollegiate athletics. The group plays an important part in the legislative politics of women's sports by evaluating legislation from, or drafting legislation for, national athletic governance organizations.

ORIGIN AND DEVELOPMENT

In 1978, a workshop was held for women in athletic administration prior to the Association for Intercollegiate Athletics for Women* (AIAW) convention. From this meeting came the formulation of the Women's Athletic Caucus (WAC). Although loosely organized, the group met annually, prior to the AIAW's delegate assembly, to discuss common administrative concerns and other athletic problems. At that time women especially were concerned with the loss of female representation through institutional mergers of men's and women's programs and mounting insistence by the National Collegiate Athletic Association (NCAA) to adopt women championships. During the year the caucus functioned as the only networking structure for women in sport and the organization also published a newsletter. In 1980, under the leadership of Judith Holland of the University of California at Los Angeles, and Barbara Hedges of the University of Southern California, twelve women formed an alternative to WAC, setting themselves up as the board of directors for the Council of Collegiate Women Athletic Administrators (CCWAA), NACWAA's predecessor.

Some AIAW members believed that the CCWAA emerged because the WAC was seen by the CCWAA's founders as too committed to the prevailing philosophy of the AIAW and not committed enough to change. For example, a small number of vocal women involved in the CCWAA urged significant rule changes in AIAW, especially with regard to the recruiting system. This dissatisfaction at least helped to precipitate the CCWAA.

The start of this alternative organization coincided with the AIAW's fight for survival. From 1975 onward, the NCAA had tried to start women's championships. The CCWAA's formation occurred in the same year as NCAA's vote to initiate women's Division II and III championships (January 1980). The following year NCAA voted to start Division I championships and to integrate women into the NCAA's governance structure. For some, but not all, in the CCWAA, the idea was to bring about a transition from the AIAW to the NCAA. After the AIAW's demise, women administrators from the WAC and the CCWAA met to explore the feasibility and desirability of a merger. The merger occurred, with the group retaining the name CCWAA; the name was changed in 1991 to the NACWAA to project a new, united image in line with other athletic administration organizations. "National" projected an all-encompassing organization rather than the regional group from which NACWAA originated.

Historically, the NACWAA has worked to establish a voice for women within the governance of intercollegiate athletics because with the AIAW's elimination, women lost their opportunity to direct women's athletics. In 1982, NCAA voting representatives were 95 percent male; in 1988. 91 percent male. The *Chronicle of Higher Education* continues to highlight these disparities and others. In addition the AIAW representation on sport national governing bodies was lost; the NACWAA acts as a forum for the discussion of issues, which, in turn, lead to legislative action in an attempt to provide leadership to help strengthen collegiate athletic programs, especially as they relate to women athletes. The NACWAA's equity resolution was instrumental in the NCAA's interest in the status of women's opportunities and the establishment of a Gender Equity Task Force, which published its results in 1992, documenting the great disparity in the treatment of men and women in intercollegiate athletic programs across the nation.

ORGANIZATION AND FUNDING

A board of directors meets three times a year: once in conjunction with the NACWAA's Fall Forum, the only national conference designed for women athletic administrators; again at the NCAA convention; and once more in the spring. The board has general power to administer the NACWAA's affairs and to initiate and carry out its programs and policies between Fall Forums. The board consists of the president, the NACWAA's official spokesperson; the immediate past president; president-elect; and twelve directors, at least four of whom come from the institutions from NCAA Divisions II and III, the National Association of Intercollegiate Athletics, and National Junior College Athletic Association. The membership currently has a 13 percent minority representation on the board. At this time the NACWAA does not maintain a permanent office or paid support personnel. The organization operates with volunteer officers and board members.

Active membership is open to women employed by a university, college, conference, athletic governance, and/or coaching organization (421 memberships), who have administrative duties in intercollegiate athletics (40 memberships) or serve as institutional faculty athletics representatives (16 memberships). Women not meeting these criteria but interested in intercollegiate athletics are eligible for associate membership. A subscription membership is open to institutions and organizations that wish to receive printed materials.

NACWAA's annual income is about $53,000; 38 percent of it is generated by membership dues, 24 percent by Fall Forum registration, and 17 percent by sponsorships. The remaining 21 percent comes from a variety of sources such as fund-raising events.

POLICY CONCERNS AND TACTICS

Two primary purposes of the NACWAA are to provide a forum for discussion and debate and to analyze, evaluate, draft, and advance, through appropriate channels, legislation for national athletic governance organizations. To facilitate action, legislative ideas are debated at the Fall Forum and, if approved, are sent forward for consideration at the NCAA convention. NACWAA also sponsors a women's roundtable at the NCAA convention; prior to the legislative business session, the roundtable reviews all pertinent legislation with potential effects, positive or negative, on women's intercollegiate programs. Primary areas of concern for this group are items related to gender equity issues and the NCAA reform ideas designed to improve the student-athlete's experience.

The NACWAA also promotes women's professional roles in athletic administration and women's athletics generally through awards recognition and special programs, such as the annual Athletic Administrator of the Year Award. The Enhanced Opportunities Award recognizes institutions that, either through a significant event or series of events, show a commitment to the achievement of equity for girls and women in sport. The Nell C. Jackson Award recognizes women who have dedicated their lives to the advancement of women through sport. Jackson devoted her life to further opportunities for women in sport, especially track and field; an Olympic sprinter, national coach, and nationally respected administrator, she served as a minority role model and mentor.

Information is disseminated to the membership through a newsletter and to the public through press releases. Testimonials by members before various action groups, such as the Knight Commission, also play an important role. The purpose of the Knight Commission was to examine growing abuses in college sports and propose a reform agenda for intercollegiate athletics. Within athletic governing organizations, the NACWAA attempts to have a representative on all important women's committees, such as the gender equity committee and NCAA committee on women's athletics. In many respects, the NACWAA's function is to provide a voice for women within the governance of intercollegiate sport.

ELECTORAL ACTIVITIES

NACWAA is a nonpartisan organization and does not have a political action committee.

FURTHER INFORMATION

Members receive the NACWAA newsletter, a quarterly publication that provides a forum for women to communicate with each other and announces news and happenings around the country.

CHRISTINE H. B. GRANT

NATIONAL ASSOCIATION OF COLORED GRADUATE NURSES
See AMERICAN NURSES' ASSOCIATION

NATIONAL ASSOCIATION OF COLORED WOMEN'S CLUBS (NACW)
5808 16th Street, NW
Washington, DC 20011
(202) 726-2044

Founded "for the benefit of *all* humanity," the National Association of Colored Women's Clubs (NACW) undertakes educational and humanitarian programs of civic and social service for the fundamental purpose of improving black women's working conditions and educational opportunity for African Americans.

ORIGIN AND DEVELOPMENT

NACW formed at the inception of the black woman's club movement. The white woman's club movement gave, at best, a diffident response to black women's efforts to integrate it. In 1894, the Chicago Women's Club found Fanny Barrier Williams's membership application confounding; it admitted her the year after. The General Federation of Women's Clubs* (GFWC) refused to accept the Women's Era Club (WEC), a Massachusetts State Federation member founded by Josephine St. Pierre Ruffin in 1893. It denied Ruffin entry to the biennial convention other than as a white club's delegate. Newspaper coverage of the slur presented Ruffin and not GFWC in a favorable light. Thereafter, WEC learned from an English female journalist and antilynching activist that Missouri Press Association president John Jacks had written a letter defaming U.S. black women. WEC informed its newsletter readers.

Black women had no intention of being derailed. NACW formed in 1896 from a merger of the National Federation of Afro-American Women (NFAAW) and National League of Colored Women (NLCW). Ruffin had created NFAAW in 1893 after a first Boston congress of black women from thirty-six clubs in twelve states; Mary Church Terrell had founded NLCW in 1893 through the Washington Women's Club. Present at the merger in the Washington, D.C., 19th Street Baptist Church, along with seventy-three delegates from twenty-five states, representing 5,000 basically upwardly mobile club members, were educator Charlotte Forten Grimke, reformer Frances Ellen Watkins Harper (who became a vice president), and Rosetta Sprague (whose father was Frederick Douglass). The legendary Harriet Tubman drew a standing ovation and later introduced to the convention Ida B. Wells-Barnett's four-month-old son, Charles Aked, the baby of the association.

After a day's heated debate and deadlocked balloting, the organizing committee elected Terrell NACW's first president; after three terms she became the group's lifelong honorary president. Ruffin was elected a vice president; and WEC's journal, *The Woman's Era,* another first for black women, became NACW's official publication. There also was conflict over whether to use "colored'' or ''Afro-American'' in the association's name. The choice made, Terrell later said, ''We refer to the fact that this is an association of colored women, because our peculiar status . . . seems to demand that we stand by ourselves.''

The organization took as its motto ''Lifting as We Climb''—as Ruffin said, addressing the first national conference, ''to teach an ignorant and suspicious world that our aims and interests are identical with those of all good aspiring women.'' NACW assumed a self-help perspective toward its community, including among its local projects day nurseries and orphanages, jail and settlement work, girls' homes, mothers' clubs, hospitals, the Phyllis Wheatley Home Association of Detroit for old black women, and the needs of black women in domestic service.

NLCW had established a kindergarten; and in 1896, NACW set up a training school for kindergarten teachers and for two years supported seven free kindergartens. In 1899, it had a national kindergarten adviser for local projects. From 1906 to 1911, Terrell served on the Washington, D.C., school board, the first black woman to serve on a school board; the school system adopted a kindergarten program.

There was substantial infighting among NACW's officers. From the beginning, tension existed between the racial uplift and antilynching factions. The ''social housekeeping'' members and those serving collective action did not always see eye-to-eye. Nonetheless, besides emphasis on rectitude and dignity, a black woman's association had priorities a white woman's did not, such as opposition to Jim Crow laws, convict lease systems, and segregated transportation services, which NACW early proposed to boycott. Danger notwithstanding and despite long-standing personal animosity, NACW founding members Terrell and Wells-Barnett deplored the racism and lawlessness characteristic of the 2,500 lynchings in the South in 1884–1900 and the annual average of 67 lynchings from 1900 to 1920. NACW figured prominently in the antilynching movement. It published statistics about the number of black women lynched since 1892 and showed that black men were neither rapists nor invariably lynched under this rubric. It persuaded the National Council of Women of the United States (NCW) to support its efforts and sought to manage over 700 state workers' efforts to halt lynching. In 1922, it set up a delegation to achieve needed state support to pass the Dyer Antilynching bill.

By 1916, NACW had 50,000 members, over 1,000 diverse affiliates, and substantial accomplishments. It partly had bridged the black working and middle classes. Its projects served as prototypes for many twentieth-century organizations, among them the National Association for the Advancement of Colored People (NAACP), founded in 1909 with ample NACW representation, and National Urban League* (NUL), founded in 1910. Before Spingarn medalist Mary B. Talbot concluded her presidency in 1922, the organization reached a membership of 300,000. It paid off a $5,000 mortgage on the late Frederick Douglass's home in Anacostia in the District of Columbia and restored it, raising

$35,000 for the project. NACW still maintains the home. The Frederick Douglass Memorial and Historical Association is an NACW affiliate.

NACW had an active suffrage department because the Fifteenth Amendment did not enfranchise black women. In a calculated move, in 1919, the 6,000-member Northeast Federation of Women's Clubs, an NACW affiliate, sought to join the National American Woman Suffrage Association* (NAWSA). NAWSA feared the application would influence unfavorably the suffrage amendment's chances for passage by southern states. The federation stood firm, demanding in exchange for the application's withdrawal NAWSA commitment to the amendment's enforcement by the U.S. Congress, not the states. Some states intended to disfranchise black women. Neither NAWSA nor the National Woman's Party* would take a forthright stand on the enforcement issue.

The original amendment had included no states' rights contingency, and the Congress sent this amendment to the states for ratification. Nonetheless, in 1920–40, southern states disfranchised black women and, as a consequence, 75 percent of all black women in the United States. In 1922, NACW encouraged its clubs to lobby to implement the amendment. A bill was introduced unsuccessfully in the Congress to decrease representation of states restricting woman suffrage. By 1928, suffrage must have seemed a lost cause, and it disappeared from NACW's agenda.

One organization that evolved from NACW—in 1924 with Margaret Mary Washington as its president—was the International Council of Women of the Darker Races. The short-lived group attracted several former NACW officers to "race literature" and an appreciation that race and sex discrimination intersected everywhere in the world. NACW leaders also worked in close association with the Women's International League for Peace and Freedom.*

In 1924, Mary McLeod Bethune became NACW president by defeating Wells-Barnett, who never held NACW office. Bethune's association with the organization began in 1909, when she went to its conference to see Washington, NFAAW's founding president and NACW president 1914–18, and her husband, Booker T. Washington. She wanted to interest them in the Daytona School for Girls. Bethune's enthusiasm and organizational skill led to her assumption of leadership roles within NACW and, during her administration, to work for the Wagner-Costigan federal antilynching bill and improved status for rural and working-class black women and women of color outside the United States, in Africa, Haiti, Puerto Rico, and the Philippines. The Congress never passed an antilynching bill; but in 1920–40 lynching became highly visible, public opinion mobilized against it, and its incidence declined.

During Bethune's administration, NACW raised $25,000 to buy a national headquarters building in Washington, D.C. Eventually Bethune became disenchanted with NACW's possibilities as an agent for nationwide change and in 1935 founded the National Council of Negro Women* (NCNW). After suffrage, NACW had turned to changing black women's economic status and giving assistance to communities under siege. In the 1940s, it took a stand favoring the equal rights amendment—in contrast to NCNW's support for protective labor legislation—and continued its traditional service projects. During World War II, NACW sold war bonds as it had during World War I and reached out to African American troops. By 1952, the organization was down to 100,000 members. When Terrell died in 1954, two months after the Supreme Court decided *Brown v. Board of Education,* she lay in state at NACW's Washington headquarters, marking a culmination of the organization's brilliant early years.

ORGANIZATION AND FUNDING

NACW has five regional federations, the central, northeast, northwest, southeast, and southwest. There are thirty-eight state federations and 1,000 local units. The clubs affiliate with the state and regional federations, which belong to the national. Biennial meetings traditionally are held in cities with large African American populations. The organization has a fourteen-member board of directors. Its current president is Savannah C. Jones. There is a legislative committee. The Washington headquarters employs three staff; Carole Early serves as executive secretary. One full-time and one part-time volunteer work at headquarters. There is an attorney on retainer.

Between 1975 and 1984, NACW's membership dropped from 100,000 to 45,000 members, continuing the decline that began with NACW's formation. Since 1984, membership has stabilized. In 1930, NACW founded an organization for young black women, ages six to fifteen, to orient them to community work and, eventually, NACW membership. Since 1976, the group has been named the National Association of Girls. NACW also has a scholarship loan fund.

Sources of funding include membership dues—fifteen dollars a year for individuals, twenty-five dollars for associates. The local clubs and state and regional associations all benefit from these moneys and forward a portion of them to the national. NACW also receives project funding.

POLICY CONCERNS AND TACTICS

Preferred strategies include educating the membership with publications and encouraging members to write legislators and committees, educating the public through press releases, conducting and publishing research on issues, and fielding public service campaigns.

Equal pay and child care are enduring items on NACW's agenda.

NACW is affiliated with NCW and the International Council of Women. It long has coordinated with NUL and worked through the United Nations Educational, Scientific and Cultural Organization.

ELECTORAL ACTIVITIES

NACW is not a partisan organization and does not have a political action committee.

FURTHER INFORMATION

NACW has a quarterly magazine, *National Notes.*

SARAH SLAVIN

NATIONAL ASSOCIATION OF DEANS OF WOMEN
See NATIONAL ASSOCIATION OF WOMEN IN EDUCATION

NATIONAL ASSOCIATION OF DEANS OF WOMEN AND COUNSEL-ORS
See NATIONAL ASSOCIATION OF WOMEN IN EDUCATION

NATIONAL ASSOCIATION OF DEANS OF WOMEN AND COUNSEL-ORS AND ADMINISTRATORS
See NATIONAL ASSOCIATION OF WOMEN IN EDUCATION

NATIONAL ASSOCIATION OF GIRLS
See NATIONAL ASSOCIATION OF COLORED WOMEN'S CLUBS

NATIONAL ASSOCIATION OF GROUP WORKERS
See NATIONAL ASSOCIATION OF SOCIAL WORKERS

NATIONAL ASSOCIATION OF MEDICAL SOCIAL WORKERS
See NATIONAL ASSOCIATION OF SOCIAL WORKERS

NATIONAL ASSOCIATION OF NEGRO BUSINESS AND PROFES-SIONAL WOMEN'S CLUBS (NANBPW)
1806 New Hampshire Avenue, NW
Washington, DC 20009
(202) 483-4206
FAX (202) 462-7253

The National Association of Negro Business and Professional Women's Clubs (NANBPW) represents working women who want to share their accomplishments, skills, and knowledge and to collaborate on improvement in their communities' quality of life, on an environment receptive to black women enacting significant life changes, on role modeling for younger women, and on options for meeting the contemporary world's challenges.

ORIGIN AND DEVELOPMENT

In 1935, Mrs. Ollie Chinn Porter, president of the New York Club, brought together Philadelphia and Atlantic City Business and Professional Women's Clubs to create NANBPW, the same year the National Council of Negro Women* formed. In 1936, Porter became its first president. For too many black women the Great Depression proved degrading: recovery initiatives either excluded or bypassed them. Despite these grim circumstances, NANBPW's founders had succeeded as owners, managers, college graduates, and professional women. NANBPW became part of the existing movement for Negroes during the period. There was movement, for example, in 1936, when President Franklin Roosevelt learned the Negro vote could be important to his victory and the Democratic national convention boasted an even ten delegates.

ORGANIZATION AND FUNDING

In 1992, NANBPW had 400 clubs in the United States, Bermuda, and Africa, up from 300 in 1984. There are six district governors and an annual convention. The board of directors has nine members. The current president is Jacquelin Washington. National headquarters is in Washington, D.C. Ellen Graves is the executive director. The office has three paid staff. Six volunteers assist them; and there is a part-time college intern paid for by PRIME Computer Company. There is a national attorney.

NANBPW membership has grown to 30,414 from a stable 10,000 between 1975 and 1984. Membership dues are seventy-five dollars. NANBPW also has several types of associate memberships: senior, young adult and youth clubs; international clubs; men's auxiliaries; and Beta Psi, the college clubs. After a forty-five-dollar membership fee, an associate member pays annual supporting dues of twelve dollars. Members join primarily for the networking possibilities.

NANBPW has a current operating budget of about $500,000; the revenues are derived from conventions, almost 40 percent; almost 31 percent from membership dues including life memberships and joining fees; a scholarship fund, 10 percent; grants, 8 percent; vocal arts and interest, both nearly 3 percent; and rent, 2 percent; with 5 percent or less coming from sales of pins and plaques, penalties, club taxes, and donations and contributions. Recently support has increased from corporations like Anheuser Busch, Avon, Blue Cross and Blue Shield of Massachusetts, Capital Cities/ABC, Coors, Ford Motor Company, PepsiCo, Philip Morris U.S.A., Ryder, and Xerox. NANBPW is a nonprofit business. It owns and operates an American Speedy Printer Center in Washington, D.C.; the Nannie Jenkins Day Care Center, also in Washington; and a federal credit union in Silver Spring, Maryland.

POLICY CONCERNS AND TACTICS

NANBPW prefers as strategies professional development; social, health, and youth programming; and education. Of special interest in recent years has been economic development among its members, as reflected by their investment in American Speedy Printer Centers as well.

Developed by President Washington with a $500,000 grant from Kellogg Corporation, the Leadership 2000 project offers apprenticeship and training to thirty-five young African American women from Louisiana, Texas, Kansas, and Colorado, with an eye to their obtaining critical local, national, and international leadership posts in the future. The award from Kellogg is the largest ever received by a major African American women's group. With a grant from the U.S. Housing and Urban Development Department, NANBPW also has offered seminars on the government procurement process for minorities and women owning businesses.

NANBPW has service projects concerning homelessness, AIDS education, and teenage sexuality (with the March of Dimes) and a child care initiative that recruits foster and adoptive parents and assists boarder babies. There are adopt-a-school and dropout programs. NANBPW also has entered into a philanthropic partnership with the National Jewish Center for Immunology and Respiratory Medicine to take action through research into asthma, lupus, and AIDS, diseases disproportionately affecting black people and, in the last two instances, women specifically.

Internationally, NANBPW takes part in such development programs as Africare and Care/Cameroon Water Wells. With Laubach Literacy, it has undertaken a significant literacy initiative for Tanzanian women. It has sponsored a Senegal grain mill and attended a conference on women's business in Harare, Zimbabwe. It also has participated in exchange delegations to both China and the former Soviet Union.

NANBPW is affiliated with the International Council on Women. It collaborates with the National Council of Negro Women,* The Links, Incorporated,* National Caucus on Black Aging, and United Negro College Fund to acknowledge with KOOL achiever awards, sponsored by the Brown & Williamson Tobacco Corporation, disadvantaged high school students striving to enhance the quality of center-city life. It also works with the National Urban League,* National Association for the Advancement of Colored People, National Association of Black-Owned Broadcasters, National Association for Equal Opportunity in Higher Education, National Newspaper Publishers Association, and Opportunities Industrialization Centers of America.

ELECTORAL ACTIVITIES

NANBPW does not see as partisan the issues that concern it and does not have a political action committee.

FURTHER INFORMATION

NANBPW publishes a monthly *President's Newsletter;* a quarterly magazine, *Responsibility;* and "The Youth Connection." It has an annual directory.

CHARLOTTE T. MORGAN-CATO

NATIONAL ASSOCIATION OF SCHOOL SOCIAL WORKERS
See NATIONAL ASSOCIATION OF SOCIAL WORKERS

NATIONAL ASSOCIATION OF SOCIAL WORKERS (NASW)
750 First Street, NE
Washington, DC 20002
(800) 638-8799
FAX (202) 336-8310

The National Association of Social Workers (NASW) is the largest professional organization representing social workers throughout the world. Its primary functions are to support professional social work standards, encourage legislative and political action, conduct policy analysis and dissemination, participate in public service campaigns to raise public consciousness, and offer various membership services and public literature related to professional social work. NASW has a legal defense fund (LDF), a research and education fund, and political action committee (PAC).

ORIGIN AND DEVELOPMENT

Seven social work organizations merged in 1955 to found NASW. Its predecessors were the American Association of Medical Social Workers, established in 1918; National Association of School Social Workers, 1919; American Association of Social Workers (AASW), 1921; American Association of Psychiatric Social Workers, 1926; American Association of Group Workers, 1936; Association for the Study of Community Organization, 1946; and Social Worker Research Group, 1949. AASW had the most comprehensive membership and functioned as NASW's major predecessor. The relationship between social change and social service was a consistent theme in defining the parameters of social work practice. These organizations merged in NASW because of a need for unity: a collective voice.

The social work profession is based on political and social action to protect all individuals' rights. Political action lay at the root of the 1881 settlement house movement; generally, the field is considered to have emerged from settlement leader Jane Addams's work. After visiting Toynbee Hall, a university settlement in England influenced by social reformer John Ruskin and the Russian novelist and Christian anarchist Leo Tolstoi, Addams founded Hull House in 1889. Located in a Chicago immigrant neighborhood, the settlement sought to raise protective walls to help industrial workers. Addams proved highly adept at fund-raising, but she and her followers soon learned that clubs and services were not enough to solve the complex problems presented. An issue agenda arose centered on the regulation of child labor, women's hours, an improved welfare process, the right of workers to organize, compulsory school attendance, and occupational safety.

Professional organizations serve as vehicles for both stability and change and restructuring. A vital element in a profession's identity, such an organization attempts to respond to political forces and societal adjustments. NASW is such a vehicle. It has attempted to adjust to constant internal and external changes within the profession as well as in society. NASW represents not only professional interests but also those groups of individuals without a collective voice in local, state, and national governments. NASW has taken on the task few interest groups or social movements have accomplished, the representation of the nonelite, nonpolitical, and voiceless in the U.S. decision-making arena. For NASW, the struggle will continue until all injustices, inequities, and social ills cease to exist.

ORGANIZATION AND FUNDING

In 1975, NASW reorganized, reducing the number of chapters from seventy-eight to fifty-five. The new structure included one chapter for each state plus the District of Columbia, New York City, Puerto Rico, the Virgin Islands, and Europe. NASW has a triennial delegate assembly, board of directors, and national officers. The assembly has 300 delegates elected by the membership and including all chapter presidents and one or more additional delegates per chapter. The twenty-five-member board, which includes the officers, makes policy, allocates resources and assembly delegates, establishes committees, determines membership policies, and selects the executive director. The current president is Barbara White. NASW headquarters is located in Washington, D.C., and includes a 4,000-volume library. It employs 135 staff. The executive director is Sheldon R. Goldstein.

The present national membership is approximately 140,000 members, up from 90,000 in 1984. Members are 71 percent women and 87 percent white, 6 percent African American, 3 percent Hispanic, 1.6 percent Asian American, and less than 1 percent Native American. Members must meet strict education or experience background requirements to enroll. The majority of members qualify through graduate education, professional experience, references, or an examination by NASW's Academy of Certified Social Workers. Individuals with an undergraduate or graduate degree from an accredited social work program qualify for regular membership. Associate members are individuals working full-time in a social work capacity and having at a minimum an undergraduate degree; voting privileges accrue to these members after five years of continuous membership. There also are student and retired/unemployed/doctoral candidate membership categories. Members pledge to abide by the Code of Ethics, which addresses the issue of the social worker's ethical responsibility to society; social work's primary obligation is the welfare of the individual or group served, which includes action to improve conditions.

Members are offered a variety of benefits and services. Members receive the newspaper *NASW News* and the journal *Social Work,* have chapter representation and membership, can join many committees (national and statewide), and have access to a legal defense fund. LDF is a service that provides financial aid to members engaged in litigation because of actions taken as professional social workers. Other benefits of membership include opportunities to improve practice and leadership skills through reduced rates for conferences, lists of social work literature, a tax-deferred annuity plan, and a professional liability and group health, life, and life disability insurance programs known as the NASW Insurance Trust.

The organization has a 501 (c) (6) tax status. The annual fee for regular members is $130; for associate members, $104; student members, $33; and retired/unemployed/doctoral candidate members, $39. The operating budget is about $14.5 million.

The NASW Legal Defense Service has operated since 1972. The service has awarded fifty-five NASW members grants totaling $75,000, raised through voluntary donations contributed along with membership dues payments. When awarding grants, service trustees consider the significance of the case to the social work profession and its principles, including the NASW Code of Ethics, and the support of the NASW chapter and other professionals in the community. The service also provides support to those involved in class action lawsuits. Among the landmark cases supported by the service are a California social worker fighting to protect the civil rights of clients and several social workers in Maryland who filed suit against county and state health departments seeking pay equal to that of psychiatric nurses and psychologists performing the same duties.

POLICY CONCERNS AND TACTICS

The association's basic positions on social and professional policy issues are determined by the delegate assembly. The assembly's agenda is determined by the members' rank ordering of policy proposals that have been screened by a committee. Proposals to the committee come from the members. There is a lobbying committee, the Education Legislative Action Network (ELAN). ELAN lobbies for responsible social policies at the state and federal levels, doing legislative analysis, preparing testimony, negotiating with legislators, and working with administrative agencies to design or implement laws.

The 1990 delegate assembly selected the following social policy and action goals for NASW's 1991–94 program: (1) advocate for a universal national policy on comprehensive health and mental health care with provision for a full range of services that include social work; (2) maintain a national peace and disarmament network among professional social workers to work toward a shift in national priorities from expenditures for armaments to adequate funding for human service needs and to promote nonviolent resolution of national and international conflicts; (3) promote freedom of choice in women's reproductive health at local, state, and national levels; and (4) implement the NASW policy statement on AIDS by pursuing action on sexually transmitted diseases in the areas of research, public education and information dissemination, psychological and social supports, service delivery and resource development, and political action.

ELECTORAL ACTIVITIES

NASW's PAC, Political Action for Candidate Election (PACE), raises money to aid legislators at all levels supporting NASW policies, especially in relation to social services. It registered with the Federal Election Commission on August 22, 1984. National PACE supports candidates if they have a strong voting pattern that reflects social work values and a commitment to human services. PACE has committees designated to examine legislators' voting records and keep report cards. Challengers must have a strong proposed agenda reflecting human service values. Office staff, the organization's chief executive officer, and elected board members also help determine which national, state, and local officials to support. The membership ranks public officials for support through a survey in *NASW News*. Some state chapters have PACs also, depending on their budget. Their endorsements are at the state and local levels. Decisions about endorsements come from member surveys.

A social work PAC is a necessary advocacy group, not only for professional self-interest and protection but also for persons disadvantaged and disfranchised. These PACs differ slightly from business and industrial ones. They may lack financial resources, a difference often mitigated by social workers' skills in interpersonal relationships, community organization, and volunteer action. These skills can assist candidates.

FURTHER INFORMATION

NASW publishes the monthly *Advocate for Human Services* and, ten times yearly, the *News*. It also publishes the bimonthly *Social Work,* quarterly *Health and Social Work Practice Digest, Social Work in Education,* and *Social Work Research and Abstracts*. It publishes a directory, an encyclopedia, and many books and pamphlets.

KRISTA L. HUGHES

NATIONAL ASSOCIATION OF SOCIAL WORKERS LEGAL DEFENSE SERVICE
See NATIONAL ASSOCIATION OF SOCIAL WORKERS

NATIONAL ASSOCIATION OF WOMEN HIGHWAY SAFETY LEADERS (NAWHSL)
7206 Robinhood Drive
Upper Marlboro, MD 20772
(301) 868-7583

The National Association of Women Highway Safety Leaders (NAWHSL) is a volunteer organization dedicated to saving lives from needless traffic crashes. It anticipates the future health and well-being that will result from reduced deaths and injuries, property damages, and lost work hours, along with reduced insurance premiums, and expects the savings to be turned to treatment and rehabilitation for those less fortunate.

ORIGIN AND DEVELOPMENT

NAWHSL formed in 1967, after passage of the 1966 National Traffic and Motor Vehicle Safety Act (NTMVSA) and the subsequent National Conference of Women Community Leaders for Highway Safety sponsored by the National Association of Counties. NAWHSL set out to create public awareness of the traffic safety measures needed to reduce deaths and injuries on the nation's streets and highways. The idea for the group was due to a few people, with no one individual acting as leader or chief organizer. The organizers did not know each other from another organizational context. They felt moved to action by the traffic death and injury toll on U.S. highways and by their support for the Transportation Department's proposed safety standards. Key founders included Georgene Havena and Agnes Beaton. Beaton, then as now, serves as executive director.

NAWHSL has as goals increasing safety belt usage, reducing alcohol and drug abuse, increasing child safety restraints and pedestrian and bicycle safety, improving traffic courts, and reducing roadside hazards. Its goals have not changed in important ways since its founding. It emphasizes heightened public understanding and support, enlightened policies ranging from high school driver education to emergency medical services, and direct contact with at-risk groups, including children and old people.

ORGANIZATION AND FUNDING

NAWHSL affiliates are to be found in all fifty states, the District of Columbia, Puerto Rico, Guam, and American Samoa. There is an intermediate structure between the national organization and state and local affiliates. The group encourages board participation by persons from lower-income strata, persons with disabilities, and older women. The president is Elaine Huttenloch; the membership elects the president. NAWHSL's Washington, D.C., office opened in 1967. Volunteers or student interns may service the office on a project-by-project basis.

The membership mixes organizations and their representatives with individuals. Since 1980, the membership has been 90 percent female, compared with 100 percent at the time of the founding. The 3 million members join to advocate important policies, communicate with peers and associate with similarly minded people, and engage in consciousness-raising sessions. They also may find as an incentive the chance to participate in public affairs, attend conferences and meetings, and develop their organizational skills. To a lesser extent, friendship ties, representation of their opinions to government, and the group's information/ research influence them to join.

NAWHSL is a nonprofit tax exempt 501 (c) (3) organization. Its initial funds came from private foundation grants. It primarily relies on government grants or contracts (60 percent) and corporate gifts (40 percent) for financing. The budget size has been reported as about $75,000 annually.

POLICY CONCERNS AND TACTICS

NAWHSL's two preferred strategies are public education and advocacy. It produces priority traffic safety publications, designs and prepares programs for family use, supports federal and state highway transportation and traffic safety legislation, and assists law enforcement officials and other groups seeking to reduce traffic crashes.

NAWHSL has continued to support implementation of the safety standards authorized by NTMVSA, works to keep uniform related programs and regulations in the states and elsewhere, stimulates effective state and local safety programs, underwrites national transportation safety policy and supportive programming, undertakes pilot projects in a timely manner, and develops advocacy positions on a regional, state, and community basis. Its accomplishments include helping to pass child passenger safety seat laws in all the states and safety belt laws in thirty-one of them plus the District of Columbia. It initiated a first national conference on women and motorcycle safety, a conference on national safety leadership, and, more recently, a program emphasizing improvement in signs, signals, and markings and in pedestrian safety. It promotes mature driving. NAWHSL was a supporter of the fifty-five m.p.h. nationwide speed limit.

ELECTORAL ACTIVITIES

NAWHSL does not see as partisan the issues that concern it and does not have a political action committee.

FURTHER INFORMATION

NAWHSL family programming is available in a video format.

SARAH SLAVIN

NATIONAL ASSOCIATION OF WOMEN LAWYERS (NAWL)
750 North Lake Shore Drive
Chicago, IL 60611
(312) 988-6186
FAX (312) 988-6281

The National Association of Women Lawyers (NAWL) has as its primary objective assisting women's advancement, especially in the legal field, by providing a professional network and celebrating female attorneys' accomplishments.

ORIGIN AND DEVELOPMENT

Women struggle to gain acceptance and equality in most professions. Although law has become the only profession more or less to integrate women, the battle for women in the legal profession has been arduous. A man's world, the legal profession defined itself as male. It also introduced distinctions by color. Until 1910, women and African Americans constituted less than 1 percent of the U.S. legal profession. The American Bar Association (ABA) admitted women beginning in 1918; however, law schools continued to resist admitting women to their degree programs. It was not until 1972 that all ABA-accredited law schools finally admitted women.

On June 4, 1899, the Women Lawyers Club (WLC) was founded in East Orange, New Jersey, by Gail Loughlin, Rosalie Loew, and twenty-three other female attorneys. The group selected officers later that month in New York City, naming Loew its first president. WLC promoted women's issues, especially women's suffrage and equality in the legal profession.

In 1911, WLC was renamed NAWL; Marion Weston Cottle was elected its first president. NAWL members actively participated in the suffrage movement, founding suffrage organizations and achieving leadership positions. The *Women Lawyer's Journal,* NAWL's publication, carried numerous articles on the progress of the suffrage movement and the women lawyers involved. After the Nineteenth Amendment was ratified, NAWL devoted its attention to the status of women in the legal profession and other substantive issues, such as children's welfare, uniform divorce legislation, and jury service for women.

NAWL gradually made inroads for women within the professional bar. In 1943, NAWL received representation in the ABA House of Delegates. NAWL president Marguerite Rawalt was the first woman delegate to this assembly. As the organization gathered power in the legal community, some questioned NAWL's existence as a separate organization. Throughout its history, NAWL has continued to justify its existence because of the discrimination facing women in the profession and under the law.

In 1969, NAWL celebrated the Women Lawyers Centennial, honoring the achievements of female attorneys since Belle Mansfield was admitted to practice in 1869. The organization sought the support of other women's groups, including the National Federation of Business and Professional Women,* Zonta,* and the American Association of University Women.* The Girl Scouts joined the celebration by developing programs encouraging girls to enter legal careers.

By 1980, women made up 12.8 percent of the legal profession and 33.5 percent of all law school graduates; a decade later, these figures were 22.2 percent and 41 percent. In 1990, 6.4 percent of female attorneys were minorities. In 1992, NAWL had approximately 1,200 members, female lawyers admitted to practice in all states and territories. NAWL finds its operation justified because of continuing discrimination by ABA, although relations between the organizations have been improving steadily.

ORGANIZATION AND FUNDING

The organization supporting NAWL's activities is minimal. NAWL is guided by an executive board composed of twelve women; the current president is Faith Driscoll. The organization has had minority representation on its executive board. The executive director is the only paid staff member in the Chicago headquarters. NAWL has fifteen state affiliates, including the Women's Bar of Illinois, Women's Bar of Maryland and Women's Bar of Florida. The state associations also operate without professional staff assistance. NAWL has a delegate to ABA and the International Bar Association. NAWL also is affiliated with the International Federation of Women Lawyers. NAWL is an accredited observer to the United Nations.

NAWL has 1,200 members, the majority of whom are engaged in private practice. Membership provides women attorneys with a national network of professionals and access to seminars and a newsletter. The network fosters communication among women and offers support when women attorneys run for public office. NAWL supports female law students and attorneys; however, it does not reach out to undergraduate women to encourage them to enter the legal profession.

NAWL receives funding primarily from membership fees from individuals and affiliates. General individual membership costs $75; membership for affiliates is $100; lifetime membership costs $1,000. NAWL offers young practitioners (those in the profession for five years or less) a special membership fee of $30; law students may join NAWL for $15. NAWL also receives revenue from registration fees at its annual conference. The organization would not disclose specific expense figures. It was estimated that the organization's operating budget is under $100,000 per year.

POLICY CONCERNS AND TACTICS

The executive board determines NAWL's issues agenda and strategies to pursue it. NAWL supports legislation directed toward equal rights and equal pay by lobbying, primarily at the state level, although it does not directly engage in lobbying and supports political activity through networking among its members. An active organization, NAWL has supported numerous women for judgeships. NAWL is also pro-choice.

NAWL occasionally files amicus curiae briefs with the U.S. Supreme Court supporting the rights of women. Two notable cases where NAWL filed amicus briefs were *Pittsburgh Press Company* v. *Pittsburgh Commission on Human Relations* (1973) and *Webster* v. *Reproductive Services of Missouri* (1989). In *Pittsburgh Press,* NAWL joined the Women's Equity Action League* in supporting the Pennsylvania Commission on Human Relations' argument that help-wanted advertisements should not be classified by gender. The U.S. Supreme Court held that gender-based help-wanted advertisements were discriminatory. In *Webster,* the U.S. Supreme Court upheld a state statute that prohibited use of public facilities or public employees to counsel a woman to have an abortion except if her life is in danger.

NAWL works closely with other professional legal organizations. It cooperates extensively with its affiliates, the National Council of Women's Bar Associations, ABA Commission on Women in the Profession, and ABA Women's Caucus. NAWL also participated in the march on Washington, D.C., sponsored by the National Organization for Women* in 1992.

ELECTORAL ACTIVITIES

As a professional organization, NAWL does not directly engage in electoral activity. Throughout its history, NAWL has endorsed qualified lawyers, both male and female, for public office, especially judgeships. In the recent past, NAWL supported Dennis Anagnost for a state judgeship in Illinois and Michelle Picard Wynne for a federal judgeship in Louisiana.

FURTHER INFORMATION

NAWL publishes the quarterly *Women Lawyers' Journal*, the quarterly *President's Newsletter*, and a biennial membership directory.

SARA ANN GROVE

NATIONAL BLACK FEMINIST ORGANIZATION (NBFO)

Recognizing the disastrous results for black women of sexism and racism both, the National Black Feminist Organization (NBFO) sought throughout its existence to improve the women's liberation movement's credibility and to strengthen the black liberation movement by facilitating economic and socio-cultural change for black women.

ORIGIN AND DEVELOPMENT

NBFO formed in 1973, when thirty black women gathered to consider what it meant to be black, female, and feminist. Attorney Florynce Kennedy, an early force in National Organization for Women—New York City* and a founder of New York Radical Feminists, and Margaret Sloan, one of *Ms.* magazine's founding editors and active on the national speaker's circuit, conceived it. Then-New York City Human Rights Commissioner Eleanor Holmes Norton generally is associated with the group's formation, having helped to announce it at a well-attended press conference three months after the first gathering. The founders were more diverse, ranging from women in the professions to women engaged in household work and from welfare rights activists to consumer activists. The first officers of the seven-member coordinating council were Sloan and Jane Galvin-Lewis, a Women's Action Group deputy director.

In 1988, a Women in the Civil Rights Movement: Trailblazers and Torchbearers 1941–1965 conference, convened by Rosa Parks and Coretta Scott King, offered as a major theme the intersection of race, class, and gender. Yet black women's absence from accounts of such struggle still may be more commented on than their critical presence in the struggles themselves. After "Freedom Summer" in 1964, Mary King and Casey Hayden drew up an "anonymous" memo comparing the position of women in the Student Non-Violent Coordinating Committee to the situation of black people. NBFO objected to the deference customarily shown black men in the black liberation movement. The task it set itself takes on additional relief when compared with National Organization for Women,* which did not insert the word "feminist" into its Statement of Purpose until after 1975. NBFO's Statement contained the following words: "Black Feminists . . . are therefore establishing THE NATIONAL BLACK FEMINIST ORGANIZATION in order to address ourselves to the particular and specific needs of the larger, but almost cast aside half of the Black race in Amerikkka, the Black Woman.''

NBFO's first project was a conference, held in the East in late 1973 and offering an array of workshops on such topics as the church, media reform, lesbianism and sexuality, culture, education, substance abuse, and child care. Among the keynoters was U.S. congresswoman Shirley Chisholm. Conferees left anticipating the independence of an organization of their own. The initial response to the group was overwhelming: 400 phone calls followed the announcement of its formation. A week after that presentation to the press, 200 black women attended an NBFO meeting; and before a year elapsed, more than 2,000 women had formed ten chapters in the states of Connecticut, Georgia, Illinois, Massachusetts, Michigan, New York, and the District of Columbia. By 1975, though, its leadership was in disarray, split by conflict over administrative style. Financial problems continued to plague it. Its issue agenda was controversial, and support from traditional black women's associations lagged. Individual chapters continued for at least four years, and possibly eight, after the New York City chapter's demise.

ORGANIZATION AND FUNDING

At its peak NBFO had fifteen chapters. It sought to provide an accessible organization ruled by consensus, to be developed during open-ended meetings. Besides the coordinating council and issue-based task forces, there were a president, Sloan, and vice president, Galvin-Lewis. Officers were not salaried; and there was no national office. The New York chapter operated out of the office of *Ms.,* and an Illinois chapter out of local president Linda Paulette Johnston's home in Harvey.

In 1983, the *Encyclopedia of Associations* reported the group still had 500 members. Incentives to join had included advocacy of black feminist ideas, development of organizational skills, particularly fund-raising, the chance to exercise influence within the organization and to associate with like-minded women, conferences and meetings, and consciousness-raising sessions.

There was a dues scale to take into account members' income. Dues collection did not yield revenues sufficient to support NBFO.

POLICY CONCERNS AND TACTICS

President Sloan sought to encourage participation by diverse women, which proved difficult to sustain, partly because of differences over NBFO's agenda. The coordinating council prepared the agenda. The question of increased centralization and also input from the New York City-based leadership eventually stymied agenda-building efforts. Reorganization effectively ended the possibility of a national-level administration. At its operational best, NBFO preferred such strategies as educating members with publications, educating the public through press releases, participating in direct action political demonstrations, and compiling statistics. It also had a speakers bureau and provided some services for children.

NBFO addressed issues that included domestic violence, black women's unemployment rate, pay equity, the needs of black women in the criminal justice system, the proposed equal rights amendment, reproductive rights, and accessible health care.

NBFO coordinated with the Women's Action Alliance and National Committee for Pay Equity,* among other organizations.

FURTHER INFORMATION

Besides a bibliography on black women and feminism, NBFO published "Standard Questions You Might Be Asked . . . Suggested Answers That Might Work" to define the group and its objectives. There was a membership packet.

SARAH SLAVIN

NATIONAL BLACK NURSES ASSOCIATION (NBNA)
P.O. Box 1823
Washington, DC 20013-1823
(202) 393-6870
FAX (202) 347-3808

The National Black Nurses Association's (NBNA) mission is to provide a forum for collective action by black nurses to review and establish black Americans' health care needs and to take steps to fill those needs, including black consumer advocacy, nursing education and recruitment, and scholarship assistance for student nurses.

ORIGIN AND DEVELOPMENT

Founded by Lauranne Sams, former dean, School of Nursing, Tuskegee University, with the shared involvement of a group of dedicated black nurses, NBNA sought to involve nurses and student nurses regardless of race, color, or creed. In the 100-year history of black nurses in this country, NBNA represents one of four distinct eras, the most recent beginning in 1970, when black nurses again came to the realization that a formal structure was needed to address largely neglected issues.

The first era (1878–1907) began when the first black nurse, Mary Eliza Mahoney, graduated in the United States. One of only four students successfully to complete the training program at New England Hospital for women and children in Boston, Mahoney became one of the American Nurses Association's* (ANA) first black members and in the next era actively recruited for the National Association of Colored Graduate Nurses* (NACGN).

In the quarter-century that followed, only a handful of black nurses were able to follow in Mahoney's footsteps. In the next era (1908–51), however, black nurses had an organization to assist them in their struggle against the flagrant and debilitating racism that daily threatened their existence. NACGN waged a gallant, heroic fight during its over forty-two years on behalf of black nurses. Believing it finally had achieved integration. NACGN dissolved in 1951 and merged with ANA.

In the third era of black nursing history (1951–70), NACGN's successors raised some haunting, troublesome questions. During those years as black nurses met and talked with others across the country, they analyzed the continuing plight of black nurses. Certain facts were indisputable: black nurses were noticeably absent in positions of leadership and power in ANA; black nurses were grossly underrepresented in the profession; and black nurses continued to fight against individual, group, and institutional racism, sometimes successfully, but too often not.

Thus, the fourth era of black nursing history, 1970–present, began. ANA was being challenged on many fronts about its responsiveness to the sociocultural-political realities impinging on nurses. At the ANA's forty-seventh annual convention in Miami, Florida, black nurses caucused about their concerns. More than 200 black nurses attended the caucus. Having come from local communities where they witnessed and/or had been a part of a black liberation movement, they felt eager to focus their energies on alleviating black nurses' plight. Sams agreed to maintain communication among caucus participants. A steering committee met in Cleveland, Ohio, in December 1971 and March 1972 for the purpose of unifying black nurses. While the loosely organized caucus had felt undecided about whether to organize outside ANA, through the steering committee it came to believe quite early that a cohesive, permanent structure outside ANA could best accomplish its objectives.

Fortunately, NBNA has a host of black nurses contributing to its development. In 1971–72, the six-member steering committee included Betty Williams, Ethelrine Shaw, and Mattie Johnson, along with Sams. For NBNA's incorporation in 1972, it established a board of directors, which included Mary Harper, Gloria Rookard, and Winnie Riddle, as well as other steering committee members. Sams served as its first president, elected in 1974. Dynamic women such as these set in motion an organization able to assist nurses to overcome some of the racism and improve the status of the black nurse in the profession and in leadership and powerful positions. Today the group's emphasis has broadened to include advocacy regarding African American people's health care needs, increasing the graduation of blacks from professional nursing programs, and recruiting and giving scholarship assistance to student nurses.

ORGANIZATION AND FUNDING

The association comprises of sixty-two chartered chapters across the nation and membership throughout the continental United States, its territories, the Caribbean, England, France, Kenya, Nigeria, and Saudi Arabia. The organization's governing structure includes a ten-member board of directors, an executive committee, and officers elected by the individual members. Linda Burns Bolton serves as president. Besides a president, the officers who help govern the organization include first and second vice presidents, a secretary, and treasurer. Besides officers, the executive committee membership consists of two members at large elected by the board from its membership. NBNA conducts its business from national headquarters in Washington, D.C. The executive director is the only paid staff member. Sadako S. Holmes is executive director.

NBNA has 7,000 members, 98 percent of them female and of African American descent. Members feel inclined to join the organization because of a belief in its goals; and membership provides an opportunity to work and network with peers and colleagues around the country. Membership also offers an opportunity to participate in research on black people's health needs. Focusing on key health care needs and issues that impact on black nurses and consumers, the NBNA National Institute and conference are designed to address black nurses' educational needs. Four annual regional conferences address two areas: health care problems identified as priority areas in the specific region and facilitating black nurses' development for leadership roles in nursing.

A nonprofit, charitable public service organization, NBNA has tax-exempt status; contributions to the organization are tax-deductible. Financial support is received from membership dues and from an annual national conference. No budget information is available.

POLICY CONCERNS AND TACTICS

Policy decisions are made at NBNA's annual meeting. The board of directors recommends policy to the membership for adoption. The executive committee makes recommendations of policy to the board. Strategies that predominate include member education, public education research, and information dissemination. A legislation committee initiates, endorses, and supports desirable health and nursing legislation. This committee also works collaboratively with chapters and/or health care providers and/or organizations in disseminating information regarding national and/or regional legislative matters.

NBNA has had a joint project with the March of Dimes, a teenage pregnancy/ infant mortality program that today is ongoing through NBNA chapters. Its purpose is to intervene directly in the black community to prevent teenage pregnancy and decrease infant mortality. NBNA is cognizant of the threat AIDS poses to young black women and as a result has implemented an AIDS public education program for the black community. The purpose of this program is to educate the community regarding the ramifications of infection with HIV virus and AIDS. A hypertension task force helps develop educational programs for use by community groups, emphasizing black nurses who train community persons to take responsibility for their peers' health education. The association is in the process of formulating added programs in the areas of child welfare, cancer, and mental health.

Policies of continuing importance to the organization include the 1963 Equal Pay Act, 1964 Civil Rights and Equal Opportunity Acts, Voting Rights Act, affirmative action orders, 1972 Equal Employment Act, proposed equal rights constitutional amendment, 1974 Women's Educational Equity Act, 1976 Day Care Act, 1983 Social Security Act, and 1988 Civil Rights Restoration Act and National Health Plan.

NBNA networks with the Black Congress on Health, Law and Economics, a federation of organizations meeting every four years to bring together theoreticians and practitioners to discuss current trends impacting directly on the black population. It has close contacts in the U.S. Health and Human Services Department and with the National Cancer Institute's cancer prevention awareness program for African Americans and is a member of the Food and Drug Administration consumer consortium on food and health policy. NBNA maintains contacts in the National Institutes of Health with programs addressing high blood pressure control and education, cholesterol education, and asthma education.

NBNA coordinates advocacy efforts with the Congressional Black Caucus, National Leadership Roundtable, ANA, National Black Child Development Institute, and National Black Caucus and Center on Black Aged.

ELECTORAL ACTIVITIES

NBNA does not find partisan the issues that concern it. It does not have a political action committee.

FURTHER INFORMATION

Official communication is facilitated through the *NBNA Newsletter,* which is published four times a year, and through the *NBNA Journal,* which is published twice a year. Articles include research reports, critical essays, in-depth interviews, resource listings, and documentation and reviews focusing on issues of black health care and nurses. NBNA also has position papers on the status of black children, entry into practice, and AIDS.

MATTIE L. RHODES

NATIONAL BLACK SISTERS CONFERENCE (NBSC)
1001 Lawrence Street, NW
Suite 102
Washington, DC 20017
(202) 529-9250
FAX (202) 529-9370

The only organization formed by and for African American women religious, the National Black Sisters Conference (NBSC) assists members to embrace their own black identity and to initiate work with self-help programs through which members can educate themselves and their black sisters and brothers.

ORIGIN AND DEVELOPMENT

Founded in 1968 shortly after the assassination of Martin Luther King, Jr., NBSC formed to enable African American women religious to work for black people's liberation. Conference founders had just participated in an international gathering of black women from various religious congregations. The founders—including several Sisters of Mercy (Mary Martin de Porres Grey, Helen Marie Christian, and Cora Marie Billings, among others), a Dominican, Shawn Copeland, and Sister Josita Colbert of the Sisters of Notre Dame de Namur—desired a permanent organization, loosely parallel to the recently formed Black Catholic Clergy Caucus, that could keep alive the international meeting's inspiration by focusing women's attention on black people's liberation.

While NBSC grew out of the immediate context of 1968 events, it had its roots in informal study groups composed of black laity, religious, and priests in the archdioceses of Detroit, Baltimore, Chicago, Washington, D.C., and elsewhere. Initial and later NBSC members came primarily from numerous, predominantly white Catholic women's religious communities of the United States but also from a few black communities, such as the Oblate Sisters of Providence. Conference goals brought members together in prayer, study, fellowship, and cooperative action aimed at confronting individual and institutional racism in church and society. Sister Mary Martin de Porres Grey (now Patricia Grey Tyree) of the Pittsburgh Sisters of Mercy ably led the conference in its first year. Her congregation subsidized the group through gifts in-kind and contributions of its members' services. In 1969, a national office was established at Mount Mercy (Carlow) College in Pittsburgh.

In 1972, Project DESIGN aimed at strengthening parochial schools in black communities through in-service training of teachers, model curricula, and programs to foster parental involvement in schools. Current NBSC work with the Religious Formation Conference promotes adaptation of congregations to black member's needs and supports black sisters conducting urban drop-ins and retreat centers.

ORGANIZATION AND FUNDING

A thirteen-unit regional structure, each with a contact person, recently began coordinating members' efforts between annual assemblies. This structure encompasses thirty-eight states, the District of Columbia, and Virgin Islands; the conference includes some members residing in Africa. A board of directors assists an elected president between assemblies with policy making and its implementation, a process further facilitated by a paid executive director and committees. Barbara Spears from the Olbates of Providence serves as the current conference president, and Gwynette Proctor from the Sisters of Notre Dame as executive director. Current committees focus on program management, black women in the Catholic Church, a response to successive drafts of the U.S. Roman Catholic bishops' pastoral letter on women, and a proactive black Catholic educational agenda for educating black children. Today the national office is located in Washington, D.C., with a paid staff of three.

The constitution adopted in 1984 confines full membership to black Catholic women belonging to any Roman Catholic congregation; associate membership is open to any black person age eighteen or older involved in some type of ministry in the black community. Anyone subscribing to NBSC's goals is welcome to auxiliary membership. Membership numbers 147. With attendance subsidized by scholarships, assemblies bring members together for mutual sharing, support, and corporate action. Annual assembly interaction enables members to act individually and corporately on legislative and other issues.

NBSC is a 501 (c) (3) organization. Income for the annual budget of $50,000 is derived principally from dues of $50 for individuals and $100 for corporations and from congregations that accept small stipends in place of full salaries for the services of sisters employed on NBSC staff.

Projects directed toward implementation of NBSC's more personal educational goals are the Institute on Black Sister Formation, which held forth regularly in the 1970s and the recently established Sojourner House in Detroit. Through the institutes, an all-black professional staff including historians, sociologists, political scientists, psychologists, psychiatrists, and theologians have assisted predominantly white congregations to rethink the way they initiated black women and have helped them recognize the identity issues, life experiences, culture, and particular needs of these women.

Conference members have extended institute influence into the 1980s by affirming black sisters' efforts at Benedict the Moor Center, Baltimore; Mariana House, Philadelphia; and Elizabeth Lang House, Louisville. Sojourner House, supported, in part, by the Detroit Archdiocese and American Board of Catholic Missions, affords blacks a place for retreat and discernment of vocational and ministry goals. Its facilities are open to men on a nonresidential basis. The conference also has called forth and warmly supported talented black women religious such as the late Thea Bowman of the Franciscan Sisters of Perpetual Adoration and many others in their use of personal gifts in ritual, prayer, and community leadership in black cultural style.

POLICY CONCERNS AND TACTICS

The board of directors implements the agenda between annual meetings. The conference consistently has favored education rather than polemics or confrontation to implement its social issues goals. Education of the membership is effected through publications and by means of workshops and dialogue at the annual meetings. Background information in the newsletter and occasional special bulletins alert and inform the membership regarding legislative issues or church matters. Action with respect to social concerns commonly takes the form of position papers and letter-writing campaigns.

Unique in the United States as a grassroots organization for black women belonging to Roman Catholic religious communities, NBSC collaborates with several other Catholic sisters' groups such as the Religious Formation Conference and the broader Leadership Conference of Women Religious,* as well as the National Office for Black Catholics. Along with its counterpart for Hispanic Sisters, Las Hermanas,* and the National Assembly of Religious Women,* it affords women who have not necessarily been elected to positions of leadership within their respective congregations opportunities to communicate with their peers, form ties of friendship, and engage in national networking around issues that concern black women.

FURTHER INFORMATION

There is a quarterly newsletter, *Signs of Soul,* and the national office issues action alerts, for example, about the situation in Africa. It issued an alert when the 1990 Civil Rights Act did not go through. NBSC has published several books, including *Naming and Claiming Our Resources: Christian Education Resources for the Black Community.*

KAREN M. KENNELLY, CSJ

NATIONAL BLACK WOMEN'S HEALTH PROJECT (NBWHP)
1237 Ralph David Abernathy Boulevard, SW
Atlanta, GA 30310
(404) 758-9590
FAX (404) 758-9661

The National Black Women's Health Project (NBWHP) empowers black women to improve their physical and mental health through education and self-help. The group advocates in the United States and internationally for better health and health care, especially addressing the particular needs of low-income black women.

ORIGIN AND DEVELOPMENT

Byllye Avery founded the Black Women's Health Project (BWHP) in 1981 after working in the women's health arena for almost a decade. In 1974, she and Judith Leavy, Margeret Parrish, and Joan Edelson opened the Gainesville [Florida] Women's Health Center, responding to a dearth of area facilities where women could obtain abortions. The center also offered general gynecological care. Realizing women's need for support in all reproductive areas, in 1978, Avery helped found Birthplace, an alternative birthing center in Gainesville. Birthplace provided prenatal care and birthing assistance in an attractive, non-institutional environment. Women exchanged information, discussed problems, and shared possible solutions in support groups that helped break down the isolation typical of twentieth-century pregnancy and motherhood. Renamed the Birth Center, the facility still existed in 1994 as a center for midwife-assisted childbirth.

Through these experiences and work with young black college women, Avery felt compelled to break the conspiracy of silence surrounding black women, especially around health issues. Avery found that the U.S. women's health movement did not effectively address black women constituents, especially those with low incomes. She discovered that compared with white women, the 14 million American black women in the United States, face shorter life expectancies, higher maternal mortality rates, higher rate of death from cervical cancer, high teenage pregnancy rates, and a high incidence of diabetes, hypertension, and cardiovascular disease. In addition, twice as many black as white infants die, and more black women and children sustain family violence. These disparities propelled Avery into action. An organization was needed to approach black women's health problems as an extension of the extreme stress caused by poverty, racism, and the high incidence of crime in low-income black neighborhoods. Avery created BWHP in Atlanta as a pilot program of the National Women's Health Network,* located in Washington, D.C., which she then served as a board member.

In 1983, BWHP sponsored the National Conference on Black Women's Health Issues at Agnes Spelman College in Atlanta. Organizers expected 200 women; over 1,700 participated. In 1984, the group incorporated and added the word "National" to its name. Other milestones in NBWHP's history include establishing a Center for Black Women's Wellness (CBWW) in an Atlanta housing project, in cooperation with the Southern Christian Leadership Conference (1988), and participating with the Morehouse Medical School and National Cancer Institute in a cancer prevention project (1989). NBWHP extended its influence around the world with the establishment of SisteReach in 1989, partly supported by the John D. and Catherine T. MacArthur Foundation. This international project fosters the improvement of women's health worldwide by educating about Third World women's health and reproductive needs and promoting intercultural exchange and networking in countries such as Nigeria, the Cameroons, Barbados, and Brazil.

National recognition of founder Avery provides one measure of the impact of NBWHP's unique approach. In July 1989, Avery personally received a five-year grant from the MacArthur Foundation of $310,000 to be spent at her discretion. The foundation awarded twenty-nine of the "genius" prizes that year; Avery was honored for independence and effectiveness. Later the same year, the publishers of the national magazine *Essence* named Avery one of seven outstanding black women in the country.

ORGANIZATION AND FUNDING

NBWHP maintains 150 chapters or self-help groups in thirty-one states and Nigeria, Barbados, and Belize. In 1992, Jean King chaired the fourteen-member board. Local chapters, self-help groups, or members may nominate candidates to serve on the board; members elect the board at the annual meeting. Board members serve at the national meeting and three quarterly board meetings. NBWHP expects board members to work at least forty hours a month for the organization. Avery holds the office of NBWHP founding president. The national office is located in Atlanta, and since 1990, there is a Public Education/Policy Office in Washington, D.C., at 1615 M Street, NW. NBWHP maintains offices in other cities, including New York City, Philadelphia, and Oakland, California. Cynthia Newbille serves as executive director; the board delegates daily management of NBWHP and its staff to the executive director. Julia Scott directs the policy office.

NBWHP has over 2,000 members.

The board controls the group's finances. Through membership dues and foundation grants, the nonprofit 501 (c) (3) organization maintains a budget of about $1.6 million to support the national office, policy office, SisteReach, and CBWW. An annual individual membership costs $60. Senior citizens and those of low income pay $25, and students pay $15. A membership for nonprofit organizations costs $150; for corporations, $250. Special membership categories exist for those wishing to make larger gifts. In 1988 and again in 1990, the W. K. Kellogg Foundation granted over $1 million to NBWHP for a project to set up and continue the services of three Atlanta housing project community centers. The organization has received moneys from such other foundations as Jessie Smith Noyes, Edna McConnell Clark, Henry J. Kaiser Family, and Ford.

POLICY CONCERNS AND TACTICS

The board generally directs NBWHP activities. Nine committees, each chaired by a board member, consider and make policy recommendations to the board. Policy statements also are brought before, and ratified by, the general membership. Within the large issue of health care reform, NBWHP deals mainly with policy issues such as violence, including sexual abuse and battering; low birthweight infants and infant mortality; early and prolonged motherhood; and reproductive health. The group informs and testifies before the Congress. The organization also works on the local level to modify policy. It maintains a speakers bureau, works to educate members, and conducts public service campaigns.

NBWHP facilitates communication between black women and their health care providers and encourages awareness about self-help approaches and available health care resources. It encourages discussion to minimize feelings of powerlessness and isolation and to foster a sense of control over physical and mental health. NBWHP tries to effect change in the health care delivery system to make it more responsive to black women's needs. The group sponsors community-based self-help programs, weekend retreats, and a triennial women's health conference.

The organization operates on the principle that clients in conjunction with providers should direct health care change. At CBWW, NBWHP offers health screening and referral, help in procuring social services, computerized learning and tutorial programs for a high school equivalency diploma, and job training.

NBWHP views empowerment as a first step. Individual wellness leads to collective wellness. The group's motto is Empowerment through Wellness. NBWHP utilizes self-help groups based on a holistic health model to facilitate communication and build self-esteem. In the self-help program, participants commit to effect change by first modifying their own lives, making lifestyle changes to prevent and detect many prevalent conditions. For example, changing one's diet and dealing effectively with stress may diminish hypertension; having regular Pap smears can detect cervical cancer. Group members determine their individual and collective health care needs and learn health management skills through shared experiences. NBWHP offers self-help groups for health care providers, as well as clients, to improve quality of care or cope with disability and death.

An NBWHP petition concerning low birth weight and infant mortality was included in a June 1984 congressional hearing on health, babies, and children. In 1987, NBWHP presented a statement to the U.S. Senate supporting the Family and Medical Leave bill (FMLA). NBWHP provided testimony in the 1990s on health issues such as the availability of mammography for lower-income women. In 1992, NBWHP supported the overrun of the gag rule on abortion and such pending national legislation as the Freedom of Choice Act, FMLA (enacted early in 1993), and Reproductive Health Equity Act.

In 1983, NBWHP joined with such organizations as the National Urban League,* National Organization for Women Legal Defense and Education Fund,* and Coalition to Fight Infant Mortality, presenting a petition to the U.S. Health and Human Services Department seeking to diminish infant mortality due to low birth weight. In 1989–90, discussions at a New York City self-help group sparked the formation of a citywide coalition, Women against Violence Everywhere. This coalition educates about violence privately and publicly, sponsoring community demonstrations and conferences besides group discussion sessions on alternatives to violence. Occasionally, local efforts exist in partnership with public health programs.

ELECTORAL ACTIVITIES

NBWHP sees women's health issues as nonpartisan and does not have a political action committee.

FURTHER INFORMATION

NBWHP issues the newspaper *Vital Signs* three times a year; it publishes articles ranging from personal accounts of health journeys to analysis of published surveys and explanation of permanent legislation. In 1992, NBWHP planned to expand the publication into a women's health newsmagazine available by subscription. The group also offers health fact sheets and brochures and has produced a ''Self-Help Group Development Manual'' (1987) to expedite new groups' establishment. It maintains a toll-free telephone line for health questions, 1 (800) ASK-BWHP. In 1987, it produced a documentary, *On Becoming a Woman: Mothers and Daughters Talking Together,* a rite-of-passage celebration film that discusses effective mother-daughter communication about sexuality, including menstruation, birth control, and reproduction. Available on videotape, the film was one of the first to deal with sexuality and motherhood from black women's perspective. Future plans include an update of the film.

JIMMY ELAINE WILKINSON MEYER

NATIONAL BLACK WOMEN'S POLITICAL CAUCUS
See NATIONAL BLACK WOMEN'S POLITICAL LEADERSHIP CAUCUS

NATIONAL BLACK WOMEN'S POLITICAL LEADERSHIP CAUCUS (NBWPLC)
3005 Bladensburg Road, NE
Suite 217
Washington, DC 20018
(202) 529-2806

The National Black Women's Political Leadership Caucus (NBWPLC) educates black women about the political process and strives for greater inclusion of black women in local, state, and national politics than now exists. Through training, communication, and networking, the caucus works to increase black women's awareness of political and economic issues and to encourage public activity around these issues. The NBWPLC encourages youth to leave high school "with a diploma in one hand and a voter registration card in the other."

ORIGIN AND DEVELOPMENT

In the fall of 1971, Nelis James Saunders, a Democratic Michigan state representative (1969–72), gathered a group of black women leaders and discussed creating an organization to educate black women in the political process. With the advice and support of Illinois state senator Richard Newhouse, Jr., a Democrat, and Ethel James Odum, Saunders' mother, the women founded NBWPLC on December 4, 1972. Women present at the original meeting included Florine James, Ohio Federation of Democratic Women president; C. DeLores Tucker, Pennsylvania secretary of state and a Democrat; Elizabeth Duncan Koontz, U.S. Labor Department Women's Bureau director; Hildagadeis Boswell, Democratic Maryland state representative; housing expert Aileen Hernandez, former president of National Organization for Women*; and Democrat Verda Freeman Welcome, Maryland's first black and first women state senator (1963–82). Thirty-three individuals from eighteen states attended the organizational meeting. People from fifteen other states expressed interest in the new caucus. First entitled the National Black Women's Political Caucus, the group soon changed its name to the present one.

These leaders founded NBWPLC out of frustration at being ignored and having little voice in U.S. politics, even after the 1964 Civil Rights Act's passage. Founders realized the necessity for training black women for political office and including black women from all economic levels through education and voter registration.

With one addition, women from the original group served as the first officers: Saunders, founder-national chairperson; Boswell, first vice chairperson; F. James, second vice chairperson; Tucker, third vice chairperson; Welcome, fourth vice chairperson; and Mary B. Williams, a former Michigan legislator, fifth vice chairperson. Other persons holding leadership positions in the new organization included Hannah Atkins, a Democrat and Oklahoma state representative; Dorothy Mae Taylor, the first black woman to serve in the Louisiana state legislature; and Pennie Doleman, state representative Alma G. Stallworth, and Avis E. Holmes, all of Michigan. Holmes served as executive director of the Detroit Non-Profit Housing Corporation. The caucus held its first executive council meeting in Washington, D.C., in January 1972. One hundred people from thirty-three states participated.

In December 1978, NBWPLC sponsored a four-day conference in Birmingham, Alabama. Directed by Juanita Kennedy-Morgan, then national executive secretary, the well-attended conference spawned eighteen resolutions. These called for revitalization and reorganization of black culture and the black community and for federal—specifically, presidential—attention to blacks' needs.

The caucus sustained an inactive period from 1979 to 1981. Restructured in 1981, it appointed Kennedy-Morgan to the new position of organizational director; Velma McEwen-Strode of Ohio replaced Saunders as national chairperson. Strode resigned after four months to direct the U.S. Labor Department Equal Employment Opportunity Office; attorney Ruth Harvey-Charity from Virginia assumed the position. Harvey-Charity, the first black woman elected to the Danville City Council (1970), served on the Democratic National Committee* (1972–80).

In August 1984, Congresswoman Shirley Chisholm (D-NY) and caucus founder Tucker formed a different organization with a similar name, the National Black Women's Political Caucus, to support candidates for political office. In February 1985, after Kennedy-Morgan initiated court proceedings on NBWPLC's behalf, Chisholm announced that her group had changed its name to the National Political Congress of Black Women. The new organization caused division among NBWPLC members and attracted potential caucus supporters. In 1992, the NBWPLC still struggled to regain momentum as a result of the split.

ORGANIZATION AND FUNDING

NBWPLC has thirty-three state caucuses and three regional caucuses. It has a board of directors made up of all national chairpersons and board members. Besides the executive council, NBWPLC is divided internally to include a women's unit and older women's, cultural youth, and men's auxiliaries. Committees include awards, cultural affairs, education, energy conservation, legislation, older Americans, registration and voting, and one for the youth directive workshop. In 1992, F. Alexis H. Robertson, retired from twenty-five years of local government service in Washington, D.C., served as national chairperson. There are offices in Washington and Birmingham, Alabama. Juanita Kennedy-Morgan holds the position of executive secretary and organizational director; she appoints the national chairperson and, together with her, the board of directors. Volunteers carry out the group's work—not even the director receives a salary.

The group encourages membership by adult black women of all ages and income levels. Members join especially for the opportunities provided for advocacy, networking, and consciousness-raising. The caucus also offers its members access to pertinent information, representation to government officials, and the chance to work and form relationships with similarly minded people.

Almost all of this nonprofit citizen organization's revenue comes from membership dues of thirty dollars, half of which goes to the national office. One percent of revenues represents conference income. Local and state groups operate on the remaining revenue from dues.

POLICY CONCERNS AND TACTICS

NBWPLC sets policy by consensus, with the group's statement of purpose as a guide; the caucus seeks to serve women working to achieve world peace, equality in the paid workforce and larger world, an increasingly representative political system and more women in political leadership roles, especially state legislative office, and an end to racism, sexism, poverty, and other factors that marginalize black women. NBWPLC encourages black women's political participation through awards, education, and communication.

In 1993, only eleven minority women—out of a total of fifty-three women—served in the 103d U.S. Congress (1 percent of the 535 legislators on Capitol Hill), including one senator, Carol Moseley Braun. The caucus works to heighten public awareness of the hurdles faced by black women candidates. By arranging meetings with state and federal legislators, the caucus provides role models for members aspiring to political office. The caucus encourages its members to write letters on pertinent issues to newspaper editors and elected officials.

NBWPLC may join other groups in testifying before the Congress. For example, in 1981, the caucus and more than twenty other organizations, including the American Association of University Women,* B'nai B'rith Women,* Mexican American Women's National Association,* and National Association of Colored Women's Clubs* presented a statement to the House Ways and Means Committee, urging rejection of President Reagan's proposed budget cuts to the Aid to Families with Dependent Children program.

ELECTORAL ACTIVITIES

This nonpartisan group does not maintain a political action committee, seeing women's issues as crossing party lines. The caucus actively promotes and participates in registering voters and publishes election tabloids featuring candidates and issues from all parties.

FURTHER INFORMATION

The caucus publishes a semiannual *Newsletter* and occasional election tabloids.

JIMMY ELAINE WILKINSON MEYER

NATIONAL CITIZENS COALITION FOR NURSING HOME REFORM (NCCNHR)
1224 M Street, NW
Suite 301
Washington, DC 20005
(202) 393-2018
FAX (202) 393-4122

The National Citizens Coalition for Nursing Home Reform (NCCNHR) provides technical support to local advocacy organizations and monitors federal nursing home policy. Since approximately seven out of every ten nursing home residents are women, concern with the quality of life of nursing home residents is an important political issue for women. Currently, over 250 community-based advocacy groups nationwide monitor the quality of care provided to nursing home residents and take part in coalition activities.

ORIGIN AND DEVELOPMENT

In June 1975, the American Health Care Association, a national association of proprietary nursing homes, sponsored a two-day conference to bring together nursing home owners, administrators, consumer advocates, and government representatives. The Gray Panthers* called consumer groups together to discuss common problems before the larger conference. At that meeting, advocates formed NCCNHR to represent their interests at the national level. Elma Holder became the new organization's executive director and has remained in that position. NCCNHR has become the central coordinating group for consumer advocacy organizations working to improve the quality of care provided to nursing home residents. Since 1975, quality of care issues have not changed to any substantial degree.

ORGANIZATION AND FUNDING

A twenty-one-member board of directors composed of representatives from consumer-controlled advocacy organizations nationwide meets four times a year to set policy. An advisory group of nursing home residents also makes recommendations on specific policy issues. The executive board is composed of twenty-one representatives of state and local advocacy organizations. Five members of the board are nursing home residents, and three are people of color. The president of the board is Susan Titus, representing Citizens for Better Care, Detroit, Michigan. Headquarters are in Washington, D.C. In addition to Executive Director Holder and Associate Director Barbara Frank, NCCNHR staff include a publications director, development director, membership coordinator, administrative assistant, legal assistant, a long-term care specialist, and support staff.

Over 250 community-based advocacy organizations are coalition members. Annual meetings held in Washington, D.C., provide opportunities for local advocates to meet, exchange information, and discuss current changes in federal laws and regulations. Members also receive mailed publications, notices of the annual conferences, discount registration fees when attending them, and discounts on publications.

During the late 1970s and early 1980s, primary funding for NCCNHR activities came from federal training grants, the Administration on Aging, and VISTA/ACTION program. In 1985, NCCNHR received funding from the American Association of Retired Persons* (AARP) to publish a newsletter. In 1986, the Health Care Financing Administration (HCFA) funded NCCNHR's study of state laws affecting nursing home residents' rights. The total annual budget is about $950,000, which includes a contract from the Administration on Aging to operate the National Long Term Care Ombudsman Resource Center. Annual dues account for only a small fraction of this budget, $50,000 per year. Membership organizations pay between $40 and $350 per year, depending upon their size. Nursing home resident councils receive discount memberships. Other sources of funding include income from the annual meeting ($120,000), donations ($40,000), foundation grants, and government contracts. In 1991, NCCNHR received grants from AARP and the Retirement Research Foundation.

POLICY CONCERNS AND TACTICS

Membership groups first identify issues and trends that impact on the quality of care that nursing home residents receive in their local communities. NCCNHR staff develop position papers on these issues and circulate them to all member organizations for comment. In addition, NCCNHR staff develop position papers on proposed regulatory and legislative changes pending in the Congress and in regulatory agencies that impact on quality of care pending and also circulate these position papers to member organizations for comment. Major policy initiatives are voted upon by the executive board. Besides serving as a clearinghouse for information dissemination to local advocacy organizations, NCCNHR monitors federal regulatory activities and legislative actions impacting on nursing home residents, testifies at legislative hearings, provides technical assistance to local advocacy organizations, and develops ad hoc coalitions to work for passage of specific legislation or oppose changes in federal regulations. The past five years, NCCNHR primarily has monitored efforts to implement the 1987 Omnibus Budget Reconciliation Act (OBRA) legislative mandates.

NCCNHR submits amicus curiae briefs in legal proceedings filed against the federal government, although it has not filed any amicus briefs in recent years. NCCNHR staff work closely with the National Senior Citizen's Law Center (NSCLC), which initiates litigation concerned with quality of care issues. Toby Edelman of NSCLC serves on the NCCNHR executive board.

In recent years, NCCNHR primarily has monitored efforts to implement the 1987 Omnibus Budget Reconciliation Act (OBRA) legislative mandates. The impetus for OBRA '87 emerged when, in 1981, HCFA developed a series of proposals to simplify and shorten the regulations for inspection and certification of nursing homes receiving Medicare and/or Medicaid funding. The response to this initiative and its consequences became NCCNHR's primary focus of activity for the next decade. The most controversial recommendation developed by an HCFA-established task force was a change in the nursing home inspection process. A state agency, usually the health or social services department, inspected nursing homes receiving Medicare and/or Medicaid reimbursement. HCFA proposed that the Joint Commission on Accreditation of Hospitals (JCAHO), a nongovernmental agency that inspects acute care hospitals, become the primary surveyors of nursing homes. This issue remained a concern for advocates in 1994.

NCCNHR felt concerned that the change would seriously compromise states' ability to enforce nursing home regulations. Under the proposed regulations, JCAH would be funded to survey nursing homes but have no power to impose sanctions. State agencies still would have to investigate complaints to impose sanctions but no longer would receive supportive federal funding. NCCNHR alerted community-based advocates of the proposed changes and organized a campaign to inform the Congress of consumers' concerns regarding such changes. NCCNHR also mobilized an ad hoc coalition of 39 national and approximately 200 local advocacy organizations to oppose them.

Reacting to mounting opposition to the proposals, the Congress adopted a ten-month moratorium on nursing home rule changes by HCFA. At the moratorium's conclusion, HCFA agreed to a congressional request not to make any changes in nursing home regulations unless consumers, providers, and regulatory representatives all concluded that they were necessary. A second provision of the agreement called for HCFA to fund a National Academy of Science Institute of Medicine (IOM) study of the survey certification process. The subsequent IOM report, *Improving the Quality of Care in Nursing Homes* (1986), includes recommendations for legislative changes.

Shortly after the study's publication, NCCNHR began a series of meetings with an ad hoc coalition of more than sixty religious, health, aging, and professional organizations to develop a legislative agenda based on IOM's recommendations. The result of these meetings was a set of policy recommendations. ''The Campaign for Quality Care in Nursing Homes,'' presented to congressional staff in April 1987. These recommendations formed the basis of proposals for nursing home reform within OBRA, enacted by the Congress on December 22, 1987. The official name of the legislation is the Nursing Home Reform Amendments; it generally is referred to as OBRA '87.

Among the law's provisions were limitations on the use of physical restraints, a requirement that state agencies develop patient-oriented nursing home inspection protocols, and mandated training for nurses aides. Facilities with more than 120 beds had to employ a full-time social worker. Other provisions included amendments guaranteeing resident rights to establish resident and family councils, examine state survey reports, and receive thirty days' notice of transfer or discharge and a more effective range of sanctions for homes found not to be in compliance with regulations. The NCCNHR-developed coalition was a significant factor in ensuring the legislation's enforcement.

Members of the coalition of organizations that NCCNHR has worked with regularly include AARP, American Nurses' Association,* American Medical Association, Service Employees International Union,* American Health Association (AHA), American Homes for the Aging (AHFA) and the National Association of Social Workers.* Both AHA and AHFA represent nursing home owners.

ELECTORAL ACTIVITIES

NCCNHR views itself primarily as an advocacy, education, and information-disseminating organization. It does not have a political action committee.

FURTHER INFORMATION

A newsletter published six times yearly, the *Quality Care Advocate,* summarizes recent state, federal, and judicial actions impacting on nursing home resident care and describes important actions initiated by local advocacy and ombudsman programs. There also are periodic information letters describing upcoming legislation and regulatory changes impacting on the quality of care of nursing home residents.

HARVEY CATCHEN

NATIONAL COALITION AGAINST DOMESTIC VIOLENCE (NCADV)
P.O. Box 18749
Denver, CO 80218
(303) 839-1852
FAX (303) 831-9251

The National Coalition against Domestic Violence (NCADV) is a feminist organization addressing the issue of domestic violence and facilitating organization among activists in the battered women's movement.

ORIGIN AND DEVELOPMENT

NCADV was founded in 1978 by a group of women who came together during a national consultation on Battered Women: Issues of Public Policy, sponsored by the U.S. Civil Rights Commission. The meeting set out to investigate denial of equal protection under the laws based on sex and to inform commissioners of the investigation's findings. The battered women's movement had been under way since the early 1970s; and much work and discussion about forming a national coalition to address domestic violence already had taken place among feminist activists in the movement. Although there was a good deal of support for a national coalition among activists, there also was concern that such an organization would detract from the movement's grassroots and feminist directions. Previous experience with co-optation of feminist organizations, as well as the tremendous struggle for resources that often accompanies national organization, contributed to early skepticism about forming a national coalition.

A number of activists felt strongly about the need for a national coalition or body for the battered women's movement. The consultation helped activists around the country to begin building such an organization. A number of women contacted battered women's organizations countrywide and encouraged activists to attend the consultation. Valle Jones initiated a meeting among sixty or so activists the night before the consultation opened officially. This served as the major jumping-off point for NCADV's formation. A steering committee formed in order to determine an organizational structure, organize a national conference, and begin monitoring national legislation affecting battered women and their children.

From the beginning NCADV has been plagued by a number of issues often faced by feminist organizations. Diversity among women, including race, class, sexual orientation, and political leanings, caused rifts among coalition activists and direct-service providers. Some activists in the battered women's movement have expressed concerns about the exclusion of women of color, poor women, and lesbians from the movement at large and from NCADV. Subcommittees drew up specific directives, ratified at the first meetings, to address these issues and plan activities to include marginalized groups. Evidence of success in addressing these issues includes eight standing task forces in place to help ensure inclusiveness and diversity, including the Battered Women and Formerly Battered Women's Task Force, Rural Women's Task Force, Women of Color Task Force, Lesbian Task Force, Jewish Women's Task Force, and Child Advocacy Task Force. Additionally, many women of color serve on the board and in other key organizational positions.

Securing a stable funding base has proven challenging for NCADV. The first year it devoted mainly to monitoring federal policy initiatives and organizing a first national conference. During this time volunteers provided labor, and operating money was virtually nonexistent. Money for the conference and to subsidize programs around the country to send representatives to it was generated by soliciting funds from private foundations, individual contributions, and registration fees. Quick and skillful proposal writing by volunteers resulted in substantial federal grants to support the organization.

Since NCADV's first national conference in 1980, the organization has continued to have difficulty generating a stable funding base. Generally, support for organizations that primarily served women and children was hard to come by under the Reagan and Bush administrations, and NCADV was no exception. From 1987 to 1989, NCADV's budget jumped substantially due to a grant from Johnson and Johnson to operate the first national domestic violence hot line. The hot line, which went into operation in September 1987, operated twenty-four hours a day taking calls and making referrals for battered women across the country. While the hot line initially proved a boon for NCADV, allowing the organization to employ nineteen full-time staff and improving the organization's fiscal picture, the breakthrough was short-lived. Because of Johnson and Johnson holdings in South Africa and its refusal to release interests there,

NCADV turned back the funds. Subsequently, the Michigan Coalition against Domestic Violence took over the hot line.

The organization's major aims have not changed since its inception and include facilitating communication and coalition at the state and regional levels, assisting battered women's organizations to secure moneys and develop services, monitoring and influencing policy developments relevant to battered women, organizing a biyearly national conference on domestic violence, and providing publications and information to a variety of groups interacting with battered women, including mental health practitioners.

ORGANIZATION AND FUNDING

While there are coalitions against violence in all the states except Utah, these coalitions do not necessarily belong to NCADV. Of the fifty-six state coalitions, twenty-eight are NCADV members, and the remaining twenty-eight are autonomous. The executive board consists of a three-member executive committee. Other board members represent the task forces and members at large. NCADV's Washington, D.C., office, address P.O. Box 34103, zip code 20043, employs one staff member, a membership specialist who also edits the newsletter, and a public policy specialist. Employees in Denver include a coordinator, resource development specialist, and an administrative assistant.

With roughly 1,500 members, NCADV has several categories of membership. Active organizational members, approximately 450 programs that work directly with battered women and their children, constitute the largest proportion of the membership. Active members' organizations are screened by NCADV to ensure that they hold to feminist principles and cultural diversity among staff and clients in the organization. Active organizational members must include women from different socioeconomic backgrounds and both heterosexual and lesbian women in their organization. Active organizational member is the only membership category that allows participation in NCADV policy decisions and grants voting privileges; NCADV carefully screens organizational members because they shape the organization's goals and direction. Other membership categories include supportive organization, supportive individual, major donor, incarcerated women, youths, and small donors.

NCADV's current budget runs between $300,000 and $400,000 annually. Approximately $90,000 of the annual budget comes from membership dues, and half from private foundations, federal grants, and individual donors. NCADV is a private, nonprofit organization. Donations are tax-deductible.

POLICY CONCERNS AND TACTICS

NCADV has a public policy advocate and a legislative committee somewhat akin to a political action committee. The policy advocate attends congressional sessions and monitors them for bills relevant to battered women and their children. She gathers information on relevant bills, analyzes their content, and analyzes the battered women's movement's interest in/stand on the bills. The policy advocate reports to the board when it meets and to the membership through a "Legislative Alert." She stays in contact with a media relations specialist who initiates media campaigns, press releases, and so on around specific bills. The policy advocate monitors national legislation but helps activists in individual states monitor state-level legislation and teaches them lobbying strategies.

As of January 1992, NCADV added a legislative committee. It sets NCADV's political agenda; and the policy advocate is the individual in Washington making the agenda happen, that is, translating it into action. The legislative committee has a four-point plan: supporting current legislation affecting battered women and their children, increasing the visibility of issues related to violence against women and children, serving as a conduit for state legislative information sharing, and strengthening the legislative capacity and understanding of the board. Although the legislative committee had not yet introduced or drafted legislation of its own for presentation to the Congress, it has this as a long-term goal.

The media specialist is in contact with the public policy advocate and often contacts the press regarding a pending bill that would affect battered women. She puts together press releases and contacts the media again when bills get passed and signed. For example, the governor of Colorado recently signed a "stalker law" that makes menacing and harassing a woman against the law. The media relations specialist contacted the family of a woman murdered by a stalker at a time no law was in place to protect her and had the family attend the bill-signing session. Standing behind the governor, the media specialist displayed a blowup of a dramatic NCADV poster. She contacted media people, who were there for the bill signing. The governor gave the signed bill to the victim's family. The media specialist gave the governor the poster, which depicted a coffin with flowers on it: "He Beat Her 150 Times. She Only Got Flowers Once."

NCADV has initiated numerous public service and information campaigns. For example, October is National Domestic Violence Awareness Month. The media specialist contacted several media organizations and persuaded "The Oprah Winfrey Show" to devote a segment to the issue, supplying Winfrey with the names of politically savvy "experts" on domestic violence, statistics, and so on. The specialist also teaches state-level activists how to initiate media campaigns in their individual states.

The organization advocated the Violence against Women Act introduced by Senator Joseph Biden (D-DE), chair of the Senate Judiciary Committee. This important piece of legislation, passed as part of the 1994 Omnibus Crime Act, also was supported by the National Organization for Women Legal Defense and Education Fund.* The National Women's Abuse Prevention Project actively lobbied for it. Several points address different types of violence against women, such as rape, domestic violence, and street harassment. The portion of the bill that NCADV most actively supported deals with domestic violence, including funds to be set aside for building and supporting battered women's shelters. NCADV tried to get the amount allotted for this purpose increased.

Other NCADV-supported legislation includes the Immigration Fraud Act, passed to allow battered immigrant women to obtain a waiver to the two-year deportation law. Previously, immigrant women battered by their partners were threatened with deportation if they went to the police or tried to divorce the partner; to stay in the United States, an individual must be married at least two years. The legislation that passed has several restrictive clauses that reduce its utility for NCADV, but it is a start. Another piece of legislation, introduced by NCADV and passed each year, is the commemorative legislation designating October National Domestic Violence Awareness Month. The Congress passed this bill for the first time in 1989.

Generally NCADV works with shelters and battered women's advocacy service organizations at the individual state level; these have specialists and task forces to monitor public policy and campaign for particular policies.

ELECTORAL ACTIVITIES

NCADV is a nonpartisan organization. It does not have a political action committee per se.

FURTHER INFORMATION

The organization has a bimonthly newsletter, *Voice*. There also is a bimonthly publication called "Legislative Alert." Other publications include a *1994 National Directory of Domestic Violence Programs: Guidelines for Mental Health Practitioners in Domestic Violence Cases* and the *Rural Resource Packet* of information concerning the needs and issues of rural battered women and suggesting services and coalition building on behalf of rural women.

BRANDY M. BRITTON

NATIONAL COALITION OF 100 BLACK WOMEN (NCBW)
38 W. 32nd Street
Suite 1610
New York, NY 10001
(212) 947-2196
FAX (212) 947-2477

The National Coalition of 100 Black Women (NCBW) empowers black women through networking, programs, and recognition, emphasizing leadership development, role modeling, and mentoring. Under the umbrella of the nonprofit National Coalition of 100 Black Women Community Services Fund (NCBWCSF), NCBW advocates heightened visibility for, and increased leadership by, black women in both the economic and political arenas on local, state, and national levels.

ORIGIN AND DEVELOPMENT

Jewell Jackson McCabe founded NCBW in 1981. She extended to a national context work begun in New York City in 1970, when twenty-six women created the original Coalition of 100 Black Women. Founders of the 1970 effort included Edna Beach, Cathy Connor, Evelyn Cunningham, and Corien Davies Drew. The women—political and corporate leaders—created the organization in order to facilitate communication among themselves and provide a forum for black women achievers. The group chose its name as counterpoint to "100 Black Men," a prominent local effort. By 1977, when McCabe became president, the coalition included 127 members. In 1981, 890 New York women belonged to the new NCBW. More than a decade later, the organization boasted over 6,000 members nationwide.

When she became NCBW president, McCabe served as president of the New York Urban Coalition. She later directed government and community affairs at WNET, TV-13. McCabe also headed the New York State Job Training Partnership Council. In the late 1980s, she started a consulting firm, Jewell Jackson McCabe Associates, to advise corporations on marketing to minorities.

ORGANIZATION AND FUNDING

NCBW has sixty chapters in twenty-two states and the District of Columbia. Delegates from each chapter elect officers at NCBW's biennial meeting. The number of delegates per chapter is apportioned according to the size of the membership. The president appoints six people every two years to the board of directors. McCabe serves as national chair of NCBW. Committees within the coalition include arts and culture, community action, economic development, education, employment, health, and political action. In 1992, Barbara DeBaptiste became national president. Headquarters are in New York City. Since 1991, Shirley Poole has held the position of executive director.

In 1994, NCBW had 6,000 members. Chapters offer both individual and group memberships. The diverse membership includes lawyers, judges, educators, community activists, legislators, psychologists, and corporate and business leaders. A 501 (c) (4) group, NCBW operates on a budget of about $200,000 a year. Chapters pay dues on a per capita basis according to their membership. Dues are $30 per member; each chapter also pays an annual assessment fee of $1,500. Chapters set their own dues structure; thus, fees vary from one chapter to another.

An Internal Revenue Service-designated 501 (c) (3) organization, NCBWCSF serves as an umbrella for programs implemented by NCBW. McCabe serves as the fund's president. As the national chair of NCBW, she biennially appoints eight members of the NCBWCSF board. The fund carries out programs while NCBW focuses on advocacy. NCBWCSF receives grants from local and national foundations such as the Ford Foundation for its budget of $300,000.

The coalition celebrates the diversity of black American women and their accomplishments worldwide, bestowing Candace awards annually to black women for outstanding achievement. The prize name, an ancient Ethiopian word, means empress or queen. Award categories vary according to the recipients chosen. They have included business, education, community service, arts and letters, communication and journalism, international affairs, philanthropy, and science and technology. One of the Candace prizes is the Distinguished Service Award, recognizing both women and men as leaders. Honorees have included *Jet* and *Ebony* publisher John H. Johnson, Harvard professor Derrick A. Bell, Jr., Camille Cosby, and Coretta Scott King. Other leaders honored by the organization include Maya Angelou and Rosa Parks. As part of its emphasis on mentoring, NCBW invites students to the annual Candace event. The award program receives national media attention.

At the celebration of the group's tenth anniversary in November 1991, the coalition presented the Ida B. Wells Award to guest of honor Anita Hill, the law professor at the University of Oklahoma who publicly accused U.S. Supreme Court nominee Clarence Thomas of sexual harassment. The award, named for a journalist/muckraker and founder of the antilynching movement, recognized Hill's strength and courage despite public disagreement.

POLICY CONCERNS AND TACTICS

Economic, health, family, employment, education, housing, criminal justice, and urban life issues concern NCBW. It stresses black women's unique and diverse achievements and the needs and the failure of the women's liberation movement to recognize those achievements or meet those needs. Solutions put forth by NCBW involve building self-esteem through leadership development, networking, mentoring, and promoting a historical awareness of black women's achievements. The coalition attempts to link the organizational, corporate, and political sectors to garner national and local support and visibility—power—for black women.

Forums for sharing between younger and older black women exemplify the coalition's high regard for intergenerational communication. Almost all chapters sponsor mentoring programs, for example, between Spelman College students and professional women. Some of these programs focus on literacy, such as tutoring adolescents in partnership with Time-Warner publishers, in a program called Time to Read. In 1992, NCBW began a pilot project on literacy and life skills development, with Maybelline cosmetic company support. This tutoring and mentoring program operates in Georgia, Florida, Tennessee, Connecticut, and New York, among other locations.

In November 1991, NCBW sponsored a national conference on reproductive health, with the Ford Foundation's support. Many other organizations, including the National Black Women's Health Project,* participated in the conference, which encouraged dialogue to increase awareness of reproductive health issues, especially those unique to black women.

Occasionally, the coalition presents its views before the Congress, as at a

1980 hearing regarding the importance of accurate representation of black Americans in the 1980 census. In 1991, the NCBW appeared before the Senate at hearings on AIDS and women's health.

ELECTORAL ACTIVITIES

NCBW does not maintain a political action committee but actively participates in voter registration. For example, in 1992, NCBW sponsored "Get Out the Vote" voter registration clinics on both the local and national levels.

FURTHER INFORMATION

The coalition publishes the semi-annual *National Coalition of 100 Black Women—A Statement,* a member newsletter reporting black women's activities and achievements.

JIMMY ELAINE WILKINSON MEYER

NATIONAL COALITION OF 100 BLACK WOMEN COMMUNITY SERVICES FUND
See NATIONAL BLACK COALITION OF 100 BLACK WOMEN

NATIONAL COALITION ON OLDER WOMEN'S ISSUES (NCOWI)
The National Coalition on Older Women's Issues (NCOWI) provided a national network of organizations and individuals specifically concerned with mid-life and older women's problems and needs.

ORIGIN AND DEVELOPMENT

NCOWI's founding members wanted to provide consistent and structured linkage between the aging network and the women's network. In 1981, these two networks were perceived as operating on parallel but often disconnected tracks. Founder Marjory B. Marvel served as president from 1981 to 1988. Four other professionals already active in Washington-based aging or women's organizations helped coalesce these disparate networks into a coalition-building force: Charlotte Conable of the George Washington University Women's Studies Program, Marxine Foreman and Pat Reuss from the Women's Equality Action League* (WEAL), and Peg Downey from the American Association of University Women.*

The coalition's network was structured to embrace the broadest possible spectrum of women's organizations, professional associations, research centers, educators, church groups, civic organizations, advocates, and individual associate members. A brochure from its early days, prioritizing problems and addressing possible solutions, lists forty-six member organizations. This carefully nurtured diversity in membership was designed to encourage breadth of research and advocacy that would yield the realistic potential for significant improvements in social and public policies. From inception NCOWI focused its attention on three major issue areas: employment, retirement income, and health and well being.

Employment issues were defined to include access to training and education, and retirement issues to encompass Social Security and pensions.

A decision to dissolve the coalition was made in 1988. The board divided all remaining assets among the Displaced Homemaker's Network, National Senior Citizen Law Center, Older Women's League,* Pension Rights Center, and WEAL. Over the seven years the group acted, numerous other organizations began serious, consistent efforts to assist midlife and older women that were meeting NCOWI's original purpose and goals. During its seven years, NCOWI's efforts did not always match its ambitious goals, but its board, under Marvel's leadership, more than met its primary mandate—to coordinate the efforts of those involved in solving problems of aging and of women and to heighten awareness of networking's value. That the coalition earned its credibility as a triggering agent and catalyst is evidenced by the current agenda and coalescing efforts of dozens of powerful Washington-based organizations.

ORGANIZATION AND FUNDING

A seven-member board of directors met monthly to appoint and oversee research committees, evaluate budget proposals, and set the agenda for future projects. It appointed task forces in its major issue areas. Originally provided at WEAL headquarters, office space later transferred to the American Association of Retired Persons* (AARP) building. The coalition had no paid staff. A volunteer intern was recruited to collect and collate material for a resource directory. A major Washington, D.C., law firm provided pro bono legal assistance.

Funding was provided by membership dues and a generous grant from United Methodist Women.* Membership categories included organizational ($35), individual ($15), and sponsor ($100) fees. The sponsor classification included both the Methodist Church* and the American Council of Life Insurance. NCOWI was a 501 (c) (3) organization.

POLICY CONCERNS AND TACTICS

The coalition honed its objectives to include the following strategies: maintaining an information network for member organizations, policymakers and the public; monitoring relevant legislative proposals; maintaining a database for use by educators, program planners, employers, and policymakers; developing resource materials within the three target areas; promoting collaboration efforts with employers to encourage hiring older women workers and retraining and promoting them; encouraging the development of affordable, accessible health care facilities; encouraging replication of the coalition at state and local levels; and promoting awareness of older women as valuable underpaid, largely untapped resource persons.

ELECTORAL ACTIVITIES

NCOWI did not see its issues as partisan and does not have a political action committee.

FURTHER INFORMATION

With the assistance and support of AARP's Women's Division* and its director Bette Mullen, the coalition's efforts culminated in a *Resource Directory for Midlife and Older Women* (1986). Hundreds of organizations were asked to select from among fifty issues those most closely approximating their objectives and concerns and to define their strategy.

PEGGY DOWNES

NATIONAL COMMISSION OF MEXICAN WOMEN
See COMISION FEMINIL MEXICANA NACIONAL

NATIONAL COMMISSION OF WORKING WOMEN
See WIDER OPPORTUNITIES FOR WOMEN

NATIONAL COMMITTEE FOR A HUMAN LIFE AMENDMENT, INC. (NCHLA)
1511 K Street, NW
Suite 335
Washington, DC 20005
(202) 393-0703

The National Committee for a Human Life Amendment (NCHLA) seeks to promote passage of a right to life amendment to the U.S. Constitution. Such an amendment would reverse the holdings of the U.S. Supreme Court's *Roe* v. *Wade* and *Doe* v. *Bolton* decisions (1973) and secure the right to life for unborn children from conception.

ORIGIN AND DEVELOPMENT

The National Council of Catholic Bishops (NCCB) facilitated the founding of NCHLA in 1974 in response to the Court's 1973 abortion rulings. Most U.S. interest groups are founded with the assistance of existing sympathetic organizations. Until the mid-1980s, the committee actively sought passage of a human life amendment (HLA) in the Congress. After years of effort, NCHLA refocused its efforts to other pro-life policies. It takes some comfort in the fact that the amendment gets debated and is supported by 45 percent of the population. NCHLA's ultimate goal still is HLA, but the committee has decided this is not viable strategy at the present time. The current goal is to ban use of federal moneys to pay for abortions (foreign and domestic). In 1993, the committee successfully opposed passage of the Freedom of Choice Act and secured enactment of the Hyde amendment, which limits the conditions for spending federal Medicaid moneys on abortion. In 1994, it opposed the inclusion of abortion coverage as a mandated benefit in health care reform.

ORGANIZATION AND FUNDING

NCHLA is not a membership organization. It exists as a service organization fulfilling the grassroots program needs of Catholic dioceses and parishes as well as Catholic lay organizations. The board of directors is open to both women and men and is racially diverse. The board accepts policy guidance from the bishops. The Washington, D.C., office has six full-time employees, including an executive director. The present executive director is Michael Taylor. In the summer, NCHLA often takes on paid interns.

The organization is funded by voluntary contributions from most Catholic dioceses in the United States. Both women and men are active as diocesan pro-life coordinators.

POLICY CONCERNS AND TACTICS

Within parameters set by the board, the Washington staff develops program strategies in consultation with church leaders on the national and local levels. When a new government policy needs to be addressed, Washington staff brainstorms a strategy to deal with the situation. NCHLA provides members and staff of both the U.S. Congress and state legislatures with information on the abortion issue. It makes presentations to other public officials. The group is set up exclusively to lobby on legislative issues. The committee has always relied on a grassroots strategy. It sends mailings to diocesan and parish officials and other church leaders and has recently inaugurated a postcard campaign to further encourage Catholic parishioners to contact their elected officials.

NCHLA coordinates activities with Catholic women's organizations, including Daughters of Isabella, the Catholic Daughters of the Americas, and the National Council of Catholic Women.* It networks with other pro-life groups. In the early 1990s, it worked with the Abortion Is Not Family Planning Coalition. As one would expect, the committee is constantly in conflict with National Abortion Rights Action League,* National Organization for Women,* and Planned Parenthood.*

ELECTORAL ACTIVITIES

NCHLA does not become involved in partisan politics or electoral activities. It does not have a political action committee.

FURTHER INFORMATION

There is no newsletter, although occasionally memos are directed to leaders in the field.

ELIZABETH ADELL COOK

NATIONAL COMMITTEE FOR THE DAY CARE OF CHILDREN
See DAY CARE COUNCIL OF AMERICA

NATIONAL COMMITTEE ON PAY EQUITY (NCPE)
1126 16th Street, NW
Washington, DC 20036
(202) 331-7343
FAX (202) 331-7406

The National Committee on Pay Equity (NCPE), the only national organization formed for the express purpose of "achieving economic equality for women and people of color through pay equity," often is recognized by those involved in the comparable worth debate as the leader of the pay equity movement.

ORIGIN AND DEVELOPMENT

The issue of comparable worth/pay equity achieved national visibility in 1977, when Eleanor Holmes Norton, chair of the U.S. Equal Employment Opportunity Commission (EEOC), identified it as a priority of her administration. Norton believed the problem of sex-based wage discrimination was a crucial one for women. Her first step was to commission the National Academy of Sciences to investigate the question of why women's jobs consistently are undervalued. In addition, under Norton, EEOC held hearings on wage discrimination and comparable worth.

These actions taken by Norton and the EEOC gave impetus to forming a national network of individuals and groups committed to the idea of implementing standards for equal pay for work of comparable worth at the national, state, and local levels. On October 24, 1979, representatives of over a dozen organizations held a national conference on pay equity in Washington, D.C., attended by at least 200 pay equity experts and activists. Participants at this conference came together to share their thoughts and concerns about the under-evaluation of traditionally female work in the United States. At the conference's end, a resolution passed to form a national coalition on pay equity, NCPE. The group's basic position is that wages should be job-related and not based on sex and race.

The first official chair of NCPE, Nancy Perlman of the Albany-based Center for Women in Government, was named in 1981. Prior to this, several individuals donated their time as acting chair. Since its creation, NCPE has engaged in various activities at all levels of government. It sees its role as providing education and advocacy and serving as a center for information and publicity. That is, the organization serves as a central clearinghouse for pay equity news and information. In 1989, NCPE celebrated its tenth anniversary at a conference in Washington, D.C. Norton, then a professor of government at Georgetown University, delivered a keynote address congratulating the coalition on its achievements and evaluating the organization's agenda for the 1990s. She praised the group for having taken a highly difficult aspect of antidiscrimination policy, bringing it to life, and keeping it alive throughout the eighties, and predicted the nineties would witness an end to most of what remains of wage differentials.

ORGANIZATION AND FUNDING

The thirty-three-member board of directors, elected at the annual meeting, consists of individuals from three categories: civil rights minority groups, trade unions/workforce representatives, and women's organizations. One-third of the board is elected from each category. In addition, the board appoints six at-large members. The current and fifth NCPE chair is Coloria Johnson of the International Union of Electrical, Salaried, Machine and Furniture Workers of the American Federation of Labor-Congress of Industrial Organizations* (AFL-CIO). NCPE's headquarters is located in Washington, D.C. Susan Bianchi-Sand currently serves as the executive director, and Meseret Alemseged as the office manager. The organization has five full-time employees. It also has internships available to students committed to pay equity for women and people of color and a speakers bureau.

When first created, the organization had 20 members. Today, it has approximately 170 organization members and 250 individual members. Membership consists primarily of labor unions such as American Federation of State, County and Municipal Employees* (AFSCME): women's groups and civil rights organizations such as the League of Women Voters*; religious, professional, and legal associations such as Catholic Churches USA Commission on Women; and state and local pay equity coalitions such as the Wyoming Commission on Women. NCPE membership also includes representatives from Canada, Japan, New Zealand, and Australia.

One-third of NCPE's support derives from membership dues and special contributions from its patrons, who contribute $5,000 (AFSCME, National Education Association and Service Employees International Union); benefactors, who donate $2,500 (AFL-CIO Women's Activities Department, Presbyterian Church USA,* and the United Methodist Church*); and sustaining members, who give $1,500 (American Library Association,* American Nurses' Association,* Office and Professional Employees International Union, United Auto Workers International Union,* United Food and Commercial International Union, and United Steelworkers of America). Individual dues are $35 except for low-income individuals, who may pay $15; organizational dues are $200 except for organizations with budgets under $200,000, which pay $100. Remaining support comes from a number of foundation grants: Alida Rockefeller Charitable Leaders Trust, Ann R. Roberts Foundation, Ford Foundation, 777 Fund of Tides Foundation, Ms. Foundation, and the J. R. MacArthur Fund. The overall budget in 1992 was $297,220, with $54,000 of this money designated for special projects. NCPE is a nonprofit, tax-exempt organization.

POLICY CONCERNS AND TACTICS

A board of directors and seven task forces establish NCPE policy. Task forces focus on separate strategies such as litigation, legislation, and research. Recommendations for action by the coalition are approved by the entire membership at its annual meeting. All organizational members are entitled to one vote, regardless of the contribution they make to NCPE. Voting privileges do not apply to individual members. In general, NCPE provides leadership, information, and technical assistance to pay equity advocates, employers, public officials, the media, and public. Recent accomplishments include congressional staff briefings, a national opinion survey on public attitudes toward pay equity, a study on women of color and pay equity, training sessions and conferences, and the filing of amicus briefs in pay equity cases. NCPE viewed the *County of Washington* v. *Gunther* (1981) as a victory when the Supreme Court ruled that Title VII of the 1964 Civil Rights Act was broader than the Equal Pay Act and could be applied to sex-based wage discrimination in jobs that were not identical. However, in *State of Washington* v. *AFSCME* (1985), where twenty-nine other organizations signed on to NCPE's brief, the Ninth Circuit Court of Appeals acknowledged that a wage gap existed between female and male employees but stated that this wage gap was not proof that the state of Washington discriminated against its female employees.

Specific policies supported by NCPE in the past few years include the 1991 Civil Rights Act, the Pay Equity Technical Assistance Act passed by the House of Representatives in 1991, and the 1992 Equal Remedies bill. Further, NCPE regularly scrutinizes the EEOC's activities and also is monitoring a General Accounting Office pilot pay equity study of the federal workforce.

As an interest group composed of organizational members, NCPE works very closely with these groups in pay equity activities. Coalition partners of NCPE include AFL-CIO. National Organization for Women* and the American Civil Liberties Union.* Some of the more influential groups to oppose the coalition include the Chamber of Commerce, National Association of Manufacturers, Equal Employment Advisory Council, and Eagle Forum.*

ELECTORAL ACTIVITIES

The coalition is not involved in electoral activities.

FURTHER INFORMATION

NCPE publishes a semiyearly newsletter entitled *Newsnotes.* The group's publication distribution exceeds 11,000 copies.

BARBARA L. POOLE

NATIONAL CONFERENCE OF PUERTO RICAN WOMEN (NACOPRW)
5 Thomas Circle, NW
Washington, DC 20005
(202) 387-4716

The National Conference of Puerto Rican Women (NACOPRW) promotes the full participation of Puerto Rican and Hispanic women in U.S. economic, social, and political life. It maintains a visible presence at the national and chapter levels.

ORIGIN AND DEVELOPMENT

Founded in Washington, D.C., in 1972 by a dynamic gathering of Puerto Rican women. NACOPRW preserved their cultural link. The early presidents and key founders represent a collective line of leadership, including Aida Berio, Ledia Bernal, Rafaela Diaz, and Ana Lopez Fontana. Early community experience connected Puerto Rican women; and they transferred their organizational skills to building a cultural forum of their own. The Puerto Rican membership affirmed life-giving relations through the family of wives, mothers, and daughters. NACOPRW affirms the empowerment of all Spanish-speaking people and women generally.

NACOPRW's founding goals aimed to attain the rights of Puerto Rican women as well as other Hispanic women in the United States, promote greater participation by all Puerto Ricans and other Hispanics in U.S. socioeconomic and political life, identify and help develop leadership among U.S.-based Puerto Rican women, and establish communication among them.

ORGANIZATION AND FUNDING

NACOPRW's seventeen chapters are located in Connecticut, Florida, Illinois, Maryland, Massachusetts, Michigan, New York, Ohio, Pennsylvania, Virginia, and the District of Columbia. Intermediate structures, between the national and local/state affiliates, enhance organizational cohesion. The national board of directors, which includes the local chapters' presidents and delegates, meets quarterly and constitutes NACOPRW's policy-making body. The current national president is Edna Banchs Laverdi. The national headquarters in Washington, established in 1975 with the aid of a Ford Foundation grant, does not employ an executive director and has one part-time staffer assisted by five volunteers.

An individual-based organization, NACOPRW has 800 members, having grown from 100 members in 1975, 500 in 1980, and 600 in 1985. Anyone supporting NACOPRW's goals may join as an active or associate chapter member or as a member at large; NACOPRW also has institutional members. Dues are $30 for individuals, $25 for affiliates, and $100 for corporations. Members are attracted to NACOPRW because it offers them opportunities to develop organizational and leadership skills and to participate in public affairs. The annual conference gives direction and leadership to a broad spectrum of women by age and occupation in such areas as health, economic development, technology, mentoring, and political empowerment. Members benefit from the education and leadership training workshops and consciousness-raising sessions conducted by the conference. Sharing information and research unifies peers and colleagues into valued friendships and associations—beneficial to members and organizations. Local chapters may provide scholarships to Hispanic students within their communities.

NACOPRW receives 60 percent of its revenues from conferences; 20 percent from corporate gifts or grants; 10 percent from the membership dues; 3 percent from gifts; and 7 percent from publications sales or advertising, merchandise sales, grants or contracts from government agencies, and fund-raising events such as concerts, parties, and theatrical events. Grants help fund the annual conferences; for example, the U.S. Centers for Disease Control provided funds for forty NACOPRW women to attend three workshops on AIDS education offered during the sixteenth conference, focusing on the consequences of the disease for Hispanic women and children, prevention and outreach, and the role of a volunteer organization in living with AIDS. Corporations and businesses also help to fund the conference, especially small ones indigenous to the local chapters. The budget recently was $40,000, down from $60,000 in 1980 but a sizable increase from the small sum of $10 with which the organization began in 1972. Contributions are tax-deductible, and this helps the group solicit yearly contributions to compensate for budget variations.

POLICY CONCERNS AND TACTICS

Board members and chapter representatives set policy at their quarterly meetings. Executive officers' decisions carry much weight, influenced by board discussion, professional staff recommendations, and the input of the delegate assembly and membership. Once policy is set, the chapters devise strategies. NACOPRW relies on educational strategies; writing comments on proposed legislation; educating the membership with publications such as research reports, a newsletter, and direct mail; encouraging members to write to legislators and committees; making press releases to educate the public; and conducting and publishing issue-oriented research. NACOPRW's education workshops, training seminars, and information dissemination at the national and local chapter levels integrate strategies overall.

In its founding year, NACOPRW joined the movement for ratification of the equal right amendment. In 1974, with the National Council of Negro Women,* it took up issues of discrimination in the sale and rental of housing and in lending practices. In 1975, it participated in the first annual celebration of International Women's Year and has worked in collaboration with the National Women's Political Caucus.* Regarding pay equity, NACOPRW was a founding member organization of the National Committee on Pay Equity.* With the Federation of Organizations for Professional Women,* that same year NACOPRW cosponsored a symposium on achieving power and change through the political system and a workshop emphasizing a legislative focus on women and the economy, preparatory for lobbying the Ninety-fourth Congress. The year after, NACOPRW prepared and conducted a program on rape and safety measures as well as participated in the National Women's Agenda Conference convened by the Women's Action Alliance.

More recently, NACOPRW's legislative interests have placed great importance on the 1963 Equal Pay Act, 1964 Civil Rights and Equal Opportunity

Acts, 1964 and 1970 Food Stamp Acts, Voting Right Act, affirmative action orders, 1968 Antidiscrimination in Housing and Revised Uniform Reciprocal Enforcement of Support Agreement Acts, 1972 School Lunch Act, Act of 1972 in which sex discrimination was added to the Civil Rights jurisdiction, 1972 Equal Employment Act, Title IX of the 1972 Education Amendments, equal rights amendment, 1974 Equal Credit Opportunity and Housing and Community Development Acts, Child Support Amendments—1974 Social Security Act, 1976 Day Care Act, 1984 Pension Equity and Child Abuse Acts, 1984 Child Support Enforcement Act, 1986 Age Discrimination Act and 1988 Civil Rights Restoration Act. Lesser importance has been placed on the cases of *Reed* v. *Reed, Frontiero* v. *Richardson, Craig* v. *Boren,* and *Roe* v. *Wade.*

Over the past ten years NACOPRW has viewed the extension of the Voting Rights Act and Title IX of the Education Amendments as two of the most important new pieces of federal legislation and amendments.

NACOPRW aligns itself with women's groups and national Hispanic organizations. To counter forces opposed to recognizing that the nation has become bilingual as well as policies adversely affecting women and families, NACOPRW traditionally has coordinated activities with similar organizations such as the Puerto Rican Forum, Puerto Rican Coalition, Puerto Rican Legal Defense Fund, Mexican American National Association, and National Association of Cuban American women.

ELECTORAL ACTIVITIES

NACOPRW sees its issues as nonpartisan. Their restriction to educational strategies has prevented a political action committee's formation.

FURTHER INFORMATION

Membership dues include a subscription to the quarterly newsletter, *Ecos Nacionales,* along with special mailings when issues require immediate attention. Local chapters have their own local newsletter as well.

MARY CHIANTA CANZONERI

NATIONAL CONFERENCE OF STATE LEGISLATURES WOMEN'S NETWORK (NCSL WN)
1607 250th Avenue
Corwith, IA 50430
(515) 583-2156
FAX (515) 583-2146

The National Conference of State Legislatures (NCSL) Women's Network (WN), a nonpartisan organization, seeks to increase the power of women in NCSL and within the state legislatures and to lift up and pursue policies of special interest to women and their families.

ORIGIN AND DEVELOPMENT

Although it had existed from NCSL's inception, the Women's Network formalized in 1985 at an NCSL conference when, during the election of officers, the nominating committee chair, a man, announced that "over his dead body" would a woman ever preside over NCSL. For fifteen years, the organization had been networking at annual meetings. After NCSL declined to promote to president a woman legislator, it prompted the networkers to decide to become more active, including as advocates for women's issues. Three chief organizers— Louise Miller (R-WA), Shirley Hankins (R-WA), and Mary Landrieu (D-LA)— and an additional ten women energized in response to the sexism. They did not know each other previously from any other organizational context except for Miller's and Hankins's membership in the Washington state lower chapter. They came together to represent the interests of women elected to state legislatures.

Initially, WN organized speakers for an annual meeting luncheon. From there it went on to request staff assistance from NCSL and brought a speaker to a State Federal Assembly dinner in Washington, D.C., that winter. Then state legislator Landrieu chaired WN and tapped corporations to help pay its expenses. Ford Foundation provided start-up funds.

In 1989, WN hired an executive director to raise funds and assist in program development. Since 1989, it has published two policy position papers annually and undertaken two national initiatives, now completed, to reduce women's deaths from breast cancer. Today WN participates in an emerging national cross-jurisdictional coalition of elected women.

ORGANIZATION AND FUNDING

WN has an annual meeting, which elects the twelve-member board of directors and three officers and approves the budget. It pays expenses to the meeting for delegates who otherwise might not attend. All officers and board members are women. Board members are 8 percent African American and 8 percent Native American. Board participation is encouraged of persons from lower-income strata, persons with disabilities, and older women elected to the state legislatures. Paula Hollinger (D-MD) chairs the group. Jane Maroney (R-DE) serves as vice chair. Through NCSL, WN has access to a Washington office and keeps one part-time person in NCSL's Denver office. Its headquarters are in Corwith, Iowa. Sue B. Mullins is the executive director, a part-time position. NCSL pays the salary of the part-time person, located in the Denver office. WN also has access to NCSL's full-time attorney.

All women in the state legislature automatically become members. Before the 1992 elections there were 1,356 members; since the 1992 elections there are 1,519, with women 24 percent of all state legislators. For the foreseeable future WN will remain a women-only group. Members feel interested in exercising influence within their organization, advocating important policies, and developing their organizational skills. Conferences and meetings, publications and information, some research-based, and friendship ties also tend to encourage members to be active. There is no membership fee.

WN receives about 50 percent of its funds from corporations or businesses and 50 percent from foundation grants. Contributions to it are tax-deductible by virtue of NCSL's tax-exempt status. The biennial budget was $250,000 in 1992 compared with $60,000 in 1980.

POLICY CONCERNS AND TACTICS

The board provides a policy agenda, but WN otherwise has not systematized its policy-setting activities. To a degree, professional staff recommendations influence the process; to a lesser extent, membership polls. Once it decides to become active on an issue, the group uses its state contacts and networks with such other private nonprofit organizations as churches, traditional women's associations, and professional organizations and also with corporations. Preferred strategies include supplying state legislators and their staff, and occasionally congresspeople and their staff, with information and educating WN members with publications. WN also conducts and publishes research on issues.

WN sees as of continuing interest the affirmative action executive orders, 1968 Revised Uniform Reciprocal Enforcement of Support Agreement Act, Act of 1972 adding sex discrimination to the Civil Rights Commission jurisdiction, 1972 Equal Employment Act and Title IX of the Education Amendments, proposed equal rights amendment, *Roe* v. *Wade,* and 1974 Equal Credit Opportunity Act.

Several times yearly, policymakers seek guidance from WN. It sees as the best national initiative of the last decade a combination of successful, breast cancer-related proposals on insurance, mammography, and personnel and equipment standards. But a Health Care Financing Authority ruling from within the U.S. Health and Human Services Department preempted two years of state-level work by women legislators by limiting Medicare coverage to a mammogram once every two years for the highest-risk group. WN sees as the three worst federal initiatives of the past decade the U.S. Supreme Court's approach to civil rights issues, President Bush's veto of the 1990 Civil Rights Act, and the rules on child care standards.

In recent years WN has collaborated with the American Cancer Society, American Association for Retired Persons,* American College of Obstetricians and Gynecologists,* and National Council of Catholic Women.* It sees as adversaries right-wing or extreme left-wing groups. It finds these adversarial groups working daily against issues of concern.

ELECTORAL ACTIVITIES

WN does not see women's issues as partisan. It does not have a political action committee.

FURTHER INFORMATION

WN produces a newsletter, *Network News,* three times yearly for its members. It also publishes research reports, including two from the recent past entitled "Family Support and Education: a Holistic Approach to School Readiness," and "Cooperative Home Care: A Win/Win for Clients and Caregivers." In May 1992, it reported on politics for HIV prevention in adolescents based on research by the Center for Population Options.

SARAH SLAVIN

NATIONAL CONGRESS OF NEIGHBORHOOD WOMEN (NCNW)
249 Manhattan Avenue
Brooklyn, NY 11211
(718) 388-6666
FAX (718) 388-1519

The National Congress of Neighborhood Women (NCNW) is an umbrella organization of local women's community groups and leaders. Together they form a national grassroots, multiethnic, multiracial, multiclass network of women active in neighborhood programs and issues encompassing housing, education, economic development, child care, and employment.

ORIGIN AND DEVELOPMENT

As has many a women's political organization, NCNW conforms to a grassroots, direct action model for reasons reminiscent of women's early political involvement. Not only have women entered the political realm to extend their domestic influence, but they have used their domestic connections as an expedient argument for their public involvement. Recognizing and seeking to alleviate what many would consider private domestic problems, NCNW's founders have developed solutions through cooperative group action and public service.

NCNW was founded in 1974 by a group of concerned women in New York City's Williamsburg community. The primary founders—Jan Peterson, Barbara Mikulski, Nancy Seifer, Geraldine Miller, and Mildred Johnson—responded to local issues such as housing, education, crime, and street maintenance. Taking a holistic approach to neighborhood problems and focusing on the needs of women in particular, the founders sought to revitalize the Williamsburg neighborhood by regaining basic city services that it had lost, offering new services such as a women's shelter, local educational opportunities, and combined child/ senior care, and combating business discrimination—such as bank redlining— against the neighborhood.

Besides addressing basic communitywide problems. NCNW focused directly on neighborhood women's individual empowerment needs, taking a bottom-up approach to determining those needs by listening to the women themselves. NCNW originated partly from the founders' desire to defend the values and confront the unique problems of white working-class ethnic women alienated by 1970s urban renewal programs that ignored their needs and desires. The media called these women racist and ignorant for protesting school busing, residential racial integration, and many urban renewal methods that dislocated long-time neighborhood residents. Understanding that these women were acting out of a fierce determination to preserve their cultural/family values, NCNW organizers concentrated on respectfully addressing the concerns of Williamsburg women, while encouraging them to recognize and deal with class, race, and ethnic diversity in a sensitive and constructive way. Within a year of its beginning, NCNW had embraced a wide range of classes, races, and ethnicities, seeking to expand all neighborhood women's opportunities through the individual empowerment provided by education and job training.

NCNW women always have paid special attention to difference, not to discriminate arbitrarily but to celebrate and preserve. Acknowledgment of difference aids them in formulating more practical, informed, comprehensive policies that take into account a wide range of neighborhood needs that often are determined culturally. As an example, NCNW has been instrumental in promoting communication between U.S. Housing and Urban Development Department (HUD) planners and neighborhood women, giving women who live in HUD homes an opportunity to influence the plans for those homes. One way they do this is by explaining the relationship between their cultural values and the housing they need to support their families and neighborhoods. NCNW fills a unique niche by addressing the problems of women marginalized by other mainstream movements claiming to include them—movements such as the predominantly middle-class women's/feminist movement and the male-dominated neighborhood movement.

Academic elements of the women's liberation movement have solicited NCNW's expertise on diversity. Several NCNW leaders moderated parts of the 1992 National Women's Studies Association* conference in Austin, Texas, in an effort to cultivate greater respect for, and sensitivity to, racial and ethnic diversity. Several years earlier the Women's Studies conference had been immobilized by racial and ethnic tension. NCNW leaders find promoting greater acceptance of diversity within academic circles integral to their ambitions to create connections between the community and the campus.

Although concentrated on the local needs of neighborhood women, NCNW has involved itself with women's needs internationally for well over a decade, primarily by sending representatives to the United Nations (UN) Women in Development conference. NCNW has become even more internationally involved through Grassroots Women Organizing Ourselves Together (GROOTS), formed in 1985 at the Nairobi UN conference. The aims of GROOTS are compatible with NCNW's. Both are committed to strengthening low-income women's participation in developing their communities; identifying and sharing, on a global basis, development projects and methods of urban and rural grassroots women's groups; and focusing capabilities. GROOTS is a natural extension for

NCNW, which sees women's leadership and collective effort as just as vital to developing countries as developing communities.

ORGANIZATION AND FUNDING

Rather than serving as a centralized body of power and decision making, NCNW is an umbrella organization, forming significant links in a grassroots nationwide women's network. The NCNW affiliate chooses its own leaders, develops its own projects, and creates its own agenda according to community concerns. Consequently, the national structure reflects NCNW's central goal of recognizing and satisfying diverse needs. NCNW women perceive that achieving broad success at extensive national reform would require them to ignore neighborhood women's diversity and the particularity of their needs. On both local and national levels, NCNW seeks to avoid general goals, focusing on the specific and changing needs of the many women it serves.

As a young, dynamic organization of ambitious women, NCNW continues to develop and diversify. In an effort more efficiently to coordinate energy, information, and decision making, leaders hope to create a delegate assembly that will hold biannual meetings. Currently, all officers and board members are women, although some men have served on the board in the past. The board, currently chaired by Maria Rivera, includes fifteen executive officers who are also working board members. As well as being regionally representative, NCNW's board embodies the organization's respect for racial and ethnic diversity: 33 percent of the board is African American, and 25 percent is Hispanic, while the remainder of European Americans include Italian, Jewish, and Swedish women.

NCNW remains rather small organizationally. From 1980 to 1982, it did seek to expand into the federal arena by operating a federally funded Washington, D.C., low-income women's network office. The office was designed to enhance the influence of these women with governmental officials, develop a women's impact statement for national neighborhood policy, and serve as a clearinghouse and resource center. This project ended abruptly, failing to regain funding when the Reagan administration took office. Currently, there are two main NCNW offices, a national office in Brooklyn and an international/GROOTS office in Manhattan, with a combined personnel of ten volunteers and eighteen professional staff members. The current coordinating executive director is Judy Ennes.

NCNW has 30 paid and 100 unpaid affiliates. Annual membership dues remain low: $20 for individuals, $50 for affiliates, and $100 for contributors.

NCNW has a local and national annual budget of $700,000 and between $70–150,000, respectively, while the international budget has soared to $250,000 due to UNIFEM support. UNIFEM represents grassroots women from different countries to the UN. At times NCNW has acquired as much as 80 percent of its funds through government grants or contracts, most notably the Comprehensive Employment and Training Act (CETA). It also receives a significant proportion of its funding from private entities such as the Rockefeller family, Chemical Bank, and smaller individual contributors.

POLICY CONCERNS AND TACTICS

A mixture of grassroots initiative and central leadership determines policy positions within NCNW. Local affiliates make policy proposals to the national board, which then accepts various proposals and calls on the local groups for support. NCNW often holds participatory conferences in which representatives from both the national organization and affiliates meet to develop problem-solving strategies. A national organization with broad national goals but no particular national agenda, NCNW prefers local groups to take whatever political action they deem relevant to their own communities. Although profoundly affected by government policies, especially federal programs such as the Johnson administration's War on Poverty, CETA, and the 1974 Housing and Community Development Act, NCNW does not attempt to influence further development of these policies. NCNW is most concerned with promoting the implementation of its own and governmental policies within specific communities.

Unfortunately, many federal programs assisting community development were severely curtailed in the 1980s. Nonetheless, using contributions from private, municipal, and state funds, NCNW has actively created educational opportunities and programs for low-income women and their families, providing on-site child care for student mothers, and organizing a teen pregnancy prevention program. In addition, as from its inception, NCNW continues to promote tenant empowerment by coordinating tenant housing groups and pressuring housing authorities to consult tenants on plans and encourage tenant management. NCNW has succeeded in acquiring municipal funding for thirty-three public housing units in Brooklyn.

Determined to operate as an independent entity with unique concerns, NCNW nevertheless often coordinates its efforts with other organizations on specific issues. It has worked with both the National Neighborhood Coalition and Association for Community-Based Education for twelve years and the Institute for Social Ecology for three years. Church groups such as United Methodist Global Ministries* and Presbyterian Church Women United* often provide assistance and resources for various NCNW programs.

ELECTORAL ACTIVITIES

As a nonpartisan political organization committed to direct personalized community action, NCNW has not formed a political action committee and does not become involved with electoral politics.

FURTHER INFORMATION

In an effort to keep its membership informed of local, national, and international activity, NCNW publishes a biannual newsletter entitled *The Neighborhood Women.* Recently NCNW has developed a ''Sourcebook'' for affiliates, designed to help them deal with issues around leadership, organization, planning, and diversity.

LEIGH ANN WHEELER

NATIONAL COUNCIL FOR RESEARCH ON WOMEN (NCRW)
The Sara Delano Roosevelt Memorial House
47-49 East 65th Street
New York, NY 10021
(212) 570-5001
FAX (212) 274-0821

The National Council for Research on Women (NCRW) is a coalition of centers and organizations that support and conduct feminist research, policy analysis, and educational programs. It works to bridge scholarship, policy, and action programs and to strengthen ties with other national and international organizations and coalitions.

ORIGIN AND DEVELOPMENT

In the fall of 1981, Marjorie Lightman, then head of the Institute for Research for History in New York, convened a meeting of women's research center directors to develop collaborative strategies for long-term survival and growth. In the late 1970s, Ford Foundation Higher Education program officer Mariam K. Chamberlain has allocated major shares of a $9 million fund to many of the first of these centers, including those at Stanford University, Wellesley College, and the University of Arizona. At the New York meeting, representatives of twenty-eight university-based centers, policy organizations, and educational coalitions established, and asked Chamberlain to head, a working alliance that would incorporate formally as NCRW in 1982. Chamberlain became the council's founding president.

As stated in the articles of incorporation, the organization's goals were to enlarge opportunities for research on women and advance collaborative research, research applications, and distribution of research findings. Sara Engelhardt, then of Carnegie Corporation, was instrumental in providing initial support for start-up expenses, and Ford Foundation followed with two three-year general support grants.

Among the first board members were William Chafe, Jane Roberts Chapman, Florence Howe, Cynthia Fuchs Epstein, Elaine Marks, Cynthia Secor, and Margaret Wilkerson. Wilkerson of the University of California at Berkeley's Center for the Study, Education and Advancement of Women was the first woman of color to serve on the board. Other women of color to serve have included Beverly Guy-Sheftall, Spelman College Women's Research and Resource Center; Bonnie Thornton Dill, then of the Memphis State University Center for Research on Women; Florence Bonner, then of the State University of New York at Albany Center for Women in Government; Florence Ladd, Radcliffe

College Bunting Institute; and Angela Ginorio, University of Washington Northwest Center for Research on Women.

The council aims to facilitate information exchange and promote links to organizations and individuals working on the broadest possible range of topics affecting women's lives. Among the projects that support this work have been a model computerized database of works-in-progress, produced in collaboration with Radcliffe's Schlesinger Library and the Research Libraries Information Network, and biennial meetings of the National Network of Women's Caucuses,* an alliance of over 200 women's groups in higher education and the disciplines.

Efforts to promote multicultural exchange in research and teaching have included a Ford Foundation project involving thirteen council member centers that integrate minority women's studies into existing liberal arts curricula. International programs include Ford Foundation-sponsored fellowships for visiting women's studies scholars and practitioners from India and Bangladesh, as well as the US/CIS (formerly USSR) Women's Dialogue. Focused on women's issues, the dialogue highlighted the need for a Russian-language newsletter for women in the former Soviet Union. Launched in 1990, the newsletter is called *Yvi i Myi,* (You and We). Colette Shulman and Katrina vanden Heuvel coedit the newsletter, which is printed in New York and distributed from Moscow to women in thirty cities in Russia.

ORGANIZATION AND FUNDING

NCRW has a fourteen-member board of directors. The current board chair is Carol Hollenshead, University of Michigan Center the Education of Women. There are five full-time and four part-time staff.

Presently, NCRW has seventy-six member research centers. Incentives to join include exchange, collaboration on research projects, information, the opportunity to attend annual meetings of member directors, access to mailing lists, referrals, and technical assistance. NCRW also has over 2,000 affiliate subscribers to its newsletter, *Women's Research Network News* and to *IQ,* a topic-specific quarterly that aims to link research, policy, and action for wider audiences.

While member centers pay minimum annual dues of $200, most of the council's funding has come from foundation grants and affiliates. The Directory Series, other publication sales, and corporate supporters of the national work/ family seminar series, Beyond Parent Tracks: Alliance for the 90s, also provide sources of income. The annual budget of this nonprofit organization was $568,000 in fiscal year 1993.

POLICY CONCERNS AND TACTICS

One of the council's goals is to encourage the translation and use of feminist scholarship into formats useful to activists and policymakers. In October 1991, immediately after the Senate Judiciary Committee hearings on Judge Clarence

Thomas's nomination to the U.S. Supreme Court, NCRW launched a sexual harassment information project.

Another example of NCRW's efforts to bridge distinctions among scholarship, policy, and action programs is the Funding Women's Project. Organized in collaboration with Women in Foundations/Corporate Philanthropy and the National Network of Women's Funds, the project has worked to develop a research agenda for better understanding issues affecting funding for women and girls and the status of women in philanthropy and fund-raising.

ELECTORAL ACTIVITIES

The council does not have a partisan affiliation and does not have a political action committee.

FURTHER INFORMATION

There are two periodicals: *Women's Research Network News,* and *IQ,* both with international distribution. A directory series includes a mailing list and the *Directory of Women's Media, Directory of International Centers for Research on Women, Opportunities for Research, Study and Internships at Member Centers,* a *Directory of National Women's Organizations,* and others. Other publications include *A Women's Thesaurus: An Index of Language Used to Describe and Locate Information by and about Women,* edited by Mary Ellen Capek (1987) and *Women in Academe: Progress and Prospects,* a major report of the council's Women in Higher Education Task Force, edited by Mariam K. Chamberlain (1989).

DEBRA L. SCHULTZ WITH MARIAM CHAMBERLAIN
AND MARY ELLEN CAPEK

NATIONAL COUNCIL OF CATHOLIC BISHOPS
See NATIONAL COMMITTEE FOR A HUMAN LIFE AMENDMENT

NATIONAL COUNCIL OF CATHOLIC WOMEN (NCCW)
1275 K Street, NW
Suite 975
Washington, DC 20005
(202) 682-0334
FAX (202) 682-0338

The national federation of Catholic women's organizations in the United States, the National Council of Catholic Women (NCCW) has been, in general, a defender of orthodox Catholic values on women's issues. NCCW is an active legislative advocacy group, exerting influence primarily by providing information to legislators and coordinating letter-writing campaigns.

ORIGIN AND DEVELOPMENT

In 1920, the National Catholic Welfare Council, composed of U.S. Catholic Bishops, founded NCCW at the urging of heads of Catholic women's organizations desiring a federation for concerted action and national representation. The formal federation evolved from the coordinated efforts of Catholic women's organizations in World War I in assisting servicemen and their families and doing relief work. Agnes Regan served as NCCW's executive secretary until 1941. During her tenure, NCCW ran the National Catholic Service School, a program to train social workers. Its responsibility for this school continued until Catholic University took over the program in 1947.

From its inception, NCCW regularly campaigned against birth control, feminism, and the equal rights amendment. It combines a traditional view of marriage and the family with a long-standing concern for social justice, advocating the 1921 Sheppard-Towner Act, minimum wage laws, unions, aid for persons with disabilities, and, in the 1930s, aid for persons fleeing Nazi persecution. Along with the Young Women's Christian Association* and National Council of Jewish Women,* it opposed restrictive immigration policies. NCCW specialized in providing services such as settlement houses and language instruction for immigrant young women to aid their adjustment to American life. Despite its antifeminist stance, NCCW's organizational activities created opportunities for women to take important leadership and administrative responsibilities in the interwar and postwar years.

The organization's stated function is to "support, empower and educate Catholic women in spiritual growth, leadership and service." In practice, NCCW provides information on church, community, family, national and international affairs, and opportunities for Catholic women to engage in social and political action in a leadership or a support role. From its founding NCCW actively has raised funds for foreign relief efforts. Through its Works of Peace programs, it serves as a collection agency for Catholic Relief Services. NCCW is also a member of the World Union of Catholic Women's Organizations and of Women in Community Service, and it has official nongovernmental organization (NGO) representation with the United Nations. In addition, NCCW develops programs in such areas as volunteer care for the elderly, alcohol and substance abuse education, and leadership training for women.

ORGANIZATION AND DEVELOPMENT

Having doubled in size since 1941, NCCW today comprises over 7,300 Catholic women's parish-level organizations and 123 diocesan-level organizations; it includes fourteen national and state organizations. It is governed formally by delegates at its biennial national convention. Between conventions, NCCW is governed by a general assembly composed of presidents of archdiocesan, diocesan, and national organizations and of the forty-two-member NCCW board of directors. The current president, elected by the national convention, is Rita

Greenwald. She serves on a seven-member executive committee, along with three vice presidents, a secretary, treasurer, and the past president. In 1967, NCCW consolidated numerous committees into a commission system concerned with family affairs, church communities, community affairs, international affairs, and organizational services; and there is a commission-level legislative information committee. Commission chairs serve on the board. The organization's Washington, D.C., office opened in 1920. Annette P. Kane presently serves as executive director. NCCW employs a professional staff of eleven supplemented by volunteers.

Organizations in NCCW are composed entirely of women, and the membership is predominantly white, typically over forty years of age. The total individual membership figure is unavailable, since membership in its affiliated groups varies. Members receive publications and opportunities to attend conferences and leadership institutes and to associate with like-minded women.

NCCW reports 1990 revenues of $605,000, 48 percent coming from dues paid by the approximately 7,300 affiliate organizations. Fees from meetings and institutes account for about 40 percent of total revenues, with grants, publication sales, and commissions responsible for the remainder. Although NCCW has experienced a recent decline in the number of affiliates, due largely to parish closings and consolidations, its 1991 revenues were $711,000.

POLICY CONCERNS AND TACTICS

Policies are set by the seven executive officers, six commission chairs, and professional staff. They are discussed at board meetings and at the general assembly, which adopts resolutions and reviews existing ones. The biennial convention also takes votes on policies. NCCW attempts to influence public policy largely by educating its members and by encouraging them to write their elected representatives and to seek elected or appointed office. Direct mailings to members, a telephone network, press releases, and, less frequently, direct lobbying are the chosen tactics. NCCW does not endorse confrontational tactics such as civil disobedience.

NCCW maintains a continuing effort to shape public policy. Since 1950 it has participated actively in the fight for equal pay legislation and generally supports legislation favorable to the rights of poor, elderly, and disabled persons. NCCW is decidedly against abortion rights and pornography. Action on these issues consists mostly of grassroots letter-writing campaigns. NCCW policy positions have included active support for the 1993 Family Medical Leave Act, which allows unpaid leave for employees of companies of fifty or more workers in cases of serious illness or if the employee has a disabled parent or a newborn to care for; and support for the 1990 Children's Television Act, which placed commercial limits on children's television programs. It supported the Americans with Disabilities Act. Recently NCCW has actively supported extensions of unemployment insurance, the Violence against Women and Brady bills, which became part of the 1994 Omnibus Crime Act, and the Family Preservation Act.

It opposes the Freedom of Choice bill. NCCW is promoting mandatory mammogram insurance bills in state legislatures. On the international front, its efforts are aimed at redirecting military spending toward hunger relief.

NCCW forms coalitions with other groups on issues of common concern, most frequently with the U.S. Catholic Conference, National Council on Aging, and National Committee for a Human Life Amendment.* It is part of the Women's Coalition for Life and often is aligned against National Organization for Women,* National Abortion Rights Action League,* and Planned Parenthood Federation of America.*

ELECTORAL ACTIVITIES

NCCW does not have a political action committee and considers itself a nonpartisan group. Its bylaws prohibit national officers from holding elective office.

FURTHER INFORMATION

NCCW publishes a bimonthly magazine, *Catholic Woman,* with a circulation of 10,5000; members receive a subscription. Three additional newsletters are published each year.

PHILIP ZAMPINI

NATIONAL COUNCIL OF GUILDS
See NATIONAL URBAN LEAGUE

NATIONAL COUNCIL OF JEWISH WOMEN (NCJW)
1101 15th Street, NW
Washington, DC 20005
(202) 296-2588
FAX (202) 452-0564

The National Council of Jewish Women (NCJW) is a volunteer organization that, both nationally and abroad, develops and implements human service programs focusing primarily on family issues, with a special emphasis on women and children. The organization has played a major role in developing the reform movement of Judaism and is the oldest volunteer Jewish women's organization in the United States. It has two active research and educational foundations.

ORIGIN AND DEVELOPMENT

This nonoccupational citizen group was founded by Hannah Greenebaum Solomon in 1893 during the Parliament of Religions at the Chicago World's Fair. Solomon brought together ninety-five representative Jewish women from throughout the United States. The story of the organization's founding speaks to its early focus on issues of sexism and women's status in society. Solomon received an invitation to organize a program for the Columbia Exposition; months of preparations were ignored by an all-male coordinating committee, which believed the women should serve tea. To this, Solomon replied, "Under these circumstances, we do not care to cooperate with you. I request that the fact of our presence at this meeting be expunged from the records."

A permanent constitution was adopted at the council's first triennial convention, held in New York City in 1896, with fifty regions represented. The council's first two decades of service activities largely targeted service to the newly arrived immigrant population and included work with Hull House and lobbying for progressive social legislation; the next two decades centered on social issues of the Great Depression and World War II. The postwar period was probably the most hectic in NCJW's history, with the formation of several new programs designed to meet the needs of a variety of populations affected by the war's devastation.

An accelerated expansion in the organization's programs marked the 1960s. Leadership training developed to reach volunteer leaders throughout the country; an extensive survey in 1960 of at-risk youth resulted in a nineteen-point action program. Services extended to elders and toward treatment and prevention of mental disorders in people of all ages. From 1961 on, a major and continuing effort has focused on educational and social services for children. These areas help distinguish NCJW from its other mainstream sister organizations, such as Hadassah and B'nai B'rith Women.* NCJW serves both the Jewish and general public, as opposed to only the Jewish community. It is further invested in women's issues, such as reproductive rights, equal pay for comparable worth, sexual harassment, domestic violence, and the equal rights amendment.

ORGANIZATION AND FUNDING

NCJW has 100,000 members in 200 regions throughout the country. All officers and board members are women. The board of directors currently consists of all white Jewish women, with much effort going toward obtaining board members diverse in economic class and age. NCJW has three main offices located in New York City, Washington, D.C., and Jerusalem; the largest of these is in New York, the smallest in Jerusalem. The Washington office is directed by Sammie Mosheburg. NCJW has seventy paid workers, of whom about one-half are professional staff. In keeping with the group's focus on the importance of volunteer membership, most of the professional staff have a voluntary counterpart. Currently, for example, the organization's paid executive director, Iris Gross, hired by the executive board, works closely with the voluntary president, Joan Bronk, elected by the membership. Directly under the executive director are eight department heads. Because NCJW is a nonpartisan group that is issue-oriented only, it does not use the term "lobbyist."

Women make up about 95 percent of the membership. Members can join at large with a yearly dues of thirty-five dollars or as members of working sections with yearly dues of twenty-five dollars. Sections are largely autonomous local bodies. There are several major benefits in joining the organization, which correspond to the level of involvement that a member wishes to have. Local members have the opportunity to meet other Jewish women (about 90 percent of the membership), form friendship ties, contribute to a national organization with both a progressive and feminist agenda, and develop organizational skills. Additionally, members can move into national leadership.

NCJW was self-funded at its start 100 years ago. Currently, the majority of its revenues are generated from individual dues and contributions, as well as contributions from the regional membership divisions, the sections. About one-quarter of NCJW's funding comes from grants for research projects. Contributions are tax-deductible, and the organization has tax-exempt status, 501 (c) (3), under the U.S. Internal Revenue Code. The budget varies between $4 million and $6 million.

NCJW conducts major research projects through its two foundations, the NCJW Research Institute and Center for the Child, and publishes reports of their results, which, in turn, influence policy decisions.

POLICY CONCERNS AND TACTICS

Policy is set for NCJW in a number of ways. The heart of the organization's basic platform for advocacy activity lies in a list of eleven principles and over 100 national resolutions. An important NCJW mission is to advance human values. All its principles relate to this mission. The national convention revises the resolutions every three years. Members periodically are polled about issues that directly pertain to them, such as a recent decision to reorganize sections from division by geography to division by size; they are unlikely to be polled about matters more removed such as bylaw or program issues. These latter issues are taken up by committee, then brought to the board for discussion and approval. An influential source of decisions is the staff/volunteer team, which, once it has agreed on a desired change in policy or bylaw, brings the proposal to the board.

The organization's political thrust is on the education of its members, the general public, and lawmakers. A major avenue for this work is to supply state legislators and congresspeople with information on specific issues through written materials, personal meetings, and testimony at hearings. Additionally, members are frequently encouraged to write legislators on different issues, as well as to participate in nonviolent direct action, such as demonstrations. Membership frequently is educated on issues through publications, and the general public similarly is educated through press releases.

Historically, NCJW has put its major emphasis into advocacy work around women's, children's, and family issues. The Work/Family project, for example, is an NCJW community development program whose goal is to help employers address their employees' child and elder care needs. A recent NCJW publication describes over twenty approaches for employers to take to funding and actively supporting child care. NCJW is involved heavily in advocating for women's rights and actively supports such feminist issues as women's reproductive rights (with a well-publicized pro-choice position), equal pay and comparable worth, the equal rights amendment, and legislation protecting women from sexual harassment and domestic violence. Significant recent policies include supporting legislation for sanctuary protection for political refugees and policies that endorse the rights of Jewish women in Jewish life.

While NCJW works on a variety of women's and children's issues domestically, it has a strong commitment to support the continuing development of family and children's programs in Israel. Its primary activity there centers on its Research Institute for Innovation in Education at the Hebrew University of Jerusalem, which annually develops, implements, or evaluates twenty-five to thirty projects concerned with the education of Israel's at-risk children, youth, and families.

NCJW often coordinates with other organizations on various issues, reflecting its strong belief in working in partnership. The partnership groups vary according to the individual issue, although National Organization for Women,* Planned Parenthood Federation of America,* and the Leadership Conference on Civil Rights are frequent coalition partners.

ELECTORAL ACTIVITIES

The nonpartisan NCJW does not have a political action committee.

FURTHER INFORMATION

NCJW publishes a twice-yearly magazine, *NCJW Journal,* as well as a twice-yearly newsletter for its members, called *Insight.* An additional resource is its list of national resolutions, which are an outgrowth of its major principles. One recent publication is "Options for the 90's: Employer Support for Child Care."

MELISSA SCHWARTZ

NATIONAL COUNCIL OF NEGRO WOMEN (NCNW)
1001 G Street NW
Suite 800
Washington, DC 20001
(202) 628-0015
FAX (202) 628-0233

The National Council of Negro Women (NCNW) is an organization representing women and dealing with women's issues. It proposes to unite national black women's organizations to address issues related to the welfare of African American women and their families.

ORIGIN AND DEVELOPMENT

NCNW, the first black organization of organizations and first national coalition of black women's organizations, was founded on December 6, 1935, by Mary McLeod Bethune. Modeled after the National Council of Women, a white association that included few black women's organizations, NCNW was proposed by Bethune as an effective structure to "harness the great power of nearly a million women into a force for constructive action."

Prior to 1935, the National Organization of Colored Women's Clubs* (NACW) was the foremost national organization of African American women. Founded in 1896 as a national coalition of black women's clubs, many of local and regional significance, it had established an enviable record of achievement and attracted a significant number of black women leaders. As a young woman seeking national support and visibility for her fledgling school, Daytona Normal and Industrial Institute, Bethune affiliated with NACW in 1912. Moving through the ranks, she served as president of the Florida State Federation of Colored Women's Clubs, as founder and president of the Southeastern Association of Colored Women, and later as NACW's eighth president. The latter experience convinced Bethune of the need for NCNW.

Beyond the issue of structure, as NACW president Bethune had experienced significant opposition to promoting and implementing her organizational agenda. Her primary goal was to have black women fully represented on national public affairs. Achievement of this purpose required that a headquarters be established in the nation's capital and an executive secretary employed. Bethune also felt concerned about the lack of a clear feminist focus and commitment in NACW to women's issues and especially to working-class and poor black women. Besides forging new relationships among black women, Bethune envisioned NCNW providing a power base that exceeded that of any black woman's national organization.

NCNW's founding was a controversial issue that effectively split the black women's club movement and led to NACW's eventual decline. Further, NCNW's founding organizations were widely differentiated in purpose, membership, and organizational strength. Bethune set about the difficult task of unifying the divergent national groups into a national council that could at once tap member organizations' expertise and harness their memberships and spheres of influence. Unanimously elected president, she served from 1935 to 1949.

During its first year of operation, NCNW consisted of life members and of national women's organizations as affiliates. Within a short time, it became apparent that this structure was inadequate for implementing a national program. In 1937, local councils, known as Metropolitan Councils (MCs), were established in communities including five or more subordinate branches of affiliates. NCNW asked affiliates to urge their local chapters to work with the MCs. Registered Councils were set up in rural areas, and Junior Councils were authorized for youth. During the 1940s, regions elected directors to aid in coordinating programming with affiliates and local councils. Regional directors functioned as the lifeline between the national and the regional and local community, because the national office could not directly address the need for field services. In the early 1950s, constitutional redefinition and common practice expanded the regional directors' broad powers. Under Dorothy I. Height, local councils became known as sections, and the state mechanism supplanted the regional system.

Bethune and her successors experienced difficulty in trying to interpret the national council concept in terms that African American women understood. Implementation of the concept also has been difficult. Lacking tax-exempt, non-profit status prior to 1966, NCNW received few major contributions from foundations and philanthropic agencies and depended on membership fees and meager, infrequent contributions. The struggle to explain and implement the national council concept and need for a more clearly defined program have been the key issues with which all four NCNW presidents have grappled. These issues have not been resolved; but Height has addressed them forcefully since 1957, when she became president.

During the early years, the council was administered by a board of directors consisting of twelve officers, four members at large, and the chairpersons of thirteen standing committees. The board comprised the president and affiliate representatives. A series of volunteer secretaries operated the national office. The council had no paid staff until 1942, when Jeanetta Welch Brown became the first paid executive secretary. A stenographer, clerk, and team of volunteers assisted her. The addition of paid staff and purchase of a national headquarters in 1943 provided the base necessary to propel the organization's goal of becoming a clearinghouse for information related to black women's organizations and for projecting NCNW's national agenda.

During Bethune's administration, NCNW's national program, administered through the committees, was carefully designed to achieve credibility for the council through affiliation and collaboration with organizations and associations in every area of American life. Besides national women's organizations, NCNW extended its contacts to every major social, educational, governmental, and community organization. Focusing upon public affairs, employment, citizenship, family life, religion, postwar planning, consumer education, rural life, membership, personnel, and publication of the *Aframerican Woman's Journal,* the committees successfully utilized the media and collaborated with key national organizations, governmental agencies, educational institutions, and individuals to educate and effect change.

Working with the Young Women's Christian Association* (YWCA), labor unions, and other organizations, NCNW collected, analyzed, and disseminated data regarding blacks' employment on federal jobs, particularly in the Civilian Conservation Corps and National Youth Administration. NCNW exposed the discriminatory practices of local communities that excluded blacks from government training programs. During World War II, the council systematically documented black employment in plants engaged in war work, and, as a result of pressures brought to bear from many sources, the Fair Employment Practice Committee was established.

NCNW campaigned for integration of blacks into the military and fought for admissions of black women in the Women's Army Corps (WACS) and other services. As a result of a series of conferences between Bethune, representatives of other black women's organizations, and army leaders, black women were accepted into the WACS. Bethune personally recruited many of these first thirty-nine WACS. She inspected training camps and, when necessary, lodged complaints against discriminatory practices. The MCs sponsored programs for WACS and took a special interest in their activities.

While NCNW closely monitored the government, it also gave strong support to government programs, and by encouraging local councils to "Buy Bonds and Be Free," NCNW members stressed their patriotism.

The council did not limit its associations to black women's organizations. It actively worked with the YWCA's national board, the National Association for the Advancement of Colored People (NAACP), National Council of Women, National Urban League,* League of Women Voters,* National Council of Church Women,* National Council of Jewish Women,* and National Council of Catholic Women* to educate and effect programs targeted to the elimination of racism and sexism. In 1944, the council sponsored a conference to address the question of the position of minorities in the United States. It was an active participant and planner in numerous conferences called by President Franklin Roosevelt and First Lady Eleanor Roosevelt; conferences on employment, child care, and women's participation in the war were attended by black women representing diverse organizations. Black women received appointments to serve on boards and conference committees for the War Manpower Commission, Women's Bureau,* and Children's Bureau, Department of Labor overall, and other government agencies.

Bethune possessed a worldview. She believed that people must be aware of, and become actively involved in, struggles for peace throughout the world. This concern led her to join the moral rearmament movement and to support the idea of a United Nations (UN). Accompanied by Dorothy Boulding Ferebee and Edith Sampson. Bethune traveled to San Francisco to witness the UN's founding. As one of two consultants to the NAACP, she not only attended this historic meeting but also projected NCNW's image and program. NCNW was the only national black women's organization represented at that meeting. NCNW sent representatives and observers to meetings all over the world and since then has maintained an official observer at the UN.

At the end of Bethune's tenure, NCNW was recognized as the major advocate for black women. From 1949 to 1952, Ferebee—a physician, former president of Alpha Kappa Alpha,* and NCNW's treasurer—served as president. By supporting UN policies of human rights and peace and through more focused programmatic thrusts aimed at eliminating both the segregation of, and discrimination against, blacks and women in health care, education, housing, and the armed forces, Ferebee's administration succeeded in maintaining the established NCNW program of advocacy and in expanding the understanding of the national council concept.

In 1953, Vivian Carter Mason, a nationally known social worker and NCNW vice president, was elected president. During her administration there was a special emphasis on interracial cooperation, constitutional development, stream-

lining the organization's administrative structure, and refurbishing national headquarters. Mason was thrust into leadership during one of the most critical periods
in U.S. history. The civil rights movement dominated her administration. NCNW
joined NAACP and other national organizations to devise strategies to implement the 1954 Supreme Court decision. *Brown* v. *Board of Education.* In 1956,
NCNW sponsored an interracial conference of women that explored how white
and black women could work to surmount barriers to human and civil rights.
Other activities included public programs supportive of Rosa Parks, Autherine
Lucy, and the Birmingham bus boycott. Mason visited Alabama to acquire first-
hand knowledge of the situation there.

Passing the presidential mantle to Height in 1957, Mason made recommendations for expanding and strengthening the local councils. After twenty-two
years of operation and having progressed under three administrations, NCNW
had built a solid base of credibility, developed an extensive network of contacts
and supporters, and created a sound constitution and operational structure that
could easily be amended and expanded. The organization needed two major
elements: money and clearly defined program service areas.

In 1957, as NCNW's fourth president, Height brought to the position eight
years as president of Delta Sigma Theta* and thirteen years' service as a YWCA
national board staff member. Introduced to Bethune and the council in 1937,
she had served for twenty years in a number of appointive positions that provided her a unique opportunity to understand NCNW's every aspect. Few leaders of organizations have been as well suited to their work when they assumed
leadership. By 1957, Height understood the many dimensions of a national organization and felt ready to assume leadership of the major national black wom-
en's organization.

A turning point for NCNW came in 1966. Many persons viewed the receipt
of tax-exempt status as the biggest news of NCNW's history. The acquisition
of this status paved the way for grants and contributions that made possible
NCNW's growth and expansion. The simultaneous announcement of two major
grants for programs to recruit and train African American women for volunteer
community service was cause for great celebration. Grants of $300,000 from
the Ford Foundation and $154,193 from the U.S. Health, Education and Welfare
Department meant that for the first time in its thirty-one-year history, NCNW
would be able to expand its quarters and staff and develop more effective community service programs. Height announced that the grants provided NCNW
with resources to mobilize ''a nationwide network of Negro women, working
with all segments of their communities, middle-class and poor, Negro and white,
to help chart and carry out needed community service and social action programs.''

ORGANIZATION AND FUNDING

NCNW has 254 community-based sections. Two representatives per section
and three representatives per affiliate attend the convention. During the 1970s

and 1980s as affiliate representation became more pro forma and its attendance and involvement more sporadic, the board expanded to include additional section leaders and nonaffiliated women of national stature. Height continues to serve as NCNW's president and board chairperson. The national staff consists of twenty-seven employees and one volunteer.

NCNW reports that membership stands at 60,000. Individual and associate dues are $25, students pay $10, and contributors, $25, and corporate memberships are $500. A life membership costs $300; a legacy life membership, $1,000.

The greatest incentive to join is the fact that this is a national coalition of women's organizations and individuals united for strength. NCNW reaches out to all women and their families to advance their quality of life through service and advocacy programs.

Major revenue sources for NCNW today include dues, government and corporate grants, gifts, bequests, publication and memorabilia sales, and fundraisers. From 1966 to 1980, the organization's funding base soared as a result of federal and foundation grants. During this period NCNW mounted major national programs, many of which could be replicated at the local level. The changing political climate and conservative fiscal policies of the Reagan administration effectively eliminated funding for many projects that NCNW and other civil rights organizations had sponsored. NCNW is a 501 (c) (3) organization.

In 1977, NCNW hired Bettye Collier-Thomas to develop the Bethune Historical Development project, a program funded under contract to the National Endowment for the Humanities (NEH). The purpose of this project was to work with national black organizations and museums to develop humanities programs and projects that could be funded by NEH. The contract was given to NCNW because of its perceived outreach to national black organizations and seeming potential for implementation of interpretive humanities programs through its local sections and affiliates. The project located at 1318 Vermont Avenue, NW in Washington. The building was Bethune's last official Washington home and held NCNW's first national headquarters. Collier-Thomas, a professional historian, saw the need to establish a museum and archives.

As director of the Bethune Historical Development project, Collier-Thomas developed NEH's first program of technical assistance, founded the Mary McLeod Bethune Memorial Museum and National Archives for Black Women's History, and developed plans and acquired NEH funding for sponsoring the "First National Scholarly Conference on Black Women." The conference coincided with the November 1979 opening of the museum and archives. In 1982, Congress passed legislation designating 1318 Vermont Avenue a national historic site, and the museum and archives located at the site were formally incorporated as a separate, freestanding institution known as the Bethune Museum and Archives (BMA). Although the NCNW continued to own property and willingly made it available to the new corporation, BMA moved forward as an independent entity with its own board of directors. In 1992, Congress passed legislation for full incorporation of the institution into the National Park Service

(NPS), which provided for purchasing the property from NCNW (1994). The institution has a dual mission, to interpret the life of Mary McLeod Bethune and to collect, preserve, and interpret the history of African American women. It is the only institution of this type in the United States.

POLICY CONCERNS AND TACTICS

After 1965, NCNW's major program priorities focused on issues related to youth employment, housing, health, consumerism, hunger and malnutrition, civil rights, volunteerism, women's issues, international problems, and family life. From 1965 to 1980, at least forty national projects related to youth; another forty targeted specific women's issues. Youth career development, health careers, national collaboration for children and youth, a national immunization program, and the Fannie Lou Hamer Day Care Center are some of the programs designed to respond to problems concerning youth unemployment, delinquency, teenage pregnancy and parenthood, and health care and to stress the need for education in areas that reflect a minimal number of black professionals. Women's issues have continued to receive major attention, including women's rights and housing, opportunity, a leadership development project, and Women's Learning Center, with exploration of problems related to lower-income women, single heads of households, household workers, sexism, employment, affirmative action, the acquisition of management skills, and education.

Under Height's direction, the traditional program expanded in several areas. The council's historic concern for working with women in the African American diaspora and maintaining advocacy on key international issues has been a key focus of Height's administration. Following forty years of international program emphasis, in 1975, NCNW, with a grant from the Agency for International Development, established an international division. It formalized NCNW work in this area and provided a unique opportunity for black American women to work with women in Africa, the Caribbean, and other parts of the world. In 1979, the division concluded an agreement with the director for educational and cultural affairs of the International Communication Agency for a "twinning" program involving NCNW and the national women's organizations of Senegal and Togo.

Employment issues have been central to NCNW's efforts to advance the economic status of black women and their families. Beginning with its earlier advocacy and the Hold Your Job campaigns of the 1940s. NCNW sponsored seminars and conferences and developed extensive program materials on this topic. The 1970 opening of the Women's Center for Education and Career Advancement for Minority Women extended NCNW's commitment to minority women employed in all levels of business. The center, located in Manhattan, offers a variety of programs and services. Education and career consultation and an educational program geared toward gaining and keeping employment are central features. In cooperation with Pace University, the center sponsors an associate degree program that emphasizes the skills and knowledge necessary for advancement in business.

These programs and many more developed since 1965 demonstrate that NCNW has moved beyond the concepts of earlier years to models utilized and replicated at the local level. Between 1965 and 1980, over forty NCNW projects developed, collaborating with national affiliates and other organizations. NCNW has sponsored numerous others. These program models respond primarily to contemporary needs of African American women and their families. Thus, there is a constant turnover in projects. Once needs are served, NCNW encourages community groups to maintain the services.

Although the NCNW's domestic program focus includes advocacy and educational projects focused primarily on black women's health issues, teenage pregnancy, older women, excellence in teaching, and AIDS and sexually transmitted diseases, the Black Family Reunion Celebration dominates its image and much of its advocacy. In the last five years NCNW's domestic program has focused on black family reunion celebrations. To address the many negative images of the black family, in 1986, NCNW launched a culturally based event emphasizing the black family's historic strengths and traditional values. The celebrations are reminiscent of the large state fairs and festivals of the past. An event consists of workshops, issue forums, exhibits, and demonstrations anchored by extensive entertainment; it has helped to renew NCNW's public roles and signifies its reentry into national public policy discourse.

Organizations affiliated with NCNW include Alpha Kappa Alpha,* Delta Sigma Theta,* the National Association of Fashion and Accessory Designers, National Association of Negro Business and Professional Women's Clubs,* Sigma Gamma Rho,* and Supreme Grand Chapter Order of Eastern Star, the Women's Convention Auxiliary to the National Baptist Convention U.S.A., Top Ladies of Distinction, Trade Union Women of African Heritage, and Women's Home and Foreign Missionary Society African Methodist Episcopal Zion Church. NCNW belongs to the Council of Presidents.*

FURTHER INFORMATION

In 1976, the Education and Career Advancement Center published a detailed curriculum guide that offered NCNW sections, affiliates, government agencies, and business training programs and instructional package useful for the development of educational programs for women employed in entry-level positions in large corporations and financial institutions. "N.C.N.W.: 1935–1980" by Bettye Collier-Thomas was published by the organization in 1981.

BETTYE COLLIER-THOMAS

NATIONAL FAIR HOUSING ALLIANCE (NFHA)
1499 I Street, NW
Suite 715
Washington, DC 20005

(202) 289-5360

FAX (202) 371-9744

The National Fair Housing Alliance (NFHA) was incorporated in 1989 after an extensive period of meeting and planning by representatives of over fifty private, nonprofit housing organizations throughout the United States. NFHA was formed partly to fill a void created as the result of the disbanding of the twenty-year-old National Committee against Discrimination in Housing (NCADH) in 1987. NFHA views discrimination in housing as a major women's issue because the 1990 census shows that women in general and women who are single heads of households are the most likely groups to be discriminated against in the housing search. In particular, black and Hispanic single female heads of households are twice as likely to be discriminated against in obtaining housing than the population at large. Fair housing is considered a key element in the achievement of basic civil rights for all citizens.

ORIGIN AND DEVELOPMENT

The history of the fair housing advocacy goes back to before the civil rights era in the 1960s. A major actor in fair housing cause has been Martin Sloan, who served as the executive director of NCADH, a research and public policy organization. During fifteen years of existence, NCADH conducted research and acted as a voice on Capitol Hill on fair housing issues. It ceased operation due to lack of funds, which left the fair housing effort without either a voice or the legal assistance provided to local fair housing agencies.

Without NCADH, the efforts of private, fair housing agencies across the United States were left without a coordinating vehicle. As a result, several fair housing groups that were served by the defunct Washington-based organization formed the NFHA. It was founded by fair housing leaders such as Marcella Brown of the Fair Housing Congress of Southern California; Connie Chamberlain of Richmond, Virginia, Housing Opportunities Made Equal; Lee Porter of the Fair Housing Council of Northern New Jersey; William Tinsdale of the Metropolitan Milwaukee Fair Housing Council; and Kale Williams of the Chicago Leadership Council for Metropolitan Open Committees. NFHA works through assistance, support, and advocacy for fair housing issues. It was instrumental in advocating for the Fair Housing Initiatives Program (FHIP) with the U.S. Department of Housing and Urban Development (HUD). Under the FHIP, HUD directly funds private Fair Housing Centers to investigate and litigate fair housing cases. For the centers, this funding meant the difference between being able to operate effectively or experience the demise of their local efforts. In addition, NFHA proposed to HUD that a direct mechanism be given to it to address relevant community issues. NFHA also acts as a communication network among fair housing advocates; develops and maintains a database of fair housing enforcement records by region, race, gender, and ethnic group; provides technical assistance to its over sixty member organizations; comments on federal regulations affecting fair housing and litigation; and coordinates the fair housing enforcement activities of member organizations.

ORGANIZATION AND FUNDING

NFHA has a twenty-person board of directors representing fair housing agencies in various regions, mid-America, the Southwest, northern California, southern California, and the Northeast. Fifty percent of board members are women, with several minority women board members. Directors are elected at the June annual meeting for a one-year term. The board is responsible for all policy decisions and program activities and for the organization's financial affairs. Additionally, at the annual meeting it elects the five officers that form the executive committee. NFHA's office is located in Washington, D.C.

Eligible for operating or voting memberships are private, nonprofit fair housing organizations that have one full-time employee and conduct investigations, enforce fair housing violations, provide assistance for victims of housing discrimination, and organize educational outreach. Others who support the goal of eliminating housing discrimination are eligible to become supporting (nonvoting) members. For tax purposes, NFHA incorporated as a 501 (c) (3) organization. The majority of its $3 million budget at the beginning of the decade came directly from contributions by member agencies, individuals supporting fair housing efforts, grants, and contracts for funding. Member agency dues range from $50 to $300, depending on the size of a member organization's budget. The majority of grants have come from HUD for fair housing enforcement and educational outreach.

POLICY CONCERNS AND TACTICS

The NFHA board assists legislators and governmental bodies with public policy around fair housing. Strategies most often used are testimony at congressional and/or agency or departmental hearings, responses to inquiries from congressional leaders, and written comments on proposed legislation. Policy is established by the board in response to the expressed needs of the private fair housing organizations that are operating members. Of growing concern for the organization is the plight of single female heads of households, the fastest growing stigmatized group in the United States. NFHA efforts have focused on this issue by its continued support with legislators for the FHIP because of the belief that remedies must come on the local level by investigating and litigating discrimination cases involving women. NFHA cooperates with groups with similar civil rights goals such as the National Association of the Advancement of Colored People. LaRaza, American Civil Liberties Union,* and Washington Lawyers Committee for Civil Rights Under Law.

ELECTORAL ACTIVITIES

As a nonpartisan organization, NFHA does not have a political action committee.

FURTHER INFORMATION

In 1992, NFHA lost its HUD funding and ceased to provide publications. Resolution to this problem is ongoing.

JEANNE A. ORTIZ

NATIONAL FAMILY PLANNING AND REPRODUCTIVE HEALTH ASSOCIATION (NFPRHA)
122 C Street, NW
Suite 380
Washington, DC 20001
(202) 628-3535
FAX (202) 737-2690

As the organization representing the entire community of family planning providers, the National Family Planning and Reproductive Health Association (NFPRHA) advocates family planning delivery system expansion through adequate governmental investment and promotion of a favorable public health climate, to assure the widest access to safe, affordable contraception.

ORIGIN AND DEVELOPMENT

Political and societal support for family planning services in the United States has varied over time from the early twentieth century's outright avoidance of the subject to broad legislative approval in the 1970s. During the past decade, public opinion and political support have retreated to a more critical and divided position on what role government should play in providing and funding these services. Intensely affected by these changes in policy and public mood, providers of reproductive health care and family planning services benefit from a central organization committed to promoting common goals. The organization that provides this centralization is NFPRHA, a diverse network encompassing over 1,000 family planning providers across the country, including state, county, and local health departments, hospital clinics, Planned Parenthood* affiliates, family planning councils, independent clinics, and health care professionals.

Initially named the National Family Planning Forum, the organization formed following a 1970 meeting in New Orleans, attended by representatives of thirty of the nation's largest publicly funded family planning programs. Joseph Beasley Louisiana Family Planning program director, and Bill Nicholas, Los Angeles Regional Family Planning Council director, are credited with the forum's founding. Both men had identified a need for communication and coordination among service providers in the rapidly growing, diverse family planning field. The New Orleans meeting and the organization that arose from it were responses to this need.

Between 1971 and 1978, a volunteer board maintained the organization and held annual meetings around the country. The majority of leaders in family planning in those years were white males, and the composition of the board reflected this, with little representation by females. A national office opened in Washington, D.C., in 1978, and the group's name changed to NFPRHA. At that time the organization's goals expanded to include the establishment of new educational programs and provision of a centralized source for information exchange. Further emphasis was placed on securing diverse leadership through minority outreach. Changes in the number of minorities and females represented on the board reflect the success of this effort.

With the decline of federal funding from the 1980s to the present, the organization has faced the monumental task of remaining viable. Its major challenges have included meeting ever expanding health care needs with sufficient funding and protecting reproductive rights while fighting the harmful regulations of unsupportive administrations.

ORGANIZATION AND FUNDING

Twenty-six individuals serve on the board of directors, about 30 percent of whom belong to racial minority groups—five African Americans, one Hispanic, one Asian American and one Native American. The board has made an effort not to exclude anyone from participation, striving toward a membership that is racially, culturally, and regionally diverse. Women now constitute approximately two-thirds of the board's membership; the president and four other females serve on the eight-member executive committee. The board's consumer affairs council seeks members from lower-income strata and encourages their participation and input in identifying needs and concerns in the delivery of family planning services.

Only one office is maintained, in Washington, with nine professional staff members. Two or three student interns from local colleges and universities also serve in the office each year. The current president/chief executive officer, selected by the executive board with full board approval, is Judith M. DeSarno. She has held this office since March 1991, having succeeded Scott Swirling, who served as executive director 1981–91. Although NFPRHA has no full-time lobbyist, staff member Deborah Horan serves as director of public affairs. An attorney serves on retainer.

From a membership of approximately 300 in the early 1970s, NFPRHA has grown to include some 1,000 members, representing both organizational and individual interests. Individuals and groups join the organization for a variety of reasons. These include the opportunity to communicate with others in their field; advocate commonly held values, ideas, and policies; receive information and publications; and attend conferences. An annual meeting is held in Washington, D.C., with approximately 350–400 members in attendance.

Membership dues, which provide about 30 percent of NFPRHA's financial support, range from individual memberships of $25, $50, and $150 for, respectively, students, consumers, and professionals, to institutional memberships of $475 and $875, depending on the institution's size. Sustaining members contribute $2,000 each. Another 60 percent of the organization's support comes in the form of private foundation grants. The federal grants received in NFPRHA's early days are no longer available. The remaining 10 percent of support is derived from conferences and meetings and the sale of publications and lists. This nonprofit organization's current budget is approximately $900,000, an increase of $700,000 over its 1970 budget.

POLICY CONCERNS AND TACTICS

NFPRHA policy is determined by its board of directors, with input from the executive director. Committees reporting to the board meet periodically on issues such as minority development, consumer affairs, development, and international and domestic public affairs. Such committees provide members with expanded opportunities to express opinion on policy matters. Staff recommendations are channeled through the executive director to the board. The board's executive committee appears to have the greatest role in developing organizational policy. It maintains the most comprehensive view of the organization's mission and therefore can develop policies most consistent with those goals.

While NFPRHA's member organizations often testify at legislative or agency hearings, NFPRHA itself serves primarily as advocate and educator, providing members and occasionally congresspersons with information, written comments, and publications. Voting records of elected officials are closely monitored, as are court decisions. When such decisions threaten the programs represented by NFPRHA, the organization may take an active role in litigation. Following the Supreme Court's decision in *Rust* v. *Sullivan* (1991), upholding the legality of the "gag rule," NFPRHA petitioned to reargue two points not covered by *Rust.* Although the First Circuit Court of Appeals denied that petition, NFPRHA's lawyers filed a petition asking the Court to reconsider its denial. In 1988, NFPRHA and the National Association of Nurse Practitioners in Public Health acted as coplaintiffs in a suit alleging that Owen Bowen, the Health and Human Services Department (DHHS) secretary responsible for the gag rule, changed his department's regulations without following the required procedures of the Administrative Procedures Act. After a district court victory for the plaintiffs, the government appealed; the appeals court delayed implementation until the incoming administration took office.

From NFPRHA's origin to the present, a primary goal has been to promote a comprehensive, *federally insured* family planning program for all needing such services. The most significant federal legislation to impact on NFPRHA and its membership has been the 1970 Public Health Service Act, with its Title X authorization of family planning services and funding. Annual appropriations bills related to this funding also have had a continuing impact, particularly during the Reagan administration, when funding repeatedly was threatened and diminished. Critical importance also must be attributed to Supreme Court decisions and legislation relating to abortion, from *Roe* v. *Wade* (1973) to *Webster* v. *Reproductive Health Services* (1989).

NFPRHA's most recent focus was on the health care legislation before the

Congress. While promoting the establishment of Title X clinics as essential community providers, the organization resisted efforts to initiate unitary drug pricing, which tends to increase the costs of providing birth control services. Efforts aimed at ensuring reauthorization of the Title X program went on hold until the next legislative session, having failed to win support in the Senate.

Although recent legislation relating to individuals with disabilities, including pregnancy, has been viewed positively by NFPRHA's membership, most legislation passed during the 1980s was much worse for this organization than legislation of the 1970s. The government's conservative mood, as expressed in the gag rule and in declining funding, presented a major obstacle to NFPRHA's effective accomplishment of its objectives. The scope of NFPRHA's concern has broadened, and the number of clients in need has increased, yet Title X funding has not significantly increased, even under the more positive atmosphere of the Clinton administration.

NFPRHA not only relies on the services of an attorney, its internal committees, and its board but collaborates as well with its sister organizations concerning strategies on issues of mutual concern. These organizations include the Center for Population Options, the Planned Parenthood Federation of America,* and the Alan Guttmacher Institute.* Cooperation with these like-minded groups has existed since NFPRHA's founding. Such antichoice organizations as the National Right to Life Committee,* Operation Rescue,* and the American Life Lobby* are seen as perennial adversaries, frequently working against policies that NFPRHA and its associates support.

ELECTORAL ACTIVITIES

NFPRHA does not have a political action committee and does not contribute to election campaigns. This lack of direct activity appears to be financially and philosophically motivated. NFPRHA views its mission as advocacy and education, and its limited funding is designated for these purposes. Member organizations and individuals are frequently part of other groups that endorse candidates for public office. More active electoral involvement appears to be contingent upon secure and consistent funding, a luxury that NFPRHA does not at this time possess.

FURTHER INFORMATION

Publications include the NFPRHA News, a periodic newsletter addressing service delivery concerns; NFPRHA Report, a monthly legislative summary with action pieces and alerts; and the executive director's monthly "Insider" letter, sent to the highest-paying members.

CATHY WERNER

NATIONAL FEDERATION OF AFRO-AMERICAN WOMEN
See NATIONAL ASSOCIATION OF COLORED WOMEN'S CLUBS

NATIONAL FEDERATION OF BUSINESS AND PROFESSIONAL WOMEN'S CLUBS OF THE U.S.A. (BPW/USA)
2012 Massachusetts Avenue, NW
Washington, DC 20036
(202) 293-1100
FAX (202) 861-0928

A traditionally structured women's organization, the National Federation of Business and Professional Women's Clubs/USA (BPW/USA) actively has pursued political and economic equality for women for more than seventy years. BPW/USA has an educational and research foundation and a political action committee.

ORIGIN AND DEVELOPMENT

The forerunner of BPW/USA was created during World War I, when the federal government felt the need to involve women in the war effort. The War Department, in May 1918, invited representatives from each state to meet and plan a national businesswomen's committee, the Women's War Council. Guided by the Young Women's Christian Association,* the group continued after the war, and in 1919 it assumed its current status as BPW/USA, an independent organization working to benefit professional women and businesswomen. Its first president, attorney Gail Laughlin, was a National Woman's Party* (NWP) member and in 1931 became a Maine state legislator. Within a year the organization attracted a membership of 25,000, found in 287 clubs in forty-seven states; by 1931, the membership had more than doubled to 56,000. From its early beginnings, BPW/USA has crusaded for working women's full participation, equality, and economic self-sufficiency.

An early supporter of the equal rights amendment (ERA), which the 65,000-member BPW/USA endorsed at its 1937 convention, the organization has stood at the forefront of most efforts to expand women's civil and legal rights in the twentieth century. While an active proponent of reforms in marriage, divorce, tax, and citizenship laws to benefit women, unlike many other women's groups BPW/USA did not support the enactment of protective labor legislation. Along with laws passed during the Great Depression limiting government jobs to one person in a married couple, BPW/USA found protective laws a threat to working women.

In the early 1960s, BPW/USA successfully led the way in establishing the President's Commission on the Status of Women* and the companion state commissions. In addition to ERA and these other early efforts, BPW/USA worked for the 1963 Equal Pay Act, The 1964 Civil Rights Act, and Title IX of the 1972 Educational Amendments Act, along with numerous other measures designed to benefit working women. It was, for instance, the first to call, in 1966, for the inclusion of sex in an executive order requiring affirmative action by firms doing business with the government.

BPW/USA's pivotal role in many of these battles can be traced to its sizable membership, often making it one of the largest women's groups in the country. Also critical has been the role of its presidents. Among the more notable have been Lena Lake Forrest and Marguerite Rawalt. The former, an early president of BPW/USA, was instrumental in creating the organization's research funding program. Rawalt, president from 1954 to 1956 and an NWP member besides, set up the tax-exempt Business and Professional Women's Foundation (BPWF) and, as a member of President Kennedy's Commission on the Status of Women,* was the only ERA supporter. Later, she helped to found several other women's rights movement organizations, including the National Organization for Women* (NOW) and NOW Legal Defense and Education Fund,* ERAmerica,* and the Women's Equity Action League.* Rawalt was also instrumental in encouraging BPW/USA to fund much of the work of ERAmerica* and in getting the amendment to the House floor for a favorable vote in 1970. Another former president, Virginia Allan, chaired President Nixon's Task Force on Women's Rights and Responsibilities; and Margaret Chase Smith, the former Democratic senator from Maine, served on the national board and as president of her local.

ORGANIZATION AND FUNDING

The bulk of the membership belongs to local clubs organized in all fifty states, as well as in Washington, D.C., the Virgin Islands, and Puerto Rico. Each of the state or regional associations has its own organizational structure, like the national, complete with a slate of officers elected by the membership at an annual convention. The national president appoints an executive board to include additional officers in charge of specific programs. The board of directors includes the executive committee as well as the presidents of all the state organizations and the immediate past president. Currently, there are sixty-seven members on the board. The method of selection requires that officers have had considerable experience in the organization at the state and local level. The president in 1994–95 was Cindy Winckler.

BPW/USA's organizational headquarters in Washington—occupying a building that has been its home since the Washington office opened in 1957—has undergone a considerable renovation in recent years. Currently, it houses BPWF and the Marguerite Rewalt Resource Center, a library used for research on working women. The executive director is Audrey Taynes Haynes. The national headquarters has a paid staff of twenty-four individuals and one or two interns. The organization employs one full-time lobbyist who works for the passage of legislation to implement its goals. Kate Premo is the public policy manager.

With a current membership of 80,000, BPW/USA represents the interests of a sizable number of women. Most who join do so for social and business connections and to be part of an organization that is a strong advocate for women's issues. A decline in membership, down from 150,000 in 1984, 154,000 in the late 1970s, and 172,000 in 1962, is a real organizational concern. Most observers believe the steep increase in dues in the last several years, needed to pay for the refurbished headquarters, is responsible for the drop-off.

This 501 (c) (3) organization has an annual budget in excess of $1.8 million. The bulk of this money (60 percent) comes from the annual membership dues, which recently have increased to thirty-one dollars for members of local clubs and fifty dollars for at-large members. Conventions, sales of advertising space, and publications provide additional sources of revenue, contributing about 20 percent toward operating costs. Besides funding the work of its national head-quarters, one of BPW/USA's other major expenses is the publication of its quarterly newsletter.

The affiliated foundation is a nonprofit education and research organization founded in 1956. It shares an executive director with BPW/USA. With a budget of $1 million, the foundation oversees a number of scholarship and loan pro-grams designed to aid women in obtaining advanced degrees. By 1994, it had awarded almost $5 million to almost 7,000 women. It also funds a wide variety of workshops, research grants, publications, and the resource center.

POLICY CONCERNS AND TACTICS

At the annual convention, representatives of the state and local clubs vote on a legislative platform. Resolutions passed by the convention also guide the organization's policy. Strategy to implement these policy choices is developed by the executive committee and the staff. The most important tactics are lobbying members of the Congress, conducting and publishing research, and educating and encouraging its own members to write to legislators. BPW/USA also has used the strategies of filing amicus briefs, presenting information and testimony to congressional and departmental hearings, and participating in marches. For several years, BPW/USA has sponsored a lobby day when members are urged to come to Washington to press their representatives to pass legislation that the organization supports. To publicize the accomplishments of working women and call attention to their needs, BPW/USA has sponsored an annual Businesswom-en's Week for over sixty years.

The organization's policy agenda usually has presented a set of focus issues on which the organization and its members concentrate the year's efforts. The key issues on its platform now are economic equity, health care, and civil rights. Included as issues under these broad concerns are the elimination of the glass ceiling on women's career progression and ending sexual harassment. BPW/USA often receives credit for playing an important role in the passage of leg-islation benefiting working women.

Perhaps the issue closest to BPW/USA's heart is ERA. In addition to being among its earliest supporters, the organization played a key role in funding the movement for ERA, tithing the members in the 1970s $1.50 per year to support the ratification effort. Because of its financial and political resources, BPW/USA was instrumental in seeing the amendment through the Congress. It also was a leading force in bringing together key organizations in ERAmerica,* which or-chestrated state efforts in a failed attempt to get the needed legislative support at that level. Since the defeat of ERA, BPW/USA has been one of the few organizations to continue with it as a major concern. Since 1985, ERA has been the preamble to the annual platform, the understanding being that immediate passage is not possible. BPW/USA is committed to making ERA a front-burner issue if and when the chances for passage again look promising. To this end, it has established a new task force to work on ERA to develop new strategies for resurrecting the amendment.

In addition to ERA, BPW/USA also has been at the forefront of a number of other legislative battles in the 1980s to expand women's rights. Among the organization's key concerns have been the 1988 Civil Rights Restoration Act, 1991 Civil Rights Act, and 1993 Family and Medical Leave bill and its predecessors. BPW/USA also has been very active in promoting the Freedom of Choice bill as a response to recent Supreme Court decisions limiting access to abortion. It considers the *Webster* decision and President Bush's vetoes of the Family and Medical Leave bills the worst actions in recent years. On all of these and related issues, BPW/USA has pursued a multipronged strategy of direct lobbying and encouraging the membership to contact their legislative representative.

BPW/USA is affiliated with BPW International; but debates over the dues the U.S. section has to pay threaten this relationship. BPW/USA works actively in coalition with other women's groups as they try to influence the policy decisions of the Congress and executive branch. Coalition partners include the American Association of University Women,* National Women's Political Caucus,* and National Women's Legal Defense Fund. Early in the century it belonged to the Joint Congressional Committee, a women's lobby; presently it belongs to the Council of Presidents.* It is also a member of the Reproductive Freedom Coalition. It counts among its adversaries Eagle Forum,* Operation Rescue,* and, on the Family and Medical Leave bill, the Chamber of Commerce.

ELECTORAL ACTIVITIES

BPW/PAC registered in 1979. Most of the money raised by the PAC comes from the membership. Its contributions to congressional races have been modest. In 1992, for instance, it gave $25,000 to eighty-nine candidates. To receive funds, candidates must fill out a questionnaire asking their views on a variety of issues of concern to the organization, including ERA, reproductive rights, family leave, and workplace equity. While BPW/USA prefers to endorse women, it has regularly supported men who endorse the BPW agenda.

FURTHER INFORMATION

The organization publishes several items, including its quarterly newsletter, *National Business Women,* and numerous information packets on workplace issues.

NANCY E. MCGLEN

NATIONAL FEDERATION OF TELEPHONE WORKERS
See COMMUNICATIONS WORKERS OF AMERICA

NATIONAL GAY AND LESBIAN TASK FORCE (NGLTF)
2320 17th Street, NW
Washington, DC 20009
(202) 332-6483
FAX (202) 332-0207
TTY (202) 332-6219
E-MAIL NGLTF @ AOL.COM

The National Gay and Lesbian Task Force (NGLTF) has an activist agenda aimed at the creation of a society where lesbians and gay men can live openly, free from bias-related violence, prejudice, and discrimination. Using conventional pressure group tactics, NGLTF has proven to be an effective agent for fairly unconventional political change. It has an educational and research foundation, the NGLTF Policy Institute.

ORIGIN AND DEVELOPMENT

Originally called the National Gay Task Force (NGTF), the organization formed on November 15, 1973, changing its name to NGLTF in 1985. Its founders and early board members came to the organization with years of experience in different subbranches of the gay and lesbian movement. Some, including Barbara Gittings and Frank Kameny, were activists in homophile organizations such as Daughters of Bilitis* and the Mattachine Society,* which has been founded in the 1950s. Others, including Barbara Love, Ginny Vida, and Sidney Abbott, came to the task force with experience in lesbian-feminist organizing of the late sixties and early seventies. Still others acted through gay liberation organizations that formed after the momentous New York City raid on June 27, 1969, on the Stonewall Inn, a gay bar in Greenwich Village. Up until this time such raids met with little resistance. That night, the police encountered strong resistance, and a riot ensured. Activists and scholars consider this event to mark the beginning of a qualitatively different era in gay and lesbian politics; and its anniversary is commemorated by pride parades in communities throughout the United States.

Both men and women have held top leadership positions in the organization. Bruce Voeller served as the first executive director. In 1976, the task force moved to a dual executive structure, and Jean O'Leary joined Voeller as co-executive director. Among the other teams that filled this codirectorate were Lucia Valaska and Charlie Brydon. By the early 1980s, the organization went back to having a single executive director. Prominent individuals who have held the position include Virginia Apuzzo, Jeff Levy and Urvashi Vaid. Vaid served as executive director from 1989 to 1992. She was one of three individuals to be honored with a first annual $25,000 Stonewall Award given by the Anderson Prize Foundation in 1991. Peri Jude Radecic was appointed executive director by a unanimous vote of the NGLTF board in 1993. In late 1994, Melinda Paras assumed the post; descended from prominent forebearers in the Philippines, Paras has an interesting and controversial history as an activist.

Since its founding, NGLTF resources have been used in efforts to end discrimination and violence based on sexual orientation. Beginning in 1983, the organization added a commitment to fighting discrimination against people with AIDS and discrimination based on HIV status.

ORGANIZATION AND FUNDING

NGLTF operates with a twenty-four-member board of directors. Before 1992, the board was elected by the membership. Since 1992, the board itself appoints new members. The bylaws mandate that at least 20 percent of the board members be people of color. In 1992, approximately 33 percent of board members were people of color, and 50 percent were women. The current cochairs are Chris Collins and Debra Johnson-Rolon. Originally, the organization was located in New York City. In 1984, as its national lobbying efforts took on greater significance, a second office was set up in Washington, D.C. In 1986, the entire organization moved to the nation's capital. The number of paid staff members has grown. Whereas in 1978, five years after its founding, there were only six paid employees, in 1994 there were twenty-one full-time and four part-time employees. Staff members report that from a pool of about 100 active volunteers in the Washington area, about ten to fifteen individuals attend each of the twice-weekly volunteer sessions held at NGLTF headquarters. Another 100 or more volunteers in different regions of the United States assist with membership and fund-raising activities. A number of college students each year do internships with the organization during breaks from school or sometimes for an entire semester.

Membership has increased more than 600 percent since 1975, growing from about 5,000 in that year to 8,000 in 1980, 14,000 in 1985, and roughly 32,000 in 1994. Approximately 35 percent of NGLTF's members are women.

Funding for NGLTF and the NGLTF Policy Institute comes primarily from membership dues and individual contributions. In 1991, for example, 35 percent of their combined total income of $1,191,673 came from membership dues, and 21 percent from individual contributions. The remaining 44 percent of the combined 1991 income came from conference proceeds (11 percent), special events (11 percent), grants (8 percent), events, honoraria and sales (2 percent), board fund-raising (5 percent), planned giving (5 percent), and other sources (2 percent). A $39,603 shortfall was covered through board-authorized use of reserve funds. This 1991 budget grew from budgets of approximately $70,000 in 1974, $300,000 in 1978, and $400,000 in 1980. NGLTF's level of financial health has varied. In the past it accumulated a long-term debt totaling over $90,000. In 1986, the task force set up an organizational development program and by 1987 paid off its long-term debt. In 1989, an excess of $232,948 in revenues over expenditures was invested in an endowment fund to support development efforts and the organization's long-term growth. In late 1994, the budget stood at $2.6 million but this was $1.4 million less than the group's estimated budget.

Officially, NGLTF and the NGLTF Policy Institute are two separate organizations. About 25 percent of the combined 1991 budget for the two groups funds NGLTF. Since NGLTF's main focus is lobbying, it is classified as a 501 (c) (4) organization, and contributions to it are not tax-deductible. The remaining 75 percent of the combined budget pays for the organizing, educational, and media efforts of the NGLTF Policy Institute. By not doing any lobbying, the NGLTF Policy Institute qualifies as a 501 (c) (3) tax-exempt organization, and contributions made to it are tax-deductible. The board of directors and officers are the same for both organizations. All staff members work for the NGLTF Policy Institute. In addition, those staff members who also lobby or provide support for lobbying do so on a contract basis for NGLTF.

POLICY CONCERNS AND TACTICS

When determining issue priorities and choosing strategies, the executive director and staff generally initiate proposals that are presented to the board for approval. NGLTF's efforts have included judicial intervention, grassroots organizing, education, serving as a media watchdog, direct action, and lobbying. NGLTF has lobbied the Congress, executive agencies, and sometimes even private associations. For example, one of the task force's first victories, 1973–74, was to convince the American Psychiatric Association to declassify homosexuality as an illness.

In the legislative arena NGLTF took part in successful lobbying efforts to defeat the 1981 Family Protection Act, increase AIDS funding and programming, remove restrictions against the immigration of gays and lesbians in the 1990 Immigration Reform Act, and include people with AIDS and HIV infection in the 1990 Americans with Disabilities Act, among others. In 1990, NGLTF earned itself an invitation to the White House signing of the Hate Crimes Statistics Act because of the leadership role it took in securing that bill's passage. In 1991 and 1992, lobbying efforts included the reintroduction of a Federal Gay and Lesbian Civil Rights Bill with a record number of cosponsors; the insertion of language into the Justice Department appropriations bill that strengthens the government's response to hate crimes; work with the Breast Cancer Coalition, which advocates for research, care, and screening; and testimony against the military's discrimination policy.

Besides its legislative victories, NGLTF has successfully lobbied various executive branch bureaucracies. In 1975, NGLTF pressure proved instrumental in the U.S. Civil Service Commission's ruling that allowed gay people to serve as federal employees. In 1978, its lobbying led the Public Health Service to end its classification of homosexual immigrants as psychopathic personalities.

NGLTF has not focused much of its resources recently on the judicial arena but in the past participated in such efforts more heavily. Perhaps its best-known effort was *NGTF* v. *Oklahoma,* in which the organization challenged a law prohibiting favorable mention of homosexuality in schools. In 1985, after years of litigation, the U.S. Supreme Court in a 4–4 decision upheld a lower court's ruling that declared the law unconstitutional.

Since 1988, NGLTF has held annual Creating Change conferences, which bring together gay and lesbian activists and grassroots groups from around the country for skill building and strategy sessions. Preconference institutes provide two-day intensive sessions on special topics. At the 1990 conference, for example, a Fundraising Institute and a People of Color Organizing Institute were held. Through the compilation and distribution of congressional voting records, periodic National Lobby Days, and an activist alert network, the task force attempts to increase the knowledge constituents have about elected officials' stands on key issues and to increase grassroots pressure on them.

Another component of NGLTF's work centers on research, education, and public information. A good example of how the research and information efforts are linked to the political ones is the work of the Anti-Violence Project. In 1982, NGLTF established the first national toll-free gay hot line, which, along with other functions, facilitated reporting violence against gays and lesbians. In 1984, the organization released the first national survey of violence directed against gay and lesbian people and since 1986 has distributed such reports annually. These reports have provided evidence for local activists trying to ensure that violence based on sexual orientation is included in municipal and state hate crime bills and for NGLTF lobbyists who successfully persuaded the Congress that crimes against gay and lesbians should be included in the 1990 Federal Hate Crimes Statistics Act.

Over the years, NGLTF has sent out numerous press releases in an attempt to reduce prejudice, increase visibility and pride, and educate journalists, broadcasters, and the general public on gay and lesbian issues. By making publications available and answering mail and phone inquiries, NGLTF has served as a clearinghouse on gay and lesbian concerns and facilitated communications within and between different segments of the gay and lesbian community. By maintaining contact with the mainstream media, NGLTF has attempted to correct biased and inflammatory reporting and to provide stories that more accurately reflect the range and diversity of gay and lesbian life in this country.

A final tactic used by NGLTF has been direct action. In recent years NGLTF has helped organize and participated in nonviolent protests primarily on AIDS-related issues in Washington, D.C. Direct action protests have not been one of the mainstays of the organization's tactical repertoire.

Potentially, NGLTF's future agenda includes such items as the extension of civil rights protections to gay men and lesbians, recognition and protection of lesbian and gay family relationships, opposition to limits on gay and lesbian artists' free expression, and elimination of discrimination in the military. These agenda items are based on long-standing liberal democratic principles of equality and individual choice. The achievement of these objectives, however, necessarily entails major revision in the ways in which society copes with human differences and even how it understands and legally defines such important concepts as family. Further, in late 1994, NGLTF announced an increased focus on technical and strategic support of community organizing.

National organizations that NGLTF views as allies include the American Civil Liberties Union,* People for the American Way, and the Human Rights Campaign Fund.

NGLTF also works closely with state and local organizations. The cooperating organization program, for example, links NGLTF with more than 100 gay/lesbian organizations, including such groups as the Illinois Gay and Lesbian Task Force, Latino/Latina Lesbian and Gay Organization, and Heritage of Pride, which organizes New York City's annual pride events. Several NGLTF projects have emphasized the development of grassroots organizing skills among state and local leaders. Among these are the Privacy Project, which works with state and local groups lobbying to repeal laws that criminalize gay and lesbian sex; the Lesbian and Gay Families Project, which advocates for legal recognition and protection of domestic partnerships and lesbian/gay parenting; the Civil Rights Project, which helps with state and local efforts to enact laws banning discrimination on the basis of sexual orientation; and the Fight the Right Project, which advises and supports campaign organizations in states facing right-wing ballot initiatives. NGLTF counts among its adversaries the Traditional Values Coalition and Concerned Women for America.*

ELECTORAL ACTIVITIES

NGLTF does not have a political action committee and is officially nonpartisan.

FURTHER INFORMATION

NGLTF has several newsletters, including the *Task Force Report,* which comes out quarterly, and the *Activist Alert,* which comes out monthly. Besides these regular newsletters, special notices sometimes are sent out to update activists on immediate concerns, such as legislation currently pending on Capitol Hill, recent outbreaks of antigay violence, and antigay legislative proposals in certain states and localities. In the late summer of 1992, an information packet entitled *Fight the Right: 1992 Action Kit* was distributed to NGLTF activists. The kit included information on voter registration and absentee voting in all fifty states, tips on media activism, and information on positions of the presidential candidates and grassroots activism. Among the other publications that NGLTF has produced and/or distributed are pamphlets that answer parents' and employers' questions about sexual orientation, a "Media Guide to Gay Issues," and a "Professional Gay Caucus List," which includes names and addresses of gay professional caucuses in such fields as nursing, teaching, and law.

DAVIDA J. ALPERIN

NATIONAL LEAGUE OF COLORED WOMEN
See NATIONAL ASSOCIATION OF COLORED WOMEN'S CLUBS

NATIONAL LEAGUE FOR NURSING (NLN)
350 Hudson Street
New York City, NY 10014
(212) 989-9393
FAX (212) 989-3710

The National League for Nursing (NLN) consistently has had the primary goal of reforming and upgrading nursing education. Its secondary goal, adopted in 1952, is to support community health nursing.

ORIGIN AND DEVELOPMENT

To standardize and improve nurses' education, the first of the existing nursing organizations, NLN, was founded in 1893 as the Society of Superintendents of Training Schools for Nurses of the United States and Canada. Impetus for founding came during a meeting in Chicago at the International Congress of Charities, Correction and Philanthropy, held in conjunction with the World's Fair. Early leadership came in association with Johns Hopkins University. In 1912, the society changed its name to the National League of Nursing Education (NLNE). Originally for nurses only, in 1943, it agreed to admit lay members. In 1952, in a reorganization of nursing organizations, the league amalgamated with the National Organization for Public Health Nursing (NOPHN) and Association of Collegiate Schools of Nursing to become NLN.

For much of its history, NLN has had to rely on voluntary compliance to reform and upgrade nursing education. To this end a series of reports was published, the first of which, *Standard Curriculum for Schools of Nursing,* was issued in 1917. NLNE recommended a three-year sequence in basic sciences and nursing along with a practicum. It also suggested that student nurses work no more than eight hours a day. Recommended curriculum was revised and updated in 1927 and 1937; but a significant number of schools continued to operate without subscribing to the standards.

To pressure some of the worst offenders, in 1926, NLNE came together with the American Nurses Association* (ANA) and NOPHN to establish a Committee on the Grading of Nursing Schools. Conditions in many proprietary hospitals were deplorable, and pressure was exerted on small, unaccredited hospitals (fewer than fifty beds) to eliminate their nursing schools. A report also recommended that all training schools have at least one instructor and a minimum of four registered nurses on their staff. Giving impetus to the report was the Great Depression, which brought about many small and large school closings, although many nurse training ''mills'' continued to operate.

Not until 1949 was the National Accrediting Service formed on an interim basis, and not until 1952 was a permanent accreditation program established as part of the newly formed NLN. Its control of accrediting recognized by various agencies, hospitals, and educational institutions, NLN finally achieved the power to do what it had organized to do in 1893. In connection with its accrediting activities, NLN provides consultation to any nursing school seeking help with its program. It also offers a testing service helpful for preimmigration screening of foreign nurses who want to practice in the United States.

ORGANIZATION AND FUNDING

NLN business sessions are held at biennial conventions. The board of directors consists of five elected officers—president, president-elect, first and second vice presidents, and treasurer—along with the council chairpersons, twelve elected directors, an executive committee made up of four members of the Assembly of Constituent Leagues for Nursing, and two board-appointed directors. The executive director is not a voting member. Council chairpersons and the executive committee are elected by their respective groups. The officers, six directors, and three members of the nominations committee are elected by the membership every two years. NLN has two types of committees, standing and special; these may be elected or appointed, depending on the bylaws.

Besides the New York City office, there are regional offices located in Chicago, Atlanta, and San Francisco. The chief executive officer is Pamela J. Maraldo, who also serves as secretary of the board of directors. NLN and its constituent groups do not have a lobbyist, but they work with lobbyists from ANA and the American Association of Colleges of Nursing (AACN).

Organized on national and constituent levels, NLN has 18,000 individual members. The first membership class is open to anyone interested in fostering the development and improvement of nursing service and education. Members of special interest forums also are individual members. Individual members normally join a constituent group while agency members join NLN directly; in 1967, the state leagues were reorganized into forty-six constituent units, which may represent a state, several states, part of a state, or a large metropolitan area, whichever best serves regional planning needs. Individuals also may join NLN directly. Individuals members pay $110 to belong.

NLN also has several forums within its membership structure, the oldest being the National Forum for Administrators of Nursing Service (1977). Membership is limited to nurse administrators as well as some faculty in graduate programs. In 1984, the National Forum on Computers in Health Care and Nursing was initiated, and in 1986, the Society for Research in Nursing Education. Membership in a forum automatically enrolls a person as an individual member in national and constituent leagues. Fees may be assessed by a forum or constituent society.

Agency membership is for organizations or groups (1) providing nursing services accredited by NLN and (2) conducting an approved educational program in nursing. By means of a recognized formula, each member agency designates two or more individuals to serve as its voting representatives. Agency members work through various councils. Four councils handle accreditation: Associate Degrees Programs, Baccalaureate and Higher Degree Programs, Diploma Programs, and Practical Nursing Programs. In addition there are councils for Community Health Services, Nursing Services for Hospital and Related Facilities,

Informatics, Nursing Centers, Nursing Practice, the Society for Research in Nursing Education, and the Constituent Leagues of local NLN membership groups. Agency membership fees depend on the agency's size and the council to which it belongs. An agency has to pay higher fees for accreditation if it does not belong to a council.

POLICY CONCERNS AND TACTICS

NLN does analysis on issues of interest to nursing, particularly actions of government agencies. In 1987, it established a Community Health Accreditation Program (CHAP), which has taken upon itself setting and monitoring standards in long-term care institutions, particularly home and community-based health care. NLN had accredited home care agencies for some twenty-five years, but previously home and community-based nursing care was ignored in the health care delivery system. A subsidiary of NLN, over 50 percent of CHAP's board of governors come from business and insurance sectors or represent consumer interests. The Joint Commission on Accreditation of Health Care Organizations also began to expand into the home health care field at the time CHAP formed, introducing an element of competition.

NLN cooperates with other nursing organizations, including ANA* and AACN, to support nursing education, nursing research, Medicare, Medicaid, home health care, and bills to improve health care delivery.

ELECTORAL ACTIVITIES

NLN is a nonpartisan organization. It does not have a political action committee.

FURTHER INFORMATION

NLN's official journal, 1952–79, was *Nursing Outlook,* published by the American Journal of Nursing Company. In 1979, NLN began publishing its own journal, *Nursing and Health Care,* issued approximately ten times a year. It also has a research division that collects data and makes them available to various publications, including its own *NLN Nursing Data Review.*

                    VERN L. BULLOUGH AND BONNIE BULLOUGH

NATIONAL LEAGUE OF COLORED WOMEN
See NATIONAL ASSOCIATION OF COLORED WOMEN'S CLUBS

NATIONAL LEAGUE OF NURSING EDUCATION
See NATIONAL LEAGUE FOR NURSING

NATIONAL LOW INCOME HOUSING COALITION (NLIHC)
1012 14th Street, NW
Suite 1200
Washington, DC 20005

(202) 662-1530

FAX (202) 393-1973

The National Low Income Housing Coalition (NLIHC) was chartered in 1978 as a nonprofit national housing advocacy organization for the purpose of lobbying the Congress and administration for improved housing programs and policies at funding levels sufficient to meet the needs of low-income people. NLIHC has earned recognition as the organization that people on Capitol Hill and candidates for public office turn to for information and assessments of the state of low-income housing. NLIHC views the housing crisis as a women's issue of major importance because women predominate among those U.S. householders most likely to be ill-housed, including abused spouses, displaced homemakers, and single mothers. Women also predominate in heading families that are homeless. NLIHC has a nonprofit research and education arm, the Low Income Housing Information Service (LIHIS).

ORIGIN AND DEVELOPMENT

Originally called the Ad Hoc Coalition for Low Income Housing, the group came together in 1974 in response to President Nixon's 1973 moratorium on federally subsidized housing programs. Its immediate goal was to protect public housing from the president's attempts to shift national priorities away from federal involvement in low-income housing. Among the groups joining the ad hoc coalition were National Organization for Women,* the National Council of Negro Women,* and National Urban League.* The need for a coalition grew out of the fact that events of the 1960s had led to the dissolution of the old alliance of church organizations, labor unions, and housing reformers, (representing housing consumers), and home builders, mortgage bankers, and real estate brokers (representing producers). That old alliance had lobbied in support of the low-income housing program since its inception in 1934 to the mid-1960s.

By the mid-sixties, many working-class members of labor unions had satisfied their housing needs with federally insured mortgage guarantees. Banks and savings and loans sought greater diversity in their loan portfolios, with less money in home mortgages. Whites had moved out of public housing and the central cities, to be replaced by blacks, and increasingly, public housing was viewed as housing for minorities. Widespread social unrest and middle-class disenchantment with the costly federal war on poverty led some to conclude that housing was not a key to resolving social problems. Thus was the former housing lobby splintered. Representatives of consumers of federal low-income housing never were a powerful lobby, and without the support of organized labor, they were almost powerless. Few voices raised in protest when a newly elected Nixon imposed his moratorium on low-income housing programs.

Housing activist Cushing Dolbeare was instrumental in organizing the ad hoc coalition and became its president and later, chief staff officer, working without pay until 1981. To enhance the organization's credibility and perceived strength among Washington politicians, Dolbeare pioneered the use of sign-on letters:

letters to the president, top administration officials, and members of the Congress that several hundred other organizations, including many not involved in housing, joined in signing. Dolbeare, whose career included a job as a speechwriter for Hubert Humphrey in 1951, became involved in low-income housing that same year when she was hired to work for the Citizen's Planning and Housing Association of Baltimore. After five years there, Dolbeare joined the staff of the Housing Association of the Delaware Valley in Philadelphia, where she worked for fifteen years.

Short of funds and with Dolbeare as its only staff member in 1974, the ad hoc coalition first used the mailing address of the Americans for Democratic Action and later the National Rural Housing Coalition, where Dolbeare was part-time executive director. The ad hoc coalition incorporated in 1978 as NLIHC, with the nation's only black U.S. senator, Edward Brooke (R-MA), as its president. Brooke and Representative Parren Mitchell (D-MD) were NLIHC's strongest supporters in the Congress. In 1981, the board named Dolbeare as its first paid executive director. She served until her retirement from the agency staff in 1984.

NLIHC is able to cite major successes since its creation in 1974. One notable success came in saving public housing from the Nixon and Reagan administrations. Dolbeare maintains that she is convinced that without NLIHC there would be no more subsidized housing. As she put it, ''We fought the Reagan administration to a draw.'' NLIHC also was instrumental in persuading the Congress to include a 30 percent set-aside for low-income families in requirements for funding under a multifamily dwelling program. Originally, NLIHC sought to ensure that 30 percent of apartment projects funded under the Section 8 New Construction program of the 1974 Housing and Community Development Act be set aside for low-income families. U.S. secretary of housing and urban development Carla Hills interpreted the agreement more broadly still to mean that in each apartment project, each landlord would choose at least 30 percent of the initial tenants from low-income families, which resulted in a sizable increase in available low-income units. (The Section 8 New Construction program was abolished by the Reagan administration.)

ORGANIZATION AND FUNDING

NLIHC operates with a 130-member board of directors, 25 of whom serve on the executive committee. About 48 percent of board members are women; 22 percent, African Americans; 6 percent, Hispanic; 4 percent, Asian Americans; and 2 percent, Native Americans. Meetings of the board are held three times a year while the executive committee meets monthly to oversee the organization's operations. Among others, the board's membership has included representatives from the American Friends' Service Committee,* Center for Community Change, Common Cause, La Raza, Leadership Conference on Civil Rights, League of Women Voters,* legal services programs, National Association of Social Workers,* National Hispanic Coalition for Better Housing, National Tenants' Organization, Rural America and the Urban Coalition, and various labor and religious groups. The acting president is Cushing Dolbeare. One of the board's responsibilities is hiring an executive director to handle day-to-day operations. NLIHC's current executive director is Barry Zigas, who is also one of two part-time lobbyists. NLIHC employs eight professional staff members in its Washington, D.C., office, which opened in 1975.

NLIHC has about 1,100 members, individuals and organizations with a common interest in advocacy, organizing, and education for decent housing for low-income people. Membership dues for individuals range from $10 to $100 and from $25 to $150 for organizations and agencies.

The recent budget of $200,000 came mainly from its annual fund-raiser (30 percent), membership dues (30 percent), contributions from churches, labor, and other organizations (20 percent), and revenues from conferences, conventions, and exhibitions (10 percent).

In 1975, NLIHC created its nonprofit research and education arm (LIHIS), to provide information and technical assistance support to individuals and organizations through a monthly newsletter and special reports on housing issues. NLIHC is supported by subscribers to the information service and corporate and foundation grants.

POLICY CONCERNS AND TACTICS

Policy and priorities are set by the broad-based board of directors representing housing advocates, organizers, tenants, and professionals in the housing field. Providing information is the chief strategy used by NLIHC to influence U.S. housing policy. This includes testifying at congressional hearings, lobbying and supplying information to members of Congress and the administration, and educating the public through press releases and reports. In 1991, NLIHC was successful in ensuring that divorced women applying for federally guaranteed loans are not penalized for the credit problems of their former husbands. NLIHC seeks to make federal and local housing policy gender-sensitive and continues to urge policymakers to pay special attention to the housing needs of low-income women who head households. Such women are jeopardized by their low incomes, by their status as renters rather than owners, and by pervasive discrimination against families with children. One major issue of concern to NLIHC in 1992 was the appropriations battle for full funding of the Home Investment Partnerships program created in the 1990 National Affordable Housing Act and designed to spur affordable housing using matching grants from the federal government to state and local governments.

NLIHC coordinates activities with similar organizations. In 1989, NLIHC joined a homeless activist, the late Mitch Snyder, the American Federation of Labor-Congress of Industrial Organizations,* Young Women's Christian Association,* and more than 200 other organizations in organizing Housing Now, an event in which an estimated 200,000 participants rallied in Washington in

October 1989 to dramatize the plight of homeless people and the growing number of low-income wage earners unable to afford decent housing.

FURTHER INFORMATION

Unlocking the Door: Women and Housing: Report by the Women and Housing Task Force of the NLIHC on the special housing needs of women was published in 1990. In 1980, the coalition published *Triple Jeopardy: A Report on Low Income Women and Their Housing Problems.* The Low Income Housing Information Service publishers *The LIHIS Roundup,* a monthly newsletter covering housing legislation, federal budget analysis, changes in federal housing regulations, and information on housing and community development efforts.

SHIRLEY TOLLIVER GEIGER

NATIONAL MILITARY FAMILY ASSOCIATION (NMF A)
6000 Stevenson Avenue
Alexandria. VA 22304
(703) 823-6632
FAX (703) 751-4857

The National Military Family Association (NMF A) views itself as a military family advocacy group that may include women's issues.

ORIGIN AND DEVELOPMENT

NMF A began in 1969 under the name, National Military Wives Association, when six military wives and widows in Annapolis met to work on survivor benefit plan dependency and indemnity compensation issues. The lack of survivor benefits—especially for widows of retired military men in all branches of services—moved the founders to action.

By the late 1970s, the group expanded into family issues such as child care and relocation. In 1980, two NMF A officers participated in a European base fact-finding tour and wrote a report for the U.S. Defense Department (DOD) Office of Family Policy (OFP). Their ''Final Report: Military Spouse and Family Issues—1982'' convinced them that the organization had import not only for military wives and husbands but also for their families. In 1984, the group took its present name.

NMF A's goals are to educate military and civilian communities about the rights and benefits of military families and their unique lives. These goals have remained constant, although the association has grown through the volunteer work of its committees to include, besides financial development and volunteer service, government relations, public relations, and a representational program.

ORGANIZATION AND FUNDING

NMF A representatives are located in military bases the world over. Rather than have NMF A chapters at these bases, in 1988, the association introduced a representational scheme. There are local, regional, and district representatives as well as representatives in Germany, Spain, and Italy. These volunteers are recruited and asked to give a significant amount of time to their post.

Thirty-one persons—serve on the board of directors, and there are twenty-one women board members. NMF A keeps no figures on the board's racial composition. The association makes every effort to ensure board representation from active duty and retired in all seven services besides reserve units: the army, navy, marines, air force, National Guard, Coast Guard, and National Oceanic and Atmospheric Administration. Board membership is not restricted to military people; civilians have served. Board members are elected by the entire membership for a two-year term and may serve no more than six consecutive years. Board members make a time commitment of thirty hours a week. Margaret Hallgren serves as NMF A president.

The association employs five part-time support staff, including its newsletter editor. Patti Bielik is the executive director, and Sydney Hickey is a registered lobbyist.

Membership is open to military families, and dues are fifteen dollars per year. The dues are kept low so that membership is affordable for enlisted and officers both. In 1994, NMF A had 10,500 members. Between 1985 and 1991, membership figures remained fairly constant at 6,000. The boost in membership is attributed to several factors—organizational outreach, the Desert Storm conflict, and most important, concern about Defense Department budget cutbacks.

The budget for fiscal year 1994 was about $200,000. Almost fifteen years ago the budget stood at $10,000, and in NMF A's early years, it ran between $5,000 and $10,000. As a 501 (c) (3) organization, NMF A has tax-exempt status.

POLICY CONCERNS AND TACTICS

NMF A acts as an advocate for military families at home and abroad. Representatives bring problems to the attention of NMF A staff, who try to get the problem solved on the local level. NMF A prefers to empower families to take care of themselves—to know their rights and benefits. This way NMF A does not take care of the family. The association formulates its action around what the representatives report as issues. The government relations department people decide which are the "burning issues" that call for obtainable changes.

The burning issues that NMF A tackles can vary due to actions by the Congress and DOD. Survivor benefits, the issue around which NMF A began, remains key. Because of defense spending cutbacks, transition benefits for those involuntary separated from military service rank high in importance. Other family-related matters include housing, DOD dependent schools, relocation, and spousal employment. Medical and dental health insurance benefits are an urgent, ongoing concern. NMF A helped get the Active Duty Dependents Plan for military families in 1987 and is working hard to expand this coverage.

Government relations staff volunteers, women and men, testify before congressional committees. Each volunteer has a particular area of expertise. Government relations staff also serve on a DOD OFP subcommittee and on DOD's

Dependent Schools Council. This service helps maintain an NMF A link with the Pentagon.

NMF A does deal with discrimination cases—especially cases of employment discrimination against the nonmilitary spouse. NMF A finds that often these women, and some men, do not know their rights under the law. Often the NMF A role starts when the individual calls the office to ask if a particular request is right. NMF A offers these individuals help and suggestions about how to deal with prospective employers. For example, it is against the law for an employer to ask where the husband or wife not applying for the job is employed.

NMF A works with the twenty-three-member Military Coalition. This coalition comprises the Council of Military Organizations, whose members include career and retired military, and an ad hoc unit that includes all the council plus the veterans' organizations. The Military Coalition was begun in 1985 to fight automatic cuts in military cost of living allotments. Members of the coalition often have divergent political views but work together on issues of common concern. When individual organizations are called to testify before the Congress, the coalition selects two or three skilled persons to speak for it. NMF A does not file court cases and would do so only as part of the Military Coalition.

ELECTORAL ACTIVITIES

NMF A does not have a political action committee. This is a nonpartisan organization. The association does not contribute to political campaigns in any way.

FURTHER INFORMATION

Besides a monthly newsletter, the association publishes fact sheets on topics such as health care. These are available only to members.

MARTHA JOY NOBLE

NATIONAL NETWORK OF HISPANIC WOMEN (NNHW)
P.O. Box 390543
Mountain View, CA 94039
(415) 962-8324
FAX (415) 962-8539

The National Network of Hispanic Women (NNHW) is dedicated to the identification and advancement of outstanding Hispanic women for positions of leadership in the public and private sectors and in civic leadership.

ORIGIN AND DEVELOPMENT

In 1985, NNHW became the first national resource center for Hispanic women. Prior to that time the network—founded in 1980 at Stanford University by Sylvia Castillo under the title of Hispanic Women in Higher Education—functioned as a support group for Hispanic women administrators at California colleges and universities. Fund-raising efforts began to focus on the corporate sector in 1983: initial and continuing board leadership by Celia G. Torres has proved significant in bringing into prominence the Hispanic woman's concerns in the corporate world.

NNHW has come to have a particular appeal to professional women, who typically participate through national and regional roundtable seminars, leadership training forums, network events, and speakers bureaus. The first national roundtables, held in Denver in 1985, and the second, held in Miami in 1987, each drew over 300 Hispanic women. The third, held in Los Angeles in 1989, had over 500 attendees. The 1993 conference in New York focused on "volunteerism and leadership." National and regional roundtables bring together opinion leaders from business, education, government, and the corporate sector to dialogue on trends and events affecting Hispanic women's future leadership and to share resources and skills. Outstanding achievement by Latinas in the areas of community and government service, higher education, and business is recognized through awards presented at the national roundtable.

Transitions, a career training program begun in 1987 for Hispanic women at the undergraduate level with aptitude for careers in business, science, and industry, as well as for graduate study, was an outreach of the 1987 roundtable. The project recruits mentors and participates through NNHW with the intent of encouraging Latinas to finish college and to pursue graduate studies as well as to seek positions in business and the professions.

ORGANIZATION AND FUNDING

NNHW plans to establish chapters in Los Angeles, Chicago, and Texas to provide continuity for its national agenda and to facilitate implementation at the local level. The network presently is structured as a full-time service organization with a volunteer board and a paid executive director located in Los Angeles, California. The eighteen-member board is representative of six regions and four Hispanic subgroups—Mexican American, Cuban, Puerto Rican, and Central American-Caribbean. Celia G. Torres chaired the board of directors.

NNHW has a paid membership of 400.

The nonprofit organization finances itself through members' dues—students, $35; professionals, $50; and corporations, $250—and contributions from corporations and foundations. NNHW has engaged in strategic planning and fundraising to enhance its capacity to meet the objectives identified at national and regional roundtables. Because it does not provide direct assistance programs, it has experienced difficulty securing funding and in 1994 went into hiatus. Activities continue at the regional level, and records are deposited at the California Ethnic and Multicultural Archives at the University of California, Santa Barbara.

POLICY CONCERNS AND TACTICS

No information is available.

ELECTORAL ACTIVITIES

NNHW does not identify its interests as partisan and does not have a political action committee.

FURTHER INFORMATION

NNHW's quarterly publication, *Intercambio,* had a subscription readership of 4,000. Unique in the United States as a magazine by Latinas for Latinas, it helped solidify NNHW by offering a valuable communication link between roundtables and forum for sharing expertise and information.

KAREN M. KENNELLY, CSJ

NATIONAL NETWORK OF WOMEN'S CAUCUSES (NNWC)
530 Broadway
10th Floor
New York, NY 10012
(212) 274-0730

A project of the National Council for Research on Women (NCRW), the National Network of Women's Caucuses (NNWC) provides a space for dialogue among representatives of disciplinary and professional caucuses and committees without the benefit of an ongoing governing body.

ORIGIN AND DEVELOPMENT

NNWC was formed as part of the NCRW in June 1988, at the Spring Hill Center in Wayzata, Minnesota. During this planning meeting, representatives of over forty women's caucuses, committees, and other women's groups in the disciplinary and professional associations met under NCRW's aegis. These groups have been instrumental in advancing the position of women in higher education and in promoting research and data collection on women's issues. Known initially as the National Network of Women's Caucuses and Committees in the Professional Associations, the objectives outlined at that initial meeting sought to advance women's status in the professions, map the substantial growth of feminist research and scholarship in and across disciplinary and professional fields, and link feminist research to international, national, regional, and local policy issues. The first biennial meeting was held in Washington, D.C., in February 1989, with fifty representatives of caucuses, committees, networks, and organizations in attendance.

ORGANIZATION AND FUNDING

NNWC is housed in the offices of NCRW, a national network of organizations formed in 1981 as a clearinghouse to bring institutional resources to bear on feminist research, policy analysis, and educational programs addressing legal, economic, and social inequities. NNWC does not exist as an independent organization, and the administrative functions necessary to maintain its database are provided by NCRW under the leadership of its executive director, Mary Ellen Capek.

NNWC has no membership roll. It is available to representatives of all women's groups within professional associations, learned societies, and other discipline-based or professional women's groups. Through these organizations, members gain access to over 10,000 scholars and practitioners and over 200 discipline-based groups and networks, all working toward women's advancement in the professions and on campus. Membership also includes referrals to resource people with expertise on gender studies and issues affecting women's status in the professions; opportunities for collaborative research and communication; access to interactive networking, policy expertise, and guidelines on such issues as sexual harassment, affirmative action, nonsexist research, and parental leave; and a resource for current feminist materials.

Funding is provided through annual institutional membership fees for NCRW, currently set at $100. NNWC has no separately defined budget.

POLICY CONCERNS AND TACTICS

NCRW has no set policy agenda and, as a nonprofit organization, is precluded from lobbying. A planning committee prepares for meetings and provides a broad-based perspective on policy issues. The committee, through a session on public policy, encourages representatives of the various caucuses, committees, and associations to address policy issues of current concern. Working closely with such organizations as the American Association of University Professors, NNWC provides the opportunity for collective action.

ELECTORAL ACTIVITIES

NNWC has neither a partisan outlook nor a political action committee.

FURTHER INFORMATION

Membership includes a subscription to *Women's Research Network News,* a quarterly newsletter of NCRW that includes a column on the caucuses.

LINDA M. WILLIAMS

NATIONAL NETWORK OF WOMEN'S CAUCUSES AND COMMITTEES IN THE PROFESSIONAL ASSOCIATIONS
See NATIONAL NETWORK OF WOMEN'S CAUCUSES

NATIONAL ORDER OF WOMEN LEGISLATORS (NOWL)
1080 Wisconsin Avenue, NW
Suite 103
Washington, DC 20007
(202) 337-2765
FAX (202) 337-3289

The oldest organization of its kind, the National Order of Women Legislators

(NOWL) seeks to arm its members to be more effective legislators and recruit more women to run for office, regardless of their policy positions, than already do. It has a research and educational foundation.

ORIGIN AND DEVELOPMENT

Julia McClune Emery, a Republican member of the Connecticut legislature (1925–29), founded NOWL in 1938 in Washington, D.C. A Connecticut Order of Women Legislators had formed in 1927; its members found it so useful that they sought to create a similar national organization. A committee of Connecticut women began the process of attempting to identify women state legislators; McClune personally wrote every secretary of state, seeking such women. Despite stymied efforts to locate many legislators. McClune summoned those she did identify to a meeting at Washington's Wardman Park Hotel.

Women attended from Massachusetts, New Jersey, Maryland, Tennessee, Ohio, New Mexico, Colorado, Michigan, Missouri, Utah, and Connecticut. They founded NOWL on the existing Connecticut order's principles. They wanted it to be adamantly nonpartisan as opposed to bipartisan. Its purposes, enshrined in the 1938 bylaws, were threefold: to stimulate a helpful attitude among past, present, and future women state legislators; encourage friendship ties and mutuality among members from state to state; disseminate information; and promote increased public participation and the election or appointment to office of qualified women. NOWL is the only such organization to permit and encourage membership of former as well as sitting members of state legislatures.

The organization's goals of education and training in legislative expertise, encouragement of women's candidacies, and promotion of friendship ties and mutual assistance have not changed from the time of its founding, but they intensified and expanded in anticipation of the 1992 elections, the Year of the Woman.

ORGANIZATION AND FUNDING

NOWL has a seven-member executive board, and a full board of directors of up to twenty-five. Historically, it has had officers ranging from president to historian and parliamentarian, including geographic regional directors. Women are 100 percent of NOWL's officers and board members. Jodi Rell of Connecticut serves as president. For years NOWL did not have a central office or a salaried executive director. The organization operated out of its officers' own personal or legislative space until January 1992, when it opened a Washington office. Robin Read began serving as a salaried executive director in spring 1992. The office now includes seven professional staff, about twenty volunteers, two student interns, and other personnel hired temporarily as particular projects require additional staff.

The core membership of 1,600 includes an active group of former legislators. They help to stabilize the group's size. The organization set annual member dues at $1 in 1938; that figure has increased to $25, and NOWL recently created associate memberships with dues of $125 and corporate membership dues of $3,500–$25,000. Men can and do become associate or corporate members, but the organization is comfortable with remaining predominantly female. Its cultural diversity is dependent on the state legislatures' cultural diversity, and its minority representation is higher than in the population as a whole because of former legislators' continuing activity. U.S. Supreme Court associate justice Sandra Day O'Connor and Harriet Woods, the former Democratic lieutenant governor of Missouri, by virtue of service in their respective state legislatures— O'Connor as Republican majority leader of the Senate in Arizona from 1973 to 1974—have been NOWL members; and all U.S. congresswomen have joined as associate members. Congresswomen also benefit from issue education and play an important mentoring role for state legislators who aspire to national office.

NOWL does not have tax-exempt status. Until recently member dues provided 100 percent of the organization's budget. The annual national meeting has been the group's largest expenditure, but the meeting recently has begun to fund itself. The total budget, including that for the meeting, had grown in 1992 to a projected $400,000. Funding in future years probably will come more frequently from commissioned research than in the past.

NOWL recently has created a 501 (c) (3) tax-exempt foundation, the National Foundation for Women Legislators, for educational and charitable activities. During the course of the year, the foundation concentrates on issue education, with particular emphasis on regions. Thus, the foundation may be running educational programs on health care in one region and on women in business in another or may bring women from several regions together for education on child care legislation.

POLICY CONCERNS AND TACTICS

NOWL takes policy positions only if they are the consensus position of members; in that case, it then attempts to support NOWL members with local press statements and information. Because the group does not lobby per se on policy questions, its interest is in behalf of its members' needs. NOWL primarily educates women legislators to be effective policymakers rather than adopting particular policy agendas. Without a fundamental change in its original nonpartisan orientation, this situation is not likely to change. Nonetheless, elected women tend to be more similar to one another than their partisanship would predict. As a result, in the future, NOWL may take more positions on issues around which members can form a consensus, as already has happened with basic equity questions. The new Washington office, with paid staff and its forays into commissioned legislative research, as well as the projected growth in membership and budget, may make NOWL considerably more visible among women's organizations than it has been in the past.

NOWL judges numerous pieces of legislation to be important to its members; these chiefly include civil rights and equality policies, such as the 1983 Equal

Pay Act and 1964 Civil Rights and Equal Opportunity Acts, and policies of significant benefit to women and children, such as the 1974 Women's Educational Equity Act and 1984 Child Support Enforcement Act.

Because NOWL seeks to support all women legislators, regardless of partisanship or ideology, it has not participated in the informal policy coalition characterizing the women's liberation movement in the last two decades.

ELECTORAL ACTIVITIES

NOWL's nonpartisan status and its mission of support for, and education of, all women legislators, regardless of their policy orientations, obviate most electoral activities.

FURTHER INFORMATION

The group publishes a monthly newsletter called *The Connection.*
                                                    SUE TOLLESON-RINEHART

NATIONAL ORGANIZATION FOR CHANGING MEN
See NATIONAL ORGANIZATION FOR MEN AGAINST SEXISM

NATIONAL ORGANIZATION FOR MEN
See NATIONAL ORGANIZATION FOR MEN AGAINST SEXISM

NATIONAL ORGANIZATION FOR MEN AGAINST SEXISM (NOMAS)
798 Penn Avenue
Box 5
Pittsburgh, PA 15221

The National Organization for Men against Sexism (NOMAS) has a wide range of goals and values devoted to achieving a gender-just society. NOMAS sponsors a wide variety of activities, from publications and conferences to demonstrations and organizations.

ORGANIZATION AND DEVELOPMENT

Men's support of women's struggle for equality has a long, if little known, history. Among its historical forebears are such pro-feminist men in America as Thomas Paine, Robert Dale Owen, Frederick Douglass, William Lloyd Garrison, John Dewey, Alan Alda, and Justice Harry Blackmun. After the beginning of the women's liberation movement, around 1970, explicitly antisexist men's groups and writings began to appear. A national conference on men and masculinity (M&M) was held in Knoxville, Tennessee, organized by male graduate students who had met in a University of Tennessee women's studies class. The next year, Robert Lewis issued a call for the second conference with a set of idealistic themes, including the personal as well as the political, and getting in touch with the strength and beauty of masculine sexuality, nurturance among men, and the experience of brotherhood. This idealism met head-on the realities of sexual politics. Less than a week before the conference began, it was banished from the university campus when an administrator noticed a workshop on homophobia included in the program. It moved to a nearby hotel.

National M&M conferences have been held annually since 1975; and NOMAS also has supported numerous regional and local conferences. In 1982, the antisexist men's movement was formalized as the National Organization for Men (NOM), with Robert Brannon, Bob Morgan, Joseph Pleck, Barry Shapiro, and Nick Tamboriello among the founders. The name later changed to the National Organization for Changing Men (NOCM) because a group supporting men's rights already had begun to use NOM to promote feminist ideas. In 1990, the organization took its current name. Two other groups, the Campaign to End Homophobia and the Men's Studies Association, have evolved from it.

The name changes encapsulated efforts on the part of pro-feminist men to define their politics clearly with regard to women's liberation, men's issues, and gay and lesbian issues. NOCM stressed that its members did not represent all men but rather men involved in a process of change and of promoting change. The direction of change was unclear. NOCM makes clear the organization's commitment to women's equality and its principled stance against sexism. Its coequal principles include full and active support for the feminist movement and women's full equality in all areas; opposition to heterosexism and homophobia, support for full equality for gay men and lesbians; and support and brotherhood with men challenging masculinity's rigid definitions and seeking to live richer, more fully expressive emotional lives. NOMAS also opposes discrimination based on race, religion, size, appearance, physical ability, and other human variations, seeing them as unjust and linked to the inequality intrinsic to patriarchy.

As NOMAS begins its second decade of activism for women's equality, gay and lesbian equality, and changes among men, it faces serious political and organizational tasks. Despite popular opinion, current administrations have eroded institutional supports for equality, including reproductive rights, and failed to respond to national emergencies such as epidemic increases in rape and battery, gay bashing, the AIDS pandemic, and widespread sexual harassment of working women.

ORGANIZATION AND FUNDING

An eighteen-member national council, elected by the membership, in turn elects or appoints members to a large number of leadership roles. All council members, alternates, task group leaders, and other officers are collectively termed the national leadership collective. There are three women and four people of color in the leadership collective, including one of the organization's cochairs; an effort is made to encourage participation on the board of persons from lower-income strata, persons with disabilities, older women, lesbians, and gay men. All the intraorganizational groups meet twice a year, and officers and committees function between meetings. The current chair committee, elected by the council to a two-year term, includes Robert Brannon, Phyllis Frank, and Jim Hannenken.

Substantive issues and activities are assigned to national task groups, which provide an organizational umbrella for the many men nationwide involved in local efforts to work toward social change in gender-related areas, such as counseling batterers, organizing date rape workshops in college dorms, and workshops on sexual harassment in corporations in public sector organizations. There are task groups on men's studies, ending men's violence, homophobia, male-female relationships, fathering, gay rights, spirituality, men and aging, pornography, men's culture, and reproductive rights.

Although an organization *for* men against sexism, NOMAS is not exclusively an organization *of* men. In 1985, it had 500 members; today it has about 1,000. NOMAS always has welcomed women members and included feminist women in its national leadership. Currently, the membership is 5–10 percent female. Provisions encourage the representation of minority members. Conferences, the chance to associate with like-minded individuals, and advocacy of important values provide the most important incentives for membership. Communication and friendship ties also are important. Since 1983, NOMAS officially has co-sponsored the annual M&M conference, which typically draws participants from around the world, with a local planning group.

Membership dues of $35 provide 60 percent of the group's revenues, and conferences, most of the rest. A 501 (c) (3) organization, NOMAS's total budget is approximately $50,000 year.

POLICY CONCERNS AND TACTICS

Policy issues and possible action strategies are raised by the general membership and brought to the national council. The council also generates policy issues for consideration. The spokesperson committee can endorse specific demonstrations or legislative activities in the organization's name. Specific action positions and task groups are organized to focus activities on specific issues; these tasks groups retain organizational autonomy and can initiate actions and strategies on their specific issues. For example, the ending men's violence task group sponsors Brotherpeace, a national day of actions held the third Saturday in October to raise public awareness about men's violence.

NOMAS remains a relatively small organization with an enormous agenda. While it always has been difficult to organize privileged persons to support the rights of persons not privileged, there is a rich legacy of men standing for women's equality, white persons supporting civil rights, and heterosexuals active in the campaign for gay and lesbian rights. Presently, the organization is concerned with a wide range of policies, ranging from parental leave to legislation to protect women's right to choose, including the Freedom of Choice Act; various state bills protecting women from losing custody; and bills on battery, date rape, and marital rape, on protecting gays and lesbians from antigay violence and discrimination, and on promoting safe sex education. NOMAS officially has endorsed a variety of state and federal laws as debated in state and national legislatures.

NOMAS is the official umbrella organization for the Men's Studies Organization, the Campaign to End Homophobia, and Men for Women's Choice. NOMAS collaborates most frequently with such feminist groups as the National Abortion Rights Action League,* National Organization for Women,* and National Women's Political Caucus* and with gay and lesbian organizations. NOMAS considers organizations that promote "men's rights"—such as National Organization for Men, Coalition of Free Men, Men Achieving Liberation and Equality, Men's Rights—as well as those organizations promoting "fathers' rights" and demanding joint custody and the elimination of alimony and child support to be adversaries and considers their underlying philosophy and policy programs to be inimical to implementing an egalitarian society.

ELECTORAL ACTIVITIES

NOMAS does not see the issues that concern it as partisan. It does not have a political action committee.

FURTHER INFORMATION

Two national publications serve the members. *Brother,* a quarterly newsletter, provides current news and notices of organizational issues. The quarterly *Changing Men: Issues in Gender, Sex, and Politics,* founded in 1980, provides full-length articles and first-person narratives as well as regular book reviews. The men's studies task group also publishes a quarterly scholarly journal. *The Men's Studies Review.*

ROBERT BRANNON AND MICHAEL S. KIMMEL

NATIONAL ORGANIZATION FOR NATIVE AMERICAN WOMEN (NONAW)
P.O. Box 7786
Albuquerque, NM 87194
(505) 766-1541

The principal purpose of National Organization for Native American Women (NONAW) is to provide a network for Native American women in the workplace and the academy. The group focuses on developing the professional competencies of Native American women and providing opportunities for them to serve as resources in their communities and to each other.

ORIGIN AND DEVELOPMENT

NONAW was chartered in 1982 in New Mexico as a professionally oriented networking and support group for Native American women from varied fields and backgrounds. It grew out of the U.S. Labor Department's Southwest Regional Task Force for American Indian women, which was headed from 1980 to 1981 by an administrator with the Indian Health Service in Albuquerque, Sophie Atencio of the San Juan tribe. Atencio's involvement with the Labor Department workshops began in the late 1970s after a telephone conversation with Mary Natani of the Oneida tribe in Wisconsin. She asked for Atencio's help in conducting the Labor Department's training workshops to educate North American Indian women about their rights. The workshops focused on the labor market experiences of Indian women as relatively newly paid workers.

Between 1970 and 1980, the percentage of American Indian women over age sixteen in the labor force increased from 35 percent to 48 percent. Despite the increased numbers of these women who were working, in 1979 their poverty rate was nearly three times higher than that of white women, since many Indian women work in low-paying jobs. The professionals participating in the Labor Department training workshops saw a clear need for an organization to give career guidance and advice to Indian women.

In 1982, Atencio joined with Caroline Harris, Indian Affairs Bureau; Clorinda Romera, Personnel Management Office; Julia Claymore, Indian Health Services; Mary Little Zuni, All Indian Pueblo Council; and Ann Kinsel, Indian Affairs Bureau. They first met during the Labor Department workshops. With Claymore serving as acting president, in 1982, NONAW began holding workshops to recruit members. In 1983, the group selected an interim board of directors, including Atencio, a Santo Domingo Pueblo, as president; Mary Little, an Islete Pueblo, as vice president; Ann Kinsel, a Navaho, as secretary; Harris, a Navaho, as treasurer; and Claymore, an Oneida/Choctaw, as public relations officer.

The group's plan was to have a national office in Albuquerque, with state chapters in New Mexico, Colorado, Arizona, Oklahoma, Minnesota, and the District of Columbia. Once established, it planned to target American women in Hawaii, Alaska, and Canada. To date, state chapters have organized in Colorado (1983), New Mexico (1984), and Arizona (date unknown); but the national office is not staffed and operates on a shoestring. Poor finances and vast geographical distances between the tribes and the reservations, coupled with Atencio's resignation to care for her grandchildren following her son's death and Zuni's subsequent transfer to Washington, D.C., left the national office in a state of disarray.

The most viable state chapter today is in New Mexico. It has sustained itself with earnings from bake sales, raffles, and membership dues. The officers of the New Mexico chapter include President Mildred H. Waller.

NONAW serves as a vehicle for organizing American Indian women to share information about educational, training, and career advancement opportunities. It also advocates for the interests of Native American women and their families; educates both Indian women and government officials about public policy issues of concern to these women and their families; and heightens the visibility of, and calls attention to, Native American women's achievements.

ORGANIZATION AND FUNDING

The national office is not operational, although Atencio maintains a strong commitment to its reactivation. When active, the national office is governed by a seven-member executive council consisting of the immediate past presidents of each regional or state chapter. According to the charter, the selection of the chair, vice chair, secretary, and treasurer is the responsibility of the executive council and accomplished at the annual meeting of the council, when functional.

The New Mexico chapter has sixty-five members who pay annual dues of twenty dollars. Members include women from the Pueblo, Navaho, Hopi, Plains, and Alaska Native tribes. Nonvoting associate members and students pay ten dollars annually. Membership in the organization is open to all women and men supporting NONAW's goals and purposes. There are three categories of membership: active members are women eighteen or older listed on the federally recognized tribal rolls; associate members are male or female over eighteen. Indian or non-Indian; and student members are enrolled full- or part-time in an educational institution. Only active members have voting rights and privileges.

Other than early encouragement from the Federal Women's Program, NONAW received no assistance from women's groups and no foundation grants.

POLICY CONCERNS AND TACTICS

Policy is set by consensus among the officers and members. Among NONAW's tactics are holding seminars and conferences; publishing newsletters to disseminate information about jobs, education and training opportunities, and funding; preparing reports and correspondence; testifying at public hearings and providing input to local, state, and federal governmental bodies and nonprofit organizations.

Of particular concern are the problems facing Native American women in rural communities, where the majority (51 percent) of Native Americans live. The rural locales of most Indian reservations generally have depressed economies and, hence, fewer jobs of any kind, especially fewer of the jobs women typically hold in the clerical or services sectors. Indian women living in rural areas experience a higher rate of unemployment than those women living in urban areas and have a lower rate of labor market participation. In many of these rural communities, the greatest issue facing Indian women is simple survival.

The New Mexico chapter is committed to giving more attention to community issues. Last year it became involved with a project of the National Eldercare Institute to address the needs of older Native American women. NONAW's initial role is to gather information about the institute. The organization is also concerned about threats to the stability of Native American families, including fetal alcohol syndrome, the high school dropout rate, gang violence, and the poor quality of the education many Native American Indians receive. In addition, the chapter has advocated for affirmative action programs in Albuquerque and helps sponsor the Albuquerque Human Rights Council annual award. In August 1992, the New Mexico chapter received a grant from the Hardin Fund to conduct a program entitled, "A Forum of Pride: A New Decade of Native American Women."

ELECTORAL ACTIVITIES

NONAW is a professional networking and support organization that has no political action committee.

FURTHER INFORMATION

At the time of this writing, NONAW was not publishing a newsletter.

SHIRLEY TOLLIVER GEIGER

NATIONAL ORGANIZATION FOR PUBLIC HEALTH NURSING
See NATIONAL LEAGUE FOR NURSING

NATIONAL ORGANIZATION FOR WOMEN (NOW)
1000 16th Street, NW
Suite 700
Washington, DC 20036
(202) 331-0066
FAX (202) 785-8576

The most important feminist women's right's association, National Organization for Women (NOW) acts on a wide issue front in government and nongovernment settings. It has a legal defense and education fund (LDEF), an educational and research foundation, and two political action committees.

ORIGIN AND DEVELOPMENT

Founded in the vortex of Betty Friedan's *Feminine Mystique* (1963), the creation of federal (1961) and state (fifty by 1967) commissions on women's status, and prohibition of sex discrimination by the 1964 Civil Rights Act Title VII, NOW represented its founders' desire for action. Seeking a National Association for the Advancement of Colored People (NAACP) for women, probably Dollie Lowther Robinson's suggestion, the twenty-eight founders met in frustration. The third national state commission conference would not resolve that the Equal Employment Opportunity Commission should reappoint a friendly member and implement Title VII.

Friedan, Dorothy Haener of the United Auto Workers Women's Department* (UAW WD) and Pauli Murray, an attorney, organized a meeting on June 20, 1966. Kathryn Clarenbach, Wisconsin Commission* chair, articulated NOW's objective; she and Friedan conceived the name. On October 22, a total of 200 individuals lent their names to NOW's formal launch in Washington, D.C. The statement of purpose provided for "action to bring women into full participation in the mainstream of American society now, exercising all the privileges and responsibilities thereof in truly equal partnership with men.''

Within a year, NOW established local chapters, then regional (1970) and state (1973) structures. After initial reluctance, in 1967, NOW pressured the Congress to introduce the equal rights amendment (ERA). Labor union women such as national secretary-treasurer Caroline Davis left NOW because their unions did not support ERA. NOW moved its office from UAW WD in Detroit to Chicago. When it pushed work-site organizing, and the American Federation of Labor-Congress of Industrial Organizations* resisted, union women formed the Coalition of Labor Union Women.*

In 1967, NOW supported abortion reform; members emphasizing educational and employment opportunities founded Women's Equity Action League* in 1968. NOW had a legal committee. Differences arose over resource allocation and direction. In 1969, two attorneys left, taking two important employment discrimination cases, to found Human Rights for Women. Because NOW's initial tax status forbade endorsing electoral candidates, it facilitated the National Women's Political Caucus* (NWPC) formation in 1971.

Despite conflict, NOW undertook an array of issues such as antiageism, antiracism, antirape reform, credit, developmental child care, educational equity, housing, the masculine mystique, nuclear freeze, poverty abatement, rural feminism, a critique of service-oriented volunteerism, sexuality, opposition to violence against women, and promotion of women through art and sports. National task forces recommended approaches; chapters established task forces as they chose.

From 15 chapters NOW grew to 604 and 40,000 members in 1975, the year it achieved a million-dollar budget. By 1983, the budget had grown six and one-half times, membership six and a quarter times. Besides in fifty states, chapters appeared in Canada, France, Guam, India, Mexico, and the Philippines. Despite bylaws change, the statement of purpose wore well. Twenty-five years later, NOW's goals remained the movement by women into powerful policy-making positions in government, labor, religion, education and media, and education and consciousness-raising.

NOW developed a third goal, a pragmatic format of identifying and mobilizing existing support for equality. The support NOW garnered through changed public opinion helped it to this end. Lobbying centralized decision making. Paid officers spoke for NOW; homemaker Eleanor Smeal became NOW's first paid president in 1975. Added change came with a right-wing backlash. NOW pursued more consciously than before a wide agenda, attacking institutions, for example, by picketing the Vatican Embassy when the pope visited. It redefined the feminist agenda. About reproductive rights, for example, it asked what let women choose to have children. It underwent a perceptual change from anxiety about vulnerability to assertion of strength.

ORGANIZATION AND FUNDING

NOW has 750 chapters in the states, District of Columbia, Britain, Germany, and Japan. There are nine regional councils of state coordinators and national board members. State boards include the coordinator, officers, and chapter representatives. The intermediate structures elect national board members. Board members and officers are women; there are two men state coordinators. One-quarter of the board is African American and Hispanic. Regions not supplying minority board members could lose a seat. Board members from lower-income strata are reimbursed for travel, hotel, and in-home child care. An annual delegate conference elects officers every three years. In 1971, founder Aileen Hernandez became NOW's first and only black president; lawyer Patricia Ireland serves currently. The president, executive and action vice presidents, and secretary lobby.

NOW has offices in Washington, opened in 1973, Boston, Chicago, Los Angeles, and New York City. Most state capitals have one. The Washington office has thirty professional staff and no executive director. In 1980, it hired a lesbian rights staffer and in 1982–85, two minority rights staffers. It has about thirty volunteers and interns. Staff reapply for their positions when officers' terms change and may change jobs at this time. They are eligible for merit increases and may gain expanded responsibility or inclusion in policy-making discussion.

NOW has about 250,000 members. At least 80 percent are women; it actively recruits women of color. Members join to advocate important policies and have their opinions represented to the government.

A 501 (c) (4) organization, NOW gets 60 percent of its financial support from individual gifts or bequests and 25 percent from membership dues, 80 percent of which come with donations. Dues are $25 for the national and about $15 for chapters; there is a sliding scale. Nominal funding comes from publication sales, conferences, and fund-raisers, with less than 3 percent from merchandise sales, insurance sale commissions, and trade unions funds. Decided at the board level, NOW's total budget is $9 million. During Judy Goldsmith's presidency, 1982–85, NOW lost $50,000 a month after ending an ERA direct mail appeal; membership dropped to 140,000. Returning as president in 1985. Smeal negotiated a $2 million loan. NOW went on a cash-and-carry basis; some staff worked six months without pay to help it through the crisis.

Founded in 1986 with 501 (c) (3) status, in 1987, NOW Foundation convened the first women of color and reproductive rights national conference and has funded a series of related regional conferences. It sponsored the 1988 Power through Action: National Lesbian Rights Conference, which developed a national lesbian rights agenda. It also funded an extremely successful young feminist conference and has been doing campus-oriented training workshops to impart organizing and advocacy skills for social change. Its Commission for Responsive Democracy called in 1991 for a new political party; and later,

NOW's national convention voted to support the 21st Century Party's formation in 1992 as the nation's equality party.

Incorporated in 1971 as a 501 (c) (3) organization, NOW LDEF has a New York City office at 99 Hudson Street. Despite a few interlocking board members, NOW LDEF and NOW today are separate organizations. The president of NOW LDEF Board is Phyllis Segal. Directed by Helen Neuborne, LDEF employs twenty-seven staff and has over a $2 million budget. Despite internal pressure, NOW long resisted creating an LDEF like NAACP's. Relying on volunteer counsel and paying out-of-pocket expenses, it hired a staff attorney in 1977. In 1980, LDEF had two staff attorneys, in 1989 five, and in 1992 six, with two in NOW's Washington office. Foundation support has surpassed funding sources such as individual contributions. One former LDEF officer, Marilyn Hall Patel, became a federal judge, and Ruth Bader Ginsburg served on LDEF's National Judicial Education Project.

NOW filed an amicus brief for *Reed* v. *Reed* (1973), argued by the American Civil Liberties Union Women's Rights Project*; the Supreme Court found the Constitution prohibited gender discrimination, a first. In the eighties, LDEF acted as amicus in nearly all major women's rights cases to reach the Court, including *Bowers* v. *Hardwick* (1986), which challenged a state sodomy law.

By 1975, NOW's legal vice president, Judith Lohnquist, had won two cases before the Court. LDEF president Sylvia Roberts and Marguerite Rawalt won *Weeks* v. *Southern Bell* (1975), the first successful Title VII case. Locally, Roberts lost *Johnson* v. *University of Pittsburgh* (1977), a tenure denial case, but applied an injunction innovatively at the pretrial stage. LDEF took several Medicaid abortion cases and in 1978 supported Marguerite Gamble's case against the University of Minnesota Medical School for race and sex discrimination. In 1980, it set up a clearinghouse for state ERA-based cases. Today LDEF litigation emphasizes employment, pension rights, insurance, and family issues such as lesbian mother custody.

In 1974, with Ford and Carnegie Foundation grants and Women's Educational Equity Act funding, Holy Knox founded NOW LDEF's Project on Equal Education Rights (PEER) to advocate for women and girls in elementary and secondary schools. The U.S. Health, Education and Welfare Department's (HEW) failure to issue Title IX regulations stimulated PEER's organization. A PEER report demonstrated graphically the HEW Office for Civil Rights' failure to respond to sex discrimination charges. PEER played a major role in the coalition to enforce Title IX. During the seventies and early eighties, PEER had state projects in Connecticut, Michigan, and Wisconsin. It also distributed a local action kit. After 1983 it shifted attention to issues such as pregnant teenagers and dropout prevention, math and science, and computer education. In 1989, it moved from its own Washington office to LDEF's New York one. Walteen Grady Truly now serves as its chief executive officer. The main source of funding for the project's $300,000 budget is LDEF. PEER in 1992 continues to work toward educational equity, K–12, in public schools. One current emphasis is the education of adolescent mothers with assistance sought from the 1988 Family Support Act.

POLICY CONCERNS AND TACTICS

The national board both makes policy and implements that set by the national conference. Executive officers' decisions contribute to policy discussion. Strategy to achieve NOW's agenda depends on perceptions of what will successfully lower barriers to it. NOW seeks creative ways to make issues credible, considers activists' comfort levels, and analyzes constituent groups for mobilization.

Favored strategies include monitoring elected officials' votes, educating members and promoting letter writing, educating the public through press releases, participating in direct action and political demonstrations, and conducting public relations and public service campaigns. NOW's impressive direct action record began early. By July 9, 1978, to persuade the Congress to extend ERA's ratification period, NOW led one of the largest Washington marches ever. Its highly visible public education campaigns also began early; and in 1973, NOW LDEF sponsored a $3 million nationwide public service advertising campaign conducted by the Advertising Council. In 1981, NOW undertook an ambitious ERA media campaign featuring Lily Tomlin and Alan Alda, among others.

NOW testifies to the Congress and state legislators, supplies legislators and staff with information, and personally presents arguments to legislators, agency heads, and staff. Policymakers seek NOW's views. In 1967, it persuaded President Johnson to amend the affirmative action executive order to include sex, and in 1968–73 it won several battles to defeat sex-segregated help wanted ads. National and local media reform task forces won many skirmishes, 1972–77. In 1975, written comments on proposed nondiscrimination amendments to revenue-sharing legislation received the Treasury Department's high praise; but during congressional Title IX hearings the education and women and sports task forces gave opposed testimony. Consolidation in the Washington office in 1976 relieved the problem. In 1975, the national conference voted to apply 1 percent of the national budget to lesbian rights; in 1977, NOW led the Houston National Women's Conference to make sexual preference a priority.

NOW increasingly turned resources to ERA, having created a national strike force in 1977 and begun annual ERA walks in 1978, and staved off an effort to have the extension it had proposed found unconstitutional. It successfully resisted charges it had violated the Sherman Antitrust Act by boycotting unratified states. In 1982, ERA failed three states short of ratification.

In 1986, NOW issued a Bill of Rights calling for ERA, enforcement of employment law banning sex discrimination, maternity leave rights, a working parent's tax deduction for home and child care expenses, child care centers, an end to education discrimination, antipoverty measures, reproductive rights, equal access to public accommodations and housing, and partnership marriages of equal rights and shared responsibility. In 1990, anticipating the twenty-first century, it expanded this Bill of Rights.

NOW supported the 1988 Civil Rights Restoration Act, 1990 Victims Services and Protection Compliance bill, 1991 Civil Rights Act, and Family and Medical Leave and Violence against Women bills. It opposed Judge Thomas's appointment to the Supreme Court—and Judge Bork's Judge Stevens's, William Rehnquist's, and Judge Carswell's; it supported Judge O'Connor's appointment. For years it has worked against the marriage tax and for child support enforcement, but not at the expense of privacy for women receiving welfare. It opposes pregnant women's preferential treatment and surrogate parenting for profit. NOW sees lesbian rights as central to action since *Webster* (1989) expanded state authority to regulate abortion. The Washington office sued Project Rescue* successfully as part of NOW's resolution to keep abortion clinics open; the Supreme Court delayed until after the 1992 elections its unfavorable ruling on *Bray, Operation Rescue et al.* v. *Alexandria Women's Health Clinic, NOW et al.*

NOW has coordinated with, to name a few groups, Planned Parenthood* and National Abortion Rights Action League* since 1970; NWPC since 1972; American Association of University Women,* League of Women Voters,* and National Federation of Business and Professional Women's Clubs,* particularly since 1976; National Black Women's Health Project* since 1985. In 1971, NOW joined the Leadership Conference for Civil Rights; in 1974 it supported the National Welfare Rights Organization* and, at Congresswoman Shirley Chisholm's (D-NY) bidding, the coalition that helped expand the Fair Labor Standards Act to domestic workers. In 1977, NOW participated in the Minority Caucus at the Houston conference. In 1981, it joined the National Anti-Klan Network. On teen pregnancy NOW has worked with the Children's Defense Fund,* National Council of Negro Women,* Young Women's Christian Association,* Delta Sigma Theta,* and Urban League.* NOW's adversaries include the National Council of Catholic Bishops, television evangelicals and their followers, Eagle Forum,* and Chamber of Commerce.

ELECTORAL ACTIVITIES

NOW sees women's issues as partisan. Much to NWPC's disappointment, NOW/Equality/PAC, formerly NOW/ERA/PAC, registered in 1977, and NOW/PAC registered in 1982. There also are forty state and local PACs. NOW/Equality/PAC does not fund federal races. Since the PACs cannot duplicate contributions, NOW/PAC would not act to fund major electoral contests unless a local welcomed the action; it makes both federal and state endorsements because of restrictions in some state electoral laws. NOW's PAC money mostly comes from direct mail solicitation, but funding strategy includes the telephone and national conference fund-raising. NOW might invite independent PACs to fund-raisers. It meets monthly with a progressive PAC network; political director Alice Cohan calls together a group of women's PACs informally. NOW's PACs also work with the Democratic National Committee* and National Committee for an Effective Congress. They stay in touch with constituents by newsletter.

Given a choice, NOW's PACs would prefer open-seat candidates but do not prefer incumbents over challengers. NOW/PAC funds congressional races and endorsed Walter Mondale for U.S. president but not Jimmy Carter, who opposed abortion. During the last several cycles, almost all its candidates were women. Office staff and the PAC board together choose national candidates; state and local PACs advise. Candidates must support ERA and abortion with no contingencies of age or money. They support civil, including lesbian and gay, rights. There also is a butter-versus-guns issue because, for NOW, military budget size relates to poverty's feminization. These criteria have limited the PAC's chance to endorse Republican women supporting ERA and abortion alone.

In 1991, NOW introduced a WomenElect 2000 project in Louisiana, the state with the fewest women (three) in its legislature. Equality/PAC coordinated a WomenElect 2000 PAC in New Orleans to recruit and train staff and political consultants to impact on over two dozen candidates; nine were elected.

In 1992, NOW PAC endorsed 132 women and men candidates. Sixty-six were elected, exactly half of them women.

FURTHER INFORMATION

NOW publishes a newsletter, *National NOW Times,* six times yearly. In 1974 its first national publication was translated into Spanish. Three to four times yearly NOW publishes research reports. For small fees, the national office has action handbooks and chapter resource kits.

SARAH SLAVIN

NATIONAL ORGANIZATION FOR WOMEN—CALIFORNIA (CANOW)
926 J Street
Suite 523
Sacramento, CA 95814
(916) 442-3414
FAX (916) 442-6942

The largest feminist women's rights association in the state, California National Organization for Women (CANOW) acts on a broad range of women's rights issues. Since 1981, it has had a political action committee, California NOW PAC, and places primary emphasis on electoral politics and legislative strategies in its promotion of women's rights.

ORIGIN AND DEVELOPMENT

CANOW, a state chapter of National Organization for Women* (NOW), with its central office in the state capital of Sacramento, began in 1971 in Los Angeles during NOW's fifth national conference. CANOW's establishment anticipated the need to lobby intensively for the equal rights amendment (ERA) passage by the California legislature. Eva Norman, the first state coordinator, led the chapter in the initial membership drives, which eventuated in forming fifteen local chapters, and in its successful effort to persuade legislators to adopt ERA, November

13, 1972. CANOW member Tony Caravello was instrumental in drawing the attention of Eleanor Smeal, then NOW president, to the concept of an ERA extension. Drawing on the work of law students and CANOW members Alice Bennett and Catherine Timlin, whose 1977 research demonstrated a difference between the equal rights and other amendments on which a time limit had been imposed, Caravello and Smeal gave the documentation to U.S. congresswoman Elizabeth Holtzman. Subsequent congressional action extending the time limit for ERA passage derived from this effort.

State CANOW board leadership was instrumental in persuading NOW to promote the Alice Doesn't Strike campaign in the midseventies. Modeled after the 1970 Alice Doesn't Strike, the California-inspired campaign had its greatest impact on the West Coast.

ORGANIZATION AND FUNDING

CANOW has remained a grassroots organization over the years. A board composed of the state coordinator and other state officers, six affirmative action delegates, and representatives from the forty-five state chapters determines the state conference agenda. This conference elects state officers and at-large delegates to the national conference. Typically, state board membership is 95 percent women, predominantly white (85 percent) but with small numbers of African Americans, Hispanics, and Asian Americans. The board manages CANOW's affairs and funds, subject to state conference decisions and the national board's purposes and policies. An executive committee is empowered to take emergency action between board meetings. Issue and administrative committees are used by both the conference and board for planning and implementation purposes. Linda Joplin serves as the state coordinator. The state chapter is headed by a full-time paid director, Joplin, assisted by a small staff and volunteers. CANOW employs the state's only independent full-time lobbyist concerned with broad-spectrum feminist issues and uses an affiliated foundation to accommodate desired political activities for the tax-exempt parent organization.

Membership in this mainly women's organization has been sensitive to abortion issues, the most dramatic sign of which is the membership increase from 25,562 (1985) to 43,295 (1990), or 17 percent of NOW's total membership, in the wake of a perceived threat to *Roe* v. *Wade*. CANOW is the largest of the state organizations in NOW, and the Los Angeles chapter the largest within the state.

A current annual budget of $190,000 comes principally from dues of $15 to $40 for individuals (60 percent of total revenues), gifts and bequests (20 percent), and special fund-raising events (20 percent). CANOW has tax-exempt 501 (c) (4) status and also has an affiliated foundation.

POLICY CONCERNS AND TACTICS

Policies established by NOW bind CANOW. An annual statewide general membership conference adopts policies and program priorities at the state level.

The state chapter has been a prime mover and advocates a range of issues pertaining to women's civil rights, including, but not confined to, reproductive rights. Strategies that CANOW considers most important in influencing public policies include testifying at state legislative hearings, supplying legislators with information, commenting on proposed regulations, encouraging members to write legislators, issuing press releases, taking direct action, and demonstrating.

CANOW takes major credit for passage in 1974 of the first bills treating rape as a serious criminal offense and halting psychological abuse of rape victims on the witness stand and cosponsored California's Title IX Educational Equity law in 1981. It backed a subsequently vetoed bill prohibiting employers and landlords from arbitrary discrimination because of sexual orientation and lobbied successfully for selection of a woman vice presidential candidate in 1984.

CANOW consistently has expressed through public stands and activities its opposition to pro-life groups and support for abortion rights. The state chapter was a major force in defeat of mandatory parental consent legislation in 1986. In 1988, it lobbied successfully in the State Assembly for Medi-Cal funding for abortion services but lost in budget negotiations between the Senate and the Assembly.

Issues cited throughout the 1980s as of continuing concern besides reproductive rights include working women's low wages, inadequate child care, most retired women's lack of pension or retirement plan income, the disproportionate number of women among elderly poor people, and failure to enforce child support laws. An emerging issue is gender disparity on boards and commissions.

CANOW collaborates with similar organizations such as the California Coalition for Reproductive Freedom (Pro-Choice), California Civil Rights Coalition, Family Equity Coalition, and the Women Family and Work Coalition. Organizations prominent in opposition to CANOW include the National Right to Life Committee,* Operation Rescue,* and the Women's Lobby.

ELECTORAL ACTIVITIES

A PAC registered in 1981 as California NOW PAC (CANOWPAC). Direct mail solicitation is used exclusively for PAC fund-raising purposes. In 1989–90, $42,000 was contributed to candidates. CANOWPAC shares information on candidates chiefly through the Women's Political Summit, a California networking group of women's PACs.

FURTHER INFORMATION

CANOW publications include *The California NOW News,* a biennial publication; *The Activist,* a legislative newsletter; *The LA Times,* for Los Angeles chapter membership; *Action Bulletin,* for Los Angeles chapter membership; ad hoc mailings; a newspaper before primary and general elections; *Highlights of CANOW History; CANOW 15th Anniversary Letter;* and Tony Caravello, *25 Years of NOW* (which traces development of feminist movement in NOW).

KAREN M. KENNELLY, CSJ

NATIONAL ORGANIZATION FOR WOMEN FOUNDATION
See NATIONAL ORGANIZATION FOR WOMEN

NATIONAL ORGANIZATION FOR WOMEN LEGAL DEFENSE AND EDUCATION FUND
See NATIONAL ORGANIZATION FOR WOMEN

NATIONAL ORGANIZATION FOR WOMEN—NEW YORK CITY (NYCNOW)
15 West 18th Street
9th Floor
New York, NY 10011
(212) 989-7230
FAX (212) 727-1961

Twenty-six years after its founding, National Organization for Women—New York City (NYCNOW) remains a leader in the fight against women's oppression. Using a multitude of tactics—from rallies and demonstrations to press conferences and electoral work through a political action committee (PAC)—the group has mobilized city residents successfully in support of such issues as reproductive choice, lesbian and gay rights, research on women's health issues, and egalitarian marital relations.

ORIGIN AND DEVELOPMENT

Within eight months of National Organization for Women's* (NOW) founding on June 30, 1966, local chapters began springing up. Muriel Fox, a NYC-NOW founder and national NOW board member, remembers sending postcards to members of national NOW residing in the New York metropolitan area and having seventy-five women and men from a three-state area show up for a house meeting. The meeting lasted four hours and covered many issues: the need to write restrictions against sex discrimination into the New York Constitution; the need for child care centers; the fact that Mayor John Lindsay's administration included no women in top posts; discrimination against women in employment, by religious institutions, and antipoverty programs; and sex-segregated listings in the help wanted ads in local papers.

National founder Betty Friedan chaired the meeting. Attending were such notables as attorney/activist Florynce Kennedy; historian Gerda Lerner; sports writer Bud Greenspan, a legislative aide to then Congressperson Ed Koch; and state lawmakers Shirley Chisholm and Constance Cook.

Within NYCNOW's first year, committees formed and consciousness-raising groups organized. Jean Faust was elected the group's first president in February 1967. It was a beginning both productive and conflict-laden. Tension between radical and establishment members grew, reaching a peak during an election for chapter officers held in October 1968. The chapter's second president, Ti Grace

Atkinson, and Flo Kennedy left afterward to form New York Radical Feminists, taking some NYCNOW members with them.

Although many members of the chapter felt disheartened by the split, a nearly simultaneous victory bolstered morale. The *New York Times* agreed to stop listing jobs by gender and to run a generic "help wanted" section instead. Members had picketed the paper and pressured the publisher to bring about this change. The matter concluded, attentions turned to developing a political base and strengthening the chapter.

The question of political direction was an extremely contentious one within the chapter. Yet it was not the only contentious issue. Some women feared that raising the subject of abortion would alienate mainstream members. Then, by the early 1970s, debate over whether lesbian liberation was a legitimate feminist issue threatened to fracture the group. Friedan resisted incorporating the fight against homophobia and heterosexism into NYCNOW's agenda; and the group became extremely polarized, with acrimonious debate and accusations coming from both sides. Although both the chapter and national NOW articulated a principled pro-lesbian and gay position by the mid-1970s, early fights over the issue made 1970–74 a particularly difficult time. Since so many NYCNOW members were lesbians, a sense of personal as well as political betrayal made it impossible for many activists to work with Friedan and her supporters.

Nonetheless, the group continued to function, producing some heady successes. On August 26, 1970, a NYCNOW-organized Women's Equality Day march brought more than 25,000 protesters into the streets to demand justice and fairness. Over the next three years many favorable changes in public opinion took place; the emergence of a national lesbian/gay presence that followed the 1969 Stonewall Rebellion in New York City made it possible for lesbians to feel more comfortable about coming out within both the chapter and the larger women's liberation movement. Phyllis Schlafly seemed an anachronism as many heterosexual feminists became, for the first time, conscious of sexual preference issues and aware of the heterosexual privilege they chose to take advantage of. Even Friedan was forced to concede that she had erred earlier in trying to exclude lesbian rights from a feminist agenda.

Despite the momentum and widespread belief that anything was possible, problems and differences continued to plague NYCNOW. Membership turnover was constant and contributed to organizational chaos. Red baiting, homophobia, and arguments over the nuances of feminist ideology divided members. Things began to quiet down by 1975, when the group rationalized its bylaws and clarified the chapter president's power over day-to-day affairs. The newfound calm also reflected national trends and sweeping local political currents. Professional women's organizations attracted the most conservative of city activists. As the demise of virtually every radical feminist organization gave way to cultural feminism, many of the area's most stalwart participants went off to form women-only collectives. Women diffused into a whole series of groups; NYC-NOW became more cohesive and homogeneous than ever. As a result of women splitting off from NYCNOW, those who remained were able to push, loudly and clearly, for an action agenda.

By 1976, NYCNOW was heavily involved in the national push for an equal rights amendment (ERA). Members also immersed themselves in a statewide push for ERA passage in the state legislature. The group's other committees continued to focus on a range of feminist issues: consciousness-raising, abortion and reproductive rights, education, employment, family relations, lesbian rights, media reform, midlife and older women's integration, and political action. With the exception of the concerted push for ERA, the same issues that galvanized members then still predominate. During the late 1980s and early 1990s a multicultural issues committee brought the fight against racism to the forefront of NYCNOW's efforts. At the present time the committee's work has been integrated into the efforts of other standing committees.

While conflicts between chapter members have a long history, enmity between NOW and NYCNOW also has limited local effectiveness. Some of the ill will is historical, based on resentment that women such as Friedan and Fox dominated the national group's early work. NYCNOW also supported both Mary Jean Collins and Judy Goldsmith against Eleanor Smeal (and Noreen Connell against Molly Yard) for the national presidency in three different races. The division between Collins and Smeal was long-standing, part of a situation that had divided national officers and board members since 1974. At that time Collins belonged to a leadership faction affected by a dues strike by some state chapters, including NYCNOW.

A walkout during a national board meeting by a minority of officers and board members, calling themselves the Majority Caucus, was directed at Collins's faction. Smeal associated with the caucus, which called for decentralizing NOW. Subsequently, Smeal became a centrist, interested in building a strong national organization. Goldsmith supported a decentralized NOW in which chapters would have maximum leeway to determine their own direction and agenda. Eventually, Goldsmith served one term as national president but lost her reelection bid to Smeal. For several years NYCNOW found itself frozen out by the national NOW power structure.

To an extent this rift has begun to heal. In 1991, the national NOW conference was held in New York City, and no public antagonism was visible. Patricia Ireland, a former vice president and then president-elect, is credited by NYCNOW's current staff with improving communications between the chapter and the national office. While some unease is still evident, a spirit of cooperation has taken hold, and the two groups work reasonably well together.

ORGANIZATION AND FUNDING

Part of New York State NOW, NYCNOW participates in a regional grouping and helps elect regional representatives to the national board. A twenty-member board of directors, which meets monthly, governs NYCNOW. All meetings are open to the full membership. Each committee has a representative on the board, along with the director of membership recruiting and processing, director of programs, the archivist, administrative staff director, newsletter editor, and speakers bureau coordinator. Presently, the board is 90 percent white, 5 percent Latina, and 5 percent Asian American. An executive committee—the president, three vice presidents, secretary, treasurer, and board chair—makes emergency decisions. Diane Welsh, a volunteer, is the elected president of NYCNOW. The chapter office has four paid staff members; and approximately 100 volunteers assist.

Boasting 10,000 dues-paying members and supporters, the NYC chapter is the largest in the country. The chapter's membership has grown significantly over its twenty-six-year history. In the 1970s, membership fluctuated between 2,000 and 4,000. Since 1980, it has climbed from 7,000 to its current 10,000 plus. The membership is mostly white, but the U.S. Supreme Court *Webster* v. *Reproductive Health Services* decision (1990) encouraged a noticeable number of women of color to become chapter members. Ninety percent of the membership is female, down from 99 percent in 1970 and 95 percent in 1980. Members join NYCNOW for a variety of reasons; political outrage, the desire to advocate feminist issues, interest in pressuring the government and participating in public affairs, and the need to associate with like-minded people. Some join to get access to information or develop organizational skills.

The annual budget, not including a service fund, runs between $300,000 and $400,000 a year. Approximately 10 percent of the budget is raised through membership dues. The budget has more than doubled in the last decade from less than $150,000 in 1980. Other than the revenue raised by dues, revenue comes from an evening telephone bank; people are telephoned and solicited for contributions. The phone banking is issue-linked and is NYCNOW's primary funding source, netting approximately one-third of the annual budget. Street fairs, tabling, house parties, and contributions by individual donors bring in added moneys.

While much of the chapter's work involves advocacy of women's rights and activism on behalf of feminism, NYCNOW, a 501 (c) (4) organization, also runs two service fund projects that address women's material needs. A Women's Helpline operates during the business week and provides between 1,000 and 1,200 women a month with information and referrals. Requests often center on the need for an attorney to help with problems such as divorce, child custody, domestic violence, sexual harassment, and discrimination in employment. Founded in 1981, Helpline is a 501 (c) (3) organization.

NYCNOW also runs a not-for-profit Direct Marketing Training Program (DMTP), a seventeen-week, full-time course for economically disfranchised women. The program teaches twenty women during a cycle the skills they need to obtain clerical work in the direct marketing field. Funded by the Job Training Partnership Act of New York City at $200,000 a year, the program is open to women whose household income is below $9,000. The chapter chose this program because of its availability to women with no college and its promise of upward mobility.

POLICY CONCERNS AND TACTICS

When NYCNOW decides to become active on an issue, it formulates strategies that incorporate educating, advocating, and changing policy. This may involve sending a mailing to members, organizing an action, leafleting, phone banking, lobbying for legislative change on a particular bill, or testifying at state or city hearings. Although NYCNOW does not have a paid lobbyist (New York State NOW does), it goes to the state capital as needed to pressure lawmakers on bills of interest.

NYCNOW also gets involved in litigation, sometimes adding its name as a friend of the court and other times litigating in its own right to stop discrimination or misogyny. In *NOW et al.* v. *NYC Police Department et al.,* the chapter won a precedent-setting victory that gives all groups the right to hold protests on the steps of City Hall. In addition, NYCNOW has joined the American Civil Liberties Union* (ACLU), National Abortion Rights Action League* (NARAL), Planned Parenthood of NYC, and the National Association for Reform of Marijuana Laws in pushing for the right to table at concerts held at the Jones Beach Outdoor Amphitheater.

A plethora of legislative arenas concerns NYCNOW members: equal pay equity, civil rights, voting rights, affirmative action, equal employment, reproductive rights, equal access to credit, bills to benefit indigent persons, child support enforcement, pension equity, and educational opportunities.

On the local level, members have been involved in the efforts to get the city to pass a domestic partnership bill and set up a functioning Civilian Complaint Review Board. On the state level, chapter members work to defeat parental consent and notification bills and in support of divorce law reform. They also have worked for federal passage of the Reproductive Health Equity Act, Freedom of Choice Act, and antiviolence bills proposed by Senator Joseph Biden (D-DE) and then-congressperson Barbara Boxer (D-CA). NYCNOW's newsletter and phone bank project publicize bills of interest to members; and they are urged regularly to write letters, make calls to their representatives, and attend rallies, speak-outs, and marches.

NYCNOW often works in coalition with NARAL, ACLU, and the Center for Constitutional Rights. It has an adversarial relationship with the Archdiocese of New York, National Right to Life Committee,* and Operation Rescue.*

ELECTORAL ACTIVITIES

NYCNOW does not believe that women's issues are partisan. It has a WomanPower PAC; the PAC's main purpose is to increase issue visibility. Founded in 1982, WomenPower PAC endorses only local candidates; rarely does it support candidates for national office. It does phone banking and Election Day palm carding. In mid-1990 the PAC had $750 in tow, most of it raised through face-to-face encounters with members and supporters. Donors may ear-mark their contributions. The PAC has no staff of its own; volunteers coordinate the PAC's work.

In its first year, WomenPower PAC raised and spent $2,300. In 1984, $1,500 was distributed. Current New York City mayor David Dinkins received several thousand dollars from the PAC in his November 1989 bid for office. In one of the most charged electoral battles of 1992, NYCNOW elected to follow the precedent set by national NOW, endorsing the primary bids of both Geraldine Ferraro and Elizabeth Holtzman against Republican incumbent Alfonse D'Amato.

To qualify for an endorsement, candidates must support abortion rights, in-cluding Medicaid funding, and oppose parental consent/notification. They also must support pay equity, efforts to include more women in construction ap-prenticeship programs, decent wages and benefits for home health workers, ex-panded availability of affordable child care, domestic partnership laws, and Family Court reform. The organization expresses no preference for Republicans or Democrats, incumbents or challengers. All things being equal, it prefers sup-porting liberal women for elected office.

NYCNOW shares information about candidates with NARAL and Citizen's Action and disseminates data on candidates to members via its bimonthly news-letter. Periodically it sponsors candidates' forums for lengthy discussions of issues and public policies.

FURTHER INFORMATION

NYCNOW publishes a bimonthly tabloid newsletter, *NOW-NYC News*.

ELEANOR J. BADER

NATIONAL RIGHT TO LIFE COMMITTEE (NRLC)
419 7th Street, NW
Suite 500
Washington, DC 20004-2293
(202) 626-8800
FAX (202) 737-9189

The National Right to Life Committee (NRLC) seeks equal protection under the law for humans from the beginning of conception of biological life until natural death and opposes abortion, infanticide, and euthanasia. It has a General Counsel's Office (GCO), a political action committee (PAC), and an educational and research foundation.

ORIGIN AND DEVELOPMENT

NRLC organized formally in June 1973 in direct response to *Roe* v. *Wade* (1973). Thirty-five state and city-level grassroots right to life organizations met in Detroit to form the national. The founding leaders included John C. and Barbara H. Willke from Cincinnati; Marjorie Mecklenburg of Minneapolis, the chairman of the board; Kenneth Vanderhoef, a Seattle lawyer; Edward Golden of Albany, New York; Judy Fink of Pittsburgh; and Mildred Jefferson of Boston. The founders did not know each other from other organizational contexts. NRLC received some of its first funds from the sale of identification bracelets for the unborn child, a fund-raiser patterned after prisoner-of-war bracelets then available. John Willke served as NRLC president for almost ten years. NRLC's third president, Jefferson, is an African American woman.

The group is a single-issue group focusing on abortion. This basic orientation has not changed over time. NRLC opposes euthanasia and infanticide. It is largely a voluntary organization. In response to criticism that the pro-life movement only cares about life before birth, local chapters now engage in counseling and give some aid to the troubled pregnant woman.

ORGANIZATION AND FUNDING

NRLC has state chapters in every state and the District of Columbia and more than 3,000 local chapters. It does not have a delegate assembly. The state organizations elect fifty of the board directors. One additional director comes from the District of Columbia. There also are three at-large directors elected by popular membership ballot. Presently, there is one black person on the board; and women make up 75 percent of board members. The organization is divided into four departments: education, legislative, news, and public relations. The board elects a nonsalaried president to a two-year term; Wanda Franz is the current president.

The national office is located in Washington, D.C. There are also a large, all-purpose office in Sacramento, California, and two satellite offices. The Alton, Illinois, office concentrates on development; and the South Bend, Indiana, office on voter identification. Executive director of the Washington office is David O'Steen. NRLC employs sixty professional staff nationally, forty-five in Washington. There are fifteen volunteers and interns in the Washington office at any given time. Employees take a fixed level of responsibility and do not rotate jobs; ability is rewarded with raises, advancement, and increased responsibility. Three persons in the organization hold the job title "lobbyist." However, all of the board members engage in lobbying. NRLC has an attorney on retainer, as does GCO.

NRLC is a white-majority organization. Women constitute 75 percent of the membership. There are estimated to be close to 500,000 dues-paying members. The local affiliates keep the dues of fifteen dollars per person and maintain membership. Members join to advocate important values or policies and represent their opinions to government. NRLC publications and information also work as incentives for them.

NRLC is a 501 (c) (4) tax-exempt organization. Ninety to 95 percent of its revenues come from direct mail solicitation of nonmembers and membership dues. The national organization receives almost no money from churches, but some state chapters receive some church funds. In the past, the Catholic Church has provided funds. The 1990 budget was about $12 million, twenty-four times the 1980 budget.

The NRLC GCO is headed by general counsel James Bopp, Jr., of Terre Haute, Indiana. Its activities are funded by the National Right to Life Educational Trust Fund. In 1990–91, GEO's legal involvement included six amicus curiae briefs, five scholarly articles, one lawsuit, and one legal analysis. All but one of these amicus briefs dealt with abortion cases; the other dealt with state guardianship laws. One lawsuit was conducted in 1990–91 and was funded by the Educational Trust Fund. The case, *Boley* v. *Miller,* was a suit to prevent West Virginia from expending money to fund abortions not permitted by the Hyde amendment. The general counsel suit was successful in *Boley.* The general counsel also filed amicus briefs in *Webster* v. *Reproductive Health Services* (1989), upholding the restrictive Missouri abortion control statue, and *Cruzan* v. *Missouri* (1990), upholding the state of Missouri's claim that the family of Nancy Cruzan (injured in a car accident and long comatose) could not instruct medical personnel to cease the intervention measures, that is, enteral therapy, that kept Nancy alive.

NRLC has an educational and research foundation, the National Right to Life Educational Trust Fund. In 1991, Geline B. Williams of Richmond, Virginia, served as chairman of the board, Willke as president, and Franz as trustee. The trust fund is located at 419 7th Street, NW., Suite 500, Washington, D.C. 20004. In 1990–91, the trust fund distributed over 341,000 pamphlets and videotapes in response to some 1,591 orders and also sent out more than 3,800 packets to students, educators, medical professionals, and members of the general public requesting information. The trust fund fosters efforts overseas to combat abortion, infanticide, and euthanasia through financial support from International Right to Life Foundation (IRLF). In 1990–91, one crucial concern for international efforts was research, speeches, and publications opposing the French abortion pill, RU 486.

POLICY CONCERNS AND TACTICS

The board of directors makes policy decisions. NRLC is pragmatic; it accepts such compromises as exceptions for rape or incest in proposed abortion policy. Other pro-life organizations such as the American Life League* have criticized NRLC for such flexibility. As a more or less single-issue group, it draws advantage from concentrating all its resources on abortion, infanticide, and euthanasia. It takes no religious stance and no position on birth control and does not work with groups such as Operation Rescue. The board of directors influences the choice of strategies to achieve the policy agenda. Preferred tactics include demonstrations on the yearly anniversary of the *Roe* decision, a speakers bureau, training in the effective use of photographs and visual aids to dramatize points, endorsement of antiabortion candidates and opposition to pro-choice ones, award presentations to NRLC's friends, testimony before congressional and state legislative committees, lobbying legislative committees, monitoring elected officials' voting records, and engaging in court cases involving abortion as either the primary litigants or amicus curia. NRLC also has sought the passage and ratification of a human life constitutional amendment (HLA), which allows exceptions to save the life of the pregnant women. It has kept its distance from groups such as Operation Rescue that engage in civil disobedience. It does not participate in actions like clinic blockades.

NRLC was active in *Cruzan* v. *Missouri Department of Health* (1990), involving the "right to die" of a permanently comatose woman, Nancy Cruzan. NRLC filed an amicus brief and held several press conferences concerning the case. Cruzan's family sought to discontinue the medical treatment of enteral feedings, which kept her alive. The state of Missouri maintained that the family did not have the authority to stop the treatment. NRLC supported Missouri. NRLC argued for the right to life of handicapped and disabled persons, critiqued the euthanasia aspects of the case, and warned of a killer ethic being promulgated by the courts. NRLC sees a connection to abortion politics in "right to die" cases, in the tensions between the individual's right to privacy and the state's interest in protecting life.

Public policymakers regularly and frequently come to NRLC for its views. Besides *Roe,* federal policies most important to NRLC include the equal rights amendment, which it opposed, and the Hyde amendments and proposed HLA. It generally supported the 1978 Pregnancy Disability Act, the Women, Infants, and Children (WIC) program, and related programs. Over the last decade, it has found most important, besides the Hyde amendment, the Mexico City policy that forbade federal aid to programs including abortion options, the Reagan administration's domestic and family planning regulations generally, and the Baby Doe Act, that is, the 1973 Rehabilitation Act and subsequent amendments. NRLC opposes the Freedom of Choice Act. NRLC supported the unsuccessful reelection efforts of George Bush in 1992.

NRLC is affiliated with the International Right to Life Federation (IRLF), which is made up of forty-four national organizations from ten different regions of the world. Willke served as the international federation's president; and NRLC helps to fund the federation. IRLF has worked recently to block access to the French abortion pill RU 486. Depending on the issue, NRLC works with other organizations, including the National Committee on Abortion. The national group does not directly work with Concerned Women for America,* Eagle Forum,* National Council of Catholic Women,* National Committee for a Human Life Amendment,* or Feminists for Life,* although the state and local organizations do. Adversaries include, above all, Planned Parenthood Federation of America*; the National Abortion Rights Action League* is seen as NRLC's antithesis. The American Civil Liberties Union* and National Organization for Women* also are adversaries, and so, depending on the candidates, are the Republican and Democratic* National Committees.

ELECTORAL ACTIVITIES

NRLC does not see women's issues as partisan. It differs from other pro-life organizations in that it does not take religious positions. It focuses strictly on abortion. It established the Washington-based NRL PAC in September 1979. The PAC's purpose is to elect the organization's friends and defeat its enemies. During the 1990 election, NRL PAC raised close to $1 million; it either directly contributed to, or spent money (through independent expenditures) on behalf of, 107 candidates. In 1979, it had a single contribution, a legacy from a person's death, of $5,000. All funds are raised by direct mail, although NRL PAC has solicited other PACs on occasion. PAC donors may earmark their contributions. NRL PAC shares information with the Free Congress Foundation and, sometimes, the two national party committees.

NRL PAC assistance is bipartisan. Endorsed candidates must support NRLC's stance against abortion. The PAC head, NRLC president, and delegate to the board from the candidate's state must agree for a candidate to receive an NRL PAC endorsement. All other things being equal, NRL PAC would prefer an incumbent over a challenger. But the crucial element in an endorsement is the degree of dedication the candidate has shown to issues of concern to NRLC. NRL PAC endorses congressional and presidential candidates; it has endorsed men and women, liberals as well as conservatives. NRLC worked with the Christian Coalition on local elections in 1992.

FURTHER INFORMATION

NRLC publishes a biweekly newsletter. *National Right to Life News,* and collects and disseminates explicit photographs and slides of fetal development and abortion procedures. It has distributed a film, *Silent Scream,* widely (including to members of the Congress, and has shown it to gatherings of anti-abortion activists. Willke records radio dispatches broadcast five days a week on 330, mostly Christian radio stations. NRLC has a legislative updates number: (202) 393-LIFE.

LAURA R. WOLIVER

NATIONAL RIGHT TO LIFE EDUCATIONAL GENERAL COUNSEL'S OFFICE
See NATIONAL RIGHT TO LIFE COMMITTEE

NATIONAL RIGHT TO LIFE EDUCATIONAL TRUST FUND
See NATIONAL RIGHT TO LIFE COMMITTEE

NATIONAL RIGHT TO LIFE POLITICAL ACTION COMMITTEE
See NATIONAL RIGHT TO LIFE COMMITTEE

NATIONAL SOCIETY, DAUGHTERS OF THE AMERICAN REVOLUTION (DAR)

Administration Building
1776 D Street, NW
Washington, DC 20006
(202) 628-1776
FAX (202) 879-3252

Members of the National Society, Daughters of the American Revolution (DAR) are linked by common heritage and genealogy. In their organization the daughters seek to preserve the artifacts, books, and records of the Revolutionary War era and to foster patriotism and an appreciation of U.S. history.

ORIGIN AND DEVELOPMENT

Patriotism and interest in American origins ran high during the years between the 1876 centennial celebration and the 1892 World Columbian Exposition. But male-only heritage groups such as the Sons of the American Revolution (SAR) barred women from membership. Several prominent Washington, D.C., women—such as Mary Desha, a suffragist who had helped organize a short-lived group called Wives, Mothers, Daughters and Sisters; Eugenia Washington, a postal department employee; Ellen Hardin Walworth, a widow of independent means active in civic affairs; and Mrs. William D. Cabell, director of the Nor-wood Institute (a school for young girls)—decided that their patriotism equaled the men's and resolved to begin their own heritage society. On October 11, 1890, calling themselves the DAR, these women invited Mrs. Benjamin Harrison, the first lady, to act as their leader.

The founders' boldness in organizing their own group drew questions from peers and newspaper commentators. To secure acceptance by Washington, D.C., society, the daughters planned a gala public reception for several hundred invited guests on George Washington's birthday celebration in 1891. Held at Cabell's home, the reception had a guest list that included the SAR. Cabell and Harrison received the guests.

In 1892, the year-old society boasted 818 members. The directors set aside funds at the annual meeting, called the Continental Congress, for a building to house their offices and display historic relics. According to minutes of the February 1892 meeting, the vice president general presiding, Cabell, declared that the society's house "should be the finest building ever owned by a woman." The headquarters houses a splendid collection of over 91,000 historical and genealogical items in a library; a museum of period rooms, decorative arts, and antiques; and displays of historic relics in the administrative building.

In 1896, an act of the Congress chartered DAR. This congressional charter requires an annual report of activities, which is printed by the government, entered into the *Congressional Record,* and presented to the Smithsonian Institution. DAR may store its collections with either the Smithsonian or National Gallery.

During the Spanish American War, DAR served as the official screening agency for all army nurses. During World War I, it served as an auxiliary to the Red Cross relief program. It helped to pass the 1921 Sheppard-Towner Maternity Act and once belonged to the Women's Joint Congressional Committee but sought to defeat extension of the act's funding. The daughters instead became involved in extreme activities against what it regarded as sedition, which raised significant First Amendment issues. In 1925, DAR passed a resolution "That the National Society recommended a definite, intensive campaign to be organized in every state to combat 'Red' internationalists and that the State Regents be asked to appoint a chairman to direct the campaign of 'Cooperation of National Defense.' " Ten years later, DAR, along with the American Legion and Chamber of Commerce, was described as a chief proponent of strict alien and sedition bills.

The DAR has yet to live down its 1939 denial of Constitution Hall to African American contralto Marian Anderson. Howard University tried to book Constitution Hall on April 9, 1939, for the Marian Anderson benefit concert but was told the National Symphony already had reserved that date. When the university asked for the dates of April 8 or 10, the hall manager admitted that the DAR had a policy of not renting to blacks. After this story reached the newspapers, DAR hid behind the excuse that a Washington, D.C., ordinance forbade integrated performances. In a September 24, 1990, article in the *New Republic* DAR president general Marie Hirst Yochim claimed that the hall was denied because of a prior booking, and not the singer's race. That excuse was discredited fifty years ago.

At First Lady Eleanor Roosevelt's request, the attorney general had looked into the matter and found that no such law existed. In a final attempt at a cover-up, DAR destroyed the minutes of meetings and records that showed the hall had hosted performances by the all-black Hampton Institute choir in 1931. The organization's white-only policy went into effect soon afterward. Media coverage of the controversy rivaled coverage of the war in Europe. The Washington *Herald* wrote a blistering editorial decrying the DAR ban. Shortly after, the *New York Times* picked up the story. The drama intensified when the Washington Board of Education denied use of all-white Central High School Auditorium for the Anderson concert. Blacks were furious. They formed a protest committee. The drama climaxed when the first lady resigned from the DAR to protest its denial of Constitution Hall to Anderson.

Anderson was very busy with concerts in California during the controversy. She learned about the Roosevelt resignation from a newspaper headline. The affair came to a conclusion when Sol Hurok, Anderson's manager, announced that Anderson would give an open-air concert on Easter Sunday, April 9, at the foot of the Lincoln Memorial. This concert has become an important symbol in the United States.

On January 7, 1943, Marian Anderson sang at Constitution Hall; and segregated seating was not in effect that night—a first for Washington, D.C. The

1943 Anderson concert is an accomplishment the DAR would like the public to remember. In fact, an unofficial goal of the society is to change the way it is perceived by a large segment of the public. The DAR wants to shed its image of stuffy clubwomen and attract younger women to its ranks.

ORGANIZATION AND FUNDING

The national society is organized on a stair-step plan of local, regional, state, and national units. These local chapters often are named for dames and leaders of the revolutionary era such as Pocahontas chapter in San Angelo, Texas; Samuel Dale chapter in Meridian, Mississippi; Frances Rebecca Harrison chapter in Vivian, Louisiana; and the Garcilaso De La Vega chapter in Lake Worth, Florida. Resolutions are voted on at the annual congress, held in April to commemorate the Battle of Lexington. They originate at the local level and progress to state and national levels for consideration. Thereafter, a committee compiles a book of resolutions by state and category; the committee discusses these items before they come to a vote.

Much DAR work is done through approximately twenty-five committees focusing on such subjects as American History Month (the committee was founded in 1956), DAR family tree genetics (1984), the U.S. flag (1909), and national defense (1926); in 1984, DAR authorized a special committee for the Statue of Liberty restoration, and members donated more than half a million dollars for this project. The president general elected in 1992 is Mrs. Donald Shattuck Blair for a three-year term; she may not succeed herself. The president general oversees a staff of about 143 at the Washington, D.C., headquarters.

DAR has approximately 205,000 members. Women may apply for membership by presenting genealogical evidence that a direct ancestor served in the Continental Army or materially aided the patriot cause. A prospective member must be sponsored by a local DAR chapter. Genealogists at society headquarters check the research's accuracy before an applicant is admitted to membership. Many daughters begin with membership in Children of the American Revolution and graduate to full DAR membership when they turn eighteen years old. Other newcomers join because of their interest in genealogical research: DAR holds one of the keys to unlocking women's genealogy, which can be difficult to trace, because, for example, married women usually have taken their husband's name. During the bicentennial period, it took further steps to facilitate this research.

The daughters do not actively seek minority members and keep no statistics on the number of nonwhite members. The first known black member, Karen Farmer of Detroit, was admitted in October 1977. She sought membership because it would enhance her standing as a genealogist. Fifteen years later, Farmer remains active, along with several of her relatives admitted to membership.

As a tax-exempt organization, DAR receives income from endowments, bequests, dues, and publication sales. The overall budget exceeds $4 million.

POLICY CONCERNS AND TACTICS

DAR has a motto, "God, Home and Country," which is part of its seal. The seal shows a dame during the time of the Revolution seated at a spinning wheel beneath thirteen stars. The spinning wheel represents the patriot woman's contributions to the revolutionary cause; they not only "fed and foraged" the troops but raised money to make the effort possible. To carry out their motto, contemporary members work in their local and state societies toward goals of patriotic endeavor, historic preservation, and promotion of education. For example, Arkansas DAR joined with other heritage organizations to help preserve the old state capitol building.

Although DAR bylaws preclude political activity, its national defense committee is led by conservative activist, Phyllis Schlafly of Eagle Forum.* Schlafly often writes on defense topics for the DAR magazine. In a March 1990 article in the magazine, Schlafly supported the Strategic Defense Initiative as highly important to arms reduction. In 1950, DAR advocated withdrawal by the United States from the United Nations (UN) and for years denounced the UN Educational, Science and Cultural Organization and UN Children's Fund. According to DAR bylaws, chapters set aside at least five minutes on their meeting agenda for a national defense report.

Despite the organization's conservative tone, local chapters have a lot of latitude in carrying out DAR objectives in their communities. Chapters often focus on a particular area of service such as veterans' hospitals, preservation of historic homes, local land conservation, literacy, classes for new immigrants, and family history research.

In its early years, DAR worked alongside the Women's Christian Temperance Union,* General Federation of Women's Clubs,* and Colonial Dames. It is a longtime ally of the American Legion and has been pictured as collaborating with the John Birch Society.

ELECTORAL ACTIVITIES

DAR does not have a political action committee.

FURTHER INFORMATION

DAR has published *Pillars of Patriotism* about its history and objectives. This lavishly illustrated book offers a guide to national headquarters, including the library and state period rooms, and a discussion of the special collections in the American area and special collections pertaining to NSDAR history. DAR also publishes books such as *Genealogical Research for Membership in NSDAR, Minor Military Service, 1773–1775* (for Rhode Island, Connecticut, and Massachusetts), and *Is That Lineage Right* to help genealogical enthusiasts with their research. The organization's magazine is published ten times a year.

MARTHA JOY NOBLE

NATIONAL URBAN LEAGUE
See NATIONAL URBAN LEAGUE GUILD

NATIONAL URBAN LEAGUE GUILD (NULG)
500 East 62nd Street
New York, NY 10021
(212) 310-9000
FAX (212) 593-8250

Housing, employment, education, social welfare, health, and civil rights are not exclusively women's concerns, yet these issues directly affect all women and their families. Throughout history, African American women have played an active role in many organizations seeking to address society's ills. Yet their position as a group in the National Urban League Guild (NULG) has been unique, for this organization has afforded college-educated African American women are rare opportunity to govern a national interracial organization whose membership includes men and women. From its founding in 1942, this nonpartisan, nonprofit service organization has derived its leadership primarily from urban, middle-class black women.

As an auxiliary of the National Urban League (NUL), the guild supports the league's work through its own separate fund-raising, publicity, and educational efforts. By creating a separate organization, the guild's founders ensured that its members would control their own leadership. Because its patronage is important to the league, the guild has been able to assert significant influence within the league's leadership ranks.

ORIGIN AND DEVELOPMENT

The guild's parent organization, NUL, was formed in 1910 to provide assistance and guidance to the large numbers of African Americans migrating to northern cities from the rural South. Its activities have included researching urban living and working conditions, analyzing policies affecting urban life, consulting with government agencies and community groups, providing direct services to disadvantaged urban dwellers, disseminating educational information about all aspects of the changing conditions of urban life, and advocating policies and programs to improve and enrich the quality of urban life. Guided by the standards, objectives, and methods of professional social work, the Urban League has been an effective national force for improving the lives of urban minorities and fostering cooperation and understanding among racial and ethnic groups.

NULG organized in New York City in June 1942, when a small group of young professionals—blacks and whites, women and men—began meeting in members' homes to organize educational, cultural, and social activities in support of the Urban League's work. While the guild's activities have helped to improve race relations and enrich community life, fund-raising has always been its main focus. In more than fifty years, the organization has never strayed from its original goals, although specific issues and emphases have always kept up with changing times.

The dynamic force behind the guild was a committed nucleus of Harlem women led by Mollie Moon. Well connected in the arts, professions, and civic organizations, they brought together an impressive array of professional expertise, leadership skills, and influence. Many of the founders were social workers and teachers, while others were artists, journalists, publicists, businesswomen, librarians, and medical professionals. The guild's membership has always included men and women of both races.

ORGANIZATION AND FUNDING

Founder Mollie Moon presided over NULG from 1942 until her death in 1990. Vice President Helen Harden has helped lead the organization for half a century. In 1991, Sylvia Hughes became the guild's second elected president. Continuity of leadership over five decades has been carefully balanced by consistently recruiting and preparing younger members to fill offices and board positions. While leadership positions have been filled by men and women of both races. African American women as a group have enjoyed the free access to prominent leadership posts that has eluded them in other interracial organizations. Today the officers and committees conduct the organization's business from a volunteer-staffed office in NULG's headquarters.

Since 1942, the Beaux Arts Ball has been the guild's most noted annual fundraiser. Celebrities and guests gather for an extravaganza of dancing, dining, and entertainment at this star-studded gala, held in the 1940s and 1950s at Harlem's famed Savoy Ballroom and thereafter at the Waldorf-Astoria Hotel. Elaborately costumed according to each year's theme, guests celebrate the Urban League's achievements while contributing thousands of dollars toward its ongoing work.

Other guild projects over the years have included art exhibitions, literary evenings with famous authors, membership drives, public relations campaigns, and educational programs, with all proceeds and publicity benefiting the Urban League. By attracting the participation and support of middle-class blacks and whites, these activities have facilitated interracial cooperation and understanding.

Early on, the guild's founders began receiving requests to help organize guild affiliates in other cities. In 1952, NULG joined with its affiliates in forming the National Council of Guilds, a confederation of autonomous local Urban League Guild chapters. Mollie Moon was elected the first of many council presidents; today Anita Marina of Carrollton, Texas, presides over this council.

As of 1992, affiliate chapters have been chartered in eighty-three cities throughout the United States. More than half have formed since 1960. Affiliate chapters function as auxiliaries to their local Urban Leagues, tailoring their programs to community needs and concerns. More than 3,000 members nationwide raise more than $200,000 annually in support of local Urban League projects.

POLICY CONCERNS AND TACTICS

The guild is not a policy-making organization; its primary purpose is to support the work of the National Urban League through fund-raising. The league's board of trustees—on which at least one guild official sits—determines its own policy priorities and tactics. It employs a variety of approaches in both the public and private sectors, advocating the needs and interests of urban minorities while addressing the problems that adversely affect urban life's quality in America. Racism, housing, employment, health care, economic opportunity, racial justice, social welfare, and education are all major areas of concern to both organizations.

ELECTORAL ACTIVITIES

As a nonpartisan organization, NULG does not participate in electoral politics, nor does it engage in lobbying or litigation. Many of its members are active in party politics and individual campaigns, as well as various allied interest groups.

LINDA NIEMAN

NATIONAL WELFARE RIGHTS ORGANIZATION (NWRO)

A social protest movement of poor women on welfare seeking an expansion of the economic rights of the poor, especially increased benefits and a guaranteed minimum income, the National Welfare Rights Organization (NWRO) worked to mobilize poor people generally and confronted the feminization of poverty long before the women's liberation movement made its eradication an agenda item.

ORIGIN AND DEVELOPMENT

NWRO was founded formally in 1967 at a Washington, D.C., convention. A number of factors nurtured the organization's growth, including the efforts of George Wiley, a black former professor dedicated to empowering poor people, and also a favorable political climate. Presidents Kennedy and Johnson supported antipoverty efforts, and Johnson launched the nation's War on Poverty, thus lending legitimacy to the antipoverty movement and resulting in NWRO's receiving the financial contributions necessary to found a national organization. The civil rights movement encouraged NWRO activists to borrow many of its principles, strategies, and tactics. The strong economy of the 1960s meant the resources necessary were available and could be channeled into NWRO policies and programs.

Despite its successes, a number of factors contributed to the organization's demise, for example, internal clashes between male staffers and women members over policy and tactics, the increasingly hostile political environment of the 1970s, and a weakening economy. When Wiley resigned in December 1972, so that he could organize a new Movement for Economic Justice, NWRO lost both a skilled fund raiser and most of its financial support. Bankrupt, NWRO closed its national headquarters in 1975.

ORGANIZATION AND FUNDING

NWRO had a nine-member executive committee and a national coordinating committee of state delegates. There was a biennial national convention. The first chief executive was Wiley; Johnnie Tillmon, a black welfare mother from California, served as the group's first national chair.

The organization vested formal decision-making power in its members, who, upon payment of a one-dollar annual fee to a local welfare rights organization (WRO), automatically became NWRO members. Membership initially was restricted to welfare recipients but later opened to anyone with a low income. Dues-paying members, peaking at 22,000, were overwhelmingly poor black women. Men not only had greater access to other sources of income than did women but also avoided joining an organization seeking benefits that would accrue largely to women. Although white women did begin to join NWRO in the mid-1970s, they made up a much smaller share of the welfare population of the inner cities where NWRO recruiters concentrated their membership drives.

Wiley wanted to make NWRO a financially self-sustaining national organization; his poverty constituency made this impossible. Instead he spent most of his time on fund-raising efforts and between 1966 and 1972 personally raised most of the organization's $3 million budget. Most of the money came from churches and private foundations. White Protestant churches, led by the United Church of Christ, responded generously to Wiley's requests for contributions. Black churches proved either unable to contribute because of their own financial difficulties or unwilling due to a strong black middle-class antipathy toward welfare. Private foundations such as the Rockefeller Brother Fund made significant contributions, as did the federal government and private individuals. Membership dues never exceeded 5 percent of the annual budget.

POLICY CONCERNS AND TACTICS

The biennial convention established NWRO policies; at other times the executive and coordinating committees met to formulate policy. In theory, the organization's dues-paying members were policymakers; in reality this theory was lost to staff dominance, which was largely white and male, at least until the early 1970s, when women began to take control of the political agenda. Abstract policy goals were not central. NWRO's interest was gaining power and access to the political system. Wiley pursued two broad strategies to achieve this goal: building a network of community-based WROs that would push for national welfare reform and creating a "crisis" in the welfare system by having all eligible persons apply for welfare entitlements in order to induce the system's fiscal collapse and force its reform. The scholar/activist Frances Fox Piven formulated this plan.

Initially, NWRO relied on the tactics of disruption. Typically, members occupied a welfare office and demanded immediate grievance resolution; often this resulted in lengthy protests, sometimes lasting for days or until members' demands were met satisfactorily. This client insurgency strategy was successful and resulted in the transfer of millions of dollars of cash and in-kind benefits to poor people. Eventually it failed as the welfare system abolished the special benefits on which recipients sought to draw.

By the early 1970s Wiley largely had abandoned a militant strategy, including protest marches and sit-in demonstrations, in favor of a more conventional one of lobbying legislators, negotiating with welfare bureaucrats, and filing federal lawsuits. Lobbying activity increased dramatically as the leadership sought to influence legislators and legislation. Generally, NWRO was more effective at blocking adverse legislation than initiating favorable policy; for example, it successfully defeated the Nixon administration's Family Assistance Plan in the Congress because NWRO leaders considered it antithetical to members' interests. Yet it offered the Congress no alternative legislation. NWRO also won a number of key U.S. Supreme Court cases, for example, *Goldberg* v. *Kelly* (1970), which held that recipients of public assistance had a right to a fair hearing before termination of benefits.

During its decade-long existence NWRO achieved a number of policy victories, for example, raising the benefit level of the food stamp program and having a cost of living clause added to its provisions. Other important contributions included more favorable welfare regulations, together with a heightened sense of self-esteem for recipients.

Major political, financial, and social support came from the National Council of Churches through its Interreligious Foundation for Social Community Organization and the United Church of Christ through its Welfare Priority Team. NWRO also collaborated with the Southern Christian Leadership Congress, Congress on Racial Equality, National Tenants Organization, People United to Save Humanity, National Urban League,* Household Technicians of America, National Women's Political Caucus,* United Methodist Women,* Coalition of 100 Black Women,* National Black Feminist Organization,* and League of Women Voters.* NWRO and its supporters fought against welfare power structures, namely, the welfare administrators, legislators, and adjudicators.

ELECTORAL ACTIVITIES

NWRO avoided mainstream electoral politics during the 1960s in favor of militant protest activity. In 1971, it entered party politics when, at the annual NWRO convention, ten officials urged members to become state delegates to the 1972 National Democratic Convention, where they would be able to shape the party's welfare platform. Although NWRO favored Democratic candidates, the organization's consistent indebtedness prevented it from contributing to party candidates.

FURTHER INFORMATION

The NWRO monthly newsletter *NOW!* was retitled *The Welfare Fighter* after an upheaval in NWRO's publication section in 1969. *NOW!* was first published on October 31, 1966. *The Welfare Fighter,* also a monthly, ceased publication in 1974.

SUSAN L. THOMAS

NATIONAL WOMAN'S PARTY (NWP)
144 Constitution Avenue, NE
Washington, DC 20002
(202) 546-1210
FAX (202) 543-2365

The National Woman's Party (NWP), known for its militant tactics during the suffrage campaign under the leadership of Alice Paul, was the only women's organization to devote itself exclusively to the passage of the equal rights amendment (ERA). As an early leader of the women's rights movement. NWP tremendously influenced development of other woman's organizations. Today, NWP has dwindled in numbers, and although it continues to work in cooperation with larger women's organizations, its importance is largely symbolic.

ORIGIN AND DEVELOPMENT

NWP's history is, in large part, the story of Alice Paul, who was the association's suffrage-era founder and an NWP activist until her death in 1977, and who in 1993 was selected by academic experts as one of the top ten women of the century. A Quaker, Paul graduated from Swarthmore College and moved to New York City for graduate work and settlement house living. She later earned her M.A. and Ph.D. from the University of Pennsylvania. In 1906, she traveled to Great Britain for additional study and became immersed in militant suffragette activity under the Pankhurst sisters' leadership. She was arrested seven times, jailed three times, and force-fed through a nasal tube twice a day for four weeks because she refused to eat. This experience influenced her life's course and led to NWP's founding.

Returning to the United States, Paul joined the National American Woman Suffrage Association (NAWSA) but felt dismayed by its reliance on conventional tactics and the use of a state-by-state approach to women's suffrage. Perceiving suffrage as a national issue, Paul convinced NAWSA's leadership to permit her to organize a national suffrage parade and revive its long-dormant Congressional Committee's (CC) activities.

Through parades and mass demonstrations, CC effectively drew attention to the idea of a national suffrage amendment and convinced the Republican Congress to debate an issue it had not considered in twenty-six years. This success and Paul's dissatisfaction with other policies led her to sever NAWSA ties after founding an independent organization, the Congressional Union, to work exclusively for a federal amendment. In 1913, the organization's name changed officially to the NWP.

Paul led NWP's largely upper-class members in protest activities to draw attention to the women's suffrage cause. Members picketed the White House twenty-four hours a day. Arrested, they were forced-fed in prison. These tactics and the government's apparent overreaction to them made women's suffrage highly visible. Paul, like NAWSA, continued to dismiss the equally visible issue of African American women's right to vote as a "radical question," not one that involved "feminist" issues. Until ratification in 1920, NWP and NAWSA remained the Nineteenth Amendment's prime movers.

After the suffrage amendment's ratification, NWP immediately turned its attention to ratifying ERA. That goal came into conflict with most clubwomen's concerns. During the Progressive era, they fought for protective legislation, as exemplified by maximum hour and minimum wage laws for women, and feared ERA would automatically invalidate it. This disagreement within the ranks came to a head in *Adkin* v. *Children's Hospital* (1923); NWP and other women's groups filed opposing friend of the court briefs in the case. NWP lawyers argued successfully that minimum wage laws for women alone should be ruled unconstitutional because they invalidated basic equal rights principles.

With the support of only the General Federation of Women's Clubs* and National Federation of Business and Professional Women* (BPW/USA) and despite U.S. labor secretary Frances Perkins's opposition in 1933–34. Paul and NWP achieved ERA's introduction in one or both houses of the Congress in every session through the 1960s. It lost ground as the preeminent pro-ERA group when National Organization for Women* (NOW) formed in 1966. Today its role largely is confined to supporting the activities of other, large groups promoting women's rights.

ORGANIZATION AND FUNDING

NWP claims eight state affiliates and is itself affiliated with the National Council of Women in the United States (NCW). (NCW serves as an information center and clearinghouse for affiliated women's organizations, conducting projects and sponsoring conferences on problems of national and international concern to women.) NWP's board of directors consists of thirty members; ten serve on the executive committee. Approximately 15 percent of board members are minorities. NWP also selects an advisory committee of three to five honorary members to advise the organization; they have no voting privileges. NWP's executive director, currently Sharon Griffith, is hired by the board as a paid employee. The number of additional paid staff varies year by year, from two to four, depending on the agenda. NWP depends on board members and volunteers to conduct lobbying; the number of volunteers varies from five to twenty, depending on the project involved. NWP also selects one intern per semester.

NWP has approximately 1,000 members. The major incentive for membership is to have an advocate of ERA and other women's issues. The Sewall-Belmont House serves as a lobbying headquarters for advocates of women's issues; and NWP hosts four to six functions a year to which members are invited to hear speakers and network with others interested in the same issues.

The Sewall-Belmont House, which dates to 1800 and earlier and is a National Historic Site, continues to serve as NWP headquarters, across the street from the U.S. Supreme Court, and Associate Justice Sandra Day O'Connor's office. (O'Connor was the first woman to serve on the Court and a proponent of a constitutional standard that would meet ERA's.) Alva Smith Belmont, NWP president 1921–33, also served as NWP's prime benefactor. She provided most of NWP's annual operating expenses and upon her death bequeathed her entire estate, including her house, to the NWP. For revenue, the contemporary NWP relies on membership dues of twenty-five dollars per year, donations, rental of the gardens and public rooms at Belmont House, and sales of jail door jewelry commemorating women incarcerated for suffrage. NWP would not release the estimates for its total current operating budget.

POLICY CONCERNS AND TACTICS

NWP's supporters still pledge themselves to issues in which women have a stake, including child support enforcement, health care, family and medical leave, civil rights restoration, and minimum wage increases. Largely a historical artifact, the organization is in a holding pattern and has not appeared before the Congress in several years. In April 1992, NWP was listed as an amicus in a sexual harassment case along with NOW, the National Coalition against Sexual Assault, and Women against Pornography. NWP works in cooperation with larger women's organizations, including NOW, the National Women's Studies Association,* and BPW/USA. In 1994, it honored U.S. Supreme Court justice Ruth Bader Ginsburg with its Alice Paul Award to mark Women's History Month.

ELECTORAL ACTIVITIES

In early years NWP campaigned against Woodrow Wilson and other Democratic candidates because they did not support women suffrage. Since the Nineteenth Amendment's ratification, NWP has engaged only peripherally in electoral activity. It considers itself a bipartisan organization in support of legislation and not candidates.

In 1993, in its application for Internal Revenue Service (IRS) classification as a 509 (a) (2) nonprivate foundation, it stated that its major purpose was education to lead to public recognition of equality of the sexes. The organization also stated that the equal rights amendment was no longer its primary concern and amended its charter to prohibit it from supporting any party or candidate for public office.

FURTHER INFORMATION

NWP publishes a quarterly newsletter, *Equal Rights,* which is free to all its members, and a pamphlet entitled *Answers to Questions about the ERA.*
                                        KAREN O'CONNOR AND LAURA VAN ASSENDELFT

NATIONAL WOMEN'S CONFERENCE CENTER
See NATIONAL WOMEN'S CONFERENCE COMMITTEE

NATIONAL WOMEN'S CONFERENCE COMMITTEE (NWCC)
c/o Gene Boyer
Winter Address:
16100 Golf Club Road
Number 201
Fort Lauderdale, FL 33326
(305) 389-1879
Summer Address:
P.O. Box 455
Beaver Dam, WI 53916
(414) 887-1078

The National Women's Conference Committee (NWCC) and its educational and research foundation, the National Women's Conference Center, act as torchbearers for the national plan of action ratified by the 1977 Houston women's conference.

ORIGIN AND DEVELOPMENT

NWCC formed as an outgrowth of the national women's conference held at Houston in 1977. The United Nations (UN) called for an International Women's Year (IWY) in 1975 with the International Decade for Women to follow, 1976–85. Initially, a U.S. commission chaired by Jill Ruckelshaus and directed by Mildred Marcy on assignment from the U.S. Information Agency undertook preparations for the UN conference to be held in Copenhagen, Denmark. The commission worked well, influenced by the women's liberation movement and its own strong beginning from within the Ford administration. Its widely distributed report, ''To Form a More Perfect Union,'' offered numerous recommendations and so disturbed movement adversaries that these adversaries temporarily stopped the reports dissemination. This commission also stimulated ERAmerica's* formation.

Subsequently, President Ford signed Public Law 94-1676, which contained a national conference call: state conferences were to elect delegates to this national conference. Leaving its advisory function behind, on short notice the National Commission on the Observance of International Women's Year coordinated the national conference effort. Again, movement adversaries sought to stymie the commissions's work. Nonetheless, 1,773 highly diverse delegates, 186 alternates and thousands of invitees, observers, and members of the public, from fifty states and six territories, attended the meeting at Sam Houston Coliseum in Houston.

The state conferences also sent resolutions to the commission, chaired by Congressperson Bella Abzug (D-NY), PL 94-1676's sponsor, and directed by Kathryn Clarenbach, one of National Organization for Women's* (NOW) founders. From over 4,000 resolutions, the commission drafted a twenty-six-point national action plan for the Houston delegates' attention. They unanimously adopted seventeen of the proposed planks and an equal credit plank. Three amended resolutions and four substitute resolutions also were adopted by large margins. The conference had, in effect, identified twenty-five "problem areas" and offered solutions for them. Although the conference failed to ratify a plank proposing a U.S. Women's Department, it did agree to a continuing committee to exercise oversight to implement the action plan.

The commission presented the plan and a report to President Carter and then appointed a continuing committee largely composed of representatives of the major national women's organizations. By issuing executive order no. 12050, in 1978, the president established a thirty-eight-member National Advisory Committee for Women cochaired by Abzug and Carmen Delgado Votaw, a commission member, to pick up where the second commission left off. Six months later Abzug was dismissed as advisory committee chair after she released to the press criticism of the president's economic program as affecting women adversely. Executive order no. 12136 (1979) established a new advisory committee, chaired by Lynda Johnson Robb and cochaired by Marjorie Bell Chambers and Elizabeth Koontz; that committee held public hearings, recommended initiatives in addition to the national action plan, and arranged meetings between equal rights amendment (ERA) advocates and President Carter. It ceased to exist at the end of 1980, leaving the continuing committee to work with women's organizations to achieve the action plan's implementation.

The continuing committee changed its name to NWCC and set up the conference center as its educational and charitable partner to implement "appropriate portions" of the national action plan. In keeping with the Houston conference's charge, it since has fostered state and regional network formation, at the time of this writing most recently in New York State, based on a model provided by the Wisconsin Women's Network (WWN). A multi-issue coalition that includes individual subscribers, WWN supports lobbying on women's issues, with the national action plan a matter of consensus. It has a decentralized representative structure, keeps an office in the state capital, raises money, does not itself lobby but facilitates, provides guidelines, and troubleshoots. NWCC also stimulated formation of the Council of Presidents* (CP) formation and helped to bring about the Soviet-American Women's Summit. Its goals have remained those of its mandate: to mobilize public support and encourage and oversee the national action plan's implementation, serve as a national network and promote coordination among groups seeking implementation, and maintain the communication of information.

ORGANIZATION AND FUNDING

NWCC has a delegate assembly. Its fifty-five-member board of directors includes the officers, ten at-large members, representatives from the twenty recognized state networks, and chairs of the conference committee's twenty-one issue task forces or caucuses. NWCC has an advisory committee, including such influential women as Abzug, Clarenbach, Catherine East, Minnette Doderer, and Votaw. There are two cochairs: Sarah Harder, a former American Association of University Women* president and convening chair of the Wisconsin Women's Council,* and Janie B. Taylor, a former Federally Employed Women* president and Black Women's Agenda member. NWCC has no headquarters of its own and no paid staff.

NWCC is a membership organization. All members are women, and the organization will remain a women-only group. Members join to share important policies, attend conferences and meetings, communicate with peers, and associate with similarly minded people and also for the sake of friendship ties; nostalgia, connections to IWY and the Houston conference, and international linkages work as further incentives to join.

Without federal funding, NWCC has proceeded as an entirely volunteer organization. Resources are those accessible to participants or personally contributed by them.

Incorporated in 1980, the conference center has its own fifteen-member volunteer board and officers. Center directors first must have served on NWCC's board; and NWCC's cochairs have ex officio seats on the board. Twenty percent of board members are African American, Hispanic, and Asian American. The center encourages board participation by persons from lower-income strata, persons with disabilities, older women, and lesbians. The center's president is Gene Boyer, one of NOW's founders and a former NOW Legal Defense and Education Fund* president. The executive officers' decisions and also public opinion influence center policy discussions. The center has as members its contributors. It is a 501 (c) (3) organization; and contributions to it are tax-deductible. Its annual budget is less than $10,000, up from $1,000 in 1980. It disseminates information and issue-oriented publications, including a newsletter, establishes communications about the national action plan, and holds an annual meeting. Recently, the center has proposed establishing a Women's Information Support Network, a clearinghouse to disseminate issue publications by women's rights groups.

POLICY CONCERNS AND TACTICS

NWCC's board of directors is its policy-making entity and also approves projects or activities that the center proposes to undertake. Preferred conference committee strategies include testifying in congressional and agency/department hearings, contributing to political campaigns, monitoring elected officials' voting records, offering written comments on proposed regulations, and seeking administrative review of agency or department decisions, along with conducting and publishing issue-oriented research through the conference center, educating members with center publications and encouraging them to write legislators and committees, and contacting public decision makers through influential members. To a lesser extent, through the center, NWCC supplies congresspeople and staff with information and educates the public with press releases.

The women's issues agenda contained in the national action plan, which NWCC is mandated to implement, includes strong support for ERA, reproductive freedom and *Roe* v. *Wade,* equality in employment and education, pay equity and effective enforcement of antidiscrimination laws, reform of family law to recognize homemakers' contributions and children's rights, greatly increased high-quality child care facilities, prevention of child abuse and treatment of victims, civil rights for lesbians, and greater representation of women in elective and appointive office.

Planks also were adopted advocating equal opportunities for women in the arts and humanities and the media, in insurance (as in credit), in business, and in formulating foreign policy. Supported were welfare law reform; extension of Social Security benefits to homemakers and programs to provide counseling and other services for displaced homemakers and assistance to battered women, women with disabilities, minority women, older women, rural women, and women in prison; greatly increased attention to women's health needs; rape law reform and increased attention to victims' needs; and the design, collection, and publication of government statistics to reflect the impact of government programs on women. The mandate to implement the national action plan precludes favoring any one issue over any other.

In 1980 and 1985, as part of its mandate, NWCC attended the UN Decade for Women world conferences in Copenhagen and Nairobi, Kenya; it organized satellite teleconferences for six cities in the United States. The national action plan established the dedication of this country to the world plan of action.

In 1982, NWCC organized a nationwide media event emphasizing grassroots activities in 300 cities to lay a base for advocacy network development. In 1989, it sponsored a summit of the state network leaders to work on strategy for matching resources and issues, and two years later it offered a coalition-building workshop aimed at focusing cross-cultural community and state action on national plan issues. In 1990, NWCC proposed a set of international networking strategies.

NWCC anticipates creating a data bank to make possible evaluation of the rate of national plan implementation; groups working on the plan as well as the U.S. government and UN, organizations at the national and international level and members of the public would have access to the data bank. NWCC also plans to enhance diversity among its members, continue its organizational skills training efforts, and consult with the state networks on education about the national plan and management skills. It expects to develop a speakers bureau.

NWCC has proposed a national women's advocacy office, to be established in Washington, D.C., for use by network leaders; it anticipates close connections between the office and the Congressional Caucus for Women's Issues.* The office also has potential as a secretariat for CP, along the lines of the one that supported the commission on IWY's observance. The thought is to share facilities with such organizations as the National Association of Commissions for Women,* Women for Meaningful Summits,* and the Young Women's Christian Association.*

NWCC has become one of the organizations most active in keeping the proposed equal rights amendment an ongoing concern and supports ratification by the United States of the UN Convention to Eliminate All Forms of Discrimination against Women. NWCC believes protections for reproductive rights and freedoms are sorely needed and sees as important arenas for future initiatives violence, health, and housing. It sees the 1988 Civil Rights Restoration Act as one of the last decade's most significant federal initiatives. The worst initiatives include attacks on affirmative action, on access to abortion, and on educational equity. NWCC attributes these attacks to right-wing and fundamentalist influence. It sees the seventies as the "golden age" for feminism and perceives itself as struggling throughout the eighties with a backlash to it.

An organization of organizations, NWCC collaborates closely with the statewide networks. These groups mostly have organizational members themselves, half of them between thirty and sixty-five organizations. The networks have an array of individual members as well. Half subsist on membership fees; six on donations, which constitute 50–100 percent of their budget; and three on foundation funding or grants, which constitute 50–100 percent of their budget. One network has three full-time and four part-time staff; five have one full-time staff member. One network has a lobbyist, and one a lobbyist when the state legislature is in session.

ELECTORAL ACTIVITIES

NWCC does not see women's issues as partisan and does not have a political action committee.

FURTHER INFORMATION

NWCC has a center-issued newsletter, the *Network Exchange Bulletin,* and an information packet. Through the center it has published *The ERA Facts and Action Guide* (1986), *The National Plan Update: 1977 Goals, 1986 Status* (1987), and *Decade of Achievement* (1988). There is a booklet by Boyer, *Coalition Building: The Wisconsin Model* (1982).

SARAH SLAVIN

NATIONAL WOMEN'S ECONOMIC ALLIANCE FOUNDATION (NWEAF)
1440 New York Avenue, NW
Suite 300

Washington, DC 20005
(202) 393-5257
FAX (202) 639-8685

To promote women's careers at the executive level of corporations and government, the National Women's Economic Alliance Foundation (NWEAF) fosters a dialogue among women and men in industry, business, and government. An important goal is to place more women on corporate boards in the framework of the free enterprise system.

ORIGIN AND DEVELOPMENT

An operating foundation, the NWEAF was established in 1983. In many respects, its creation and survival can be explained by the interest group theories proposed by the late political scientist Jack Walker and other scholars. They emphasize the importance of a social entrepreneur who can gain the backing of private and public benefactors. With respect to the NWEAF, this leader emerged in Patricia de Stacy Harrison, founder and current president. An alumna from American University, she is the cofounder and partner of E. Bruce Harrison Company, a business consulting firm, and president of AEF/Harrison International, a public affairs firm. For NWEAF, Harrison secured start-up funds from large corporations such as Clairol, American Brands, and Nestle Enterprises. On the government side, Harrison enlisted an important patron in former Republican congresswoman Margaret Heckler, who at the time of the NWEAF's founding was the U.S. secretary of health and human services.

To further its objectives, the NWEAF conducts leadership seminars, offers placement services, maintains biographical archives, and bestows awards. It also nurtures foreign contacts and maintains an international advisory board. Since the collapse of Communism in Eastern European countries, it has held conferences there in conjunction with the U.S. Labor Department to help female entrepreneurs obtain a share of the emerging business opportunities.

ORGANIZATION AND FUNDING

The foundation is governed by a board of directors. All present board members are women who own their own companies or hold important positions in corporations. One member is a Native American, but no special efforts are made to recruit minorities. Additional deliberating bodies are an advisory board of governors drawn from the executives of major corporations and an international advisory board consisting of members from various countries. The president of the NWEAF is Patricia Harrison. NWEAF's office is located in Washington, D.C. The NWEAF has about four paid employees and usually two to three interns, who may receive a small stipend.

NWEAF's constituency consists of 750 female and male associates holding leadership positions in the private and public sectors. Anyone supporting the foundation's goals can join as an associate. The annual contribution is $100. In return, associates are entitled to participate in a variety of ongoing programs and special events. Associates also receive the books and newsletter published by NWEAF and become part of an information exchange about other publications of interest to businesswomen.

The foundation's budget varies. The core income of about $150,000 comes from corporate sponsors. Additional revenue is obtained from the annual contributions by associates. Unlike many other foundations, the NWEAF does not have an endowment. It is a 501 (c) (3) tax-exempt educational foundation.

POLICY CONCERNS AND TACTICS

The board of directors and the advisory board of governors, on the advice of the president and staff, set the organization's agenda and determine strategies. NWEAF uses several tactics to achieve its objective. It sponsors regular and special events to provide a forum where associates can practice their leadership skills and demonstrate their talents. These same events then are used to invite corporate and government representatives to enable role modeling, mentoring, and networking. The leadership also networks in the capital, around the country, and abroad. Under the Bush administration it had contacts with the federal administration almost on a daily basis. Since its mission is of an educational nature, an important strategy is to disseminate information.

NWEAF has one primary policy concern, the executive personnel actions of corporations and government. Its premise is that women are underrepresented in top-level offices and on corporate boards, and many more are capable of assuming leadership positions than they presently do. NWEAF holds the view that the free enterprise system offers the best route for increased career and economic opportunities for women and that women leaders in business, industry, and government have a critical contribution to make to a thriving free enterprise system. Otherwise, on specific policy issues, the foundation remains neutral to accommodate divergent opinions among the board members.

NWEAF affirms its support for executive women through public forums, research, scholarship, leadership, and management programs. Ongoing programs include leadership development, media outreach, a speakers bureau, awards for excellence in leadership, a directors' resource council and a resource database, and Alliance International. NWEAF distributes its publications to corporate and government decision makers to highlight the outstanding women available for executive and board appointments. When the Bush administration came into office in 1989, for example, it used the NWEAF database to identify women for leadership positions in the new government.

Through its president, the alliance is part of various policy networks in the capital. Harrison is, for instance, a member of the Women's Network for Entrepreneurial Training, which is part of the National Advisory Council of the U.S. Small Business Administration. A coalition partner is the National Association of Women Business Owners. An annual convention with forum also serves networking purposes.

ELECTORAL ACTIVITIES

As a foundation, NWEAF is prohibited by law from participating in partisan activities. It does not have a political action committee.

FURTHER INFORMATION

NWEAF distributes a semiannual newsletter, *NWEA Outlook,* and periodic *Policy Papers.* It also publishes an annual directory of women serving on corporate boards of Fortune 1000 companies: *Women Directors of the Top 1000 Corporations,* which costs $100. Among its other publications, NWEAF offers self-help pamphlets and a book, *America's New Women Entrepreneurs: Tips, Tactics and Techniques of Women in Business* (1986). A computerized database of women on corporate boards is also available.

SIEGRUN F. FOX

NATIONAL WOMEN'S HEALTH NETWORK (NWHN)
514 10th Street, NW
Suite 400
Washington, DC 20004
(202) 628-7814 (Information Clearinghouse)
(202) 347-1140 (Administration)
FAX (202) 347-1168

The National Women's Health Network (NWHN) is dedicated to reorienting basic values of the U.S. health care system. It seeks to shift the system's focus from medical treatment to prevention and to sensitize consumers and health care providers to women's needs as a special health interest group.

ORIGIN AND DEVELOPMENT

Women are the principal health care consumers in the United States, but, for the most part, women are absent from health care decision makers' ranks. This imbalance has affected American women's health negatively as they all too often have found themselves in a system modeled on, and responsive to, primarily male health needs. In an attempt to address this imbalance, five women—Barbara Seaman, Berlita Cowen, Mary Howell, Alice Wolfson, and Phyllis Chesler—laid the groundwork for NWHN during 1974 and 1975. Initially, they attempted to recruit members through advertisements in women's newspapers. Their first public event, a demonstration at the Food and Drug Administration (FDA), was held in December 1975. NWHN was officially launched in May 1976 at a conference attended by 150 people.

NWHN's goals have remained consistent throughout its history: to work for improved health care for women and better access to health and to promote participatory relationships between women and health professionals and increased, improved research on women's health issues. From the beginning NWHN has included the health needs of rural women, women of color, and

low-income women on its agenda. The National Black Women's Health Project*
evolved from NWHN. Initially, NWHN funded several rural women's health
initiatives as well as a Black Women's Health Project. Since the mid-1980s,
reductions in foundation funding have forced cutbacks in such programming.

ORGANIZATION AND FUNDING

The group's structure is fairly uncomplicated. There is a national office, and
there are no state affiliates. NWHN's sensitivity to the diversity of women's
health needs is reflected in its organization and decision-making structure. There
is a racially mixed board of directors, and efforts are made to encourage board
participation by low-income women, women with disabilities, lesbians, and
older women. Jane Sprague Zones serves as chairperson. The executive director
is Beverly Baker. The Washington, D.C.-based group employs five professional
staff and has seven volunteers and student interns. Each has fixed responsibilities
and does not rotate jobs. Ability is rewarded through praise, although at times
job descriptions are revised to promote a meritorious employee.

The diversity of issues occupying NWHN's agenda reflects its broad-based
membership, which numbers some 17,000 individuals and 500 organizations,
such as Family Planning Perspectives, Every-woman's Center, and the East Carolina University Health Science Library. NWHN functions as a coalition and
counts among its members consumers of health care, activists, providers, researchers, and educators. Historically, the membership has been overwhelmingly
female; and women still constitute over 90 percent of the members. NWHN
intends to remain a group of women for women.

At its inception, NWHN had two principal sources of funding, private foundations and small contributions from a number of individuals. Most recently,
annual membership dues of $25 and gifts or bequests from individuals account
for 90 percent of its annual income. Publication sales, foundation grants, and
loans constitute the remainder. The annual budget is $655,000.

POLICY CONCERNS AND TACTICS

Policy is set by the board, and members vote on changes in bylaws. Board
discussions and executive officers' decisions are the most influential factors in
setting policy. NWHN employs a number of strategies in its efforts to influence
public policy. Foremost among these are testifying at agency and department
hearings, making written comments on proposed regulations, and educating
members with publications and the public through press releases. NWHN also
testifies at congressional hearings, supplies members of the Congress and their
staff with information, and makes personal presentations to members of the
Congress, agency heads, and staff.

One of the first issues NWHN addressed was contraceptive pill safety. Since
its founding, it has worked for manufacturer's liability for such products as the
Dalkon Shield, warnings on birth control pills and menopausal estrogen drugs,
and emergency room protocols for rape victims. Today NWHN is involved in

a broad spectrum of women's health issues. It won FDA approval for the cervical cap and continues to work to lower the high rate of cesarean section births. It also has become heavily involved with the campaign to educate the public and health professionals about the specific problems of women and AIDS. NWHN's ongoing breast cancer prevention project stresses education, self-examination, safe mammograms, and research on breast cancer and dietary fat.

Even as consumers and health care providers along with policymakers become more sensitive to women's health issues than before, NWHN continues to mount an aggressive campaign to showcase such issues and keep them in the public's consciousness. It intends to continue to monitor developments concerning RU-486, the so-called abortion pill, and fetal protection policies. NWHN has been involved for ten years with the campaign to disclose the dangers of breast implants. It has been developing three regional forums on women and AIDS and was a key player in the establishment of an office for women's health research within the National Institutes of Health.

NWHN frequently works on issues of common concern with organizations such as the Older Women's League,* Boston Women's Health Book Collective, and Alan Guttmacher Institute.* It often finds itself in an adversial relationship with groups such as the National Right to Life Committee* and Moral Majority.

ELECTORAL ACTIVITIES

NWHN does not have a political action committee.

FURTHER INFORMATION

There are a bimonthly newsletter entitled *Network News* and a series of pamphlets and booklets on women's health issues.

GERTRUDE A. STEUERNAGEL

NATIONAL WOMEN'S POLITICAL CAUCUS (NWPC)
1275 K Street, NW
Suite 750
Washington, DC 20005
(202) 898-1100
FAX (202) 898-0458

The National Women's Political Caucus (NWPC) is an influential group best known for recruiting women to serve in elected and appointed political offices. From its earliest years, the caucus has had Democratic and Republican task forces to work with political parties in support of women's issues. Its political action committee (PAC), the Campaign Support Committee (CSC), contributes money to women candidates who support the NWPC agenda of feminist concerns. It also has a research and educational foundation.

ORIGIN AND DEVELOPMENT

Approximately 300 politically active women from across the country formed NWPC in 1971. These women saw a need for a ''multipartisan women's membership organization that would promote the election and appointment to public office of women with progressive, feminist goals.'' NWPC's object was to increase the number of women in all aspects of politics.

During the early years, NWPC worked to ratify the equal rights amendment (ERA) to the Constitution as its key issue. NWPC members believed that placing more women in the Congress and state legislatures would not only improve chances to pass ERA but also brighten the prospects for other legislation favored by the organization, including bills equalizing women's and men's legal treatment, funding child care, and assuring reproductive rights for all.

The original members were well-known public officeholders such as Representatives Shirley Chisholm (D-NY) and Bella Abzug (D-NY) and women affiliated with existing women's groups, including National Organization for Women,* the League of Women Voters,* and American Association of University Women.* They came together to form NWPC, realizing that no one had seriously examined either how few women held political office in the United States or what the consequences of this lack of direct representation of women might be. Through the efforts of NWPC and other groups, such as the Center for the American Woman and Politics* at Rutgers University, a great deal now is known about how many women serve in public office. Increases in the number of women officeholders have been dramatic since NWPC's founding. In 1971, 344 or 4.5 percent of state legislators were women. By the start of 1990, 1,261 or 16.9 percent were women, almost a fourfold increase. NWPC periodically publishes national directories of women elected officials. Overall, NWPC can boast of helping place women in public office and claim credit for helping to win a variety of legislative and internal party struggles. NWPC is one of the groups that have raised women's awareness of themselves as a political interest group, forcing politicians to recognize women as a constituency.

ORGANIZATION AND FUNDING

The caucus has 300 state and local affiliates in forty-six states. The head of the organization is elected at the national biennial convention made up of delegates from state caucuses. Delegates at national conventions elect officers, consider amendments to the bylaws, and adopt resolutions defining the group's policies and objectives. Delegates also concern themselves with NWPC's internal workings, helping determine how it raises money, disseminates information about key issues, and heightens members' organizational and political skills. NWPC's national steering committee, made up of officers and representatives of state caucuses, acts on recommendations for candidate support submitted by the organization's political planning committee.

The organization's chair is Harriet Woods, former lieutenant governor and Democratic nominee for the Senate from Missouri. By tradition, the leader of the group has alternated between Democrats and Republicans. NWPC is one of the few national women's organizations to have had women of color serve as past chairs. Since 1973, NWPC has had its national headquarters in Washington,

D.C. The executive director, Jody Newman, and staff of twelve salaried employees work at the headquarters.

From its founding, NWPC has included influential feminists as members, including NOW founder Betty Friedan and *Ms.* magazine's first editor, Gloria Steinem. NWPC membership has increased substantially from the original 300 to 30,000 in 1975, 50,000 in the late 1970s, 77,000 in the mid-1980s, and down to about 70,000 in 1992. All members are women. Eighty-five percent of the membership is Caucasian, 10 percent African American, 3 percent Hispanic, and 2 percent Asian American. Attempts are made within the caucus to encourage participation by persons of lower socioeconomic status and younger women. NWPC's lesbian caucus encourages lesbians to become members. Individuals join and participate in the organization for a wide variety of reasons. First, the caucus advocates values and policies that most of its members support, giving them the opportunity to contribute to a group of like-minded people. Second, NWPC represents member's opinions to government. Third, the caucus provides publications, such as its national newsletter, *Women's Political Times,* conferences, and meetings where members may communicate with each other and form new friendships. Finally, it is a place to learn political organizational skills.

Nationally, NWPC receives funds from the following sources: approximately 25 percent from contributions made in response to direct mail appeals; 20 percent from membership dues (individual members pay an average of $35); 18 percent from gifts and grants from corporations or businesses; 12 percent from conventions, conferences, or exhibitions; 10 percent from foundation grants; 8 percent from fund-raising events; and 4 percent from trade unions. The caucus budget for the last year was $1.5 million.

NWPC has established a nonprofit foundation called the Leadership Development Education and Research Fund. The foundation runs training programs for women seeking to run for public office or to manage political campaigns.

POLICY CONCERNS AND TACTICS

The NWPC board of directors and the delegate assembly exercise approximately equal influence over policy decisions. Professional staff, executive officers, and members of the group help determine issue priorities. After the delegates to NWPC's conventions pass resolutions defining policy positions for the organization, directors on the national staff in cooperation with the president and appropriate committee members work to implement them. The principal tactics used to influence public policy are personal presentations to legislators and financial contributions to those political candidates supporting key NWPC policy concerns. NWPC representatives also routinely testify in congressional hearings.

The Capitol Hill Caucus of NWPC plays a unique role in monitoring the working conditions of House and Senate staff members. Because the Congress exempts itself from federal antidiscrimination laws, this is one of the few ways for women employed on Capitol Hill to draw attention to their grievances.

NWPC also conducts annual surveys of governors' appointments to cabinet positions, tracking the number of women appointees. The caucus runs a Presidential Candidates Information project in presidential election years, soliciting information from the candidates about their stances on women's issues and publicizing past votes and actions that seem to indicate their priorities on these issues.

Over the past decade NWPC claims a number of legislative achievements. The organization worked to improve conditions for women in the military, to help pass the 1988 Civil Rights Restoration Act and 1991 Civil Rights Act, to extend the health insurance benefits of people leaving employment as well as women whose spouses die, and to minimize the impact of Reagan administration budget cuts on women and children. Some of the policies that the group has opposed unsuccessfully are Hyde amendments blocking the use of government funds for abortion, nonratification of ERA, and Supreme Court decisions weakening employment protection against sex discrimination.

The caucus works regularly with those groups and organizations concerned with similar issues—other women's groups, education organizations, and certain labor, civil liberties, and civil rights groups. Specific organizations that NWPC frequently works with are the American Association of University Women,* National Federation of Business and Professional Women,* National Women's Law Center, Older Women's League,* American Nurses' Association,* National Education Association, and the Women's Legal Defense Fund. Normally, NWPC joins and assists an existing coalition of interest groups concerned with a particular policy. If such a coalition does not exist around an issue, the caucus takes the lead and forms one. These ad hoc issue coalitions, common to politics in Washington, divide the tasks of lobbying according to the relative advantages of the specific group. Caucus officials believe that they are best at working with their members at the grass roots, educating them about issues and helping them communicate with legislators. NWPC worked in coalitions to help extend the Fair Labor Standards Act to domestic workers. It was part of a large coalition to pass the 1978 Pregnancy Discrimination Act barring employment discrimination against pregnant workers. It was also an important part of the coalition to extend the deadline for ratifying ERA. NWPC itself organized a coalition for women's appointments. For more than two decades NWPC has been central to most feminist issue coalitions in Washington.

The caucus regards the following organizations as generally adversarial—the U.S. Chamber of Commerce, National Federation of Independent Business, and National Right to Life Committee.*

ELECTORAL ACTIVITIES

Given the caucus's purpose, to increase the number of women elected to public office, setting up a PAC was a logical development. CSC is tied to the membership, which raises money in a variety of ways. Sixty percent is raised through direct mail solicitation; 30 percent by telephone solicitation, personal appeals, and special events; and an additional 10 percent is raised by other sources. NWPC PAC gave more than half a million dollars to candidates in 1982 and 1984. In the 1991–92 budget cycle, the CSC distributed about half that amount ($250,000).

Mary Beth Lambert is the political director of the caucus. Through the use of newsletters and meetings, constituents stay informed about the PAC's activities.

CSC does not solicit money from other PACs; and donors cannot earmark their contributions to particular candidates. The PAC board decides which politicians to support. Before any money is given, the candidate's voting records are monitored. Those candidates endorsed by the PAC must support NWPC goals, including backing ERA, retaining the Supreme Court decision *Roe* v. *Wade* (1973), which legalizes abortion, and a mix of public and private funding for child care programs. NWPC states that no preference is given to incumbents, challengers, Senate or House candidates, Republicans or Democrats. There is a preference for liberals over conservatives because they most often support women's issues, for candidates in close races, and for women candidates over men. The national PAC gives only to women candidates, and there has not yet been an endorsement of a presidential candidate.

FURTHER INFORMATION

NWPC puts out a variety of publications, including *Women's Political Times,* a quarterly newsletter; *The Appointment of Women: A Survey of Governor's Cabinets,* an annual publication; and occasional books, such as Cathy Allen, *Political Campaigning: A New Decade,* a guide to women's campaigning written in 1990. Many state caucuses have newsletters as well. The caucus runs a Presidential Candidates Information project in presidential election years, using questionnaires to get information from candidates about their stances on women's issues. The caucus also publicizes the candidates' past votes and actions that seem to indicate their priorities on these issues.

ONEIDA MASCARENAS AND ANNE COSTAIN

NATIONAL WOMEN'S STUDIES ASSOCIATION (NWSA)
University of Maryland
7100 Baltimore Avenue
Suite 301
College Park, MD 20740
(301) 403-0525/0524
FAX (301) 403-4137

The National Women's Studies Association (NWSA) seeks to support and promote scholars and scholarship in women's studies. NWSA has a legal defense fund (LDF).

ORIGIN AND DEVELOPMENT

Designed primarily by academic women working with their students in campus and community centers focused on women's issues, NWSA was from its inception different from the traditional disciplinary-based organization. In the late sixties, women had begun organizing to promote a feminist agenda in colleges and universities, including issues of equality in student admission criteria, equal pay, equal access to tenure line positions, and increased opportunities for promotion in teaching ranks and other professional positions. Students also began agitating relatively early, in connection with the student movement for relevance in curriculum context, for courses that addressed women's issues and lives. Some of the first women's studies courses emerged in English and history departments. Survey courses multiplied in many disciplines throughout the seventies, and each year there were geometric increases in courses, in students registered, and in campuses having women's studies offerings, changes well chronicled in Feminist Press periodicals edited by Florence Howe, one of the NWSA founders, and by KNOW, Inc., which grew out of Pittsburgh National Organization for Women.

In the midseventies talk began, among people by now five years or more into this work, about the next steps to take to bring this interdisciplinary area into recognition by mainstream scholars. In 1974–75, informal discussions took place at the Modern Language Association, American Historical Association, Organization of American Historians, and the Berkshire conference at Radcliffe College. No one individual acted as a leader or chief organizer. A steering committee received a Ford Foundation grant to help in getting established. In June 1976, representatives from an organizing committee based at San Jose State met with East Coast organizers at the Berkshire conference at Bryn Mawr to plan strategies for including diversity among delegates to the founding convention at the University of San Francisco in January 1977. State delegations received specific instructions to include in their membership representation of faculty, staff, and students, with appropriate racial diversity.

From conception, a particularly salient NWSA feature, inclusivity, has meant a struggle to bring sisterhood, solidarity, and empowerment to all participants. It also has meant struggle to design forms of governance that facilitate rather than impede attainment of such goals, to keep the organization's base wide and encourage widespread participation. The first constitution, drawn together from the resolutions created and approved at the founding convention by the specifically diverse delegates, reflected these principles. From the beginning NWSA committed formally to ensuring that minority viewpoints received more than token consideration. These goals have not changed appreciably. The most recent mission statement, approved February 1991, presents a vision of all persons developing to their greatest potential, free of oppressive and exploitative ideologies and structures, by means of feminist education—including teaching, research, and service—from prekindergarten through postsecondary levels. Nor were the political implications of this commitment neglected; governance structures making the vision possible are incorporated in the 1992 constitutional revisions.

Over the last decade NWSA leadership has developed semihierarchical structures to operate effectively between the governing board's semiannual meetings. Work groups during the coordinating council's meetings and discussion groups during the first part of the delegate assembly promote discussion on initiatives and equitable access to decision-making participation at the grass roots. A formal governance reorganization was completed during 1990–92 and fully in place in 1993.

Within NWSA, members have felt confronted by tensions between commonalty and difference and between empowerment and efficiency in their attempts to make practical the ideals of equality, unity, inclusivity, and participation. Current tensions exist between those emphasizing the need for an organization that validates their work as women's studies students, teachers, and scholars/ researchers and those emphasizing work to develop the widest diversity.

ORGANIZATION AND FUNDING

NWSA has affiliates in most states and twelve regional organizations. Effort is made to encourage governing council participation by persons of color, persons from lower-income strata, persons with disabilities, older women, and lesbians. All the officers and board members are women. Headquarters is located at the University of Maryland at College Park. NWSA employs one full-time staff member, an office manager, Loretta Younger.

NWSA has 2,000 members, down from 4,000 in 1990. In 1980, it had 2,000 members. There are some members abroad. From the beginning, the membership has been 99 percent female. The organization's status as a mainly-women group has come under discussion, and it will remain a women-mainly group. Incentives to join include conferences but also advocacy of important ideas, communication with colleagues, friendship ties, and the chance to associate with similarly minded people.

NWSA is a 501 (c) (4) organization. Sixty percent of its revenues come from conventions and membership dues, ranging from $25 to $75, and 40 percent, from government and corporate or business grants, with negligible returns on merchandise sales. The total budget for 1991–92 was $250,000.

The NWSA Academic Discrimination Task Force Legal Defense Fund is funded by donations. Annette Kolodny's settlement from the University of New Hampshire endowed it. Annis Pratt serves as the LDF's chief executive officer. The fund provides litigants with partial financial assistance; recipients return the money if they win. Despite the Reagan and Bush administrations' opposition to affirmative action, it has not kept these litigants from winning. The LDF filed for 501 (c) (3) status in 1992.

Among the most important cases that LDF has backed is Katherine Gutzwiller's suit in the seventies against the University of Cincinnati, which led to her reinstatement and tenure in the classics department as well as a settlement of around $350,000. Another significant case was Louise Witherell's against the University of Wisconsin at Green Bay for long-standing salary disparities; the grievance was settled after an internal process. LDF also deals constantly with sexual harassment issues.

POLICY CONCERNS AND TACTICS

NWSA policy is initiated through the delegate assembly and established by the board of directors. Executive officers' decisions also exercise influence. Strategically, NWSA seeks to educate its members with publications; it also encourages them to write legislators about appropriate political issues. NWSA conducts and publishes research on issues and works to educate the public through press releases. To a lesser extent, it participates in such direct action political demonstrations as the 1978 pro-choice march and contacts public decisions makers through influential members.

The most important federal law to NWSA today is the 1974 Women's Educational Equity Act. Its LDF finds the 1991 Civil Rights Act quite helpful.

NWSA collaborates with some like-minded groups on such projects as research on the women's studies major.

ELECTORAL ACTIVITIES

NWSA does not see women's issues as partisan, and it does not have a political action committee.

FURTHER INFORMATION

NWSA publishes a quarterly newsletter for its members, *NWSAction,* and offers a journal three times yearly to subscribers, the *NWSA Journal.* It publishes research reports such as one with AAC by Caryn McTighe Musil, *The Courage to Question: Women's Studies and Student Learning.* Another publication is *Liberal Learning and the Women's Studies Major,* completed in cooperation with a national review of art and sciences majors initiated by AAC.

BARBARA W. GERBER

NATIONAL WOMEN'S STUDIES ASSOCIATION ACADEMIC DISCRIMINATION TASK FORCE LEGAL DEFENSE FUND
See NATIONAL WOMEN'S STUDIES ASSOCIATION

NETWORK: A NATIONAL CATHOLIC SOCIAL JUSTICE LOBBY
806 Rhode Island Avenue, NE
Washington, DC 20018
(202) 526-4070
FAX (202) 832-4635

Through lobbying activities, NETWORK: A National Catholic Social Justice Lobby seeks fair access to economic resources, equitable allocations of national funding, and justice in international relations. There is a NETWORK Education Program.

ORIGIN AND DEVELOPMENT

NETWORK, the first registered national Catholic social justice lobby, formed at a meeting held at Trinity College in Washington, D.C., in December 1971. The idea for the organization grew out of several people's realization that Catholics needed a social justice lobbying arm. Sisters Mary Hayes and Josephine Dunne wanted the Washington, D.C., chapter of the National Assembly of Religious Women* (NARW) to get involved in lobbying. Dominican sister Marge Tuite—who had worked with civil rights advocates at the Urban Training Center in Chicago, taught social analysis to many Catholic sisters' groups, and was a board member of the Catholic Committee on Urban Ministry (CCUM)—shared similar feelings with urban policy activist Monsignor Geno Baroni and Sisters Claire Dugan and Mary Riley at a CCUM meeting. They knew the energy and commitment that sisters brought to social justice work and dreamed of using that energy to influence national policy.

Baroni convened the December meeting that would give substance to that dream, under the auspices of the National Center for Urban Ethnic Affairs, and gave staff assistance from his office. Tuite, with Josephine Dunne of the Campaign for Human Development, and Mary Hayes of Trinity College, sent invitations to the members of the Leadership Conference of Women Religious* (LCWR), to NAWR and other interested sisters to join in forming a network of sisters to lobby for resolution of social policy issues.

Forty-seven women religious from twenty-one states attended the meeting. Audrey Miller took over the leadership role from Monsignor Baroni on the last day, after asserting that religious women were capable of organizing themselves. After much discussion of issues and strategy, Carol Coston moved that the sisters present should establish a political action network to disseminate information and facilitate communication. The vote in favor was almost unanimous. A steering committee was empowered to make concrete plans, with Coston at its head.

LCWR gave enthusiastic support to NETWORK's formation at its assembly in 1972, assuring its existence. The first offices were in an apartment of the Religious of the Sacred Heart, in the low-income Sursum Corda housing project near the Capitol. Coston and Margaret Hohman were the first full-time staff members. Starting in 1972, Dominican sister Coston served as executive director for the network's first eleven years. Nancy Sylvester held the office for the next nine years.

NETWORK's formation culminated a process begun in the sixties, when sisters became more active in civil rights, antiwar, and other social justice issues, particularly after the Second Vatican Council asked them to promote gospel values in their contemporary culture. As sisters left classrooms to work among the poor and powerless, many came to see that the political process is often the route to bringing about systematic change in a democracy. Sisters were often very effective in dealing with issues on a local or state level; but it became evident that the Congress was the center for policy formation. To influence it, one needed to have a Washington presence and to lobby congresspersons, as did other interest groups. Church documents pointed to the importance of political ministry in dealing with social issues.

ORGANIZATION AND FUNDING

NETWORK has a governing board with nineteen members, all of whom must be women, chaired by a president with a three-year term. The board includes two African American and one Haitian women and three Hispanic American women. In 1989, Dorothy Ettling general superior of her congregation, became president, succeeding Barbara Aldave, dean of the Law School at St. Mary's University in Texas. Kathy Thornton became national coordinator in the fall of 1992. In 1992, there was a staff of ten in the Washington office, including coordinators for finance, education, and development, an organizer, and two lobbyists. To reflect the principle of equality of persons, all staff members receive the same compensation; accountability within the organization is horizontal, and an effective peer evaluation process has developed. There are three associates or interns.

In the 1990s, membership has stood around 10,000. A 1983 survey showed that each individual membership actually represented an average of thirteen people. NETWORK functions as a means for active participation in public policy formation toward a more socially just society. It provides up-to-date, carefully researched information and analysis on the issues it follows. Further incentives to membership include access to staff members for specific research and contacts; participation in a local congressional district network and/or as an issue activist on specific issues; receipt of a bimonthly magazine with information, analysis, and resource suggestions as well as action alerts; and voting records published at the end of each Congress for all congresspersons and senators.

NETWORK is a registered lobby, a 501 (c) (4) organization and as such is a taxable entity. Religious congregations and other groups such as Catholic hospital systems support NETWORK financially, as do individual memberships and donations. Annual dues are $30, $15 for low-income persons. The 1992 expense budget totaled $734,000.

NETWORK Education Program is a 501 (c) (3) organization, which is tax-exempt because it has an educational purpose. Funds raised for this organization support much of its specifically educational work.

POLICY CONCERNS AND TACTICS

Decisions as to which issues to stress are made jointly by board, staff, and members every four years, during the U.S. presidential election year, when all members are polled as to their preferences. Decisions are made in NETWORK in a participative rather than hierarchical manner. One of the organization's goals is to make the internal management processes reflect the same values for which it advocates in public policy—mutuality, coresponsibility, participation. Decisions on the organization's issue focus are made every four years through a referendum process involving board members, staff, and the full membership.

Strategies for implementing the issue agenda are developed consensually by a staff issue-organizing committee. NETWORK integrates its lobby work on Capitol Hill with strong field action to bring constituent pressure to bear on members of the Congress. Its organizers keep its congressional district contacts and its 800 issue activists updated on the progress of legislation. When key votes on NETWORK issues are pending, phone alerts and a rapid response network activate constituent contacts to lawmakers. NETWORK provides educational materials and processes on issues, on lobbying, and on political participation as an expression of faith-based values. It also produces educational resources on specific issues and on the social teachings of the Catholic Church.

An important vehicle for promoting political awareness has been the legislative seminar, which educates people about the legislative process and justice issues and trains them to lobby and organize for political change. An average of 200 people from across the nation attend each seminar. Such major Washington figures as Adlai Stevenson, Hubert Humphrey, John Gardner, and Patricia Schroeder have been featured seminar speakers. Many participants have become justice and peace coordinators for their congregation or diocese.

NETWORK derives its positions on issues through reflection on the values in Catholic social teaching. It always has striven to be a voice for people rendered voiceless. Among the issues it has emphasized are health care, housing, income support, changes in military spending and Latin American policy, sanctions in South Africa, Salvadoran refugees, immigration reform, reordered budget priorities, and equitable and sustainable development in the so-called Third World. It seeks global collaboration with special focus on the Philippines, Central America, and South Africa.

Some of NETWORK's successes include helping block the MX missile system, curbing spending for Star Wars, ratifying the Intermediate Nuclear Force Agreement to eliminate the intermediate-range missiles of the United States and the Soviet Union from Europe and Asia, winning passage of the 1988 Civil Rights Restoration Act, lobbying for creation of the Consumer Cooperative Bank, and helping to defeat aid to the contras. Issues on which NETWORK worked hard in the last decade, in conjunction with the District of Columbia interreligious community, include the 1990 National Affordable Housing Act, ending U.S. military intervention in Nicaragua and El Salvador, and beginning the decline of military spending. Three failures include campaign finance reform, the Family and Medical Leave bills during the Bush administration, and military buildup and concomitant draining of domestic social programs in the early eighties.

NETWORK celebrated its twentieth anniversary in 1992 with the theme, Twenty Years of Creating Alternatives. Staffers, interns, members, and friends sharing in social justice political activities over the years gathered to celebrate NETWORK's accomplishments and chart future directions. As issues to be addressed, NETWORK's publication, *NETWORK Connection,* noted concern about the new world order and questions about what kind of nation America wants to be economically, racially, militarily. Among the seeds of hope for the future that NETWORK members note are women bonding to achieve common goals—a seed of hope for the future to which NETWORK itself has contributed.

Staff members join with other groups in lobbying, organizing protests, and so on. NETWORK collaborates with the following coalitions: the Citizens Budget Campaign, which includes groups such as Sane/Freeze, Jobs with Peace, Friends Committee on National Legislation, and Church Women United*; the Interreligious Task Force on Health Care, which includes all the mayor religious denominations; the National Neighborhood Coalition; National Low Income Housing Coalition*; and National Commission for Economic Conversion and Disarmament. It also collaborates with the Women's International League for Peace and Freedom,* Religious Network for Equality for Women, National Women's Law Center, Central America Working Group, and Philippine Development Forum.

ELECTORAL ACTIVITIES

NETWORK does not see as partisan the issues that concern it. It sees its issues as justice issues, human needs issues that especially affect the most disadvantaged in society. It lobbies both Democrats and Republicans. It does not have a political action committee and does not endorse candidates for election. In presidential election years it produces nonpartisan information on candidates' positions on issues and conducts voter education workshops around the country. Many sisters participating in the annual legislative seminar have gone on to run for political office, including Clare Dunne, who served in the Arizona state legislature from 1975 until her death in 1991; Elizabeth Morency, a state representative in Rhode Island from 1978 to 1988; Ardeth Platte, who served on the Saginaw, Michigan, City Council; and Arlene Violet, attorney general of Rhode Island.

FURTHER INFORMATION

NETWORK publishes a bimonthly magazine, *NETWORK Connection,* and a bimonthly newsletter, *NETWORKer,* for its activists. Subjects of recent action alerts have included opposition to a balanced budget amendment, to military aid or sales in Central America, and to political restrictions on aid to Nicaragua, extension of the low-income housing tax credit, support for comprehensive rather than piecemeal health care reform, and increase in funding for housing assistance to low-income persons.

MARY EWENS

NETWORK EDUCATION PROGRAM
See NETWORK: A NATIONAL CATHOLIC SOCIAL JUSTICE LOBBY

9to5, NATIONAL ASSOCIATION OF WORKING WOMEN (NAWW)
238 W. Wisconsin Avenue, Suite 700
Milwaukee, WI 53203
(414) 274-0925
Job Problem Hotline (800) 522-0925
FAX (414) 272-2870

9to5, National Association of Working Women (NAWW), a membership organization, advocates for the rights of American office workers. In conjunction with the 9to5 Working Women Education Fund (WWEF), 9to5 addresses issues such as the future of office work, automation, health, and safety and the elimination of harassment and discrimination based on sex or race.

ORIGIN AND DEVELOPMENT

9to5 evolved from a local grassroots effort. Karen Nussbaum, Janet Selcer, Ellen Cassedy and seven other women published the first issue of 9to5 *News* in Boston in December 1972. The newsletter expressed the concerns of a group Nussbaum and Cassedy organized earlier that year, women working with them in Harvard University offices. Grievances included salary inequities, inability to advance, a preponderance of male supervisors (often trained by women), and generally a lack of respect for office workers. They represented the largest segment of American workers. *9to5 News* emphasized the power of collective action to enhance clerical workers' self-respect and treatment by management.

Late in 1973, newsletter organizers sponsored a public forum in Boston for women office workers and a month later announced the formation of 9to5, a group for Boston area clerical staff. The group had the twofold purpose of correcting workforce inequities through education and action and building a women's network to make these corrections. Joan Tiqhe served as the first chairperson.

In 1974, Boston 9to5 held a public hearing for 300 women office workers from seven different industries; it concluded by reading the new "Bill of Rights for Women Office Workers." Other early activities concentrated on affirmative action generally and fair treatment in the publishing, insurance, and banking industries specifically. A 1975 hearing on the publishing industry attracted much attention to Boston 9to5 and the sponsoring committee, Women in Publishing (WIP). Late the same year, Boston 9to5 filed suit against publishers Allyn and Bacon, Houghton Mifflin, and Addison-Wesley, winning $1.5 million dollars in back pay. In 1975–76, it launched an affirmative action campaign involving hearings, press releases, and congressional testimony. The organization joined Women Employed (WE) of Chicago and the Boston chapter of National Organization for Women* in opposing proposed revisions in U.S. affirmative action policy.

In 1977, Boston 9to5 joined with such affiliates as WE, Women Working (Cleveland), Women Organized for Employment (San Francisco), and Women Office Workers (New York City) to create a national Working Women Organizing Project, headquartered in Cleveland. Nussbaum became its director in 1978. In 1982, the name changed to Working Women, National Association of Office Workers. The national organization became 9to5, National Association of Working Women, in 1983.

To gain collective bargaining power for office workers, 9to5 helped organize the first 925 Local of the Service Employees International Union (SEIU) for private sector office workers in the Boston area in 1975. Nussbaum and other 9to5 leaders carefully selected SEIU as most amenable to NAWW's goals. In 1981, this effort expanded nationwide with the formation of SEIU District 925, in cooperation with NAWW and its affiliates. The two groups maintain a close affiliation: in 1991 9to5 trained 100 District 925 leaders to advise 9to5 hotline callers.

In January 1977, 9to5 joined with the Cleveland, San Francisco, and New York City working women's groups in the National Women's Employment Project (NWEP) to underscore the need to broaden and enforce federal equal employment policy. The monitoring, research, and implementation effort raised money to educate women about the federal equal hiring bureaucracy (the Equal Employment Opportunity Commission, and Contract Compliance Program) and to push for stronger enforcement. Interest and membership in 9to5 increased after the first convention held in Boston in 1978. Over 800 women attended the event, which featured workshops, crisis counseling, and keynote speaker Senator Edward Kennedy (D-MA). 9to5 sponsored the first Summer School for Working Women at Kent State University in 1979, addressing topics such as fund-raising and organizing skills. The summer school has become an annual event.

Nussbaum's acquaintance Jane Fonda drew public attention to female office workers' concerns in her 1980 feature film *Nine to Five*. A comedy, the film drew upon meetings Fonda and the film writers had with 9to5 members. Campaigns on career development, higher pay, modern workplace hazards, and continuing efforts on behalf of affirmative action occupied 9to5 through the early 1980s.

ORGANIZATION AND FUNDING

In 1993, 9to5's administrative offices, located in Cleveland since 1977, moved to Milwaukee. At that time, Ellen Bravo became Executive Director, following Nussbaum's appointment by President Clinton to the U.S. Department of Labor. 9to5 maintained its membership office and Job Problem Hotline in Cleveland.

There are twenty-five local 9to5 chapters. Chapters elect representatives (one for every fifty members) to the board of 9to5 for renewable one-year terms. The size of the board varies with chapter size.

Fifteen thousand people representing 100 cities and every state belong to 9to5. Annual dues are twenty-five dollars. A man or woman interested in promoting the issues may join a chapter or, if one is not available locally, the 9to5 Field Rep program. The organization supplies resource materials to Field Reps on topics such as family leave, health care coverage, computer monitoring, discrimination, child care, and sexual harassment; Field Reps contact the media or political officials about pertinent issues and meet with other nearby 9to5 members. Anyone not an office worker can become a friend for a tax-deductible donation to 9to5 WWEF.

Women often join 9to5 in response to job-related frustration or anger. Members feel attracted by the attention 9to5 pays to such daily concerns as maternity leave, medical benefits, equal pay, and equal treatment. All members receive the newsletter and benefits such as discounts on publications and opportunities for low-cost credit cards, insurance, travel, and a pharmacy discount.

The budget of about $600,000 is raised by membership fees and publication sales.

The 9to5 WWEF, until 1989 known as the Working Women Education Fund, maintains a 501 (c) (3) status, while 9to5 NAWW's status is 501 (c) (5). The education fund, which conducts research and training, has a separate, eight-member board and receives its funding from foundation grants and other donations.

POLICY CONCERNS AND TACTICS

9to5 utilizes grassroots activism, research, and the media to accomplish its goal of better working conditions. Specific strategies include surveys, congressional testimony, and education through public hearings, conferences and workshops, research, and media publicity to address and improve unfair and/or unsafe working conditions affecting the country's clerical workforce. Surveys on subjects such as marginalization of older workers, hazards of video display terminal (VDT) use, and electronic monitoring in the workplace often have provided a base for advocacy. In its early days, 9to5 leaders implemented the organizing approach of the Midwest Academy, a Chicago school for community organizers, emphasizing empowerment of the community as well as individuals. Through class action suits, 9to5 has won over $25 million in back pay and pay equity raises for office workers in industries such as publishing, insurance, and banking.

In the late 1980s and early 1990s, 9to5 congressional testimony concentrated on issues of workplace privacy, family and medical leave, day care, employment and poverty, and equal pay. Earlier testimony focused on workplace technology, especially VDTs, home-based workers and women, work and aging. Occasionally, 9to5 representatives testify on behalf of both 9to5 and SEIU, as in Nussbaum's 1987 appearances before the House and Senate advocating improved day care. Local 9to5 chapters give testimony before state legislatures. For example, in Georgia in 1992, local leaders' four-year effort culminated in the passage of a state family leave bill.

As part of its educational effort, 9to5 has presented training and workshops on sexual harassment almost since its inception. In 1987, 9to5 pioneered another education program, the Job Retention Project (JRP) in Milwaukee. JRP provides training in skills such as managing time and stress, setting and reaching objectives, and resolving conflict, to enable low-income women to obtain and keep jobs.

9to5 also uses the media to modify policy, spotlighting unfair treatment of working women. In the spring of 1992, it organized a press conference to help Melissa Fojtik of Racine, Wisconsin, publicize the sexual misconduct of a mayoral candidate. The previous year, 9to5 joined with the American Civil Liberties Union* (ACLU) in drawing attention to the fact Continental Airlines fired employee Terri Fishette for not wearing makeup. In both cases the media blitz succeeded: the candidate lost the election, and Continental rehired Fishette (who later resigned to become an advocate). Local and national 9to5 representatives often use radio and television appearances. In 1989, 9to5 initiated a labor press conference following the second international scientific conference on VDTs, uniting with labor groups in calling for action to prevent future occurrences of injuries, illnesses, and stress problems related to prolonged use of computer terminals. The organization highlights National Secretaries' Week and Day in April each year, calling for "raises AND roses," and since 1990 has sponsored a National Bosses Contest, where employees nominate candidates in the categories of "good," "bad," or "unbelievable." The contest began in 1975 as local "Pettiest Office Procedure" contests.

Through its toll-free Job Problem Hotline, 9to5 has counseled more than 75,000 women and men from every state about their job rights, tabulating information about the frequency and types of concerns. It initiated the hotline in May 1989 to broaden the knowledge base about working women's problems and to assist women office workers more directly. More than 1,400 women called the hotline in five business days about job-related sexual harassment during the 1991 confirmation hearings for Supreme Court appointee Clarence Thomas.

Concerned with physical working conditions, 9to5 works with employers in changing offices and task distribution to improve job efficiency, performance, and satisfaction. The organization encourages including employees in such efforts, promoting job redesign by workers on a team basis. Along with Communication Workers of America* and ACLU, in 1991, 9to5 introduced legislation in four states and the Congress to restrict electronic monitoring of workers.

ELECTORAL ACTIVITIES

In 1981, 9to5 entered electoral politics, developing a "working women's platform" of concerns such as comparable worth, flextime, and job sharing. During the 1992 presidential campaign, 9to5 hosted opportunities in Cleveland for Hillary Rodham Clinton to meet and speak with working women.

FURTHER INFORMATION

9to5 issues *9to5 Newsline* five times a year to members—twenty-five dollars a year for nonmembers and forty dollars for institutions. Through the newsletter, it educates members about workers' legal rights, for example, the right to work while pregnant, and upcoming legislation. It offers many published resources, including *"Business as Usual": Stories from the 9to5 Job Problem Hotline* (1991) and reports on topics such as job performance, wage replacement for family leave, electronic monitoring, and VDT syndrome. In 1992, 9to5 compiled *The 9to5 Guide to Combatting Sexual Harassment* by Ellen Bravo and Ellen Cassedy. 9to5 also publishes fact sheets, including an annual profile of working women, and pamphlets.

JIMMY ELAINE WILKINSON MEYER

9to5 WORKING WOMEN EDUCATION FUND
See 9to5, NATIONAL ASSOCIATION OF WORKING WOMEN

NOW/EQUALITY/PAC
See NATIONAL ORGANIZATION FOR WOMEN

NOW/ERA/PAC
See NATIONAL ORGANIZATION FOR WOMEN

NOW FOUNDATION
See NATIONAL ORGANIZATION FOR WOMEN

NOW/PAC
See NATIONAL ORGANIZATION FOR WOMEN

NURSES' ASSOCIATED ALUMNAE OF THE UNITED STATES AND CANADA
See AMERICAN NURSES' ASSOCIATION

NURSES' COALITION FOR ACTION IN POLITICS
See AMERICAN NURSES' ASSOCIATION

NURSES UNITED
See COMMUNICATIONS WORKERS OF AMERICA

O
/

OLDER WOMEN'S LEAGUE (OWL)
666 11th Street, NW
Suite 700
Washington, DC 20001
(202) 783-6686

An educational and grassroots community action organization, the Older Women's League (OWL) has addressed the intersection of feminist and age-related public policy issues.

ORIGIN AND DEVELOPMENT

OWL grew through feminist and grassroots organizing from the displaced homemaker campaigns of Tish Sommers and Laurie Shields in the 1970s. By 1978, with the Displaced Homemaker Network in place, Sommers and Shields moved on to broader issues affecting older women through the nonprofit Older Women's League Education Fund (OWLEF). Their grey paper, "Older Women and Public Policy," described the combined effects of age and sex discrimination. A series of grey papers on Social Security, health care, pensions, and welfare built OWLEF's reputation as an educational resource.

By the end of the 1970s, the potential for a new kind of national organization was evident. Some age activists felt angry that their organizations ignored women; some older feminists felt their organizations ignored age. The catalyst for the next step was the White House Conference on Aging set for 1981. Sommers and Shields, through contacts established during the displaced homemaker campaign and through the National Organization for Women* (NOW) Task Force on Older Women, built a coalition with the Western Gerontological

Association to win a grant for a miniconference on older women. Old friends from early campaigns received invitations; and Maggie Kuhn of the Grey Panthers* (GP) agreed to be the keynote speaker. The organizers chose Des Moines, Iowa, as the conference site both because a strong organizer lived nearby and because they wanted OWL to be seen as an organization grounded in middle America.

Sommers became president of the board, Shields the executive director. The meeting and board's composition were orchestrated carefully to include minority representation, geographical diversity, and political clout. Eugenia Hicks and Dorthy Pitts served as founding board members and later organized the first national conference on black women and aging. Three hundred charter members signed up for OWL on October 13, 1980. OWL's formation was featured in Sylvia Porter's syndicated column and drew more than 4,000 letters. Among the first chapters organized was a southern one in Louisville, Kentucky; within two years there were over seventy chapters and nearly 5,000 members.

From the onset, the idea was to build OWL chapters across the country to focus on three core issues: access to health care insurance, Social Security reform, and pension rights. The goals were political, but the context, including warm folksy reports in the newsletter from chapter correspondents, embraced the wholeness of women's concerns. OWL chapters have a mixed membership in that some came to OWL as experienced activists, eager to convert their energy to older women's interests, whereas others had no political background. Many also experienced the consequences of divorce, widowhood, loneliness, poverty, and invisibility. Each chapter faced with this combination of interests had to find a balance and did so, as business meetings paired with a meal or social occasion and as support manifested for those sick or depressed, urging them to share in the political excitement. The grassroots chapters flourished, their strength grounded in this mixture, although it also led to frustration on many occasions as more experienced activists pushed for a faster pace than newcomers could maintain.

OWL's Washington, D.C., office opened in 1983, staffed by Alice Quinlan, a worker on the displaced homemaker campaigns, and Shirley Sanbage, who moved from a Des Monies displaced homemeker center to become OWL's second executive director. The change to a bicoastal operation, with the national office on the East Coast and the board president and both cofounders in Oakland, California, was a difficult one. Sommers shaped and guided OWL, feeling reluctant to let either the board or Washington staff operate totally independently, and remained at the center of decision making until her death in 1985. An uneasy transition followed. After ten years there has been much turnover—a hazard of organizing a population over age sixty-five—and OWL is no longer the only organization paying attention to older women's issues. Sommers and Shields both are gone from OWL now, but their legacy continues. The feminist personal networking that generated both the displaced homemaker network and OWL continues to renew itself as each new generation of women ages and sees the problems.

ORGANIZATION AND FUNDING

OWL has 117 chapters in thirty-seven states and nearly a dozen state chapters across the country. There is a national delegate convention. The board of sixteen directors is elected by mail ballot by members. Two board members are African American; one is Hispanic. Lou Glasse has served as president of the Board since 1985. Joan Kuriansky is the executive director of the Washington-based office. In that office there are eight full-time and seven part-time staff as well as several interns and volunteer workers.

The 20,000 members are primarily women older than fifty, a high proportion of whom are or have been displaced homemakers. OWL's national membership dues were and are low, fifteen dollars a year, to attract a wide range of members; most members also are active in local chapters. Incentives to join include advocacy of important values, ideas, or policies; representation of member's opinions to government; communication with peers and the chance to associate with similarly minded people.

Initially, Sommers and Shields raised funds from private philanthropic organizations, their first concern a strong financial base. Sommers paid the Oakland office staff's wages in the first years and eventually set up an OWL endowment of more than $700,000. OWL also has been successful in direct mail campaigns. It is a 501 (c) (3) tax-exempt organization and in 1991, had a budget close to $900,000.

POLICY CONCERNS AND TACTICS

Decision making has become less centralized than originally, and the executive director and board members take a more direct role in shaping policy. When a new policy issue is selected by delegates to the national convention, an issue action alert is sent from the national office, which also implements a nationwide telephone tree to local chapters and develops model legislation. Chapters and new state organizations continue to press on OWL's issues, with some tension between the locally based grassroots chapters and the more bureaucratically structured national office. As preferred strategy, OWL presents legislative testimony, educates the public, and organizes campaigns to promote positive shifts in aging policies. OWL representatives testify frequently before state and federal legislators, repeatedly raising older women's interests.

One important OWL accomplishment is the increased visibility of older women. For example, its 1990 Mother's Day Report on Social Security drew national media attention that resulted in a federal legislative hearing on older women's retirement incomes, which, in turn, led in 1992 to formation of a congressional working group to develop recommendations for pension and Social Security legislation reform.

At the state level, OWL members have supported the extension of health insurance to women over sixty and legislation on health plans and mammography screening. In many states, OWL members have pushed for living will and right to die legislation, as well as spousal impoverishment waivers now enacted in about half the states.

Nationally, OWL has been influential in passage of the Health Insurance Continuation Act, spousal impoverishment legislation, and inclusion of elder and spousal care under the Family and Medical Leave bills vetoed by President Bush. It continues to serve as a strong voice for older women; and legislative leaders seek information from OWL.

OWL finds of continuing importance the 1965 Administration on Aging Act; 1968 Revised Uniform Reciprocal Enforcement of Support Agreement Act; Act of 1972 adding sex discrimination to the Civil Rights Commission jurisdiction and 1972 Equal Employment Act; 1974 Equal Credit Opportunity and Women's Educational Equity Acts; the Child Support Amendments—1975 Social Security Act; and 1984 Child Support Enforcement Act. It finds the 1983 Social Security, 1984 Pension Equity, and 1986 Age Discrimination acts to be the most important federal initiatives of the last decade.

OWL benefits from relevant coalitions with such organizations as GP, NOW, the National Council of Senior Citizens, National Women's Law Center, National Association of State Units on Aging, Women's Legal Defense Fund, and American Association of Retired Persons.* To strengthen alliances with women of color, at its 1992 national convention OWL sponsored a Women of Diversity: Coming Together conference. Its primary focus for the 1990s is coordination of the Campaign for Women's Health, a coalition of seventy national and local organizations with a combined membership of 8.4 million. Its purpose is to help women's organizations unite around the priority of women's health needs and to ensure that public policy discussion about health insurance programs and government budgets adequately considers women's voices and priorities. The coalition works with the Congressional Caucus for Women's Issues* as well, assisting in agenda setting and identification of priorities and principles.

FURTHER INFORMATION

Besides the *Owl Observer,* which carries news to members, balancing local initiatives and concerns with columns by legal counsel, OWL publishes special-topic grey papers and an annual Mother's Day report on some economic/political aspect of older women's lives.

PATRICIA HUCKLE

OPERATION RESCUE NATIONAL (ORN)
P.O. Box 1180
Binghamton, NY 13902

Operation Rescue National (ORN) protests the 1973 *Roe* v. *Wade* decision by organizing and conducting direct action demonstrations at abortion clinics.

ORIGIN AND DEVELOPMENT

Although ORN is a different organization from Randall Terry's defunct Operation Rescue (OR), both organizations share a common history. In 1988, in protest of legalized abortion, Terry organized "rescue" missions: direct action political demonstrations in which he and other protesters blocked entrances to abortion clinics to women seeking abortions. Terry at the time of this writing hosted a radio program, "Randell Terry Live," and was a speaker on Christian activism, primarily pro-life activities. The first series of clinic rescues that Terry led took place in Cherry Hill, New Jersey, and in New York City and Atlanta. The demonstrations in Atlanta occurred during the Democratic National Convention and brought the first national media attention to Terry's activities. These rescues led Terry to organize OR formally; and the publicity resulted in the formation of more than 200 autonomous local rescue groups.

In 1989, OR went underground because of lawsuits that resulted from its protest activities and eventually disbanded as a formal organization. Early in 1991, the Reverend Keith Tucci founded ORN. Before coming to ORN, Tucci was a pastor for different churches; his last pastorship was for Greater Pittsburgh Word and Worship Fellowship. ORN maintains the same organizational principle as its predecessor: to serve as the voice of unborn children. It has two goals. First, it seeks to prevent the slaughter of as many unborn children as it can. The second goal of this nondenominational Christian organization is to stimulate contriteness in the Christian church for not doing all it could to prevent the *Roe* decision as to change to active and constant participation.

ORGANIZATION AND FUNDING

ORN is not affiliated with local rescue groups. The 200-plus local organizations, which exist in forty to fifty states and the District of Columbia, are autonomous. ORN has headquarters in Binghamton, New York. The personnel structure of ORN consists of a small group of volunteers. The executive director is Tucci. Filling out the staff are three volunteers, wearing many hats and experiencing different levels of responsibility within the organization. Legal services are supplied pro bono.

ORN does not have a membership base.

ORN is a nonprofit group. All its funding comes from small donations from individuals. Gifts are received at rallies, rescues, and other events, as well as through the mail. Any requests to earmark contributions for specific ORN activities are granted. Donations are not tax-deductible, although ORN has tax-exempt status under the U.S. Internal Revenue Code because it is considered a religious group. ORN's budget for 1991 was $295,000. Expenditures include direct mailings, newsletters for contributors, information packets, rent, office necessities, and the costs associated with organizing major demonstrations. Local groups have their own budgets and organize their own rescues.

POLICY CONCERNS AND TACTICS

ORN is a grassroots organization because it seeks to "change the hearts of the people," so it chooses the location of its protest activities by going to locations where there are good, strong local groups and support. ORN tries to get to all of the ten zones in which the country is divided. Such major rescue events as the ones held in Wichita, Kansas, and Buffalo, New York, last a week or two and include protests by day and rallies at night. These events are large, and for this reason, ORN organizes only a few major "rescues" each year. ORN also has an adoption project, in which it will link applicants and an adoption clearinghouse.

ORN has not sustained any fines. At the 1992 Buffalo rescue event, six pro-life leaders went to jail for violating a federal injunction. A case concerning an event, *Bray, Operation Rescue et al.* v. *Alexandria Women's Health Clinic, NOW et al.*, made it to the Supreme Court and ended favorably for ORN in January 1993. The Court found that Bray did not violate the rights of pregnant women as a class by opposing/protesting abortion. The appellants argued that the original law, the "Ku Klux Klan Act," was meant to apply to blacks; and J. Scalia found it to be applied wrongly against individuals blocking abortion clinics, because they sought to protect victims of abortion, not discriminate against women per se. Scalia also found no right existed that could have been encroached upon.

An initiative that would be counterproductive to ORN goals would be passage of the proposed Freedom of Choice bill; it has not yet passed the Congress. This bill, if passed, would prohibit a state from restricting a woman's right to an abortion, under certain requirements. ORN sees this initiative as antifamily. The passage of such laws and initiatives as the Freedom of Choice Act is attributed to the "culture war" that has taken place since the 1960s between "cultural elites" advocating "individual freedoms" and the conservative establishment supporting what it considers basic social tenets, originally based on the Bible. It also is attributed to the liberal Congress and pandering special interests that are highly influential due to their money. ORN believes the decisions made and laws passed in the 1980s are better than those of the 1970s, since they have placed greater restrictions on abortion's availability.

National and local groups may work together at rallies and rescues. ORN coordinates with these groups to bring protesters to the events. It also counts on local groups to provide sidewalk abortion counselors, as well as to disseminate information. ORN is not affiliated with the rescues that have taken place in Europe, Australia, South America, Mexico, or Puerto Rico, among others. It considers itself allied with groups that share its pro-life perception: the sanctity of life. ORN has an adversarial relationship with Planned Parenthood,* National Abortion Rights Action League,* and National Organization for Women.* These groups support the two issues ORN staunchly opposes: the equal rights amendment and *Roe* v. *Wade.* Confrontation with these groups peaked over the *Web-*

ster v. *Reproductive Health Services of Missouri* (1990) and *Planned Parenthood of Southeastern Pennsylvania* v. *Casey* (1992) decisions. ORN does not wholly support these decisions, because the Supreme Court did not overturn *Roe,* but does praise the limitations that the decisions placed on women's ability to obtain abortions.

ELECTORAL ACTIVITIES

ORN is a nonpartisan group. It does not engage officially in electoral politics. It does not have a political action committee, nor does it endorse candidates for political office.

FURTHER INFORMATION

ORN has a monthly newsletter, *National Rescue Update,* which has 8,000 recipients. It also has available two informational packets, one offering a general history of the rescue movement, pictures of abortion's results, and the biblical and legal basis for opposing abortion. The second packet, for college students, offers a more detailed version of the first.

CAROLYN JESKEY

ORGANIZATION OF CHINESE AMERICAN WOMEN (OCAW)
1300 N Street, NW
Suite 100
Washington, DC 20005
(202) 638-0330

The first national Asian American women's association, the Organization of Chinese American Women (OCAW) seeks to advance the cause of Chinese American women in the United States and to foster public awareness of their talents, activities, needs, and concerns. It supports equal participation by Chinese American women in all aspects of life and integration into mainstream women's activities and programs as well as leadership and policy-making posts.

ORIGIN AND DEVELOPMENT

OCAW formed in 1977. Pauline W. Tsui, a member of the Advisory Committee of the U.S. Center for the Observance of International Women's Year, helped to found it, along with Julia Chang Bloch, the first Asian American ambassador, serving in Nepal and female. The idea occurred to Tsui and Bloch in 1975 during International Women's Year. OCAW had 22 charter members. By 1990 membership had risen to 2,000.

Since 1977, OCAW has consistently worked to increase public awareness of the special needs of Asian American women, monitored institutional adherence to guidelines as related to job opportunities for Asian women, developed models for professional leadership and skills training, and worked to integrate immigrant women into American society and to overcome racial stereotypes. These goals are accomplished through conferences and workshops, cultural events, research activities, and technical assistance workshops.

OCAW has among its general goals training immigrant Chinese women for employment, networking to serve such needs as legal representation, and providing English language education and support and outreach systems. The group's national office has trained and placed over 100 refugees and recent immigrant women in jobs. A former Women's Education Equity Act program director, U.S. Education Department, has honored OCAW as a "model of networking." Members work actively to enlarge college admission opportunities for Asian Americans. Since the group's inception, these goals have not changed but rather have expanded to include international linkage through a Women to Women program endorsed by the White House in 1987. The program encourages exchange visits, lectures, and tours between women of various countries, including the People's Republic of China (PRC), Republic of China (Taiwan), and Hong Kong.

ORGANIZATION AND FUNDING

OCAW has seven chapters located in Maryland, Louisiana, Texas, California, Hawaii, and the District of Columbia. It coordinated the first national conference of Chinese Asian women in 1978, now a biennial occurrence. A seventeen-member volunteer board of directors and an elected volunteer president head the organization. The board contains two lawyers and a certified public accountant, who donate their expertise. Most board members are professional women. The current president is Katherine Chang Dress, manager of Minority and Women, Owen Business Procurement. Functioning committees deal with program, finances, membership, community, and public relations. National headquarters is located in Washington, D.C., close to Chinatown, in order best to serve the community. The executive director is founder Tsui, who administers the organization as volunteer, and a part-time secretary, Ivy Wong. OCAW hires special consultants as workshop coordinators for individual projects.

Professional women constitute most of the membership, and recent immigrant women, the rest. Several members are influentially placed, including Elaine Chao, president of United Way, formerly deputy secretary of the U.S. Transportation Department; Linda Tsao Yang, ambassador and U.S. executive director of the Asian Development Bank; Nancy Linn Patton, deputy assistant secretary of the U.S. Department of Commerce; Esther Yao, former deputy director of Bilingual Education, U.S. Education Department; and Pearl Chow, director of World Trade in Baltimore. All Chinese dialects, especially Mandarin and Cantonese, are represented within the membership; and many members are bilingual. Bylaws are written in both English and Chinese. Age of members extends from traditional college students to senior citizens. Members pay annual dues of twenty-five dollars for adults and fifteen dollars for students. They join to enjoy strong friendship ties, participate in public affairs, and generate opportunities to exercise influence and advocate for Asian American women. They also engage in consciousness-raising exercises and seek to develop a group identity.

OCAW is a nonprofit, tax-exempt 501 (c) (3) organization. It has secured federal and District of Columbia grants to award scholarships to young women seeking to major in math and science, as well as such private foundation grants as support from the *Washington Post*'s Philip Graham Fund. Other revenue derives from the Li Foundation, annual banquets, corporate donations, and special fund-raising events, for example, a concert held at the Kennedy Center for Performing Arts and the Lisner Auditorium, featuring international vocalists from PRC, (ROC) Taiwan, and Belgium. Information on total budget size is not available.

POLICY CONCERNS AND TACTICS

The national board of OCAW sets the group's action agenda. The organization uses a number of different strategies to achieve its goals. The choice of strategy is influenced by the national board of OCAW. OCAW serves as a clearinghouse on matters concerning Asian American women and has earned a reputation as a major minority organization in the political process. It acts as a consultant to various federal departments and bureaus, in such issue arenas as health, economics, and welfare, and to the Transportation Department when its actions and policies affect women and minorities. OCAW testified against unequal immigration bills and college admission ceilings for Asian American students at a forum convened by Senators Paul Simon (D-IL) and Thomas A. Daschle (D-SD). They held a White House briefing on OCAW policies and goals as part of the fourth national conference in 1985 and for the OCAW Women to Women delegation in 1987, before its tour of ROC (Taiwan), PRC, and Hong Kong to strengthen educational, economic, and cultural ties with counterparts abroad. The sixth biennial conference, 1988, included another White House briefing.

A high-visibility organization, OCAW was designated by the Immigration and Naturalization Service as an agency to assist undocumented migrants in applying for legal status in the United States, 1987–88. Through these efforts, many migrants obtained interim permanent resident status. Subsequently, OCAW established classes for these immigrants in English, job training, Western culture, and counseling. OCAW also has supported the national Summer Youth Employment program sponsored by the U.S. Labor Department.

Between 1977 and 1990, OCAW held six national training conferences and three regional conferences preparing professional women for leadership roles in their communities and focusing on Asian Americans' issues and concerns, conducted six workshops for nonprofessional Chinese American women, conducted five courses in job placement and skills training and three seminars on management and money management, and conducted six essay contests. Emphasizing self-help, the organization created six training models of Chinese women, two of which were recommended, in 1983, by a national panel associated with

Wellesley College Women's Research Center to the U.S. Education Department for publication and general public distribution.

OCAW addresses issues of racial and sexual discrimination, breaking down stereotypes and restrictive traditional behavior and beliefs. It supports equal employment opportunity for professional and nonprofessional women and assists impoverished immigrants. It celebrates National Women's History Month and supports the Women's Hall of Fame. It encouraged the Senate's 1985 bill on Women's Economic Equity and the House's 1985 bill on retirement for Foreign Service wives and former spouses of the military services.

The issues addressed by OCAW link it to other national women's organizations and causes; and it works to construct bonds of common interest. OCAW opened the plenary session of the second women's agenda conference, held in 1989. It networks with the American Association of University Women,* Young Women's Christian Association,* and the various Commissions on the Status of Women.

ELECTORAL ACTIVITIES

A nonpartisan organization, OCAW seeks support from men and women at all levels of government and in electoral politics for the advancement of Asians. It does not have a political action committee. OCAW members Oregon state senator Mae Yih, formerly a school board member; Judy Chu, council member of Monterey Park, California; and Lily Lee Chen, former mayor of Monterey Park, California, enjoy considerable political recognition.

FURTHER INFORMATION

OCAW communicates with its members through a quarterly newsletter, *OCAW Speaks,* and an annual report. OCAW position papers are reprinted in the *Congressional Record,* and its issues of concern statements are listed in the Senate Committee on Human Resources Sourcebook, 1977. OCAW's purpose is further defined in *Celebrating a Decade of Excellence,* published by the office of the executive director, Washington, D.C., 1989. The *1993 Survey of Needs of Low-Income Elderly Housing* for the metropolitan Washington, D.C., area was also published and available for distribution.

BARBARA BENNETT PETERSON

ORGANIZATION OF PARENTS THROUGH SURROGACY (OPTS)
7054 Quito Court
Camarillo, CA 93012
(805) 482-1566

A volunteer association, the Organization of Parents Through Surrogacy (OPTS) provides information about assistive reproductive technology, referrals, and a support network for the infertile community and seeks to influence related legislation to protect the rights of all parties to the surrogacy process.

ORIGIN AND DEVELOPMENT

OPTS formed in 1987, in response to proposed legislation in California that would have banned commercial surrogacy. All the organizers were clients of the Center for Surrogate Parenting* (CSP) in Beverly Hills, California. The center, headed by attorney William Handel, is among the best-known centers for commercial, or "contractual," surrogacy in the United States. Fewer than ten people were involved in OPTS's organization. To some extent it emerged as an outgrowth of an earlier support group for surrogates and infertile couples at the center. This group, the National Association for Surrogate Motherhood (NASM), was facilitated by Hilary Hanafin, head psychologist at CSP. NASM is now inactive, but OPTS serves some of its functions. Unlike NASM, OPTS focuses primarily on the needs of infertile couples, although it welcomes participation by surrogates.

Founded by parents whose children were born through surrogacy or assisted reproduction, OPTS describes one of its goals as seeking to keep open the options made available by advances in reproductive technology to those unable to have children in the conventional manner. Founders Kathe Linden and Elisabeth Tilles served as national directors, as did Shirley Zager. Although initially OPTS focused on providing information and support, it now has developed broader goals and includes a commitment to political action. It remains committed to providing information about surrogacy to infertile couples and to provide emotional support throughout the surrogacy process.

ORGANIZATION AND FUNDING

All the organizational officers are women. Participation by persons from lower-income strata, persons with disabilities, older women, and lesbians is encouraged, although no data are available on the degree of participation by these groups. At present there are OPTS chapters in California, Illinois, Massachusetts, New York/New Jersey, and Texas. Informal support groups meet in Los Angeles, San Francisco, Chicago, Boston, New York City, and Dallas. The current unsalaried director at headquarters is Fay Johnson; she obtained her office through a feminist consensus approach. Tilles edits the newsletter.

Despite a limited source of income, OPTS has 550 members throughout the United States and also in Australia and Canada, countries where new reproductive technologies have been utilized to a significant degree. Membership is predominantly white. About half of OPTS members are men, reflecting the group's focus on the needs of infertile couples. In recent years, both gay and heterosexual men have joined OPTS to explore the possibility of becoming biological fathers through a combination of surrogacy and artificial insemination.

The two primary reasons persons join OPTS are a chance to associate with other persons considering or involved in alternative reproductive methods and to give help specifically related to the surrogacy process. Since the organization formed, U.S. legislation related to surrogacy (mainly contractual and commercial surrogacy) has increased greatly. Consequently, secondary goals of OPTS members include advocacy of values and policies supportive of surrogacy and, specifically, support of well-regulated commercial surrogacy with enforceable contracts, communication with peers and colleagues sharing these values, information provision and help with research, and representation of members' views to government. Membership in OPTS includes a subscription to the newsletter, a directory of legal and health care providers for those involved with surrogacy, a reading list, and a legislative update on the status of commercial surrogacy in each state.

The nonprofit group is supported primarily by membership dues of fifty dollars per year for new individual/family membership, and twenty dollars for membership renewals. At this time dues are not tax-deductible. The newsletter invites contributions from friends of OPTS who do not choose to become active members; such contributions are suggested to celebrate a pregnancy, birth, or adoption and to honor a surrogate, egg donor, or physician.

POLICY CONCERNS AND TACTICS

Policy is set by the three directors. The most important sources of policy discussions are recommendations by professional staff involved with surrogacy, discussion among the board of directors, and the executive officers' decisions. Membership polling also enters into discussion of policy recommendations.

Among the most important strategies for influencing public policy are testifying at state and federal legislative hearings, providing legislators with information, making personal contacts with legislators, and encouraging members to write their political representatives. Second in importance are monitoring elected officials' positions, testifying at hearings and seeking legislative review of agency decisions, commenting on proposed regulations, educating members, participating in direct political action and demonstrations, and contacting public decision makers through influential members.

Commercial surrogacy has become an increasingly frequent subject of state legislation; and OPTS accordingly has developed more fully its ability to serve as a political advocate of regulated, legal surrogacy. (OPTS uses the term "contractual surrogacy" to refer to surrogacy that involves payment to the surrogate under the terms of a contract between the surrogate and the infertile couple.)

In general, feminist bioethicists have tended to view commercial surrogacy as commodifying of both women and children and as potentially racist and classist. OPTS regards the option of participating in regulated commercial contractual surrogacy as a fundamental reproductive right and observes that the infertile community has lacked legal rights analogous to those granted the fertile community by *Roe* v. *Wade*. OPTS clearly considers the right to participate in regulated commercial surrogacy contracts as a fundamental reproductive right and portrays critics of surrogacy as failing to recognize the ability of surrogates to make informed decisions for themselves.

Federal laws viewed by OPTS as most important to the organization are the

1972 act adding sex discrimination to the Civil Rights Commission's jurisdiction, the equal rights amendment, and *Roe* v. *Wade*. Second in importance are the 1963 Equal Pay Act and the 1972 Equal Employment Act (by OPTS's calculations, surrogates are paid well below the minimum wage); the 1964 Civil Rights and Equal Opportunity Acts; the Voting Rights Act; and affirmative action orders. At the time of this writing, no federal legislation regarding surrogacy has passed, although a number of states have passed laws, some favoring and some opposing surrogacy.

Coordinating work with organizations sharing OPTS's goals is important. Groups perceived as sharing these goals are surrogacy agencies such as the Beverly Hills center and legal firms handling surrogacy contracts. The organization has worked with these groups since its founding, but only in the past year has it begun to define a position as part of a reproductive rights agenda. OPTS members are typically pro-choice with respect to abortion. However, they have limited affiliation with groups focusing on abortion rights, since the latter do not generally regard facilitating commercial surrogacy as part of the reproductive freedom agenda. Groups viewed as adversarial include the Catholic Church, adoption agencies, and antisurrogacy coalitions, all of which are seen as working against OPTS goals.

ELECTORAL ACTIVITIES

OPTS does not see its issues as partisan, nor does it have a political action committee.

FURTHER INFORMATION

OPTS uses its newsletter to share information on national legislative issues relating to surrogacy. Zager and Johnson are frequent newsletter contributors.

DIANA E. AXELSEN

P
/

PAN-PACIFIC AND SOUTHEAST ASIA WOMEN'S ASSOCIATION—U.S.A. (PPSEAWA—USA)
P.O. Box 1531
Madison Square Station
New York, NY 10159
(212) 228-5307

The Pan-Pacific and Southeast Asia Women's Association—U.S.A. (PPSEAWA—USA) is devoted to issues that is believes bind together women everywhere, such as peace and infant and maternal care. PPSEAWA—USA, through its chapters, provides women a forum for research and discussion of international issues and has nationally established significant links with United Nations organizations, such as the International Children's Emergency Fund (UNICEF) and the Economic and Social Council (UNESCO).

ORIGIN AND DEVELOPMENT

PPSEAWA-USA is a member association of the International Pan-Pacific and Southeast Asia Women's Association, originally founded in Hawaii in 1928, during the upsurge of efforts to strengthen international peace after World War I. The organization, first called the Pan-Pacific Women's Association (PPWA), developed out of international conferences supported by the Pan-Pacific Union of Honolulu; these conferences included both men and women. The union was committed to both peace and mutual understanding among nations and was composed of distinguished representatives from each major country in the Pacific and Southeast Asia. Alexander Hume Ford founded the union and served as its first director. In 1924, Mark Cohen of New Zealand suggested that an all-women's meeting be called to discuss women's questions and especially children's health care. The first PPWA conference convened in Honolulu in August 1928 and was chaired by Jane Addams, the founder in 1889 of Chicago's Hull House. Addams received the 1932 Nobel Peace Prize for committing her energies to the doctrine of peace, a doctrine shared by PPWA, renamed PPSEAWA in 1955.

At the first PPWA meeting, thirteen countries were represented: Australia, Canada, China, Fiji, Japan, Korea, Mexico, Netherlands East Indies, New Zealand, Philippines, American Somoa, the United States, and Hawaii, then a U.S. territory. Hawaii continues to have a women's association separate from the mainland U.S. organization because of its special status as a founder of the organization on the international level. Since the founding, international conferences have convened every three to five years, with twenty-five delegates and five alternates from each country sharing national experience on topics ranging from maternal and child welfare and day care facilities to legal reform and women's wages. These conferences explore women's role in preserving cultural heritage and issues of overpopulation, the environment, and family health and seek practical ways to promote peace and answer questions of social and economic concern. Women from many racial, religious, and ethnic groups have always constituted the organization, to work to solve common problems.

Between 1928 and 1930, Mrs. A. H. Reeve of Philadelphia founded the PPWA of USA on the mainland. This group then formed chapters to attract individuals as members throughout the United States. There were, at one time, chapters in Washington, D.C., and Valdosta, Georgia.

In 1930, Reeve chaired the second international meeting, in Honolulu, during which PPWA's constitution was written, and it separated from the Pan-Pacific Union. PPWA's goal's were to strengthen the bonds of peace among Pacific peoples by promoting a better understanding and friendship among the women of all Pacific countries and to initiate and promote cooperation for the study and betterment of existing social, economic, and cultural conditions. The international president, 1930–34, was Georgina Sweet of Australia. Reeve served as vice president, and Ann Satterthwaite of Hawaii served as secretary.

After the 1930 conference, the delegates returned home and formed national committees composed of representatives from the major women's organizations in their countries. PPWA—USA originally worked with the League of Women Voters,* Young Women's Christian Association,* and American Association of University Women* (AAUW), among many others. Prewar international conferences were held in 1934 and 1937. At the third international meeting, PPWA's original sponsor, the Pan-Pacific Union, cut back its financial support; and volunteerism became more important to PPWA. By 1937, all financial ties to the parent union were cut, and PPWA became independent. Its focus then included education, home economics, health, and national and international relations, soon followed by labor and living standards, population, emigration, education, and prostitution.

With the outbreak of World War II, conferences ceased until 1949, when the group reconvened in Hawaii with the theme, Pacific Women Unite for the United Nations. Topics of food and agriculture, health and welfare, education for international understanding, and women's status dominated the discussions. Seventy women representing ten Pacific Basin countries attended the Hawaii meeting. Postwar presidents included Josephine Schain of the United States, 1949–55; Clorinda Lucas of Hawaii, 1964–68; and Grace Stuart Nutley of the United States, 1975–78. PPSEAWA has pioneered networking in the Pacific Basin through international conferences, blending women of diverse races and ethnicities, finding common ground in advocating education, health, population control, and international relations.

In 1957, Ella P. Stewart, the first black woman to pass a Pennsylvania State Board Pharmacology Exam, formed a chapter in Toledo, Ohio. She toured twenty-three countries as a goodwill ambassador for the U.S. State Department and was present at the signing of the United Nations Charter in San Francisco in 1945. To this day, PPSEAWA—Toledo invites other women's organizations to come together to celebrate United Nations Day, and many of its members serve on the governing boards of other women's organizations throughout Ohio.

In 1961, a Stockton, California, chapter was established by Marion O. Pease and Lorraine Knoles after they attended the international conference in Tokyo, Japan, in 1958. The New York City area chapter formed in 1972 with Ruth Satzman as its first president; the home of the United Nations (UN), New York, has proved an ideal place for PPSEAWA members to forge bonds of friendship and international goodwill through hospitality and social events. Phyllis Ellis and Royal Buscombe founded the Chicago chapter in 1980; in 1988, Ann Aurelius founded a chapter in Minnesota and became its first president. Elizabeth-Louise Girardi, a member of the Chicago chapter, eventually became national president. The Minnesota area chapter had one of its first meetings honored by a visit from the international president, Khunying Sumalee Chartikavanij of Thailand.

ORGANIZATION AND FUNDING

PPSEAWA has five chapters, in Illinois, Minnesota, New York, California, and Ohio, and members at large throughout the United States. Election of officers is held every two years at the annual membership meeting. The U.S. organization also sends delegates to the international conferences. The current president is Ann Aurelius. The national headquarters is located in the president's home, currently in St. Paul, Minnesota.

PPSEAWA—USA had approximately 350 members in 1991. The membership is entirely female. Through the chapters, members devote themselves to expanding friendship networks around the world and strengthening bonds of peace and sisterhood. Incentives to become members include the numerous opportunities to meet similarly minded women from other countries.

PPSEAWA—USA is financed by dues. Each individual member pays dues to her chapter; and each chapter sends a percentage of the dues collected to the national organization. Dues are kept low—between ten dollars and thirty dollars/ year (set by each chapter)—so that as many women as possible may join. A total budget figure is not available.

POLICY CONCERNS AND TACTICS

Policy is established by the board of directors, with occasional recommendations from the executive committee. Members work to educate themselves and members of the communities they serve through informational programs and speakers on topics of interest. PPSEAWA—USA has held a number of special events, such as "Tell Me Mr. Ambassador" in New York, wherein the ambassadors from countries of the Pacific Rim address members and friends, and instructive programs such as "Modes and Mores of the Orient." In 1988, PPSEAWA—USA sponsored a reception and program with Sadato Ogata, High Commission for Refugees, as speaker at the UN, in celebration of the fortieth anniversary of the Universal Declaration of Human Rights; PPSEAWA was the only accredited nongovernmental organization to sponsor such a function.

In 1981, PPSEAWA—USA hosted the first international conference to be held on the U.S. mainland with activities at Skidmore College in Saratoga Springs, New York, and in New York City and at the UN. It continues to move toward the twenty-first century with vigor after being received in 1990 in Thailand by Queen Sirikit at an audience granted to PPSEAWA delegates to the eighteenth international conference and, in 1994, in Torga by Queen Halsevala Mataho.

PPSEAWA—USA, like its predecessor, PPWA, has involved itself with the UN since its inception. Four members witnessed the UN Charter's signing. Both PPSEAWA—USA and International PPSEAWA have their own representatives to the UN. Janet Nixon and Francesca Todd represent PPSEAWA—USA to the UN in New York. Girardi serves as the representative to the UN Commission on the Status of Women; Elizabeth Buckett is representative to the UN in Geneva; Marie Eslinger is representative to UNICEF in New York; Shirley Munyan is representative to UNESCO in Paris; and Chaiskran Hiranpruk is representative to the Economic and Social Commission for Asia and the Pacific in Bangkok. Leoni Pynappel represents PPSEAWA to the UN; she is a member of PPSEAWA—USA. Representatives present resolutions or statements to UN agencies on such issues as an end to nuclear testing and dumping in the Pacific and promotion of breast-feeding in developing countries. At the UN End-of-Decade conference held in Nairobi in 1985, a PPSEAWA-sponsored song was presented, written by Addy Fieger, a famed composer and then a PPSEAWA—USA member.

PPSEAWA—USA is a member of the National Council of Women and the United Nations Association. It works with many other organizations, including the Asia Society, with which it collaborated in administering classes and cultural programs for newcomers. It continues to work actively for peace not only with other women's groups such as the national and international councils of women but also through diplomats, artists, students, scientists, scholars, and businesspeople throughout the world.

FURTHER INFORMATION

There are a semiannual *USA Newsletter* and semiannual *International Bulletin.* In 1981, PPSEAWA—New York produced a cookbook offering recipes from countries belonging to the international organization.

BARBARA BENNETT PETERSON

PAN-PACIFIC WOMEN'S ASSOCIATION
See PAN-PACIFIC AND SOUTHEAST ASIA WOMEN'S ASSOCIATION—U.S.A.

PEACE LINKS (PL)
747 8th Street, SE
Washington, DC 20003
(202) 544-0805
FAX (202) 544-0809

Peace Links (PL) is an organization founded to limit the threat of nuclear war. In recent years it has focused increasingly on a broad agenda that includes the environment and reordering U.S. budget priorities.

ORIGIN AND DEVELOPMENT

In 1982, Betty Bumpers, wife of Senator Dale Bumpers (D-AR), founded Peace Links-Women Against Nuclear War (the name was shortened in 1990). She started the organization because of the fear her teenage daughter expressed about nuclear war. Responding to this concern, Bumpers called together other congressional wives and a few close friends from Arkansas, including Elinor Bedell, Deborah Harding, Deba Leach, and Theresa Heinz. They decided to create an organization that would focus on mobilizing middle-class women to work for the peace cause. Bumpers's rationale for focusing on women centered on mothers' socialized maternal instincts and the need to include women in the political arena. Her intention was not so much to exclude men as to project women's tendency to nurture into the foreground of the political process.

PL serves as a conduit linking women concerned about limiting nuclear war's threat. The initial, and still important, goal was to put peace on mainstream women's groups' agendas. Since its founding, PL has broadened its focus to include citizen diplomacy, conflict resolution, peace education, environmental issues, and global awareness. Women are urged to take political action encouraging elected officials to listen to women's concerns.

Bumpers has continued to serve as PL's leader and president. For her efforts in founding PL and other peace activities, she has received several awards, including the first Wilton Peace Prize given by the Unitarian Universalist Peace

Network and the first National Peace Institute's National Citizen/Grassroots Peacemaker Award.

ORGANIZATION AND FUNDING

PL has seven affiliates. It has always worked from a loose organizational structure. Originally, it had no officers, meetings, or dues. Currently, it has a sixteen-member all-women board of directors, an executive director, and a president, who serve as the leadership. PL maintains its primary office in Washington, D.C., and has a smaller office in Philadelphia. The current director is Carol Williams. There are also three paid staff and generally two or three interns.

PL is not a membership but a grassroots organization. Favorable media attention, including early articles in *McCalls* and *Parade* magazines and other press coverage, has helped it recruit supporters. Over 30,000 individuals, 90 percent of them women, subscribe to PL's newsletters, and this number has remained almost constant since 1986. PL also counts among its national links many congresswomen and wives of members of Congress.

Foundation grants played a major role in PL's founding and in sponsoring some of its exchanges with Soviet women. PL's budget in 1992 was $189,000. Much of the money (40 percent) comes from individual contributions to this 501 (c) (3) organization. The other major source of funds is the Annual Peace Links Gala, a dance attended by many Washington insiders. The gala, along with other funding activities, also raises about 40 percent of the annual operating budget. Foundation grants contribute another 20 percent. Merchandise sales make up the remainder of income needed to finance the organization.

POLICY CONCERNS AND TACTICS

PL policy is set by the board of directors, with professional staff providing input. Its goals generally have concentrated on efforts to induce supporters to become informed and active. PL also has adopted a number of strategies designed to influence members of the Congress and the White House. In 1986, it sponsored a petition campaign to encourage President Reagan to support arms control. In 1988, it delivered almost 10,000 signed postcards to the two candidates for the White House, urging them to foreswear nuclear hardware in favor of such constructive approaches as a healthy economy, education, jobs, housing, health, and day care. During President Bush's first year in office, PL sponsored another postcard campaign exhorting him to make ending the arms race his highest priority. In 1992, it organized a letter-writing campaign directed at both presidential candidates and urging each to focus his campaign on pressing domestic issues. In 1993, letters were sent to President William Clinton in support for a Comprehensive Test Ban.

Initially, PL developed a number of educational kits designed to help the middle-class women it wanted to reach to become better informed about the issues. Early kits included such topics as peace, presenting a peace panel, global awareness, the process of talking to children about nuclear war, formation of a community group, fund-raising, and elementary and high school students' education about peacemaking. Subsequent kits have discussed conflict resolution and understanding the Soviets. In 1990, PL began a new initiative, Action Network, to inform its members of a variety of things they can do to promote peace.

Besides educating its members through kits and action alerts, the organization also has undertaken a major effort to improve relations between Soviet and U.S. women. To this end, since 1986, PL has sponsored several exchanges between these women. The arrangement was formalized in 1987 when an Agreement of Cooperation was signed by Betty Bumpers and Zoya Pukhova, the Soviet Women's Committee president. The agreement stated that the two groups would facilitate the dissemination of correct information about their counterparts, strive to establish direct contact between the women, and continue the exchanges. Since the breakup of the Soviet Union, PL continues to work for a closer understanding between the two peoples with a Pen Pals for Peace campaign and leadership training for women from newly independent states. PL works on many of its goals in cooperation with several other groups, including Alliance for a Common Future and Peace Institute Federation.

ELECTORAL ACTIVITIES

While PL is a nonpartisan group, its leader and many of its activists have ties to elected officials, especially in the Democratic Party. PL does not have a political action committee, nor does it endorse individual candidates for political office.

FURTHER INFORMATION

PL publishes one newsletter, *Connection,* a quarterly. It also mails *Action Alerts* to members of its Action Network.

NANCY E. MCGLEN

PHI BETA SIGMA
See ZETA PHI BETA SORORITY

PLANNED PARENTHOOD FEDERATION OF AMERICA (PPFA)
810 7th Avenue
New York, NY 10019
(212) 541-7800
FAX (202) 293-4349

Planned Parenthood Federation of America (PPFA) is the largest provider of contraceptive health care in the United States. Planned Parenthood doctors are known for their treatment of sexually transmitted diseases, their work with at-risk teenagers, and their sponsorship of medical research. PPFA also has achieved prominence among government policymakers, becoming an uncompromising advocate of abortion rights and sexual education. Moreover, the organization has held to these priorities through the loss of corporate donations and government grants. The Alan Guttmacher Institute (AGI), an independent, nonprofit corporation that engages in research, policy analysis, and public education, is a PPFA special affiliate; Planned Parenthood Action Fund (PPAF) is another independent organization, devoted to political and electoral activities on behalf of PPFA priorities.

ORIGIN AND DEVELOPMENT

PPFA traces its origins to Margaret Sanger's work. At a time when the federal Comstock laws classified birth control materials as obscene, Sanger campaigned for women's reproductive rights and medical research into reproductive issues. In 1921, she established the American Birth Control League (ABCL) to generate revenues for her work. Two years later, Sanger founded the Birth Control Clinical Research Bureau, the first doctor-staffed birth control clinic in the United States. Sanger viewed this as a politically expedient maneuver, given the opposition her work was encountering from the medical profession. Some of her colleagues believed this approach disempowered women. In *U.S.* v. *One Package* (1936), a test case largely engineered by Sanger, the Second Circuit Court of Appeals constructed the Comstock laws to open the mail to contraceptive materials.

Relations between Sanger and ABCL leadership always were strained: Sanger was a policy entrepreneur unwilling to consult others, and ABCL leaders considered her fiscally irresponsible. When all ties between the two were cut in 1928, ABCL found that the loss of Sanger's endorsement crippled fund-raising. In 1939, following protracted negotiations with Sanger, ABCL merged with the Research Bureau and created the Birth Control Federation of America. In 1942, the name was changed to Planned Parenthood Federation of America to facilitate fund-raising.

PPFA has experienced steady growth throughout its history. With the support of PPFA, the International Planned Parenthood Federation (IPPF) was established at a 1952 conference in Bombay; Sanger served as its first president. ABCL had strongly resisted this expansion. The IPPF endorsement pointed up the American organization's new fiscal and political strength. Under Presidents Nixon and Carter, PPFA benefited from funding for Title X of the Public Health Service Act and for various Agency for International Development programs.

More recent PPFA political activism reflects a significant change in its contraceptive services policy. Until the 1960s, Planned Parenthood was a firm opponent of abortion, viewing the procedure as dangerous and unnecessary, given reliable contraceptives. In 1969, in response to the increasing number of deaths from illegal abortions, PPFA publicly supported the repeal of criminal abortion statutes. Following *Roe* v. *Wade* (1973), PPFA opened clinics to provide safe, low-cost abortions.

In 1978, Alyce Faye Wattleton became PPFA president. Known for her fund-raising skills, work on national PPFA committees, and reproductive rights stance, Wattleton was the first woman and the first African American to head the organization. Though Wattleton's appointment caused considerable controversy among board members, it was widely perceived as a statement about PPFA's status as a social movement with diverse membership. Wattleton's politics and management so dramatically altered PPFA that there is little institutional memory of the pre-Wattleton Planned Parenthood. Wattleton resigned the presidency in 1992; and her executive vice president, David J. Andrews, was appointed acting president by the board.

ORGANIZATION AND FUNDING

PPFA has 172 affiliates and 911 clinics. As part of a periodic recertification program, national staff conduct through reviews of each affiliate's policies, programs, and medical practices. Affiliates are therefore only quasi-autonomous, and policy-making power remains with the national office. Members of the board of directors are elected through mechanisms designed to balance the power of the national organization and the affiliates, sustain regional diversity, and protect the institutional independence of such special affiliates as the Alan Guttmacher Institute. Thus, board elections are held at the regional level and within the organizations that constitute the PPFA network, in addition to the at-large elections held at the PPFA annual meeting. In early 1992, 54 percent of the board of directors were women; the board's racial distribution was 68 percent white, 23 percent African American, 6 percent Hispanic, and 3 percent Asian American. Pamela J. Maraldo succeeded Wattleton as PPFA president. An author and lecturer on health care, Maraldo received her Ph.D. in nursing from New York University and has served on a number of councils, boards, and government commissions. The chief executive officer of the National League of Nursing since 1973, she comes to PPFA with an established reputation in fundraising and programmatic reform. Maraldo hopes to draw Planned Parenthood into greater efforts on behalf of national health care reform, though she has publicly stated that she will not change the organization's existing commitment to abortion rights.

Shortly after her appointment by the board of directors, Wattleton reorganized PPFA headquarters and put a hierarchical layer of vice presidents between herself and the staff. In restructuring PPFA, Wattleton sought to professionalize management, achieve closer relations with state and local affiliates, and gain greater prominence for the organization. In 1981, as a branch to national headquarters in New York City, Wattleton created the Legislative and Public Information Office in Washington, D.C. In all, there are eleven executive staff members. PPFA currently employs ten staff in the Washington office, five of whom are registered lobbyists. An unusual staff incentive program sustained Wattleton's priorities in the national headquarters: individual employees annually set personal objectives and receive raises according to manager's assessments of staff development. The apparent success of this arrangement caused

Business Week in 1990 to select Wattleton as one of five top managers in U.S. social service agencies.

PPFA's strength is evident in its financial development. In 1977, PPFA headquarters had an operating budget of $11.3 million; by 1991 (the most recent year for which data was available), the budget had risen to $43.4 million. PPFA national and affiliate offices had total revenues of $406.3 million. The increase was all the more significant because Planned Parenthood increasingly relied on direct mail solicitation of private donations during the Reagan-Bush years: corporations cut their PPFA giving when pro-life groups threatened economic boycotts; and federal funding for family planning programs diminished after implementation of the Hyde amendments and the Mexico City policy. The latter denied U.S. government funding to most foreign nongovernmental organizations that engaged in abortion-related activities, even if those activities were financed from other sources and were legal in the host country. In compliance with this rule, the Agency for International Development terminated a $9.9 million cooperative agreement with the international division of PPFA, ending support for ninety-four projects overseas.

Approximately 500,000 individuals gave to PPFA in 1991, over half giving amounts smaller than $300. With 1991 revenues noted, the following is a complete list of funding sources: clinic income ($140.9 million), government grants ($124 million), private contributions ($113.7 million), indirect support from affiliates ($4.2 million), Planned Parenthood Action Fund ($2.9 million), Alan Guttmacher Institute funding ($4.2 million), and miscellaneous operating revenue ($16.4 million).

The Alan Guttmacher Institute (AGI) was founded in 1968. Originally the Center for Family Planning Program Development, the organization served as the research division of PPFA until 1977. In that year it was renamed and became a wholly independent nonprofit corporation with 501 (c) (3) tax status. AGI conducts research and advocates on behalf of reproductive health, family planning, prenatal care, and reproductive rights. The New York staff numbers forty-four, with ten additional staff in Washington. In 1991, the most recent year for which data are available, the organizational budget totaled $4,061,203.

POLICY CONCERNS AND TACTICS

PPFA policy statements are issued by its board, acting with the advice of professional staff. PPFA and its affiliates engage in four types of political activism, the combination used in any instance set by the national board of directors in response to policy priorities and the political climate. Contacts with educators and the media are deemed the best route to informing the public about Planned Parenthood's concerns. Legislative lobbying occurs at both national and local levels. PPFA has an in-house legal department whose seven attorneys file amicus briefs, conduct research, and design model legislation; affiliates also appear in court to secure injunctions against protesters. Electoral politics are the Planned Parenthood Action Fund's province.

The legal division of PPFA is active at all levels of the court system. Attorneys litigated in *Rust* v. *Sullivan* (1991) and *Planned Parenthood of Southeast Pennsylvania* v. *Casey* (1992). Pending are cases that challenge the Tennessee abortion laws and the Jacksonville, Florida, school district "abstinence only" curriculum of sex education programs. Litigation efforts are tied closely to legislative lobbying: *Rust* led to a focus on "gag rules," while the Freedom of Choice Act is intended to eliminate state-by-state litigation.

Planned Parenthood claims that its political efforts are on behalf of the clients using its clinics, 68 percent of whom have incomes below 150 percent of the poverty level. Wattleton especially linked her work for reproductive rights with civil rights concerns of the women's liberation movement, focusing upon African American women's circumstances. Describing the respective contributions of PPFA donors and clients, Wattleton maintained that donors finance the pro-choice movement, whose outcomes are endorsed by client's reproductive health care decisions. She also argued that the stakes of the abortion debate are disproportionately high for African American women because they belong to a demographic cohort with limited access to medical care.

PPFA, guarding its tax-exempt status, undertakes little legislative lobbying and constrains the action fund's activities. All lobbying is strictly focused on reproductive rights. Of ongoing concern is the proposed Freedom of Choice Act, statutes or regulations that prevent doctors from informing their patients about abortion, and provisions for the availability of new contraceptive technology such as RU 486. The last issue receives less attention from PPFA than the previous two.

In abortion politics, Planned Parenthood strongly allies with National Organization for Women,* National Abortion Rights Action League,* Fund for the Feminist Majority,* American Civil Liberties Union,* and the National Women's Law Center. Opponents of Planned Parenthood include Operation Rescue,* which organizes protests outside Planned Parenthood clinics; and the Christian Action Council, which coordinated the consumer boycotts that cut PPFA corporate sponsorship.

ELECTORAL ACTIVITIES

In 1989, PPFA incorporated a 501 (c) (4) organization, the Action Fund, for electoral activities, including voter registration drives and media campaigns. Concerned for its tax status, the parent organization did not allow the fund to issue blanket endorsements, although it financed three affiliate voter education programs during the 1992 elections.

FURTHER INFORMATION

In addition to a biweekly newsletter and a quarterly report tracking federal and state reproductive health legislation, AGI publishes two peer review journals on family planning. Recent AGI reports examine how aggressively states have implemented congressional expansions in Medicaid coverage for low-income pregnant women, the effectiveness of teen pregnancy prevention programs, reasons for contraceptive failure and rising rates of sexually transmitted diseases in women, and the use and practice of abortion in Latin America and the Caribbean. PPFA has an extensive list of publications and bibliographic resources. Affiliates commonly issue a newsletter, in addition to maintaining their own libraries.

MARYANNE BORRELLI

POLITICAL ACTION FOR CANDIDATE ELECTION
See NATIONAL ASSOCIATION OF SOCIAL WORKERS

PRESBYTERIAN WOMEN (PW)
100 Witherspoon Street
Louisville, KY 40202
(502) 569-5000

To support Christian mission, Presbyterian Women (PW) has pursued national and global issues of peace and justice. It has helped to fund and build projects and institutions that have touched significantly the lives of millions, especially women and children. It has created an essential role for women in the church, gradually approaching an equality that still is transforming it and contributing to the women's rights struggle in the wider world as well as bringing about ''an inclusive caring community of women'' to strengthen the church and give witness to God's kingdom.

ORIGIN AND DEVELOPMENT

From the early decades of the last century to the present, women in Presbyterian churches have applied leadership and helping skills through their mission organizations. PW had its origins in the nineteenth century, when women of Presbyterian persuasion began banding together to support their churches' missionary activity. After the Civil War and into the twentieth century, this work increasingly took on national dimensions, and several women's organizations were created with associations to what were called ''home'' and ''foreign'' missions and to the different Presbyterian denominations that had emerged because of doctrinal quarrels and the debate over slavery. The women's missionary organizations took different forms over the years, sometimes because of decisions made by the male-dominated general church, but, led by indomitable individuals such as Katherine Jones Bennett and Hallie Winsborough, they thrived.

In 1983, when denominational dialogue promised the reunion of the United Presbyterian Church in the U.S.A. and the Presbyterian Church U.S. after more than a century's division, United Presbyterian Women and Women of the Church, respectively, began their own dialogue. They already had begun in 1978 to work together by creating a joint Bible study, and over the next decade a joint committee on women and the church hammered out the framework for a new organization. Leaders in that process were Jeanne C. Marshall, Catherine

S. Vaughn, and Patsy Correll, assisted by staff Gladys Strachan and Jean Guy Miller. Nannie Alston, Barbara Mann, and Diana Lim helped assure minority participation.

ORGANIZATION AND FUNDING

PW operates at every level: local, synodical, presbyterial, and national. It is present in every state plus Puerto Rico. Every three years a churchwide gathering is held with several thousand women from across the church, including voting representatives from every presbytery, attending. The official voting representatives, their way paid by the organization, vote for new national leadership and a triennium budget and set policy directions for the next three years. In July 1991, Sara Cordery succeeded Cleda Locey as PW moderator; she served a three-year term. Headquarters for PW is in Louisville, Kentucky, where headquarters for the whole denomination lodges. Staff includes Strachan as executive director. An associate for mission participation and publication staff assist her. In addition, the denomination pays for an administrative assistant and treasurer.

PW is open to all the women of the church and currently has a membership of more than 350,000. Members are predominantly white, middle-class, and over fifty years old. The age level largely has to do with the volunteer nature of the organization and lack of leisure experienced by increasing numbers of women working and raising families. Great attention has been given to including women of all races and women with disabilities in the membership, especially in membership roles.

While PW received some financial support from the general church in its beginnings, then and now most of its financial support comes in the form of gifts from its individual members. Presently that means 80 percent from individual women. Twenty percent comes from church sources. The organization is tax-exempt, and gifts are deductible, but for most members, the gifts extend their Sunday church offerings, just as belonging to PW is another aspect of their lives as church members. PW raises close to $6 million a year. Two major offerings in the course of each year, the birthday and the thank offerings, help fund an impressive number of projects. Thirty-three percent of the thank offering goes to health-related programs. In a recent year, $1,078,990 went to hospitals and health care institutions in nineteen countries on four continents and to sixty-six projects running the gamut from an AIDS case management program in Florida to a Native American coalition against family violence in Wisconsin.

POLICY CONCERNS AND TACTICS

On a national level, policy is set by the voting representatives to the triennial churchwide gathering. Ideas for PW policy can emerge from a number of places: the churchwide coordinating team that provides ongoing leadership between gatherings, staff recommendations, women on a presbyterial or even local level, or such ecumenical partners as Church Women United* (CWU). The organization frequently cooperates with other parts of the church, for example, in efforts to change legislation affecting Central American refugees. Letter-writing campaigns around national issues affecting women and children are not unusual, but PW's greatest influence comes at the level of education and communication with its very wide membership and several million denominational members.

PW has taken a stand on many issues, especially those relating to women and children, such as the Nestle and American Home Products boycotts, instituted when the corporations refused to stop heavy promotion of infant formula in Third World countries. PW has shared in efforts to get the U.S. Congress to ratify the United Nations Conventions on the Elimination of All Forms of Discrimination against Women and on the Rights of the Child. The organization has found laws enforcing racial or sexual equality or benefiting women and children among the most important issues over the years, including, for example, the 1964 Civil Rights Act, Food Stamp Act of the same year, and the Act of 1972, adding sex discrimination to the Civil Right Commission's jurisdiction.

PW also belongs to the Religious Coalition for Abortion Rights.* Within the Presbyterian Church there is strong opposition to PW's position on abortion rights, through Presbyterians Pro Life.

ELECTORAL ACTIVITIES

PW is nonpartisan, has no political action committee, and plays no direct role in electoral politics.

FURTHER INFORMATION

Brochures and videos, occasional newsletters for leadership at all levels, and *Horizon* magazine, published seven times a year, enable the organization to be an effective educator and communicator with its constituency. A typical issue of *Horizon* may contain articles about the economic conditions of women farmers in Africa, a Presbyterian-related community center, or refugee project. It also includes Bible study and provocative articles on spiritual growth.

ELAINE MAGALIS

PROJECT ON EQUAL EDUCATION RIGHTS
See NATIONAL ORGANIZATION FOR WOMEN

PUBLIC EMPLOYEES ORGANIZED TO PROMOTE LEGISLATIVE EQUALITY
See AMERICAN FEDERATION OF STATE, COUNTY AND MUNICIPAL EMPLOYEES

R

---- / ----

RELIGIOUS COALITION FOR ABORTION RIGHTS (RCAR)
100 Maryland Avenue, NE
Suite 307
Washington, DC 20002
(202) 543-7032
Legislative hot line—(202) 543-0224
FAX (202) 543-7820

The purpose of the Religious Coalition for Abortion Rights (RCAR) is to preserve reproductive freedom as an intrinsic element of religious freedom and to oppose any attempt to enact into secular law restrictions on abortion rights based on one theological definition of when a fetus becomes a human being. RCAR has an educational and research foundation.

ORIGIN AND DEVELOPMENT

Founded in spring 1973 in response to attempts to weaken or nullify *Roe* v. *Wade,* RCAR comprises thirty-five interdenominational groups. The founding occurred under the auspices of the United Methodist General Board of Church and Society. RCAR representatives have worked to prevent the passage of legislation espousing a particular religious viewpoint, because the abortion decision relates to religious considerations on which there is no consensus. In certain instances, such as its inability to reverse the Hyde amendment, RCAR proved unable to prevent legislative approval of restrictions on abortion rights. Consequently, it began to argue in court the legislation's unconstitutionality, finding in it state endorsement of a particular religious viewpoint of fetal personhood and hence an abridgment of the first amendment establishment clause. This argument was made in such cases as *McRae* v. *Califano* (1977).

ORGANIZATION AND FUNDING

RCAR has twenty-four state affiliates. It is controlled by a board of directors composed of one person from each of the thirty-five member organizations. The racial composition of the board is 14 percent African American and 86 percent white. Chiquita G. Smith is the present president. Other officers include two vice presidents, a secretary, and treasurer. RCAR has an eight-member staff in Washington, D.C., to oversee its national legislative, communications, and state affiliates programs. The executive director is Patricia Tyson; Beverly Hunter heads the legislative program.

Among the membership organizations are the American Ethical Union, B'nai B'rith Women,* Episcopal Women's Caucus, Lutheran Women's Caucus, Na-'amat U.S.A., National Council of Jewish Women,* Women's Ministry Unit Presbyterian Church,* Unitarian Universalist Women's Federation,* Coordinating Center for Women United Church of Christ, Women's Division General Board of Global Ministries United Methodist Church,* Women's American ORT, Young Women's Christian Association National Board.* There also are individual members, including 4,000 clergypersons. People join RCAR because of the organization's representation of their view that reproductive rights are an intrinsic element of religious liberty.

In the 1980s, RCAR became incorporated independently as a 501 (c) (4) nonprofit advocacy organization with a supporting 501 (c) (3) educational fund. RCAR receives its funding from individual contributions, funds from the member churches, foundation grants, and list sales amounting to $467,254 in 1990.

The fund spent $434,426 in 1990 on a state affiliate and communications program, fund-raising, a women of color partnership program, and general and administrative expenses. The state affiliate program, directed by John H. Evans, works to prevent the passage of bills that restrict reproductive rights in the different states. Liz Castro directs the partnership program, which is designed to enhance minority representation in the abortion debate. RCAR also has a library.

POLICY CONCERNS AND TACTICS

The policy of the RCAR and the strategies it uses are set by the board of directors in consultation with the organization's staff. The most common strategies performed by RCAR include filing amicus briefs, testifying at congressional hearings, monitoring voting records of elected officials, providing information to the organization's members, and educating members with publications. The organization has a legislative hot line. It also has a speakers bureau. RCAR continues to argue cases before the courts, as indicated by its amicus briefs in the *Webster* v. *Reproductive Services* case (1990). RCAR did not submit a separate brief in *Casey* v. *Planned Parenthood* (1992) but signed a brief that was submitted by another organization.

In the past few years, RCAR has undertaken several new approaches. The first is the National Clergy for Choice Network, a network of 4,000 clergy believing in freedom of conscience regarding abortion. The clergy members of this group advocate the organization's goals by participating in public speaking events, testifying before state legislators, contacting their elected officials, or keeping informed on the issues to keep their congregants up-to-date. Operation Respect was established to create a peaceful religious response to abortion opponents blocking the clinics. The Words of Choice Program attempts to clarify and correct such frequently used but misused terms in the abortion debate as "beginning of life" or "person."

RCAR works against restrictive abortion legislation and limits on abortion funding. It gives high priority to the Freedom of Choice bill, Title X of the Public Health Services Act, and the 1991 Reproductive Health Equity Bill.

RCAR works with its state affiliates to prevent restrictions being placed on abortion rights in the states. It is likely, in pursuit of its policy goals, to go into coalition with different pro-choice organizations, such as National Organization for Women.* RCAR opposes groups that argue for restrictive abortion legislation and limiting abortion funds, especially those organizations that espouse a particular religious doctrine such as the National Conference of Catholic Bishops.

ELECTORAL ACTIVITIES

RCAR does not participate in electoral politics for two reasons. A small organization, its priorities lie in the legislative and judicial arenas. Second, as a group of religious organizations, it cannot get involved in electoral politics because the groups would lose their tax-exempt status.

FURTHER INFORMATION

RCAR publishes two quarterly newsletters. *Religious Coalition for Abortion Rights Newsletter* focuses on the entire organization, and *Common Ground, Different Planes* discusses the Women of Color Partnership Program.

ANDREW R. HART

REPRODUCTIVE FREEDOM PROJECT
See AMERICAN CIVIL LIBERTIES UNION

SERVICE EMPLOYEES INTERNATIONAL UNION DISTRICT 925
See 9to5, NATIONAL ASSOCIATION OF WORKING WOMEN

SERVICE EMPLOYEES INTERNATIONAL UNION 9 TO 5 LOCAL
See 9to5, NATIONAL ASSOCIATION OF WORKING WOMEN

SEXUAL PRIVACY PROJECT
See AMERICAN CIVIL LIBERTIES UNION

SIGMA GAMMA RHO SORORITY
8800 S. Stony Island Avenue
Chicago, IL 60617
(312) 873-9000
FAX (312) 731-9642

A black Greek-letter organization, Sigma Gamma Rho Sorority works to enhance the quality of life of its members and society. It has an education fund.

ORIGIN AND DEVELOPMENT

Sigma's founders—Nannie M. Johnson, Mary Lou Little, Vivian White Marbury, Bessie Martin, Cubena McClure, Hattie M. Redford, and Dorothy Whitside—wanted to give educators a chance to experience fellowship and professional growth through networking. The founders were schoolteachers in Indianapolis; the sole survivor among them, Marbury, remains an active member. The prime founder and ''first rose'' was Gardner-Little, who died in 1992. Seven years after its founding in 1922 at Butler University, a largely white institution, the group incorporated. Prevailing conditions were neither supportive nor communal; and the organization felt a commitment to the black community, which it owed so much. The founders' foresight led to a legacy of service and achievement by means of higher education, not only for teachers but also for psychologists, legal and health care professionals, and all the other talented individuals interested in Sigma.

The group's motto is "Greater Service, Greater Progress." Community service, leadership training, and youth education still provide priorities for Sigma action. These priorities have heightened as government funding has declined, and substance abuse problems have increased. A Butler University chapter reactivated in 1992 to help keep the dream alive.

ORGANIZATION AND FUNDING

The organization has 350 chapters for undergraduates and alumnae in the United States, the Caribbean, and Africa. Its organizational structure includes five areas and regions. There is a biennial boule or national conference. The national board has thirty members, including the national officers. There are eleven officers; Katie K. White serves as grand basileus. Sigma's headquarters is in Chicago. Bonita M. Herring serves as executive director. In all, four staff people serve the national office.

Sigma has over 71,000 members, up from 38,000 in 1984. It emphasizes activities designed to foster its diverse members' social, moral, and intellectual advantage. Incentives to membership include friendship ties and social contacts, development of organizational skills, support for high scholastic attainment, advocacy of important values, and the promotion of dignity.

Sigma Gamma Rho is a nonprofit organization.

The Education Fund, formed in 1984, focuses on perpetual support for Sigma's commitment to education and promotes higher education, education-related research, and collaboration with individuals and organizations similarly oriented. It awards over $20,000 in scholarships annually and makes contributions to the United Negro College Fund, the Assault on Illiteracy Program, and other groups. Its work to stimulate and assist research in education, health, and related areas comes, for example, through the National Association for the Study of Afro-American Life and History and the National Mental Health Association.

POLICY CONCERNS AND TACTICS

Working with the March of Dimes through Project Reassurance, Sigma offers teenage parents counseling and referral and health and parenting information and seeks to prevent birth defects. The project itself is nearly twenty years old and addresses teen pregnancy and its influence on families' economic well-being.

Sigma also directs the Vocational Guidance and Workshop Center in New York City, which provides youth programs to encourage creative activities. Sigma has a drug, alcohol, and substance abuse awareness project.

Sigma, in conjunction with Africare, has participated for almost a decade in Project Africa, a national program focused on agricultural assistance for African women, who produce over three-quarters of the food grown in Africa. They also lack equitable access to land, credit, and resources and basically are not recognized by existing development programs. Further, malnutrition is common in Africa, and starvation is familiar. Yet the continent has the potential for self-sufficiency. One recent Sigma project involved fund-raising to assist in buying diesel-powered, hand-operated grain grinders for the women who hand-process meal in rural Zimbabwe. Besides members' individual contributions, chapters subscribe to assistance packages.

Sigma collaborates with such organizations as the National Association for the Advancement of Colored People, Leadership Conference on Civil Rights, National Council of Negro Women,* National Urban League,* Black Women's Agenda, and Southern Christian Leadership Conference.

FURTHER INFORMATION

Sigma's quarterly magazine is *The Aurora;* this is a membership publication.
CHARLOTTE T. MORGAN-CATO

SIGMA GAMMA RHO EDUCATION FUND
See SIGMA GAMMA RHO

SOCIAL WORKER RESEARCH GROUP
See NATIONAL ASSOCIATION OF SOCIAL WORKERS

SOCIETY OF SUPERINTENDENTS OF TRAINING SCHOOLS FOR NURSES OF THE UNITED STATES AND CANADA
See NATIONAL LEAGUE FOR NURSING

SOROPTIMIST
See SOROPTIMIST INTERNATIONAL OF THE AMERICAS

SOROPTIMIST FOUNDATION
See SOROPTIMIST INTERNATIONAL OF THE AMERICAS

SOROPTIMIST FOUNDATION OF CANADA
See SOROPTIMIST INTERNATIONAL OF THE AMERICAS

SOROPTIMIST INTERNATIONAL ASSOCIATION
See SOROPTIMIST INTERNATIONAL OF THE AMERICAS

SOROPTIMIST INTERNATIONAL OF THE AMERICAS, INC. (SIA)
1616 Walnut Street
Philadelphia, PA 19103
(215) 732-0512
FAX (215) 732-7508

Soroptimist International of the Americas (SIA), an association of federations of women's classified service clubs, formed to promote and engage in community service. It is the world's largest classified service organization for executive and professional women of all ages and all ethnic, cultural, and economic groups.

ORIGIN AND DEVELOPMENT

The first Soroptimist club was founded in 1921 in Oakland, California, by eighty women in professions that included medicine, laboratory technology, education, and printing. Key leaders were Violet Richardson Ward, the founding president, and Adelaide E. Goddard, a preliminary advocate. Other clubs in North America quickly followed. The founding of Soroptimist reflected heightened optimism following the 1920 passage of the Nineteenth Amendment. In the organization's name, the Latin *soro* means sister; *optima,* meaning "best," is interpreted as "the best for women."

This optimism fueled expansion. In 1923, the first clubs abroad were chartered, in greater London and Paris. Women networking felt empowered through their mutual association. By 1928, there were enough clubs to form two federations—American and European—and to establish the Soroptimist International Association. In 1934, a third federation—Great Britain and Ireland—formed. By 1978, the number of countries with Soroptimist clubs had grown to fifty-five. The organization had come to embody considerable cultural diversity. A fourth federation—South West Pacific—was established in 1991. Headquarters of Soroptimist International (SI) is located in Cambridge, United Kingdom. SI has accreditation with the United Nations (UN), having a voice at UN centers in New York, Geneva, Vienna, and Paris. As a nongovernmental organization, SI has had official links with the UN Economic and Social Council since 1951, including connections to the UN Educational, Scientific, and Cultural Organization, the Children's Fund or UNICEF, and the International Labor Organization.

SI demonstrates the possibility of building bridges of global consciousness across class, race, and gender lines. Internationalism has engendered diversity in the more than 3,500 occupations and professions represented in Soroptimist, for example, university presidents, farmers, office managers, business owners, physicians and other health care professionals, educators, accountants, and attorneys. Members are known as leaders in their fields, actively engaged in the private or public sector in a management or professional capacity or in an occupation with comparable status or responsibilities. Women join after accepting an invitation to membership from the local club and are classified by profession, assuring broad occupational representation.

Objectives and principles established in 1921 by the first Soroptimist remain strong today: to maintain high ethical standards in business and professional life; to strive for human rights for all people and particularly to advance women's status; to develop a spirit of friendship and unity among Soroptimists of all countries; to develop interest in community, national, and international affairs; to contribute to international understanding and universal friendship; and to develop the highest concept of patriotism.

ORGANIZATION AND FUNDING

There are currently around 95,000 SI members in over 2,800 clubs in ninety-five countries and territories, with membership rapidly expanding in developing countries. SI's organizational hierarchy is reinforced by voting procedures and standing committees. All clubs established within the federation's regional geographical limits are permitted one vote per club to select a regional governor and to elect a board of directors within the designated electoral area, that is, Brazil, Canada, Japan, South Korea, Mexico, the Caribbean, Spanish-speaking South American nations, the Philippines, and United States. Clubs also choose the president-elect and international president by mail ballot and may amend the constitution. There is a biennial convention of clubs; each club designates a delegate.

Above the club level stands the governor's roundtable, which represents every regional governor. In even-numbered years the president calls a meeting of incoming governors. Governors also may meet in odd-numbered years if a majority of them decide to. SI's thirteen-member board of directors includes a racial/ethnic mix of members, and has full power to conduct, manage, and direct the federation's business and affairs. Directors serve two-year terms. Meetings are held at least three times a year at Philadelphia headquarters. Directors, except for the president and president-elect, serve on at least one committee. Standing committees include service programs, communications, finance, legislative, and international. The current president is Joyce E. Byrne; she supervises the federation's activities and operations subject to broad control.

Program coordinators take responsibility for direction; they serve for two years and may be reappointed by the board. The six worldwide service programs include economic and social development, education, environment, health, human rights/status of women, and international goodwill and understanding.

Each of the four federations' constitutions have maintained an all-women membership—except within the United States federation, which has a waiver accepting twenty-one men members. Total SIA membership includes 50,000 representatives from the United States, Canada, South Korea, Panama, Brazil, Japan, Philippines, and Mexico, up from 35,000 members in 1984. Membership dues are set by the club; regional fees are set by the region. The federation annual fee is $40, of which $4 goes to SIA. SIA revenue derives from dues, charter dues, profits from sales, interest income, foundation reimbursement, venture reimbursement, and convention fees. The annual Canadian foundation budget totals $48,000; the Soroptimist Foundation Service Fund, $566,283. The total overall budget totals $918,045.

The Soroptimist Foundation (SF) and Soroptimist Foundation of Canada

(SFC) were established for charitable, scientific, literary, and educational purposes to support SIA programs—SF by deed of trust in 1958 and incorporation in 1988, SFC as a corporation under Canada's laws in 1963. Leigh Wintiz is the chief executive officer for SF and SFC. Foundation directors are charged with investment, management, and distribution of funds for projects recommended by SIA federation board and approved by the biennial convention body. Interest and dividends earned from the principal in the endowment funds come to more than $200,000 annually and are transferred to the foundation's service fund.

The funds support SIA-identifying projects, including a training awards program, youth citizenship awards, the Soroptimist Youth Forum, and, in Canada only, Soroptimist grants for women. Individual members clubs, regions, and other interested parties send contributions to the foundations. Income also is generated from memorial gifts and bequests. In addition, the foundations receive Founders Pennies collected through a voluntary program whereby Soroptimists celebrate the organization's founding by donating two cents per member for each year of Soroptimist's existence.

POLICY CONCERNS AND TACTICS

Policy concerns shaped at the SI board take all levels of development into account, for example, focusing on family planning rather than abortion rights. In turn, the SIA's general program interests are adapted to local areas' needs. Policy is shaped at the convention through resolutions about programmatic policy. Overall policy and approaches are still at the stage of organizational development. Favored tactics involve the media, use of UN committees, and lobbying state and local governments. In general, programs foster economic justice such as equal pay for work of equal value—in the United States, for comparable value—and the use of resources for peaceful ends in pursuit of common ground among women. Soroptimist works with other women's groups such as Zonta* and with such coalitions as the National Alliance for Child Survival and Women against Entertainment Violence.

ELECTORAL ACTIVITIES

Soroptimist does not see its agenda as partisan and not have a political action committee.

FURTHER INFORMATION

The Soroptimist of the Americas is published six times annually and provides information on SIA's financial and program states as well as program features on refugees, literacy and the environment, and a recommended reading and viewing section.

MARY CHIANTA CANZONERI

SOUTHERN ASSOCIATION OF COLLEGE WOMEN
See AMERICAN ASSOCIATION OF UNIVERSITY WOMEN

STOP ERA
See EAGLE FORUM

STOP ERA POLITICAL ACTION COMMITTEE
See EAGLE FORUM

U
—————————————— / ——————————————

UNION WOMEN'S ALLIANCE TO GAIN EQUALITY (UNION WAGE)
The Union Women's Alliance to Gain Equality, known as Union WAGE, was notable not only for its feminist aims, labor programs, and organizing projects but as a defender of the rights of working-class women and women of color. Union WAGE's newsletter and business office formally closed in 1982.

ORIGIN AND DEVELOPMENT

Established in California during the equal rights amendment campaign in 1971, Union WAGE formed as a labor organization to represent women's interests in the workplace. WAGE's 1975 organizing convention featured over 500 women discussing unions, affirmative action, and other women's issues. WAGE's accomplishments included a Household Workers Rights Project and programs aimed at safeguarding working women's health. Not affiliated with any particular union, in 1982, Union WAGE became a victim of dwindling funds and a fundamentally antilabor political and social environment and closed its doors.

ORGANIZATION AND FUNDING

Union WAGE had its headquarters in San Francisco. Its membership included both union and nonunion members, as WAGE organizers believed that limiting membership to the unionized female workers would be self-defeating. The way to organize the unorganized, according to WAGE, was to create an organization open to nonunion women. The organization depended on grassroots financial support.

POLICY CONCERNS AND TACTICS

As a labor organization, WAGE distinguished itself by a creative, dynamic approach to organizing female workers as well as by including nonunion and union women both. Organizing working women did not seem to be a top women's liberation movement (WLM) priority; and many women's organizations were then, as now, middle-class in orientation. WAGE sought a dual role— labor organization during a difficult time for the labor movement and feminist organization dedicated to improving working women's lives at a time support for feminism was eroding, and WLM was becoming less visible.

WAGE noted that issues raised by women workers, not strictly limited to wages and hours and extending beyond the workplace, demanded a major commitment by unions if they were to be resolved. Traditional male leaders strongly resisted making this commitment. WAGE organizers maintained that feminist issues such as child care or comparable worth could not be solved quickly or easily by negotiation.

In 1972, WAGE established a Household Workers Rights Project to publicize and seek enforcement of new laws covering household workers. The project assisted workers in collecting back pay and overtime and held conferences in black and Latina communities. WAGE also spearheaded attempts to organize clerical workers. Its Health and Safety Project focused on hazards clerical workers face on the job. Lack of funds forced WAGE to defer a project for women factory workers, which would have included monitoring electronic shops employing women in "Silicon Valley," California, and Mexico. WAGE also envisioned a worker-controlled employment service.

ELECTORAL ACTIVITIES

A nonpartisan organization, Union WAGE did not engage in electoral politics, and its financial situation kept it from founding a political action committee.

FURTHER INFORMATION

WAGE had a bimonthly newsletter, *Union W.A.G.E.* One of its publications, *Bargaining for Equality,* introduced the use of legal and collective bargaining techniques for women in the workplace and discussed expanding labor organizing to include nonunionized working women. WAGE also chronicled the lives of female labor organizers and documented the work of black and immigrant women who fought for unions. WAGE had planned a bilingual newsletter.

MARTHA BAILEY

UNITARIAN UNIVERSALIST WOMEN'S FEDERATION (UUWF)
25 Beacon Street
Boston, MA 02108
(617) 742-2100, ext. 692
FAX (617) 367-3237

The Unitarian Universalist Women's Federation (UUWF) serves a dual purpose: to support the national feminist policy agenda within mainstream American politics and to advocate internally for a equitable role for women within the denominational affairs of the parent Unitarian Universalist Association.

ORIGIN AND DEVELOPMENT

An autonomous membership organization within the Unitarian Universalist Association (UUA), UUWF formed in 1963 by a consolidation of the Alliance of Unitarian Women, established in 1880, and the Association of Universalist Women, founded in 1869. This merger mirrored that of the American Unitarian Association and the Universalist Church of America in 1961.

The earliest activities of these churchwomen centered around traditional mission work, at home and abroad, and charitable service. Because many early feminists belonged to Unitarian or Universalist churches—for example, Susan B. Anthony, Lucy Stone, Julia Ward Howe, Lucretia Mott, and Elizabeth Cady Stanton—social justice and reform were also of group concern. These issues included women's suffrage, prison reform, Prohibition, protective labor legislation, and world peace. Since the 1960s, UUWF actively has supported the national feminist agenda while working internally for an equitable role for women within UUA. One notable UUWF project includes the ownership and operation of Universalist and American Red Cross* founder Clara Barton's birthplace as a museum and camp for diabetic girls.

The Unitarian Universalist Service Committee, formed in 1939, is now the primary associational unit for traditional charitable activities at home and abroad. Many UUWF members are also active in this group.

ORGANIZATION AND FUNDING

Four officers and an eight-person board are elected for two-year terms and take responsibility for implementing policy adopted at the conventions. Kay Aler-Maida assumed the presidency in 1991. One woman of color currently serves as a board member. In a denomination based on complete individual freedom of belief, local self-governing congregations, and democratic participation in church affairs, one purpose of UUWF has been to bring UUA institutions into compliance with these historic principles; to be consistent, since 1987, the UUWF board has explored a less hierarchical, more feminist system built on the principles of shared leadership. Federation responsibilities are organized by function, with one board member serving as the initiator along with one or more other board, nonboard, and staff members. This system's implementation has proceeded so successfully that the membership directed that UUWF bylaws be amended by 1993 to reflect these changes.

UUWF headquarters is in Boston, although the federation has a Washington, D.C., representative and can draw upon the resources of the UUA Washington office. The board and officers are supported by a paid staff of three full-time and two part-time employees and a varying number of volunteer interns. Mairi Maeks, the executive director, and administrative assistant Ellen Spencer provide organizational continuity with their more than two decades of combined service. One staff position is filled by a woman of color. UUWF relies solely on volunteer lobbyists.

In 1991, the federation had approximately 5,300 primarily female members who joined either as individuals or as groups in local UUA congregations. Until recently, with liberal Protestant churches generally, the group has suffered a yearly loss of members and church units. Demographically, the membership reflects the UUA; predominantly Euro-American and among the most affluent of American religious bodies. UUWF enables Unitarian Universalist women to join a network for leadership training, mutual support, and personal and spiritual growth. In addition, UUWF affords members an opportunity to advance a common social and political agenda. UUWF offers scholarships that support lower-income women and women of color at biennial conventions.

The annual budget—in 1990, $2,680,669—comes from membership dues ranging from $500 for a lifetime membership to $10 annually for unit members, donations, fund-raising campaigns, conference fees, publication sales, and grants from UUA and foundations. Individual dues for those not joining as part of the church unit begin at $25 and may be set at $50 for contributing members and $75 for supporting members. UUWF currently operates at a deficit by using cash reserves and borrowing against endowment funds of $1.5 million. In part, this shortfall stems from the special costs of creating Clara Barton Camp as an independent entity.

POLICY CONCERNS AND TACTICS

The annual meeting adopts the agenda; and the elected board/staff play a role in suggesting and implementing it. Broadly stated, UUWF's policy goals are to advance women's role in society and to include women fully in the denomination's affairs. In pursuit of UUA-related goals, UUWF sponsors feminist theology awards to encourage work from the UUA perspective; a circuit rider program, reminiscent of the rural church tradition of ministers riding circuit to preach at various isolated churches too small for a full-time minister, which provides UUA groups with women program leaders; and the Ministry to Women Award. Two recipients of this last award have been Planned Parenthood Federation of America,* in 1990, and the National Coalition against Domestic Violence,* in 1991. UUWF also develops program materials and presents workshops and resolutions at the UUA general assembly. In the fall of 1991, a Clergy Sexual Misconduct Task Force was formed in conjunction with the UUA women and religious committee.

Throughout the denomination, UUWF members work together in their local churches and at district meetings. One particular strategy is to initiate resolutions on women's concerns that are submitted as a high-priority item by the congregation for consideration at the associationwide annual meeting.

UUWF works in coalition with a total of fifteen national organizations—including the Children's Defense Fund* and National Abortion Rights Action League*—that share its social justice concerns. These include women's equality, reproductive choice, AIDS, older women, children, and world peace. Confronting violence against women and opposition to limitations on choice are current priorities. As an affiliate of all fifteen organizations, UUWF makes an annual donation, cosigns amicus briefs in cases such as the *Webster* and *Casey* decisions of 1990 and 1992, attends meetings, and cosponsors projects such as marches. UUWF's adversaries in the political arena are those common to liberal groups: conservative and antifeminist organizations. Within UUA, a faction opposes all social action by the denomination. This includes passing resolutions, maintaining a lobby in Washington, D.C., funding social projects, and publishing literature with a liberal bias. Currently this viewpoint is voiced by Unitarian Universalists for Freedom of Conscience.

ELECTORAL ACTIVITIES

As a nonprofit organization, UUWF has no political action committee and does not participate in electoral politics.

FURTHER INFORMATION

The membership receives a bimonthly newsletter, *The Communicator*, devoted to local and national UUWF activities. The presidents of local units receive the quarterly bulletin, *The Women's View*, containing program ideas.

JANET K. BOLES

UNITED AUTO WORKERS WOMEN'S DEPARTMENT (UAW WD)
8000 East Jefferson
Detroit, Michigan 48214
(313) 926-5212

To deal with the special employment problems of women members and encourage their participation in the union, in 1955 the United Auto Workers (UAW) established a separate Women's Department (WD). In meeting its fundamental commitment to ensuring that "a woman's place is in her union," WD has followed a two-pronged strategy. On one hand, WD has vigorously attacked discriminatory practices. On the other hand, WD has tried to make women aware of their own strengths.

ORIGINS AND DEVELOPMENT

At World War II's beginning, women composed approximately 7 percent of UAW's membership, but by 1944 the percentage of women members had increased to 28 percent. As part of UAW's War Policy Division (WPD), in 1944 the Women's Bureau (WB) was established. Placement of the WB within WPD indicates the union's limited, short-range commitment to its women members. In 1947, WB was shifted to the newly created Fair Practices and Anti-

Discrimination Department, whose primary mandate was to counteract racial discrimination within the industry. In 1955, UAW became the first major union to establish a separate women's department.

Led by its first director, Mildred Jeffrey, WB tried to educate both men and women members about the problems experienced by women workers, published a bulletin for women members, and provided consultants to union negotiators working on contract language pertaining to women workers. WB's first educational campaigns dealt with equal pay for women workers and an end to separate male and female job classifications. When WPD in 1944 came out against job classification by sex, its primary motivation was to ensure not equal treatment for women but that lower-paid women's jobs would not be used by management against male UAW members after the war.

Although 86 percent of women autoworkers indicated that they would like to continue working, women were fired wholesale after the war. Both the male members and union leadership divided over whether to support women in their efforts to keep their jobs and what tactics to employ on their behalf. In many cases employers had the support of local union leaders in negotiating contracts with separate male and female seniority lists; separate job classifications and clauses permitted the discharge of married or pregnant workers. In other cases the union locals filed grievances and, with WB's assistance, helped women win their jobs back. As a result of the exclusionary practices, however, the percentage of women members dropped almost to prewar levels. Feeling betrayed by union leaders, in 1945 some women picketed UAW headquarters in Detroit to demand that WB be upgraded to a department with all-female staff and that female staff throughout the union be increased. Under Caroline Davis's leadership, WD continued to push for equal pay for equal work, single seniority lists, and an end to sex discrimination in hiring and promotion.

ORGANIZATION AND FUNDING

Currently, 150,000 women make up approximately 13 percent of UAW's membership. In 1962, WD succeeded in getting UAW's convention to amend the UAW Constitution to require the establishment of women's committees in all union locals with female members. Another way that WD sought to educate and train women members is through weeklong annual women's conferences and smaller regional women's conferences. These conferences combine consciousness-raising with classes designed to teach women the skills necessary to become union activists and leaders. Since 1975, over 3,500 UAW women have attended annual conferences, and thousands more have attended regional ones.

As a result of these efforts, today there are 144 women presidents of the 1,432 union locals compared with 74 in 1973, and over 1,500 other women hold top offices in union locals. Women have occupied top positions within the national union leadership since 1966, when Olga Madar, WD's national director, became the first woman on the International Executive Board. In 1970, Madar was elected international vice president. In 1974, when Madar resigned, she was replaced by Odessa Komer, who still holds the post as well as serving as WD director. In 1973, only 20 out of the approximately 800 international represen- tatives of the union were women. Today, with more than 90 women serving as international representatives, UAW has more women in national leadership po- sitions than any other major union, including those with predominantly female membership. Almost all these women have come up through the ranks from the shop floor.

In addition to members involved at the local level, WD has two professional staff and two clerical staff working out of the headquarters in Detroit. UAW's strong commitment to racial equality is reflected in the racial composition of the permanent staff, which is half African American. The director, who is elected every three years at the constitutional convention and is now Komer, shares leadership with assistant director Dorothy Jones.

POLICY CONCERNS AND TACTICS

Besides educating its own members, WD since its inception has seen itself as an actor within the broader political arena. Even though WD has no paid lobbyists, it has been deeply involved in legislative politics. WD has been in- strumental in getting its union to endorse legislation dealing with women. Be- cause WD is isolated organizationally from the rest of the union's leadership structure, Komer plays a particularly important role as a bridge between WD and the executive board. WD's earliest lobbying efforts were on behalf of the passage of the 1963 Equal Pay Act and the 1964 Civil Rights Act. Since then, WD has lobbied on behalf of the equal right amendment (ERA) and the 1978 Pregnancy Disability Act. Currently, its top legislative goals are federally funded child care and family leave policy; other issue concerns are sexual harassment, comparable worth, child abuse, and violence against women. WD has supported women members in legal cases involving equal pay, seniority, pregnancy dis- crimination, and fetal protection plans. When Johnson Controls Company began excluding women of childbearing age from working with lead, UAW filed suit on behalf of its women members. In 1991, the U.S. Supreme Court in *UAW* v. *Johnson Controls* ruled that the firm was guilty of sex discrimination under Title VII of the 1964 Civil Rights Act.

A final way WD has played a political role within society is through involve- ment in the broader women's liberation movement. When asked about their relationship with feminism, one WD director described union women as "the first women's libbers." While there is some truth in this statement, it does not reflect the cross-pressures union women have felt. The story of the relationship between WD and the National Organization for Women* (NOW) provides an excellent example of the ways union women deal with these cross-pressures.

At least one year prior to NOW's formation, WD leaders were involved in discussions with a representative from the government's Women Bureau about the need to form an "NAACP for women." Present at the small 1966 meeting establishing NOW were WD director Davis and Dorothy Haener, a WD staff member. Haener was elected to NOW's temporary steering committee, and Davis later became its first secretary-treasurer. For the first year, NOW's national headquarters was in WD Detroit headquarters. In 1967, NOW's decision to endorse ERA severely strained this close relationship. All labor unions opposed ERA on grounds that eliminating protective legislation would hurt women workers. Although women said that they personally supported ERA, they opposed NOW's formally endorsing the amendment because their union was on record opposing it. When the NOW conference endorsed ERA, NOW had to find new headquarters because UAW temporarily withdrew from active participation.

When one of its own studies showed that protective legislation most often was used against women rather than on their behalf, WD led a major educational campaign about ERA within UAW and in 1970 became the first major union to endorse it. Representing UAW, Madar testified for ERA in congressional hearings. WD also mobilized women within other labor unions to work in its favor. Much of the credit for the AFL-CIO's decision to reverse itself and come out in favor of ERA belongs to WD. In 1978, UAW joined a NOW-initiated boycott of the fifteen states that had not ratified the amendment.

WD also provided a moving force behind the creation of the Coalition of Labor Union Women (CLUW). Two of the eight women present at the 1973 meeting that laid the basis for CLUW's formation were from the UAW's WD. From 1974 to 1979, WD director Madar served as CLUW's president. When Madar retired, Komer, WD's new director, was elected CLUW's corresponding secretary. UAW also was a founding member of the National Committee on Pay Equity.* Dorothy Jones, WD's current director, serves on its board and also as the president of the National Association of Commissions for Women.* WD's major adversaries are hate groups, right to work organizations, and right-wing politicians.

ELECTORAL ACTIVITIES

WD is not a politically partisan organization. WD does not have a separate political action committee or lobbying presence in Washington, D.C. Because its interests are represented by regular lobbyists, the issues dealing with women may take second place to more general labor legislation. For example, federal plant closing legislation is the top priority of lobbyists. Civil rights and minimum wage legislation have also been important recent initiatives.

FURTHER INFORMATION

Since education has been one of the Women's Department's primary aims from inception, it has devoted a great deal of attention to providing its members with information. The informational material can be divided into two broad categories: that dealing with traditional labor union issues and that with a strong feminist focus. UAW administrative letters on sexual harassment and occupational and workplace exposure to lead, along with the *Local Union Women's Committees Handbook* and the "UAW Women's Department Annual Report," are very similar in form and content to other UAW publications. More strongly feminist publications include a pamphlet on sexual harassment entitled *When I Say No, I Mean No* and other pamphlets summarizing Title VII guidelines dealing with sex discrimination, highlights from all the major laws dealing with sex discrimination and sexual harassment, copies of the Pregnancy Disability Act, a fact sheet on women's issues, and tips for preventing assaults. In addition, the department has produced films and videos on the history of the women's movement, sexual harassment, rape's aftermath, the advertising industry's devaluation of women, pregnancy discrimination, and women's involvement in the labor movement. The video *Would You Let Someone Do This to Your Sister?*, chronicling five women's struggles against workplace sexual harassment, has won national awards and has been shown to thousands of trade unionists in this country and abroad.

JEAN REITH SCHROEDEL

UNITED CHURCH WOMEN
See CHURCH WOMEN UNITED

UNITED COUNCIL OF CHURCH WOMEN
See CHURCH WOMEN UNITED

UNITED METHODIST CHURCH
See UNITED METHODIST WOMEN

UNITED METHODIST CHURCH GENERAL BOARD OF GLOBAL MINISTRIES WOMEN'S DIVISION
See UNITED METHODIST WOMEN

UNITED METHODIST WOMEN (UMW)
Room 1504
475 Riverside Drive
New York, NY 10115
(212) 870-3600, ext. 3752
FAX (212) 870-3736

United Methodist Women (UMW), a laywoman's membership organization related to the Women's Division (WD) of the General Board of Global Ministries, United Methodist Church, seeks to become educated around specific issues affecting women and children and to provide leadership development opportunities to enable informed citizen participation.

ORIGIN AND DEVELOPMENT

UMW traces its life through fourteen women's missionary societies from 1869 to the present. The organizing purpose of the societies was proclamation of the Christian gospel to women and to children: by Christian presence, direct service ministries and advocacy on behalf of women and children in church and society. To fulfill this purpose, women founded and operated schools, hospitals, community centers, orphanages, and hostels. Women were recruited, educated, and trained to be leaders of the institutions; others were educated and encouraged to undertake social change in areas impacting on women's and children's lives. In the United States and abroad, programs were designed to serve those isolated and segregated by culture, social norms, and/or geography.

The founders of the earliest societies, 1869–93, were white women. As the organization grew and spread, black, Asian, and Hispanic women became members and leaders at regional levels, and much later at the national level. Also, a few of the earliest societies were established among German immigrants, and fluency in two languages was a condition of leadership.

Beginning in 1940, church structures assured black women proportionate membership at the division or national level. The Charter of Racial Policies committed the division intentionally to seek black women as national officers and staff. Subsequent charters in 1962 and 1978 addressed other groups of marginalized women.

From 1868 to 1940, women in the United States administered mission institutions worldwide. Since 1964, WD's primary functions have been mission education, advocacy, spiritual nurture, leadership development, and financial support for ministries with women and children.

ORGANIZATION AND DEVELOPMENT

UMW has 27,000 units throughout the United States. There are four levels of regional structures with a full complement of officers and operating funds. WD, a corporation of sixty-five directors, is the national policy-making body for the UMW. Directors are elected for four-year terms; elected officials must be United Methodists. At present 40 percent of directors are Asian, Hispanic, Native American, and black. Inclusiveness among directors, staff, and members is a high priority. The current president of WD and the national president of UMW is Carolyn E. Johnson. Thirty-eight executive/professional staff are located in ten cities, including an Office of Public Policy in Washington, D.C., and the church center at the United Nations in New York. Joyce D. Soyl, WD's deputy general secretary, is the chief staff officer.

UMW has approximately 1.2 million members. Membership is open to any woman supporting its purpose.

The division's 1994 budget was $20,565,318. Permanent, that is, endowment, funds are in excess of $80 million. Funds are secured by annual member contributions, special gifts, and investment income.

POLICY CONCERNS AND TACTICS

The national policy-making body is WD, with headquarters in New York City. A facet of the division's total program, public policy is set within UMW's history as a woman's missionary society, the changing conditions of women, and the denomination's social policy positions. Recommendations for work on specific issues may be initiated by directors, staff, or local members. Social policy resolutions are adopted every four years and forwarded to the UMW's general conference for consideration as general church policy. WD directors set policy, which staff and directors implement in concert with UMW's elected leaders. The criterion for engagement is the degree to which an issue impacts on women's and children's lives. Persons at every level of the organization— volunteers called mission coordinators of Christian social involvement—form a comprehensive national communications network. Differences of opinion about work on social policy issues center in two groups: those believing the church should not involve itself in politics and those in disagreement with a particular topic or strategy undertaken by the division.

Preferred strategies include letter-writing tables at various meetings, which serve to urge members to contact congressional representatives about particular legislation. Direct action such as boycotts and shareholder resolutions has been undertaken; and division policy permits submitting amicus briefs as the occasion warrants.

Ongoing work on domestic policy resolutions can be categorized broadly in the following areas: racial justice/inclusiveness, status and role of women, child care and family life, environment and health, and economic justice. In the 1970s, the division was an active participant to secure ratification of the equal rights amendment. It has monitored and supported legislation such as the proposed 1990 Act for Better Child Care.

WD celebrated the International Year of the Child in 1971 and authorized a child advocacy program in 1972. A renewed effort, a five-year Campaign for Children, was launched in 1989 in cooperation with the Children's Defense Fund.* A second five-year program extends through 1998. Endorsement of the Valdez principles affirms the division's belief that corporations and shareholders have a direct responsibility for the environment. The Law of the Sea project, initiated in 1974, continued through 1982, when the Law of the Seas Treaty opened for signing in Montego Bay, Jamaica. Representatives of the division were invited to be present as observers.

WD sees its task in a global context and works in coalition or as a member of religious and secular groups sharing common concerns. It long has been a member of IMPACT, an interreligious network. It has continuing contact with women's organizations in many countries and intentionally makes a domestic-international link in such issue arenas as infant formula or apartheid. In the United States, since the 1970s, the division has worked with the Religious Coalition for Abortion Rights.*

ELECTORAL ACTIVITIES

As a nonprofit corporation, WD does not engage in partisan politics or support individual candidates. Instead, in 1960 it launched a National Citizen's Roll Call to help shore up the foundation of a government believed to be imperiled by unwholesome secular campaigning. A political action primer was published, and thousands of local citizenship brunches were held for the purpose of discussion and planning for local involvement. In 1972–74, just prior to national elections, WD sponsored a series of national legislative training events for designated UMW conference leaders. During 1984–86, the division sponsored fifty-seven one-day political skills workshops with a theme, Making a Difference. Over 2,200 women attended. Work was done in cooperation with the National Women's Education Fund. A 1989 follow-up survey revealed that among 390 respondents, 18 percent had run for office at least once, and 7 percent following the workshop. Nine percent had managed or taken major responsibility in a campaign for the first time; 46 percent reported working in at least one campaign; 27 percent worked in two campaigns, and 14 percent in at least three.

FURTHER INFORMATION

There is an annual journal published after division meetings. WD *Annual Reports* summarize its work the previous year. Topical publications, for example, on the Law of the Sea project, are available.

BARBARA E. CAMPBELL

W
/

WASHINGTON GAY ACTIVISTS ALLIANCE
See GAY AND LESBIAN ACTIVIST ALLIANCE

WASHINGTON OPPORTUNITIES FOR WOMEN
See WIDER OPPORTUNITIES FOR WOMEN

WASHINGTON RESEARCH PROJECT
See CHILDREN'S DEFENSE FUND

WIDER OPPORTUNITIES FOR WOMEN (WOW)
815 15th Street, NW
Suite 916
Washington, DC 20005
(202) 638-3143
FAX (202) 638-4885

Wider Opportunities for Women (WOW) is a private, nonprofit organization that promotes employment opportunities for women in nontraditional jobs through information, training, and advocacy services. Its aim is to help women and girls achieve economic independence and obtain well-paying work. Since 1987, the National Commission on Working Women (NCWW) has been part of WOW.

ORIGIN AND DEVELOPMENT

WOW started as a local self-help effort in the nation's capital. More specifically, it developed from a vocational conference held in 1963 for the alumnae of Barnard, Bryn Mawr, Mt. Holyoke, Radcliffe, Smith, Vassar, and Wellesley colleges in Washington, D.C. Among the early organizers were Jane Fleming and Mary Janney. Conference participants identified lack of part-time educational programs and part-time professional employment as a severe obstacle for female college graduates to combine a homemaking job with outside work or additional schooling. Participants also believed that perhaps there were more opportunities than people knew, and they decided to research the options available. They recruited volunteers in the capital area, who in turn compiled a book on part-time and educational opportunities for women in Washington, D.C.

Following the success of the book, WOW—an acronym that originally stood for Washington Opportunities for Women—branched into other employment services, such as job counseling, skill assessment, job-hunting strategies, and interview techniques. It listed job openings and maintained a talent bank for employers.

In the early 1970s, WOW expanded its efforts to meet the needs of less-educated women having to cope with sex stereotyping, discrimination, and job segregation. WOW's new programs provided job preparation and training for low-income and unskilled women as well as technical assistance for employers. Simultaneously, WOW evolved from a local to a national organization. In 1977, it founded the Women's Work Force Network (WWFN) to serve as an information exchange, provide leadership development opportunities, facilitate technical assistance, and coordinate public policy advocacy. By 1994, the Network comprised more than 500 women's employment programs and advocacy groups in forty-eight states, reaching more than 300,000 women seeking employment information, counseling, training, and jobs.

Changes in WOW's leadership reflected the organization's changed focus. The original founders mostly had graduated from the "seven sisters colleges." Subsequent leaders closely reflected the ethnic and racial diversity of society at large. The change in focus and leadership took the organization on the same course as NCWW, and they merged in 1987.

Founded in 1977, NCWW focused on the needs of 80 percent of women in the workforce, concentrated in traditional, lower-paying, dead-end jobs. The commission targeted as policy concerns such issues as pay equity and the non-traditional learner. Elizabeth Koontz, the first chair, had formerly served as head of the Women's Bureau* in the U.S. Labor Department. She also was the first woman to head the National Education Association and served as vice-chair of the President's Advisory Committee for Women in 1979.

ORGANIZATION AND FUNDING

WOW is governed by an eighteen-member board of directors. The chair is Anna Padia. Board members reflect the racial and ethnic composition of society and are affiliated with business, education, unions, advocacy, and the media. Additional guidance comes from the Industry Advisory Council. WOW is located in Washington, D.C. Cynthia Marano is the executive director. The organization has a staff of about eighteen and accepts four to six unpaid interns annually.

NCWW and the WWFN have retained distinctive identities within the organizational structure. A national advisory board of the commission is chosen from five interest areas: corporations, labor, advocacy, the media, and Congress. In 1994, the congressional representation consisted of Senator James Jeffords (R-VT) and Congresspeople Matthew Martinez (D-CA), James Leach (R-IA), and Constance Morella (R-MD). The chair of NCWW is Irene Natividad, former chair of the National Women's Political Caucus.*

WWFN has a national advisory board of ten regional leaders, who meet twice yearly in Washington, D.C. Membership in the Network is open to women's employment or educational programs, advocates, employers, unions, and all others supporting WWFN's work and wanting to stay informed. Private industry councils are WOW's largest customer, followed by state agencies dealing with vocational education and community colleges. Affiliation allows WWFN members to receive the newsletter and other WOW publications. Additional membership benefits include consultation with the staff on program and policy issues and attendance at regional and national conferences.

WOW is a nonprofit educational organization under section 501 (c) (3) of the Internal Revenue Code. Thus it is tax-exempt, and donations are tax-deductible. Funding for its programs comes from grants and contracts with government agencies, grants from corporations and foundations, and contributions from individual donors. Additional income derives from book sales and, in the case of WWFN, a membership fee of $55. In 1994, the organization had a budget of about $1 million.

POLICY CONCERNS AND TACTICS

WOW's board, with recommendations from the staff, determines the policy agenda. Tactically, the organization is a public interest group in the classical pluralist sense: it articulates the interests of providers of training or job search services and of recipients of such services. WOW primarily tries to influence the political process by documenting problems and recommending strategies for solutions. It emphasizes research into salient issues and education about legislative or administrative actions. WOW's official congressional delegation, consisting of four senators and representatives from either party, also can be utilized for the information exchange in the policy network.

Of all the federal laws passed and administrative regulations issued, WOW considers legislation and rules involving women and employment important. This list includes the Equal Pay Act of 1963, Title VII of the Civil Rights Act of 1964 and subsequent amendments, Executive Order 11246, the Elementary and Secondary Education Act of 1965 as amended in 1972 and subsequent years, the Higher Education Act of 1965 and amendments, the Age Discrimination in Employment Act of 1967 as amended, the Equal Rights Amendment, the Equal Employment Opportunity Act of 1972, the Pregnancy Discrimination Act of

1978, the Job Training Partnership Act enacted in 1982 and amendments, the Retirement Equity Act of 1984, the Displaced Homemakers Self-Sufficiency Act enacted in 1990, the Carl D. Perkins Vocational and Applied Technology Education Act of 1990, the Civil Rights Act of 1991, and the Nontraditional Employment for Women Act of 1991. WOW also supports the Family and Medical Leave legislation, which was vetoed by President Bush but signed into law by President Clinton in 1993. Among its top legislative priorities in the current year are universal health care coverage and school-to-work legislation involving training of women in nontraditional apprenticeship programs.

For maximum effectiveness, WOW has formed coalitions with other organizations, each taking a lead role in tracking major policy areas of concern to women. Among the coalition partners are the National Committee on Pay Equity,* Council of Presidents,* and the National Coalition for Women and Girls in Education.

But the policy monitoring is only part of WOW's strategy. Since its inception, it has also pursued a self-help approach and actually expanded into a multifaceted women's employment organization. As a result WOW is well positioned to help implement the policy initiatives in the area of vocational-technical education introduced by the Clinton administration. WOW is especially concerned that women are included in apprenticeship programs that promise a higher earning potential than in traditional female occupations. WOW's agenda for 1994 included eight types of self-help activities:

The WOMANLINC Project: staff development workshops and technical assistance for organizations interested in teaching literacy in the context of employment or intergenerational programs

Leadership Development Project: state-based institutes and follow-up support designed to increase the effectiveness of women's advocates in community-based employment and training organizations

Nontraditional Employment Training Project: technical assistance for the JTPA system on improving the access of women to nontraditional occupations

Educational Equity Options Project (EEOP): consultation with school systems to improve vocational education opportunities for women and girls

The Women at Work Awards: a recognition event to celebrate exceptional contributions to working women in the media, public policy, the workplace, and individual leadership

The Sexual Harassment Solutions Project: a best-practices project identifying programs and policies that prevent or address sexual harassment in the workplace

The Family Literacy Project: a program for local area women integrating basic skills, introduction to nontraditional and technical jobs, and family learning activities

The DC NEW Act Project: a local public education and technical assistance project to increase the numbers of low-income women entering and succeeding in training for nontraditional jobs.

ELECTORAL ACTIVITIES

As a nonprofit educational organization, WOW is limited in the extent to which it can engage in partisan political activities. It does not have a political action committee.

FURTHER INFORMATION

A newsletter, *Women at Work,* is published quarterly. The *WWFN Directory* of 500 employment and training programs from across the country is issued annually, and public policy action alerts are distributed as warranted. Other WOW publications fall into five categories: (1) public policy resources, (2) literacy resources, (3) program resources, (4) media reports, and (5) a fact sheet series. Public policy resources include the *Risks and Challenges: Women, Work and Future* (1990) and *A More Promising Future: Strategies to Improve the Workplace* (1991). Among the literacy resources, WOW offers *Wider Opportunities: Combining Literacy and Employment Training for Women—an Action Kit* (1988), a study on *Teach the Mother and Reach the Child* (1991), and a five-volume workbook series: *Combining Literacy and Employment Training* (1992), *Functional Context Education: A Primer for Program Providers* (1992), *Introduction to Integration Literacy* (1992), *Making the Nation Smarter* (1992), and *A Road Map to Funding* (1992). Program resources involve videos, such as *Into the Working World* and *Consider a Nontraditional Job,* and manuals, such as *Step by Step: The Educational Equity Options* (1992) and the *Training, Placing and Retraining Women in Non-traditional Jobs* (1994). Media reports are produced periodically, for instance, *What's Wrong with This Picture? The Status of Women on Screen and behind the Camera in Entertainment TV* (1990) and *Growing Up in Prime Time: An Analysis of Adolescent Girls on Television* (1993). The fact sheet series has issued such pamphlets as *Women and Nontraditional Work* (1989), *An Overview of Women in the Workforce* (1990), and *Women, Work and Health Insurance* (1991).

SIEGRUN F. FOX

WISCONSIN WOMEN'S NETWORK
See NATIONAL WOMEN'S CONFERENCE COMMITTEE

WOMANPOWER PAC
See NATIONAL ORGANIZATION FOR WOMEN—NEW YORK CITY

WOMAN'S CHRISTIAN TEMPERANCE UNION (WCTU)
1730 Chicago Avenue
Evanston, IL 60201
(708) 864-1396
    Members of the Woman's Christian Temperance Union (WCTU) believe that

the sale and consumption of alcoholic beverages are a menace to women and their homes and must be fought with determined, steadfast, and organized effort.

ORIGIN AND DEVELOPMENT

The post–Civil War temperance movement began in small towns in New York and Ohio. Alcoholism ran rampant across the United States, especially among working-class men; and temperance workers, especially women of the middle and upper classes, reached out to help their working-class sisters in crisis. During the early months of 1874 this crusade spread, and in Jamestown, New York, women formed a Ladies Temperance Society. In August 1874, three eminently practical women delegates to a Sunday school convention in nearby Chautauqua, New York—Jane Fowler Willing, a faculty member at Illinois Wesleyan University; Emily Huntington Miller, a juvenile fiction writer from Evanston, Illinois; and Martha McLellan Brown of Alliance, Ohio, and a member of the Good Templar temperance women—issued a call for a formal organization of temperance women.

The organizing convention gathered in November; among the founders was Sojourner Truth. The newly formed WCTU elected Annie T. Wittenmeyer as president. A wealthy, well-educated conservative women, she remained cool to the ideas of women's suffrage. That same year, educator and WCTU founder Frances E. Willard became president of the Chicago women's temperance organization. Recently resigned from Northwestern University, Willard found a cause in temperance. In 1879, she became president of national WCTU and, exerting energetic leadership, linked temperance to women's suffrage under the banner of home protection. This link made the idea of suffrage palatable to many hesitant churchwomen. Willard's motto was "do everything"; and by 1890, WCTU boasted forty departments with superintendents at the national, state, and local levels. Further, in 1883 Willard founded the world WCTU, the first international women's organization.

Membership peaked at about 1 million women when the Prohibition amendment was added to the U.S. Constitution in 1920. After the amendment's rescission, in 1933, membership declined across the decades to 150,000 in 1960 and a low of 40,000 in 1991. Nonetheless, in 1990 twelve newly elected state presidents were women under the age of fifty years. Young mothers, concerned about controlled substance and alcohol abuse among children and teenagers, are joining the union. The group's continued relevance also may be measured by alcohol-related crime statistics and the stop-driving-while-intoxicated movement, which the media sometimes refer to as "neotemperance."

ORGANIZATION AND FUNDING

WCTU has an interlocking organization plan, from the local union through the county, district, state, and national levels; each level has its own officers. WCTU has several boards. The board of presidents is made up of the state presidents. The official board of directors consists of the presidents' board and the national officers—president, vice president, promotion director, treasurer, and recording secretary. The two boards together form the executive committee, which includes eight department directors, an honorary president, the chairman of the national board of education, a narcotic education consultant, and leadership training director. In addition, the executive committee includes adult representatives of the youth clubs. The legislative correspondent, who monitors congressional legislation, has a seat on this committee, as does the national field service executive secretary, who is in charge of sending workers to organize local unions. These women do not receive a salary but are reimbursed for expenses.

President Rachel B. Kelly, who has served since 1988, is eager that WCTU reach out to ethnic women and women with disabilities and bring them into leadership roles within the union. The segregated Sojourner Truth unions were phased out in the mid-1960s. The Michigan president, Kleo Johnson, is an African American woman; and the national education director and Loyal Temperance Legion director posts are held by an African American mother-daughter team—Colleen Wilson and Natalie Wilson.

The national president is elected for a two-year term and may be reelected. The president, promotion director, and treasurer are required to live in Evanston. A Washington, D.C., office closed in 1989. President Kelly supervises a paid staff of twenty-one at the Evanston headquarters.

Women made up 92 percent of the 1989–90 membership of approximately 40,000, located in forty-eight states and fifty-three countries. Each member signs a pledge of total abstinence. Like-minded women on the local, state, regional, and national levels join the organization to advocate a value important to them, temperance; they also find incentive in the chance to gain leadership training by participation in public affairs. Women may begin in WCTU as white-ribbon recruits: A mother can enroll her child with a white ribbon, which stands for abstinence, and when the child is in grade school, she may be enrolled in the Loyal Temperance Legion. A Youth Temperance Council for teenage girls and boys sponsors summer encampment in many states.

WCTU is a 501 (c) (3) organization. Members pay dues of $3.65 a year; their literature calls this "a penny and a prayer a day." Churches contributed to the founding; today national and local unions get along with small contributions from members in towns and villages across the United States. The total budget is $600,000.

POLICY CONCERNS AND TACTICS

Not a fashionable stand, total abstinence from alcohol is WCTU's hallmark, and pledge cards for total abstinence are circulated by the organization. WCTU interests always have extended to related causes, such as substance abuse. In keeping with Willard's do-everything motto, the union has eight departments: Christian outreach; education, which sponsors drug and alcohol abuse workshops; home projection, which focuses on child abuse and pornography; protection methods, which promotes nonalcoholic beverages; publications; public relations; social service, which fosters friendly relations with similar groups; and legislation and citizenship to get members involved in working on legislation of concern to the union. WCTU locals are described as autonomous but expected to follow national programs and the departments. They also may concentrate on a particular issue in their community.

In 1992, WCTU reinstated the position of director for petitions. This director, who serves in the Legislative Department, is in charge of circulating petitions on topics and legislation important to the temperance cause. Petitions were a vital part of WCTU history, as Willard believed that petitions gave a significant voice to voteless women and helped to educate them on public issues.

WCTUers have testified at congressional and state legislative hearings and also keep legislators and their staff informed, monitor voting records, and engage in letter-writing campaigns. Members also testify at local public hearings on liquor licenses.

WCTU plays a large role in educating the public about its issue agenda. One local chapter in Canton, Ohio, presented drug programs and materials to 5,000 students in twenty-one schools over a three-month period, 1990–91, as well as participated in five church services about a drug-free life and three programs at a juvenile detention center. Maryland WCTU participated in the 1991 Greater Washington Education Association convention and distributed 3,137 pieces of literature. Although the national WCTU took a pro-life stance in 1989, its main priority remains alcohol and drug education. Besides its opposition to *Roe* v. *Wade* and, support for Hyde amendments and a human life constitutional amendment, WCTU supported the 1984 Child Abuse and Child Support Enforcement Acts.

Many groups shy away from working with WCTU, despite its willingness to go into coalition. The union and Mothers against Drunk Driving* (MADD) work together often. But, where MADD says, Don't drink and drive and accepts funds from the alcohol industry, WCTU says, Don't drink at all. WCTU also has close ties with the Center for Science in the Public Interest in Washington, D.C., the National Temperance Council, and National Council on Alcoholism.

ELECTORAL ACTIVITIES

The union does not have a political action committee. Electoral activities are educational, coming through publications and public programs such as Youth Temperance Council Week proclamations in states, cities, and towns.

FURTHER INFORMATION

WCTU has a bimonthly magazine, *Union Signal,* which includes a "Washington Letter" about proposed legislation of interest to members. Union Signal Press is owned by WCTU. Since 1990, the WCTU national board of education has written or revised 126 pieces of literature—posters, activity sheets for children, booklets, and alcohol and narcotic educational materials for schools. A catalog of publications is available from the press. The Frances E. Willard Memorial Library houses approximately 5,000 volumes on Willard, WCTU, alcohol, and related topics and is open to researchers.

MARTHA JOY NOBLE

WOMEN FOR MEANINGFUL SUMMITS/USA (WMS/USA)
624 9th Street, NW
3rd Floor
Washington, DC 20001
(202) 393-1009

Women for Meaningful Summits/USA (WMS), a coalition of women's peace groups, has focused its energies on presenting women's opinions at international summits, beginning with the first Reagan-Gorbachev meeting.

ORIGIN AND DEVELOPMENT

WMS was originally formed in 1985 as a coalition of women's groups. The organization sought to represent women's opinions at the first Reagan/Gorbachev Summit, held in Geneva in 1985. To this end, Women Strike for Peace* (WSP) called together representatives from many (mostly women's) peace groups. The meeting's outcome was Women for Meaningful Summits, which was expected to be a temporary network of women's groups desiring to influence the summit's outcome. As the relationship between Presidents Reagan and Gorbachev developed, and the meetings between the two nations' leaders increased, WMS evolved into a more permanent organization, adopting a statement of purpose in 1986 focusing on the upcoming summit that year between the United States and the Soviet Union and urging the two nations to negotiate "verifiable weapons' reductions" and a Comprehensive Test Ban Treaty.

In 1987, WMS moved even further than it had in the direction of becoming a permanent organization, establishing a board of directors and rewriting its statement of purpose to recognize a broader set of goals. While the new statement continued to focus on summits between the United States and the Soviet Union, it also gave WMS support to all meetings among nations that worked toward peace and to equitable development of all nations. In recognition of its broader goal, the organization's name changed. The rewritten statement noted the need to include women in all such summits, offering the belief that women's leadership is essential to the achievement of common security.

ORGANIZATION AND FUNDING

Figures for 1986 indicated WMS had fifty-nine affiliated organizations; by 1994 the permanent board of WMS consisted of fifty-one women with representatives from dozens of women's organizations, including the Young Women's Christian Association of the USA* (YMCA), Women's Foreign Policy Council,* League of Women Voters,* Women's International League for Peace and Freedom* (WILPF), Women's Action for New Directions* (WAND), Mothers Embracing Nuclear Disarmament (MEND), WSP, and Grandmothers for Peace.* From its founding, WMS has attempted to include members from organizations representing women of color. Currently serving on the board are women from Hispanic Women in the Network and Americans for Indian Opportunity.

When it was first established, WMS was loosely run by its constituent organizations through a coordinating committee, with WSP and the Committee against Nuclear War (CAN) providing the major support. Karen Mulhauser, executive director of CAN, served as the chair; and WMS shared office space with CAN. The current president is Sarah Harder, a former president of the American Association of University Women,* and the honorary members are Senator Barbara Boxer (D-CA), Coretta Scott King of the Martin Luther King, Jr. Center for Nonviolence and Social Change, former representative Claudine Schneider Representative Connie Morrella (R-MD), Representative Maxine Waters (D-CA), and the actress Joanne Woodward. WMS's Washington office shares space with the YMCA. Currently, there is no executive director, nor is there any paid staff or interns. Linda Weber serves as chair and editor of the newsletter.

There is no membership category for individuals, although there are contribution categories ranging from $10 for students to $500 for benefactors. Organizations may join for $50, and so may endorsers of the statement of purpose.

Originally, contributions to WMS were funneled through CAN's foundation arm. Initial funding came through the contributions of a few large donors and several foundations, including the Rockefeller Family Association, Plowshares, and Paul Newman's Salad King. Today the main source of funds is the individual constituent organizations. The 1990 budget totaled $150,000. WMS is a 501 (c) (3) organization. Virtually all contributors are women, although some men have supported the organization's activities. Contributions from foundations are tied to WMS programs and prove important in some budget years. The largest expenditures are tied to specific WMS programs.

POLICY CONCERNS AND TACTICS

A coordinating committee initially set WMS policy decisions; today the board of directors makes policy for the organization. The board, with the advice of the president, also determines strategy choices for implementing the policies. Past projects have connected to the group's goals of reducing nuclear weapons and the threat of nuclear war. To this end, WMS has observed at all the summits between the United States and the former Soviet Union. At the first summit, WMS members were able to meet with Gorbachev to present their statement and petitions. In addition to the superpower summits, WMS has participated in, or sent observers to, numerous other international gatherings, including meetings of the North Atlantic Treaty Organization and the Five Nation Peace Initiative Meeting in 1986. At these meetings, WMS brings a woman's perspective to bear on negotiations, often by meeting with delegates and presenting questions that represent the women's perspective.

Since the cold war's end, WMS has broadened its concerns to women's needs in developing countries, to the environment, and to international cooperation more generally, especially among women. For instance, WMS's representatives helped to found the Women's International Network for Development and Democracy in El Salvador and the International Pacific Policy Congress. WMS also has organized several broader international conferences of women, often with representatives from countries around the world. The first such meeting was a women and global security conference, held in Washington, D.C., in 1986. This meeting brought together women working at all levels for peace. The other major conference was the Soviet/American Women's Summit held in 1990. This meeting involved women from the former Soviet Union and the United States. Out of their discussions came the document, ''From Disarmament to Day Care: Women's Vision for the 21st Century.'' Conferees sent this agenda to Presidents Bush and Gorbachev. Included on the list of priorities were calls to guarantee women's full participation in all dimensions of decision making, demilitarize societies, convert from militaristic to socially and ecologically responsible economies, implement a worldwide plan for the environment, respect human rights, adopt nonintervention principles of international law, and promote citizen diplomacy.

In all its activities, WMS works closely with its affiliate organizations and often with other groups, especially the Alliance for Our Common Future.

ELECTORAL ACTIVITIES

WMS does not have a political action committee, nor does it endorse candidates for public office. It does, however, support having more women elected officials.

FURTHER INFORMATION

WMS regularly sends letters to its supporters detailing its activities. Starting in winter 1991, it began to publish a newsletter, *Just Peace.* WMS also has produced several documents out of its conferences, most notably *Women's Vision for the 21st Century: Disarmament to Day Care.*

NANCY E. MCGLEN

WOMEN FOR RACIAL AND ECONOMIC EQUALITY (WREE)
198 Broadway
Number 606
New York, NY 10038
(212) 385-1103

Representing the interests of working-class women, women of color, and their children, Women for Radical and Economic Equality (WREE) holds that the struggle for women's rights must be founded on, and continue the fight against, racism, which divides women among themselves and reduces their ability to achieve equality. WREE has an educational and research fund.

ORIGIN AND DEVELOPMENT

WREE was the idea of a group, with no one individual acting as chief organizer. Among the key founders were Georgia Wever, Alva Buxembuam, Carmen Ristorucci, Carmen Teizidor, and Norma Spector. The organizer/founders knew each other from such organizational contexts as the Committee for a Sane Nuclear Policy, Women Strike for Peace,* and other peace groups; community groups, including the Parent Teacher Association and block associations; and political groups, among them Democratic clubs and the Communist Party. The catalyst for the founders was the sudden burgeoning of the women's liberation movement in the early seventies. The founders attended meetings of various movement groups and found themselves isolated because the issues they wished to deal with were not on the agenda of women involved in the new organizations: racism, poor and welfare women, child care, health care, and so on.

The founders met, then contacted friends and political associates in other cities to plan for a conference. In 1976, an organizational conference met in Chicago to plan for a founding convention. The founding convention was held in Chicago in 1977 and attracted nearly 600 women from thirty-two states and fifty organizations and trade unions. As the U.S. affiliate of the Women's International Democratic Federation (WIDF), a United Nations (UN) nongovernmental organization in consultative status with the Economic and Social Council, WREE's first convention also drew women from Canada, Chile, Cuba, Mexico, Palestine, Puerto Rico, South Africa, the Soviet Union, and Vietnam, this latter a first. WREE's first chair was Josetta Lawns, an elderly domestic worker from Philadelphia; she served until her death in 1981, when Cheryl Allen Craig, then a Pittsburgh lawyer, now a judge, succeeded her. Craig served until 1990.

WREE produced a Women's Bill of Rights listing twelve demands for national legislation to guarantee racial and economic equality to women, among them, peace and security, a safe job at a living wage, equal pay and pay equity, affirmative action, union membership for all working women, a multicultural environment, child care and public education, a national health care plan, reproductive freedom, housing, and a sustainable environment. WREE revised this bill of rights once and in 1990 revised it again for a change in emphasis; today it also includes rights to an unbiased judicial system, equal access to the democratic process, and diversity in lifestyle. The primary goals have not changed and have become agenda items for mainstream women's organizations.

ORGANIZATION AND FUNDING

WREE is a membership organization with members in many states across the country. It has a national convention; the last one was held in 1992. Over 50 percent of the ten national executive board members are African American. Participation on the board is encouraged of persons from lower-income strata.

All the officers and board members are women. Until 1990, the membership elected the chairs of the organization at the national convention; since then they have been chosen by mail ballot to the entire membership. The current chair is Rudean Leinaehg. WREE's national office is in New York City. Two volunteers work in the national office.

Presently WREE has about 1,000 individual members, down from 2,000 in 1985 and 2,500 in 1980. Women are 99 percent of the membership. The group has discussed its status as a women-mainly group and plans to remain so. Members join to advocate important values or policies and for the conferences and meetings WREE convenes. WREE publications also provide an incentive to membership, and, to a lesser extent, so does the chance to associate with similarly minded people.

Sixty percent of WREE revenues come from membership dues, ranging from $7 to $20 to $50, with fund-raisers producing about 30 percent of remaining revenue. Merchandise sales, corporate grants, individual contributions, and church and trade union funds may together yield 10 percent of WREE's revenue. This is not a tax-exempt organization, and contributions to it are not tax-deductible. The total budget is around $35,000, compared with $20,000 in 1980.

POLICY CONCERNS AND TACTICS

Proposals, suggestions, and ideas for policy come from chapters, officers, and committees. Discussion on them takes place at board meetings, after which they are forwarded to the chapters for discussion as well as featured in the group's newspaper. Feedback is sought. Major policy is discussed thereafter at council meetings and, when decisions can wait, national conventions. Sometimes voting or consensus is achieved through mail solicitation of the membership. The convention and council are most influential in policy discussions, although executive officers' decisions and membership polls play a role. Once WREE decides to become active on an issue, a committee is formed to work out the campaign. The committee presents its aims and actions to the board, and suggestions for actions are sent to the chapters, members at large, and other organizations.

Preferred strategies for achieving WREE objectives include making written comments on proposed regulations and letter-writing campaigns by the members, educating the membership with publications and the public through press releases, and participation in direct action political demonstrations. WREE also may conduct and publish research on issues. Less frequently it gives testimony at congressional and state hearings; supplies congresspeople, state legislators, and staff with information; testifies at agency/department hearings; and files amicus briefs. WREE filed as friend of the court in *Rust* v. *Sullivan* (1990) and *Planned Parenthood of South Eastern Pennsylvania* v. *Casey* (1992).

WREE has participated in the Penicillin for Vietnam Campaign. It also has collected and made clothes for the children of South African fighters against apartheid, raised funds and foods for striking miners, demonstrated and organized against racism and bias, petitioned and lobbied for every issue on its bill of rights, protested interventionist U.S. foreign policies that have hurt women around the world, and urged U.S. support for a peace initiative in Central America.

WREE has worked in recent years, through election campaigns and legislative campaigns and for the UN, on its Campaign against Human Rights Violation in the U.S. This work has included hearings on the impact of racism in Birmingham, Alabama, and Boston, Massachusetts. New York WREE has sought to bring a major banking institution to terms with affirmative action. Whenever necessary, Dayton WREE takes to the City Council instances of institutional racism or police brutality; Montgomery County, Pennsylvania, WREE organized a coalition to assert the rights of a woman whose prison experience caused her to miscarry. WREE also supported ratification by the U.S. Senate of the UN Convention on the Elimination of All Forms of Discrimination against Women and the UN Convention on the Rights of Children. Individual legislators on the local level may seek WREE views.

WREE finds of continuing importance the 1964 Equal Pay Act; 1964 Civil Rights, Equal Opportunity and Food Stamp Acts; the Voting Rights Act; affirmative action orders; 1968 Antidiscrimination in Housing Act; 1970 Food Stamp Reform and School Lunch Acts; the act of 1972 in which sex discrimination was added to the Civil Rights Commission jurisdiction; the 1972 Equal Employment Act and Title IX of the Education Amendments; the proposed equal rights amendment; the Strategic Arms Limitations Treaty agreements; *Roe* v. *Wade;* the 1973 War Powers Act; 1974 Office of Economic Opportunity, Social Services and Women's Educational Equity Acts; Child Support Amendments— Social Security Act of 1975; 1976 Day Care Act; opposition to the Hyde amendments; 1978 Pregnancy Disability Act; 1982 Welfare Act; 1983 Social Security Act; 1983 Pension Equity Act; 1984 Child Abuse and Child Support Enforcement Acts; and 1986 Age Discrimination and 1988 Civil Rights Restoration acts.

WREE considers the most important new federal policy initiatives of the last decade to be extension of minimum wage; Head Start reauthorization, if only for one year; the Americans with Disabilities Act; and the parental and medical leave bills vetoed by President Bush and, similarly, the 1990 Civil Rights bill, along with child care, clean air, and other relevant efforts. WREE mobilizes members to write, phone, and visit their legislators and support, endorse, and participate in demonstrations and marches on behalf of these initiatives.

It sees as the worst initiatives of the last decade regressive Supreme Court rulings, the savings and loan wholesale rip-off of the U.S. working people, and appropriations of funds to help the contras of Nicaragua, El Salvador, the invasion of Grenada and Panama, and war with Iraq. It attributes their onset to the atmosphere of fear and racism encouraged by the Reagan-Bush administrations, a deteriorating economy engendered by profit-mode corporations that run the government, and the contribution of these factors to increasingly rightward movement by U.S. society. WREE sees the eighties as having been a legislative desert, with retreat from affirmative action, civil rights, and reproductive rights.

WREE has formed and worked in coalition with women's labor, peace, justice, and religious groups, including the Coalition of Labor Union Women,* Church Women United,* Women's International League for Peace and Freedom,* Citizens against Nuclear War, and chapters of National Organization for Women.* It participates in a twenty-six-member coalition to boycott Beatrice, a transnational corporation doing business in South Africa. It was part of the Coalition for Nairobi Conference and helped to produce the UN document, "The Effects of Racism and Militarization on Women's Equality." In 1987, it organized the U.S. delegation to the World Congress of Women. As a WIDF affiliate, it has access to the 142 national women's organizations in 135 countries that also have affiliated with the group and is a member of the UN Children's Fund International Year of the Child national organizations advisory committee. WREE sees as its adversaries the present and for the foreseeable future Supreme Court of the United States; skinheads, the Ku Klux Klan, Nazis, and so on; and Operation Rescue* and other right-to-lifers. It constantly finds these groups working against issues of concern to it.

FURTHER INFORMATION

WREE VIEW is a quarterly newspaper published by WREE. In 1990, WREE published a factbook, *191 Facts about U.S. Women.* WREE and the Indigenous Women's Network are currently working together on a book about Native American women.

NORMA SPECTOR

WOMEN IN COMMUNICATIONS, INC. (WICI)
3717 Columbia Pike
Suite 310
Arlington, VA 22204-4255
(703) 920-5555
FAX (703) 920-5556

Women in Communications, Inc. (WICI) is a membership association of 10,000 women and men who work in all areas of communications across the United States and around the world. For more than eighty-five years, WICI members have worked to advance women in their communications careers, protect First Amendment rights and responsibilities, recognize distinguished professional achievements, and promote high professional standards throughout the communications industry.

ORIGIN AND DEVELOPMENT

WICI was founded as Theta Sigma Phi, a women's honorary journalism society, by seven sophomore students at the University of Seattle in 1909, the same year the Washington state legislature amended the state constitution to give women the right to vote. In 1919, two years before the Nineteenth Amendment's ratification, Theta Sigma Phi held its first convention at the University of Kansas in Lawrence. Local chapters and networking were the mainstays of membership structure, enhanced in 1934 by the executive secretary. Right through the decades to 1960, Theta Sigma Phi struggled to reduce women's marginality in journalism.

During the decade of the 1960s, the organization became more involved than before in public policy and social issues, especially equality legislation affecting women. By 1972, the dynamic of change led to the decision to adopt the name Women in Communications and also to admit men members on other than an honorary basis. For most of the years between its founding and the present, the national headquarters was in Austin, Texas. In 1980, a national public affairs office opened in the Washington, D.C. area to monitor legislation and represent the organization to the Congress and other Washington publics. The national headquarters relocated to the Washington, D.C., area.

ORGANIZATION AND FUNDING

WICI has 186 professional and campus chapters throughout the United States. These chapters provide programs, seminars, and job referral services for members. Structurally, WICI is divided into eight regions governed by a single board of directors composed of the president, president-elect, immediate past president, vice presidents of finance, professional development, programs, and student affairs, and eight regional vice presidents. The current president is Carol Fenstermacher.

Communications touches all of social life, and WICI membership reflects the broadly gauged nature of communications, with 11,500 members drawn from the fields of print journalism, broadcasting, education, public relations, advertising, magazines, technical writing, business communications, photojournalism, publishing, film, and graphics. The overwhelming majority of members are women.

Professional dues of $90, student onetime fees of $51, and corporate contributions support an annual budget that is about $1.2 million. WICI is a 501 (c) (6) organization.

POLICY CONCERNS AND TACTICS

National board decisions advance basic policy. Issues may arise from anywhere within the organization: local chapters, national headquarters staff, the board itself, or delegations to the national annual business meeting held in conjunction with the national professional conference. WICI positions on public issues develop through resolutions at the business meeting. These positions tend to dictate potential partners and adversaries on issues such as pay equity for women, the equal rights amendment, women in public office, employers' parental support programs, child care, gender balance, family and medical leave, reproduction rights, and free speech. WICI consistently has supported policies that would extend equity, access, and support for women. The advancement of WICI positions is handled through a combination of formalized and ad hoc lobbying, by both Washington staff and active members.

WICI maintains an ongoing annual program with workshops on First Amendment freedom of the press and free flow of information issues. Examples of recent initiatives include work on access to court proceedings and on sexism in advertising. During the last decade the organization's most important work has come in three areas: the growth in prestige of the Clarion Awards for excellence in communications, begun in 1973 with 34 entries and completed in 1991 with 1,400 entries from an international field; the growth and high quality of the national conference now bringing to itself a national trade show; and advocacy for women in the workplace on issues including pay equity, sexual violence against women, civil rights, family medical leave, health care, and First Amendment issues.

WICI regularly joins forces with a wide range of organizations sharing goals on issues, such as the National Commission on Pay Equity,* National Women's Law Center,* American Association of University Women,* and National Women's Legal Defense Fund.

FURTHER INFORMATION

The Professional Communicator, published five times a year by Women in Communications, Inc., is a magazine that gives members and subscribers an overview of issues, trends, and news in all areas of communications. The publication features communications management practices, how-to material, membership news, legislative updates, job networking ideas, career advancement tips, and information affecting communicators and the communications industry. Subscription to the magazine is free to members, $18.50 to nonmembers.

WICI also publishes an annual membership directory, called the *WICI Membership Directory and Buyer's Guide.* The *Membership Directory* is a valuable networking took for members looking to do business across the country and around the world. This publication also is free to members, $49.95 to nonmembers.

MILDA K. HEDBLOM

WOMEN IN GOVERNMENT RELATIONS (WGR)
1325 Massachusetts Avenue, NW
Suite 510
Washington, DC 20005
(202) 347-5432
FAX (202) 347-5434

Women in Government Relations (WGR) sees as its mission a commitment to women's professional and educational development in the government relations field. It has a philanthropic foundation and a Government Relations Institute.

ORIGIN AND DEVELOPMENT

In 1976, twelve women, professionals in government relations, formed an organization for purposes of networking and improving their effectiveness on the job. No one person acted as the group's leader or chief organizer, but founder Nancy Benson of American Cyanimid Company became its first president; founder Susan Friday of the University of Connecticut, its second; and founder Bettie S. McCarthy of Bettie McCarthy & Associates, its third. In 1988, Sally J. Patterson, Planned Parenthood Federation of America,* served as president.

In recent years WGR has achieved visibility via C-Span and ABC's "Working Women" show, through such agency newsletters as the Federal Energy Regulatory Commission's and *Broadcasting Magazine.* It seeks to become "known as the preeminent association of government relation professionals," a challenge set forth in its vision statement, with its current educational component an enlargement on the original objective, Presently, it is implementing a five-year strategic plan that includes management of continued growth, enhanced member participation, excellence in membership services, financial stability through a reserve account and capital budget policy, and enhanced acknowledgment and esteem.

ORGANIZATION AND FUNDING

WGR has an eight-member board of directors and eight officers. All the officers and directors are women, 12 percent are African American, and 6 percent are Hispanic. Millicent Gorham of the National Rural Health Association serves as president and is African American. The treasurer is Kathy Bryant of the American College of Obstetricians and Gynecologists.* WGR has twenty-four internal committees and eleven task forces. The organization's Washington office opened in 1990. Janet Allen serves as administrative director. The office employs two professional staff; they take a fixed level of responsibility. One of WGR's officers is the group's general counsel.

Membership has reached 750, up from 600 in 1985 and 300 in 1980. Ninety-nine percent of the members are women. Discussion has concerned the group's status as a mainly women's group; it will remain as it is. Thirty-four members live outside the District's metropolitan area. New members are sponsored by three members and must be active in the group. They also must meet three of five standards as professionals: actively assess the effect by any government or partisan activity on their employer; draft testimony, position papers, and so on for related issues; represent an employer on such an issue; manage an employer's decisions, strategizing, or policy making; or play an active part setting and administering fund-raising and solicitation for a political action committee or organization. There is a onetime $100 initiation fee. Members join to communicate with their peers and for the conferences and meetings, which may offer professional learning opportunities. Friendship ties also offer an incentive to membership, as do, to a lesser extent, publications, association with similarly minded people and the chance to exert influence within the organization. There is a job bank.

WGR's first budget was $75; it received financial support from the founders and early member employers and government agencies and small contributions from many people. In 1992, this 501 (c) (6) organization had income of $289,687, 52 percent of it generated by the task forces and committees, 36 percent by membership dues of $150, and 8 percent by interest. Publication sales or advertising and corporate or business gifts or bequests provided nominal revenue. Contributions are not tax-deductible. Total expenses were $248,946.

Since 1979, a 501 (c) (3) WGR LEADER foundation has created Leadership, Education, Advisement, Development, and Endowment programs and opportunities. A midcareer fellowship program seeks not only to stimulate access to leaders in business, government, and academe but also to increase the proportion of women to men in influential posts. There is a seminar for women high school students, which, among other things, points the way to government relations careers; in 1991, the program expanded to include both District and New Jersey students. The many foundation contributors include American Express, Chanel, Chrysler Corporation, Corning, Distilled Spirits Council, Dow Chemical, Good Housekeeping, Johnson & Johnson, Kraft General Foods, Metropolitan Life Insurance Company, National Restaurant Association, Procter & Gamble, RJR Nabisco, and Tobacco Institute.

In 1988, the foundation and WGR together formed the WGR Government Relations Institute to offer training, develop relevant educational materials, and promote improved understanding of the government relations profession. The institute makes available such courses as advanced lobbying and legislative process taught by experts, practitioners and academic both, in the field. Public-speaking skills and career development are among the available emphases. A Women in Leadership program first manifested through the Junior League.* Its focus has shifted from community service to public policy. It draws on the methodology of Coro, an institute providing public affairs training through hands-on experience.

POLICY CONCERNS AND TACTICS

The board sets WGR policy. This activity's intensity varies, depending on who serves as president. The organization expects the board to put more time into policy considerations in the future.

The task forces assess major issues, including banking and finance, taxes, telecommunications, the environment, health, labor and human resources, education, foreign relations and international trade, energy, and political action committees. Among the specific issues concerning them in recent years are the General Agreement on Tariffs and Trade, North American Free Trade Agreement and European Community banking directives; economic recovery; the 1991 Resource Conservation and Recovery Act, 1990 Clean Air Act Amendments regulations and Clean Water Act reauthorization; food safety and nutrition labeling, Medicaid, medical liability, AIDS-related ethical dilemmas, and the Canadian health care system; the 1991 Civil Rights Act and Striker Replacement bill; and "mega" notice of proposed rules on natural gas pipeline service and electric regulatory policy comparability.

As professionals WGR members take many issue stands; WGR is known not to take issue stands as an organization. WGR most likely would coordinate with the American League of Lobbyists and American Society of American Executives.

ELECTORAL ACTIVITIES

WGR is not a partisan organization and does not have a political action committee.

FURTHER INFORMATION

WGR publishes a membership newsletter six times yearly; *On the Record* includes features on such topics as sexual harassment and financial planning. Nonmembers may subscribe for thirty-five dollars. The *WGR Membership Directory* is revised annually and is well received by government relations professionals. There are a *Policies and Procedures Manual* and a *WGR Historic Policies* book.

SARAH SLAVIN

WOMEN IN GOVERNMENT RELATIONS, GOVERNMENT RELATIONS INSTITUTE
See WOMEN IN GOVERNMENT RELATIONS

WOMEN IN GOVERNMENT RELATIONS LEADER FOUNDATION
See WOMEN IN GOVERNMENT RELATIONS

WOMEN IN MEDICINE PROGRAM
See ASSOCIATION OF AMERICAN MEDICAL COLLEGES WOMEN IN MEDICINE PROGRAM

WOMEN LAWYERS CLUB
See NATIONAL ASSOCIATION OF WOMEN LAWYERS

WOMEN OFFICE WORKERS
See 9to5, NATIONAL ASSOCIATION OF WORKING WOMEN

WOMEN ORGANIZED FOR EMPLOYMENT
See 9to5, NATIONAL ASSOCIATION OF WORKING WOMEN

WOMEN'S ACTION FOR NEW DIRECTIONS (WAND)
691 Massachusetts Avenue
Arlington, MA 02174

(617) 643-6740
FAX (617) 643-6744

Women's Action for New Directions (WAND) seeks women's empowerment to undertake political action to decrease violence and military buildup and to redistribute military resources for human and environmental purposes. In the decade of the 1980s, WAND played a key role in the peace movement. WAND has an educational fund and a political action committee (PAC).

ORIGIN AND DEVELOPMENT

WAND has gone through several name changes since it was founded in 1980. Originally called the Women's Party for Survival, it sought to serve as a third political party in the United States to mobilize women in opposition to nuclear weapons. In 1982, the organization incorporated as Women's Action for Nuclear Disarmament. The change signified a move away from the idea of a political party to a more broad-based organization; the goal of organizing women in opposition to nuclear weapons proliferation continued. After many years of discussing the need to alter the group's name to reflect an expanding set of goals, the organization adopted its current name in 1992. With the new name came a refined mission statement focusing on empowering women for broader goals. Throughout these transformations, WAND has continued to serve as a vehicle for women interested in changing the foreign policy of the United States, especially respecting the use of nuclear weapons.

The founder of WAND is Helen Caldicott. Born in Australia and trained as a pediatrician, she first became active politically when she organized the Australian protest to French atmospheric tests in the South Pacific. In addition to working in WAND she also has served as president of Physicians for Social Responsibility. Caldicott's motivation to undertake this effort was the fear that nuclear weapons and their potential use would destroy the world for the next generation. Caldicott believed that women could be mobilized to work to save the planet for their children. In her best-selling book, *Missile Envy,* she wrote that women needed to empower themselves so that they might play a worldwide role in local, national, and international politics, using their special connection with children in their efforts to save the world for future generations. A powerful speaker as well as author, Caldicott served as WAND's guiding light for many years. Today she spends most of her time in her home country of Australia, occasionally coming to the United States for speaking tours. She also continues to have a position on WAND's board.

ORGANIZATION AND FUNDING

WAND's governing board of directors is composed of fifteen women, all of whom, except Caldicott and Sayre Sheldon, president emeritus, are elected by mail ballots of the members. The board has three representatives from its home base in the Boston area, four at-large delegates and one representative from each of the four national regions. A president, vice president, secretary, and treasurer are selected from the board. The current president is Arlene Victor. Besides the board of directors, WAND has an advisory board composed of twenty-seven notable women and two men, including the president of Peace Links,* Betty Bumpers, actress Sally Field, Harvard psychologist Carol Gilligan, and comedienne Lily Tomlin. In addition to its headquarters in Arlington, Massachusetts, it has an office in Washington, D.C. The executive director serves as the group's day-to-day leader. Since 1980, WAND has had four women serve in this position. The current director is Susan Shaer. On the staff of seven are two lobbyists.

WAND is an organization primarily of women. With a membership of 10,000, it is one of the largest women's peace groups in the country. Members may join at large or through one of its thirty-five local or regional groups. In 1986, WAND had 15,000 members and 100 affiliated groups; thus, the end of the cold war apparently weakened support for the organization, a problem its new name and mission statement may help overcome. Most members join to work with like-minded women on important causes and to have a voice in national politics.

WAND's budget is in excess of $220,000, with the bulk of the money coming from annual dues of $35 and contributions from its members through a pledge program. Some funds also come from the sale of merchandise and subscriptions. Twenty-five percent of the annual dues goes to the local organization.

WAND's Educational Fund, a 501 (c) (3) organization with a budget of $240,000, publishes informational materials designed to educate the public about issues of importance to WAND. Among its recent projects has been a billboard advertising campaign. It also sponsors the annual Mother's Day for Peace and conducts workshops and training sessions for activists. The book *Turnabout* was published by the WAND Education Fund as a careful evaluation of how the peace movement might better influence public opinion and public policy. The Education Fund shares an executive director and president with WAND.

POLICY CONCERNS AND TACTICS

Policy stands are made by the board of directors at its four annual meetings. Member input is sought on a regular basis, including an annual meeting and ballots on some key issues. The executive director and the staff implement the decisions of the board and exercise influence over the choice of strategies.

From its beginning, WAND focused its energies on changing U.S. policy on nuclear weapons. To this end it has worked actively for a ban on all nuclear testing. It also has supported negotiated arms agreements. Recently, it concentrated on reducing the defense budget and shifting national budget priorities to environmental and human needs. A major policy initiative in 1987 was the constitutional peace campaign designed to focus on the bicentennial of the U.S. Constitution and to draw a link between the themes of the Constitution and the cause of nuclear disarmament. A peace dividend petition campaign, conducted during the 101st session of the Congress, aimed to gather citizens' signatures in a call to reorient budget priorities away from military to human needs. During the Persian Gulf War, WAND organized a movement urging all persons opposed to the war to wear white ribbons as a way of protesting against it. WAND actively participates in a number of budget priority change coalitions, including Citizens Budget Campaign, Common Agenda, Campaign for New Priorities, and Invest in America Working Group. It also works closely with other peace groups, including Peace Links* and Campaign for a Livable World.

A firm supporter of grassroots lobbying, WAND has organized a network of activists who are ready to lobby at the local and national level. One of WAND's most original initiatives was the recent creation of the Women's Legislative Lobby (WiLL), a coalition of women state legislators working to reduce the military budget and redirect funds to important human needs. The organization has mobilized more than one-fifth of all women state legislators and has held several successful annual lobby days in the nation's capitol. WiLL and WAND have lobbied in opposition to the B-2 stealth bomber and in support of a nuclear test ban, economic conversion, and especially a redirection of budget priorities.

ELECTORAL ACTIVITIES

Since March 1984, WAND has had a separate WAND PAC. Its director is Nila Bolus. It lists as its major functions educating candidates on the arms race, contributing to presidential and congressional campaigns, and keeping the media focused on the arms race. Before 1990, WAND PAC contributed money to the campaigns of both women and men who worked to reduce reliance on nuclear weapons. Since then, WAND PAC has limited its contributions to women candidates only. Another change in policy begun in 1990 was to contribute more money to fewer candidates. In addition to direct contributions, it actively has encouraged its members to write checks to endorsed women candidates' campaigns. WAND PAC then "bundles" the checks and sends them to the candidate. This new strategy of supporting only women candidates coincides with a major effort on WAND's part to increase the number of women in the Congress by the year 2000. In 1992, because of the large number of women running for office, WAND PAC endorsed thirty-eight women and funded fifteen for the House and Senate. Contributions to WAND PAC also increased between 1990 and 1992.

FURTHER INFORMATION

WAND publications include its quarterly newsletter for members, *The Bulletin,* and a monthly legislative and action update, *WAND Action.* The latter is available by subscription for thirty dollars to WAND members. WAND also publishes numerous educational and informational pamphlets.

NANCY E. MCGLEN

WOMEN'S ATHLETIC CAUCUS
See NATIONAL ASSOCIATION OF COLLEGIATE WOMEN ATHLETIC ADMINISTRATORS

WOMEN'S CAMPAIGN FUND (WCF)
120 Maryland Avenue, NE
Washington, DC 20002
(202) 544-4484
FAX (202) 544-4517

The Women's Campaign Fund (WCF) is the largest bipartisan political action committee (PAC) dedicated to supporting progressive women running for public office. It has a research and education fund.

ORIGIN AND DEVELOPMENT

Founded in 1974, WCF was the first bipartisan PAC to raise significant funds solely to elect women. The idea to create WCF came from political activists who had worked with women candidates and witnessed their difficulty raising money from traditional sources. Frustrated at seeing women candidates not taken seriously by the "old boys' network," the founders decided to start a PAC just for women candidates. WCF was launched. Ann B. Zill, then funding representative for philanthropist Stewart Mott, and Sandra Kramer, a Washington activist, led the effort. Others involved in WCF's early days included Susan King, Barbara Williams, Arvonne Fraser, Marge Tabankin, Jill Ruckelshaus, and Elise duPont. Fraser and duPont served briefly as the first cochairs. Fraser, a Democratic activist from Minnesota, and du Pont, a Republican activist from Delaware, were trying nationally and within their states to increase the power that women held within the ranks of their respective political parties. In 1975, Zill became WCF chair and served until 1979.

WCF came into existence because these women's liberation movement activists realized that to move their policy agenda, they needed to increase their political clout. Several new political organizations already had started to this end. The National Women's Political Caucus* (NWPC) formed in 1972 to increase women's participation in party politics and their election and appointment to public office. In 1973, the National Women's Education Fund formed to provide political training for women. The following year, WCF was created to raise money to elect more women to office. From the beginning, WCF supported only women candidates holding progressive issue stands. To be endorsed, candidates had to be both pro-equal rights amendment and pro-choice. Later candidates also were required to support federal funding for abortions to win support.

Initially WCF focused on congressional and key state races. Starting in 1978, it expanded into state legislative races in important unratified states. In 1981, realizing that the women eventually running for state and federal office first would run for state legislative and local office, WCF made a commitment to increase its support for candidates running at this level. WCF also stated that one of its goals would be to recruit and support minority women candidates. Candidate viability also became a more important factor in evaluating candidates for endorsements.

Although it took several election cycles to became established, WCF has grown into the largest bipartisan national PAC supporting women candidates running for office at all levels of government. WCF has become well known for its success in helping women candidates master the complex art of Washington, D.C., PAC fund-raising. It is credited with not only teaching women candidates to raise money but also teaching women in general to give money to women running for office.

ORGANIZATION AND FUNDING

WCF has an unpaid bipartisan, racially mixed board of directors consisting of forty members from all regions of the country. Cochairs, for the most part, have headed the board. By custom, one is a Democrat (D), and the other a Republican (R). Cochairs during the 1993–94 election cycle were economist Ann Kinney and businesswoman Elaine LaRoche. Past cochairs have included teacher Molly Raiser (D) and businesswoman Candy Straight (R); Sandra Kramer (D), active in national Democratic reform efforts to include more women in party affairs; Dorann Gunderson (R), active in national Republican Party politics; Frances Barnard (D), writer and fund-raiser; Sharon Percy Rockefeller (D), board of directors, Corporation for Public Broadcasting; and Janet Hill (R), attorney and first woman of color to serve as a WCF cochair. WCF maintains an office in Washington, D.C., which serves as a home away from home for WCF candidates. Its staff primarily include an executive director, Amy Corroy; political director, Amy Simon; and various support personnel. Those serving as executive director in the past have included Carol Randles, Ranny Cooper, Stephanie Solien, and Jane Danowitz. Jody Newman, Pam Fleischaker, Celinda Lake and Julie Tippens were former candidates services or political directors.

WCF started with a $15,000 loan and office space provided by Mott. In its first year, WCF used two direct mail appeals and a small Washington fund-raiser to solicit additional funds. It raised enough money to repay Mott's loan, hire a staff person, and make candidate contributions. Since 1974, WCF has developed a sophisticated national fund-raising operation. It raises most of its money through direct mail appeals and from fund-raising events such as its highly successful series of small dinner parties. Funds also are raised from other progressive PACs. Corporate money is accepted for contributions to certain state and local races.

To develop a talent pool of women to run for higher office, WCF added a research and training component. Formed in 1983 as a 501 (c) (3), the Women's Campaign Research Fund (WCRF) is charged with helping women candidates develop leadership, policy, and political skills. Corporate money and other tax-deductible contributions are raised to fund WCRF. The author could not obtain a figure for the budget. Directed by Danowitz, WCRF sponsors off-year candidate training schools, maintains a candidate recruitment talent bank, sponsors conferences, and conducts research on such campaign-related issues as fundraising for women candidates and long-term strategic political career planning.

POLICY CONCERNS AND TACTICS

WCF has remained committed to its goal of electing progressive women to public office; at times the organization has been criticized by some Republican board members and elected women, such as former congresswoman Mary Rose Oakar (D-OH), who was not pro-choice but a strong supporter of women's economic and health issues, for not having a more flexible endorsement policy. These critics argue that women candidates good on such women's issues as economic ones should receive support despite their opposition to abortion or federal funding for abortion. WCF board also has debated the policy of not endorsing female challengers running against progressive male incumbents. These debates often have partisan overtones because the male incumbents tend to be Democrats, the female challengers Republicans.

Nor will WCF support more than one progressive woman candidate in a particular race, another source of controversy. Such an exception was made in the 1992 New York Democratic Senate primary race. The race involved former Democratic vice president candidate Geraldine A. Ferraro and New York City comptroller Elizabeth Holtzman, as well as several male candidates. WCF supported both women in the past when they ran for the Congress. In this race, WCF refused to choose between them. The fund believed that both women had distinguished political careers and were eminently qualified to serve in the U.S. Senate. EMILY's List,* faced with the same dilemma, agreed both women were well qualified but decided to endorse Ferraro on the grounds that she was the more viable candidate for this particular race. Both organizations were criticized for their actions. Nonetheless, most endorsement decisions have not been shrouded in controversy.

ELECTORAL ACTIVITIES

Although the board approves all candidate endorsements, it relies on staff for recommendations. To develop these recommendations, staff evaluate candidate questionnaires and interview candidates. They also discuss races with political consultants and with representatives from other PACs. Some of the PACs consulted include the American Nurses' Association,* EMILY's List, Committee on Political Education,* National Committee for an Effective Congress, and those representing Republican or Democratic party interests. Priority goes to races in which women candidates are running for open or newly created seats.

Besides direct dollar contributions, WCF provides candidates with technical services. These services include polling, extensive help with fund-raising, and strategy sessions with media and campaign consultants.

In its first election year, WCF contributed a total of $22,500 to twenty-eight women candidates for federal and statewide office. In the 1976 elections, contributions rose to $63,000. In 1978, WCF contributed over $103,609 to candidates, and in the 1980 elections, contributions totaled $115,000. In 1982, WCF spent a total of $270,000 in cash and in-kind contributions.

In 1984, ten years after WCF's founding, numerous other organizations and independent groups across the country raised money for women candidates. Both National Organization for Women* and NCWP had national and local PACs. The Republican and Democratic parties had special funds targeted for their respective women candidates. In 1985, EMILY's List, which operates as a fund-raising network, was created to raise money for pro-choice Democratic women candidates. In 1991, Women in the Senate and House (WISH) was formed to do the same for pro-choice Republican women. Despite the competition, WCF has continued to make significant contributions to women candidates. In the 1990 election cycle, WCF gave over $.5 million in cash and technical assistance to 113 candidates in thirty-six states. As of 1991, one-half its financial and technical assistance was earmarked for women running at the state and local level. In the 1992 elections, WCF had over 18,000 contributors and distributed more than $1 million to candidates in direct and technical services to 242 candidates.

WCF taught those interested in increasing the number of progressive women in political office to target resources effectively into well-run campaigns. A diverse number of women officeholders—including Democratic U.S. senators Barbara Mikulski of Maryland and Carol Moseley-Braun of Illinois; Democratic governors Ann Richards of Texas and Barbara Roberts of Oregon; Congresswomen Patsy Mink (D-HI), Maxine Waters (D-CA), Eddie Bernice Johnson (D-TX) Susan Molinari (R-NY), and Connie Morella (R-MD); Cherokee Nation chief Wilma Mankiller; state treasurers Mary Ellen Withrow (D-OH), Janet Rzewnicki (R-DE), and Kathleen Brown (D-CA); state legislators Susan McLane (R-NH), and County Supervisor Gloria Molina of Los Angeles—cite the technical assistance and early contributions they received from WCF as critical in winning their elections.

FURTHER INFORMATION

During the election years WCF periodically publishes a *Women to Watch* newsletter, which highlights women candidates and their races.

JOAN E. MCLEAN

WOMEN'S CAUCUS
See AIDS COALITION TO UNLEASH POWER

WOMEN'S CAUCUS FOR POLITICAL SCIENCE (WCPS)
c/o Professor Toni M. Travis
Department of Public Affairs
George Mason University

Fairfax, VA 22030

FAX (703) 993-8714

The Women's Caucus for Political Science (WCPS) is an organization of predominantly white academic women, most with the Ph.D. in political science or in the process of earning it. One current goal of the organization is to become more inclusively diverse in terms of race and ethnicity. Organizationally independent of the American Political Science Association (APSA), WCPS meet annually at the same time and place as APSA. It has a Legal Defense Fund (LDF).

ORIGIN AND DEVELOPMENT

Founded in New York City in the summer of 1969 by five white, female political scientists who decided to organize a women's caucus "to promote women within the APSA," WCPS immediately began to bring its concerns to the floor of APSA business meetings. The founders—Carol Barry, Berenice Carroll, Kay Klotzberger, Judith Stiehm, and Audrey Wells—spread the word at the APSA annual convention and met to elect officers. Klotzberger became the group's first president and served two terms through 1971.

WCPS membership is international, although most members are affiliated with institutions of higher education in the United States. The purposes of today's not-for-profit organization, as stated by its constitution, include upgrading the status of women in the profession of political science; promoting equal opportunities for women in graduate school admission and financial assistance and in employment, promotion, and tenure; promoting the development of nonacademic professional careers for women political scientists; encouraging the application of political science-based skills to promote equal opportunities for all women; and obtaining these goals by cooperating with APSA and other professional political science organizations.

A first item of business in 1969 was a resolution, offered by Kirsten Amundsen, condemning the meeting site of the APSA convention, the Roosevelt Hotel, for sexism because it would not allow her to enter the "men's bar" unescorted, although it was the only place in the hotel serving food in the late hours following the previous evening's business meeting. Met with gasps from several male members, the resolution passed and called upon APSA to see to it that "generous facilities" were provided at future meetings "so that members can organize to deal with problems of women in the profession." Other examples of sexist convention culture were soon forthcoming. For example, Virginia Gray reported visiting the display booth of the University of North Carolina to examine books on mathematical models, only to be shown "something brought for the little ladies—a book on *The Wild Flowers of North Carolina.*"

ORGANIZATION AND FUNDING

From an initial membership of 42, including 11 men, the membership has grown to over 800. A number of regional caucuses for women political scientists exist independently of, but cooperatively with, WCPS and regional political science associations: the southern, midwest, western, southwest, and northwest. WCPS officers are elected at the annual meetings. The executive council is made up of the group's president, president-elect/program chair, secretary, treasurer, and membership director, along with the immediate past president and two regional caucus presidents. Presidents since Klotzberger have been Evelyn Stevens, Marie Rosenburg-Dishman, JoAnne Aviel, Ruth Cowan, Naomi Lynn, Maria Falco, Susan Tolchin, Betty Nesvold, Sarah Slavin, Ann Matasar, Marianne Githens, Jeanne-Marie Col, Marian Lief Palley, Diane Fowlkes, Rita Mae Kelly, Janet Clark, Arlene Saxonhouse, Kay Lawson, Karen O'Connor, Margaret Conway, and Anne Schneider. The WCPS has no paid staff or permanent residence, but work is under way to archive organizational records at Radcliffe College Schlesinger Library.

Main sources of funding are individual and institutional membership dues and contributions. In 1990, general revenues totaled about $20,000. Supported by tax-deductible contributions, the Women's Caucus Legal Defense Fund offers funds to enable any member to consult an attorney in the event she perceives that a tenure or promotion decision affecting her was discriminatory.

POLICY CONCERNS AND TACTICS

Policy initiatives come from the leadership as well as the membership and usually reflect emerging membership needs as well as responses to events in the political environment, for example, the emphasis on addressing the problem of sexual harassment or need to make the organization inclusive and sensitive to needs beyond those of the white majority. Interests have included stimulation of research about women and politics through WCPS panel presentations and appointment of appropriate reviewers by scholarly journals for research in the field. WCPS was instrumental in setting up the APSA Organized Section on Women and Political Research, which subsumed the field of political socialization. Another concern was securing child care at annual APSA meetings.

In 1975, James MacGregor Burns came to the caucus for its endorsement of his candidacy for APSA president. Since that time, WCPS has, on a yearly basis, offered suggestions to the APSA president-elect of professional women to hold appointed office in APSA and generally has achieved greater than parity representation in the process. In 1983, William Riker was asked to come to a WCPS business meeting and explain his having failed to maintain this record. In 1980, WCPS offered its one and only slate of nominations for APSA office, including Betty Nesvold for president; two of its candidates, Betty Glad and Lucius Barker, were elected. It was not until 1990 that the first woman was elected to the APSA presidency, Judith Shklar.

WCPS has worked closely with the APSA Committee on the Status of Women in the Profession (CSWP), which it helped to establish; generally the two organizations have shared elites. One mutual project, 1975–76, included a survey of professional associations' grievance procedures and culminated in reform of the APSA's procedure. Another CSWP project, underwritten by the Fund for the Improvement of Post Secondary Education, created a Task Force on Women and American Government to integrate feminist scholarship into introductory American government courses. WCPS members chaired or constituted the bulk of the task force's membership. In its first decade WCPS became a member of the Federation of Professional Women's Organizations,* from which it subsequently withdrew, and of a short-lived umbrella organization, funded by the Ford Foundation, for women in the social and natural sciences.

In 1978, when National Organization for Women* undertook a boycott of convention sites in states that had not ratified the equal rights amendment, it enlisted—through women's liberation movement founder and longtime WCPS member Jo Freeman—WCPS to help. WCPS stimulated passage of a resolution during an APSA business meeting to break the association's contract to hold its next convention at a Chicago-based Hilton; APSA became one of two organizations (the other was the American Library Association*) later sued by the Hilton hotel and paid substantial damages as a result.

During the mid- to late 1980s, through the leadership of Kay Lawson, WCPS began evaluating American government textbooks for their treatment of women and politics and sharing these evaluations with publishers. WCPS so far has cited two textbooks for their positive integration of women, and members are encouraged to choose these textbooks over others found wanting in this regard. In 1988, also through Lawson's leadership, WCPS began to work on developing a women's agenda, identifying policy priorities of the women's liberation movement that political scientists could address through policy-relevant research.

ELECTORAL ACTIVITIES

WCPS does not engage in politics for public office and hence does not have a political action committee.

FURTHER INFORMATION

WCPS publishes a quarterly newsletter and from time to time a membership directory.

DIANE L. FOWLKES

WOMEN'S COLLEGE COALITION (WCC)
1090 Vermont Avenue, NW
Washington, DC 20005
(202) 234-0443
FAX (202) 234-0445

The Women's College Coalition (WCC) has a single focus, the promotion of women's colleges and women's educational needs.

ORIGIN AND DEVELOPMENT

WCC was founded in 1972 as a response to two trends of the late sixties and early seventies. During that period a number of selective men's colleges decided to admit women, and a number of women's colleges closed or merged. Both factors prompted several education leaders, including Jill Ker Conway, Paula Brownlee, and Irene Hecht, to band together to make the case for single-sex education. One early activity of this advocacy group for women's colleges was the engagement of a public relations firm to gather statistics on women's college graduates and to initiate studies that would compare and contrast outcomes for women's college graduates and women graduates of coeducational institutions. Such data still are collected for the coalition, but its agenda now focuses on public policy issues such as women in science, women and leadership, and gender equity in higher education.

ORGANIZATION AND FUNDING

Of the eighty-four women's colleges in the United States and two in Canada, sixty-seven are presently coalition members. Each institution is represented by its president; in 1992, 79 percent of the presidents at women's colleges are women, and two are African American. Ten presidents constitute a governing board, which functions as an executive committee with staggered three-year terms. The governing board president serves a two-year term. Currently the president is Helen R. Washburn, president of Cottey College. Three standing subcommittees address member services, public policy, and outreach and promotion. The WCC staff includes Jadwiga S. Sebrechts as the executive director, with an administrative assistant. A public relations counsel also is retained on an annual basis. WCC's affiliation with the Association of American Colleges* (AAC) provides some administrative and financial assistance.

The membership services committee makes recommendations on internal studies, media relations, and other support activities, such as disseminating information, on members' behalf. The coalition also provides its members with the opportunity to communicate with colleagues, with advocacy on issues related to women's education, and with publications and conferences. The total 1992 budget came to $250,000.

POLICY CONCERNS AND TACTICS

The governing board sets the coalition's policy, and the public policy committee defines the WCC agenda within the programmatic concerns. With a constituency of single-sex institutions, WCC concerns itself with identifying those issues relating to women's higher education where women's colleges can lend expertise and offer leadership. Currently, there are three such policy areas: women in science, women and leadership, and gender equity in the classroom. The outreach and promotion committee recommends collaboration with other organizations advancing women's educational opportunities and recommends a national promotion strategy to follow. Preferred strategies include educating members through publications, educating the public through press releases and public service campaigns, and conducting and publishing research on issues.

Current initiatives include sponsorship of research that addresses ways to optimize women's educational environment, whether single-sex or coeducational; the fostering of women's selection of, and persistence in, math and science career paths; and the development of models for women's leadership in the public and private sectors. To these ends, the coalition has supported gender-equity research as part of a four-year project funded by the DuPont Foundation. The research aims to define those characteristics generally necessary to promote equal opportunity for all women regardless of the particular characteristics of their alma mater. The coalition has organized a national conference on women in science, for an audience of undergraduate women students majoring in math and sciences and faculty who teach these disciplines.

WCC's affiliation with AAC has facilitated an exchange of ideas with other higher education institutions. The outreach and promotion committee recommends which other groups to collaborate with on certain issues. Among those groups are the American Association of University Women,* National Association of Colleges and Universities, Independent College Office, Girls Inc.,* and National Coalition of Girls Schools.

ELECTORAL ACTIVITIES

WCC does not see women's issues as partisan and does not have a political action committee.

FURTHER INFORMATION

Individuals may order directly from the coalition publications such as *A Profile of Women College Presidents, A Study of the Learning Environment at Women's Colleges, Alumni Giving at Women's Colleges: A Ten-Year Study, A Profile of Recent Women College Graduates, Enrollment Trends in Women's Colleges,* and *Expanding Options: A Profile of Older Graduates.* In preparation for publication are *What Works: Women in Math, Science and Engineering* and the results of the DuPont Foundation-sponsored research on women's education. A periodical entitled *Women's Education Quarterly* has been released.

LINDA MATHER

WOMEN'S DIVISION OF THE GENERAL BOARD OF GLOBAL MINISTRIES, UNITED METHODIST CHURCH
See UNITED METHODIST WOMEN

WOMEN'S EQUITY ACTION LEAGUE
See MARGUERITE REWALT LEGAL DEFENSE FUND

WOMEN'S INSTITUTE FOR FREEDOM OF THE PRESS (WIFP)
3306 Ross Place, NW
Washington, DC 20008
(202) 966-7783
FAX (202) 363-0812

The Women's Institute for Freedom of the Press (WIFP) works to widen the female majority's access to male-owned mass media and to help promote women's own media.

ORIGIN AND DEVELOPMENT

Because freedom of the press belongs to those owning one, access became key to media activism. WIFP was established in April 1972 by five women concerned about women's access: Karen Lunquist, a musician and editor-publisher; Sara Alterr Reitz, a *Washington Post* reporter; Margot Burman, an artist and video producer; Martha Leslie Allen, who became WIFP's executive director; and Donna Allen, its president. The five original board members were white. They were acquainted with women working within the media and women outside them who felt their substantial impact. Convinced that something needed to be done about a paucity of women among media owners and of programming and news relevant to women's lives, they founded WIFP to learn what could be done about this situation. Because the founders knew women already active in the media reform movement, they introduced *Media Report to Women* to put activists in touch with each other, recruit help for their efforts, and interest others in participating.

Since 1972, WIFP has served a vital information function within American feminism. Its primary constituency is media workers—both in mainstream mass media and in women's media—concerned about the fact that men control the means of communication and women have difficulty putting forward their own views and experiences. WIFP also serves scholars, activists, and others interested in media issues. It has offered important networking resources through its associates program, sponsored seven conferences on developing a new communications system, and managed satellite teleconferences from the 1980 and 1985 United Nations women's conferences in Copenhagen and Nairobi. Neither WIFP's policy goals nor the ways its goals are set have changed over its more than two decades.

ORGANIZATION AND FUNDING

Most remarkable are the stability and frugality of this all-volunteer organization. The six-member board has reelected author Donna Allen, a labor economist by training, as president since 1972; and she has managed the organization without salary or paid staff for more than twenty years. For this steady advocacy she has received numerous awards from journalism, broadcasting, and feminist groups, including the Women in Communications* 1979 Headliner Award and the 1983 Wonder Woman Award. Similarly, Martha Allen has served since 1978 as WIFP's director. (The two women are mother and daughter.) Interns and part-time volunteers assist these two professional staff. The office is run on a shoestring. WIFP employs neither lobbyists nor legal counsel.

The group's approach to the membership issue is unusual. It networks with hundreds of organizations and does not have dues-paying members as such.

Instead, women affirming WIFP's goal of mass media democracy through access and participation may become associates; donations are optional. Of around 500 associates, about 50 live outside the United States. Associates support WIFP because it offers opportunities for action on media issues, networking, access to information, and participation in conferences and public affairs. WIFP always has been all-women and represents a variety of economic classes. Volunteers and associates include minority women at least in proportion to their presence in the population; the late Audre Lorde was an associate. WIFP projects are highly inclusive.

WIFP has nonprofit status, qualifying for tax-deductible contributions under federal 501 (c) (3) guidelines. Its budget grew from a $2,000 at start-up to $70,000 in 1980. WIFP since has scaled back to $5,000 per year by passing on its two major periodicals, *Media Report to Women* and *The Directory of Women's Media,* to Communication Research Associates, Inc., in Silver Spring, Maryland, and the National Council for Research on Women in New York City. Originally, WIFP did its own editing, pasteup, and typesetting.

Without conventional membership, WIFP publications bring in most of the organization's income, but they are sold at cost. Other income comes from individual and institutional grants and from loans. Under WIFP's umbrella, associates have undertaken new projects, such as the African Outreach Project and International Tape Exchange Project. The former, chaired by Yahne Sangarey, seeks to enable connections with African media women. In the latter, originating in Nairobi, women taped their own lives and concerns, with the purpose of exchanging tapes with U.S. women.

POLICY CONCERNS AND TACTICS

Ways to implement WIFP's policy concerns always are of interest, although in line with the continuity of board membership and the associates network, means have gone unchanged. Strategies are determined by discussions among the incorporating members. Issues are aired through WIFP's publications, above all, the newsletter/magazine, or by letter to associates and through one-on-one discussion. Priorities include conducting and publishing research, coordinating with other organizations, writing and distributing press releases, encouraging members to write legislators, monitoring selected officials' voting records, and supplying members of congress and staff with information. WIFP also occasionally has testified in congressional hearings.

WIFP has filed amicus briefs. In the mid-1980s, it filed as an amicus against a successful challenge by the American Booksellers Association and American Civil Liberties Union* of a referendum passed by two-thirds of the voters in Bellingham, Washington; at issue was an ordinance similar to the Indianapolis ordinance that Catharine MacKinnon helped to draft.

WIFP takes a strong stand on the pornography issue, which has provoked bitter controversy within feminist organizations. It states that both its networking with women's organizations and interest in women's media access preclude attacking women, demeaning their intelligence and independent thinking, or subjecting them to violence. Such debasement falls short of constructive information and would result were WIFP to take other than an antipornography stand. The group regrets that this side is not being heard and believes that if the story of women damaged by pornography were known, people would know what to do with pornography.

Public policymakers solicit information and opinions from WIFP. Although most concerned with communication issues, three federal initiatives have been most relevant to WIFP's goals: the 1972 Equal Employment Act, which led the Federal Communications Commission (FCC) to mandate women's employment in broadcasting; the Freedom of Information Act, which made it possible to learn the employment patterns of women employed at media such as United Press International; and the affirmative action executive orders, which led to charges of discrimination against the media. To assist women in applying them, WIFP publicized these laws.

WIFP has found reprehensible the FCC ruling that it had no enforcement responsibility for equal opportunity, cable systems' discretion to reject public access channels, and the Equal Rights Amendment's (ERA) failure. Equating public outreach and power, WIFP believes that if women had access to mass media commensurate with that of its owners, ERA would have been ratified.

WIFP collaborates with many groups on common interests, among them Mediawatch on portrayals of women, the National Women's Political Caucus* on surveys of media coverage of women candidates, and the National Woman's Party* on media coverage surveys made of newspaper coverage of ERA. WIFP was a founding member of the National Women's Studies Association* and the National Women's Agenda Coalition formed in 1975–76 by the Women's Action Alliance. Its only adversaries are pornography publishers; but the male owners of the mass media who delete women's news and resort to stereotypes are perceived by WIFP as playing a role adversarial to its end of eliminating these practices.

ELECTORAL ACTIVITIES

WIFP has no political action committee because it is nonpartisan and concerned with the process of communication, not its substance.

FURTHER INFORMATION

WIFP published an excellent monthly newsletter/magazine, *Media Report to Women*. It also provided the 1,000-entry *Index/Directory of Women's Media*.

VALLAURIE CRAWFORD

WOMEN'S INTERNATIONAL LEAGUE FOR PEACE AND FREEDOM, UNITED STATES SECTION (WILPF/US)
1213 Race Street
Philadelphia, PA 19107

(215) 563-7110

FAX (215) 864-2022

The Women's International League for Peace and Freedom, United States Section (WILPF/US) has organized women actively in the cause of peace and human rights for over seventy-five years. It has a research and education foundation, the Jane Addams Peace Association (JAPA).

ORIGIN AND DEVELOPMENT

WILPF grew out of the First International Congress of Women, which met at The Hague in 1915 to protest the war in Europe. Out of this meeting, an International Committee of Women for Permanent Peace was established; after the war the organization adopted its current name. The U.S. section of WILPF has its origins in the Women's Peace Party (WPP). In January 1915, Jane Addams and Carrie Chapman Catt brought together over 3,000 women from a variety of women's groups to discuss what women could do to end the war in Europe; the result was WPP. Another notable early activist was Emily Greene Balch, WILPF's first international secretary. Both Balch and Addams received the Nobel Peace Prize, the only U.S. women ever to do so. The most prominent executive director of the U.S. section was Mildred Scott Olmstead, who held the position for forty-three years and helped the organization celebrate its seventy-fifth anniversary the same year she turned 100.

From its founding, WILPF has had a dual focus on women's rights and peace. Participants at the Hague congress had to agree to women's suffrage and peaceful settlement of international disputes. WPP organizers were equally adamant about the need for women's equality and opposition to war. Since 1915, WILPF/US has expanded its agenda to include a variety of related issues, among them support for a nuclear ban treaty and opposition to U.S. intervention in other nations' affairs. WILPF/US also has broadened its concerns with women's rights to include advocacy for the equal rights amendment and freedom of choice on abortion. Its policy stands extend to calls to end racism and demands to free all people to determine their own economic and political systems.

ORGANIZATION AND FUNDING

Organized into four regions composed of thirty-three state groups and 110 branches, WILPF/US maintains its affiliation as the U.S. branch of the international organization, which has active sections in thirty-four nations. The leadership is composed of a thirty-three-member board of directors, twenty-two of them elected. In 1992, 20 percent of the board was African American. The current president is Jean Gore. With nine staff and three interns, WILPF/US maintains an office in Philadelphia. There is an attorney on retainer.

Composed almost entirely of women (95 percent), WILPF/US has grown from a few hundred to over 15,000 members. Most join to communicate and interact with women of similar views in the advocacy of important causes.

The 1991 budget was over $550,000. Most of the money was used for program, member, and support services. An international assessment to WILPF and office expenses compose the other major outlays of money. Income to WILPF/US comes mainly (60 percent) from membership dues of $35. Other income sources includes sales of merchandise and pamphlets (15 percent), gifts or bequests (8 percent), foundation grants (1 percent), and transfers from the tax-exempt education fund (12 percent).

With a budget of about $240,000 JAPA funds most of the educational works of WILPF/US. In addition to publishing numerous pamphlets on peace, racism, and budget priorities, it supports a number of conferences and training sessions. Each year JAPA selects the winner of the Jane Addams Children's Book Award, a prize given for the book that best portrays the issues of peace. JAPA's long-time executive director, Ruth Chalmers, retired recently.

POLICY CONCERNS AND TACTICS

Policy decisions and strategy choices are set by the board of directors in concert with the executive director and staff. Meetings of the national membership congress also are important in setting long-range policy. Strategies employed by WILPF/US to obtain its policy goals include educating its members and encouraging them to write to public officials, taking direct action, conducting and publishing research on important issues, supplying members of the Congress and state legislatures with information, and monitoring elected officials' voting records.

From its beginning, WILPF/US has been at the forefront in demanding an end to the use of force in international relations and equal treatment for all. Besides opposing World War I, the Vietnamese conflict, and other instances of U.S. intervention in the affairs of other nation states, WILPF/US has taken an active role in supporting the League of Nations, the United Nations (UN), and a Limited Test Ban Treaty. In recent years, it called for a revision of U.S. budget priorities away from military to human needs. WILPF/US also has continued its call for a Comprehensive Test Ban Treaty and an end to the U.S. embargo to Cuba. In the area of human rights, WILPF/US in the 1990s is focusing on violence against women, empowerment of women and an end to sexism, and elimination of racism both in the United States and in the Western Hemisphere more generally.

WILPF/US has observer status as a nongovernmental organization at the UN, a position held for many years by a volunteer, Ruth Sillman. Currently Paula H. Tasso is the director liaison with the UN. WILPF/US finds its policy allies among the peace groups, including the American Friends Service Committee,* War Resisters League, Mobilization for Survival, and Common Agenda. It also has fostered the growth of other women's peace groups, including Women Strike for Peace* and the Seneca Falls Peace Encampment. It numbers among its opponents Operation Rescue* and the Moral Majority.

ELECTORAL ACTIVITIES

WILPF/US currently does not have a political action committee, nor does it endorse candidates for political office. It prefers to continue its work at the grassroots level.

FURTHER INFORMATION

The organization publishes several items, including its magazine, *Peace and Freedom;* a bimonthly action bulletin, *Program & Legislation Action;* and *The Women's Budget,* an analysis of the defense budget.

NANCY E. MCGLEN

WOMEN'S LAW FUND (WLF)
3214 Prospect Avenue
Cleveland, OH 44115
(216) 431-4850
FAX (216) 431-6149

The Women's Law Fund (WLF) secures and protects the civil rights of American women in this country and abroad by working to eliminate gender-based discrimination. WLF does not directly litigate but provides legal assistance to individuals in gender discrimination cases.

ORIGIN AND DEVELOPMENT

Attorneys Jane Picker and Lizabeth Moody, Yale Law School classmates and then associate professors at the Cleveland-Marshall School of Law, Cleveland State University (CSU), founded WLF in 1972 in Cleveland as a pilot project funded by the Ford and Cleveland foundations. Picker and Moody created the fund to address issues of discrimination based on gender—issues cloaked in sexism. In their private practices, both lawyers had received many requests to handle discrimination cases, their clients complaining that no one else would tackle them. WLF was the first nonprofit agency in the country to address the legal issue of gender discrimination. Picker, realizing the litigation training gap around gender bias issues, helped CSU secure a grant from the Equal Employment Opportunity Commission to open the Sex Discrimination Clinic (now the Fair Employment Practice Clinic) for CSU law students and has served as the clinic's director.

Picker and Moody served on the first WLF board and selected other board trustees to represent national organizations with similar interests, such as the Women's Rights Project of the American Civil Liberties Union* (ACLU).

The fund's first case became a landmark, reaching the Supreme Court in 1974 as *LaFleur* v. *Cleveland Board of Education.* WLF funded the successful lawsuits of Jo LaFleur and Ann Elizabeth Nelson, Cleveland public school teachers forced to take maternity leave in 1971. Following this success, WLF supported many other cases involving pregnant women's employment rights. WLF funded a series of lawsuits in 1972–73 against Cleveland on its hiring quota for policewomen and the restriction of female police officers to desk jobs in the Cleveland Police Department's Women's Bureau. Most were settled before trial. The City Council repealed the quota ordinance in January 1973 and disbanded the Women's Bureau in January 1975, responding, in part, to WLF pressure. WLF also helped eradicate an Ohio law prohibiting male or female cosmetologists (rather than barbers) from cutting men's hair. In the 1970s in Ohio and elsewhere, WLF litigated against gender-based discrimination in other police departments, the Ohio State Bureau of Employment services, public school athletic programs, and volunteer fire fighting.

In the late 1980s, WLF funded a plaintiff who charged Cleveland with discrimination in the hiring of professional firefighters (also an issue in such other cities as New York City and Columbus, Ohio, at the time). Although the plaintiff lost the case, the Cleveland Fire Department hired ten women firefighters—the first in its history—during the proceedings. Also in the 1980s, WLF began focusing on two areas that would occupy much of their attention in the next decade—discrimination against American women employed by American companies overseas and against older women.

ORGANIZATION AND FUNDING

In 1993, the WLF board of fourteen members underwent restructuring in preparation for hiring of Caryn Groedel as executive director. Most board members have been women attorneys, with one or two men serving in an average year. Board candidates are chosen by a nominating committee and elected by the outgoing board. Picker, now professor of international and employment law at CSU's law school, serves as president of WLF's new six-member board of trustees. Other 1993 officers included Santiago Feliciano, Jr., vice president; Denise Knecht, treasurer; and Sister Mary Brudenski, secretary. Headquarters is in Cleveland.

WLF does not offer memberships. Gifts from local fund drives such as Community Shares, receipts from fund-raising events, and private donations support WLF's budget of under $25,000. It is a nonprofit organization with a 501 (c) (3) status.

POLICY CONCERNS AND TACTICS

Not a law firm, WLF is rather an agency supplying funds and helping secure attorneys for plaintiffs with sex discrimination charges pending before state and federal governmental bodies. Within its single-issue focus, WLF concentrates on discrimination in employment but also addresses the areas of government benefits, housing, and education, including sports participation. WLF supports litigation to try to eradicate discriminatory policies, using the judicial system as a change agent. Occasionally, WLF files amicus curiae briefs. It does not lobby and testifies only when particularly requested to do so.

A litigation committee decides which cases WLF will support, based on the importance of the issues, the resources needed, and potential number of people to benefit. Many suits involve multiple types of discrimination. WLF selects some cases that impact on women's civil rights, although not directly concerned with gender discrimination, such as cases of age discrimination.

Two WLF-funded cases address gender bias directed at young girls. In one, which began in the late 1980s and continues into the 1990s, WLF supported a plaintiff who has charged the Ohio Chapter of the Future Farmers of America (FFA) with discrimination for forcing a teenage girl to give up her position as FFA secretary, allegedly because of her recent marriage. In another case, against the city of Cleveland Heights, WLF funded the defense of a girl who charged that, because of her gender, she was placed on an inappropriate level of a hockey team and then not provided with a suitable place to dress. The plaintiff lost this case.

The WLF has also acted in the interests of American women working overseas for U.S. companies, for example, filing an amicus curiae brief in a 1990 U.S. Supreme Court case, *Boureslan* v. *Aramco.* The plaintiff lost the case. In 1991, the U.S. Congress amended the Civil Rights Act, effectively overturning the verdict, by ensuring extraterritorial rights for American citizens employed by U.S. companies overseas, unless those rights would violate host country's laws.

WLF still works closely with the CSU Fair Employment Practice Clinic. Among many other organizations, it has consulted with the Women's Legal Defense Fund, especially on cases of discrimination in sports and with the League of Women Voters Education Fund* on a case involving the right of a married woman to vote using her maiden name; and it communicates regularly with ACLU. Especially in early cases, labor unions generally sided with employers against the plaintiffs supported by WLF.

ELECTORAL ACTIVITIES

The nonpartisan WLF does not support candidates for public office or maintain a political action committee.

FURTHER INFORMATION

WLF has no publications.

                                                            JIMMY ELAINE WILKINSON MEYER

WOMEN'S LOBBY (WL)

An activist organization that followed legislative issues impacting on women in the 1970s, the Women's Lobby (WL) was a complete lobby of feminist women seeking to apply their principles to lawmaking.

ORIGIN AND DEVELOPMENT

WL was an outgrowth of an ad hoc coalition of women's groups that came together to work for passage of the equal rights amendment (ERA). Its birth was announced publicly at a press conference on Capitol Hill in June 1972 under the late Carol Burris's guidance and skill. Burris came to Washington, D.C., from Montana and proceeded to galvanize a group of women from disparate organizations into a cohesive lobbying power. Flora Crater, a longtime Democratic Party activist and leader in National Organization for Women,* assisted Burris, becoming WL's first vice president. Many of these women had initiated their lobbying careers with organizations such as the American Association of University Women* (AAUW), church groups, legislative arms of unions, Republican and Democratic politics at all levels, and other social groups with a legislative agenda. Also represented were homemakers, university students, and retirees. After its organizational meeting in 1972, the lobby quickly became involved in issues of educational and employment opportunity, health care, and pension reform and followed this agenda throughout the seventies.

The lobby refined its skill in coalition building and successfully reached out to make common cause with numerous, wide-ranging interest groups with policies coinciding with women's agenda in all legislative arenas. By this means WL intended to achieve congressional attention. During the time the coalition worked successfully for ERA, it realized there were other greatly significant contemporaneous issues whose resolution would benefit women's future and opportunities generally. These included the creation of an Equal Employment Opportunity Commission (EEOC) with enforcement powers and the 1972 Higher Education Act, which would open doors for women on university campuses throughout the country. ERA's successful passage through the House in October 1971 and the Senate in March 1972 freed WL to concentrate on the enactment of EEOC enforcement powers, which was achieved.

From the ranks of poorly paid and, in many cases, unpaid workers volunteering with WL were born new professionals, as women, flush with new achievements, went on to other careers and permeated the professional and business environment with a confidence generated by their WL activities. The lobby well may have been a victim of its own success in identifying and promoting these women into new careers. Their legacy was a new awareness among the 535 members of the Congress of organized women's clout in pushing a new political agenda to transform the U.S. social organization in the twentieth century's last quarter.

ORGANIZATION AND FUNDING

WL had a board of directors. Burris served as WL's president. The lobby operated from a small headquarters on Capitol Hill. Through its doors came student interns, suburban homemakers, professionals, and academics, and women with interest representation experience under their belt through prior work with unions, church groups, and corporate offices located in Washington. There was no executive director. Sally Determan, now in the American Bar Association leadership, advised WL; and Gladys Kessler, now a judge, represented it against the U.S. Catholic Conference.

During WL's eight-year existence, funding was generated from small individual donations as well as larger grants, some corporate aid, and the attention of wealthy, prominent women across the country.

POLICY CONCERNS AND TACTICS

Burris led, and members followed, somewhat driven by legislation because WL's clout was not enough to introduce its own bills. WL periodically reviewed pending legislation to assess its impact on women, then sought liaison with sympathetic committee staff and congressional office legislative and administrative assistants and in the process conserved lobbying staff and resources. WL preferred giving testimony in congressional hearings and also supplied congresspeople with information, made personal presentations to them, and monitored their voting records. Education of members and the public rounded out its strategic repertoire. Legislators and their staff frequently solicited WL's views.

WL worked centrally to influence the Health Education and Welfare Department to produce regulations for the 1972 Educational Amendments Act Title IX, confronting the National Collegiate Athletic Association over women's role in sports. WL's successes in this regard helped demonstrate women's potential in making their voice heard. It worked in a large coalition including labor, facilitated by Representative Shirley Chisholm (D-NY), to add domestic workers to the Fair Labor Standards Act. In 1974, the Congress overrode President Nixon's veto of the enrolled bill. WL played a significant part in passing equal credit opportunity legislation through the House in 1972, after the Consumer Affairs Subcommittee had declined to hold hearings on it the previous year. In 1977, it entered a pro-abortion coalition. WL found of continuing importance the affirmative action orders, act of 1972 in which sex discrimination was added to Civil Rights Commission jurisdiction, 1972 Equal Employment Act, the proposed ERA, and women's rights decisions, such as *Reed* v. *Reed,* (1972) and *Roe* v. *Wade* (1973).

WL often collaborated with such like-minded groups as AAUW, American Federation of Labor-Congress of Industrial Organizations,* B'nai B'rith Women,* Catholics for a Free Choice,* League of Women Voters,* National Federation of Business and Professional Women,* Methodist* and Presbyterian* women's organizations, National Association for the Advancement of Colored People, National Councils of Jewish* and Negro* Women, and National Organization for Women.* Its adversaries included Eagle Forum* and antiabortion groups.

FURTHER INFORMATION

WL published a monthly newsletter, *Women's Lobby Alert,* and also *Women's Lobby Quarterly.*

ELLEN PATTIN

WOMEN'S NATIONAL DEMOCRATIC CLUB (WNDC)
1526 New Hampshire Avenue, NW
Washington, DC 20036
(202) 232-7363
FAX (202) 986-2791

The Women's National Democratic Club (WNDC) supports the politicization and participation of Democratic women through action and education. Formed by and for Democratic women, its current organization shows that its agenda focuses broadly on Democratic Party issues.

ORGANIZATION AND DEVELOPMENT

In 1922, two years following the suffrage amendment's ratification, WNDC formed. On the premise that suffrage recognized women's expanding role in politics, a national club was intended to advance women's political participation, including service in elected and appointive office. WNDC formed to provide a Democratic forum for the informed exchange of ideas and continues to function on this premise today. Daisy Harriman, along with Eleanor Roosevelt, Edith Wilson, and Emily Newell Blair, founded the nonprofit group.

Between 1922 and 1960, WNDC began efforts to strengthen its organization. To that end, WNDC hired a paid staff and began its speaker luncheon series. WNDC also instituted life memberships and endowments during this time in order to facilitate long-term funding resources.

Currently, the club functions as an educational, cultural, and social organization for Democratic women and men. "Democracy Encompassing the Globe" is their motto. All WNDC activities promote, and are consistent with, Democratic Party principles. To that end, the club gives Democrats the opportunity to share and explore their views on a wide array of issues, including current national problems, democratic processes, and governmental procedures. WNDC also works actively to provide the Washington community with educational and social services, such as fund-raising for local elementary schools.

ORGANIZATION AND FUNDING

A board of officers and governors oversees the club. The typical board includes twenty governors, who meet monthly. Three members of the board of governors are nonwhite, and one is male. Club members elect these officers, while the club's programs, policies, and functions are administered by twenty committees with appointed chairs. Committees focus not only on public policy but also on the group's programs, that is, international and legislative affairs; such organizational functions as membership, fund-raising, finance, procedures, and policies; and club administration, that is, hospitality, library, lounge, and seating. The club president typically serves for one to two years; past presidents have included Lindy Boggs (1958–59) and Mildred Pepper (1940–41). Former Democratic presidents' wives hold honorary presidencies. The current president is Sacha Millstone. A small administrative and professional staff and a director implement club operations. Its general manager is Jeffrey Watkins. WNDC club-house is, and always has been, located in Washington, D.C. WNDC purchased the Club House, which was designed by architect Harvey Page, in 1927. In 1973, the Club House was entered into the National Register of Historic Places.

Membership is open to Democrats sponsored by a current member and approved by the governing board. Currently, there are 2,000 members, many of whom are the spouses of Democratic officeholders and party officials. Males normally make up 5–10 percent of the total membership roster.

The organization's budget is $1.3 million. Its primary funding source is membership dues and initiation fees. Annual membership dues range from $500 for Washington, D.C., residents older than thirty-six, to $100 for residents outside the District; initiation fees range from $250 for members, to $50 for members' spouses. Other funding sources include the Sign of the Donkey boutique located at the clubhouse. Members may also rent club meeting rooms and employ the in-house catering service for business and personal use. The club arranges for other contributions such as endowments and legacies. Classes, luncheons, and seminars are offered, and WNDC collects fees for them.

POLICY CONCERNS AND TACTICS

Policy is set for the organization through its committee structure. Each committee focuses on administrative, programmatic, or procedural concerns.

A public policy committee primarily concerns itself with WNDC issue positions. It comprises nine task forces that research and prepare position papers for dissemination to the Democratic National Committee* (DNC), Democratic congressional leaders, the *New York Times,* the *Washington Post,* and Democratic party platform committee (in presidential election years). The WNDC public policy committee researches policy issues and formulates positions consistent with its parent organization's views.

Recent position papers encompass a wide range of national and international economic and social issues. Because WNDC is a partisan group, its policy concerns change with political and legislative tides. Its positions are in general agreement with the DNC's official positions. Arms control is promoted through a ban on development, testing, and deployment of sea-based, air-based, and mobile systems. Also supported are other arms control efforts that extend the Outer Space Treaty to ban all weapons, resume negotiations and ratify a Comprehensive Test Ban Treaty, and eliminate entire classes of nuclear weapons in Europe in cooperation with North Atlantic Treaty Organization.

Economic aid and trade concessions are endorsed as the means to restore peace and promote democracy in Central America. Further efforts in Central America should focus on a reduction and eventual removal of all military forces in Panama. WNDC also wants the U.S. government to reaffirm its commitment to human rights by protesting human rights violations here and abroad and to implement the United Nations Universal Declaration of Human Rights.

On the domestic front, WNDC feels especially concerned with the federal budget. Efforts to solve the current budget crisis include support for a temporary tax increase for business and personal incomes above the poverty line, substantial decreases in defense spending, an income tax increase on Social Security benefits for those earning over $25,000 annually, and a gasoline tax increase. WNDC also would like to see funding for education increased at all levels. Prekindergarten students will benefit from increased Head Start funding whereas college students should have greater access to loans and scholarships.

WNDC endorses strengthening the Environmental Protection Agency and implementing the Clean Air Act. Oil drilling in environmentally sensitive areas should be controlled; and the government is encouraged to implement a conservation-oriented energy policy that stresses renewable natural resources.

Other policy goals include strict gun control legislation that limits handgun availability and a federal public information campaign to prevent gun violence. On health issues, the group supports a comprehensive health insurance plan that would provide services through a decentralized state-centered system. An expansion of the Medicare program to protect elderly persons from the high cost of long-term care also is supported.

The group addresses domestic social issues, including a focus on access to public housing. Finally, WNDC supports ratification of the equal rights amendment, access to the full range of family planning services, economic equity for women, and resumed congressional support for the International Planned Parenthood Federation.

WNDC is a member of the National Federation of Democratic Women. Its parent organization is the DNC. It does not coordinate activities with other similarly minded groups, although it maintains relationships with feminist organizations such as the National Abortion Rights Action League* and National Organization for Women.*

ELECTORAL ACTIVITIES

WNDC believes that women's issues are partisan. It does not have a political action committee.

FURTHER INFORMATION

Communication of WNDC's policy goals and other club news are achieved through two primary publications. Members and friends receive the monthly *WNDC Calendar Notes* and the *WNDC News.*

TERRI SUSAN FINE

WOMEN'S NETWORK
See NATIONAL CONFERENCE OF STATE LEGISLATURES WOMEN'S NETWORK

WOMEN'S RESEARCH AND EDUCATION FOUNDATION
See NATIONAL ASSOCIATION OF COMMISSIONS FOR WOMEN

WOMEN'S RESEARCH AND EDUCATION INSTITUTE (WREI)
1700 18th Street, NW
Room 400
Washington, DC 20009
(202) 328-7070
FAX (202) 328-3514

The Women's Research and Education Institute (WREI) is a nonpartisan policy research organization. It serves as a link between researchers and policymakers on issues of interest to women and as an information clearinghouse for legislators and women's research centers. WREI monitors the administration of existing laws, submits information to the Congress about pending legislation, suggests issues that the Congress should address, and sponsors policy fellowships and internships on Capitol Hill.

ORIGIN AND DEVELOPMENT

The institute formed in 1977 as a research arm of the newly created Congresswomen's Caucus and initially took as its name the Congresswomen's Caucus Corporation (CCC). The caucus, which in 1981 admitted congressmen and changed its name to the Congressional Caucus for Women's Issues* (CCWI), was founded by a bipartisan group of congresswomen—notably, Elizabeth Holtzman (D-NY), Margaret Heckler (R-MA), Shirley Chisholm (D-NY), Barbara Mikulski (D-MD), Lindy Boggs (D-LA), and Patricia Schroeder (D-CO). Congresswomen Heckler and Holtzman were named caucus cochairs. These women determined that, since their Capitol Hill staffs were occupied with administrative and constituency-related responsibilities, a new agency was required to help them gather and analyze information about U.S. women's progress.

Needed, for example, was a watchdog research group to monitor the extent to which the recently inaugurated Carter administration recruited and promoted women to responsible executive branch positions. This agency also would conduct studies useful for promoting legislation addressing women's goals. Caucus founders believed ideas about how to deal with domestic violence were especially important.

The founders thought initially to finance CCC by contributions from representatives' staff and office allowances. Caucus membership did not exceed fifteen, and annual dues were nominal. Additional funds were solicited from corporate, labor, and other private sector donors. A few contributions were realized from these sources, but many private foundations decided not to support the research efforts of an organization closely tied to politicians. Accordingly, in October 1978 the caucus changed its research arm's name to WREI and separated administratively from it. The caucus also created a nine-member WREI board of directors. Nonpoliticians replaced the congresswomen serving until then as CCC board members. Former congresswomen Martha Griffiths (D-MI) initially chaired the new nonpartisan board. In 1980, actress Jean Stapleton succeeded Griffiths as chair and has continued to hold the position.

CCC's executive director, Betty Dooley, became WREI's executive director; and in 1980 the organization moved from its public quarters in the Rayburn Building to private offices close to the Capitol. At the same time it severed its financial relationship with the caucus and began relying exclusively on private donations. Changes in the House rules in 1982 forced WREI to sever all legal ties with CCWI.

ORGANIZATION AND FUNDING

WREI's board of directors has grown from nine to nineteen. In 1992, besides Stapleton, the board included former congresswomen Boggs and Helen Stevenson Meyner; former congresswoman, Health and Human Services secretary, and ambassador to Ireland Heckler; California state senator Diane Watson; Washington, D.C., mayor Sharon Pratt Kelly; former Dallas mayor Annette Strauss; AT&T vice president for public affairs in Washington Martina Bradford; International Ladies Garment Workers Union* vice president Evelyn Dubrow; American Express vice president for government affairs in Washington Denise Ferguson; Paquita Vivo of the Puerto Rican Foundation; Hispanic women's activist Celia G. Torres; homemakers Esther Coopersmith, Dorothy Gregg, and Alma Rangel; JoAnn Heffernan Heisen, treasurer of Johnson and Johnson; Teachers Insurance and Annuity Association-College Recruitment Equities Fund director Matina Horner; National Council of Negro Women* president Dorothy Height; Juanita Kreps of Duke University; and United Auto Workers vice president Carolyn Forrest.

Dooley serves as WREI's president, although her assistant in earlier years, Susan Scanlan, is no longer with the organization. Dooley heads a full-time paid staff of six, which in 1994 included research director Cindy Costello, director of congressional fellowships on women and public policy Shari Miles, director of women's health project Barbara Krimgold, director of women in the military project Georgia Sadler, and office manager Kathy Pagano. Former research associate Anne Stone serves as a consultant. Staff salaries are augmented each year, and fringe benefits are generous. Two unpaid interns are recruited annually.

Although the institute continues to cooperate with caucus members, it is an independent research organization, retaining 501 (c) (3) status for tax purposes. During the last decade, most WREI activities have been supported by the Ford, Revson, and Rockefeller foundations, by about 30 percent of the 1990 fiscal year budget, and by business (50 percent) and labor unions (5 percent). The organization also has relied on fund-raising events (15 percent). Its annual budget has increased from $50,000 in 1977, to $150,000 in 1980, to a projected $870,000 in 1994. Initially financed by a three-year Charles H. Revson Foundation seed grant, since then support for the fellowship program has come from the General Mills and Helena Rubenstein Foundation, Philip Morris Companies, RJR Nabisco, Sea-Land Corporation, Johnson and Johnson, the Communication Workers of America, and a consortium of other labor unions.

POLICY CONCERNS AND TACTICS

Policy decisions are made by the board of directors after consultation with staff members, CCWI leaders, whose needs continue to enjoy the highest priority, and representatives of such groups as the American Association of University Women,* National Council for Research on Women,* and National Organization for Women.* Research reports are distributed widely, with members of the Congress, executive branch officials, media, scholars, and women's groups constituting the principal audiences. WREI has sponsored conferences and symposia designed to call attention to important economic and social problems women encounter and to generate information that can be used to address them. A symposium on the low wages most working women are obligated to accept was held in 1984, and a Capitol Hill conference on the impact tax policy has on women and families was conducted the following year. WREI conferences on health care and on housing were convened in 1986 and 1988, respectively.

A grant from the Rockefeller Family Fund has helped the organization underwrite a series of papers by experts on such subjects as older women at work and home-based employment. In addition, WREI staff regularly issue special reports and fact sheets for the edification of congressional and executive agencies, the media, and women's groups. Occasionally, WREI disseminates studies prepared by other individuals and organizations.

Since 1980, WREI has awarded fellowships to graduate students. It has placed them in CCWI members' offices and on the staffs of strategically important Senate and House committees. Students receive annual stipends for tuition and living expenses. The program is designed to encourage effective participation by women in policy making and to impart a better understanding of how policies affect women and men differently. It also is calculated to encourage appreciation of the belief that issues often defined as women's are of equal importance to men. Fellows are selected in a national competition and pursue master's and Ph.D. degrees in a variety of academic and professional specialties, including public health, nutrition, and law. They represent a broad spectrum of age, race, and ethnic backgrounds and are geographically diverse. Past classes have included an Army sergeant, a nun, and a Texas rancher. Many of the more than 130 women participating in the program through 1994 held professional staff positions on the Hill; others decided to return to their home states to put their knowledge of public policy to direct use.

Issues of greatest importance to the organization have been reflected in such laws as the 1984 Child Support Enforcement Act and the 1988 Civil Rights Restoration Act. WREI has monitored consideration, passage, and enforcement of affirmative action proposals and efforts to overturn *Roe* v. *Wade* (1973). It has felt most disappointed by the underfunding of education, health, and social service programs during the 1980s and by restrictions imposed on International Family Planning agencies, many of which were lifted in 1993.

FURTHER INFORMATION

In 1987, WREI began annual publication of *The American Women: A Report in Depth,* which describes each year's important events that have affected women. Articles in the volume are written by specialists in such fields as education, health, employment, political participation, and family life. Other WREI publications include *Older Women: The Economics of Aging* (1984), *Parental Leave and Women's Place* (1989), *Family and Medical Leave* (1989), and *A Directory of Selected Research and Policy Centers Working on Women's Issues.*
IRWIN N. GERTZOG

WOMEN'S RIGHTS PROJECT
See AMERICAN CIVIL LIBERTIES UNION

WOMEN STRIKE FOR PEACE (WSP)
110 Maryland Avenue, NE
Suite 302
Washington, DC 20002
(202) 543-2660
FAX (202) 546-0090

Women's Strike for Peace (WSP) was organized to limit the testing of nuclear weapons. Since its founding, it has continued to concern itself with eliminating nuclear tests, preventing the use and spread of nuclear weapons, and reducing the threat of war.

ORIGIN AND DEVELOPMENT

WSP grew out of one of the largest demonstrations by women in the twentieth century. On November 1, 1962, between 12,000 and 50,000 women staged a one-day strike to protest aboveground nuclear testing. Many of the women participating and most of the organizers became WSP's nucleus. The strike organizers were women known to each other through the Committee for a Sane Nuclear Policy (SANE) and Women's International League for Peace and Freedom* (WILPF). Discouraged by the male-led SANE's unwillingness to consider women's fears about the effects of nuclear fallout on their children's health, Dagmar Wilson and four other women conceived the idea of the strike. A network of female organizations and friendship circles sent the message to other women. For two years the women demonstrated for the test ban cause, even capturing President Kennedy's attention. When the United States and the Soviet Union agreed to a limited Atmospheric Test Ban Treaty in 1963, many observers attributed the achievement to WSP's efforts.

The most dramatic event in WSP's early years occurred when it was called before the House Committee on Un-American Activities (HUAC) in December 1962. Refusing to be intimidated by the committee's Red-baiting, the WSP women subpoenaed to appear—Blanche Posner, Ruth Meyers, and Lyla Hoffman—won the public's and the media's praise. Their lecture to the committee on WSP's maternal rationale for opposition to nuclear testing surprised HUAC members and inspired WSP members. Some commentators date the demise of the influence of HUAC to this hearing.

WSP has continued its efforts to reduce the threat of nuclear war and international conflict generally. An organization of mainly women, WSP has remained viable and active in the cause of peace, arguing for the presence of women's voice in international issues discussions.

ORGANIZATION AND FUNDING

WSP has ten local branches in California, Illinois, Pennsylvania, Washington state, and New York. Since its beginning, WSP has aimed to develop an organizational structure with an emphasis on participatory democracy and the absence of hierarchical structure. It continues to be WSP's practice to allow its locals to plan their own events and actions. There is a national consultative committee of about twelve women to represent the various national regions. For many years, Ethel Taylor has served as WSP coordinator. Edith Villastrigo also has a long career with WSP as head of the legislative office in Washington, D.C. Both women serve in a volunteer capacity. One part-time staffer in the legislative office is assisted by other volunteers and one of three interns.

WSP claims a membership of 2,000 individuals, 95 percent of whom are women. Members also are encouraged to take independent action. Most join to work with like-minded persons and participate in the political actions WSP organizes.

In 1990, the WSP budget was $60,000. Most of this money was used to fund legislative work and publications and to maintain the Washington office. At-large dues are $25, and they, with a few larger contributions from individuals, are the main source of operating funds. Local branches have separate dues schedules.

WSP has a Research and Education Fund with 501 (c) (3) status to which tax-deductible contributions can be made. The president of the fund is Riva Aaron, who works in the New York City area. In recent years the fund has produced a number of educational materials, including videos and pamphlets on Star Wars and the need to clean up nuclear weapons plants.

POLICY CONCERNS AND TACTICS

Policy decisions and strategy choices of WSP are determined by the national consultative committee, which meets every three months in Philadelphia. Local chapters may decide their own activities through meetings of the branch members. Besides urging its members to write their elected officials on the issues, WSP has undertaken an innovative Lobby by Proxy program that allows members and others to sign peace proxies, which the legislative office takes to the representative or senator from the signer's district or state. The goal is to show members of the Congress that people in their district support or oppose certain peace-related issues. WSP also has testified before congressional committees, publicized the voting records and policy statements of elected officials, and directly lobbied members of the Congress. WSP also has written to the secretary general of the United Nations on issues of importance.

Since 1961, WSP has undertaken a number of stands and actions, including opposition to the war in Vietnam and other instances of U.S. intervention in Latin America and the Persian Gulf. WSP has continued its focus on arms control, undertaking a major campaign in opposition to Star Wars, which included the publication of a booklet, *A Basic Primer on Star Wars for the Legitimately Confused.* It has mounted campaigns in support of a Comprehensive Test Ban Treaty, an international conference on the Middle East, and a boycott against General Electric as a major manufacturer of nuclear weapons. Most recently it has expressed opposition to the use of force in Korea and support for limitations on the sale of U.S. armaments. It still considers its efforts to achieve a total nuclear test ban an unfinished goal. In all these causes, members' efforts to write their elected officials and the legislative office's activities are WSP's most important strategies.

WSP also was the key player in forming a coalition of women's peace groups, Women for Meaningful Summits.* Actions often are taken in concert with other peace groups, including WILPF and Women's Action for New Directions.*

ELECTORAL ACTIVITIES

WSP does not have a political action committee, nor does it endorse specific candidates.

FURTHER INFORMATION

WSP publishes a bimonthly *Legislative Alert,* which details current issues before the Congress and the executive branch. Included with each discussion of an issue is a suggested action, generally a recommendation to write to the reader's representative or senator urging opposition or support for some piece of legislation. Individuals who are not members of WSP can subscribe to this publication for fifteen dollars, and more than 2,000 people do.

NANCY E. MCGLEN

WOMEN'S VOTE
See COUNCIL OF PRESIDENTS

WOMEN'S WAR COUNCIL
See NATIONAL FEDERATION OF BUSINESS AND PROFESSIONAL WOMEN'S CLUBS OF THE U.S.A.

WOMEN U.S.A. FUND (WA)
835 Third Avenue
15th Floor

New York, NY 10022
(212) 759-7982
FAX (212) 759-8647

Women U.S.A. Fund (WA) is a nonmembership organization that focuses on encouraging women to take an active role in public policy making. Its two main projects have been the Women's Foreign Policy Council and the Women's Environment and Development Organization (WEDO).

ORIGIN AND DEVELOPMENT

WA started in 1980. The founder was Bella Abzug, who convinced a few colleagues from the women's liberation movement, especially those in the National Women's Political Caucus* (NWPC), of the need for an organization to mobilize women. Abzug is one of the greatest figures in the women and peace movements in the last three decades. Trained as a lawyer at Columbia University when few women were allowed into law school, Abzug participated actively in the civil rights movement. Later she became a founder of Women Strike for Peace.* Elected as a Democrat to the House of Representatives in 1970, she became known as a leading opponent of the Vietnamese conflict. She also worked actively for the women's rights cause, helping to organize NWPC and the Congressional Women's Caucus.* Defeated in her attempt to join the Senate, Abzug was appointed by President Carter to cochair his National Advisory Committee for Women. After the 1980 election she called together a group of prominent women to discuss the gender gap's implication and the need to organize women to prevent the elimination, under a Reagan presidency, of gains made during the previous decade. The outgrowth of these meetings was WA.

WA originally focused on increasing women's involvement with a voter education and registration program. Later it undertook projects designed to include women in foreign and environmental policy making.

ORGANIZATION AND FUNDING

The president of WA is Brownie Ledbetter. Abzug is the secretary. Abzug and Mim Kelber have cochaired one of the major projects, the Women's Foreign Policy Council, and cofounded the other project, WEDO. The latter also has an International Policy Action Committee (IPAC) of fifty-five women from thirty-one countries. IPAC has ten cochairs from ten nations. There is one staff member in the New York City office.

WA has no members. It is an educational 501 (c) (3) organization. Funds have come largely from private foundations and a few large and many small contributors.

POLICY CONCERNS AND TACTICS

The officers determine both the policies and strategies of the organization and its affiliated groups. The first project was begun during 1982. Based on research on the gender gap by Kelber, WA undertook a number of pilot projects to mobilize women in the election. In 1984, Abzug, with Kelber, published the results of these projects and their research on the different voting preferences of women in the book *Gender Gap.*

Dismayed by the absence of women from the debates over foreign policy, Women's Foreign Policy Council was established in 1985. It published the *Women's Foreign Policy Council Directory.* Listed in the directory are the names of women experts on arms control, disarmament, and other international issues.

In the last few years, WA mainly has focused on the environment and development. It called together women from around the world in October 1990 to discuss the need to have a women's input on these issues. The resulting organization, IPAC, held a conference in November 1991 to discuss the necessity of including women in the United Nations Conference on the Environment and Development in Brazil. More than 1,500 women from eighty-three countries attended, passing an action agenda that they later presented at the meeting in Brazil. WEDO has organized women's caucuses for most of the UN's major international meetings.

ELECTORAL ACTIVITIES

WA is a nonpartisan organization that does not endorse candidates. It does not have a political action committee.

FURTHER INFORMATION

WEDO under the auspices of WA publishes a newsletter, *News & Views.* It also has reports and cassettes from its conference.

NANCY E. MCGLEN

WOMEN WORKING
See 9to5, NATIONAL ASSOCIATION OF WORKING WOMEN

WORKING WOMEN, NATIONAL ASSOCIATION OF OFFICE WORKERS
See 9to5, NATIONAL ASSOCIATION OF WORKING WOMEN

WORKING WOMEN, NATIONAL ORGANIZING PROJECT
See 9to5, NATIONAL ASSOCIATION OF WORKING WOMEN

WORLD YOUNG WOMEN'S CHRISTIAN ASSOCIATION
See YOUNG WOMEN'S CHRISTIAN ASSOCIATION

YOUNG WOMEN'S CHRISTIAN ASSOCIATION OF THE U.S.A. (YWCA)

726 Broadway
New York, NY 10003
(212) 614-2700
FAX (212) 677-9716

The pluralism, diversity, and dedication to service of the Young Women's Christian Association of the U.S.A. (YWCA) combine to make it an important instrument of progress. Other women's organizations often use the YWCA network to enhance their outreach. Meeting women's and girls' critical needs, the YWCA has become a bellwether for the nation, harbinger of change, and catalyst for social evolution—for America's women and girls—as vital to the future as it was to the past. The YWCA story is a chapter in women's civil rights history. Operating at over 4,000 locations throughout the country in more than 400 associations, in all fifty states, the YWCA serves girls and women with flexible programs that span their lifetimes. Its outreach extends internationally through its membership in the World YWCA, at work in ninety other countries.

ORIGIN AND DEVELOPMENT

The YWCA of the U.S.A. began its work in 1858, three years after the organization formed in England. Carolyn D. Roberts brought together thirty-five women at New York University's chapel to establish the New York YWCA. At about the same time, Lucretia Boyd, a city missionary in Boston, was working with a group of churchwomen to develop interest in the plight of employed young women. Opposed by male clergy, the movement nevertheless took hold, and soon YWCAs formed in a number of cities in the East and Midwest. In

1871, national meetings began at the same time that student YWCAs were established. By 1909, Grace Hoadly Dodge, a New York City philanthropist, brought 616 member associations together in a national structure, the YWCA of the U.S.A. national board, and was elected its first president.

The organization's history is voluminous, abounding in social service landmarks, public policy successes, and enduring contributions to U.S. cultural, political, and economic life. The YWCA is the oldest and largest women's organization, with more than 2.5 million participants nationwide and programs that touch 20 million individuals annually. Its programs and locations have changed many times over the years, but the YWCA's basic purpose has not.

The YWCA literally began as a movement; its name came later. In each instance the founding of a member association came about because a small group of concerned, caring women would begin the task of making life better for other women. The nineteenth century's Industrial Revolution provided dramatic changes that saw women migrating from Europe and Asia as well as internal migration from farm to city. YWCA founders realized that women needed a safe haven, a place to eat, live, relax, and learn new skills, particularly about the handling of financial matters related to living away from home. YWCAs provided boardinghouses with safe, clean rooms and affordable meals. The Traveler's Aid Program, established in the Boston YWCA in 1866, soon became involved in meeting trains and ships to protect traveling women and girls. Because many factories were poorly ventilated, YWCAs became concerned about women's health and recreation needs. Many YWCAs set up recreational programs at factory sites during lunch hours.

It soon became apparent that women needed specialized training to compete in the marketplace. Because so many women continued to work at home, YWCAs provided instruction on the earliest sewing machines, bringing women new freedom at home and greater earning power. YWCAs also offered the first instruction in typewriting for women. The YWCA industrial program attracted many women nationally prominent in the labor movement, like Florence Simms, a YWCA staff member responsible for many women's finding their way into the trade union movement, where they rose to leadership positions.

Professional women were not ignored by the YWCA. In 1919, the St. Louis YWCA organized the National Federation of Business and Professional Women's Clubs* (BPW/US). Among their concerns were equal pay for equal work, education for personal and professional advancement, and the value of a feeling of solidarity among women with similar occupational interests.

Interest in reaching rural women demanded new methods of outreach. Besides its urban "secretaries," the YWCA national board employed county field staff to do its work. Based on this model, services were brought to farms, mining towns, black women, and foreign-born workers. The YWCA denounced programs intending to strip the foreign-born woman of her native culture; YWCA programs were designed to help her adjust to American life while maintaining her cultural values. The YWCA International Institute, founded by Edith Terry

Bremer, worked from Ellis Island and spread outward, offering adult education classes, sponsorship of ethnic folk festivals, and lobbying for more humane immigrant legislation. Fifty-five institutes developed and in 1934 formed the National Institute of Immigrant Welfare.

Since the 1880s, programs for teens have been administered locally; in 1918, the Girl Reserve Program was established. During World War I, the program was confined to war-related activities that dovetailed with YWCA. The YWCA's responsibility was to serve 1.5 million women workers in war plants. It continued its work during World War II and changed the name of its adolescent component to YTEENS. While teen programs have focused on civil rights issues, feminism, international affairs, youth unemployment, citizenship training, and the like, the teen program has embodied the tradition of YWCA emphasis on sex education. Founders of the YWCA movement were concerned that immigrant and rural women moving to the cities to work would be lured into prostitution in their effort to be self-supporting. That concern precipitated the YWCA's lobbying for a new minimum wage law for women in 1911. Today's concept of human sexuality expresses the traditional YWCA vision of open, frank discussion about sexual matters, and YWCA teens are leaders today in educational programs dealing with rape, incest, AIDS, and other related topics.

While the wording of the YWCA's mission has changed with the times, its essential components have remained: "to join women and girls of diverse experiences together so that they may struggle for peace, justice, freedom and dignity" for all. At the core of the YWCA's work over the decades has been the recognition that not all women are treated equally, and therefore the YWCA has pioneered in the task of working against racial discrimination and toward full integration, fighting obvious segregation practices and exposing hidden patterns of discrimination in legislation, institutions, and systems.

Some firsts in its radical justice history include the student division's establishment of the Haworth Institute in 1890 in Oklahoma to fight discrimination against American Indians. As early as 1908, the national board hired a black woman, Eva Bowles, to work with "colored" women in the cities, and she was instrumental in creating the same administrative structures for white and black YWCAs that had been operating separately in the same city. The first interracial conference in the southern United States was held by the YWCA in Louisville, Kentucky in 1915. In 1938, the YWCA called for an investigation of segregation in YWCAs and community life.

During World War II, the YWCA extended its service to the relocation centers for Japanese Americans who had been forced from their homes and deprived of their citizens rights. In 1946, the Interracial Charter of the YWCA was adopted, thus committing the entire organization to work toward racial justice. In 1958, the YWCA began its Institutes on Racism Program, and in 1965 a Racial Justice Center was established, headed by renowned civil rights activist Dorothy Height, who was and remains president of the National Council of Negro Women.* During the 1960s, the YWCA's work of promoting racial justice in all aspects of the association's life culminated in the mandate for full integration. Some southern YWCAs did not comply and were disaffiliated.

Prior to the 1970 national convention, black women held a conference that culminated in the YWCA's adoption of One Imperative: the association will thrust its collective power toward the elimination of racism, wherever it exists and by any means necessary. As recently as 1989, under threat from neo-Nazi groups, the YWCA held a racial justice convention at its Leadership Development Center in Phoenix. The organization's vision to empower women by eliminating racism and sexism remains its driving force today.

Another important thread of YWCA history deals with its social and public policy initiatives, both nationally and internationally. The YWCA has always included the dual emphasis of direct services to women and girls and sociopolitical action to improve their environment and living conditions. The formal YWCA public affairs program began in 1911, when convention demanded legislation to regulate hours and wages of women workers. Its work on behalf of women workers made it instrumental in establishing the Department of Labor's Women's Bureau,* an agency with which it still works closely today. Florence Kelley and the National Child Labor Committee publicly acknowledged the YWCA's work to prohibit child labor in the 1920s. In the 1930s, the YWCA was in the vanguard of the New Deal, supporting the rights of workers (particularly women) to organize for collective bargaining, compulsory unemployment insurance, national health insurance, public housing, Social Security coverage, and minimum wages. The YWCA worked tirelessly to expand civil rights and conserve national resources and worked for the equal rights amendment (ERA) and gun control; repeatedly during the last decade abortion as women's private choice was its first public policy priority. The YWCA policy reads: A woman has the right to choose in the matter of abortion based on her own religious and ethical beliefs and her physician's guidance. YWCA opposes mandatory parental consent.

Women's health, in terms of exercising control of her body or being fit, always has been a YWCA concern. As early as 1890, YWCAs offered classes in first aid, and summering in YWCA's camps known for their physical fitness training is legendary. The first classes in calisthenics started in Boston in 1877 to counter the attack that women could not endure six weeks of typing classes and were not strong enough for sports. In 1988, YWCA became the first and only women's organization to sit on the U.S. Olympic Committee. YMCA has pioneered not only using sports to enhance women's self-esteem and confidence but also rehabilitative health services through the ENCORE program to support postmastectomy patients. Another important health component is the national teenage pregnancy prevention program, which since 1913 has provided support services and education ranging from relationships to AIDS prevention.

YWCA's work on an international level has been far-reaching. Starting in the 1920s with demands that the international community outlaw war and urging entry into the League of Nations (the YWCA formed the National Conference on the Cause and Cure of War), YWCA has continued its international priority of seeking world peace and caring for the aftermath of war. At various points in its history, YWCA has withstood smear campaigns because of its antiwar position, most notably the one conducted by the National Society, Daughters of the American Revolution,* which attempted to link it with radical political elements. During each world war, it formed a Work Council, which financed research studying the effects of war and its aftermath on women workers. It also has established refugee funds for war victims, a practice that continues today. YWCA has taken a lead in recent international conferences, such as the United Nation's Decade Women's Conferences; for example, Dame Nita Barrow, the then-immediate past president of the World YWCA, presided over the Nairobi conference. She was succeeded to the World YMCA presidency by Jewel Graham, the then-retiring president of YMCA of the U.S.A. The Nairobi workshops were organized by YWCA of the U.S.A. staff. YWCA conventions have prioritized working for world peace as the first international policy.

As YWCA women move into the twenty-first century, their response to the need for public leadership training has been the Institute for Public Leadership (IPL). This is a national, nonpartisan program that trains women to be effective candidates, campaign managers, and issue advocates. This type of leadership training, which includes research, marketing, strategic planning, and networking techniques, has resulted in women's entering and winning their local primaries and setting their sights on state and federal offices. Over 400 women are now IPL graduates.

Because YWCA was founded to offer services to working women, child care has proved a major concern. In 1864, the Philadelphia YWCA organized the first day care center in the United States. Today YWCA is one of the largest providers of day care in the country. Eighty-five percent of YWCAs now provide day care. YWCA day care is more than just a place for a child to stay; it is an important, educational component of the child's earliest experience, recognized by early childhood specialists as such, particularly because of the opportunity to understand children from all backgrounds.

Other typical YWCA services linked to its public policy priorities include extensive programs pertaining to violence against women, rape crisis support, all forms of women's support groups, and educational and job training and development programs.

Well known nationally and internationally for its educational and training programs, the YWCA built a Leadership Development Center in Phoenix, Arizona, in 1983. It houses a state-of-the-art media center that provides satellite transmissions of teleconferences to YWCAs nationwide. The goal of YWCA education and training is to ensure that volunteers and staff understand the mission of YWCA of the U.S.A. the meaning of racism and sexism, and how advocacy on behalf of girls and women leads to social change. Participants learn the meaning of empowerment and how to deal with controversy and take action on issues. They learn that the YWCA is more than an association; it is a women's membership movement. That philosophy provides the basis for YWCA's exclusively female membership. Many organizations are working in areas cited in the history of YWCA, but the YWCA is unique in that from the beginning women have owned, led, and managed it.

ORGANIZATION AND FUNDING

Made up of some 400 community and student associations operating at over 4,000 locations, YWCA services over 20 million girls, women, and their families annually. That membership reflects diversity in age, ethnicity, religion, race, lifestyle, and interests. Member associates meet triennially to determine legislative mandates, which then are implemented by a fifty-five-member national board, also elected by the legislative convention. Member associations are free to work on those issues of greatest concern to their own members, while the national board is accountable to its members to provide a national presence for the organization. Ann Stallard of Atlanta, Georgia is the current president.

The YWCA has national offices in Washington, D.C., Chicago, and Phoenix. The national executive director is Gwendolyn Calvert Baker, expert in multicultural education and recent chair of the New York City Board of Education. There is a public policy staff in the Washington office led by Beverly Stripling, director of public affairs. Currently, the YWCA is undergoing a massive reorganization to better serve its members and member associations. It is downsizing its central staff and relying more on computer-assisted information for support.

YWCA is reviewing its participant criteria as more women become involved with YWCA because of a personal crisis. While technical membership has decreased to about 300,000, the participant base constantly has increased during the last decade. Women and girls join YWCA for a variety of reasons, for example, to get child care for their children, learn to swim, join a travel club, or take assertiveness training. Women and girls stay within the YWCA family because they learn the meaning of empowerment and become dedicated to the elimination of racism and sexism. They are YWCA women because they are committed to an advocacy role on behalf of women, locally, nationally, and internationally.

Member YWCAs are funded through United Way allocations, membership fees and dues, endowments, government grants, and private and corporate gifts. The national board is supported from member associations (38 percent); contributions from individuals, corporations, and foundations (11 percent); income from investment (32 percent); government (2 percent); and other sources (18 percent). The YWCA national board's 1990 operating budget was approximately $10 million, and its assets were approximately $46 million. The total assets of the entire YWCA of the U.S.A. are approximately $5 billion.

POLICY CONCERNS AND TACTICS

The national board has a public policy committee that interprets convention policy. In carrying out its convention mandate, the YWCA national board uses a variety of strategies to influence public and social policy. It monitors federal legislation and works in collaboration with other national organizations (particularly closely with other national women's organizations) to share information and action. There is not a political strategy that it does not engage in. It testifies at congressional and state hearings and works closely with legislative staff. It works with agency and department staff and appeals directly to the president, governors, mayors, and so on. It participates in political demonstrations and has been prominent in the Washington marches on behalf of choice. Members engage in strong grassroots lobbying efforts, coordinated by the national office. It files court cases and amicus briefs. It regularly testifies at both Republican and Democratic platform hearings.

Since the 1963 Equal Pay Act and 1964 Civil Rights Act, there has not been a piece of legislation or administrative policy affecting women and girls that YWCA has not supported. Dedicated to ERA as a main public policy priority since 1973, YWCA has participated in every public demonstration and march regarding its passage. It has been active at every turn in every issue pertaining to reproductive freedom and has testified at U.S. Supreme Court appointment hearings, including the Clarence Thomas hearings.

YWCA has also been very active regarding the 1988 Civil Rights Restoration Act, 1991 Civil Rights Act, and the Voting Rights Act. The YWCA effort has been persistent and aggressive, providing the central administrative place for the coalition working in defense of abortion clinics during 1992 wherever necessary (e.g., Albany, Brooklyn), with both the national executive director and president doing time "on the line." During the past decade, YWCA of the U.S.A. has spent an enormous amount of time and energy on public policy initiatives, attempting to hold the line on what it perceives as an erosion of hard-won rights for women under the Reagan and Bush administrations.

The YWCA consistently participates in various lobbying and voter registration activities in collaboration with other organizations that share its political agenda. In 1988, as a member of the Voter Registration Project, the YWCA registered more voters than any other participating organization.

The YWCA of the U.S.A. works in collaboration with more than fifty coalitions, primarily focused on women's public policy and economic and human service issues. A member of the Council of Presidents,* YWCA also works with National Organization for Women* and its Legal Defense Fund,* the National Women's Political Caucus,* National Abortion Rights Action League,* American Association of University Women,* Girls, Inc.,* and the Girl Scouts. Other well-known collaborations include Federally Employed Women,* the Religious Coalition for Abortion Rights,* National Women's Law Center,* Older Women's League,* National Council of Jewish Women,* and National Committee on Pay Equity.* Important alliances also include the National Council of Negro Women,* National Puerto Rican Forum, National Council La Raiza, Pan-Asian Council, and MANA, A National Latina Organization.*

FURTHER INFORMATION

Each month in *Communique*, mailed to member associations, there is included a comprehensive public policy bulletin. Developed by the Washington, D.C., office, it includes detailed analysis of federal legislation affecting women and girls. Lobbying strategies are outlined for individual YWCAs to undertake. It uses its quarterly publication *Interchange* and *Communique* to keep its membership informed.

RITA DUARTE MARINHO

Z

ZETA PHI BETA NATIONAL EDUCATION FOUNDATION
See ZETA PHI BETA SORORITY

ZETA PHI BETA SORORITY
1734 New Hampshire Avenue, NW
Washington, DC 20009
(202) 387-3103

Zeta Phi Beta Sorority staffs community outreach programs, funds scholarships, supports charities, and promotes legislation for social and civic change. It has a National Education Foundation.

ORIGIN AND DEVELOPMENT

Zeta Phi Beta was founded in 1920 at Howard University in Washington, D.C., by five women—Arizona Cleaver-Stemmons, Myrtle Tyler-Faithful, Viola Tyler-Goings, Fannie Pettie-Watts, and Pearl Neal. Rather than follow the path of existing black sororities, the organization they chartered was intended to meet high standards of scholarship through scientific, literacy, cultural, and educational programs, stimulate service on campus and in the community, promote sisterhood, and "exemplify the ideal of Finer Womanhood."

Since its inception, Zeta Phi Beta has focused on the needs of minorities, women, and children. Before 1960, it targeted housing and the prevention of juvenile delinquency. Talent shows, vocational guidance clinics, youth clubs and camps, and cotillions were the staples of sorority efforts. In 1965, Zeta incorporated these efforts into a national umbrella project focusing on education, poverty, and health issues.

The sorority prides itself on being the first among the established black sororities to charter chapters outside the United States, to form constitutionally affiliated adult and youth groups, and to maintain a central national office with a salaried staff. In addition, it is the only one constitutionally bound to a fraternity, Phi Beta Sigma.

The membership is college-educated with degrees in all areas. Among its honorary members are the late congresswoman Florence Dwyer (D-NJ), Indiana state senator Julia Carson, the leading song stylist Dionne Warwick, and the late jazz great Sarah Vaughn. Zora Neale Hurston, a leading writer of the Harlem Renaissance, was a chapter member.

Approaching the twenty-first century, Zeta has undertaken new strategies to meet future challenges. Its rapid growth attests to its success in reaching contemporary women supporting its objectives. Fostering community ideals of service, charity, scholarship, civic and cultural endeavors, sisterhood and "Finer Womanhood" remains the sorority's goals.

ORGANIZATION AND FUNDING

Zeta Phi Beta has 560 college and graduate chapters located in forty-five states, the District of Columbia, Virgin Islands, Bahamas, Germany, Liberia, Sierra Leone, and Nigeria. Another first was the formation of international chapters, originally in Germany and West Africa. In the United States, chapters are divided into nine regions. Governing policies and procedures and national officers are voted upon democratically at biennial conventions. Board members attend, expenses paid. There is a national, voluntary executive board of elected and appointed officers, all of them African American women. Board participation is encouraged of women from lower-income strata, persons with disabilities, and older women. The president and chief executive officer is called the grand basileus. Each basileus develops a programmatic plan for her tenure. The current president is Gylla Moore Foster.

A paid professional staff, headed by an executive director, is located at the Washington, D.C., office, which opened in 1959. The current executive director is Linda Thompson. Staffers assume a fixed level of responsibility but acquire experience in other areas; they are rewarded with bonuses and annual pay increases. There is an attorney on retainer.

Zeta Phi Beta presently has a membership of more than 75,000 predominantly African American women. In 1960, there were 40,000 members. The membership grew by over 20 percent between 1970 and 1985, on the heels of the civil right movement. Members join to advocate important values, ideas, or policies; communicate with peers; engage in consciousness-raising sessions; experience friendship ties and the chance to associate with similarly minded people; and engage in community service. Development of organizational skills; local, state, and regional conferences and meetings; information and research; representation of a member's opinions to government; and the chance to participate in public affairs and exercise influence within the organization also provide incentives to membership. Membership is seen as a lifetime commitment, as exemplified by

Faithful, the sole surviving founding member, now past ninety years old and still active.

Affiliate membership is available through the organization's *Amitae* units to women without college degrees. Zeta's youth groups, the Archonettes and Amicettes, aquaint young people with the sorority's ideals and give sorority members the opportunity to role-model and mentor women in the middle and high schools and promote leadership, academic achievement, and community service.

The sorority is a 501 (c) (4) organization. It is supported by membership donations and dues ranging from $23.50 to $48.50, as well as by revenues obtained from public meetings, merchandise sales, and government and foundation grants from the U.S. Education, Health and Human Services and Labor Departments, National Institute of Drug Abuse, and March of Dimes Foundation. Zeta's total budget in 1992 was $300,000.

In 1975, Zeta Phi Beta established the National Education Foundation, a tax-exempt 501 (c) (3) corporation, to encourage and promote educational efforts. It has a board of managers with nine trustees and is funded by contributions and gifts from chapters and members. Among its projects is the annual undergraduate and graduate scholarship program.

POLICY CONCERNS AND TACTICS

Discussion by the board of directors, executive officers' decisions, and the delegate assembly help build Zeta's agenda. There also are membership polls. Zeta sees itself as a community catalyst with individual chapters conducting voter registration campaigns, distributing information, sponsoring programs on legislative initiatives in education, employment, child care, public health, and social services, and offering workshops on lobbying and campaigning. In 1987, Zeta joined three other black sororities in sponsoring a Black Women's Political Action Forum in Atlanta, Georgia. That forum subsequently became the prototype for other such efforts.

Zeta has directed special efforts in the areas of prenatal care, child development, and substance abuse counseling. One example of such efforts is a Stork's Nest program, which originally offered prenatal care, parent education, and clothing; since 1985, its focus has expanded to include teen mothers, AIDS and safe-sex information, and drug and alcohol abuse education and prevention. Begun in Atlanta in 1972, this project now has 300 units nationally and one in Haiti.

In the 1980s, illiteracy and drug abuse became targets of Zeta efforts to improve community life. Individual chapters sponsored tutorial services and affiliated with national programs such as the National Assault in Literacy. Project Zeta, a national effort to combat substance abuse, led to sorority participation in, and cosponsorship of, national and regional conferences addressing this issue. Individual chapters sponsored Just Say No clubs, information resource centers, and peer counseling in cooperation with local schools and colleges, churches, and other civic and community efforts.

Zeta stands as a forerunner among groups endorsing the civil rights legislation of the sixties. Today its community-based projects extend to old people, training for successful entrepreneurship, and support for developing cultural awareness.

Since its founding, Zeta Phi Beta has collaborated with like-minded groups on health issues, political awareness, and community service. These organizations include the Black Women's Agenda, Children's Defense Fund,* Leadership Conference for Civil Rights, National Association for the Advancement of Colored People, National Council of Negro Women* (with which Zeta is affiliated), National Council of Women in the United States, National Urban League,* and United Negro College Fund. Zeta belongs to the President's Council.*

ELECTORAL ACTIVITIES

The sorority does not sponsor partisan political activities. It is nonetheless interested in increasing the number of black women elected to political office. Many Zetas serve in elected or appointed office on the federal, state, and local level.

FURTHER INFORMATION

Zeta Phi Beta has a national quarterly newsletter and a semiannual magazine, *Arcon,* and has published books and pamphlets.

CHARLOTTE T. MORGAN-CATO

ZONTA INTERNATIONAL (ZI)
5S7 West Randolph Street
Chicago, IL 60606
(312) 930-5848
FAX (312) 930-0951

Zonta International (ZI) is a worldwide classified service organization of business and professional executives exercising leadership in their communities and countries. It seeks to advance women's legal, political, economic, and professional educational status and dedicates itself to friendship and peace. There is a Zonta International Foundation (ZIF).

ORIGIN AND DEVELOPMENT

Founded in 1919 in Buffalo, New York, with Marian DeForest as the charter president, the first Zonta club sought to provide women with an outlet for community service and humanitarian relief activities denied them by existing service organizations. The founders felt empowered by the Nineteenth Amendment's ratification to increase the scope of their public service participation. The name Zonta comes from a Sioux Indian word for "honest and trustworthy." During 1919, Mary E. Jenkins became president of a confederation of these clubs, advancing the service club movement that began in 1917; and Zonta achieved international status through its clubs in Canada.

During the Great Depression, Zonta campaigned against bills sure to limit married women's employment in government if their spouse also was a government employee and took a position opposing federal legislation to the same end.

ZI gave direct aid to Hungarian refugees in 1956 and ushered in the sixties by aiding refugee families in West Germany. It helped underwrite a vocational and teacher training center for Jordanian women (1962–74), mobile pediatric units for Ghana (1972–74), a training and research center for Pan African women to enhance their life quality and their children's (1974–76), and ten Colombian health and education centers (1976–82). Since the sixties, ZI has increased its service activities on the international front, including support for the United Nations Development Fund for Women (UNIFEM). Zonta clubs also have formed in many nations outside North America. ZI is a nongovernmental organization (NGO) at the United Nations (UN).

ORGANIZATION AND DEVELOPMENT

In 1975, there were 600 Zonta clubs; in 1984, 850. Today there are over 1,050 Zonta clubs in fifty-eight nations, including Argentina, Australia, the Bahamas, Bangladesh, Canada, Costa Rica, Denmark, Egypt, England, Finland, France, Ghana, Greece, Honduras, Hong Kong, Iceland, India, Indonesia, Israel, Italy, Ivory Coast, Japan, Kenya, Korea, Mexico, New Zealand, Nigeria, Norway, Peru, Philippines, Poland, Puerto Rico, Scotland, Senegal, Sri Lanka, Taiwan, Thailand, Togo, and Uruguay. In 1991, ZI's first Eastern European chapter formed, in Szombathely, Hungary. Clubs are divided into a total of twenty-six districts worldwide.

A biennial delegate assembly can amend the bylaws and set the dues and fee schedule; it elects board members, officers, and the nominating committee. The board has nine members. Ninety-eight percent of the board and officers are women; 9 percent are African American, and 9 percent are Asian American. In 1993, the president was Sonja Renfer. National headquarters is in Chicago. The current executive director is Bonnie Koenig. The national office employs fifteen professional staff. The organization has an attorney on retainer.

ZI's membership is made up of individuals. In 1991, there were 35,000 members, up from 32,000 in 1984 and 23,500 in 1975. Women constitute 98 percent of the membership. Zonta has discussed its status as a mainly women group and will remain as it is. Members join to advocate important values, communicate with peers or colleagues and associate with similarly minded people, and engage in consciousness-raising sessions. To a lesser extent, they find as incentives to membership friendship ties, the publications and other information Zonta provides, and opportunity to develop organizational skills and exercise influence within the group and to have their opinions represented to government and participate in public affairs.

There are Z clubs for high school students and Golden Z clubs for college and university students; they emphasize leadership, career development, and service. ZI distributes awards to stimulate female high school students' attention to policy making and entrance into community service and careers and leadership posts in government, business, and volunteer groups. Friends of Zonta do not belong to ZI but help with fund-raising or a particular service project. The Century Club helps clubs deal with revitalization issues; a push to increase membership by 10 percent in the nineties is under way.

Originally, ZI received large contributions from a few persons and small contributions from many people for help in getting established. Today its financial support comes almost entirely from membership dues (38 percent), with nominal support coming from revenues other than dues for publication sales or advertising; conventions, conferences, or exhibitions; and merchandise sales. ZI is a 501 (c) (3) organization. Contributions to it are tax-deductible. In 1991, the budget of this not-for-profit group was $1.3 million.

From a bequest, ZIF administers scholarships for Irishwomen seeking technical degrees. Since 1988, it has increased funding for the Amelia Earhart fellowship program for graduate women in the aerospace sciences and engineering; aviator Earhart was a Zontian. Women from forty-four countries have received 589 fellowships valued at $2.7 million. ZI also has a building fund intended to pay off the World Headquarters Building mortgage; a contribution of $22 constitutes a "brick."

POLICY CONCERNS AND TACTICS

The international board of directors sets ZI policy. Also influential in policy discussions are professional staff recommendations, executive officers' decisions, the delegate assembly (which sets program policy) and membership polls. Preferred strategies includes making personal presentations to congresspersons, agency heads, or staff; contacting public decision makers through influential members; conducting and publishing research on issues; educating members with publications and encouraging them to write legislators and committees; and educating the public through press releases and fielding public relations or public service campaigns. ZI also may testify in congressional and state legislative hearings; supply congresspeople, state legislators, and staff with information; make written comments in proposed regulations; and seek administrative review of agency or department decisions. Occasionally it monitors elected officials' voting records, testifies at agency/department hearings, participates in direct action political demonstrations, and files court cases.

Any relationship between federal law and a women's issue is taken into consideration by ZI. It has taken special note of the feminization of poverty. ZI seeks to promote the World Decade for Women Conference recommendations and guidelines, as well as the Nairobi Forward-Looking Strategies. Together with other NGOs, ZI has sponsored joint statements about women in the paid workforce, their development role, guidance abuse, and AIDS. Deploring the "cultural bias" that contributes to women's low status and working to implement article B of the UN Human Rights Commission Right to Development

Declaration, which mandates "effective measures . . . to ensure . . . women . . . an active role," ZI emphasizes training and education, as well as dissemination of information about the right to development. ZI sought with other NGOs to enter the environment and population growth, and related problems onto the 1992 UN Environment and Development Conference (UNICED) agenda. Along with guidance abuse and literacy, ZI believes that environmental problems get in the way of world peace.

ZI's primary impact on policy making comes through the UN. Taking an emphatic advocacy role in international dialogue, it seeks the allocation of development resources to women as a significant aspect of sustainable development. By 1991, it had contributed $1.5 million to self-help projects for women in developing countries through UNIFEM. These projects included training in labor-saving technologies, vocational training, and credit techniques, all meant to enhance women's roles as farmers, entrepreneurs, managers, and technicians. During the years 1990–92, ZI with UNIFEM committed more than $500,000 to projects in Egypt, India, and Togo. Each club sponsors a woman for the biennium. ZI also has a literacy program with the UN Education, Scientific and Cultural Organization (UNESCO) International Children's Emergency Fund. It observes that over 25 percent of the world's people are illiterate and that women's educational level is related inversely to infant mortality. The UN regularly polls its consultative body representatives for information.

Besides encouraging the clubs to network, ZI coordinates with Soroptimist International* and Project Five-O. It has worked with these groups throughout its existence. It has consultative status with UNESCO and the International Labor Organization. In 1990, it participated in the Women's Foreign Policy Council* international meeting of women to prepare for UNICED and particularly to pressure for women's equal representation at the conference.

ELECTORAL ACTIVITIES

ZI does not see women's issues as partisan and does not have a political action committee.

FURTHER INFORMATION

ZI has a quarterly magazine for its members, the *Zontian;* an annual subscription is seven dollars. It publishes an annual directory and issues research reports.

SARAH SLAVIN

ZONTA INTERNATIONAL FOUNDATION
See ZONTA INTERNATIONAL

APPENDIX I:
GOVERNMENTAL WOMEN'S
ISSUES GROUPS

———————— / ————————

THE CITIZENS ADVISORY COUNCIL ON THE STATUS OF WOMEN (CACSW)

The Citizens Advisory Council on the Status of Women (CACSW) served as a primary means for suggesting and stimulating action with private institutions, organizations, and individuals working for improvement of conditions of special concern to women. Its directive enabled the council to distribute without prior approval of government officials its recommendations and position papers to state and city commissions on women's status, to women's organizations, the press, and individuals. This provision enabled the council to be influential.

ORIGIN AND DEVELOPMENT

In November 1963, President Kennedy, acting on a recommendation of his Commission on the Status of Women* (PCSW), signed executive order no. 11,126, establishing the Interdepartmental Committee on the Status of Women and CACSW. The interdepartmental committee included heads of the federal departments and agencies represented on PCSW. The private citizen members of the president's commission, with a few additions, constituted the council.

Council priorities varied with each chair due to her interests and personality and the political beliefs of the members. The rapidly changing climate of opinion and political opportunities influenced action on the council. In 1962, women's advocates in government justified their suggestions for change in terms of women's status and the loss to society of women's talents. By 1969, a Republican White House had established a Task Force on Women's Rights and Responsibilities (PTFWRR). CACSW was abolished on April 4, 1978, by executive order no. 12,050, which established the National Advisory Committee for Women.

ORGANIZATION AND FUNDING

Margaret Hickey, a past president of the National Federation of Business and Professional Women's Clubs* (BPW/USA) and editor of *Ladies Home Journal,* chaired CACSW until June 1966, when Senator Maurine Neuberger (D-OR) succeeded her. Jacqueline Gutwillig, a reserve army colonel, chaired the Nixon administration council. Kennedy's executive order directed the Labor Department to furnish the intergovernmental committee and citizen council with staff, space, travel expenses, and other services. The two-member committee and council staff were located in the Women's Bureau* (WB) and on that payroll; a staff of three full-time and one half-time employees served, while Senator Neuberger chaired CACSW. Catherine East, a career civil servant, served as executive secretary of the committee and council both, until April 1975, when she was detailed to the newly established National Commission on the Observance of International Women's Year (NCOIWY) in the State Department. Fran Henry then served as executive secretary until 1976.

The seventeen original members of CACSW generally represented women's organizations, unions, progressive employers, civic leaders, and educators. Five members were men. There were representatives from the National Council of Negro Women,* National Council of Jewish Women* (NCJW), National Council of Churches,* National Council of Catholic Women,* and BPW/USA. In 1969, President Nixon appointed new council members. All the members were women, chosen largely from the women's advisory group for the Nixon campaign, including women business and civic leaders, attorneys, a deputy assistant secretary of state who had shown leadership in establishing state commissions on women's status, an African American editor and publisher, a leading pro-choice member of the Hawaii state legislature, a leading authority on Social Security, and representatives of the National Council of Catholic Laity, BPW/USA, General Federation of Women's Clubs,* and NCJW.

POLICY CONCERNS AND TACTICS

From 1963 to 1966, assistant secretary of labor and interdepartmental committee vice chair Esther Peterson, WB director Mary Keyserling, and Hickey set the committee's and the council's agenda. From 1969 to 1977, the interdepartmental committee did not function. Secretaries of labor Shultz and Hodgson supported the council; and lack of committee activity left the newly appointed council members free to pursue their own goals rather than react to committee direction. Elizabeth Duncan Koontz, a feminist appointed WB director on Secretary Shultz's recommendation, also encouraged and supported CACSW and its recommendations; she played an important role in securing the equal rights amendment's (ERA) passage in the Congress. During Hickey's tenure, CACSW sponsored 1964, 1965, 1966, and 1967 conferences of state and city commission members that they might exchange information and ideas and form networking and support groups. National Organization for Women* (NOW) formed at the

1966 conference, its founding members composed largely of state commission and council members. A policy paper on major issues presented by the inclusion of sex in Title VII of the 1964 Civil Rights Act presented criteria for a strict interpretation of the bona fide occupational qualification and a recommendation that newspaper advertising not be permitted under separate columns for males and females. In a suit sought by NOW and the Women's Equity Action League* (WEAL), the federal courts upheld these interpretations, and the Equal Employment Opportunity Commission (EEOC) adopted them in its guidelines. Council and committee together recommended that the affirmative action executive order, no. 11,246, prohibiting discrimination in federal employment and employment under government contracts, be amended to include sex. President Johnson revised the order in October 1967; the change became effective the following year.

During Senator Neuberger's tenure, four task forces were established to review and update PCSW's recommendations. Most task force members appointed by the senator were private citizens, leaders in their professions. The task forces were staffed by highly qualified federal employees detailed from other agencies at Neuberger's request. The Family Law and Policy Task Force and Social Insurance and Taxes Task Force offered the most radical reports.

A leading ERA supporter and former BPW president, Marguerite Rawalt chaired the Family Law and Policy Task Force, which recommended revision of domestic relations laws based on the premise that marriage is an economic partnership. It suggested major changes in state family laws. Convinced that women's right to determine her reproductive right was a basic human right, the task force also recommended repeal of laws that made abortion a criminal offense and of federal laws restricting access to birth control devices and information. CACSW was the first and only government body to recommend repeal of criminal abortion laws five years before the Supreme Court decided *Roe* v. *Wade*. Senator Neuberger ultimately gets credit for this recommendation; she wanted to update PCSW recommendations. Harriet Pilpel and Alice Rossi, members of the family law task force, were leading proponents of repeal of abortion laws.

The task force also declared that so-called illegitimate children should have the same rights as legitimate children and that custody of children in divorce cases should be granted in accordance with the child's best interests. The report, including supporting position papers, was distributed widely and used extensively in state legislatures in which abortion law reform was active. Major reforms have occurred in the arena that concerned this task force.

The Labor Standards Task Force, chaired by Voit Gilmore, recommended major reforms in the protective labor laws applying to women only. Judicial decisions holding that Title VII superseded them were taken. The state "protective" labor laws soon overtook the Labor Standards recommendations.

The Health and Welfare Task Force, chaired by Ellen Winston, gave primary attention to reinforcing community institutions and services, particularly day care facilities, homemaker services, and consumer education. It argued that services such as family planning should be available under the same conditions to all women regardless of economic status. There has been more regression than progress in provision of these services.

The Social Insurance and Taxes Task Force, chaired by Selma Mushkin, recommended major changes in the unemployment insurance system to eliminate discrimination against women. Also recommended was a federal-state system of temporary disability insurance tied to the unemployment insurance system and including maternity coverage. The task force also supported legislation to permit some couples to combine earnings for the purpose of computing Social Security benefits and to provide an allowance for all employed persons. Little came of these reforms, except in unemployment insurance discrimination.

During Gutwillig's tenure, CACSW played an active, influential role in the fight for ERA, provided a theory of maternity leave under Title VII that resulted in increased benefits for women employees, researched and publicized for the first time in lay language the discrimination against wives and children in family law, published papers on discrimination against women in employee benefit plans, and urged reform in health care for female offenders. The council made other recommendations but did not have the staff to provide backup research and technical assistance to help state commissions and volunteer organizations to act effectively.

The Republican CACSW, with no ties to the labor movement, endorsed ERA at its second meeting in February 1970. The chair asked the attorney general to detail Mary Eastwood from the Office of Special Counsel to work with CACSW on legal issues. Eastwood had staffed PCSW's civil and political rights committee and prepared the legal memo on which NOW based its endorsement of ERA. Eastwood drafted a comprehensive memo outlining a legal theory for interpreting ERA, which CACSW published. Over 250,000 copies were distributed by 1975 to state and city commissions, women's organizations, to the press, to local organizations for conferences, and in lobbying packets to state legislators. As CACSW could not lobby the Congress, it did not send publications but instead furnished members with any publications or assistance requested. Most supporting witnesses in Senate and House hearings used the legal theory. CACSW's chair testified in the Senate hearing held during May 1970 by Senator Bayh (D-IN) and keynoted WB's fiftieth anniversary conference in June. The council's paper and the PTFWRR report endorsing ERA were distributed to participants, who, in turn, endorsed the amendment and other task force recommendations.

After ERA passed the Congress, CACSW prepared and distributed widely a paper interpreting ERA in accordance with its legislative history. Gutwillig sent a letter to the leadership and women members of the state legislatures outlining this history's importance in interpreting ERA and listing sources for obtaining the relevant documents. CACSW's executive secretary actively participated in meetings of the informal coalition of organizations supporting ERA before and after congressional approval and also testified in ERA's support in several state legislatures. During these years, CACSW was the chief source of information for reporters and television and radio producers seeking background material and suggestions for supporters to appear on programs.

CACSW also undertook a review of data available on maternity leave practices because the subject generated so much interest. No uniformity of practice and practically no data were found. Since the Social Security system did not include health or temporary disability insurance, it left employers free to exclude childbirth and complications of pregnancy from any health or temporary disability insurance they carried on employees. By way of contrast, European countries provided maternity benefits within their social security systems, with health and temporary disability insurance for all; employers in these systems did not pay a higher contribution or tax for female employees. CACSW found that some U.S. employers and state governments partially or wholly treated medical costs and leave because of pregnancy and childbirth as they treated other temporary disabilities. Some considered it a "normal physiological condition" and treated medical costs and absence from work differently from the way they treated other disabilities—to women's disadvantage.

CACSW concluded that a woman about to give birth is temporarily disabled from work, under professional medical care, and usually hospitalized. Therefore, she should be entitled to all the benefits the employer provided for other disabilities. This theory meant that any difference in treatment would constitute sex discrimination under Title VII. CACSW also concluded that women should not have any special benefits not provided for other disabilities. Any special treatment would lead inevitably to situations in which men and women with disabilities that were not pregnancy-related would have fewer benefits than pregnant women. This was not sociologically or economically justified and potentially divisive in the workforce. In addition, in the United States, where the employer usually pays all or part of the costs, such policies could result in reluctance to hire or promote women of childbearing age. The EEOC in its sex discrimination guidelines issued in 1972 adopted CACSW's position, later ruling that any leave for child rearing must be available equally to women and men employees.

The executive secretary of the CACSW testified as an expert witness in several court challenges by employers to the guidelines. Four federal courts of appeal upheld the guidelines, but the Supreme Court in an opinion written by J. Rehnquist held that discrimination because of pregnancy is not sex discrimination. The decision, *Gilbert* v. *General Electric* (1976), later was overturned by an act of the Congress.

At the request of John McLaughlin, then a presidential assistant, East researched and prepared a paper on ERA's impact on women's and children's legal support rights. Contrary to conventional wisdom, the full-time homemaker without independent resources, virtually always a woman, largely was dependent on her husband's generosity, goodwill, and character. In January 1972, CACSW published a paper in the area, the first time women's and children's rights to support were stated in lay language from a feminist perspective.

After further research, in November 1973, CACSW recommended that state, county, and city commissions and other concerned organizations seek recognition of these rights through amendments to state divorce laws, adopting at a minimum the economic protections of the Uniform Marriage and Divorce Law. The recommendation came with a position paper that was distributed to the press, women's organizations, and status of women commissions. Only one reporter, Vera Glaser of the Knight Ridder Washington Bureau, wrote a story based on the paper, although the data supplied and case law quoted contradicted prevailing views that all divorced women received alimony and that divorced fathers supported the children. Despite a lack of media attention, state laws in this area improved on the heels of debate about ERA in the state legislatures and follow-up activities of NCOIWY.

ELECTORAL ACTIVITIES

CACSW members were appointed by the presidents, but there was little partisanship exhibited; Republican councils generally did not approve changes that would require new government activities, and Democratic councils would not approve ERA because of opposition by AFL-CIO and some women's organizations. CACSW engaged in no electoral activity.

FURTHER INFORMATION

CACSW's publications were its hallmark and included the widely recognized and utilized *Interpretation of the Equal Rights Amendment in Accordance with the Legislative History* and *The Equal Rights Amendment and Alimony and Child Support Laws.*

CATHERINE EAST

PRESIDENT'S COMMISSION ON THE STATUS OF WOMEN (PCSW)

The President's Commission on the Status of Women (PCSW) was created by President John F. Kennedy in December 1961 to make recommendations for overcoming sex discrimination and enabling women to meet both traditional family roles and new roles as workers and citizens.

ORIGIN AND DEVELOPMENT

Women activists representing civic and labor organizations, such as the National Consumers' League and the National Women's Trade Union League, first had proposed in 1947 a federal commission on the status of women, to be created by the Congress. For decades this group of women had sought protection for women working in factories, and their proposal for a commission came out of their opposition to the proposed equal rights amendment (ERA), which appeared to be gaining new support from the Congress in the wake of World War II. ERA, they argued, would sweep the good protective laws away with the bad;

a federal commission would be able to make specific recommendations to ameliorate women's condition without the negative consequences they saw in a constitutional amendment. The split between ERA supporters and advocates of a commission doomed whatever chance either measure possessed in the Congress.

Esther Peterson, a labor lobbyist in the 1940s, belonged to this group of activists and supported the proposal. By 1961, Peterson had become a member of the Kennedy administration. As director of the Women's Bureau* (WB) and assistant labor secretary, she took the opportunity her position afforded to implement the proposal for a commission on women. Labor secretary Arthur Goldberg proposed that the commission be established by executive order, and President Kennedy agreed.

Acting on Peterson's suggestion, the president established PCSW in December 1961. Kennedy's executive order no. 10,980, drafted at WB, traced the commission's establishment to discrimination and outworn traditions barring women's "full realization" of their rights; he charged the commission with developing recommendations to eliminate sex discrimination in both public and private institutions and to propose ways in which the government and the private sector could assist women in meeting their traditional responsibilities as wives and mothers while expanding their opportunities for employment and public service. The commission's report was to be transmitted to the president by October 1963.

A commission on women's status fit Kennedy's liberal agenda: to energize the sluggish American economy, which increasingly relied on women workers, and to improve the American position vis-à-vis the Soviet Union, in part by calling forth women's talents in the public interest. Moreover, the commission would be a powerful tool to express John Kennedy's interest in women as voters. With the commission operating under Peterson's watchful eye, it would not embarrass him by its recommendations. During PCSW's life, President Kennedy acted upon its recommendation to eliminate selection by sex in the civil service; on November 1, 1963, as the commission had recommended, the president signed executive order no. 11,126, establishing two continuing federal committees on women.

The commission, although it expired after less than two years of active work, had several important lasting effects. First, by acknowledging a need for constitutional equality, it broke a long-standing stalemate among women's organizations over ERA, thereby narrowing the gap between opposing camps of activist women. It enunciated a federal policy against sex discrimination, legitimating the concern about the prejudice women faced, until then the target of ridicule; it formulated a cogent set of proposals to begin ameliorating the difficulties women faced; it built up networks of support among women's organizations and served as the model for analogous commissions on the state level; and it provided for a continuing federal presence through the continuing committees. All these outcomes contributed in an important way to the first independently organized expression of feminism's new wave, National Organization for Women,* which was founded by women associated with PCSW and the state commissions on women at their third annual meeting in 1966.

PCSW's membership was prestigious, including the labor, commerce, agriculture, and health, education, and welfare secretaries, the attorney general, Civil Service Commission chairman, and four members of the Congress—Senator George D. Aiken (R-VT), Senator Maurine B. Neuberger (D-OR), Congresswoman Edith Green (D-OR), and Congresswoman Jessica Weis (R-NY). It also included the presidents of the National Council of Negro Women* (NCNW), National Council of Catholic Women, and National Council of Jewish Women* and representatives of such educational institutions and labor organizations as Radcliffe College and the American Federation of Labor-Congress of Industrial Organizations.*

A series of subgroups, called "committees," enlarged the membership to incorporate a cross-section of the nation's white reform elite. To help establish PCSW's eminence, the Kennedy administration asked Eleanor Roosevelt to serve as "chairman," an invitation she accepted.

A handful of commission and committee members were African American. Dorothy Height, NCNW president, was the only black member named to the commission itself. Pauli Murray, a black lawyer and civil rights activist, sat on the committee on civil and political rights, which considered ERA, and Rosa Gragg, president of the National Association of Colored Women's Clubs,* accepted a position on the committee on home and community. Dollie Lowther Robinson, a black civil rights activist, lawyer, and unionist, served on WB's staff.

As executive chair, Peterson retained the key administrative role; Katherine P. Ellickson was executive secretary. WB provided additional staff and services; other staff members were "detailed"—that is, loaned—from such federal agencies as the Civil Service Commission and the Justice Department.

POLICY CONCERNS AND TACTICS

PCSW reached policy decisions by consideration of the committees' proposed recommendations; and its liberal centrist membership readily deferred to administration preferences. Peterson had intended the president's commission to divert attention from ERA, which she opposed. To permit PCSW to function effectively, it announced no position on the amendment at the beginning of the effort, and a special committee undertook a two-year study to examine the amendment and alternatives. Ultimately, the commission adopted Murray's proposal to seek constitutional equality under the Fourteenth Amendment, with litigation aimed at Supreme Court review—a strategy pioneered by the National Association for the Advancement of Colored People.

With ERA's consideration sequestered in the civil and political rights committee, PCSW and its six additional committees could consider other areas that affected women's lives: employment in both the public and private sectors,

Social Security and taxation, home and community, education, and protective labor laws. Special meetings (''consultations'') were held to assess media's impact on women's status, to address the role of volunteerism in women's lives, to encourage businesses and labor unions to expand women's opportunities in private employment, and, with a small number of prominent African Americans, to discuss the ''problems of Negro women.''

When PCSW submitted its report to President Kennedy in October 1963, it laid out an agenda for public and private institutions that, were it implemented, would expand opportunities for women, diminish discrimination in both law and custom, improve the care of working parents' children, and provide greater economic security for women dependent on male breadwinners. Recommendations included an executive order enunciating a federal policy against sex discrimination in employment, extension of minimum wage and equal pay laws to all men and women not already covered, paid pregnancy and maternity leaves, publicly supported child care services for all needing them, educational opportunities for older women, extension of unemployment insurance to household and agricultural workers, equalization of jury service rules, removal of all legal disabilities from married women, recognition of nonmonetary contributions by married women, thereby giving them the right to property, a greater role for women in political life, and continuation of federal efforts to monitor and stimulate action toward these ends.

In keeping with the group's liberal ideology, the commission report acknowledged the dual burden and especially hurtful circumstances that racism produced for women of color. It explicitly deplored programs that required mothers of small children to work in order to receive public assistance.

ELECTORAL ACTIVITIES

PCSW, although heavily Democratic in membership, made a concerted effort to avoid partisan behavior. It engaged in no electoral activities.

FURTHER INFORMATION

PCSW publications included the commission report, reports of the committees, and a summary of the four ''consultations,'' all published by the U.S. Government Printing Office in 1963.

CYNTHIA HARRISON

PRESIDENT'S TASK FORCE ON WOMEN'S RIGHTS AND RESPONSIBILITIES (PTFWRR)

One of the task forces advising President Nixon on the legislative program for 1970, the President's Task Force on Women's Rights and Responsibilities (PTFWRR) produced a series of recommendations that served as a federal legislative agenda for the women's movement.

ORIGIN AND DEVELOPMENT

A White House press release on October 1, 1969, announced PTFWRR's establishment. The task force resulted from an earlier meeting arranged by Vera Glaser, a veteran reporter with extensive contacts among Republican leaders, with Arthur Burns, counselor to the president, with responsibility for task forces. At this meeting Glaser and Catherine East, executive secretary of the Interdepartmental Committee and Citizen's Advisory Council on the Status of Women,* presented facts about discrimination against women that the federal government could correct and proposed corrective action.

The task force met frequently between October I and December 15, 1969, when its report was submitted to President Nixon. The strong report included a ringing declaration in the cover letter that huge "dividends of productivity" and women's respect and loyalty awaited the leader allocating opportunity to women; it also reaffirmed the appropriateness of U.S. leadership worldwide to achieve human rights. Although many PTFWRR recommendations have achieved adoption, and none seem radical now, they were too advanced for the White House. It did not release the report until June 1970, after Marie Anderson, *Miami Herald* women's editor, secured a copy, printed it in the newspaper, and distributed it in tabloid form for twenty-five cents. Elizabeth Duncan Koontz, the Women's Bureau* AWBA director, used the report in WB's fiftieth anniversary conference as the agenda for all workshops. Conferees endorsed the report, and the recommendations became the women's movement agenda at the federal level for a number of years.

ORGANIZATION AND FUNDING

The businesswoman, educator, and past president of the National Federation of Business and Professional Women's Clubs* (BPW) Virginia Allan was named chair. Allan, a veteran Michigan feminist and a Republican, had led Michigan BPW in supporting Democrat Martha Griffiths in her first campaign for the Congress in 1954. During Allan's national BPW presidency in 1963, she had worked closely with Esther Peterson, vice chair of President Kennedy's Commission on the Status of Women,* in a successful program to establish status of women commissions in every state. The task force met in Washington, D.C., at the Labor Department. East and assistant Bertha Whittaker volunteered to staff it.

In fulfilling his responsibility for nominating task force members, Charles Clapp of Burns's staff saw to it that highly qualified persons, mostly prominent Republicans, were appointed and later took strong interest in the task force meetings. Sixteen members besides Allan were appointed, including Patricia Hutar, former cochair of the Republican National Committee ARNCA; William Mercer, vice president for personnel relations, American Telephone and Telegraph; Anne Blackham, an RNC member; Sister Ann Ida Gannon, president of Mundelein College; Evelyn Cunningham, director of the Women's Unit in the

New York governor's office; Glaser; and a labor union official, Dorothy Haener of United Auto Workers.*

The organization had no official budget. Members were paid expenses for attending meetings. The Labor Department covered the expense of printing and distributing the report when it finally was released.

POLICY CONCERNS AND TACTICS

At the chair's request, East proposed an agenda, based on the paper earlier prepared for Burns, and arranged with top-level government officials to meet with PTFWRR to discuss the issues. East also drafted most of the report, and Glaser edited much of it, preparing the cover letter to the president. The report, *A Matter of Simple Justice* recommended that the President establish an Office of Women's Rights and Responsibilities in the White House and call a White House conference in 1970. The report also recommended that the president change many executive branch policies, including reforming administration of executive order No. 11,246, prohibiting discrimination by government contractors and "manpower" training programs and requiring collection and publication of all statistical data by sex.

The task force also recommended, justifying each action, that President Nixon propose legislation to ratify the equal rights amendment (ERA), strengthen Title VII of the 1964 Civil Rights Act and the Equal Pay Act, provide remedies for discrimination in education and public accommodations, remove sex inequities in the Social Security Act, provide federal assistance for child care, guarantee women employees' husbands and children the same fringe benefits provided for male employees' wives and children, provide federal grants on a matching basis to state commissions on the status of women, and allow tax deductions for employees with responsibilities for child care or dependents with disabilities.

The White House ignored the report, not publishing it at the time other task force reports were published. There were rumors that some adviser to the president thought it was Communistic. The Congress, led by the women members, nonetheless adopted many of the recommendations, including ERA, passage of Title IX of the 1972 Education Amendments prohibiting sex discrimination in education, and tax deductions for child care. The White House did not oppose these laws.

A warning, never heeded until recently, was made in support of the recommended reforms in "manpower" training programs to give young women equal attention with young men, lest girls living in disadvantaged circumstances find their path to employment blocked and they and their children forced into welfare. PTFWRR noted that stability for low-income families and any hope of moving into the middle class depended on two-paycheck families and hence on training women as well as men for employment.

WB's fiftieth anniversary conference in 1970 brought together 1,100 women, the largest, most widely representative, best-informed group of women yet assembled in the United States to consider women's status. PTFWRR's report was distributed and discussed by an assemblage including members of the Governors' Commission on the Status of Women, leaders of women's organizations, minority women, union women, women on welfare, and students. Conferees approved most of the task force's recommendations, among them the one minority recommendation to extend Fair Labor Standards Act Coverage.

On January 22, 1971, Congressman Abner R. Mikva (R-IL) introduced H.R. 916, a bill to carry out PTFWRR's recommendations. Hearings in the ninety-second Congress in March and April were held on it at the same time as House hearings on ERA. Some opponents of the amendment sought unsuccessfully to have it considered as a substitute for ERA. The committee took no action on H.R. 916. ERA was reported with a recommendation for passage.

ELECTORAL ACTIVITIES

A governmental organization, PTFWRR engaged in no electoral activity.

FURTHER INFORMATION

The PTFWRR report was published by the Government Printing Office. It is now out of print. A copy appeared in the hearings before subcommittee No. 4 of the Committee on the Judiciary, House of Representatives, 92d Cong., 1st Sess. on H.R. Res. 35, 208, and Related Bills, and H.A. and Related Bills, March 24, 25, April 1, 2, and 5, 1971.

CATHERINE EAST

U.S. DEPARTMENT OF LABOR WOMEN'S BUREAU (DOL WB)
200 Constitution Avenue, NW
Room S3002
Washington, DC 20010
(202) 219-6611
FAX (202) 219-5529

Working out of the U.S. Department of Labor (DOL), the Women's Bureau (WB) serves as the principal spokesperson for the country's over 52 million working women.

ORIGIN AND DEVELOPMENT

During the forty years leading up to WB's establishment, studies carried out by private foundations, reform groups, and newspapers revealed the ways in which wage work posed a threat to adequate mothering. This investigatory impetus peaked in 1910–14 with the publication of the nineteen-volume Senate-commissioned report, *Women and Child Earners*. During World War I, the federal government created the Women-in-Industry Service Women's Bureau to facilitate women's insertion into war industries. Reformers seized on this experiment's success to press for a permanent office to monitor and advocate for working women. Organizations such as the Women's Trade Union League

(WTUL) and National Consumer's League (NCL) successfully lobbied the Congress, which reluctantly voted to create WB.

WB's establishment in June 1920, within DOL, created a bureau responsible for investigating and improving opportunities, wages, and working conditions for women in the labor force. The appointment as WB's first director of Mary Anderson, a former shoe worker and WTUL leader, established the agency's activist credentials. Throughout its more than seventy-year existence, WB has developed numerous program initiatives, some responding to governmental needs and others to concerns expressed by working women.

Throughout the 1920s, WB focused many of its efforts on supporting protective legislation for women workers and opposing the equal rights amendment (ERA) proposed by the National Woman's Party.* Toward this end, WB initiated a study, released in 1928, *The Effects of Labor Legislation on the Employment of Women,* which concluded that in the majority of cases protective legislation benefited women workers. Many experts questioned the validity of these conclusions; but the fact they affirmed the prevailing ideology of women's primary responsibility in the home guaranteed the study's acceptance by workers, labor leaders, and reformers alike. Neither WB staff nor their supporters understood that protective legislation had the effect of isolating women workers from the mainstream labor movement and continuing their segregation into low-wage, lower-status job categories.

The Great Depression shaped the types of studies that WB undertook during the 1930s. The public discourse during the early 1930s posited that one way to remedy overall unemployment would be for working women to give their jobs to men. In fact, Norman Cousins thought it *the* way in 1939. DOL secretary Frances Perkins and WB director Anderson countered this argument with statistics demonstrating that most working women were single, widowed, or supporting disabled, unemployed husbands. Nevertheless, the 1932 amendments to the federal Economy Act, (section 313) decreed that in the event of personnel reductions, women would lose their jobs if their spouse held a job with the federal government. The act was misused, and many employers fired women indiscriminately.

Other bureau studies during the period pointed out the paradox of occupational segregation emerging from the 1920s and protecting women in the 1930s as employers often preferred women over men for certain jobs in the domestic and clerical areas as well as in the growing light manufacturing areas brought about by modernized equipment's introduction. Bureau director Anderson spoke out frequently about the continuing, widespread problem of differential wages and wage distinctions made on the basis of artificial job classifications. She pointed out that even government employers such as the Civil Works Administration and Works Progress Administration had gender-based wage differentials. Moves to drive women back into the home during the 1930s did not prevent women from solidifying their place in the workforce.

WB had little success influencing policies on women's labor during World

War II or in the immediate postwar period. The powerful War Manpower Commission denied the bureau representation, forcing Anderson and her successor, Frieda Miller, to go through the Women's Advisory Committee and Management-Labor Committee with their suggestions. Undaunted, WB continued its investigations on women's wages and working conditions and explored ways to prepare women workers for the inevitable layoffs at war's end. In 1945, WB joined with WTUL to mount an energetic, but for years unsuccessful, campaign in support of an Equal Pay Act. In the early postwar period, Miller aggressively looked for ways to keep women in the workforce; she used the cold war mentality to convince policymakers that it would be a disaster to lose the skills of trained women workers who might be necessary for future war production. The recognition of women workers as essential for national economic well-being marked a major shift in attitude for WB and DOL, which would become more pronounced in subsequent decades.

During the 1950s under the leadership of Alice Leopold, WB increasingly became more a part of DOL's bureaucratic structure and less a maverick agency supported by a coalition of outside interest groups such as WTUL and NCL, as had been the case in the past. WB began to develop studies and programs aimed at understanding how the nation could better use its women workers and how assumptions about women's role limited their opportunities. It began to include representatives from women's civic organizations and organized labor as well as from management in discussions such as the 1955 White House Conference on Effective Uses of Womenpower. In 1954, it signaled another shift from the past when it dropped its opposition to ERA, but it came short of endorsing it.

During the 1960s, the civil rights movement and burgeoning women's rights movement brought equity issues to the fore as they had not been for several decades. In 1961, John Kennedy created the President's Commission on the Status of Women,* which Dollie L. Robinson helped to set up. In 1962, the Kennedy administration outlawed discrimination in the federal civil service and in 1963 pushed the Equal Pay Act through the Congress. When the 1964 Civil Rights Act came to a vote, the word "sex" was left in the legislation because two women legislators threatened to hold up the entire bill unless it was left in. These and other pieces of job equity legislation that WB supported during the 1960s forced WB to confront its traditional support of incremental equality and protective legislation for women workers. This position had kept WB from advocating for ERA, even though it dropped its opposition in 1954. Finally, in 1970, WB endorsed the concept of ERA. Reflecting the anti-ERA bias of the Reagan administration, the first Reagan appointee as WB director was Leonora Cole-Alexander, an African American woman opposing ERA. Throughout the eighties and into 1992, WB officially opposed ERA.

ORGANIZATION AND FUNDING

In the 1970s, the WB director was raised to the level of assistant secretary of labor but did not have the title or pay associated with that position. The director is a political appointee; during the Bush administration the director was Elsie Vartanian. WB's headquarters are located in the DOL building in Washington, D.C. It has ten regional offices scattered throughout the country and employs about eighty people. The annual budget for it ranges between $7 and $8 million, with approximately half a million going to fund the National Network of Displaced Homemakers.

POLICY CONCERNS AND TACTICS

WB's ability to influence top policy decisions at DOL is very much determined by the director's relationship to the labor secretary. The current secretary, Lynn Martin, does not have free rein to select her own top policy people but rather must select them from a list of approved candidates sent to her by White House staff. The federal Paper Reduction Act of the early 1980s had a chilling effect on WB's ability to influence policy, because it cut down on the bureau's ability to assess women workers' needs and conditions through surveys and conference feedback forms.

In the decades 1960–80, women entered the workforce in ever growing numbers. WB began to focus more on its efforts to develop programs enhancing women's educational level and providing job-related skills for professional and unskilled workers alike. Recognition of the need to move women into nontraditional jobs, which often have higher pay and fringe benefits, has become another focus for WB. Especially during the 1970s, WB took an important role in working with minority and unemployed women, helping them to find and keep jobs, often through developing model programs. During the 1980s, WB facilitated, through grants, a series of conferences on the new Job Training Partnership Act to focus on women's needs. This was the only federal money available to train low-income people, and the level was dramatically lower than for similar earlier programs in earlier administrations.

In recent years WB has moved into working on issues such as balancing the often conflicting demands of work and family, employer-sponsored child care systems, older women's and displaced homemakers' needs, and women veterans' employment needs. The director mandated that the regional offices organize during fall 1992 presentations on the glass ceiling.

In the 1980s, WB took a position in opposition to affirmative action, pay equity, and mandated maternal/family leave policies. Generally, WB's positions on policy issues have reflected those of the administration in the eighties and early nineties.

During the eighties WB lost status within government and with its natural constituent groups. The Paper Reduction Act made it impossible to conduct significant current research on working women's conditions. The turnover rate and caliber of WB directors did not add to the bureau's prestige to influence decisions at top levels. The positions the administration forced WB to adopt on a range of issues diminished the bureau's status and effectiveness among traditional constituent groups in the women's liberation movement and among labor groups. Consequently, in 1992, it was not clear where there was organized support for WB because so many of its official policies ran counter to the position of constituent groups, such as women's rights and service organizations and the labor movement.

ELECTORAL ACTIVITIES

As an agency in the executive branch of the U.S. government, WB participates in no electoral activities. Although technically nonpartisan, in reality WB programming and the policies it advocates or ignores reflect the current administration's ideology.

FURTHER INFORMATION

WB has available without charge single copies of booklets, including a *Directory of Nontraditional Training and Employment Programs Serving Women* (1991) and fact sheets such as "Women Workers: Outlook to 2005" (1992), "Earning Difference between Women and Men" (1990), and "State Maternity/ Paternity Leave Laws" (1990). Other fact sheets concern black women and women of Hispanic origin in the workforce ("La Mujer de Origin Hispano en la Fuenza Laboral") and women business owners of Native American/Alaska Native, Asian American, black, and Hispanic origin. WB also distributes a pamphlet, *Preventing Sexual Harassment in the Workplace.*

CYNTHIA J. LITTLE

WISCONSIN WOMEN'S COUNCIL (WWC)
16 North Carroll Street
Suite 720
Madison, WI 53702
(608) 266-2219
FAX (608) 266-5046

The Wisconsin Women's Council (WWC), which succeeded after six years the Wisconsin Commission on the Status of Women (WCSW), has provided leadership for women by identifying problems, creating public awareness, influencing policy, and cooperating with other organizations.

ORIGIN AND DEVELOPMENT

Following President Kennedy's Commission on the Status of Women* (PCSW), Wisconsin governor John Reynolds, a Democrat, created the Wisconsin commission in May 1964 when asked by a small group of women. The thirty-four-citizen/member commission was charged to investigate the conditions and quality of life of Wisconsin women and to work toward substantive changes designed to improve their status and ability to participate in society. Throughout WCSW's existence, membership represented diverse constituencies including labor, education, farming, religions, and public servants, with minority representation increasing over time. Minority members of the first commission were

Edith Finlayson, Ardie Halyard, and Sarah Scott. Other members include Catherine Conroy, Ervin Bruner, Nancy Knaak, Cynthia Stokes, and Geraldine Hinkel. Kathryn Clarenbach chaired the commission throughout its existence; and Norma Briggs served as executive director during the 1970s. Appointments were neither contentious nor highly partisan. Four governors of both parties selected members primarily from lists developed by the commission's executive committee.

Republican governor Lee Dreyfus terminated the commission June 30, 1979, substituting the Governor's Advocacy Office for Women and Family Initiatives, headed by Marlene Cummings; but Democratic governor Anthony Earl and the legislature created the WWC in 1983 through Wisconsin Act 27. The act stipulated a three-way appointing authority for WWC's fifteen members; first, the governor or his designee and six public members appointed by the governor, then two public members appointed by the president of the Senate, and two Senate members and two assembly members. Thus configured, the legislature and governor share control of the council and take an active part in it. The agenda and debate have become decidedly partisan as a result. Also, institutional politics enters through bicameral and legislative/executive routes. This model makes the council quite different in character from the commission, yet both have served as models for other states.

Importantly, as WCSW chairman, Clarenbach attended the national meetings for the commissions sponsored by the federal government from 1964 to 1968. At the 1966 meeting, when conference organizers refused to allow commission representatives to introduce a motion for action, Clarenbach joined others in forming the National Organization for Women* (NOW). For a time, Clarenbach housed both NOW and WCSW in her University of Wisconsin Extension office.

ORGANIZATION AND FUNDING

As a statutory body, WWC has certain advantages over an executive entity. WCSW survived by the governor's graces. WWC takes an act of legislature to abolish. Additionally, statutory bodies have longevity and improved operating resources. WWC began operation in 1984 in an office adjacent to the capitol. Hannah Rosenthal served as WWC executive director from its inception until 1992, when Eilene DeGrand Mershart assumed the position. Longtime program assistant, Donna Chan, and a retinue of interns continue.

Like WCSW, WWC has benefited from diverse membership, and up until recently at least one farm woman, African American, Hispanic, and Native American have served simultaneously. Of the forty-five members appointed from 1984, 29 percent have been women of color. Initial appointments included Tresa Malone, Alma Rose Gonzales, and Ada Deer. Under the smaller WWC, the stakes have increased for council seats; appointment responsibility is shared; and partnership is central. WWC has attracted more political interest, but the price may be diminished diversity.

WCSW struggled for resources. Initially, the University of Wisconsin system provided most operating expenses, although WCSW was granted $1,000 annually from 1968 to 1972. For the 1973–74 biennium, WCSW was allocated $40,000 in general funds and received a substantial increase in 1975 that garnered opposition from groups such as Happiness of Women. The 1984 WWC budget of $95,300 has been sustained since.

POLICY CONCERNS AND TACTICS

WWC plays a central role in policy development, as did WCSW. Legislators and the governor's surrogate, usually a key staff aide, now dominate agenda formation and choice of tactics, although other members continue to contribute meaningfully. This tendency has exacerbated since Republican governor Tommy Thompson began a practice of appointing Republican legislators as commission chair. Similarly charged to eliminate barriers to women's equality, the council followed the commission's practice of enabling policy development by monitoring agency rules and legislation; providing information through published reports; educating the public, agencies, and elected officials through speaking engagements, public forums, dialogues, and jawboning; passing resolutions; and mobilizing constituencies. Moral suasion and timely, accurate information remain primary resources for influence. The formal involvement of elected officials and WWC's explicit charge to initiate legislation distinguish its influence tactics from those of WCSW. Interaction with the legislative agenda has increased; and the executive director is charged to lobby, testify, and advocate for women. A formal and close working relationship exists between WWC and branches of state government.

WCSW always provided leadership for women. In 1971, it took positions on bills pertaining to birth control, protective labor laws, divorce reform, and unemployment compensation for maternity, among others. It initiated action on issues including abortion law repeal, maternity leave, welfare, sex education, day care, services for pregnant schoolgirls, and the appointment of women to state board commissions as well as high executive office. It held seminars and conferences for tribal women and homemakers. Broad activism, quiet negotiation, and use of media were essential. Legislators now frequently ask WWC to take stands, but with increased partisanship, deadlocks on the council have become more common in arenas of reproductive freedom and welfare reform especially. Nonetheless, WWC has provided leadership in arenas that include removing the barriers of poverty, comparable worth, teen pregnancy prevention, farm women, family leave, and women in business and the economy.

Since its inception WCSW/WWC have focused on politics to assure economic opportunities and women's independence. This area figures as Director Mershart's top priority. Educational opportunities and job training persist as critical areas, although the issues continue to evolve. Reproductive freedom, especially teen pregnancy prevention, has dominated the last decade.

WWC, like WCSW before it, coordinates issue advocacy with other groups. Sarah Harder, the first WWC chair, set the tone for joint efforts, especially with such consistent allies as the National Women's Political Caucus,* National Organization for Women,* League of Women Voters,* and Wisconsin Women's Network. Labor, farm, minority, and children's advocacy groups have figured predominantly since WCSW's inception.

ELECTORAL ACTIVITIES

As an agency in the state executive branch, WWC engages in no electoral activity. The partisan composition of the governorship and legislature determines the extent to which discussions become partisan battles since the council member appointments are now split between the institutions.

FURTHER INFORMATION

WCSW first report, *Wisconsin Women* (1965), included recommendations for disadvantaged persons, education, family, employment, citizen participation, and legal rights. Handbooks were published in 1968 and 1974 to guide other commissions. WCSW published landmark works about women and the law, marital property, credit, economic concerns, careers, and a directory of women's groups. Many of these works continue to be revised by the council.

GEORGIA DUERST-LAHTI

APPENDIX II:
QUESTIONNAIRE SENT TO
WOMEN'S INTEREST
GROUPS

———————— / ————————

History

1. Some background on your organization will be helpful. Would you briefly describe your organization's founding?

    _____

    _____

    _____

    _____

    _____

    _____

2. In what year was your organization founded?_____

    _____

3. In talking about your organization's development since 1960, which statement listed below best describes how your organization began? Choose the statement that best describes your organization's beginning.

    ❑ A. The idea for the group and much of the original organization was due to one individual.

    ❑ B. The idea for the group and much of the original organization were due to a few people (less than ten) with one individual acting as a leader or chief organizer.

    ❑ C. The idea for the group and much of the original organization were due to a few people (less than ten) with no one individual acting as leader or chief organizer.

    ❑ D. The idea for the group and much of the original organization were due to several people (over ten) with one individual acting as leader or chief organizer.

    ❑ E. The idea for the group and much of the original organization were due to several people (over ten) with no one individual acting as leader or chief organizer.

    If B, C, D or E, did the organizers know about each other in another organizational context?   ❑   YES   ❑   NO

    If yes, please tell me the name of the earlier organization, or describe it?

    _____

    _____

    _____

    _____

    _____

4. Did any particular issue or event move the organizers to action?

□   YES   □   NO

If yes, please describe what moved them.

_____

_____

_____

_____

_____

_____

5. Would you name a few key founders?

_____

_____

_____

6. If your is a majority white group, then please name any minority founders.

_____

_____

_____

7. If your organization is no longer active, in what year did it become inactive?

_____

Why did it become inactive?_____

_____

_____

_____

8. How would you characterize the group whose interests your organization represents?

_____

_____

_____

9. How would you describe the general goals of your organization?

_____

_____

_____

10. Since your organization was founded, have its goals stayed about the same, or have they changed in important ways?

    ❑ Goals have <u>not</u> changed.

    ❑ Goals have changed.

    If goals have changed, please tell me why and how they have changed.

    _____

    _____

    _____

    _____

    _____

    _____

11. Have new organizations evolved from yours?

    ❑   YES   ❑   NO

    Their names?

    _____

    _____

12. Would you tell me something about your organization's historical development, especially since 1960? Please use the back of this page if you need it.

    _____

    _____

    _____

    _____

    _____

    _____

    _____

    _____

    _____

    _____

    _____

    _____

    _____

Organization and Founding

1. In their early stages, organizations often are helped in getting established by financial grants and other kinds of assistance. Did your organization receive help from any of these sources in getting started?

	YES	NO	If 'YES,' please identify the sources.
A. Private foundation grants	❑	❑	_____
B. Trade unions	❑	❑	_____
C. Churches	❑	❑	_____
D. Other associations	❑	❑	_____
E. Corporations or businesses	❑	❑	_____
F. Government agencies	❑	❑	_____
G. Lg. contributions from a few persons	❑	❑	No identification necessary
H. Sm. contributions from many people	❑	❑	No identification necessary
I. Other (please specify)	❑	❑	_____

2. After getting started, organizations receive financial support from many different sources. For each of the sources listed below, please estimate the percentage which seems most like that source's contribution to your group's total financial support during the last fiscal year.

A. Membership Dues	none	1%	20%	40%	60%	80%	100%
B. Revenues other than dues for publication sales or advertising	none	1%	20%	40%	60%	80%	100%
C. Conventions, conferences or exhibitions	none	1%	20%	40%	60%	80%	100%
D. Sale of merchandise	none	1%	20%	40%	60%	80%	100%
E. Commission from insurance sales	none	1%	20%	40%	60%	80%	100%
F. Grants or contracts from gov. agencies	none	1%	20%	40%	60%	80%	100%
G. Gifts or grants from corp. or bus.	none	1%	20%	40%	60%	80%	100%
H. Gifts or bequests beyond dues from individuals	none	1%	20%	40%	60%	80%	100%
I. Foundation grants	none	1%	20%	40%	60%	80%	100%
J. Loans	none	1%	20%	40%	60%	80%	100%
K. Funds from churches	none	1%	20%	40%	60%	80%	100%
L. Funds from trade unions	none	1%	20%	40%	60%	80%	100%
M. Fundraising events such as concerts, parties, or theatrical events	none	1%	20%	40%	60%	80%	100%
N. Other (please specify) _____	none	1%	20%	40%	60%	80%	100%

3. Does this association have tax exempt status under the U.S. Internal Revenue Code?

   ☐ No   ☐ Yes, 501 (c) (3)

   ☐ Yes, 501 (c) (4)   ☐ Yes, Other (please specify) _____

4. Are contributions to your organization tax deductible? _____

5. Some organizations like yours are made up of organizations or organizational representatives, such as chief officers or professional caucuses, and other organizations are made up of individuals representing themselves. Some organizations are a mixture of both of these. Which membership classification describes your organization best?

   ☐ Membership made up of organizations or organizational representatives.

   ☐ Membership that mixes organizations/organizational representatives and individuals.

   ☐ Membership made up of individuals.

   ☐ Not a membership organization.

6. Presently, what is your organization's total membership count? _____

7. How many members did your organization have during the years listed below?

   1960 _____   1975 _____

   1965 _____   1980 _____

   1970 _____   1985 _____

8. Does your organization have any state and local chapters?

   ☐   YES   ☐   NO

   How many local/state affiliates does your organization have? In how many different states?

   _____

   _____

9. Does your group have any intermediate structure between the national and local/state affiliates?

   ☐   YES   ☐   NO

10. Is your organization represented outside the U.S.? If so, where?

   _____

   _____

11. Is there a Washington, D.C. office? _____ Date opened? _____

12. Does your organization have other offices? _____ Where?

_____

_____

_____

13. Do your headquarters have an executive director? _____

14. How many professional staff does your organization employ? _____
    In Washington, D.C.? _____ Nation-wide? _____

15. How many volunteers or student interns serve in your organization's
    Washington, D.C. office?

    _____

16. Some organizations find it useful to give their workers a chance to fill jobs in
    which the level of responsibility varies. Other organizations describe their
    jobs in terms that basically do not change. Choose the description below that
    best characterizes your organization's Washington, D.C. office.

    ❐ Our workers rotate jobs and experience different levels of
       responsibility.

    ❐ Our workers take on a fixed level of responsibility and do not rotate
       jobs.

    ❐ Other (Please specify) _____

       _____

       _____

17. How is ability rewarded in your organization's Washington, D.C. office?

    _____

    _____

    _____

    _____

18. How many people in your organization hold the job title, lobbyist? _____

19. Does your organization have an attorney on retainer?

                          ❐   YES   ❐   NO
    A legal defense-education fund?
                          ❐   YES   ❐   NO

20.   Members join an organization for many reasons. Benefits or activities may encourage them to join. Other benefits or activities either will not be available or do not play a large role in encouraging people to become members. Please mark on the scale below the significance you believe a given benefit or activity may have in attracting members to your organization. A '5' indicates one of the Most important benefits/activities and a '1' indicates that you feel it is one of the Least important benefits/activities.

	most important 5	4	3	2	least important 1	not provided
A. Publications or other information	O	O	O	O	O	O
B. Development of organizational skills	O	O	O	O	O	O
C. Conferences and meetings	O	O	O	O	O	O
D. Low cost insurance	O	O	O	O	O	O
E. Advocacy of important values, ideas or policies	O	O	O	O	O	O
F. Communication with peers or colleagues	O	O	O	O	O	O
G. Consciousness-raising sessions	O	O	O	O	O	O
H. Information/research	O	O	O	O	O	O
I. Legal help	O	O	O	O	O	O
J. Representation of member's opinions to gov't	O	O	O	O	O	O
K. Chance to participate in public affairs	O	O	O	O	O	O
L. Friendship ties	O	O	O	O	O	O
M. Opportunity to exercise influence within your org.	O	O	O	O	O	O
N. Chance to associate with similarly minded people	O	O	O	O	O	O
O. Other (please specify)_____	O	O	O	O	O	O
_____	O	O	O	O	O	O

21. A. Women make up what percentage of your organization's membership?

%_____   1989-90

%_____   1980 (or first year thereafter that organization existed)

%_____   1970 (or first year thereafter that organization existed)

%_____   1960 (or first year thereafter that organization existed)

B. At present, what percentage of your organization's officers and board members are women?

_____

C. Is your board of directors racially mixed?

1) Percentage of board members who are African American? _____

2) Percentage of board members who are Hispanic? _____

3) Percentage of board members who are Asian-American? _____

4) Percentage of board members who are White Anglo-Saxon? _____

D. In your organization, is effort made to encourage participation on the board of persons from lower income strata?   ☐ YES ☐ NO

of persons with disabilities?   ☐ YES ☐ NO

of older women? ☐ YES ☐ NO

of lesbians? ☐ YES ☐ NO

22. Has one issue discussed in your organization concerned its status as a women-only or women-mainly group, if it is either of these?

☐ YES   ☐ NO

23. If your organization is a women-only or women-mainly group, will it remain so?

☐ YES   ☐ NO

24. Is the head of your organization salaried?

☐ YES   ☐ NO

If yes, size of her salary? $_____

Year organization began paying a salary: _____

25. How does the head of your organization obtain her office?

_____

_____

_____

26. Would you please name persons particularly successful in holding
     since 1960?

     _____

     _____

27. Do you have a delegate assembly?

                     ❏   YES   ❏   NO

     If so, briefly, what is its role?

     _____
     _____
     _____
     _____
     _____
     _____

28. Does your organization pay any percentage of expenses for any persons
     attending the delegate assembly?

                     ❏   YES   ❏   NO

     If your organization does help pay people's expenses for the delegate
     assembly, who would be eligible to have their way paid?

     _____

     _____

29. At present, how large is your organization's budget? _____

30. Please would you state the size of your organization's budget for any of the
     following years it was in existance?

     $_____ 1980 (or first year thereafter that organization existed)

     $_____ 1970 (or first year thereafter that organization existed)

     $_____ 1960 (or first year thereafter that organization existed)

31. What are the annual dues for your group?

     $_____ for individuals

     $_____ for corporations

     $_____ for affiliates

Electoral Politics

1. Does your organization see women's issues as partisan ones?

   ☐   YES   ☐   NO

2. If your organization sees women's issues as partisan, are they of greatest interest to:

   ☐ Democrats

   ☐ Republicans

3. Does your organization have a Political Action Committee (PAC)?

   ☐   YES   ☐   NO

4. If your organization does not have a PAC, would you tell us briefly why it has stayed out of this kind of political action?

   _____

   _____

   _____

   _____

   _____

5. If your organization does have a PAC, what is its name?

   _____

   Date of registration with the Federal Election Commission: _____

   Address of PAC office in Washington, D.C.:_____

6. Some background about your PAC would be helpful. Would you briefly describe your PAC's founding?

   _____

   _____

   _____

   _____

7. In talking about your PAC's founding, which phrase below best describes your PAC? Choose the phrase that best describes your PAC.

   ☐ Independent or nonconnected PAC

   ☐ PAC associated with a trade/membership/health organization

   ☐ Labor PAC

   ☐ Other (please specify) _____

8. A. If you are an independent or nonconnected PAC, have you established a nonprofit educational and research foundation as authorized by section 501 (c) (3) of the U.S. Internal Revenue Service Act?

    □ YES   □ NO

    If you have established a nonprofit educational and research foundation, what is its name?

    _____

    B. If you are an independent or nonconnected PAC, have you established a lobbying group as authorized by section 501 (c) (4) of the U.S. Internal Revenue Service Code?

    □ YES   □ NO

    If you have established a lobbying group, what is its name?

    _____

9. A. At present, what are the assets of your PAC?

    _____
    _____
    _____

    B. What were the assets of your PAC in its founding year?

    _____
    _____
    _____

10. After getting underway PACs may raise money in different ways. For each of the methods listed below, please choose the percentage that seems best to describe the amount of the time your PAC relies on that method of raising money.

    A. Personal, face-to-face   none 1% 20% 40% 60% 80% 100%
    B. Direct mail/letters   none 1% 20% 40% 60% 80% 100%
    C. Group seminars   none 1% 20% 40% 60% 80% 100%
    D. Telephone   none 1% 20% 40% 60% 80% 100%
    E. Other (please specify)_____ none 1% 20% 40% 60% 80% 100%

11. A. Does your PAC solicit other PACs?

    □ YES   □ NO

    B. May donors earmark their contribution, that is, specify for what their contribution may be used?

    □ YES   □ NO

12. In recording your PAC's growth, some information about the total
     contributions your PAC has received will be helpful. Please tell us the total
     contributions received by your PAC for each of the election years marked
     below that your PAC was in existence.

$ _____	1960	$ _____	1970	$ _____	1980
$ _____	1962	$ _____	1972	$ _____	1982
$ _____	1964	$ _____	1974	$ _____	1984
$ _____	1966	$ _____	1976	$ _____	1986
$ _____	1968	$ _____	1978	$ _____	1988

13. Many PACs share information about candidates. Does your PAC regularly
     receive information from or go to meetings of any of the organizations listed
     below?   YES NO

     A. Business-Industry PAC (BIPAC)   ❏ ❏
     B. COPE (AFL-CIO)   ❏ ❏
     C. Democratic National Committee (or other Democratic committees)   ❏ ❏
     D. Republican National Committee (or other Republican committees)   ❏ ❏
     E. National Committee for an Effective Congress (NCEC)   ❏ ❏
     F. Free Congress Foundation   ❏ ❏
     G. Other groups (please specify) _____   ❏ ❏

14. Are there standards that candidates must meet to qualify for support from
     your PAC?

                     ❏   YES   ❏   NO

     If there are standards that candidates must meet, would you please briefly
     describe them?

     _____

     _____

     _____

     _____

15. Different PACs may decide in different ways which candidates to support.
     Please choose any of the sources of decision about which candidate to support,
     as listed below, that apply to your PAC.

     ❏ Office staff
     ❏ Head of organization
     ❏ Combined decision by office staff and PAC board
     ❏ PAC board or committee
     ❏ Other (please specify) _____

16. Many PACs communicate regularly with their constituents. Does your PAC
     regularly use any of these means of communication to stay in touch with its
     constituents?   YES NO

     A. Newsletter   ☐ ☐

     B. Meetings or seminars   ☐ ☐

     C. Annual report   ☐ ☐

     D. Other (please specify) _____   ☐ ☐

17. In talking about the decision of which candidates to support, if all else were
     the same between two candidates in the same race, which of the candidates
     listed below would your PAC prefer to support? Choose the candidate
     description that seems best to describe your PAC's decision of which candidate
     to support.

     A. ☐ An incumbent
        ☐ A challenger
        ☐ An open-seat candidate
        ☐ No preference

     B. ☐ A U.S. Senate candidate
        ☐ A U.S. House candidate
        ☐ No preference

     C. ☐ A Republican
        ☐ A Democrat
        ☐ A third-party candidate
        ☐ No preference

     D. ☐ A liberal
        ☐ A conservative
        ☐ A moderate
        ☐ No preference

     E. ☐ A candidate in a marginal race
        ☐ A candidate in a safe race
        ☐ No preference

     F. ☐ A woman
        ☐ A man
        ☐ No preference

18. Does your PAC endorse a candidate for U.S. President?
                              ☐   YES   ☐   NO

Policy and Approaches

1. Could you briefly tell me how you see policy as being set for your organization?

_____

_____

_____

_____

_____

_____

2. There can be a variety of people who influence discussions about policy in an organization. For each of the following possible sources of influence, please give me your best estimate of the importance of that source in policy discussions. A '5' indicates one of the Most important sources, and a '1' indicates that you feel the source is one of the Least important.

		most important 5	4	3	2	least important 1
A.	Professional staff recommendations	○	○	○	○	○
B.	Board of directors discussion	○	○	○	○	○
C.	Executive officers' decisions	○	○	○	○	○
D.	Delegate assembly	○	○	○	○	○
E.	Poll of membership	○	○	○	○	○
F.	Other (please specify)_____	○	○	○	○	○

3. There may be many strategies adopted to influence public policy. Among the following strategies for influencing public policy, how important is each for your organization? A '5' indicates one of the Most important strategies, and a '1' indicates that you feel the strategy is one of the Least important.

		most important 5	4	3	2	least important 1
A.	Testify in congressional hearings	O	O	O	O	O
B.	Supply congresspeople and staff with information	O	O	O	O	O
C.	Testify in state legislative hearings	O	O	O	O	O
D.	Supply state legislators and staff with information	O	O	O	O	O
E.	Make personal presentation to Congressperson, agency head, or staff	O	O	O	O	O
F.	Contribute to political campaigns	O	O	O	O	O
G.	Monitor voting records of elected officials	O	O	O	O	O
H.	Testify at agency/department hearings	O	O	O	O	O
I.	Make written comments on proposed regulations	O	O	O	O	O
J.	Seek administrative review of agency or department decisions	O	O	O	O	O
K.	Educate membership with publications	O	O	O	O	O
L.	Encourage members to write legislators and committees	O	O	O	O	O
M.	Educate public through press releases	O	O	O	O	O
N.	Participate in direct action, political demonstrations	O	O	O	O	O
O.	Contact public decision-makers through influential member	O	O	O	O	O
P.	Conduct and publish research on issues	O	O	O	O	O
Q.	Field public relations or public service campaign	O	O	O	O	O
R.	File court cases	O	O	O	O	O
S.	File amicus briefs	O	O	O	O	O
T.	Litigate cases	O	O	O	O	O
U.	Coordinate with similar organizations	O	O	O	O	O

4. Once your organization decides to become active on an issue, tell me how you would develop strategy for the specific problem.

_____

_____

_____

_____

5. Organizations sometimes coordinate with similar groups. Tell me three groups your organization would most likely work with on issues of common concern.

_____

_____

_____

6. How long would you say your organization has worked with each of these groups on issues of common concern?

_____

_____

7. Please name three groups you would see as adversaries of your organization on women's issues.

_____

_____

_____

8. How often do you find one or more of these adversarial groups working against issues of concern to your organization?

_____

_____

9. Sometimes members of a legislative body, agency heads and their staff will come to an organization to solicit views on a policy matter. How often do public policymakers come to your organization for views on a policy matter?

_____

_____

_____

_____

_____

10. For each of the following federal laws, please indicate on the scale provided the law's importance to your organization today. A '5' indicates one of the Most important laws, and a '1' indicates that you feel the law is one of the Least important.

		most important 5	4	3	2	least important 1
A.	Equal Pay Act of 1963	O	O	O	O	O
B.	Civil Rights Act of 1964	O	O	O	O	O
C.	Equal Opportunity Act of 1964	O	O	O	O	O
D.	Food Stamp Act of 1964	O	O	O	O	O
E.	Administration on Aging Act of 1965	O	O	O	O	O
F.	Voting Rights Act	O	O	O	O	O
G.	Federal Jury Reform Act of 1968	O	O	O	O	O
H.	Affirmative Action Orders	O	O	O	O	O
I.	Antidiscrimination in Housing Act of 1968	O	O	O	O	O
J.	Revised Uniform Reciprocal Enforcement of Support Agreement Act of 1968	O	O	O	O	O
K.	Food Stamp Reform Act of 1970	O	O	O	O	O
L.	School Lunch Act of 1970	O	O	O	O	O
M.	Act of 1972 in which sex discrimination was added to Civil Rights Commission jurisdiction	O	O	O	O	O
N.	Equal Employment Act of 1972	O	O	O	O	O
O.	Title IX of the Education Amendments of 1972	O	O	O	O	O
P.	Equal Rights Constitutional Amendment	O	O	O	O	O
Q.	SALT Agreements	O	O	O	O	O
R.	Reed v. Reed, Frontiero v. Richardson, and Craig v. Boren	O	O	O	O	O
S.	Roe v. Wade	O	O	O	O	O
T.	War Powers Act of 1973	O	O	O	O	O
U.	Equal Credit Opportunity Act of 1974	O	O	O	O	O

		most important 5	4	3	2	least important 1
V.	Housing and Community Development Act of 1974	O	O	O	O	O
W.	Legal Services Act of 1974	O	O	O	O	O
X.	Office of Economic Opportunity Act of 1974	O	O	O	O	O
Y.	Social Services Act of 1974	O	O	O	O	O
Z.	Women's Educational Equity Act of 1974	O	O	O	O	O
AA.	Child Support Amendments– Social Security Act of 1975	O	O	O	O	O
BB.	Day Care Act of 1976	O	O	O	O	O
CC.	Hyde Amendments	O	O	O	O	O
DD.	Human Life Constitutional Amendment	O	O	O	O	O
EE.	Pregnancy Disability Act of 1978	O	O	O	O	O
FF.	Welfare Act of 1982	O	O	O	O	O
GG.	Social Security Act of 1983	O	O	O	O	O
HH.	Pension Equity Act of 1984	O	O	O	O	O
II.	Child Abuse Act of 1984	O	O	O	O	O
JJ.	Child Support Enforcement Act of 1984	O	O	O	O	O
KK.	Age Discrimination Act of 1986	O	O	O	O	O
LL.	Civil Rights Restoration Act of 1988	O	O	O	O	O

11. In the past ten years, what would you say in your organization's view have been the three most important new pieces of legislation or amendments to earlier laws passed on the federal level?

_____

_____

_____

12. What level of influence would you say your organization has had in the passage of these acts or amendments?

_____
_____
_____

13. In the past ten years, what would you say in your organization's view have been the three worst initiatives or changes made to federal laws?

_____
_____
_____

14. To what do you attribute their passage?

_____
_____
_____

15. In the view of your organization, would you say the laws and amendments passed in the 1980s were better or worse than legislation passed in the 1970s?

_____
_____
_____

16. Sometimes organizations produce publications. Please tell me what kinds, if any, of publications your organization produces.
   ❐ Research reports
   ❐ Newsletter for membership
   ❐ Journal for public sale/consumption
   ❐ Direct mail
   ❐ Other (please specify)_____

INDEX

/

Page numbers in **bold** refer to main entries.

CONTRIBUTORS

/

Davida J. Alperin is an assistant professor at the University of Wisconsin—River Falls, where she teaches political science and women's studies. Her essay ''Social Diversity and the Necessity of Alliances'' appears in *Bridges of Power*, edited by Lisa Albrecht and Rose M. Brewer.

Carol J. Auster is associate professor of sociology at Franklin and Marshall College, with interests in gender and occupations. She is currently working on a longitudinal Study of Woman in Engineering funded by a grant from the Alfred P. Sloan Foundation.

Diana E. Axelsen taught philosophy for twenty-three years at Spelman College (Atlanta) and California Lutheran University. She now is a production editor at Sage Publications in Thousand Oaks, California.

Eleanor J. Bader is a journalist and teacher whose writing often appears in ''Belles Lettres,'' ''The Guardian,'' ''New Directions for Women,'' and other progressive feminist publications.

Martha Bailey is an assistant professor in the political science department, Southern Illinois University at Edwardsville. Her research interests include class, politics, and social movements.

Robert W. Bailey is associate professor of political science, Rutgers University. His main research interests include urban politics, education policy and public sector financial management. He has held several positions in New York City government and has been active in the Gay and Lesbian Caucus for Political Science.

Anne L. Barstow taught European history at the State University of New York College at Old Westbury for over twenty years and has written a gender analysis of the European witchcraft persecutions, *Witchcraze: A New History of the European Witch Hunts.*

Janet Bickel joined the American Association of Medical Colleges in 1977 and currently is Assistant Vice-President for Women's Programs. She has published extensively in medical education and teaches a course on issues in health care at George Washington University Health Sciences Center.

Robert E. Biles is professor of political science, Sam Houston State University. He has published *Inter-American Relations* and *Texas Government Today* and has in progress a study of Colombian women and politics. He has served as the Southwestern Social Science Association Women's Caucus President.

Janet K. Boles is associate professor of political science, Marquette University, and a member of the Milwaukee First Unitarian Society. She has written extensively on the equal rights amendment, including *The Politics of the Equal Rights Amendment* (1979).

MaryAnne Borrelli is assistant professor of government, Connecticut College, with interests in abortion politics, lobbying and interest groups.

Robert Brannon is professor of psychology and Director, Center for Sex Role Research, Brooklyn College, City University of New York. He co-edited *The Forty-Nine Percent Majority* (1974). A founder of National Organization for Men Against Sexism,* he co-chairs the organization.

Brandy M. Britton is affiliated with the Institute for Scientific Analysis, San Francisco. She has involved herself in the battered women's movement for several years and has, as one research interest, activism in this movement.

Bonnie Bullough was Dean, School of Nursing, State University of New York at Buffalo. She has written extensively on nursing history and organization. She is affiliated with the department of Nursing, University of Southern California.

Vern L. Bullough, a State University of New York distinguished professor of history, State University College at Buffalo, currently is a visiting professor at the University of Southern California. He has written extensively on nursing history and organization.

Frances Burke is professor of management, Suffolk University, with interests in public administration and organization behavior.

Barbara E. Campbell, Women's Division Assistant General Secretary in Administration, has served since 1985 as a staff member at the General Board of Global Ministries, United Methodist Church.* She authored *United Methodist Women: In the Middle of Tomorrow.*

Mary Chianta Canzoneri is an adjunct social science faculty member, Erie Community College South in Western New York, and an interdisciplinary historian/theorist of labor and women's history.

Patricia Anne Carter teaches and serves as Associate Director of Women's Studies, University of Connecticut at Storrs. Her teaching and research interests include the history of American women teachers, feminist pedagogy, and American women artists.

Harvey Catchen is associate professor of community health and gerontology, State University College at Old Westbury. He has published papers on the politics of aging and health care.

Mariam Chamberlain is an economist by training. She is currently the Founding President and Resident Scholar at the National Council for Research on Women, a working alliance of centers and organizations for feminist research, policy analysis, and educational programs for women and girls.

Joyotpaul Chaudhuri is professor of political science, Arizona State University, and teaches and studies political theory, Amerindian/Native American politics, and South Asia. Together with his family, he is involved in community issues including those involving American Indians on and off reservations.

Bettye Collier-Thomas is associate professor of history and Director, Temple University Center for African American History and Culture. Previously she served as founding Executive Director, Bethune Museum and Archives* National Historic Site. She is project director for "African American Women and the Church: A History," a Lily Endowment funded project to research and write the first narrative history of black church women. Author of over twenty-five scholarly articles, Collier-Thomas has completed a book on *The Howard Theatre and the Black Theatre Movement* as well as a biography of Frances Ellen Watkins Harper.

Elizabeth Adell Cook is visiting assistant professor, American University, co-author of *Between Two Absolutes: Public Opinion and the Politics of Abortion* and co-editor of *The Year of the Woman: Myths and Realities.* She has in progress a book on feminist consciousness in the United States.

Anne Costain is associate professor of political science, University of Colorado, and author of *Inviting Women's Rebellion: A Political Process Interpretation of the Women's Movement.* She currently directs a National Science Foundation sponsored project examining the relationship between the gender gap in voting and mobilization of a U.S. women's movement.

Flora Crater is co-author and publisher of *The Almanac of Virginia Politics* and editor and publisher of ''The Woman Activist.'' A long-time Democratic party activist and leader, she also convened the Northern Virginia chapter of National Organization for Women* and Virginia Women's Political Caucus.* She served as Vice President of the Women's Lobby,* chaired the National Women's Political Caucus* committee for equal right amendment ratification, and in 1973 ran as an independent for Virginia Lieutenant Governor. She is presently serving as Chief Strategist for the ERA Summit Committee.

Vallaurie Crawford is a political scientist working in news journalism since 1978. Her research in the Philippines and Taiwan focuses on the political significance of local literary genres and on censorship issues.

Madeline Davis is the Chief Conservator/Head of Preservation, Buffalo and Erie County Public Library System. A gay rights activist for over 20 years, she co-authored *Boots of Leather, Slippers of Gold: The History of a Lesbian Community* (1993) and has authored and co-authored fiction, short stories, and articles on lesbian history.

Susan Davis is associate professor of economics, State University College at Buffalo, and studies professional sport economics and women's economic status in industrial and post-industrial economics.

Peggy Downes is a professor of American government, Santa Clara University, and has designed nationally recognized pilot courses on the politics of aging, intergenerational conflict and double jeopardy: the politics of age and gender.

Georgia Duerst-Lahti is assistant professor of government and women's studies, Beloit College. She researches questions of gender and power in bureaucracy.

Catherine East served in a senior staff capacity with all the presidential advisory commissions on women, 1962–77, taking responsibility for research and preparation of position papers, publications and reports on many women's issues. From 1983–86, she served as the National Women's Political Caucus* Legislative Director.

Mary Ewens, a Sinsinawa Dominican sister, serves as Executive Director, Conrad Hilton Fund for Sisters. The fund supports Catholic sisters' work among poor people worldwide. Ewens has written studies on the history of Catholic sisterhood, and helped found the History of Women Religious Network, which promotes research and conferences.

Marianne C. Ferguson is assistant professor of philosophy and religious studies, State University College at Buffalo, and writing a textbook, *Women and Religion.*

Terri Susan Fine is associate professor of political science, University of Central Florida. Her teaching and research interests include women and American politics, political parties, public opinion, and research methodology. She has published several articles and book chapters.

Diane L. Fowlkes is professor of political science and director of women's studies, Georgia State University. She has authored *White Political Women: Paths from Privilege to Empowerment* (1992), as well as numerous articles and chapters on women and politics, and co-edited *Feminist Visions: Toward a Transformation of the Liberal Arts Curriculum* (1984). She chaired the American Political Science Association Task Force on Women and American Government, 1981–85, and served the Women's Caucus for Political Science* as President, 1984–85. She was a senior Fulbright Scholar in the United Kingdom, 1985–86.

Siegrun F. Fox is assistant professor of political science and public administration, Texas Tech University. Her research on urban politics, third sector and public personnel has been widely published.

Colleen Frey is an associate professor of consumer and family studies, State University College at Buffalo. She helped establish a national clothing resource center for individuals with physical disabilities.

Shirley Tolliver Geiger is assistant professor of political science, University of South Carolina. She has conducted research and presented papers on the influences of race, gender and class on federal and local housing policy making. She is currently researching the politics of housing policy and welfare reform.

Barbara W. Gerber is Distinguished Service professor of counseling and psychological services, State University College at Oswego. She served the National Women's Studies Association* as Treasurer, 1982–85.

Irwin N. Gertzog teaches political science at Allegheny College. He authored *Congressional Women: Their Recruitment, Integration and Behavior* (1995), among other works.

Ellen Giarelli teaches graduate research methods at Seton Hall University and "Women, Schooling and Society" at Rutgers University. She is a registered nurse, independent scholar, wife, and mother of two. She has contributed to the Women's Project of New Jersey.

Christine H.B. Grant is Athletic Director, University of Iowa, and served as President of both the Association for Intercollegiate Athletics for Women* and National Association of Collegiate Women Athletic Administrators.*

Mary W. Gray is professor of mathematics and statistics, American University, and the author of many books and papers in such fields as mathematics, economic equity, discrimination law, and opera. Gray chairs the American Association of University Professors committee on the status of women in the profession and was the first President of the Association of Women in Mathematics. She also served as President of the Women's Equity Action League.* She is a member of the District of Columbia and U.S. Supreme Court bars.

Sara Ann Grove is assistant professor of government, Shippensburg University. She served as Co-Director of Women's Studies at Frostberg State University from 1991–92.

Sarah Harder serves in the Associate Chancellor's Office, University of Wisconsin at Eau Clair. She has served as President of American Association of University Women* and of Women for Meaningful Summits/USA,* presides over the National Women's Conference Committee,* and helped found the Wisconsin Women's Council.*

Cynthia Harrison serves as Chief of the Federal Judicial History Office, Federal Judicial Center, Washington, D.C. She authored *On Account of Sex: The Politics of Women's Issues 1945–1968* (1988).

Andrew R. Hart has been working toward a graduate degree, University of South Carolina.

Milda K. Hedblom is professor of politics and media, Augsburg College. A lawyer and political scientist, most recently she has served as a policy analyst with the Federal Communications Commission.

Patricia Huckle is Associate Dean, College of Arts and Letters, San Diego State University, where she also teaches women's studies. She authored *Tish*

Sommers, Activist, and the Founding of the Older Women's League (1991), and has published research on affirmative action and public policy issues affecting women.

Krista L. Hughes is employed by Warner Brothers Records.

Megan Isaacs began graduate studies in women's history in the New York City area.

Carolyn Jeskey is a University Fellow, Georgetown University. Her primary interests lie in gender politics and political behavior.

Roberta Ann Johnson is professor of politics, University of San Francisco, where she created and chairs the Public Service Program. She has authored numerous political science articles and a book, *Puerto Rico: Commonwealth or Colony?* She has been a Fulbright Scholar.

Nancy Douglas Joyner directs the Lutheran College Washington Consortium. A former Executive Vice President of the American Association of University Women,* she also has chaired the Women's Conference Network.*

James R. Kelly is professor of sociology, Fordham University. He has published many articles on the social history of the right to life movement.

Mary Lou Kendrigan is professor of social science, Lansing Community College, Michigan. She has authored *Political Equality in a Democratic Society: Women in the United States* and *Political Equality, Women, and the Military,* and edited *Gender Differences: Their Impact on Public Policy.*

Karen M. Kennelly, CSJ, serves as President, Mount St. Mary's College, Los Angeles. She has authored and edited various books and articles on American women on religion.

Michael S. Kimmel is associate professor of sociology, State University of New York at Stony Brook. His books include *Men's Lives* (1989; 2d ed., 1991), *Men Confront Pornography* (1990), and *Against the Tide: Profeminist Men in America, 1776–1990, A Documentary History* (1992). He serves as spokesperson for National Organization for Men against Sexism.*

Dorothy I. Lansing is a medical doctor and Archivist and Librarian to the Philadelphia Obstetrical Society.

Susan Rimby Leighow is an assistant professor of history at Shippensburg University of Pennsylvania. She completed her dissertation "Nurses' Questions/

Women's Questions: The Impact of the Demographic Revolution and Feminism on United States Working Women, 1946–1986'' in 1992. She is the author of ''An 'Obligation to Participate': Married Nurses' Labor Force Participation in the 1950s'' in *Not June Cleaver: Women and Gender in Postwar America, 1945–1960* (1994).

Cynthia J. Little serves as Vice President for Interpretation, The Pennsylvania Historical Society. She has published in the fields of U.S. and Latin American women's history and in public history.

Nancy E. McGlen is a professor of political science and Director of the Social Science Program, Niagara University. She co-authored *Women's Rights: The Struggle for Equality in the 19th and 20th Centuries* (1983) and *Women in Foreign Policy: The Insiders* (1993), as well as *Women, Politics, and American Society* (1995). She has published articles on women in politics and women in political science. She has a book on women and politics in progress.

Joan E. McLean teaches at Ohio Wesleyan University. She has worked for several national organizations including the National Women's Political Caucus,* ERAmerica,* and Women's Campaign Fund.* She advised Geraldine Ferraro during her campaign for Vice President.

Elaine Magalis is a freelance writer and video producer working often for women's national church organizations.

Christine Marin is Curator-Archivist of the Chicano Research Collection in the Hayden Library, Arizona State University, where she also teaches courses in the history of Mexican-American women.

Rita Duarte Marinho is professor of political science and women's studies, University of Massachusetts—Dartmouth. She served as First Vice President of the Young Women's Christian Association* National Board (1986–91).

Oneida Mascarenas is assistant professor of political science, Metropolitan State College in Denver. She has completed a book on Native American Indian political activism in the United States.

Linda Mather is a principal in the consulting firm, Beacon Associates. Previously Interim Dean of the School of the Arts and Communications at William Paterson College, she was also associate director at the New Jersey Department of Higher Education and associate professor of communications at Rowan College. She chaired the New Jersey College and University Coalition on Women's Education. Active in the League of Women Voters, she has served as president of the Princeton Area chapter and as chair of the LWV New Jersey Nominating Committee.

Janna C. Merrick is professor of government and international affairs and Associate Dean for Academic Affairs at the University of South Florida at Sarasota. Her research area is public policy and reproductive rights.

Jimmy Elaine Wilkinson Meyer co-edited, with David D. Van Tassel, *U.S. Aging Policy Interest Groups: Interest Group Profiles.* She is Associate Editor of the *Encyclopedia of Cleveland History/Dictionary of Cleveland Biography.*

Charlotte T. Morgan-Cato is associate professor of black studies, Lehman College, City University of New York at Bronx, where she teaches African history and African American women's history. Current research interests include the adult education efforts of national black women's organizations.

Katherine C. Naff is a senior research analyst with the U.S. Merit Systems Protection Board and is completing a Ph.D. at Georgetown University. Her areas of interest include women and minorities in politics and public administration.

Linda Nieman is a cultural historian, curator, and educational consultant specializing in African American Art. She has underway a biography of Aaron Douglas.

Martha Joy Noble has interests in unusual, sometimes forgotten reform movements. She has led historical and architectural tours and done research for Boston by Foot. She received a master's degree in history from Binghamton University.

Karen O'Connor is professor of political science, Emory University, where she teaches courses on women and the law and conducts research on interest group litigation. Among her many publications are *Women's Organizations' Use of the Courts* (1980), *Public Interest Law Groups: Institutional Profiles* (with Lee Epstein, 1989), and *American Government: Roots and Reform* (with Larry J. Sabato, 1993, 1994, 1995). She has served as President of the Women's Caucus for Political Science* and is an attorney.

Laura Katz Olson is professor of government, Lehigh University. Her publications include *The Political Economy of Aging* (1983), *Aging and Public Policy* (1983), and most recently *The Graying of the World.* She has been a Fulbright Scholar and a Gerontological Fellow.

Jeanne A. Ortiz is Dean of Student Life, Incarnate Word College in San Antonio. She has worked to promote fair housing.

Ellen Pattin is an attorney in private practice since 1978 specializing in family law. She formerly was a lobbyist for National Organization for Women* and the Women's Lobby* and worked with Representative Patricia Schroeder's (D-CO) staff during major federal pension law reform and with Senator Mark Hatfield's (R-OR) office on U.S. Foreign Service pension reform.

Barbara Bennett Peterson is professor of history, University of Hawaii, and the editor of *Notable Women of Hawaii* (1984), author of *America in British Eyes* (1988), co-editor of *The Pacific Region* (1991), and editor of *American History: 17th, 18th and 19th Centuries* (1993) and *America: 19th and 20th Centuries* (1993). She has published over 100 professional journal articles. She was a Senior Fulbright Scholar teaching in Japan and the People's Republic of China.

Barbara L. Poole is associate professor of political science, Eastern Illinois University. Her current research focuses on the role played by women serving in the Illinois General Assembly.

Peter V. Rajsingh is a research fellow, Center for Labor-Management Policy Studies in New York City and an American Civil Liberties Union* equality committee member. He adjunct lectures on politics and constitutional law at City University of New York and New York University.

Mattie L. Rhodes is clinical assistant professor of nursing, State University of New York at Buffalo. Her specialty areas include acute care of the medical surgical adult patient and health care delivery issues.

Alice Sardell is associate professor of urban studies, Queens College, City University of New York. She has authored *The U.S. Experiment in Social Medicine: The Community Health Center Program, 1965–1986* and numerous articles on health care issues and the politics of social policy.

Joan Sayre serves on the Hunter-Bellevue School of Nursing faculty, Hunter College, City University of New York. Her interests include women's history, deviance, and the chronic mentally ill and social movements.

Jean Reith Schroedel is assistant professor of political science, Claremont Graduate School. She authored *Alone in a Crowd: Women in the Trades Tell Their Stories* (1985) and more recently *Congress, the President and Policy-Making Over Time.* She has published numerous articles on race and sex discrimination in employment and decision making within congressional committees.

Debra L. Schultz served as Assistant Director, National Council for Research on Women* from 1990 to 1993. Her current research concerns Jewish women in the southern civil rights movement.

Melissa Schwartz teaches in the psychology department, Sonoma State University. Her teaching and research interests include the psychology of women and women's adult development. She is also a clinical psychologist in private practice.

Mary C. Segers is professor and chair of the political science department, Rutgers University at Newark. Her most recent book is *The Catholic Church and the Politics of Abortion: A View from the States* (co-edited, 1992).

Sarah Slavin is professor of political science and a former Women's Studies Unit Coordinator, State University College at Buffalo. She has authored an intellectual history of feminism in the United States (1979) and co-authored a history of attitudes toward women (1988), as well as published articles and chapters about public law and jurisprudence and women and politics. She edited Volume 8 of the *Female Studies Series* (1975) and the journal *Women & Politics* (1979–86). She has served as President of the Women's Caucus for Political Science* and Seneca Falls National Women's Center and Educational Institute, Co-president of Remove Intoxicated Drivers* Niagara Frontier chapter and Co-coordinator of the Gay and Lesbian Caucus for Political Science. In the mid 1970s she was part of National Organization for Women's* national leadership. She is working on a volume on lesbian and gay citizenship politics in the United States.

Gertrude A. Steuernagel is professor of political science at Kent State University. She is co-editor of *Foundations for a Feminist Restructuring of the Academic Disciplines* and co-author of *Women and Public Policy: A Revolution in Progress*.

Genie L. Stowers is a political scientist and associate professor in the Public Administration Program, San Francisco State University. Her research concerns how politically marginalized groups such as women and ethnic, racial and life-style minorities are able to influence public policy and the political process. This work emphasizes domestic violence policy issues.

Yolanda Tarango, CCVI, serves as Councilor in the General Administration, Sisters of Charity of the Incarnate Word. She has co-founded and co-directed Visitation House, a transitional residence for homeless women and children. As former National Coordinator of LAS HERMANAS* and co-author of *Hispanic Women: Prophetic Voice in the Church* (1988), Tarango is recognized nationally for her work on issues of Latina women in church and society. She is active in the National Assembly of Religious Women.*

Susan L. Thomas is assistant professor of political science, Oakland University. Her research interests include gender politics, women in poverty and public policy and she wrote a book on *Gender and Poverty* (1994).

Joan Hulse Thompson co-chairs the political science department, Beaver College. She worked at the Congressional Caucus for Women's Issues* during summer 1983 on research funded by the American Association of University Women.* In 1985–86, she was an American Political Science Association Congressional Fellow.

Sue Tolleson-Rinehart is professor of political science, Texas Tech University. She authored *Gender Consciousness and Politics* (1992), and most recently co-authored *Claytie and the Lady: Gender in the Political Crucible* (1994). She has written numerous articles and book chapters on women and politics.

Laura Van Assendelft is an assistant professor of political science at Mary Baldwin College, where she teaches courses on women and politics and conducts research on state politics.

Judy Vaughan is National Coordinator, National Assembly of Religious Women.* She identifies herself as a feminist and an activist.

Richard A. Wandling is assistant professor of political science, Eastern Illinois University. He has practical experience in labor, serving as a chapter executive board officer in an American Federation of Teachers affiliated local.

Cathy Werner has done research for the Maternal and Child Health Bureau, South Carolina Health and Environmental Control Department, and served on state and local boards of the American Association of University Women* and League of Women Voters.* She volunteers in a local Planned Parenthood* affiliate.

Leigh Ann Wheeler did doctoral studies in history at the University of Minnesota, including dissertation research on women's antipornography activism.

Lynne M. White taught in the consumer science field for nine years and worked with Cornell Cooperative Extension of Erie County, New York, before her untimely death in 1992.

Clyde Wilcox is associate professor of government, Georgetown University. He has co-authored *Between Two Absolutes: Public Opinion and the Politics of Abortion* and co-edited *The Year of the Woman: Myths and Realities.* He writes on gender politics, religion and politics, and campaign finance.

Leonard Williams is associate professor of political science, Manchester College, where he chairs the history and political science department. He writes often on the subject of political ideologies and co-edits *Political Theory: Classic Writings, Contemporary Views.*

Linda M. Williams is a senior research specialist at Arizona State University. Prior to entering the academic community, she served for fifteen years in policy positions within the federal government, most recently at NASA Headquarters in Washington. Her research interests are in the areas of ethics and public policy and organizational policy, specifically focusing on the impact of policy on individuals within society. She is currently working on a book on controversial issues surrounding ethics policy.

Leslie R. Wolfe serves as President, Center for Women Policy Studies.* Previously she directed the Project on Equal Education Rights* of the National Organization for Women Legal Defense and Education Fund.* From 1985–87, she directed the Women's Educational Equity Act Program in the U.S. Education Department. She chaired the National Coalition for Women and Girls in Education.

Laura R. Woliver is an associate professor of political science, University of South Carolina. Her specialties include American political interest groups and social movements.

Philip Zampini is associate professor of political science, Westfield State College.

Eleanor E. Zeff is an adjunct associate professor of political science at Drake University in Des Moines, Iowa. She received her Ph.D. in political science from the Graduate Faculty of the New School of Social Research in New York City. Recently she has taught courses on comparative politics and on women and politics at both Drake and Iowa State Universities, and she has published articles on women in the United States and in Europe. She is also a member of numerous women's organizations.

ISBN 0-313-25073-1

9000 0>